Shakespeare Studies

Advisory Board

Shakespeare Studies

AN ANNUAL GATHERING OF
RESEARCH, CRITICISM, AND REVIEWS

III

Edited by

J. LEEDS BARROLL

Inaugurated under the Sponsorship of
THE UNIVERSITY OF CINCINNATI
1967

All correspondence should be addressed to:
The Editor, Shakespeare Studies, The University of Cincinnati,
Box 2198, Cincinnati, Ohio 45221.
Contributions offered for publication
should be accompanied by unaffixed return-postage.
Annual subscription is ten dollars

Contents

Contributors

Gates K. Agnew.
> *Assistant Professor of English, Indiana University.*

Sylvan Barnet.
> *Professor of English, Tufts University.*

Herbert Berry.
> *Professor of English, the University of Saskatchewan.*

James L. Calderwood.
> *Associate Professor of English, the University of California, Irvine.*

Joseph S. M. J. Chang.
> *Assistant Professor of English, the University of Wisconsin, Milwaukee.*

Maurice Charney.
> *Professor of English, Rutgers University.*

Thomas Clayton.
> *Associate Professor of English, the University of California, Los Angeles.*

R. W. Dent.
> *Professor of English, the University of California, Los Angeles.*

John R. Elliott, Jr.
> *Assistant Professor of English, the University of California, Santa Barbara.*

G. Blakemore Evans.
> *Professor of English, Harvard University.*

Charles R. Forker.
> *Associate Professor of English, Indiana University.*

Thelma N. Greenfield.
> *Associate Professor of English, the University of Oregon.*

Sherman Hawkins.
> *Associate Professor of English, the University of Rochester.*

Charles K. Hofling.
> *Associate Professor of Psychiatry, the University of Cincinnati.*

Cyrus Hoy.
> *Professor of English, the University of Rochester.*

Patricia Ingham.
> *Fellow and Tutor in English, St. Anne's College, Oxford.*

Paul A. Jorgensen.
> *Professor of English, the University of California, Los Angeles.*

R. J. Kaufmann.
> *Professor of History and English and Chairman of the Department of History, the University of Rochester.*

Alvin B. Kernan.
> *Professor of English, Yale University.*

Hilton Landry.

Professor of English, Kent State University.

Carol MacClintock.

Professor of Musicology, the University of Cincinnati.

Kenneth Muir.

King Alfred Professor of English Literature, the University of Liverpool.

Leonard Nathanson.

Associate Professor of English, Vanderbilt University.

Ruth Nevo.

Senior Lecturer, The Hebrew University of Jerusalem.

Norman Sanders.

Professor of English, the University of Tennessee.

Samuel Schoenbaum.

Professor of English, Northwestern University.

Alice Lyle Scoufos.

Assistant Professor of English, California State College at Fullerton.

Charles H. Shattuck.

Professor of English, the University of Illinois.

J. D. Shuchter.

Assistant Professor of English, the University of Colorado.

Rolf Soellner.

Professor of English, the Ohio State University.

Adolph L. Soens.

Assistant Professor of English, the University of Notre Dame.

W. F. Staton.

Associate Professor of English, Purdue University.

J. M. Steadman.

Senior Research Associate, The Henry E. Huntington Library.

Robert K. Turner, Jr.

Professor of English, the University of Wisconsin, Milwaukee.

Peter Ure.

Joseph Cowen Professor of English Literature, University of Newcastle Upon Tyne, England.

John W. Velz.

Assistant Professor of English, Rice University.

Herbert Weil, Jr.

Assistant Professor of English, the University of Connecticut.

Frances A. Yates.

Fellow of the Warburg Institute, the University of London, England.

Abbreviations

In the interest of uniformity, a list of abbreviations of the titles of Shakespeare's poems and plays has been agreed upon by the editors of a number of important editions and periodicals. These include the Oxford Shakespeare, edited by Dr. Alice Walker; the New Variorum Shakespeare; the *MLA Style-Sheet*, now again revised by Professor William Riley Parker; *Shakespeare Studies*; *Shakespeare Quarterly*, edited by James G. McManaway; and *Shakespeare Newsletter*, edited by Professor Louis Marder. Dr. Howard-Hill has written that he will use the same abbreviations in the computer concordance to Shakespeare that he is now compiling. The advantages of uniform abbreviations in scholarly publications are too obvious to require comment. Contributors to *Shakespeare Studies* are requested to use these abbreviations in footnotes and documentation.

Ado	Much Ado about Nothing	MV	Merchant of Venice
Ant.	Antony and Cleopatra	Oth.	Othello
AWW	All's Well that Ends Well	Per.	Pericles
AYL	As You Like It	R2	Richard II
Cor.	Coriolanus	R3	Richard III
Cym.	Cymbeline	Rom.	Romeo and Juliet
Err.	Comedy of Errors	Shr.	Taming of the Shrew
Ham.	Hamlet	TGV	Two Gentlemen of Verona
1H4	1 Henry IV	Tim.	Timon of Athens
2H4	2 Henry IV	Tit.	Titus Andronicus
H5	Henry V	TN	Twelfth Night
1H6	1 Henry VI	TNK	Two Noble Kinsmen
2H6	2 Henry VI	Tmp.	Tempest
3H6	3 Henry VI	Tro.	Troilus and Cressida
H8	Henry VIII	Wiv.	Merry Wives of Windsor
JC	Julius Caesar	WT	Winter's Tale
Jn.	King John	LC	Lover's Complaint
LLL	Love's Labour's Lost	Luc.	Rape of Lucrece
Lr.	King Lear	PhT	Phoenix and Turtle
Mac.	Macbeth	PP	Passionate Pilgrim
MM	Measure for Measure	Son.	Sonnets
MND	Midsummer Night's Dream	Ven.	Venus and Adonis

Dr. Fludd's Engravings and Their Beholders

by Herbert Berry

I

The five engravings of what appear to be stages in Robert Fludd's *Ars Memoriae* (1619) have recently become important in speculations about English stages during Jacobean times. The work is part (Volume II, part 2) of a much longer work, *Utriusque Cosmi . . . Historia* (1619-21) in which Fludd developed the macrocosm (vol. I) and the microcosm (vol.II), often along the Hermetic, hence occult lines used chiefly by Giordano Bruno in Fludd's lifetime. In the part concerning memory, Fludd described the ancient practice of memorizing with the aid of memory rooms, but, as Bruno and others had done before him, Fludd connected the practice to astrology and the more abstrusely occult. One of Fludd's innovations is that his rooms are theaters or stages. Of the five engravings, two show relatively little beyond the peculiarities of Fludd's method, so that writers have been inclined to discount them as having much to do with actual stages. Two others are crude and very small. The fifth, however, is large, carefully drawn, and detailed in many ways not peculiar to Fludd's method. It is this engraving which has mainly engaged the attention of Mr. Richard Bernheimer (1958), Miss Frances Yates (1966, twice), and Mr. I. A. Shapiro (1967).[1] It was Miss Yates who first noticed that the engravings might have something to do with Renaissance stages.

At first they caused little stir among historians of the English stage, because Fludd's book was published in Germany and written in Latin, and because quite important parts of the structure its engravings portray are alien to the present evidence about English stages. Chiefly, Fludd's stages do not have portions of the pit at their sides, but side walls containing at stage level either something like boxes, or doorways; and three of Fludd's stages have a large oriel hanging above the stage in the middle of the back wall. Besides Mr. Bernheimer decided that the engravings do not represent an English stage at all, and Miss Yates, in arguing that the detailed engraving represents the second Globe, had to defy too many probabilities and not a few facts (as Mr. Shapiro convincingly shows).[2]

A discovery of mine, however, has recently lent two of these engravings an impressive English relevance. I found that in the season of 1631-32, at least, boxes at Blackfriars were contiguous to the stage and on a level with it (1966),[3] though whether at the sides, the back, or both the evidence does not show. In the detailed engraving and in one of the tiny ones, what seem to be boxes are just so— at the sides. Mr. Shapiro made the association and has confidently announced that "Fludd's large illustration shows the stage of the Blackfriars." If Mr. Shapiro is right, English stage history has taken a mighty step forward. But as with so many assertions about the English playhouse, cogent reasons for caution suggest

11

themselves at once. Important parts of the case are far from proved or are even, it seems, at odds with the evidence.

At the outset, one might argue that the detailed engraving shows a room or courtyard and not necessarily a stage at all; that the word Fludd regularly used to describe his structures is not *scaena* (stage), but *theatrum* (the whole building); that in any case the passage in which Fludd described these structures as theatrical is murky at best and probably signifies a more general understanding of stage or theater than we should have;[4] that the two little engravings, which show theaters or stages according to Fludd's text and, more important, show them as raised and paled in, bear no necessary relation to the detailed one; and that it is logically shaky, at least, to pitch on one engraving which suits one's argument and to dismiss the two or four which do not, especially when one bears the legend, *"Forma Theatri,"* and another *"Sequitur figura vera theatri."*[5] Treacherous as these possibilities seem, however, I believe that Mr. Shapiro has rendered most of them quibbles, at least as far as the preliminary arguments go. As he contends, the detailed engraving is very likely of a stage, and the two little ones are very likely crude versions of the detailed one. The two others are probably stages, too, but because the artist has juggled details to suit Fludd's exposition, one can properly discount them in the preliminary arguments, though he does so at his peril in the arguments which must follow.

The next steps in Mr. Shapiro's case, and in Miss Yates' too, are not so easy to accept: 1) Fludd would have wished his engravings to show a particular, existing theater, 2) it would have been an English one, and 3) he could have seen to it that his continental publishers carried out his intentions accurately. Neither writer has much doubt. As Mr. Shapiro says, the detailed engraving shows "a stage that actually existed, in or before 1619" and in England. These matters, he says, are "now beyond reasonable doubt." For both, the chief question remaining is which English stage the engraving shows. But both have leapt very lightly into these contentions, and both omit apparently fatal evidence against the playhouses they have chosen.

II

Most of our information about Fludd's stages comes from the engravings. His prose specifies only that his stages have three or five doors, approximately equidistant from one another, that when they have five a post be in front of each, and that the posts be round (the two outside ones), hexagonal (the center one), and square (the two others). Structurally speaking, that is all. He wrote nothing about the shape or size of the stage, nothing about boxes, oriels, or galleries. He did not say how far in front of the doors the posts might be. Nor did he say whether the stage was the "open" sort common in England or the enclosed sort common on the Continent, nor whether his theater was roofed or unroofed. One must argue about these things, but one's evidence is the work of engravers, not typesetters. Fludd did give the colors of his doors and posts, and he specified that one theater generally be light and another dark. Each door and its post are the same color. The colors in turn are white, red, green, blue, and black.

If Fludd had much choice about the theaters engraved for his book, he probably would not have chosen English ones. Quite likely he had little choice, and in that event his theaters almost certainly would not have been English. One must at least suspect that the engravings show no actual theater.

That Fludd knew both the Globe and Blackfriars is quite reasonable, but his audience must have been a continental one, and such an audience would have found such things uncongenial. We have ample evidence that whatever the London stages were like, they were different from the Italian sort common on much of the Continent, the sort Fludd's educated readers in France, the Low Countries, and Germany would have taken for granted. Fludd surely knew the difference, for he had spent six years travelling on the Continent around the turn of the century. Moreover, Fludd says in his book that the idea of using the stage occurred to him in Nîmes, that he explored it in Avignon, and that he expounded it, finally, to the Duc de Guise, his brother, and their followers in Marseilles (p. 48). Those surroundings and that audience would hardly have sorted in Fludd's mind with London stages. No more, I believe, would the surroundings and audience of 1619. He wrote his book in Latin and had it published by the Dutch-German firm of de Bry in Oppenheim. Fludd also wrote nearly all his other works in Latin and published them on the Continent, often as part of controversies with continentals (at the end of the volume of which the *Ars Memoriae* is a part is a reply to Kepler about music). As one of Fludd's biographers observed, "His writings obtained more attention abroad than at home" *(D.N.B.)*.

Fludd did write one book specifically for Englishmen. It was the only one he wrote in English and the only one he published in England. In that work he described the audience for one of his books as being "as well in *Germany* as in *France,*" and boasted that another was "verie acceptable" to Frenchmen. He complained that he had received encouragement not from his countrymen, but from Poles, Swedes, Prussians, Germans, Transylvanians, Frenchmen, and Italians. He complained, too, that English physicians, at least, were no supporters of his. Fludd's fascination with the occult was neither new nor unique in England, but it was not very saleable there, and it bordered on being illegal and heretical, as an English parson, William Foster, rudely pointed out in 1631. English printers, therefore (as Fludd also complained), demanded great sums to print at least one of his books "and to find the cuts in copper," but continental printers actually paid him for the privilege.[6] Fludd, then, knew very well that his audience for the *Ars Memoriae* as for his other books was a continental one, and if he had any choice, he would have been wise to use for the book some generalized idea of the continental stages.

Besides, Fludd used the expression "in theatro publico" (n.4 above), referring to professional theaters in general. He would hardly have done so if he had an English audience in mind, and especially if the theater he had in mind were Blackfriars.

One Englishman did write a memory book for English readers and printers. He was John Willis, who published his *Mnemonica* in Latin in 1618 and a part of it in

English in 1621, having altered it *"with all libertie"* to make it easier for *"the common sort."* He not only avoided the occult, but apologized in his English introduction for including *"some conceits which are phantasticall,"* by which he meant mostly familiar classical myths. He too spoke of stages, and he too had an engraving (in both editions). Miss Yates thinks his engraving (which she has twice reproduced) shows the same sort of stage as Fludd's engravings, and she calls Willis' structure a "Memory Theater." But Willis nowhere used that term, and the way he did use theaters and stages seems devious. He began with them in mind, it appears, then soon dropped the first and eventually dropped the other. In Latin, in his first sentence, his structure was an imaginary "aedificium," cunningly built "ad formam theatri scenici" (p. 57). Then he often referred to a marble "proscenium" in the building. But he never again used the word "theatrum" and did not.give his proscenium any particularly theatrical qualities. Indeed, he seems to have used the word to mean merely floor. His regular word for the whole structure was "repositorium," or the phrase, "in loco memorialis." In English three years later, he omitted the phrase about the form of a theater. Instead, the structure was a "house or building . . . hauing no wall at all vpon the hither side which is towards vs"; and where in Latin he had alluded to the three walls as "proscenium terminantes," he now mentioned "all the three walls of the house." His proscenium became "stage," by which he clearly meant floor (*OED,* "stage," sb., I, 4), and his English word for the whole structure was "Repositorie."[7] Such a structure is what his engraving shows, quite exactly to the letter. He must have known from the start, as one is tempted to conclude, that his engraving would not look much like a theater, even to his learned audience, much less to his *"common"* one. Nor does it look much like anything we have seen among the reliable evidence about the playhouses of his time.

How much choice did Fludd have about the drawings in his book? Not nearly so much, it seems, as Miss Yates and Mr. Shapiro would like.[8] The firm of de Bry were engravers first, booksellers second, and printers not at all. They farmed their printing out, but did their own engravings, as they often claimed on their title pages, including the two in the first volume of Fludd's book. How closely were they likely to follow their artists and authors? They made one set of engravings from a famous collection of drawings which survive, John White's and Jacques Le Moyne's "American drawings." These were cut in 1589-90 by the founder of the firm, Theodor (d. 1598), and his two sons, Johann Israel (d. 1611) and Johann Theodor, who was head of the firm when they did Fludd's book. These engravings are remarkable as engravings, and they are even surprisingly accurate at times. But except, perhaps, for one celebrated example, the de Brys regularly Europeanized White's and LeMoyne's Indians, often extensively, and added or altered background very freely. For drawings of buildings, they not infrequently altered such details as doors and windows. Even in their more accurate engravings, one can rely upon them to represent truly only major features. It is obvious that, as the old man wrote in limping English, they had executed the engravings "the most diligentye and well that wear in my possible to doe," or as he added with more luck, "I and my sonnes hauen taken ernest paynes in grauinge the pictures there of in Copper."[9] But accuracy of detail was not one of the tasks they had set themselves.

Even though we do not have the drawings from which the firm took Fludd's engravings, it seems clear that their methods had not greatly changed. Many of the hundreds of engravings in Fludd's two volumes show what Fludd's text demands *plus* backgrounds of rural scenes, seascapes, flora and fauna, and the like, much of it characteristically Dutch or German. Besides, Fludd's engravings of stages are not among the firm's more accurate work. The de Brys missed even some of the most important demands of his text. Fludd specified that the two little stages be identical in design; they are not. He specified that one be light and the other dark; they are the same. He specified that one group of his stages have five posts; one stage has two, one none. He specified that the center post in these stages be hexagonal; that in one engraving is round. He specified that these stages have five doors equidistant from one another, and that each have one of the posts in front of it; neither is the case in the detailed engraving, nor in the two little ones.[10]

Mr. Bernheimer convinced himself that much of Fludd's detailed engraving is German, and that, therefore, a German artist did the drawing behind it—a conclusion Mr. Shapiro seems to accept. No matter what the artist's nationality, however, it is a fair guess that the engravers were responsible for a good deal in those engravings, including, probably, everything in the two little ones, and the engravers' nationality is clear. They were the two senior men in the firm, Johann Theodor de Bry and his son-in-law, Matthäus Merian, and their workmen.[11] De Bry was a native of Liège who had moved with his father to Frankfurt in 1590 and to Oppenheim in 1609. He was about to return to Frankfurt. Merian was a Swiss who had learned his craft in Zurich, Nancy, Paris, Stuttgart, and the Low Countries. He had married de Bry's eldest daughter in 1618, and would some two years after de Bry's death in 1623, take over half the firm. As Mr. Bernheimer pointed out, the firm had English connections. The elder de Bry had engraved plates of a procession of the Knights of the Garter in 1576, others of the funeral of Sidney in 1587, and still others for an English book of 1588. He may have seen Sidney's funeral, for he had visited London in search of White's and LeMoyne's drawings in 1586/7 and again the next year. When he had published the firm's engravings of White's drawings in 1590, he had accompanied them with Thomas Hariot's account of the Virginia Colony (first published in London in 1588), and he had issued an English edition as well as others in Latin, German, and French. The firm had reissued the Latin and German editions, not the English one, numerous times up to 1620. Another of the younger de Bry's daughters (the third) would marry William Fitzer in 1625, an Englishman who left England about a year earlier and soon took over the other half of the firm, including Fludd's custom.[12] But it would be difficult to argue on these accounts that this de Bry, his son-in-law, and their workmen would have thought of English stages in 1619 or so.

It is distinctly likely, then, that the engravings are the work not of one mind but many, all of whom have thought of stages along continental lines. The artist(s) and engravers could have got everything which ties their engravings to Fludd's method from Fludd's text, and a good deal more.[13] They could equally easily have done all the rest without any instruction from Fludd or anybody else who had ever seen a London stage. As Mr. Bernheimer allowed, the detailed engraving could even have been in the publisher's hands for years and then given to someone to add further details which would make it more or less suitable for Fludd's book. The only details which do accord with Fludd's text (the posts) seem clumsily added. Perhaps we should not be surprised, therefore, to find that Fludd's stages are much closer to the drawings we have of continental stages than to those we have of professional English stages. Like Fludd's stages, many continental ones were enclosed at the sides. The oriel and the area around it in Fludd's detailed engraving are not much different from that portion of those continental stages which had a "throne of honour" and an open room above it, like one in Brussels and another in Ghent in the sixteenth century and even the Schouwburg in Amsterdam in 1658. Much of that engraving is closer still to drawings of the courts of chivalry, especially to an engraving of the Cortile of the Pitti Palace in Florence.[14]

III

Mr. Shapiro has explained why the detailed engraving is probably not of the Globe, but he has ignored altogether at least three important reasons why it is probably not of Blackfriars either.

First, space, which has inhibited everybody from Wallace (1908) to Mr. Irwin Smith (1964) and me from putting the boxes in Blackfriars where they are in the drawing, at the sides. (I suggested they were at the back. The usual suggestion is that they ran along the sides of the auditorium and stopped at the front of the stage.) The house was 46 feet wide. If the boxes were at the sides, and if we are to take Fludd's engraving as of Blackfriars, we must subtract from that distance room for, 1) two passageways, since, as we have long known, the boxes had effective keys, hence doors, which do not appear on the stage side in the engraving, 2) four walls, the two of which in the engraving seem quite thick, 3) two rows of boxes for the most prominent people in the kingdom, and 4) numerous sitters[15] and at least a few standers in front of the boxes. I have put all this at a minimum of 20′, leaving about 26′ for acting. If one allows only the narrowest dimensions into which a smallish frame will fit, he can probably assert that 16′ would do, leaving 30′ for acting. But considering the prices exacted for those seats at Blackfriars and the people who sat in them, one is inclined to allow much more than even 20′ and thus leave an unacceptably small space for acting. The stage at the Fortune was 43′ wide.

Second, the persons responsible for the details in Fludd's engravings seem to have thought they were showing all five places without roofs. Blackfriars, of course, was very much an enclosed room. Not only did they show no signs of roofs nor of the artificial lighting which at Blackfriars was so famous and expensive, but also they organized their shading quite consistently to show light coming from quarters where no artificial lighting would.[16] That place is very high over and well *behind*

16

the left stage wall. In Fludd's three larger engravings it is also somewhat toward the back of the stage. The light floods these structures consistently and widely from the same direction, as neither one chandelier nor a string of them could do without creating shadows not in the drawings or dispelling one or another of those which are. Mr. Shapiro may think of windows. But to let in the light on Fludd's stages, windows would have to be very wide and of a fantastic height. Besides, Mr. Shapiro has spent a long paragraph convincing us that the windows at Black-friars would have been boarded up. Light in the detailed engraving also trickles in behind the boxes on the left at the same angle as the light which floods the stage from above them, implying that the boxes too are open to the sky.

Yet another difficulty confronts those who would argue that Fludd's detailed engraving represents Blackfriars or any particular stage, especially an indoor one. It is the explicit indication in both the engraving and the text that five posts stand in a row across the front of that stage, though the posts themselves are not shown.[17] One post is in the very middle. What could these posts hold up? And would not an audience have trouble looking around them? If the stage was indoors like that of Blackfriars, surely no roof would require so many posts in such difficult positions. If the stage was in an open courtyard or otherwise outdoors, the posts could support a roof like those over the stages of English public playhouses—but five of them, one dead center? The English houses had only two, one on each side (as, indeed, one of the little engravings has). Some continental theaters had posts holding up affairs like the oriel, but hardly five, and those a long way from the front of the stage. Those posts must support a proscenium arch, another device unknown so far in regular English playhouses before the Restoration. Many continental theaters, however, had a row of such posts supporting such an arch. Those theaters were erected outdoors, where a substantial arch was necessary to hold the main members of the stage together because the walls of buildings could not serve the purpose. Four posts were common, but not one in the middle. The stages of indoor theaters on the Continent—or anywhere else—were supported from the walls and roof beams of the building which housed them. Hence they had no elaborate proscenium arches and no posts. The Schouwburg had for its arch merely a curtain rod, which ran from wall to wall. The only English design presently known for a theater on continental principles, that for the quite special (and indoor) Cockpit-in-Court, shows no formal arch and no posts.

IV

Having satisfied himself that Fludd's detailed engraving is of Blackfriars, Mr. Shapiro examines the use of the oriel and the battlemented area on each side. He finds the one to be the music room and the other the upper stage. In order to support these findings he turns to de Witt's drawing of the Swan, where he finds two musicians in the middle of the gallery above the stage and a woman on the left side. Thus the musicians are in a music room and actors on either side of them. But one "musician" who is "holding up, at face level, . . . some wind instrument such as a cornett or hautboy," projecting "forward across" one of the posts is actually doing no such thing. The two lines which persuade Mr. Shapiro are level with the person's armpits rather than his face, and his hands do not seem to touch them. The point at which one of those lines crosses the post is the same as that at which a line crosses each of the other posts to form a base for them. The other line does not cross the post. Mr. Shapiro has been deceived, probably, by a slightly errant piece of cross hatching, as he almost certainly has been with his other "musician," who "seems to hold some object under his left arm." The "object" is surely the person's armpit on one side (like that of the person on the left) and cross hatching on the other. And to see that person on the left as a woman is very likely to confuse an arm for a breast. In any case, Mr. Shapiro's argument for acting on an upper stage in Fludd's detailed engraving and in de Witt's drawing of the Swan implies a new shift in the inner-upper stage advocacy—that Elizabethan stages (or at least two of them) had one but not the other.[18] For Mr. Shapiro wisely does not attempt to argue that an inner stage lies behind either Fludd's double doors in the back wall or de Witt's pair of them. But if the oriel was used for music and the battlements for acting, there was little means for sound to get out of the one and little room for acting on the other. The oriel seems more suitable for yet another box, as it would be in the courts of chivalry.

Whoever invented the details in the five engravings had in the back of his mind, or their minds, a fairly consistent idea of the stage. Above all, the stage was enclosed at its sides, as the continental ones were and modern ones are. Like those stages, it amounted to two sides and a back joined together at right angles, with, probably, an arch across the front. This structure was made of flimsy materials (two of Fludd's stages are faced with stuff painted to look like masonry,[19] another with boards). It could stand inside another, such as an open courtyard. In at least one instance (the detailed engraving and two little ones), this structure backed against a wall of masonry which had a gallery running along well above the floor and two doorways giving onto the gallery. Here the back wall of the stage was cut off so that it formed the railing of the gallery, leaving the side walls to go much higher. This gallery continued beyond the stage on both sides, and the side walls did not cross it, nor did the oriel—as one gathers from the light which catches the uprights of the battlements on the right. That oriel may have been part of the gallery or of the back wall of the stage: its inscription, "THEATRVM ORBI," suggests the latter. The shading against the masonry wall behind the gallery and in the boxes on the left suggests that other walls ran behind the boxes so as to cut off part of the sun, hence that the stage was in the courtyard.

The stage was probably rectangular, perhaps twice as wide as deep. The perspective in the engravings is very elaborate, especially in the detailed one, but not always accurate. The focal point in the detailed one, for example, wanders about in a circle some quarter of an inch across in the corbel under the oriel.[20] The stages look square, or even deeper than they are wide: the whole stage area in the detailed engraving could be a cube. But if one looks carefully at the blocks in the floors of Fludd's stages, comparing them to the blocks or boards in the backs and sides, one will find first that the floor blocks in the detailed engraving and in one other are wider than deep, and, more important, that the stages measured in blocks are about twice as wide as deep, the one in the detailed engraving somewhat more than twice as wide. In all three larger engravings, the side walls (by both tape measure and the blocks) are not quite so high as the stage is wide. The top course of artificial masonry visible in the detailed engraving is probably the last, for the light is streaming over a wall which if it were the stage wall would be only half a course higher still.

The back wall of Fludd's stage, finally, had one to three doorways at stage level. Its floor was usually a parquet affair. It had no curtains visible anywhere. It had neither roof nor artificial lighting. It had boxes or doorways in the side walls, and often an oriel in the back wall.

Some of this is familiar enough from the drawings we have of English stages: the doorways in the back wall at stage level, the gallery in the back wall above the stage, the rectangular stage, perhaps the parquet floor. Other details are not familiar, and they are very important, especially the enclosed sides and the oriel.

What, finally, are we to make of the stages shown in Fludd's engravings? We should, I believe, be chary of attempts to read English practice into them, and especially chary of attempts to read English practice into them at particular playhouses. Perhaps we should suspect that they are a mélange which is generally continental. Two things we should not do. We should not juggle the details of the engravings to fit other evidence or our own theories—omit, for example, the shading and the posts, supply a roof, change the size of the windows in the oriel and of the central door at stage level, move the boxes away from the stage, and the like. Miss Yates has played this game so diligently that in her reconstruction almost nothing remains of Fludd's detailed engraving save four doorways, the general shape of the oriel, the battlements, and the facing on the walls. Nor should we run intricate circles with the evidence in the engravings—argue, as Mr. Shapiro does, that boxes would have been at the sides of the stage at Blackfriars because they are in the detailed engraving; show, as Miss Yates does, how English plays were staged on Fludd's structures; "safely conjecture" and "confidently assume," as Mr. Shapiro does, that this or that device convenient to Blackfriars and English actors would have been built behind Fludd's facade—before we have unbegged some obstinate questions.

Notes:

(1) *SQ*, IX (1958), 19-29; *New York Review of Books*, May 26, pp. 16-22 (and two replies, July 28, pp. 28-29; Nov. 17, pp. 41-42); *The Art of Memory* (London, 1966), ch. XV, XVI; *Shakespeare Studies*, II (1966), pp. 192-209. The engravings appear also in this issue. See the article by Yates.

(2) See also the useful objections in letters to *NYRB* by Frank Brownlow (July 28, 1966, p. 28) and Glynne Wickham (Nov. 17, 1966, pp. 40-41), and the reluctance of even her generous reviewer in *TLS* (Nov. 10, 1966, p. 1025).

(3) *SP*, LXIII (1966), 163-86.

(4) Miss Yates (*NYRB*, May 26, p. 17; Nov. 17, p. 41; *Memory*, p. 331) and Mr. Shapiro (p. 193) frequently assure us that in this passage Fludd described his stages as "a public theatre in which

comedies and tragedies are acted." But the matter is not that simple. Fludd's words are, *"THea-trum* apello illud, in quo omnes vocabulorum, sententiarum, particularum orationis seu subjectorum actiones tanquam in theatro publico, ubi comoediae & tragoediae aguntur, demonstrantur" (p. 55).

(5) Mr. Shapiro (n. 9) takes Miss Yates to task for translating this as "the figure of a true theatre." Interestingly, the entry in the index for the engraving reads, *"Theatri veri in arte memoriae figura."*

(6) Foster's *Hoplocrisma-Spongus*, sig. A3, p. 37, etc., and *Doctor Flvdds Answer vnto M. Foster (1631)*, "Members" 1 and 2, pp. 14, 21-22, 24, 124-29.

(7) *Art of Memory*, Sigs. A4ᵛ-A5, pp. 2-7, 11, and esp. 55, 60, 99. He once used "stage" in a theatrical sense, but meant the theater in general (p. 47). See Yates, *NYRB*, May 26, p. 16; *Memory*, pp. 336-37.

(8) Miss Yates (*NYRB*, May 26, p. 16; *Memory*, pp. 324, 325) says Fludd "was satisfied that the illustrations" in the *Ars Memoriae* "carried out his intentions" and cites a remark in his reply to Foster. But that remark (pp. 21-22) alludes specifically and only to Fludd's "first Volume," presumably either his first book, *Apologia Compendiaria* (Leyden, 1616), or, since he was thinking elsewhere in the passage of his replies to Mersenne, the first of those, *Sophiae cum Moria Certamen* (Frankfurt, 1629).

(9) Paul Hulton and David Beers Quinn, *The American Drawings of John White* (London, 1964), I, 11, 41, etc., and the engravings and drawings in II (both parts of the exception are reproduced in pl. 145); de Bry's prefatory remarks to Raleigh and the reader in his English edn. of *America*, pt. I (Frankfurt, 1590); A. M. Hind, *Engraving in England* (Cambridge, 1952), I, 124-26.

(10) Miss Yates (*Memory*, p. 326) points out that the picture on the title page of the *Ars Memoriae* contains five images, none of which is alluded to in the text.

(11) Both title-pages in the first volume read, "Aere Johan Theodori De Bry," meaning, no doubt, the firm, because the second of those title-pages is an engraving actually signed by Merian, and de Bry himself would hardly have done the many hundreds of engravings in the two volumes. The elder de Bry's name similarly appears on his English title-page in 1590, but in his preface to the reader he wrote that he and his sons had done the work.

(12) Moriz Sondheim, "Die de Bry, Matthäus Merian und Wilhelm Fitzer," *Philobiblon*, VI (1933), no. 1, pp. 10-14; Ernst Weil, "William Fitzer, the Publisher of Harvey's *De Motu Cordis*, 1628," *The Library*, Dec. 1943-March 1944, pp. 146-50.

(13) Mr. Bernheimer supposed that the inscription in the oriel of the detailed engraving, "THEATRVM ORBI," signifies Globe Theater and is one detail which would have come from Fludd himself. Neither Miss Yates in her book (p. 332, but see one of her replies in *NYRB*, Nov. 17, p. 41, where she misquotes and mistranslates the phrase) nor Mr. Shapiro, however, has pressed the point, because the inscription is thoroughly appropriate to Fludd's astrological methods.

(14) C. W. Hodges, *The Globe Restored* (London, 1953), pp. 135, 142, 157, etc.; Wickham, *Early English Stages* (London, 1959), I, pl. xxiv, and his letter to *NYRB*. Perhaps the curtained box in the gallery above the late English stage shown in the frontispiece of Kirkman's *The Wits* (1662) derives from such structures as the oriel.

(15) "Gallants" still sat on the stage at Blackfriars in 1626-32, and the boxes were nearby: see Massinger's *The City Madam*, II,ii,156-59, and T. A. Dunn, *Massinger* (London, 1957), pp. 29, 31, 34.

(16) Some of the shading in all five engravings of stages shows depth rather than shadow, especially that on the right walls, the floors, and perhaps the back walls of the three larger engravings. This is a practice followed by the de Brys in many of their other engravings.

(17) Miss Yates (*Memory*, pp. 332 & n., 348) points out that Fludd used the verb *fingo* in his passage about the posts, by which she would have us understand that they were only feigned, not a real

part of the structure. But Fludd did not intend that distinction. He used such indefinite language for everything he mentioned in his theater, verbs like *fingo* and *existimo*, or these and others in the future or subjunctive. On p. 55, he has for the light and dark theaters, "*Primum* ergo theatrum habebit colorem album . . . . *Secundum* vero fingetur imbutum colore nigro," and for the doors, "Quodlibet autem horum theatrorum habebit *quinque portas*." On p. 63, just before Miss Yates' passage, Fludd has a long string of these devices for the places in front of the doors, then, just after, more for the shapes and colors of the posts. (I am indebted to Professors L. M. Murison of the University of Western Ontario and P. M. Swan of the University of Saskatchewan for help with Fludd's Latin.)

(18) Mr. Harbage has done the same: *Theatre for Shakespeare* (Toronto, 1955), p. 29.

(19) The detailed one and one of the other larger ones. This latter looks like real masonry until one considers the arches, which could not have stood if the material were stone.

(20) One looks at the stage of the detailed engraving from somewhere on the left in front. The artist made allowance for being on the left in the side walls and in the placing of the back wall, but not in the floor or elsewhere.

The Language of Paradox in Romeo and Juliet

by Joseph S. M. J. Chang

Critical insight has foundered in the case of *Romeo and Juliet*,[1] in part because critics restrict their readings to the level of understanding defined by the two choric sonnets, and in part because students of the play have misread Shakespeare's major artistic tool here, making it subserve their own penchant for analysis of character. For example, since Dowden, it has been commonly accepted that Shakespeare employs a low order of Petrarchanism in the first act to indicate the shallowness of young Romeo's conventionalized devotion to Rosaline.[2] Petrarchan oxymorons tediously issue from the boy, when he is not playing the role of the melancholic, only to give way under the pressure of true emotion to genuinely moving poetry. From a man in love with love, he becomes a truly persuasive and compelling instance of romantic love in a play which demonstrates the inherent dangers of such love. It is my purpose here to raise some objections to this analysis by noting its inconsistencies and to demonstrate that the play is controlled by the Petrarchan contrarieties, which are realized both rhetorically and by the action.[3] Finally, the tragedy is not primarily concerned with love, any more than first-rate *carpe diem* poetry is about actual seduction. As in the Elizabethan sonnet tradition,[4] the play exploits a love-centered situation to explore problems of larger import, the abiding concerns of time, death, and immortal aspiration.

The fact is that the "bad" poetry of *Romeo and Juliet* is not reserved for young Romeo of Act I. While it may be convenient to think Shakespeare uses two poetic voices as an instrument of characterization, showing growth through the experience of love, in truth, he does not. Even if we forgive lines 181-88 of the first scene as deliberately hyperbolic—Romeo self-consciously mocks himself before his friends do[5]—there is the evidence afforded by Benvolio's and Montague's descriptions, all picturing Romeo as the love-struck melancholic. This understanding of Shakespeare's use of poetry to indicate growth in character might be acceptable were it not for Juliet's lines in Act III, after the lyrical experience of the banquet, after the rhapsody of the balcony. Awaiting her husband, she is frustrated with the news of Tybalt's death and breaks out with this fine piece of oxymoronic blubbering:

> O serpent heart, hid with a flowring face!
> Did ever draggon keepe so faire a Cave?
> Bewtifull tirant, fiend angelicall,
> Dovefeatherd raven, wolvishravening lamb,
> Despised substance of divinest showe:

Just opposite to what thou justly seem'st,
A damned saint, an honourable villaine.   *(III.ii.73-79)*

By the criterion applied to Romeo's

> o brawling love, o loving hate,
> O any thing of nothing first create,
> O heavie lightnesse, serious vanitie,
> Mishapen Chaos of welseeming formes,
> Feather of lead, bright smoke, cold fier, sicke health,

Juliet is obviously not truly in love with Romeo, only with the idea of love. No one suggests this of course; the answer is that Shakespeare, still a developing artist, cannot control his language. The patent error of such gratuitousness is in supposing the clever artist can in one instance deliberately resort to poor poetry for the subtle end of character development but in another, when true poetic energy is called for, he can only muster forth the same species of language he supposedly knows to be unworthy. The poet capable of *Antony and Cleopatra's* intensity and concentration is barely evident here, but surely, no poet who can consciously use bad poetry in Act I will two acts later use the same devices and believe them good.

Had it been Shakespeare's intention to write a tragedy of character, based on moral choice, illustrating the dangers of either love or youth,[6] he might have chosen to represent the Friar as one of the "superstitious friars (the naturally fit instruments of unchastity)" Arthur Brooke speaks of as abetting "unhonest desire."[7] What Shakespeare did to his source was to heighten Fortune's role, first by carefully removing the stain of sin and secondly by defining Fortune in terms of time and mortality. Moral guilt in Romeo and Juliet is averted by the propriety of their conduct and by the development of the feud. Thus, the "wicked lust" Brooke charges his lovers with is absent, and the "neglecting the authority and advice of parents and friends" is rendered meaningless in view of the inveterate feud. The Prince's condemnation of the feud deprives both sets of parents of all moral authority with the audience. As for the suicide, not to mention the two killings, Shakespeare had a greater problem in managing his play, since self-slaughter is a manifest sin. It seems however that Shakespeare intended to ignore this fact. The Friar's recapitulation does not refer to the cause of Romeo's death and only surmises on Juliet's. The man makes no judgment on the sinners; the Prince directs his wrath toward their parents. Critics have urged, not unreasonably, that lyricism supplants theology, poetic lapses and structural defects. That Shakespeare was unwilling to depend entirely on this resource is evident in III.v.207-210 and in IV.i.55-59. In these speeches Juliet declares her will to abide by a contract sealed in heaven, and she places suicide in the context of fidelity. As Friar Lawrence says, "vice sometime by action [is] dignified" (II.iii.22). There is a paradox, if there ever was one, and Shakespeare makes good on it, not by overwhelming a weak story with poetic energy, but by giving it shape, texture and meaning.

Whether or not we care for oxymorons, their function in the play, in Act I and in

Act III, is development of theme, not character, and to this end they are consistent, using the same polarities despite fluctuations in poetic quality.[8] The effect sought by the use of oxymorons and paradoxes is the same intended by Petrarch—to indicate the irreconcilable oppositions of love, or, indeed, of life itself. "O brawling love!" is certainly third-rate Petrarchanism; it is also the most succinct statement of the play's action, which is so contrived that for every moment of love, there is one of hatred.[9] The significance of Tybalt's death extends beyond the inconvenient timing of the event and the problems it creates for the newly married couple. It is precisely timed to intervene the two acts of marriage, the ceremony and the consummation. The killing of Tybalt is the fulfillment of the first scene's comic treatment of brawling love: Samson intended to "push *Mountagues* men from the wall, and thrust his maids to the wall" (I.i.21-22). That Romeo kill Juliet's cousin, in effect shedding her blood, is as inevitable as her singling out a hated enemy to love. The same understanding may be applied to the killing of Paris, which Granville-Barker believes "wanton" and with "little dramatic purpose."[10] But again, Romeo is on his way to the ultimate consummation of his love for Juliet, and attending this act of love is one of hatred. Again, rhetoric is realized in action, though at the peril of character.

These instances of brawling love and loving hate are supplemented by poetry, both fine and tedious. The latent aggressiveness of love is revealed in the imagery of Juliet's speech describing how she would possess her Romeo:

> I would have thee gone,
> And yet no farther than a wantons bird,
> That lets it hop a litle from his hand,
> Like a poore prisoner in his twisted gives,
> And with a silk threed, plucks it backe againe,
> So loving Jealous of his libertie.   *(II.ii.177-82)*

When Romeo responds approvingly, Juliet concedes the fatal possibility, "Yet I should kill thee with much cherishing" (l. 184). Awaiting her husband with a bride's eagerness, Juliet represents herself in the figure of a falcon whose destructive powers shall remain restrained until the proper moment (III.ii.14-16). With these details in mind, it is therefore difficult to allow her ambiguous remarks to her mother to remain at the simplest level of understanding:

> O how my heart abhors
> To hear him namde and cannot come to him,
> To wreake the love I bore my Cozen
> Upon his body that hath slaughterd him.   *(III.v.100-103)*

Here is fine jesuitical practice, but beyond that, there is the same element of contrariety, touched upon in many ways other than love and hate. The wedding night is not unmitigated ecstasy; the anticipated passion of the soliloquy, "Gallop apace, you fierie footed steedes," is darkened and substantially altered by the news of Tybalt's death. The ambivalence of

24

> But wherefore villaine didst thou kill my Cozin?
> That villaine Cozin would have kild my husband   *(III.ii.100-101)*

is, in spite of what may strike us as false notes because of false poetry, entirely proper to the play.

The contrarieties in love, and in life generally, are touched upon in many more instances than can be here discussed. It must suffice to recall quickly that we find oxymorons in the punning before the ball, opposing heavy and light, nimble soles and soul of lead. The gallants burn their lamps by day; they come too late and they come too early, simultaneously. At the feast, the imagery of light and dark, of doves and crows, is pursued. The sweetness of new love will by Tybalt be converted to bitterest gall. In the lover's sonnet, pilgrims do wrong, faith turns to despair, one sin purges another. On the balcony, parting is sweet sorrow. When Benvolio and Mercutio catch up with Romeo the following morning, they all jest on good whores, the new form and the old bench, on Romeo's wit—"a very bitter sweeting." The copiousness of Shakespeare's invention suggests that the theme of loving hate is not exactly predicated on the modern psychologist's love-hate relationship, though there is indeed a strong resemblance. Rather, loving-hate is the primary instance of a series of paradoxes, and it serves as a focal point for a wider problem. This is verified in the two speeches which develop in detail the problem of life's bitter sweetness, the Nurse's monologue and the Friar's disquisition on herbs.

Far more than a comic set-piece, the Nurse's speech helps define the meaning of the tragedy in placing the action of the play—Juliet's relinquishing to Romeo—within a specific context. In the celebrated speech, the Nurse introduces an abundance of details—the now dead Susan, the earthquake, a pratfall, a bawdy joke, a dead husband—all in reference to another apparently irrelevant detail, Juliet's weaning. The weaning is the central incident, and it is described appropriately enough, in terms of bitter-sweet experience. The wormwood on the dug alters what had been sweet and palatable to something henceforth to be rejected. The point of the anecdote lies in the symbolic import of weaning, a milestone attained in the infant's progress to death. Juliet, at that time, indicated her growing independence in another way,

> For then she could stand hylone, nay byth roode
> She could have run and wadled all about:
> For even the day before, she broke her brow,
> And then my husband (God be with his soule,
> A was a merrie man) tooke up the child,
> Yea quoth he, doest thou fall upon thy face?
> Thou wilt fall backward when thou hast more wit.
> Wilt thou not *Jule*?   *(I.iii.36-43)*

Though colored by the low imaginations of the nurse and her husband, the three events—walking, weaning, and capitulating to love's invitation—are of a piece. Neither walking nor weaning is achieved without pain and distress; the same is true of love, whether one understands its pain in Mercutio's or the Nurse's terms, of groaning and bearing the burden of love, or in terms of the exquisite sorrows of parting. Conversely, for the reason that the child must stand alone and never more palate the dug, Juliet must yield to love, when she has wit enough to do so. In reducing Juliet's age from what it had been in the source[11] to nearly fourteen, Shakespeare may have increased the pathos of the tragedy, but he also fixed the events at the stage when the heroine passes physically from girlhood to maturity.

The Friar's speech (II.iii.5-30) is congruent with the Nurse's in a number of ways. Both make references to time, of which more will be said later. The Friar contrasts weeds and flowers, sententiously describes the earth as both womb and tomb, and he comments on the wonder that what heals may poison as well. The speech is built of the same antitheses found throughout the play, of light and dark, birth and death, good turning evil. Moreover, both speeches have in common the image of the child at suck, one actual and the other metaphoric:

> We sucking on [earth's] naturall bosome finde:
> Many for many vertues excellent:
> None but for some, and yet all different.

Construed from both speeches, the implication of the image is, clearly, that eventually man must, in the process of attaining maturity, cut himself first from the womb, and then the earth, though, ironically, in so doing he must return to the womb, now a tomb.[12]

However, the Friar's speech says much more than this, raising the problem which faces the man who seeks to find his destiny. As Romeo enters the stage, the Friar proceeds with his speech:

> Within the infant rinde of this weake flower
> Poyson hath residence, and medicine power:
> For this being smelt, with that part cheares each part,
> Being tasted, slaies all sences with the hart.
> Two such opposed Kings encampt them still,
> In man as well as hearbes, grace and rude will:
> And where the worser is predominant,
> Full soone the Canker death eates up that Plant.

Here, the paradoxical equipoise is represented in a state of uneasy tension, and the wonder is not that man is compounded of warring elements, but that ultimately one or the other must prevail. The passage obviously applies to the lovers, who have been represented as buds and flowers;[13] and we recall that Romeo speaks of the apothecary's poison as medicine (V.i.85), and Juliet kisses Romeo for the restorative yet on his lips (V.iii.166).

The difficulty of the speech is that it does not weigh the alternatives as clearly as the nurse's does. No parent would deny the inevitable need for walking or weaning. But the Friar raises the problem of finding the "true qualities" he so teasingly refers to:

26

O mickle is the powerfull grace that lies
In Plants, hearbes, stones, and their quallities:
For nought so vile, that on the earth doth live,
But to the earth some speciall good doth give:
Nor ought so good but straind from that faire use,
Revolts from true birth, stumbling on abuse.
Vertue it selfe turnes vice being misapplied,
And vice sometime by action dignified.

The simple contradiction of love and hatred is expanded to include the despised substance which is beneficial, or the vicious act, such as suicide, which under certain circumstances escapes condemnation either as evidence of a womanish disposition or as a sin. One can condemn Romeo and Juliet as having loved immoderately or too hastily, but one must keep in mind that until the point of death, they do nothing without the pious father's consent. In any case, the dualities in men and herbs must eventually be resolved for good or ill. Although the speech does not explicitly provide the scale by which we may evaluate the lovers' actions, it does help advance our ability to cope with the play in reminding us that man is a thing of parts, grace and rude will, senses and heart, even as the love between Romeo and Juliet is a thing of parts.

When Juliet attempts to dissociate Romeo from his name, she claims Montague has no part of his being;

> it is nor hand nor foote
> Nor arm nor face, nor any other part
> Belonging to a man.   *(II.ii.40-42)*

The problem of identity is not so easily solved; Juliet is as wrong as Mercutio is in supposing that he can conjure Romeo by·

> *Rosalines* bright eyes,
> By her high forehead, and her Scarlet lip
> By her fine foot, straight leg, and quivering thigh,
> And the demeanes that there adjacent lie.   *(II.i.17-20)*

If Romeo's being is in his physical parts, then so too is Juliet's, and their love nothing more than Mercutio supposes. Shakespeare is using for dramatic purpose the same device employed in the famous mock-blazen of sonnet 130. In the conventional sonnet tradition, the blazon of love attempts to evoke the essential beauty of the beloved. But in his sonnet and in this play, Shakespeare modifies tradition so that his reader and his audience can realize love has nothing to do with either coral lips or reeking breaths. Thus, the nurse can find no urgent basis for loving Romeo though she concedes his desirability in physical endowment:

> Well, you have made a simple choyse, you know not how to
> chuse a man: *Romeo*, no not he: though his face be better than
> any mans, yet his leg excels all mens, and for a hand and a foote

and a body, though they be not to be talkt on, yet they are past
compare: he is not the flower of curtesie, but ile warrant him,
as gentle as a lamme.   *(II.v.38ff.)*

In short, though there is every reason, objectively speaking, for a girl to love Romeo, the Nurse does not find him appealing. Capulet is, for this reason, foolish in supposing that Paris can be attractive to Juliet because he is

Of faire demeanes, youthfull and nobly liand,
Stuft as they say, with honourable parts.   *(III.v.182-83)*

The participle *stuffed* betrays the shallowness of such an appeal, essentially no different from Mercutio's conjurations by flesh. Paris does not exist in his parts, any more than does Romeo, whose name cannot be cut from his body (III.iii.107-109).

Well, then, what's Montague, if it is no part belonging to a man? This question, or some variation of it, is at the core of the tragedy, and lest we forget it, the playwright keeps it before us. Mercutio, finding Romeo able to keep pace with his own wit, presumes his friend to be his old self again: "now art thou sociable, now art thou *Romeo*: now art thou what thou art" (II.iv.93-94). But when despair overwhelms the youth, who seeks to destroy his identity by seeking its mansion, the Friar denounces him,

Art thou a man? thy forme cries out thou art:
Thy teares are womanish, thy wild acts denote
The unreasonable furie of a beast.   *(III.iii.109-111)*

Juliet asks, "O God! did *Romeos* hand shead *Tybalts* bloud?" and the nurse, with grammatical precision, replies, "It did, it did, alas the day, it did" (III.ii.71-72). This is guilt evaded by a reversal of metonymy, where the part is not equivalent to the whole. Similarly, when Juliet threatens suicide, she dissociates hand and heart:

God joynd my heart and *Romeos*, thou our hands:
And ere this hand by thee to *Romeos* seald
Shall be the Labell to an other deed,
Or my true heart with trecherous revolt,
Turne to an other, this shall sley them both.   *(IV.i.55-59)*

With minor variations, the theme of parts, with some more truly of a person than others, is developed in Juliet's rejection of the nurse,

Go Counsellor,
Thou and my bosome henceforth shall be twaine.   *(III.v.239-40)*

and in Romeo's euphoric statement,

My bosomes Lord sits lightly in his throne.   *(V.i.3)*

Of no less importance to the play are the many references and allusions to sexual organs, for they too are parts by which identity may be created. That is, one may either pursue the fulfillment of sexual gratification or the wishes of his bosom's lord. The current of sexuality in the play, extensive though limited to the scenes prior to Mercutio's death, has led to the misunderstanding that Shakespeare obliquely undercuts the lyrical innocence of young love by showing it to be motivated by sexual appetite. As in the standard romantic formula, it is love at first sight for Romeo and Juliet, with the often forgotten difference that neither actually has a direct view of the other, for it is at a masked ball that they meet, and Romeo most assuredly is masked.[14] If not literally true that the lovers are veiled from each other's view, the symbolic importance of the masks must be recognized, inasmuch as in the balcony scene, the lovers are muffled by the dark. Juliet questions Romeo thus,

> What man art thou, that thus beschreend in night
> So stumblest on my counsell? *(II.ii.52-53)*

As for herself "the mask of night is on my face" (l. 85). The effect is, I believe, to minimize the physical attraction each holds for the other. Without denying the urgency of Juliet's longing for her husband's coming, I think Shakespeare intends to contrast the love to which sexual activity is but an important incidental, to the preoccupation with physical gratification marked by Mercutio and the Nurse.[15]

The Balcony Scene is so managed that, while free from bawdry and eroticism itself, it is framed by these elements. Mercutio, by his conjurations, sets up in the audience's mind the expectation of sexual encounter between Romeo and Juliet. Later, both his friends and Friar Lawrence suppose Romeo to have spent the night with Rosaline. In the company of the gallants, Romeo can match jest for jest with Mercutio, but never in his conversations with Juliet is there a suggestion of sex. The single exception occurs during the Balcony Scene, and its presence there is intended to recall to the audience its expectation—prepared by Mercutio—so that it may recognize the essential purity of the present moment. The exchanged questions,

> O wilt thou leave me so unsatisfied?
> What satisfaction canst thou have to night? *(II.ii.125-26)*

provoke, for the audience, the obvious answer. Instead, Romeo returns to the language of the pilgrim and begs "Th' exchange of thy loves faithful vow for mine" (l. 127). Love of this sort—and despite our own cynicism, it exists in this play—is consummated in death, not in copulation.

Tumescence and the phallus are referred to repeatedly by the characters of low imagination. In one series of speeches the subject is elaborated upon particularly. Mercutio, before the balcony scene, offers this bit of bawdry:

> twould anger him
> To raise a spirit in his mistresse circle

Of some strange nature, letting it there stand
Till she had laid it, and conjurde it downe.   (II.i.23-26)

Still better and still worse, these parts of love's blazon are incessantly repeated,
until they are inescapable when the nurse admonishes Romeo, who at this point
has been banished and is in despair:

Stand up, stand up, stand and you be a man,
For *Juliets* sake, for her sake rise and stand:
Why should you fall into so deepe an O?   (III.iii.88-90)

Though the language is the same, the virility Romeo is called upon to exercise is
of a different order from Sampson's (I.i.20-22). It is with an erect spirit that Romeo
will save his beloved, and only in this sense is the Friar's axiom valid: "Woman
may fall when theres no strength in men" (II.iii.80). For Sampson and Gregory,
for Mercutio and the Nurse, for Susan's prophetic father, it is otherwise; when
men have strength to stand, then may women fall. The Friar's consolation might
well have been used at the play's end, since it bespeaks the dramatic truth of the
tragedy. For Shakespeare persuades us by his art that the physical decay of our
heroes is no more significant than the artificial death Juliet takes on wilfully. Juliet's
"death scene" of Act IV is an anticipation of the actual suicide, as is the Friar's
description of how his herb will divest all her parts of life's image.[16] Juliet's speech
is better placed there than in Act V, for at the later moment, swift action is demanded. Moreover, the fear before artificial death is as valid as that inspired by
an actual threat to life. This is so, not simply because Juliet's terror is manifest,
but because actual death, according to the play, attacks only those parts to be
numbed by the potion:

Each part depriv'd of supple government,
Shall stiffe and starke, and cold appeare like death.   (IV.i.102-103)

The upshot of the tragedy is obliquely stated in Friar Lawrence's consolation to
the Capulets, who suppose their daughter dead. Because the speaker is a cleric,
the tendency is to take his remarks as referring to Christian salvation, though, as
has been noted, the problem of salvation and damnation are not insisted upon at
the play's close. The speech is coordinated with the play in its reliance on Juliet's
parts, that which has its place in heaven, above the clouds, and those which may
be claimed by death.

heaven and your selfe
Had part in this faire maide, now heaven hath all,
And all the better is it for the maid:
Your part in her, you could not keepe from death,
But heaven keepes his part in eternall life:
The most you sought was her promotion,
For twas your heaven she should be advanst,
And weepe ye now, seeing she is advanst

30

Above the Cloudes, as high as heaven it selfe? *(IV.v.66-74)*

The opposition of mortal and immortal parts is reiterated explicitly in Balthasar's report to the banished Romeo:

> Then she is well and nothing can be ill,
> Her body sleepes in *Capels* monument,
> And her immortall part with Angels lives. *(V.i.17-19)*

For those who would pursue the ends of their sexual parts, there is a fool's paradise offered (II.iv.176); for Romeo and Juliet, a place among the immutable stars.

The play's movement is not from sinfulness to salvation through either grace or Divine Providence,[17] but rather from an alien existence as mortals to one's true abode, figuratively represented in the stars or in heaven. The conflict focusses on the traditional antagonism between body and soul, modified however so that the conflict is not in terms of subordination of the passions. The play instead opposes the irreconcilable modes of being manifest by body and soul, the mortal and the immortal. The crisis is not whether reason can moderate passion, but whether the immortal part can survive in an earthly prison. The theme of parts is eventually brought to the implied opposition of Friar's Lawrence's rebuke,

> Why raylest thou on thy birth? the heaven and earth?
> Since birth, and heaven, and earth all three do meet
> In thee at once. *(III.iii.119-21)*

Romeo longs for death, as will Juliet, and by the play's end, they will have attained it. Birth and death are the moments marking the conjunction and divergence of heaven and earth. The play is so constructed that for Romeo and Juliet, and for the audience which shares their experience, the union is an impossible one.

Capulet misunderstood the truth he spoke in describing Juliet, not yet fourteen, as a stranger in the world (I.ii.8-9). So are all men, whether they have the sensitivity to perceive that fact or not. Romeo's banishment is a felicitous stroke, balancing Juliet's alienation. Benvolio is, therefore, half-right in saying of the dead Mercutio,

> That gallant spirit hath aspir'd the Clowdes,
> Which too untimely here did scorne the earth. *(III.i.122-23)*

All death is timely, since time is death's instrument. Hence the propriety of the Nurse's lamentation, which curses the day and not the supposed fact of Juliet's death, a woeful, lamentable, hateful day, a day never so black as this (IV.v.49-54).

The Friar's long recapitulation of the tragic sequence (V.iii.229-69) at the play's close is, thematically if not poetically, valid, in its continual placing of events in the context of time. The Friar refers to time, now early, now late, now exact. The marriage day is stolen, the potion loses its power on "this dire night," the Friar returns "some minute ere the time" of "the prefixed hower." Death however is consistently referred to as untimely, and the Friar's speech thereby fulfills a theme already established in the play. Romeo had been apprehensive about the "vile forfeit of untimely death" (I.iv.111) before his meeting with Juliet, and Capulet, gazing on his daughter's still form, had believed that

> Death lies on her like an untimely frost,
> Upon the sweetest flower of all the field.   *(IV.v.28-29)*

For the Friar, "*Tybalts* doomesday" brought his "untimely death," and side by side in Capel's monument,

> here untimely lay
> The Noble *Paris*, and true *Romeo* dead.

As for himself, he is willing to "be sacrific'd, some houre before his time." Wiser far than the Friar and Benvolio, who had thought Mercutio's death untimely, Ben Jonson understood that his own son's death was timely, being "Exacted by [his] fate, on the just day" ("On My First Son").

The general note of death touching all the principals which marks the play's end is therefore entirely valid thematically. Lady Capulet hears her death knell, Lady Montague has died, and the Friar, like Capulet early in the play, anticipates his own death. In the First Quarto, moreover, Benvolio's death is reported. Juliet is not singular; no man may "weare out the everlasting flint" (II.vi.17). For these reasons, the Friar's words to Romeo,

> Affliction is enamourd of thy parts,
> And thou art wedded to calamitie.   *(III.iii.2-3)*

apply generally, for all men await the calamity of death which will claim their mortal parts. By the play's end, the strangers are all gone, even as they departed from Capulet's residence, itself a metaphor for the world. On the occasion of the party, when earth-treading stars invaded his home, "well appareld Aprill" supplanted "limping winter," and "fresh fennell buds" inherited his house (I.ii.27-30). Winter still attends, though, as does the canker, and such a mansion must be abandoned, and the soul's mansion must be sacked for a mansion of love.

What's Montague, then, but that singular part which can escape time's ravages, all else being but "a forme of waxe, Digressing from the valour of a man" (III.iii.126-127)? No less than for the sonnets, time is a major factor in the play, and Shakespeare's careful manipulation of sequence goes beyond the plotter's preoccupation with timing.[18] True, timing creates the plot,[19] but time in the play is not used to illustrate the youthful vice of impetuosity, but to develop a tragic action centering on the conquest of time.

The preponderance of critical investigations into time in *Romeo and Juliet* have been concerned with the intervals between events, from the relatively simple matter of the duration of the represented events, to the number of hours between the individual incidents. Among the judgments arising from these inquiries is that the play exhibits "double time"[20] with the lovers hasty and precipitous,[21] and their parents and the older characters cautious and deliberate. The inconvenient fact that Old Capulet later contradicts himself by insisting upon a quick marriage for Juliet is explained as a relinquishing to the impetuosity of youth.[22] Actually, the treatment of time is more complex than the simple association of haste with youthful impatience and deliberation with mature action. For one thing, the elder Capulets do not always move in conjunction: at first, Old Capulet is reluctant to allow Paris' suit, while his wife favors it. The reason he urges Paris to wait is the same his wife uses to promote the match: the girl is nearly fourteen. At that age, Juliet's mother, as did many "ladies of esteeme" in Verona, bore a child (I.iii.70-74); Paris agrees with the proposition that Juliet is at the proper age for marriage. Old Capulet, of course, feels otherwise (I.ii.8-11). However, at another point touching on time, the parents are coordinated in their unawareness of its passage. Remarkably, Lady Capulet is uncertain of Juliet's precise age, a fact which the Nurse provides. Similarly, Old Capulet cannot properly fix the years since last he masked; he grossly underestimates the years since Lucentio's wedding (I.v.31-41).[23] In each case, Shakespeare provides a character who is able to define the forgotten date with precision. The dramatic point is clearly that these two individuals, and not older people in general, live their lives unaware of time, though time takes its toll. Before he knows it, Old Capulet must give up his sword for a crutch (I.i.82-83). Rather than instances of sober judgement, the Capulets are the unwitting victims of time's ravages.

> But old folks, many fain as they wer dead,
> Unwieldie, slowe, heavie, and pale as lead.   *(II.v.16-17)*

Better instead to feign death by yielding one's mortal parts to death so that one may "bound a pitch above dull woe" (I.iv.21).

In contrast to Lady Capulet's unawareness of time is the Nurse's sharp recall of its passage, precisely measured in terms of disaster.[24] Susan, who should be Juliet's age, is dead, as is her father. The weaning itself is well fixed in time by the earthquake. Though the event has escaped Lady Capulet's memory, the nurse will remember it a thousand years because of her husband's little joke. Even Old Capulet is not so caught up in the present that he cannot realize his advanced age, and in his best line in the play, he confesses of his youth, "'Tis gone, 'tis gone, 'tis gone" (I.v.26). Reason enough to call throughout the scene, "more light, more light" (I.v.29,89,127), for soon enough the darkness comes to swallow his last hope.

Until he too is caught up in the frantic events, the Friar is singularly free in his own mind of time's pace, standing apart to comment on haste, now in Romeo, now in Paris. It is instructive that despite his self-discipline, his careful planning, and his conscientious observing of his appointed hour at Capel's tomb, he is no more successful in controlling time than any other character. His oft-quoted maxim, "Wisely and slow, they stumble that run fast," (II.iii.94) must be counterbalanced by the paradoxical, "Too swift arrives, as tardie as too slowe" (II.vi.15). Slowly done is not always wisely done; one may as well proceed swiftly, for the results are the same. And, as is consistent with the play's thematic structure, there is no middle ground of moderation, though the Friar thinks there is (II.vi.14). His own utter failure as benevolent intriguer is sufficient testimony of his error.

In the sonnets addressed to his friend, Shakespeare offers two resources against fell Time, heirs and art. After the manner of the sonnet tradition, Romeo laments the barren course followed by Rosaline, and he complains of love's effect upon him, fettering him to dull earth. As the play proceeds to demonstrate, Romeo is wrong in both respects. In the tragedy, if not in the sonnets, beauty will survive by the love it inspires, since love is its own value. It can overwhelm its antagonist, death, since death holds power over dull earth alone. That love frees man — rather than burdening man with a soul of lead or staking him to the ground (I.iv. 15,16,19-22) — is symbolically demonstrated in the easy movement of young Romeo climbing the stony limits of Capulet's walls (II.ii.66-67). Later, before Balthasar brings news of Juliet's interrment, Romeo speaks of his dream (V.i.1-11), the point of which is too often taken for simple dramatic irony. Shakespeare does not merely wish to sharpen the anguish of Balthasar's news by first having Romeo anticipate joyful news. The imagery is too carefully coordinated with earlier speeches to allow for so limited an intent. He has had a dream; his bosom's lord — that is, that part above all other parts — sits lightly in his throne, and he is again lifted above the ground; and the dream itself represented Juliet's reviving him from death, for even as he prepares to take his deadly "Cordiall and not poyson" (V.i.85), Romeo experiences a lightening before attaining "A datelesse bargaine to ingrossing death" (V.iii.115), a "timelesse end" (V.iii.162). Juliet, in perfect harmony with her beloved, kisses Romeo, paradoxically, to "dye with a restorative" (V.iii.166). For each, the other is quick despite all contrary appearances:

> Death that hath suckt the honey of thy breath,
> Hath had no power upon thy bewtie:
> Thou art not conquerd. *(V.iii.92-94)*

> Thy lips are warme. *(V.iii.167)*

Not only does love have the power to lift man above the limits imposed by his gross body, but it can confer a vitality beyond death. Romeo's error in complaining of Rosaline's cold chastity is that love's immortality is understood in terms of its secondary effects, the propagation of children. Romeo thinks as Old Capulet does when he charges

> O she is rich in bewtie, onely poore,
> That when she dies, with bewtie dies her store.
> . . . . .
> and in that sparing, makes huge waste:
> For bewtie sterv'd with her severitie,
> Cuts bewtie off from all posteritie. *(I.i.221-26)*

True as this conventional proposition is, it bespeaks a lower order of truth than that apprehended by Romeo as he first catches sight of Juliet at the ball. On that occasion, there are present "Earthtreading starres, that make dark heaven light" (I.ii.25), and Juliet is manifestly

34

>   a rich Jewel in an Ethiops eare,
>   Bewtie too rich for use, for earth too deare.   *(I.v.48-49)*

Shakespeare creates the conflict between mortality and immortality in a variety of ways, either by the opposition of time and eternity, or by reference to other symbols suggestive of one or the other. The lovers themselves seek night and create an artificial day, making actual the reported conduct of Romeo, who, while pledged to Rosaline, "away from light steales . . . locks faire day-light out, And makes himselfe an artificiall night" (I.i.143-46). Though Romeo's affection will change, he is nevertheless correct in his conduct, as Juliet well knows, for

>   Lovers can see to do their amorous rights,
>   By their owne bewties,   *(III.ii.8-9)*

Miss Spurgeon missed this essential point about Shakespeare's light imagery, equating as she does "the irradiating glory of sunlight and starlight in a dark world."[25] The difference depends upon a realization of the symbolic import of sun and stars, one as the measure of time and the other as the symbol of timelessness. It is by the self-created rays of love that our young heroes can attain a stellar constancy.

There are in the play two schemes of time, that of the real world—incessant and implacable, now too soon, now too late, but ever true to itself, and that measured by the lovers. These timepieces are metaphorically represented, the one traditionally as Phoebus' chariot, and the other, by Queen Mab's chariot. The sun is represented in all its ruthlessness by Romeo's image:[26]

>   The grey eyde morne smiles on the frowning night,
>   Checkring the Easterne Clouds with streaks of light,
>   And darknesse fleckled like a drunkard reeles,
>   From forth daies pathway, made by *Tytans* wheeles.   *(II.iii.1-4)*

In addition to the picture of relentless force overwhelming all in the sun's path, there is the promise that the night's dew will be consumed as the sun progresses (II.iii.6), an ill omen for the lovers who have just created the rhapsody of the balcony scene by night, that time when "the earth doth drisle deaw" (III.v.127).

Romeo and Juliet can never exist under the servitude imposed by time, for the rhythms of their lives, now one, are measured by Queen Mab. Far from a poetic but dramatically irrelevant outburst, Mercutio's speech (I.iv.53-95) is central to the play's meaning. Like the sun, Queen Mab too courses through the skies in a chariot, but unlike her opposite,

>   she comes
>   In shape no bigger than an Agot stone,
>   On the forefinger of an Alderman,
>   Drawne with a teems of little attomie,

> Over mens noses as they lie asleep:
> . . . . .
> Her waggonspokes made of long spinners legs,
> The cover, of the wings of Grashoppers,
> Her traces of the smallest spider web,
> Her collors of the moonshines watry beams,
> Her whip of Crickets bone, the lash of philome. *(I.iv.54-63)*

In the delicacy of detail, Queen Mab's vehicle is like the chariot Juliet imagines will transport love to her. Love is drawn by "nimblepiniond doves" (II.v.7), and

> loves heraulds should be thoughts,
> Which ten times faster glides then the Suns beames,
> Driving backe shadowes over lowring hills. *(II.v.4-6)*

Juliet would toy with her imprisoned bird, using nothing more than "a silken threed" (II.ii.181) to confine it.

Queen Mab is not the goddess of love; rather she is the figure of subjective reality, bringing to men the dreams they dream. To the soldier, and to quarrelsome men like Mercutio and Tybalt, she brings the desired realities

> of cutting forrain throates,
> Of breaches, ambuscados, spanish blades,
> Of healths five fadome deepe. *(I.iv.83-85)*

But for such as Romeo, who dream of love, love comes.[27] As with so much else in this play, Mab is a figure of ambivalence, for her confusions, however mischievous, must be yielded to:

> this is that very Mab
> That plats the manes of horses in the night:
> And bakes the Elflocks in foule sluttish haires,
> Which once untangled, much misfortune bodes.
> This is the hag, when maides lie on their backs,
> That presses them and learnes them first to beare,
> Making them women of good carriage. *(I.iv.88-94)*

With more meaning than Romeo perceives, he charges Mercutio with talking of nothing; but everything in the play is built on nothing, from the "three civill brawles bred of an airy word" (I.i.96) to the love so pure that it transforms Juliet to one like him who

> bestrides the lazie passing Cloudes,
> And sayles upon the bosome of the ayre. *(II.ii.31-32)*

and enables Romeo to master his gross element, to

> orepearch these walls,
> For stonie limits cannot hold love out,

36

And what love can do, that dares love attempt.   *(II.ii.66-68)*

After all,

> A lover may bestride the gossamours,
> That ydeles in the wanton sommer ayre,
> And yet not fall.[28]   *(II.vi.18-20)*

Indeed, Juliet's love for Romeo is for that part which is nothing, being no physical part of the man. The inevitable direction of the drama is that forecast by Juliet for Romeo:

> when I shall die,
> Take him and cut him out in little starres,
> And he will make the face of heaven so fine,
> That all the world will be in love with night,
> And pay no worship to the garish Sun.   *(III.ii.21-25)*

Love, Romeo's "any thing of nothing first create" (I.i.183), confers immortality because it is generated from nothing and cannot share in the corruption and decay awaiting all things.

Love, measured by the standards of the world, is inadequate. Fragile because it is compounded of ephemeral realities, love is suspect. Those who know of the secret love—Romeo, Juliet, the Friar—all at one or another time warn of its dangers. When it appears that Romeo will never claim his bride, the Nurse suggests a reasonable expedient. The Friar, though he lends his counsel, sanctions the relationship on peripheral considerations, the feud between the houses. Otherwise, he is dubious. Even Romeo and Juliet have their misgivings. There is a point of divergence, nevertheless, which carries Romeo and Juliet beyond the simple realities of the Friar and the Nurse. Significantly, Juliet first weans from the Nurse, at whose breast she sucked wisdom, and later, from her ghostly father.

The love between Romeo and Juliet is just such a dream as Mercutio spoke of,

> Begot of nothing but vaine phantasie:
> Which is as thin of substance as the ayre,
> And more inconstant then the wind who wooes
> Even now the frozen bosome of the North:
> And being angerd puffes away from thence,
> Turning his side to the dewe dropping South.   *(I.iv.98-103)*

Spoken just before Romeo meets Juliet, these lines figuratively anticipate his erratic progress from old love to new love. Moreover, they suggest that the change of affection is not rooted in fickleness, but is rather generated by obvious wisdom in turning from a barren suit to one which is promising. As in Capulet's apprehensions, contrasting barrenness and fertility, the dream of love, though an airy nothing, cannot be satisfied with the nothingness of rejection and must turn to more hospitable climes. There, love can truly come into being, for until it is requited, it is only devotion.

37

In the management of the imagery, the evanescent nature of love is freely confessed. It is begot of nothing, it is, like the dew, the spider's thread. Moreover,

> It is too rash, too unadvisd, too sudden,
> Too like the lightning which doth cease to bee,
> Ere one can say it lightens.   (II.ii.118-20)

Love, as Romeo is well aware,

> is but a dreame,
> Too flattering sweete to be substantiall.   (II.ii.140-41)

These lines, among others, are often thought to serve as foreshadowing of tragic consequences for the youth's hasty and immoderate love. In support of this contention are offered the complementary images of gun-powder and explosions.[29] Nevertheless, as in the Friar's long speech on herbs, there is an ambiguity in the comparison of love to lightning. Although the enveloping darkness instantly prevails over the brief moment of illumination, that moment itself is precious. The paradox is that however slender the experience afforded by love, it can in its brief span create values otherwise forever obscure. This is the limitation Romeo accepts, and quite rightly, regardless of what the Friar has to say. The Friar, in terms of the perspectives created for this play, speaks a simple contradiction, and not a paradox, in advising Romeo to "love moderately," for "long love doth so" (II.vi.14). Being outside of time, love is neither long nor short, and Romeo has the higher truth. As an absolute value, it can hardly be moderated without being vitiated.

An understanding of the dramatic use of the devices and themes of Elizabethan sonnet conventions yields an approach to the tragic meaning of the play. Though defective in several respects—one recalls Schücking's charge that Romeo, unlike Troilus, is not truly masculine[30]—the play creates its tragic effects despite inconsistent levels of poetic accomplishment and inadequate character development. For the tragic issue lies in the exposure of life's impossibility. Death for the Elizabethans was feared "as the conclusion to all accomplishment. It was," Theodore Spencer explains, "a kind of horrible joke which grinned at impotent desire and mocked all achievement into air. Because death destroyed them, beauty and power and wealth were hollow on their own account, not in comparison to the pleasures of heaven."[31] The play uses love to create a value for life and a means of sustaining it. When that value is threatened by death, the center of the tragedy moves to mortality, an area of experience far more comprehensive than young love. Because the play does not revolve around the eccentricities of the principal characters, it can transcend supposed weaknesses in their conception or execution. Critics have recognized that the play generates pity and pathos, while withholding the final constituent, fear or terror, by which the play achieves stature as tragedy.[32] I would claim both effects for the play, for there is a terrible beauty in the inevitable course toward ruin, yet transcended.[33] In its own way, the tragedy of *Romeo and Juliet* is built around the same awareness which in *Hamlet* is expressed as the consummation devoutly to be wished, in *Antony and Cleopatra* as immortal longings, the shackling of accident, and the bolting up of change.

The tragic basis of the drama does not lie in moral or personality defects. *Romeo and Juliet* is not a tragedy of character. As in the sonnets, love is used as a vehicle for representing, simultaneously, man's subjection to time and decay and man's ability to transcend the limits prescribed by his mortal nature. Paradoxically, by seizing the day, lovers can triumph over time. It is precisely because man is born to die that the play moves inexorably to its conclusion, dateless death. What distinguishes Romeo and Juliet is not their impetuosity, for so too are Mercutio and Tybalt, Lady Capulet and her husband, and the County Paris impetuous. The tragic experience is exclusively reserved for the lovers because they alone perceive, gradually, that the scope and compass allotted by time is not enough. With such an awareness, there is no recourse for a man

But to rejoyce in splendor of mine owne.   *(I.ii.106)*

Notes:

(1)   All citations are taken from George Walton Williams' critical edition, *The Most Excellent and Lamentable Tragedie of Romeo and Juliet* (Durham, N. C., 1964).

(2)   See his note to I.i 180 of the Arden edition, as well as Shakespeare: *A Critical Study of His Mind and Art*, 3rd ed. (New York, 1881), p. 94. See also, Wolfgang Clemen, *The Development of Shakespeare's Imagery* (Cambridge, Mass., 1951), p. 79, and Irving Ribner, *Patterns in Shakespearian Tragedy* (London, 1960), p. 32. According to Miss Lu Emily Pearson, in this play "Shakespeare shows first the break between Petrarchan love and natural love" (*Elizabethan Love Conventions*, Berkeley, 1933, p. 291). George Ian Duthie holds "the poetic inanities of the lamentations of Capulet, his wife, and the Nurse in 4.5 are no doubt intended by Shakespeare to symbolize the poverty of their emotional life and the smallness of their spiritual stature, as contrasted with the richness and greatness of the emotional and spiritual being of the hero and heroine" (Introduction to the edition by John Dover Wilson and George Ian Duthie, Cambridge, 1955, p. xxxiv). E. E. Stoll, commenting on Juliet's lamentation over Tybalt, attributes the lines to "the immaturity of Shakespeare's art," though he mitigates this criticism by allowing for the dramatic requirements of the situation (*Shakespeare's Young Lovers*, New York, 1966, pp. 32-33; first printed, 1937).

(3)   Especially useful are essays by M. M. Mahood, in *Shakespeare's Wordplay* (London, 1957), pp. 56-72, and by John Lawlor, in *Early Shakespeare, Stratford-upon-Avon Studies* III (London, 1961), 123-43. Lawlor amplifies G. Bullough's observation in *Narrative and Dramatic Sources of Shakespeare*, 1957, I, 278) that Shakespeare "makes Romeo's conventional passion express itself in contradictions and paradoxes suited to the pattern of the whole play." Robert O. Evans, *The Osier Cage: Rhetorical Devices in Romeo & Juliet* (Lexington, Ky., 1966), offers a detailed study of the play's rhetorical figures. Like others, he believes language (specifically, rhetoric) is used "to emphasize the development of character" (p. 97). His originality lies in defending many passages which have been faulted. Juliet's speech (III.ii. 73-79, given below), is "a subtle and extensive complex of figures . . . [which] serve[s] to refine her intellect and make her a fitting equal for Romeo (if they do not make her his superior)" (p. 36). As with many others, Mr. Evans seems prejudiced in Juliet's favor, though the girl does nothing that Romeo does not do.

(4)   On the Elizabethan sonnet, see J. W. Lever's discussion of "the conflict of Love With Time" in *The Elizabethan Love Sonnet* (London, 1956), pp. 246-72. On Shakespeare's sonnets, see G. Wilson Knight, *The Mutual Flame* (London, 1955), esp. Chapter IV, "Time and Eternity," pp. 69-103).

See also Kenneth Muir's chapter on *Romeo and Juliet* in *Shakespeare's Sources* (London, 1957), I, 21-30. Though too precise in identifying sonnet 85 in Sidney's *Astrophel and Stella* and Daniel's *Complaint of Rosamund* as influences, Muir is correct in the affirmation, "into his play Shakespeare infused the quintessence of Elizabethan love-poetry" (p. 30).

(5) Ernest William Talbert, *Elizabethan Drama and Shakespeare's Early Plays* (Chapel Hill, 1963), p. 287.

(6) For a recent presentation of this view, see Franklin M. Dickey, *Not Wisely But Too Well* (San Marino, 1957), pp. 63-117.

(7) *Romeus and Juliet*, ed. J. J. Munro (London, 1908), p. lxvi.

(8) Presumably Professor Virgil K. Whitaker had the standard of poetic excellence in mind when he warned "that it is unwise to search the implications of Shakespeare's language too closely, simply because his language is not consistent," *The Mirror up to Nature* (San Marino, 1965), p. 111. J. M. Nosworthy attributes the stylistic inconsistencies to Shakespeare's reliance on *The Two Angry Women of Abingdon*, though the lines of clearest indebtedness to Porter's play are not the worst by any means at all. "The Two Angry Families of Verona," *SQ*, III (1952), 219-26. Others have suggested revisions by the playwright to explain variations in poetic quality. I am not here concerned with the problem; regardless of inconsistencies, there is an overriding uniformity based on paradoxical oppositions.

(9) Or of comedy and violence, as Talbert points out with respect to the opening scene (p. 297).

(10) "Romeo and Juliet," *Prefaces to Shakespeare* (Princeton, 1946), IV, 50, n. 10.

(11) In Brooke she is sixteen; in Painter almost eighteen.

(12) See below, n. 29.

(13) Imagery depicting the lovers in terms of flowers and fruit is found in the following passages: I.i. 157-58, I.ii. 10-11, II.v. 44, IV.i. 99, IV.v. 29 and 37. Floral imagery is also applied to their love (II.ii. 121-22) and to Paris (I.iii. 77-78). Eventually the image merges with that of sucking: "Death that hath suckt the honey of thy breath, Hath had no power yet upon thy bewtie" (V.iii. 92-93).

(14) The Stage Direction for I.iv. reads, "*Enter Romeo, Mercutio, Benvolio, With five or six other Maskers, torchbearers.*" The text indicates that Mercutio puts his mask on (I.iv. 29-30) and that Old Cauplet has his on (I.v. 34-35).

(15) By another avenue, Irving Ribner comes to the conclusion, "it is not really the sight of Juliet which causes [Romeo] to change" (p. 29). Paul N. Siegal concludes, "Intense though their passion is, however, it is exalted." "Christianity and the Religion of Love in *Romeo and Juliet*," *SQ*, XII (1961), 380. Gordon Ross Smith places the tragedy in the context of neo-Platonic aspiration ("The Balance of Themes in *Romeo and Juliet*," *Essays in Shakespeare*, ed. G. R. Smith, Univ. Park, Pa., 1965, pp. 15-66). See also Duthie, p. xxxvii.

(16) The Friar's speech is derived from the medieval tradition and, in one sense, entirely conventional (Cf. T. J. Spencer, *Death and Elizabethan Tragedy*, New York, 1960, pp. 26-34). Shakespeare's innovation is in use of a secular context. The lovers overwhelm death, not by reason of their own virtuousness or God's redeeming grace, but because of their commitment to the values threatened by death.

(17) See Ribner, pp. 28-35.

(18) Tom F. Driver finds the handling of time in this play to be Shakespeare's means of "creating on stage the illusion of passing time," meaning that the young dramatist is concerned with realistic effects. "The Shakespearian Clock: Time and the Vision of Reality in *Romeo and Juliet* and *The Tempest*," *SQ*, XV (1964), 363-70.

(19) Whitaker claims that coincidence and chance weaken the plot (p.109). Some critics have preferred to speak of fatality, rather than chance. Examples are J. W. Draper, "Shakespeare's 'Star-Crossed Lovers,'" *RES*, XV (1939), 16-34; G. L. Kittredge, in his Introduction to *Romeo and Juliet* (Boston, 1940), p. xii; and Duthie (pp. xvii-xix). Georges A. Bonnard makes an important contribution in demonstrating that "Shakespeare himself is responsible for most of the incidents that render the catastrophe inevitable." "*Romeo and Juliet*: A Possible Significance?" *RES*, n.s. II (1951), 325.

(20) Granville-Barker, IV, 40.

(21) Brents Stirling, *Unity in Shakespearian Tragedy: The Interplay of Theme and Character* (New York, 1956), p. 19.

(22) "The leisureliness of the time of the older generation forms a background which makes the tragedy of haste even more tense by contrast. The older generation is part of the tragedy too, however, since it becomes ineffective and doomed to failure when forced to act with the speed of youth." G. Thomas Tanselle, "Time in Romeo and Juliet." *SQ*, XV (1964), 360-361. H. Edward Cain, on the contrary, finds an opposition between "Crabbed Age and Youth in 'Romeo and Juliet,' "*SAB*, IX (1934), 186-191. Bonnard's experience of tragic fatality is prompted by the heroes' isolation "in the evil of their world, being unable to understand and participate in the feelings and prejudices of their relatives" (325).

(23) There is some doubt as to whether Capulet knows Juliet's age. When he says to Paris, "Shee hath not seene the chaunge of fourteen yeares, Let two more Sommers wither in their pride, Ere we may thinke her ripe to be a bride" (I.ii. 9-11), he may mean, "I will consent when she is fourteen; but since she is only twelve, I must deny your suit." In this case, he would be in agreement with his wife in thinking fourteen a proper age, and he would be giving further evidence of his inability to keep track of the years.

(24) In tone and content, the Nurse's speech is faithful to Brooke's poem, ll. 652-660, with the significant difference provided by Shakespeare's addition of the three disasters.

(25) *Shakespeare's Imagery and What It Tells Us* (Cambridge, 1935), p. 310.

(26) Williams follows Hosley in assigning these lines to Romeo rather than to the Friar, contrary to the practice of most editors. On literary and dramatic grounds, the decision is, I believe, fortunate. See Williams' note on the passage, pp. 119-121.

(27) Norman N. Holland, applying psychoanalytic techniques to Romeo's dream, speaks of it in terms of wish-fulfillment. "Romeo's Dream and the Paradox of Literary Realism," *Literature and Psychology*, XIII (1963), 97-104.

(28) True, the Friar goes on to add, "so light is vanity," but his pejorative remark may be tested against the play's imagery, which approves of lightness, and the play's effects.

(29) Though an instrument of death, the cannon, when compared to poison, is described in paradoxical terms, its breech being compared to a womb: poison takes its effect "As violently, as hastie powder fierd / Doth hurry from the fatall Canons wombe" (V.i. 64-65).

(30) *Character Problems in Shakespeare's Plays* (New York, 1948), p. 55. First published, 1922.

(31) Spencer, p. 231.

(32) Some instances are Brents Stirling: "There is no tragic guilt in this play except the plague of both the houses; no such complexity as Aristotle held essential to tragedy. This play has pity only, no purgation by pity *and* terror" (p. 17). Whitaker finds the issue of moral culpability confused, and so the principal effect is pathetic: tears are shed "over the needless sacrifice of young love to a cruel world" (p. 113). See also, H. S. Wilson, *On the Design of Shakespearian Tragedy* (Toronto, 1957), p. 30.

(33) Though Professor Ribner goes further than I am inclined in his Christian reading of the play (pp. 25-28), he comes closer to the truth than most in placing the play in the context of Stoic tragedy. For an excellent discussion of this subject, see Hardin Craig, "The Shackling of Accidents: A Study of Elizabethan Tragedy," *PQ*, XIX (1940), 1-19. In his too brief discussion of this play, Donald A. Stauffer declares, "Love conquers death even more surely than it conquers hate. It sweeps aside all accidents, so that fate itself seems powerless." *Shakespeare's World of Images* (New York, 1949), p. 58.

A Crux and No Crux in Hamlet I.iii:
Safty: Sanctity (21) and Beguide: Beguile (131)

by Thomas Clayton

I

The first pair of variant readings is a well-known crux, the second is of paleo-graphical and linguistic interest otherwise. In line 21 of *Hamlet* I.iii (wanting in Q1), Q2 and F1 contrast thus:

> The *safty* and health of *this whole* state,   *(Q2, sig. C3ᵛ)*
>
> The *sanctity* and health of *the weole* State.   *(F1, sig. nn6ᵛa)*

In addition to the crux, the line contains two more substantive and two accidental variants. Charlton Hinman notes that F1's signature nn6ᵛ, which was not proof-corrected, was set from case x by Compositor A, or if not by A probably by C, "about whom, from a qualitative point of view, we know almost nothing."[1] If our evidence were confined to this line, however, we should have to infer that Compositor A or C was careless at either distribution or composition, or both, whatever the nature of his copy, because "weole" is plainly a manual error resulting from foul case (the *e* types are located immediately above the *h* types in the case).[2]

As for *the: this*, there are "a number of passages where F1 reads the definite article or the possessive and Q2 a demonstrative pronoun, . . . and it is easy to see the hand of the careless transcriber in these weaker F1 readings"; but in a note Dover Wilson also cites examples that "warn us to remember the possibility of interference by the compositor of 1605" (*MSH*, II, 262-263), and it seems no coincidence that, of seventeen demonstrative pronouns in Q2 for articles or possessives in F1, Compositor X, the worse of two, is responsible for all but three (Q2-Compositor Y's "this" for F1's "his").[3] These variants clearly have value as evidence for inferences about the nature of copy and the process of composition, but Wilson, remarking (inaccurately, as it now seems) that "it is an editor's duty to follow Q2," adds with some justice "though Shakespeare would not as a matter of fact take much harm if he did not" (*MSH*, II, 263).

In his New Cambridge edition of *Hamlet*, Wilson admitted, in place of Q2's "safty" and F1's "sanctity," the emendation "sanity," which was first suggested by Theobald and later endorsed by Johnson, on most of the grounds noted in the New Variorum *Hamlet*.[4] "Sanctity" was rejected because it is, here, a virtual nonsense word; but "safty"—rejected chiefly on metrical grounds—could only be retained by supplying (with Warburton) a second "the" before "health" or by reading (with Singer) "saf[ĕ]ty" as a trisyllable, notwithstanding that it is always disyllabic elsewhere in Shakespeare (and probably was so in conventional pronunciation).[5] Wilson adds that "sanctity" is misprinted for "sanity" ("Sanitie," F1) in Q2 at II.ii.212, where "sanity" has a "mental" cast, as it cannot sensibly here, and is of unique occurrence with substantive authority in Shakespeare.

Wilson's paleographical defense of "sanity" is based on the peculiarity of F1's "sanctity": "There is no graphical basis for supposing it to be a misreading of 'safety' on the part of Scribe P, while though Scribe C is capable of anything his tendency is to give us easier readings than Shakespeare intended rather than more difficult ones. Is it not possible, therefore, that the F1 nonsense word conceals the true reading? It might well enough be a minim-misprint or mistranscript for 'sanity,' which in its turn, if spelt 'sanety' by Shakespeare, might equally well have been misread 'sauety,' an old but recognised spelling of 'safety,' and set up as 'safty' by the Q2 compositor" (*MSH*, II, 316). It is worth noting in Q2's hypothetical defense that "sanctity" might just as "well enough be a minim-misprint or mistranscript" for "sauety," correctly retained but spelled "safty" in Q2.

A preponderance of the minim- or quasi-minim-letters of the Secretary hand— *m, n, u, i, c, r, w*; and sometimes, in effect, *a, e, t*—invariably increases the likelihood of manuscript illegibility and scribal or compositorial misreading, guesswork, or sophistication, and enforces especially careful consideration by the editor or critic of both textual variants and conjectural alternatives. "Sanctity," "safty" (as "sauety"), "sanity" (or "sanety"), and—a new alternative I wish to suggest for consideration—"surety," all abound in such characters, and as Wilson notes there is evidence in Q2 of compositorial misreadings resulting from confusion in the copy between—among other letters—*a:u, n:u,* and *r:n* (*MSH*, I, 106-108); and the possibility of minim-letter confusion is amply demonstrable, as in many other contemporary English hands, in Addition III (D) to the manuscript play, *Sir Thomas More*, which I accept as being in Shakespeare's hand.[6]

The still vexed question of the precise relationship between *Hamlet* Q1, Q2, and F1 enters here, but no hypothetical answer to it is of much help in deciding between some textual alternatives. Whether Act I of Q2 was set partly from Q1 or not is irrelevant: since the appropriate passage was wanting in Q1, Q2 had to have it from manuscript copy, that is, from Shakespeare's foul papers, as most textual critics agree with Dover Wilson. Nor does it much matter whether we suppose that F1 was set from a copy of Q2 annotated by collation with a manuscript (Alice Walker), or from a playhouse prompt-book, or a transcript of it, supplemented and corrected by reference to printed copy (Dover Wilson and Harold Jenkins).[7] Where two ambiguously substantive texts diverge, we are left—as we should be with certainly independent substantive texts—to decide the matter by the respective merits of the readings and by whatever inferences from the bibliographical facts we can adduce in support of one or the other, or against both. And the evidence of such variant readings is often equivocal: besides the possibility of derivation of the later from the earlier, each could accurately or inaccurately reflect either a common original or a variant copy reading. As for the variants under discussion, if we were to postulate different copy readings as the cause of variation, there would be no paleographical argument either to explain or to support the textual (and conjectural) alternatives, and—"sanctity" being dismissible as nonsense—"safty" would have to be accepted or rejected virtually on its criti-

44

cal merits alone as presumptively authoritative or sophisticated. If, however, we suppose with Dover Wilson that the same reading does—or could—lie behind the variants, either one or both may be wrong.

Certainly but not only through Wilson's conjectural "true" reading, "sanety," the argument from paleography militates against Q2's "safty." If Q2's copy infer-ably was and *More* Addition III is in Shakespeare's hand, the evidence of the latter is decisive: unlike many of hand D's words, "safer" (l. 112) is unambiguous, and the formation of his *f* would have left it so whether he spelled "saf[e]ty" with or without the *e*.[8] If "safty" were authorial, "sanctity" would have to be wrong, either through misreading of "saf[e]ty"—an apparent impossibility (whether by a scribe or a compositor is irrelevant)—or through sophistication, of which "sanctity" is, as relative nonsense for good sense, a very unlikely example. If "sanctity" does reflect the true reading, as its very wrongness suggests, then "safty" is certainly wrong, either through misreading or sophistication; and, owing to their extensive if not exactly equal "minimization," "sanctity" itself, "sanity," and "surety" are about equally defensible on paleographical grounds.

Confidence in "safty" is not increased by the suggestion of a conspectus of Q2's errors that "Roberts [Compositor] X was more prone to error than Roberts Y" and the fact that no "sheet set by Y [is] so manifestly careless as X's sheet G," as Alice Walker notes; she concludes that "the errors in Q2 must . . . be laid to the charge of the compositors."[9] If Compositor X misread his copy (and he apparently did mis-read "sanctity" for "sanity" on F1[v]), he did not misread an eccentric spelling of "safty"; and there remains, *prima facie,* a paleographical case for Wilson's "sanity" as well as for the other alternatives.

But there are also semantic considerations at stake here. "Sanctity" does not require extended dismissal. Although it is doubtful, Shakespeare may have in-tended no more than metrical expletion, and Theobald's "sanity" is an intelligent and satisfactory emendation of Q2's metrically deficient "safty." Nevertheless, if "sanity" means only—as Wilson glosses it—"welfare, soundness," and "soundness of condition generally" (New Cambridge *Hamlet,* pp. 155, 284), then it is rather more expletive than Warburton's metrically remedial interpolation of "the" (be-fore "health") and is indeed substituted "with what is surely undue insistence on the Ministry of Health in Denmark," as Sisson remarks.[10] He pointedly adds, more-over, that "the *safety* of the state in Elizabethan thought was in the forefront, and dependent upon the Prince. Cf. the *Book of Common Prayer,* 'the safety, honour, and welfare of our Sovereign and her dominions.' Shakespeare went to church."

If "sanity" is most defensible on metrical, and "saf[e]ty" on general semantic grounds, "surety"—metrically more defensible than "safty"[11]—is so from the immediate context of the scene and passage, in which a number of the figures, both explicit and implied, and the overall drift of sense, are prominently legal and financial:[12]

Perhaps he loves you now,
And now no soil nor cautel doth besmirch

The virtue of his will. But you must fear,
His greatness weighed, his will is not his own,
For he himself is subject to his birth.
He may not, as unvalued persons do,
Carve for himself, for on his choice depends
The *surety* and health of this whole state,
And therefore must his choice be circumscribed
Unto the voice and yielding of that body
Whereof he is the head. Then if he says he loves you,
It fits your wisdom so far to believe it
As he in his particular act and place
May give his saying deed, which is no further
Than the main voice of Denmark goes withal.

(Lines 14-28; for convenience of
interpretation, I have substituted—and italicized—"surety")

Certainly, "will," in lines 16 and 17, is Hamlet's 'disposition' and 'inclination,' and "deed," in line 27, the 'act' that fulfills the promissory word; but part of what gives the passage—as well as others in the scene—its peculiar life and strength is the simultaneous metaphorical expression of essentially the same tenor through intermediate legal-financial vehicles. Most explicitly, the *will* is also a 'testament,' and the *deed* an 'indenture,' to which there were two or more parties (in this context, one Hamlet, the other the people: head and body);[13] and "cautel" (legal wile), in line 15, and "virtue" (efficacy, legal power), in line 16, work in close semi-technical consonance with them. Furthermore, even the metaphor in "He may not . . . / Carve for himself" (lines 19-20), which with the complementary metaphors of "body" and "head" appears more akin to the parable of the belly than to the actions of the law courts, is closely associated with the law: for "it is not lawful for legataries to *carve for themselves,* taking their legacies at their own pleasure, but must have them delivered by the executors," according to Henrie Swinburn, in *A Briefe Treatise of Testaments and Last Willes* (London, 1590), p. 50, in which "cautel" also figures prominently.[14] In this connection Hamlet is figuratively said to be a "legatary" in the choice of a wife, and of the matrimonial legacy of his will the people are executors.

"Surety" includes all the relevant senses of "safty," and would have here the opposite of the pejorative emphasis in "The wound of peace is surety, / Surety secure" (*Tro.,* II.ii.14-15). It has, in addition, a legal and contractual basis—as 'a formal agreement entered into, a pledge, bond, guarantee, or security given for the fulfilment of an undertaking'[15]—that is complemented by the quasi-legal "circumscribed" in line 22. Also relevant here is *Sonnet* 134, which shares, though not in the same degree, the legal-financial figuration of these lines (as well as the double entendre later in the same conversation between Laertes and Ophelia):

So now I have confess'd that he is thine,
And I myself am mortgag'd to thy will;

My self I'll forfeit, so that other mine
Thou wilt restore to be my comfort still.
But thou wilt not, nor he will not be free,
For thou art covetous, and he is kind;
He learn'd but *surety-like* to write for me
Under that bond that him as fast doth bind.
The statute of thy beauty thou wilt take,
Thou usurer that put'st forth all to use,
And sue a friend came debtor for my sake;
So him I lose through my unkind abuse.
    Him have I lost; thou hast both him and me;
    He pays the whole, and yet am I not free.[16]

The collocation of similar vehicles and analogous tenors in the two passages is highly suggestive. The sense of *surety* in "surety-like"—'a person who undertakes some specific responsibility on behalf of another who remains primarily liable; one who makes himself liable for the default or miscarriage of another, or for the performance of some act on his part (e.g., payment of a debt, appearance in court for trial, etc.)'[17]—is somewhat different from the primary legal one urged in the *Hamlet* passage, but it is not altogether extraneous there. The function of a *surety* (person) is to assure the *surety* (security, interest) of the person(s) he represents: in amatory transactions, John Alden's is to speak for Miles Standish; in the business of monarchy, the king's is to act for his people. In the *Sonnet*'s "He [who] learn'd but surety-like to write for me," the emphasis falls on the innocent surety who hast lost his various worth through seduction by a creditor's cautel. In *Hamlet* I.iii, Laertes emphasizes Hamlet's courtship as a kind of matrimonial power of attorney: as prince and future king, he is truly bound to circumscribe his choice "unto the voice and yielding" of the people in order to guarantee their surety (safety, security) and perhaps, too, to maintain his virtue and identity as their regal surety.

The case for "surety" as emendation seems to me a strong one: it has paleographical equality with both textual alternatives and Theobald's emendation, probable metrical equality with the others and superiority over "saf[e]ty," and semantic superiority over all the alternatives. Q2's "saf[e]ty" is certainly defensible, but if it is rejected "surety" would seem to be its strongest emendation.

II

In the substantive variant readings in line 131,

The better to *beguide*: this is for all,	*(Q2, sig. C4ᵛ)*
The better to *beguile*. This is for all:	*(F1, sig. nn6ᵛ b)*

there is no real textual crux, and F1's "beguile" is so manifestly "right" that it must be accepted, whether the reading is supposed to have manuscript authority or to be a compositor's or corrector's sophistication.[18] The standard lay of the case and the easy distinguishability of *d* and *l* types virtually preclude typographical error, but since the often careless Compositor X set sig. C4^v the error is not surprising (nor is it especially noteworthy that on H2^v [at III.ii.236], where it is the rhyme word for "while," Compositor Y correctly set "beguile"[19]).

If "beguide" is a curious misunderstanding, it is an understandable and not necessarily careless misreading of such forms of "beguile" as might have been written in Shakespeare's own hand and could lie behind the readings of both Q2 and F1.[20] And it is possible that "beguide" is itself a sophistication of an illegible form, perhaps even one related to the infinitive verb of *Lucrece*, in

> To me came TARQUIN armed to beguild
> VVith outward honestie, but yet defild
> VVith inward vice.
> $\qquad\qquad\qquad\qquad\qquad$ *(Q [1594], sig. L1^v)*

which has much bedeviled editors but is almost certainly right and authorial.[21] But sophistication in *Hamlet* Q2's "beguide" is improbable, and the matter of terminal *e* vs. *d* is in any case somewhat academic, because in Shakespeare's cursive hand (and many others of the period) these letters are often indistinguishable.[22] The most serious paleographical ambiguity is likely to have arisen with the preterminal characters, *uid:uil*. Thompson notes of the handwriting of *More* Addition III that *i* is "in no position... a conspicuous letter," and "in the middle of a word it is often reduced, in hurried writing, to a very small scale"; that *ul* and *id* may easily be misread for each other; and that *u* is "often written negligently small" ("Handwriting," pp. 82, 94, and 100). Shakespeare was apparently often careless also in supplying the correct number of minims to several minim letters in sequence, and one cannot be certain what stood in Q2's copy: "begule" (or even "beguld") would have resulted most excusably in the misreading, "beguide," but it is as likely that a hastily written "beguile" was the copy reading as anything else.[23]

I am persuaded that "surety" is the strongest possible emendation of *safty: sanctity* in line 21, and I agree, as probably few have ever doubted, that "beguide" is a misreading of "beguile," in Shakespeare's own hand. I am also convinced that it is unfortunate that the kind of paleographical study and even speculation practiced so ardently and so well by Sir Edmund Maunde Thompson and Dover Wilson has fallen relatively far from favor during the past three decades, because there is a great deal still to be learned by critic and editor alike from close study of *More* Addition III and comparison of its characteristics with the extant substantive texts of Shakespeare's plays.[24]

Notes:

(1) *The Printing and Proof-Reading of the First Folio of Shakespeare* (Oxford, 1963), I, 300; II, 217-219, 512-514, 516.

(2) On the other hand, missettings of *r* and *t* (on opposite sides of the case) are the result of visual errors, which Compositor B, from case y, commits on sigs. nn5a ("ir" for "it," I.i.140), pp2a ("patt" for "part," III.iv.97), qq1b ("rhis" for "this," V.ii.350), and qq1^{v}b ("ro" for "to," V.ii.388).

See J. Dover Wilson, *The Manuscript of Shakespeare's Hamlet* (Cambridge, and New York, 1934), II, 345 (hereafter abbreviated "*MSH*"), and Hinman, I, 300, 302, 304; II, 516-517. General references are made to and quotations taken from the New Cambridge Shakespeare *Hamlet*, ed. J. Dover Wilson (Cambridge, 1934), except where otherwise noted.

(3)   My F1:Q2 examples—*the: this* (5), *his: this* (7), *the: their* (1), *the: those* (3), and *the: that* (1)—are taken from Wilson's Appendix E, "A Table of Variants in the Dialogue of *Hamlet*, Q2 and F1" (*MSH*, II, 370-426), and the division of work on Q2 by Compositors X and Y (Wilson thought there was only one compositor) from John Russell Brown, "The Compositors of *Hamlet* Q2 and *The Merchant of Venice*," *Studies in Bibliography*, VII (1955), 19 (cf. Fredson Bowers, "The Printing of *Hamlet*, Q2," same issue, p. 42). Brown divides the work as follows (for convenience I have added the standard act-scene-line numeration of the Globe edition as used in *Shakespeare Quartos in Collotype Facsimile Number 4: Hamlet Second Quarto 1604-5*, introd. W. W. Greg, Shakespeare Assoc. [London, 1940]): *Compositor X*: B1-D4^v (I.i.1-v.184), F1-4^v (II.ii.161-605), I1-4^v (III.iii.21-iv.210), L1 (IV.v.90-121), L4 (IV.vii.101-136), and N1-O2 (V.i.306-ii.414). *Compositor Y*: E1-4^v (I.v.185-II.ii.160), G1-H4^v (II.ii.606-III.iii.20), K1-4^v (III.iv.211-IV.v.89), L1^v-4 (IV.v.122-vii.100), and M1-4^v (IV.vii.137-V.i.305).

(4)   Ed. H. H. Furness (New York, 1877; repub. New York: Dover Publications, Inc., 1963), I, 62.

(5)   "Always" is of course tentative; Bartlett's *Concordance*, derived from the Folio-based Globe edition, is the chief authority for these assertions. Eighteenth-century scholars were especially prone to editorial meretricity in metrical matters.

(6)   Of this portion of the manuscript, ff. 8-9^r of BM MS. Harl. 7368, there are reproductions in Sir Edmund Maunde Thompson, *Shakespeare's Handwriting* (Oxford, 1916), between pp. 32 and 33, and *Shakespeare Survey*, II (1949), between pp. 48 and 49. Cf. Thompson's "The Handwriting of the Three Pages Attributed to Shakespeare Compared with his Signatures," and the illustrations of individual letters in the signatures and the *More* Addition, in *Shakespeare's Hand in the Play of Sir Thomas More*, introd. Alfred W. Pollard (Cambridge, 1923), pp. 57-112 and pls. v-vi, between pp. 80 and 81, and pl. vii, between pp. 102 and 103. For the immediate purposes, particularly noteworthy in *More* Addition III are the ambiguous *ur*[e]:*an*[e] in "figure" (l. 102) and "nature" (l. 126); *n:u* in "Comaund" (l. 52), "offend" (l. 61), "Ingland" (l. 73), "sound" (l. 89), and "hound" (l. 122); and *u:r* in "Comaund" (l. 99). A minim (apparently of *n*) is wanting in "sounde" (l. 117) and "found" (l. 147). The *a*, following initial *s*, is generally connected and unambiguous (and *u* would be an unlikely misreading of it), but the *u* following initial *s*, which is generally unconnected, often resembles and might easily be misread as an open *a*, and as Thompson notes "the forms (closed and open) of the *a* . . . are used indifferently in the Addition" ("Handwriting," p. 86).

(7)   See Alice Walker, ch. vi, *Hamlet*, in *Textual Problems of the First Folio* (Cambridge, 1953), pp. 121-137, and Jenkins, "The Relation Between the Second Quarto and the Folio Text of *Hamlet*," *Studies in Bibliography*, VII (1955), 69-83; and cf. Dover Wilson, *MSH*, I, 66-67.

(8)   See the examples of *f* in pl. v in *Shakespeare's Hand* (n. 6).

(9)   "Collateral Substantive Texts (with Special Reference to *Hamlet*)," *Studies in Bibliography*, VII (1955), 57, 60, 65.

(10) *New Readings in Shakespeare* (Cambridge, 1955), II, 209.

(11) Although the word is commonly disyllabic in Shakespeare, it would seem to have been often trisyllabic, or virtually trisyllabic, in contemporary pronunciation (see E. J. Dobson, *English Pronunciation* [Oxford, 1957], I, 103; II, sec. 218 [pp. 760-762]).

(12) The passage is analysed in detail in my article, "The Quibbling Polonii and the *Pious Bonds*: the Rhetoric of *Hamlet* I.iii," *Shakespeare Studies*, II (1966), 59-94.

(13) See Paul S. Clarkson and Clyde T. Warren, *The Law of Property in Shakespeare and the Elizabethan Drama* (Baltimore, 1942), p. 120.

(14) Quoted from William Lowes Rushton, *Shakespeare's Testamentary Language* (London, 1869), p. 43 (quoted in part in the Variorum *Hamlet*, I, 61).

(15) See *OED* s.v. *Surety, sb.* 1, 3, and 5.

(16) *Works*, ed. Peter Alexander (London and Glasgow, 1951).

(17) *OED* s.v. *Surety, sb.* 7, ll. 7-8 above given as example.

(18) This pair of variants, like so many others, is of little help to a solution of the F1-copy problem, since "beguile" may be argued as an easy sophistication of "beguide," though it is by no means certainly so.

(19) Moreover, the words of the Q2 line are substantively identical in Q1 (F3^v).

(20) Dover Wilson long ago briefly noted Q2's "beguide" as a misreading of "beguile" (*MSH*, I, 112).

(21) In "The Compositors of *Hamlet* Q2" (n. 3), p. 31, John Russell Brown remarks that "it would seem that either these workmen [Compositors X and Y] were abnormally rushed while setting *Hamlet*, . . . or else their copy was abnormally illegible." On *Lucrece*'s "beguild," see the New Arden Shakespeare *Poems*, ed. F. T. Prince (London and Cambridge, Mass., 1960), p. 136, where the editor, quoting Pooler's explanation that "an excrescent 'd' or 't' is common," suggests that "'beguild' is simply a colloquial variant of 'beguile.'" Cf. Helge Kökeritz, who, in *Shakespeare's Pronunciation* (New Haven, 1953), p. 300, defends and cites parallels of "beguild"; and Dobson, *English Pronunciation*, II, sec. 437 (pp. 1003-4), where excrescent d and t are treated generally. In *Lucrece*, "beguild" is likely to be—more than simply a colloquial form—at least in part the result of the orthographical homogeneation of rhyme words that was common during the late sixteenth and early seventeenth centuries, and it seems at any rate significant that the compositor was apparently untroubled by what he saw in his copy.

(22) Thompson points out, for example, that in *More* Addition III the terminal letters of "braule" (l. 78) and "clothd" (l. 79) may "be declared identical" ("Handwriting," p. 88).

(23) On minim omissions see n. 6 above. As Fredson Bowers puts it, "Palaeographical 'explanations' have a marked tendency to take it for granted that every letter must be confused with another," but "error results usually from the influence of only a few letters that transmit an erroneous picture of the whole word to the brain" (*Bibliography and Textual Criticism* [Oxford, 1964], p. 92).

(24) I hope shortly to be able to make available, in a form more finished than that of an experimental preliminary processing, three computer-produced aids to Shakespearean textual study from *More* Addition III: a concordance; an orthographical index alphabetized by modern spellings, which will immediately indicate (within the limits imposed by the brevity—and still doubtful date—of the Addition) Shakespeare's range and preference of spelling for a given word; and an *index litterarum*. The latter is in effect an initial-medial-final, letter-word concordance ordered alphabetically and vertically aligned by subject-letter and, within listings for a given letter, alphabetized from left to right following the letter and from right to left preceding it. The preliminary "output" for the *index litterarum*, with three columns of entries per page of standard 11 x 15 computer-paper, runs to an unwieldy eighty-four pages, a number that can be substantially reduced by modifications in the printing program, which at present begins a new page wherever a given group—e.g., "C, TERMINAL," for which there are only eleven entries—ends.

A Re-Examination of the "Patient" Pericles

by Thelma N. Greenfield

Recent interpretations of *Pericles* present fairly consistently the view that the hero is a type of the patient man. We find, for example, this of J. F. Danby's: "In *Pericles* it is patience in adversity which is the dominating motif."[1] D. A. Stauffer writes of the moral significance of the play, "Not only integrity, then, but patience, may make a man ruler over himself, and worthy of salvation."[2] Kenneth Muir finds in *Pericles* "the triumph of patience."[3] In his introduction to the New Arden edition, F. D. Hoeniger extensively develops the concept of patience as central both to the play's characterization of the hero and to its theme.[4] Closely related to this patient hero is the "passive" and "resigned" Pericles of John Arthos and D. A. Traversi.[5] Most influential among presentations of this view is J. M. S. Tompkins' "Why *Pericles*?" Tompkins finds Pericles more an example of patience than any other of Shakespeare's heroes and sees the conclusion of his story in terms of payment for this virtue: "As a character [Pericles] is almost static; he is the sport of fortune; the years and the great seas break over him; at last he turns his face to the wall, but in a despair that is silent and unrebellious; and then the gods restore to him the treasures they have reserved, and reward his patience."[6]

The prospect of taking exception to such an array of opinion must give one pause, yet my own examination of the evidence leads me to suggest that the patient Pericles be supplanted by the wise and learned one, the Renaissance descendant of the wily Greek traveler, a solver of riddles, a master of escape and incognito, skilled in the arts, and in his accomplishments and understanding a born ruler of men. This Pericles has a genius for coming out alive and, ultimately, on top, from the threats and disasters of a long, adventuresome life however much, like the storied philosopher, he can be bowed by inner griefs which his shrewdness and learning find no defence against. In all his wisdom, this Pericles willingly admits the power of the gods ("I am son and servant to your will") but he is a little short on faith in their benignity (see below).

To proceed further with the wise and adroit but sometimes desolated Pericles, we must assess the evidence critics have set forth for the patient one. Although his patience is more often remarked upon than demonstrated, the evidence offered for the case is of two kinds, those instances where the word *patience* is spoken, implied, or enacted in the play—as when Helicanus or Lychorida or Marina adjures Pericles to be patient—and those instances where the play's relation to its sources shows by similarity or difference that Shakespeare's (or some other's) hand shaped the play toward the theme—as the impatience exhibited by Twine's Apollonius or the patience demonstrated by Plutarch's Pericles.[7]

Hoeniger's arguments on the use or implications of the word, appearing importantly in the New Arden edition of the play, may be considered first. He begins
with a comparison to *King Lear,* a play which surely comes to mind when we read
Pericles. Hoeniger observes that Pericles (II.i and III.i) and King Lear (III.ii) react
differently to the storms to which they are exposed—Lear encourages the storm,
admits that he is its slave, and rebukes it, while Pericles patiently submits to it.
This contrast bears a second look and doubtless goes deeper than Hoeniger indicates. Lear's immensely complicated responses to his storm are individual and
varied, but clearly that storm becomes to the audience and to the hero an imaginative extension of Lear's own emotional state and simultaneously symbolic of his
daughters' savagery. Pericles' storms, additional episodes in a series of adventures, have no such connections with pre-existent conflicts and inner tensions,
and although the diction of Pericles' description of the turbulent elements may
call Lear's speeches to mind, we cannot safely say that here are two characters
reacting differently to the same thing. The storms in *Pericles,* completely external,
lead the hero to new conditions and contemplations, unrelated, except as reversals, to his previous state. Pericles' reactions to the storm in Act II are those of a
virtuous but thinking man: first, he says that man is helpless in the face of the
angry heavens, and second, he designates himself as obedient, as man must be,
to the powers above, and desires only a chance to die undisturbed. Interesting
here is the use of logical patterns.

The passage, in full, reads as follows:

> Yet cease your ire, you angry stars of heaven!
> Wind, rain, and thunder, remember, earthly man
> Is but a substance that must yield to you;
> And I, as fits my nature, do obey you.
> Alas, the seas hath cast me on the rocks,
> Wash'd me from shore to shore, and left me breath
> Nothing to think on but ensuing death.
> Let it suffice the greatness of your powers
> To have bereft a prince of all his fortunes;
> And having thrown him from your wat'ry grave,
> Here to have death in peace is all he'll crave. *(II.i.1-11)*[8]

Pericles, even in his extremity, thinks like a scholar: man must yield to you powers
of nature; I am a man; therefore I do obey you. You have left me breath only to think
of death; therefore, I (who must obey you) think of death and having been deprived
of a grave at sea only desire to die on land in peace. Lear, by contrast, speaks in
imperatives, moral assessments, and the dawning of new perspectives. Pericles,
distressed as he is, plays the learned disputant. He argues with the heavens even
in praying: "Yet cease your ire . . . remember . . . Let it suffice." The point of his
argument is that since he has suitably cooperated in this demonstration of heavenly strength, he should now be tormented no further.

One sees here something other than patience: Pericles' tendency to rely on wit and to retreat in the face of odds greater than himself. Such was his method in the adventure with Antiochus and such will be his way of winning (almost accidentally) Thaisa at her father's court. In the second storm scene, where Thaisa suffers in childbirth, Pericles again introduces the argumentative note in addressing the heavens, although now with a stronger tone of remonstrance. His first argument is that the gods, having called the storm from the deep, should now further exercise their power to quell it:

> The god of this great vast, rebuke these surges,
> Which wash both heaven and hell; and thou that hast
> Upon the winds command, bind them in brass,
> Having call'd them from the deep! *(III.i.1-4)*

On hearing of the queen's death, Pericles expresses his passion of grief in argumentative reproach to the gods—man's example is better than theirs:

> Why do you make us love your goodly gifts,
> And snatch them straight away? We here below
> Recall not what we give, and therein may
> Use honour with you. *(III.i.23-26)*

Hoeniger notes that Lychorida twice charges Pericles to be patient and that Pericles soon turns to care for the newborn baby,[9] but nowhere in the play is the hero actually described as patient. His only striking use of the word is applied to Marina, "Yet thou dost look / Like Patience gazing on kings' graves, and smiling / Extremity out of act" (V.i.137-139). Hoeniger here can apply the virtue to Pericles by remarking that Marina, as Pericles' daughter, is "part of Pericles' own personality"[10] but one can argue for significant differences between this father and daughter, as does John Arthos. Pericles' next use of the word, he does apply to himself, "Nay, I'll be patient" (V.i.145); however, Marina's subsequent rebuke and threat to stop talking (ll. 150-152) indicate more a temporary concession on Pericles' part than a genuine revelation of character or philosophy.

Pericles' quick surrender of Thaisa's body to the waves Hoeniger calls patience and Tompkins "courtesy"[11] but the action may be interpreted differently. In light of the first sailor's terse ultimatum, "Therefore briefly yield'er, for she must overboard straight," Pericles' assent may be as easily attributed to discretion as to patience. In fact, the several critics who deplore the absence of guilt and retribution in this play here could find a point at which Pericles' lack of faith and his hasty withdrawal from threatening situations make him responsible for a very human but serious error.[12]

In certain speeches Pericles sounds like the long-suffering Edgar in *King Lear*. Hoeniger cites:

> We cannot but obey
> The powers above us. Could I rage and roar
> As doth the sea she lies in, yet the end
> Must be as 'tis *(III.iii.9-12)*

which he compares to Edgar's "Stoical resignation." We seem to hear Edgar again in Pericles'

> Courage enough: I do not fear the flaw;
> It hath done to me the worst   *(III.i.39-40)*

for Edgar more than once welcomes his misfortunes because they have brought him to "the worst" (II.iii.11-12 and IV.i.1-9) and "the worst returns to laughter"; but Danby, while finding in Pericles' speech "new balance" and "re-established manliness" later points out that there is something wrong with Edgar's view, which he calls a "complacent" patience, since Edgar must soon admit, "I am worse than e'er I was . . . / And worse I may be yet: the worst is not, / So long as we can say this is the worst"(IV.i.28-30).[13] Pericles is equally wrong. He has called Thaisa's death "the worst" but Marina's loss will be more staggering, the thing which drives him to utter desolation. And the question may be raised as to whether these statements really represent patience. They seem to be more a kind of dialectical talisman which the sufferer presents to Fortune, a rationalizing formula to create fortitude within himself or to "magic" into being the return of better times. Pericles' analysis here reminds us of his earlier argument to the heavens: "Let it suffice the greatness of your powers / To have bereft a prince of all his fortunes"; by contrast, Marina steadily calls upon the gods in her time of trial.

If one examines this contrast in the light of Danby's excellent distinction between active Christian patience and classical Stoicism in his chapter on "'King Lear' and Christian Patience," one finds Marina much closer to what Shakespeare probably understood as Christian patience in its fullest sense—a deep capacity for suffering combined with the realization that adversity comes from God, and the retention of faith and hope. I do not wish to identify Marina as a type of Christian patience but I think if one looks for patience in the play it appears more clearly in her than in Pericles. Although she feels great sorrow (even before her life and virtue are threatened), as her sufferings multiply she refuses to blame the gods ("I accuse them not," IV.ii.67) and she continues to call on them (IV.ii.86, 147; IV.vi.98-101, 107, 146, 178-179). Her persistence in attempting to penetrate Pericles' terrible darkness is, of course, the most dramatic enactment of patience in the play, and the ultimate discovery of her father in the stricken king is indeed patience rewarded.

Pericles, by contrast, does occasionally go astray in his reservations of faith; and Marina, at the point where she offers him the solution to his suffering, several times persistently demands of him his willingness to believe: "If I should tell my history, 'twould seem / Like lies, disdain'd in the reporting"; "Patience, good sir, / Or here I'll cease"; "You said you would believe me; / But, not to be a troubler of your peace, / I will end here"; "You scorn; believe me, 'twere best I did give o'er" (V.i.118-119; 144-145; 150-152; 166).

Although the technique here is reminiscent of Prospero's interrupting his recital of past woes to tell Miranda she is not listening, the point of the lines is close to Paulina's telling Leontes in *The Winter's Tale,* "It is required / You do awake your faith" to see the statue of Hermione move. Not until Pericles promises (ll. 167-168), "I will believe you by the syllable / Of what you shall deliver," does he receive the revelation which shows Marina incontrovertably to be his daughter. Similarly, his wife is restored to him by an act of faith, when Pericles changes his course from Tarsus to Ephesus at the bidding of the visionary Diana; but these things come at the end of the play. Early in the play, Pericles seems more than simply resigned in his combinations of retreat and near despair; threatened by Antiochus, he runs away, falls a victim of "dull-ey'd melancholy" and dread, and flees again from his own country; the single survivor of his wrecked fleet, he wishes only to die in peace; in Pentapolis he conceals his full identity in spite of the honors given him; at Thaisa's "death" he hastily accedes to the sailors' demands for instant sea burial; at Tarsus, he immediately accepts the story of Marina's death and undergoes his most violent retreat from life.

To turn now to the evidence concerning the patient Pericles taken from the play in relation to its sources: Hoeniger writes, "... in neither Gower nor Twine, nor in any other possible source, is the idea of enduring suffering with patience emphasized," and he cites Apollonius, with tears and outcry, rending his clothes, swooning, etc. He continues,

> These quotations should suffice to convince anyone that the conception of the character of Pericles in Shakespeare's play, at any rate from the beginning of Act III on, differs considerably from that in his sources. To clinch the argument, in Gower, Twine, and Wilkins, immediately before the recognition the hero gives a more violent expression to his anger at his daughter's persistence. He does not merely push her off: he smites her with his hand. In Twine's and Wilkins' novels, she falls to the floor and wounds her cheek.[14]

Hoeniger might have put it even more strongly. Twine's Apollonius, as in versions older than Gower's, "stroke the maiden in the face with his foote" when she "threw her selfe uppon him" and he repeats the same pattern in his reunion with his wife. Lucina, recognizing her husband, embraces and tries to kiss him, but he "was mooved with disdaine, and thrust her from him, much misliking such lightnesse."[15] Shakespeare rejects the repeated response of anger. His Thaisa (Lucina) simply faints, as does Gower's, but, recovering, unlike Gower's, hesitates, promising that her "sanctity / Will to my sense bend no licentious ear" if this be not Pericles. Shakespeare must have had Twine's detail of seeming light behavior in mind when the word *licentious* came to him, but he chose neither Twine's thrusting away of Lucina nor Gower's quick recognition between husband and wife. Having passed through his initial vigorous rejection of Marina, Shakespeare's Pericles displays no more violence (I use the word *violence* because it is Marina's) or indifference. The old shrewdness is there, however; as he had done with Marina, Pericles collects piece after piece of evidence to solve the riddle of his wife's identity—her body was deposited in the waters near Ephesus, there are identifying jewels from her coffin, her voice is familiar, she recognizes his ring as a gift from her father, she knows Helicanus' name. Though the recognition is not handled this way in either of his main sources, Shakespeare found the clues for it in both. In his sources, part of Marina's therapy offered to her unknown father is comprised of riddles. Thus Gower:

> For in proverbe and in probleme
> Sche spak, and bad he scholde deme
> In many soubtil question *(Book VIII, 1681-83)*[16]

while in Twine, her three riddles are actually set down and Apollonius answers them.

Shakespeare transmutes this element in his sources into the riddle of Marina's identity and the riddling nature of her answers about herself: born on no shore yet mortal, where she lives she is a stranger, her griefs are equal to the king's, she is Marina alive yet Marina is dead. Marina herself must solve the final question—what is the name of her mother. It is this engagement of the wits that Shakespeare uses in both the Marina and Thaisa recognition scenes.

Central to both Hoeniger's and, before him, Tompkins' case for the patient hero is, as I have said, the absence of violent expressions of grief. Unfortunately, stage directions, often cryptic in plays of the time, are particularly limited in this one, and we simply do not know what an actor of Pericles may have done on the stage. Such descriptive details from the sources as Apollonius weeping, tearing his clothes, or throwing himself on his wife's body are not part of the dialogue; they may or may not have been enacted. The point can scarcely be argued, except that there is Lychorida's "do not assist the storm" (III.i.19) to reckon with. She obviously refers at least to sighs (winds) and tears (rain), since Pericles' spoken line is only "How? how, Lychorida?" The dumb show of IV.iv calls for Pericles "in a mighty passion" and here a strenuous demonstration of grief is clearly demanded.

Hoeniger and Tompkins both attempt to mitigate whatever it is that Pericles exclaiming "Hum, ha!" does to Marina at V.i.83. Tompkins calls it "the push that the barely conscious Pericles gives to Marina."[17] Hoeniger inserts "pushing her back" as a stage direction and includes a footnote arguing rather circularly, since he has already used this detail as evidence of Pericles' gentleness, that Shakespeare's Pericles is not one who would "roughly repulse" Marina, as Maxwell has it in the Cambridge *Pericles*. The play itself makes two references to the action. Marina says, "if you did know my parentage, / You would not do me violence" (V.i.99-100). Hoeniger again inserts an interpretive note: "These words do not indicate any crude behavior on Pericles' part." Marina's words, however, can easily indicate "crude behavior." More supporting to Hoeniger's case is Pericles' own "when I did push thee back" (l. 126), at least as a justification for Hoeniger's stage direction. But there are gentle pushes and hard pushes and if Marina felt this push was violence, there is no need to discount her reaction. Nevertheless, Shakespeare often improved upon the taste of his sources and of his contemporaries and here is a case in point. We can safely say that Pericles certainly does

56

not knock Marina to the floor and kick her as in Twine. That what he does do, however, demonstrates patience by comparison is seriously open to question.

On this matter of sources, Tompkins makes another point which requires scrutiny. His answer to the question of Shakespeare's choice of the name *Pericles* is that the playwright, happy to avoid the five-syllable *Apollonius* and presenting here the most patient man of all his heroes, chose *Pericles,* not from Sidney's *Pyrocles* in the *Arcadia,* but from Plutarch's *Lives:* "For Plutarch stresses the patience of Pericles strongly."[18] Plutarch begins thus, "For they [Pericles and Fabius Maximus] were both men very like together in many sundry vertues, and specially in curtesie and justice: and for that they could patiently beare the follies of the people."[19] Tompkins cites first the "naughtie busie fellow" who railed on Pericles all day and received only kindness in return. Remarking that Shakespeare passed quickly over the large central portion of the "Life," Tompkins notes next the one occasion where Pericles does lose his equanimity, weeping for his dead son, "which they never saw him do before all the dayes of his life."

These similarities to Shakespeare's Pericles have severe limitations. The hero of the play is placed in no situation where calumny or "the follies of the people" put him to the test. Furthermore, he often loses his composure. He suffers melancholy after the Antiochus adventure, near-despair in the shipwreck, and sorrow at Simonides' feast (although Tompkins diagnoses Pericles' reaction in this last instance as "constancy and cheerfulness;" see the references to his melancholy II.iii.54 and 91). Shakespeare's Pericles also feels fear at Thaisa's pursuit of him and grief at Thaisa's dying before he enacts his "mighty passion" at the news of Marina's death, whereas the Athenian leader is quite a different case. Although he lost many of his friends and kinfolk, "al this did never pull downe his countenance, nor any thing abate the greatnesse of his mind, what misfortunes soever he had sustained. Neither they saw him weep at any time, nor mourne" except for the death of his youngest son.[20]

There are, nevertheless, other extensive matters where Plutarch's story would call to mind the story of Apollonius, and this with no skipping over the middle part. One similarity is that the Athenian Pericles roved and sent expeditions throughout the Mediterranean area, moving through the islands as well as the mainland. More important, and tying Plutarch's Pericles to Gower's as well as Twine's Apollonius, is the point that they are men of excellent education, wisdom, and eloquence. In the *Confessio Amantis* we find this of the hero:

> Of every naturel science,
> Which eny clerk him couthe teche,
> He couthe ynowh, and in his speche
> Of wordes he was eloquent. (*Book VIII, 390-94*)

Twine gives still greater development to Apollonius as the wise scholar. His hero is "very well learned." Quickly solving Antiochus' riddle and returning home, he, scholar-fashion "withdrawing himselfe into his studie, perused all his bookes concerning the kings probleame." Questioned in Pentapolis, "Apollonius answered little or nothing, wherein his wisedome the rather appeared according to the saying of the wise man: *in many words there wanteth discretion.*" (The passage continues at some length, concluding with the mention of Socrates.)[21] The hero's musical skill is, of course, an important part of the story and he becomes a teacher to Lucina. To penetrate his gloom, Marina stirs his interest with "subtle questions" and "parables" and Twine's Apollonius brilliantly answers her riddling. Also in that version, Tharsia (Marina) "wondering at his wisdome, and the rather ['therefore the more quickly'] lamenting his discomfortableness," embraces him and exclaims upon how unworthy it is "that so wise a man should languish in griefe, and die in sorrow." At Ephesus, Apollonius tells how he "attained unto all kinde of knowledge." Lucina reveals herself by reminding Apollonius that she loved him, "not for concupiscence sake but for desire of wisdome." And after his adventures, Apollonius, still the scholar, settles down to write his life's story, making sure there are two copies.[22] George Wilkins' *The Painfull Adventures of Pericles Prince of Tyre,* combining Twine's account with the play (if recent opinion is correct), continues with the wise and learned Pericles, even in its brief summarizing "argument of the Whole Historie."

Plutarch's account of the education of the Athenian Pericles begins with reference to his training in music and proceeds from there to his instruction in philosophy and oratory. From his great teachers and his own natural wit, Pericles developed a "great mind," an "eloquent tongue," "ready utterance," and "knowledge of naturall things, and of those specially that worke above in the ayre and firmament."[23] It would be too time-consuming to pursue all of Plutarch's references to Pericles' mastery of "natural philosophy" and "artificial rhetoric" and their happy combination with his "natural excellent wit and capacity," for the theme runs throughout the account. I shall pause only over one point. Plutarch probes the possible intellectual aspect of Pericles' association with the wise and witty Aspasia, to whom many of the Athenians came to learn the art of rhetoric, and who possessed a deep understanding of affairs of government. Lucina's learning, which Twine tells us soon surpassed Apollonius' own under his tutelage, and Tharsia's remarkable "cunning" in the arts provide a link with the most important woman in the "Life." Perhaps, also, Aspasia as a wise prostitute who marries the governor linked the story in Shakespeare's mind with the learned Tharsia's emergence from a brothel to marry the governor, Athanagoras (Lysimachus). Of Aspasia we are told that "those that used her company also, brought their wives many times with them to heare her talke," a detail reminiscent of Gower's Thaise emerging from the brothel to teach the daughters of lords. (Twine's Tharsia, even more academic, from the market place displays her skill in music and her eloquence, answering all such questions as are propounded from among the people.)

It seems to me that these are the elements which most clearly connect Plutarch's "Life" with the story of Apollonius. These rather than Pericles' composure may have led Shakespeare to give the name of the Athenian governor to the Prince of Tyre.

Many a commentary alludes to the inevitable suggestion in Shakespeare's Pericles of Odysseus and Oedipus but little has been made of the fact that beyond sharing their travels and the hard blows of fortune, all three are men who use their wits. More than men who face adversity, they are clever men who face adversity. The dangerous riddle-solving aside, Pericles is especially close to Odysseus, and like the shrewd Ithacan king, Pericles' methods of coping with problems include "showing a clean pair of heels" (to use a phrase from Rieu's translation), remaining incognito, and depending on his personal skills in competitions. Like Odysseus grieving on Calypso's island or washed ashore in misery in Phaeacia, Pericles suffers deep sorrow under Fortune's buffets. In his story we find the special pathos of the virtuous and shrewd hero struck at again and again by hostile forces, some human and some natural or supernatural. Each is detained away from his homeland while affairs there are kept in abeyance waiting for the king's return. Also Odysseus is from time to time a helpless victim of his men's folly, and Pericles must submit to the sailors' superstitious insistence on getting rid of Thaisa's body. Pericles is not so much a Job, patiently enduring God's testing. He is the seeker, the traveler, and the fugitive who even in his greatest suffering remains a voyager, letting the winds blow him where they will.

Shakespeare's Pericles displays much less of the learned clerk than we find in Twine's Apollonius or Gower's Appolinus, but the flavor of the scholarly disputation appears in his addresses to nature and his use of wit is important in the adventures in Antioch, Tarsus, and Pentapolis, as well as in the recognition scenes with Marina and Thaisa. I have already touched upon the first and last of these points. It remains to look briefly at the Antioch, Tyre, Tarsus, and Pentapolis scenes in the light of Pericles' shrewd insights and evasions and to mention Shakespeare's resurrection of the overt academic emphasis of his sources in Marina.

Pericles' immediate solving of the riddle does not prove, as Arthos has it,[24] that the other suitors were fools, for Pericles immediately, too, has the guile and wisdom to answer in veiled terms. He also has the wisdom to penetrate at once Antiochus' hypocritical courtesy and to read murder in his intentions. The scene ends with his determination to flee: "By flight I'll shun the danger which I fear." In the melancholy that overtakes Pericles after his return to Tyre, he thinks cannily upon the futility of trying to elude Antiochus by silence or lies and upon the possibility of war and the suffering of his subjects. He wisely picks Helicanus, the best of his lords, to confide in (after putting him to the test) and takes his advice to leave Tyre. The episode of Pericles relieving the Tarsus famine is difficult to integrate with the spirit of the rest of his adventures except insofar as it prepares for Marina's later coming there, but one may see two other connections: first, Pericles is put, like Antiochus, into a position of power. As Tyre would be helpless to withstand the Syrian armed might, Cleon, expecting an attack on Tarsus, bewails the helplessness of the city. Unlike the tyrant, however, Pericles generously provisions the starving city. Second, his typical foresight is exhibited in his choice of repayment. With a kind of fairytale exactitude, he asks for "love and harbourage," which are precisely what he will need in a few months to save his infant daughter.

In Pentapolis, Pericles conceals his identity from the fisherman, saying of his father's armor only that it belonged to a king who loved him dearly. He enters the lists as a rustily-armored stranger whom the people call "the mean Knight." He sits down at the feast, a "melancholy" stranger, and asked to give his name and parentage, conceals his high degree, saying only

> A gentleman of Tyre; my name, Pericles;
> My education been in arts and arms. *(II.iii.81-83)*

In addition to his skill in armed combat and dancing, he demonstrates that he is "music's master" (II.v.25-30). Alert and cautious, as he was in the Antioch and Tyre scenes, his immediate reaction to Thaisa's letter telling of her love for him is one of fear: "'Tis the king's subtlety to have my life."

Marina repeats her father's story by undergoing dangerous adventures and by being a child of the sea in birth, name, and destiny. In addition to this and to the virtuousness she shares with Pericles, Marina is primarily shown as the heir her father has sought from the beginning and as a paragon of learning. When she moves to the center of the action, the Chorus (Act IV) first remarks on her training in "music's letters" and her possession of "all the grace" of education. Her mastery of the arts is further expanded here and later: her skill is great in weaving, sewing, singing, poetry, and dancing. "Deep clerks she dumbs," and her arguments with the assassin and the frequenters of the brothel and the brothel keepers testify to her eloquence. Marina's safety depends totally on the defense provided by her learning and there she contrasts with her father, who with his wisdom has also the freedom of flight. Marina must and does stand her ground. She does so finally in the presence of the forbidding king. By engaging his mind with the riddle of her identity she brings him at last the "issue" he had sought even in solving that first riddle, when

> against the face of death
> I sought the purchase of a glorious beauty,
> From whence an issue I might propagate,
> Are arms to princes and bring joys to subjects. (I.ii.71-74)

In conclusion, I feel that certain weaknesses appear in the arguments which support Pericles (however virtuous he is) as an extraordinary example of patience, for too often the play emphasizes his avoidance of and retreat from misfortunes rather than his patient endurance of them. While Pericles' character is far from being the whole story, if one keeps in mind the engagement of wits and the exercise of skillful "cunning" which most major episodes in the play reveal, then a significant continuity becomes apparent throughout the hero's adventures and between his parts of the story and Marina's. The concept of the wise and learned hero is important in the sources Shakespeare drew upon and his own utilization of it is worth attention.

Notes:

(1) *Poets on Fortune's Hill* (London, 1952), pp. 101-102.

(2) *Shakespeare's World of Images* (New York, 1949), p. 271. See also pp. 269, 274.

(3) *Last Periods of Shakespeare, Racine, Ibsen* (Detroit, 1961), p. 36.

(4) The New Arden *Pericles*, ed. F. D. Hoeniger (London, 1963), pp. lxxix-lxxxviii.

(5) John Arthos, "*Pericles, Prince of Tyre*: A study in the Dramatic Use of Romantic Narrative," *SQ*, IV (1953), 269, and D. A. Traversi, *Shakespeare: The Last Phase* (New York, 1954), p. 32.

(6) *RES NS*, III (1952), 317.

(7) Lawrence Twine, *The Patterne of Painfull Adventures* (1576, 1607), is, along with John Gower, *Confessio Amantis*, Book VIII, a positive source of the play. Plutarch's *Lives* is a possible source for the name *Pericles* which the play substitutes for *Apollonius* (or Gower's *Appolinus*). Twine's romance appears in W. C. Hazlitt, ed., *Shakespeare's Library*, 2nd edn., IV (London, 1875).

(8) Quotations from *Pericles* are as they appear in the New Arden edition.

(9) Hoeniger, p. lxxxiii.

(10) Hoeniger, p. lxxxvi.

(11) Hoeniger, p. lxxxiii; Tompkins, p. 321.

(12) G. Wilson Knight suggests guilt for Pericles in his being enticed by Antiochus' daughter, *The Crown of Life* (New York, 1966), p. 38. Kenneth Muir guesses that Thaisa's broken vow to Diana or there being no vow when Simonides said there was accounts for Thaisa's being taken from her husband. He offers his theory to "prevent the play from being a series of accidental misfortunes," "*Pericles* II.v," *N & Q*, 193 (1948), 362. J. C. Maxwell in the New Cambridge *Pericles* remarks, as do other critics (see for example Stauffer, p. 279, and Tompkins, pp. 316-317), on the absence of expiation and forgiveness in *Pericles*. There has been, in short, a wide-spread search for an equation between the play and some external moral system or a feeling that something is missing if one is not found. The patient Pericles has helped to fill this felt need of a moral rationale; whether that need is real is another question.

(13) Danby, pp. 96, 123.

(14) Hoeniger, pp. lxxxvi-lxxxvii.

(15) Hazlitt, p. 311.

(16) *The English Works of John Gower*, ed. G. C. Macaulay, II, EETS (London, 1901, reprinted 1957).

(17) Tompkins, p. 320.

(18) Tompkins, p. 323.

(19) Hazlitt, p. 337.

(20) Hazlitt, p. 388.

(21) Hazlitt, pp. 257, 275.

(22) Hazlitt, pp. 311, 319, 333.

(23) Hazlitt, pp. 341-345 and *passim*.

(24) Arthos, p. 260.

The Two Worlds of Shakespearean Comedy

by Sherman Hawkins

The New Criticism has now grown old. Paradoxically, the criticism that now seems new, with its stress on archetype and genre, is really older still. It represents a badly needed modern revision—an archetypal critic might say "resurrection"—of the traditional doctrines of imitation and the kinds. The New Criticism taught us to analyze each literary work in isolation; it made little distinction between a novel or a play or a poem, and it was ill equipped to deal with the total corpus of an individual author, much less with any wider range of works. Generic criticism, in contrast, analyzes individual works as members of a class: epic, tragedy, lyric, and so on. Archetypal criticism explores narrative and thematic patterns which unite even these major divisions, recurring in various genres and different authors. In this essay, I shall outline two basic patterns which seem to shape Shakespearean comedy; then, more briefly, I shall try to suggest their archetypal connections with Shakespeare's other plays and a spectrum of non-Shakespearean works. So described, the undertaking sounds dry and flat—another exercise in critical method. I can only attest that the patterns to be described are to me inherently fascinating and evocative, and that the possibilities for further application seem real and exciting.

As everyone knows, the choice of genre was a primary and definitive factor in the Renaissance poet's intention. The Elizabethan concept of genres was flexible and often imprecise, but it was universally accepted, and grounded in an equally universal conception of reality. Indeed, I prefer the native and Elizabethan "kind" to the French "genre" precisely because the word points to the naturalness of such formal divisions. Art, we are assured on good authority, holds the mirror up to "Kind," to Nature. God creates in genera and species; so does the poet. As the natural creation is ordered by the supreme Maker in hierarchical classes and categories, so the poetic microcosm, the golden world of art, has its analogous "chain of being," ranging from the lofty forms of epic and tragedy down to the lowly farce and humble epigram, each in its proper style: the high, the middle, or the low. Decorum, the canon of appropriateness, is the literary equivalent of natural law, which assigns to every creature the mode of working proper to its form and end. Distinctions of genre, then, are natural, not arbitrary. The dictates of decorum are "artificial" only in the good Elizabethan sense of artful and elegant— decorum being, as Milton declares, the grand masterpiece to observe. There is always the danger, of course, that form may harden into stereotype and decorum may stiffen into rules. We observe this petrifaction in neoclassic criticism, as the organic universe of *Paradise Lost* gives way to the cosmic clock, and man the microcosm becomes *l'homme machine.* But Elizabethan poetic is still biology rather than physics. Its lively conception of the kinds is shown by those experiments in grafting and cross breeding that produce the hybrids listed by Polonius. It demands a strong and profound understanding of genre, not a weak or superficial one, to produce the tragical-comical-historical-pastoral that is *King Lear.* On the other hand, Shakespeare repeats certain motifs in plays of a given kind with as little embarrassment as great creating Nature endows man after man with nose and eyes and mouth, always in the same approximate relation. Shakespeare, like Nature, is creating one member of a species; with plays as with men, we need to recognize the general pattern as well as the individual variations. To know that man is a featherless biped, omnivorous, rational, and sociable, capable of laughter, speech, and prayer, helps us distinguish him from a fish, but it does more than that: these preliminary distinctions are also final and definitive. So too the basic and recurring patterns in Shakespeare's plays form part of our final understanding of them.

The generic method seems especially promising as an approach to comedy. For comedy is—next to tragedy and epic—the most distinctive and conservative of literary kinds. But Aristotle's treatise on the subject has been lost, and comic theory remains largely unformulated, leaving the kind of vacuum that nature and critics both abhor. It is one of Northrop Frye's major achievements that his investigations of comic form help to develop a poetics for comedy, and for Shakespearean comedy in particular.[1] Shakespeare's comedy is seen as a variant of the comic formula which the English Renaissance inherited from the New Comedy of Menander, Plautus, and Terence. This traditional comedy dramatizes the victory of young lovers over the opposition of parents and rivals. The hero's opponents, the *senex* and his allies, are slaves to some form of mental bondage: a ruling passion or humor, the rigidity of social codes or the tyranny of wilfulness and personal eccentricity. These figures dominate the comic society at the beginning of the play, but in the end a new society forms itself around the hero and his bride. The movement, then, is from bondage to liberty: "The normal individual is freed from the bonds of a humorous society, and a normal society is freed from the bonds imposed on it by humorous individuals." But we should notice (and Frye does not) that, at least in Shakespearean comedy, this new freedom expresses itself in the voluntary "bond" of wedlock.[2] The conflict between the sexual desires of the individual and the conventions of society is resolved: society needs the energy of youth for its own renewal and continuance; the individual seeks the assent of age, which gives his private wishes the public sanction and stability of social institution. Comedy is thus a dramatic *rite de passage,* in which the young assume their proper place in the adult world and society renews itself through the cycle of the human seasons. The marriage in which comedy ends is both freedom and bond, the fulfillment of the individual will and the nexus of a new social order.

Shakespeare adapts this traditional pattern to what Frye calls the drama of the green world. The action begins in a "normal" world, moves into a "green" world where the comic resolution is achieved, and then returns to the normal world (though this return is often indicated without being acted out). The drama thus turns on the contrast between two worlds, two orders of experience, two perspectives on reality. Even the primary, "normal" world is a heightened and romantic version of the world we know. The initial action is set in a court or city which is real but long ago or far away. The ruler of the city is a duke, placing this romantic comedy midway between the royalty proper to tragedy and the bourgeoisie proper to satiric comedy like that of Jonson. The city is conceived as a close-knit community of families where marriage is a matter of social and even civic import, where parental will has the force of law, where the duke himself may be called upon to discipline a rebellious son or daughter. The hero and heroine are usually of different social or financial standing. They find themselves opposed by an older figure who is parent or prince or both, and sometimes by a law against lovers, as in *Midsummer Night's Dream*. This opposition, like the law which embodies it, is felt to be foolish or tyrannical, but the only way to escape its threat is to leave the old world altogether. For beyond the walls of cities known at least by name to the Elizabethans stretches another and magical world: forests where fairies dance by moonlight, the pastoral landscape where shepherds woo their loves, the beautiful mountain where is a lady richly left, awaiting the right hero. This green world takes on different meanings in the thematic dialectic of each play: it is the order of grace opposed to the old order of law in *Merchant of Venice*, the moonlit world of fancy (in its Elizabethan double meaning of imagination and desire) opposed to Athens, city of reason, in *Midsummer Night's Dream*. But always it is the world as we wish it were instead of as it is, reality refashioned "as you like it." The hero or heroine must sometimes undergo hardships to enter the green world, and there he faces ritual trials or tests, but these serve only to reveal or perfect his essential good nature. Orlando worries about his lack of gentle breeding, but the tests of court and forest confirm the strength and kindness that are his by nature; Bassanio appears to Shylock a younker and a prodigal, but the casket test reveals the true inner sense of values his extravagance concealed. In the green world identities are frequently changed or disguised: Rosalind as Ganymede surrenders the gifts of nature, Celia as Aliena those of fortune. Yet in the end all that was lost is more than restored. The very defects and dangers of the green world permit us to enjoy its dream-like reality without losing our intellectual self-respect: we believe in Arden, as we do not in more perfect Arcadias, because it is winter there. Our assent is important, for the green world incarnates the essential optimism of comedy, which makes the happy ending the only right one. The realism of romantic comedy is a matter of perspective: it is a "vision in the form of youth," whose pattern of trials leading to a happy ending is a myth which all of us believe —so long as we are young.

Frye's green world theory seems to me both true and useful; it isolates a recurring psychological and mythic pattern in Shakespeare's comedies which is clearly deliberate and which helps to account for the perennial fascination of these plays. There is one obvious limitation to the theory, however. It fits only four of the comedies: *Two Gentlemen of Verona, A Midsummer Night's Dream, The Merchant of*

Venice, As You Like It. Frye also claims *The Merry Wives of Windsor,* but I hope to show that *Merry Wives* is written in a mixed mode. If we include the late romances, we can add *Winter's Tale* and *Cymbeline* to our list. But what about the rest of Shakespeare's comedies? Frye has suggested a group of "sea" comedies, including *Comedy of Errors, Twelfth Night, Pericles,* and *The Tempest,* but I do not find this classification helpful or convincing. Is there no other pattern which accounts for all or most of the remaining plays?

Critics ask such questions only when the answer is affirmative. And indeed, it would be surprising if Shakespeare, having constructed half his comedies as variations on a basic pattern, had written all the rest at random. If, on the contrary, he employed another recurring pattern, we might expect it to bear some significant relation of analogy or contrast to the green world motif. What is the essence of that pattern, the basic dramaturgical device? Clearly, the double setting: the whole convention depends on the juxtaposition of two strongly contrasted locales, representing two different orders of reality, and the movement of the action from one to the other. What, then, do we find when we examine the use of setting in the remaining comedies? It strikes us at once that the majority are limited to a single basic locale. The court of Navarre, the streets and homes of Ephesus or Messina, the mansions of Illyria are all essentially single settings. The action may move from one street or dwelling to another, and there may even be significant contrasts between them, as between the court where Navarre and his scholars shut themselves up and the open fields were the Princess of France is lodged. But these places are closely related imaginatively and physically: they belong to the same order of reality, the same "world." So in *As You Like It,* there is a contrast between the orchard where we meet Orlando and the palace where we first see Rosalind. But the usurpation of tyrant brothers in both places makes us aware of the likeness between court and country: both exhibit the disorder of an age of iron, contrasted to the magic forest where courtiers and rustics together fleet the time carelessly in a golden age. But for Navarre and the Princess, there is no forest, no green world, no different reality. So too in most of the remaining comedies. Against the four comedies of the green world, we can set *The Comedy of Errors, Love's Labors Lost, Much Ado About Nothing,* and *Twelfth Night.* These belong to what for the present I shall call the "alternate pattern," whose distinctive mark is unity of place. *The Tempest* is a late variation of this pattern, as *Cymbeline* and *Winter's Tale* are variations of the green world formula. The two remaining comedies, *The Merry Wives* and *Taming of the Shrew,* are mixed, combining features of both patterns in their double plots; and I shall use them only for purposes of illustration.

The unity of place in comedies of the alternate pattern produces a striking difference in their plot and action. In green world comedies, the hero and heroine begin by leaving the old world behind them: whether they are exiled or elope or set off to seek their fortune, the first phase of the action is an exodus. In the comedies we are now describing, the characters stay put, but they are visited by outsiders, who upset the routine of the community into which they come. These plays begin not with expulsion but intrusion, not exodus but advent. Thus the King of Navarre at the beginning of *Love's Labors Lost* receives an untimely visit from the Princess of France, and *Much Ado* opens with the arrival of Don Pedro in Messina. The Prince himself is Spanish; Claudio is Florentine and Benedick a Paduan: all three young men are aliens, foreigners; and in impact their entrance is more like an invasion than a homecoming. So in *Twelfth Night*, Viola and Sebastian, shipwrecked in Illyria, turn Orsino's dukedom upside down; and Dromio and Antipholus create as great a stir in *Comedy of Errors* when they land at Ephesus. The mixed comedies, *Taming of the Shrew* and *Merry Wives*, employ the same motif. Falstaff, staying (appropriately) at the Garter Inn, is very much a fish out of water in the quiet village: "What tempest, I trow, threw this whale, with so many tuns of oil in his belly, ashore at Windsor?" Petruchio's motives resemble Sir John's: he comes to wive it wealthily in Padua. Contrasted to these unlikely wooers, the heroes of the subplots are conventionally romantic, but they too are aliens: Lucentio is Florentine, and Fenton is a courtier, a companion of the wild Prince and Poins: "He is of too high a region; he knows too much," says Master Page.

In the subplots of these "mixed" comedies, as in the green world plays, we find the conflict of amorous youth and oppressive age: Fenton and Lucentio must each win his bride against her father's will. There is even an echo of the law against lovers in Baptista's resolution to marry off his elder daughter first. But this is not the source of conflict in the main plot, and in the other comedies no conflict of generations occurs. Fathers, when they appear at all, are sympathetic or even pathetic figures, like Leonato and Aegeon. Indeed, the unreasonable law which normally threatens young lovers is, in the *Comedy of Errors*, turned against their father. But the twins do not even discover their parents till the last scene; they are independent agents, free from all constraint. So Navarre in *Love's Labors Lost* rules his own kingdom, and the Princess' father is an off-stage character whose main function is to die. In Illyria, the young are wholly in control: Orsino is a duke and Olivia a countess; she governs her household as firmly as he his dukedom; Sir Toby and Malvolio are subjects merely.[3] Her dead brother and father have not even (like Portia's cautious parent) left a will to direct her fancies. In these plays, the young have it all their own way.

In any case, there is little social disparity between the lovers to which a tyrannic father might object. Leonato would gladly marry Hero to a prince, but he is contented with a count; and Beatrice and Benedick, as their friends realize, are destined for each other even by alliteration. The dynastic logic which matches the King of Navarre and the Princess of France is as obvious as the family link which attracts the brother of Antipholus to the sister of Adriana. The social status of Sebastian of Messaline is left ambiguous; his blood is "right noble," but we do not know whether his son is a fit husband for a countess or his daughter the proper partner for a duke. Though Olivia has resolved not to marry above her station, there seems to be a romantic mingling of classes when Olivia falls in love with a servant and Viola becomes her master's mistress. But the traditional New Comedy *cognito* proves, as usual, that these apparent misalliances are socially acceptable. In these plays generally, the union of the lovers is socially desirable; and age, when it appears at all, acts as the benevolent ally of youth.

The obstacles to love in comedies of this alternate pattern are not external—social convention, favored rivals, disapproving parents. Resistance comes from the lovers themselves. The premise from which the green world comedies begin is sexual attraction: whoever loved that loved not at first sight? The answer is, of course, Benedick and Beatrice. They belong to a different type of comedy, whose premise is sexual antagonism. Instead of the conflict of generations, we watch the war between the sexes. Instead of age versus youth, the dramatic patterning pits male against female. Thus in *Love's Labors Lost* and *Much Ado*, the "intruders" belong to one sex, the "natives" to the other; men visit women or women visit men. In *Love's Labors Lost*, as we have seen, this sexual opposition is further emphasized by setting: Navarre has his court, the Princess her tents, and the action consists of raids, sorties, and ambushes between these hostile camps. In *Much Ado*, Don Pedro and his courtiers break in upon the quiet seclusion of Messina, where young women joke and gossip with old men. The aged Leonato, like the effete Boyet, is a being of a middle state, free of both sides, but the advent of a Benedick or Claudio among the ladies produces instant effervescence. The developing action of *Much Ado* sets scenes involving women in contrast and parallel with scenes involving men; attempts to bring the sexes together in a masque or marriage produce comic mistakes or tragic mishaps almost to the end of the play. So in *Twelfth Night*, Orsino's household is set against Olivia's in a kind of amatory stalemate, with a girl in boy's clothing as ambassador and go-between.

Such contrasts of place and character-groupings emphasize sexual oppositions which may take the form of marital conflict, as in *Comedy of Errors* and *Merry Wives*, or of warring lovers, as in *Much Ado*. In the marital comedies, husband and wife attack each other, directly or through a surrogate. Thus Ford incites Falstaff to prove his wife's infidelity and beats him in a woman's form, while Mistress Ford punishes his masculine lust by having him cleansed and beaten and frighted with fairies and hobgoblins. *The Taming Of the Shrew* stands midway between these plays about marriage, comedies of experience, where conflict springs from the sexual distaste and disillusionment of middle age, and plays about wooing, comedies of innocence, where the conflict springs from the shyness or hostility of adolescence. Boys go off in one corner, girls in another; the sexes shun or plot against each other. The reluctant bachelor confronts the shrewish spinster, and their witty skirmishes are both flirtation and aggression. Petruchio and Katherina, Berowne and Rosaline, Benedick and Beatrice face each other in a courtship which is part dance, part duel. In *Twelfth Night*, Orsino and Olivia seem as hard to bring together as Cesario and Sir Andrew: they do not even meet till the last scene. One loves, the other mourns, and love and grief are counterpointed throughout the play. But the alliteration of their names points to the likeness in these apparent opposites: the grief of love and love of grief alike betray a certain self-involvement, an emotional solipsism: both Orsino and Olivia are withdrawn into the self-centered privacy of melancholy. These plays reveal a spectrum of sexual hostility and inhibition; in none of them is the force opposed to love social convention or parental tyranny. Love is denied by lovers; husband turns upon wife; youth is divided against itself.

We have seen that in the green world comedies, the social opposition that thwarts young love is sometimes dramatized as an actual law or threat of punishment. In plays of the alternate pattern, the lovers, free from external frustrations and restrictions, proceed to bind themselves with their own wilful bonds. In *Comedy of Errors,* marriage itself has become such a bond: for Antipholus, the ornamental "chain" which he promises first to his wife and then to a courtesan; for Adriana, the literal bonds in which she binds her errant husband and imprisons him at home. In the comedies of wooing, the bonds are psychological, but they are sometimes objectified as an oath or vow: the law against lovers is replaced by a law against love. So Navarre and his bookmen swear not to see a woman for three long years: Olivia has "abjured the company and sight of men" to live like a "cloistress" for seven. Less formally articulated but just as binding is Benedick's determination to die a bachelor. In these vows, as in the attitude that begets them, there is inhibition as well as exclusion, "shutting in" as well as "shutting out." The scholars plan to deny themselves food and sleep; Olivia will "water once a day her chamber round / With eye-offending brine." It is as if society's distrust of sexual love and all the energies of appetite and emotion had here become internalized: young men and women turn ascetic, warring against each other, their own affections, the "huge army of the world's desires." The father's jealous hostility towards his daughter's wooer has likewise been internalized, transferred to the heroine herself. So Beatrice scoffs at Benedick and Katherina rages against the whole race of men. It needs no Bradley to detect the real interest Beatrice feels for Benedick; no Freud to see that Katherina, jealous of Baptista's fondness for her sister, yearns for someone who will combine the dominating authority of a father with the exclusive absorption of a lover. Their surface aggressions are "humors," forms of compulsive and irrational behaviour which deny and thwart their deepest wishes, their natural selves. In the green world comedies — as in New Comedy generally — the humor characters are the opponents of the hero. In comedies of the alternate pattern, the heroes and heroines themselves sometimes resemble humor characters, imprisoned in their inhibitions and aggressions, isolated by fear or repugnance from the general life, cut off not merely from others whom they ought to love but even from themselves. Their "laws" are only whims, but to the compulsive personality whims are law: there is no bondage stricter than bondage to the self.

By now it should be clear why these comedies begin with an intrusion into what is in some sense a closed world. The public and social equivalent of the attitudes we have discussed is the law which in *Comedy of Errors* makes it death for anyone from Syracuse to enter Ephesus (or vice versa). A law which thus blocks traffic between these "adverse towns" is cruel and unnatural, for they are mercantile communities, whose life depends upon the intercourse of trade. Such a law punishes its agents and victims: the Duke of Ephesus, who "Excludes all pity" to enforce it, must resist a natural and growing sympathy for old Aegeon's suffering and search. But life keeps breaking in: not only Aegeon but Antipholus and Dromio come to Ephesus from Syracuse. And within the city itself, we see the other Antipholus hammering at the doors his wife has shut against him, and Adriana in her turn preparing to storm the abbey and regain her husband. Something there is that does not love a wall, that seeks to break down the laws that divide city from city, the barriers that "separate the husband and the wife." And we recall how Navarre, true to his vow, denies the Princess admission to his court, how Olivia, who "will admit no kind of suit," refuses to receive Orsino's messengers till Viola threatens to remain forever at her doors. So Bianca's lovers disguise themselves to gain admission to her father's house, and Falstaff insinuates himself in Master Ford's. The motif of gaining entrance to a closed house or dwelling repeats in miniature the major pattern of these comedies, in which intruders force their way into a closed world and draw its thwarted or random emotional forces to themselves. In green world comedies where houses are shut up, like Shylock's, they are places to escape from, not to break into; so Orlando is warned to flee from Duke Frederick's court and his own home. *The Merry Wives* stands between the two conventions: Falstaff's problem is to escape from Ford's house, but he is an intruder in a home which should be shut against him. In general the distinction seems clear: one pattern turns on escape, the other on invasion. And as one group are comedies of the green world, so we may call these others comedies of the closed world.

The closed world is a metaphor, a symbol for the human heart. The force which knocks at its closed door is love. And in these comedies, love finally gains admittance: Navarre and Olivia renounce their vows: Katherina and Beatrice fall in love with men they thought they despised. The happy ending comes about not by perseverance through trials and changes of fortune, as in the green world comedies, but by a reversal, by conversion, by a change of heart. This is the work of love: one of these plays is named *Love's Labors Lost,* and almost any of the others could be called *Love's Labors Won.* For Cupid here becomes a Hercules, performing the seemingly impossible task of changing negative to positive, hostility and inhibition to normal human affection. This is not accomplished by supernatural intervention, by a Cupid from a machine. Love enters the closed world wearing a human face, the face of Viola or Benedick, of Rosaline or Petruchio. And there is nothing sentimental about the way these unconscious agents of love set to work. They come speaking the language of judgment: "I see you what you are—you are too proud. . . ." The beginning of regeneration is the conviction of sin:

> What fire is in mine ears? Can this be true?
> Stand I condemn'd for pride and scorn so much?
> Contempt, farewell! And maiden pride, adieu!

In contrast to such self-recognition, Navarre and his friends undergo a *peripeteia* without an *anagnorisis.* They resolve to conquer "these girls of France" as confidently as they formerly resolved to war against their own affections: "Saint Cupid then! and, soldiers, to the field!" Hence when these "brave conquerors" mock a pedant in the role of Judas Maccabaeus or a braggart soldier playing Hector, they do not realize that they are indirectly making fun of themselves. There has been no real conversion, no change of heart: the same comic hybris inspires their studies and their wooing; the owls have turned to cuckoos, that is all. Thus at the end, they must hear the words of judgment: "Your Grace is perjur'd much, / Full of dear guiltiness."

Love's labors are not really lost. Berowne and his fellow "Worthies" are saved by grace, not merit; the ladies love them despite their guiltiness. Still, penance is necessary to bring about the happy ending and turn "sport" into "comedy." The usual penance comedy imposes is the ridicule involved in a drastic reversal of behavior or attitude. Olivia, the cruel fair who refuses a duke, must humble herself to woo a servingman; she who shut her doors against all men now rushes forth into the street and almost carries off the bewildered Sebastian. So Benedick, the cynical woman-hater, must pose as champion of feminine virtue and challenge Claudio in defense of Hero's honor.

Sometimes, however, the penalty is more drastic. In a "demonic" inversion of the green world motif, Katherina is dragged off to what editors call "Petruchio's country house," a place of hunger, cold, and wrath; a purgatory where Katherina is punished, with Dantesque justice, by suffering Petruchio's caricature of her own shrewishness. But Katherina throughout is in the hands of love: this topsy-turvy world, where old men become maidens and the sun becomes the moon, is the point of reversal and unbeing on the path to a rebirth. Petruchio insists that Katherina really is what Bianca pretends to be: gentle, submissive, lovable. Thus "Kate the curst" is freed from a role which was always a form of protest, freed to become her true self—if by "true" we understand not what she is "underneath," but what she and (according to the play) all women are meant to be. Her metamorphosis is parodied in Christopher Sly, who is never truly himself whether "disguised" in drink or as a lord.

What happens to Kate is less a catharsis than an exorcism. She is freed from the spirit of shrewishness which was her curse. Beatrice too is "cursed," despite her name: she is "possessed by a fury," and the "infernal Ate" must be driven out of her if she and Benedick are ever to be blessed. So Rosaline rebukes Berowne's gibing and bids him to

> throw away that spirit,
> And I shall find you empty of that fault,
> Right joyful of your reformation.

Metaphor becomes dramatic action in *Comedy of Errors*, where Doctor Pinch conjures Antipholus:

> I charge thee, Sathan, hous'd within this man,
> To yield possession to my holy prayers,
> And to thy state of darkness hie thee straight.

The scriptural symbolism of demons "hous'd" within a madman fits well in plays where a closed house or dwelling is often the emblem of the mind or heart. Thus Ford in *Merry Wives* hunts through his house for his wife's lover but is told he

70

exists "nowhere but in your brain." Ford is "possessed" by his jealousy: it is a demonic self, projected in "Master Brook," who "wrongs" the true Ford. But it is not enough to exorcise Ford's jealousy and scare the "spirit of wantonness" out of Falstaff. These are manifestations of a larger madness, a spirit of discord that possesses the closed world as a whole and expresses itself in the quarrels and humors of the different characters.

The dramatic exorcism necessary to subdue or expel the anticomic spirit seems to proceed on two principles. One is "acting out" its latent impulses: Ford is encouraged to act out his jealousy and Falstaff his lust—up to a point. So in *Much Ado*, the pervasive suspicion of women which exploits Claudio's gullibility as well as Benedick's cynicism must be acted out in the accusation of Hero. So in *Twelfth Night* Malvolio is tricked into acting out his egotistic fantasies, and the device of twins in *Comedy of Errors* permits Adriana to act out her ambivalence towards her husband: one brother she welcomes and feasts; the other she alternately locks out and locks up.

The second principle is "fixing the blame." "Acting out" is expansive and cathartic: it allows the anticomic spirit its full and often violent expression. Only after sexual antagonism has expressed and spent itself in the cruel verbal assault which "kills" Hero can Benedick be detached from the masculine party or declare his love for Beatrice. Fixing the blame, on the other hand, is a focusing; it locates the general lunacy or evil in a criminal or a scapegoat in whom it can be overpowered or driven out. So the blame which attaches itself to Hero is finally traced to Don John; and Antipholus, escaping from his madman's bonds and darkness, binds and manhandles Doctor Pinch. The conjurer is fit scapegoat for a society which an outsider like Antipholus of Syracuse sees as bewitched, and we observe a similar thematic decorum with Malvolio and Falstaff. Malvolio's "madness" and imprisonment is an intensification of the isolating melancholy that afflicts Olivia and Orsino. Like them, but far more fatally, he is "sick of self-love," a spirit Feste cannot exorcise either as clown or curate. "Let me enjoy my private," cries Malvolio, and his wish is granted; the loneliness and darkness of his prison only dramatize what has been his spiritual condition from the start. Falstaff is not imprisoned but expelled— twice from Ford's house, finally from the village to the forest in animal disguise. The first time his bodily grossness merges with the smell and grease of foul linen in a disgusting and undifferentiated "first matter," a cumulative image for all the stench and soilure of the flesh. His second metamorphosis is as a monstrous woman —hag, witch, polecat, runnion—and his last as a yet more monstrous man, bestial in lust and crowned with cuckold's horns. In his feminine role of Mother Prat he is beaten and vilified by Ford; in his masculine role as Herne the Hunter he is scolded and pinched by the Queen of Fairies and her following. *Merry Wives*, as its title suggests, is much concerned with marriage; there is more discussion than is usual in comedy about which wooer will make the best husband, and the main plot deals with conflicts among those already wed. What is driven out in Falstaff, then, is all that makes for dissension in marriage, the physical distaste, the sexual antagonism that sometimes grow up within an outwardly respectable and happy union.[4]

Reversal, recognition, penance, exorcism: the form of these plays seems closer to the conventions of tragedy or the punitive logic of satire than to romance. This is not to deny that similar motifs occur in both green and closed world comedy. But their function, tone, and meaning differ in ways appropriate to each kind. Consider, for example, the "anticomic" figures, those antagonists of love who refuse or are refused the happy ending. Malvolio and Jaques are both anticomic in their melancholy; Shylock and Don John are both branded by their very lineage as villains. But Jaques and Shylock in the green world plays are figures of parental opposition to love.[5] Malvolio and Don John in the closed world plays represent extreme forms of the self-love or skepticism that afflicts the lovers themselves. Thus Jaques contrasts with the lovers but Malvolio mimics them. Jaques stands outside and over against the lovers' world, criticizing and commenting objectively upon it. Malvolio, inside the household of love, embodies—as his name implies— a subjective distortion in "what you will," a misdirection of love itself. Characteristically, the anticomedians are let off more easily in green world comedy. *As You Like It* suggests by its title that the dramatic conflict within the Forest of Arden is a dialectic of tastes and attitudes. The melancholy wisdom of Jacques is refuted, but he is allowed to withdraw with dignity intact, while the narcissism of Malvolio must be exposed and exorcised by ritual humiliations. In the great trial scenes of *Merchant of Venice* and *Much Ado,* the villainies of Shylock and Don John bring green and closed world comedy to the verge of tragedy and death. But Shylock's feeling for his dead wife and his daughter allies him—however distantly—to the community of love; whereas Don John loves nobody, not even himself. Hence Shylock can be baptized, while Don John can only be punished. The new law offers to fulfill and liberate the old, a promise we see prefigured in Jessica. But the lonely malice of Don John must be expelled or imprisoned; it is the eternal adversary of love. Or again, compare the amatory confusions caused by the heroine's disguise in *Twelfth Night* and *As You Like It.* In each play, both a man and woman fall in love with a girl in boy's attire. In both, the attraction felt by the man grows and deepens till it is confirmed when the seeming boy is revealed as the heroine. In both, the sudden passion of the woman can have no natural fruition: it serves to reverse and punish her initial refusal to love. The green world comedy typically emphasizes the positive and evolving love of Orlando for the disguised Rosalind; the conversion of Phebe is only a subplot. The closed world comedy stresses the abrupt and humiliating conquest of Olivia by the aptly named Cesario, while Orsino's growing affection for Viola is more lightly sketched. It is characteristic that the mock wooing of Orlando and Ganymede is a delightful game, a form of erotic play, whereas the erroneous wooing of Viola by Oliva is one of Cupid's practical jokes, parallel at a higher level with the trick that converts Malvolio from puritanism to love. Both practical joke and play are native to the comic spirit, but one is "funny" while the other is "fun": they tend, like closed and green world comedy, towards the opposed poles of corrective satire and romantic idyl. Hence the lyricism of Olivia and the witticisms of Rosalind may seem indecorous. But the more impassioned Olivia is, the more nearly ridiculous she becomes, whereas Rosalind's "cure" for love actually nourishes and fosters it: she can make even satire promote romance.

The theme of love itself is handled less romantically in closed than green world comedy. Orlando and Rosalind in the springtime of their passion are ourselves as we wish we were; Benedick and Beatrice are wittier versions of what we actually are, and their problems are ones we know too well: to be humble, to trust and forgive, to learn at last to love. Yet for these very reasons, the happy ending in these comedies remains an act of faith in life — the life which comedy teaches should be grasped. Nor is this faith blind. The fact of sexual antagonism did not dismay Shakespeare or Spenser. The progression from conflict to reconciliation is not a distortion of love but its essential pattern, the *discordia concors* or harmony of opposites. In *Faerie Queen* IV, we find that the sons of Concord are Hate and Love; Hate is the elder, but he is constantly mastered by his younger brother. They are contrary but kindred principles, and the overcoming of hate by love is the way order is brought from chaos. Creation is an act of reconciliation, atoning the warring qualities of hot and cold and wet and dry in a harmonious cosmos; and the agent of creation is Love. Without discord, there can be no concord; without hatred, the instinctive opposition of things different in kind, there can be no love to atone them. So Arthegall and Britomart fight before they woo.[6] The sexes, like the elements, are at war; and in marriage, which unites woman (according to Renaissance physiology, cold and moist) to man (who is hot and dry), there is always a sense of creation. It is the making of a new world or — as Frye puts it — a new identity: the true self of the individual, the union of lovers, a society made one in charity. This new creation is the labor of Love, a task too large for any hero — or even for the Shakespearean heroine. The felt presence of a power working through semitragic errors and comic confusions is at the center of the comic faith in life, the intuition that apparent catastrophe, instinctive hostilities, and seeming chance alike direct us to our happiness. The secret meaning of Shakespeare's comedy is joy.

It only remains to see whether we can fit the two patterns of Shakespearean comedy together. Two possible ways suggest themselves: the closed world may correspond to either the first or second phase of the green world pattern, the "real" or "normal" world or the green world itself. And we observe that the primary, "real" world in green world comedies is often in some sense closed. The lovers are divided; the hero must overcome barriers which separate him from his mistress. But these obstacles are not internal: they are barriers of social convention or parental prejudice. The heroine is shut up in her father's house, and we find the familiar motif of the closed dwelling as her lover comes to her window by night to woo and win her. So Egeus complains that Lysander has "bewitched" his child: "Thou hast by moonlight at her window sung / With feigning voice verses of feigning love." So Proteus serenades Sylvia, and Valentine carries the motif one step further in his plan to scale her window with his rope ladder. The penetration of the lady's chamber has its obvious sexual analogy: in that play upon words, *Much Ado About Nothing*, it is enough for Hero to talk with a man at her chamber window to be proved unchaste. But in green world comedies, as we have seen, escape rather than intrusion is the lover's aim: Valentine intends to use his ladder to "enfranchise" Sylvia. Lorenzo does not climb to Jessica's window; she comes down to him. He is drawing her out of Shylock's house, the closed world of the old law, its "ears" locked shut against the music of Christianity and comedy, which Lorenzo can teach her to hear and understand only in the gracious world of Belmont.

When no such escape is possible, tragedy results. Romeo overcomes the hatred that divides Montague and Capulet, makes his way into his enemies' feast, surmounts the "stony limits" of their orchard walls, and discovers—in the greatest of such wooing scenes—that he is already in Juliet's heart. The sexual analogue is completed when he later climbs to her chamber to consummate their love. But for these star-crossed lovers there is no green world. Mantua is another Verona to which Romeo is "banished"; Juliet remains behind in the over-protective confines of her family and home, a womb that turns into a tomb, that ultimate closed world which Romeo invades only to die. Yet the sexual parallel persists: it makes the grave a wedding bed, the vault a feasting presence full of light. *Romeo and Juliet* is thus a closed world tragedy which corresponds to the primary phase of the green world pattern, a reality which in tragedy can only be escaped or transcended through death. But as we find in *Midsummer Night's Dream,* even the green world itself, the second phase, has its tragic possibilities. Pyramus and Thisbe also find ways to communicate through the wall that parts their fathers—a psychological division materialized in loam and plaster much as the sexual analogies materialize in jokes on "hole" and "chink." Like Hermia and Lysander, these lovers run away to meet by moonlight. But it needs only the substitution of Lion for Puck to turn dream into nightmare, the lucky accidents and confusions of comedy into the fated misfortunes of tragedy. Pyramus and Thisbe, like Romeo and Juliet, are united in death, but this time the tomb is appropriately Ninny's.

If the primary phase of green world plays resembles a closed world, the setting of closed world plays resembles the courts and cities of the primary phase. The crucial difference remains: there is no need to escape Messina or Illyria or the court of Navarre. They suggest a world potentially green or golden, but somehow at odds with its own happiness. Romeo and Juliet declare their love in an orchard where moonlight tips with silver all the fruit tree tops: within the city walls of Verona, Capulet's garden creates an "internalized" green world. And there are other orchards in Leonato's house and in Olivia's, where Benedick and Beatrice, Olivia and even Malvolio can fall in love. These gardens with their "arbor" or "box tree" are certainly tamer, more domesticated than the forest of Arden; nevertheless, they stand for the latent fertility, the source of potential life, at the heart of the closed world. And while the settings of these comedies are less romantic than the green world, that is partly a matter of perspective: they present a green world seen, as it were, from inside. To those who enter this world, it often seems a place of romantic wonder or romantic peril: Antipholus, landing in Ephesus, like Sebastian in Illyria, assumes that the people are bewitched, that he is dreaming. But for Olivia or Adriana, who live there, Illyria or Ephesus is about as magical as Boston. Rosalind is enchanted by the pastoral world of Arden; for Corin, Arden is a place to tend sheep, where one's present master is stingier than the last. The natives of the green world, like those of the closed world, seem unable to love: Silvius woos Phebe, who scorns him; Titania and Oberon quarrel over a changeling; Portia is besieged by suitors she detests. But into this world of discord comes a stranger—Rosalind or Bassanio or the egregious Bottom—and soon we have a happy ending. To turn the pattern into tragedy, however, we need only substitute for the invading power of love the coming of retribution or the encroachments of demonic evil.

Audience perspective finally determines which is a green world and which is closed. Whatever Corin thinks of Arden, we see it as Rosalind does; for us Ephesus is a closed world, since we see the humdrum causes for the bewitchment of Antipholus. But, of course, we are dealing with the continuum of a creative imagination, not the rigid oppositions of a system. Illyria, though closed, is nearly a green world, while Hermia, Helena, Lysander, and Demetrius in their alternating attraction and repulsion are not unlike the lovers of a closed world comedy. The patterns interlock in *Merry Wives* and *Taming of the Shrew*, and in the "problem" comedies Shakespeare went on to experiment with sophisticated and ironic versions. *All's Well* is a green world comedy but deals with sexual antagonism; *Measure for Measure* is a closed world comedy in which a law against lovers is averted by an intruder who turns out to be the lover, the father, and the ruler of us all. The two patterns merge in *The Tempest*, where the green world and the closed world are definitively one, as reality becomes indistinguishable from dream.

Perhaps the relation of the two patterns may be clarified by examining the archetypes they represent. Both suggest basic story forms familiar to us in those fairy tales where a younger son sets out to seek his fortune in a magic world of adventure, or a princess lies locked in enchanted sleep until the prince comes to wake her with a kiss. The archetypes—and by "archetype" I mean simply a narrative pattern that recurs in different periods, cultures, and literary kinds—are the journey and the siege. The latter is the less familiar: we find it whenever the action centers on a city, palace, garden, house, or room besieged or invaded from without. The siege may be military, amatory, or moral and psychological, may enact wooing or temptation or armed assault. *The Rape of Lucrece* illustrates all these modes at once: Tarquin penetrates Lucrece's home, her chamber, her bed and body, but never her heart. It is a rape, not a seduction, which finds its painted analogue in the siege and sack of Troy.

The analogy is not only apt but inevitable, for these archetypes of quest and siege go back to the *Odyssey* and *Iliad*. The *Odyssey* is an epic of quest: in his travels, Odysseus visits many lands, all of them magical, multiple versions of the green world. Some are "comic": dream lands of ease and luxury and sexual delight; other are "tragic": nightmare places of terror and death. The epic rounds out the pattern by employing a double hero. It begins with Telemachus, virtually expelled from Ithaca, setting off to seek his father, and ends with Odysseus' return home. We notice a characteristic difference of perspective between protagonist and audience: the courts of Pylos and Sparta are real for us but magical to young Telemachus, whereas the strange worlds Odysseus encounters are enchantment for us but hardship, peril, temptation to him. Both are tested, but the visits of Telemachus to foreign courts are part of his princely education: the son is achieving his identity while the father struggles to preserve his. Each of the green worlds, viewed independently or from inside, is a closed world into which Odysseus intrudes. His problem is always to establish some human link with inhabitants, a link which is often —as with Circe, Calypso, and Nausicaa—sexual or romantic. Even the hero's return home is presented as intrusion into a closed world: Odysseus comes secretly to Ithaca and crosses his own threshold disguised as a beggar; there he must "exorcise" the usurping suitors and reclaim his identity as king and husband.[7]

The *Iliad*, on the other hand, is an epic of siege. But as the quest of the *Odyssey* is a series of closed world episodes, so the siege of the *Iliad* is the central episode in a larger epic cycle of departure and return, the saga of the Greeks who went to Troy. At least on the human level, the poem observes unity of place, the plains between the walls of Troy and the sea wall of the Greeks. Each is besieged in turn, but neither is destroyed: it seems a war that no one really wins. The to and fro of the action underlines for the reader the likeness of Greek and Trojan where they themselves see hateful difference. Dominating all is the figure of Achilles, shut up in his tents as in his wrath, impervious alike to the embassies of friends and the assaults of foes. Only at the conclusion of the poem does the old Trojan king, divinely guided, make his way past guard and wall and gate to Achilles' tent, and finally to the savage heart of the young warrior who slew his son. Each alone in his grief but united by their grieving, Trojan father and Greek son share their tragic moment of community.[8] As smoke rises at the end from the pyres of Hector and Patroclus, we cannot tell victor from victim in the shadowing doom that waits for all men equally.

The interconnection of patterns is still closer in the *Aeneid*, which divides into six books of quest and six of siege. Even more clearly than in the *Odyssey*, the quest is made up of closed world episodes: the sack of Troy with the climactic invasion of Priam's palace, the advent of the Trojans in Carthage and the conquest of its queen, the descent into the forbidden regions of the underworld. Conversely, the double siege of city and camp in the last six books is remarkably mobile, and it is punctuated by Aeneas' river journey to the green Arcadia that will be Rome. But Virgil's epic reverses Homer's: the siege (though not the poem) ends in a marriage that unites natives and aliens in a new and international Troy.[9]

These poems are the fountainheads of Western story-telling, and their basic patterns persist when epic gives way to romance and then to novel. In the *Divine Comedy*, the pilgrim spirit pursues the quest for salvation from Hell to Heaven, while that other great medieval allegory, the *Romance of the Rose*, turns on intrusion into a garden enclosed: the fleshly lover must pass its wall and hedge of thorn, besiege and invade its castle, before he finally penetrates the rose itself.[10] So Chaucer follows his human comedy on the pilgrimage from London to Canterbury, Babylon to Jerusalem, and circumscribes his tragedy of wooing with the analogous action of the siege of Troy. Spenser and Milton, like Virgil, are eclectic: *The Faerie*

Queene intersperses its quest motif with scenes of siege like the Castle of Alma, Acrasia's Bower, and the House of Venus, while Milton balances Satan's quest against his invasion of Eden and the seduction of poor Eve.

When we turn to the novel, whom do we encounter but Don Quixote, on quest to green worlds of his own imagining? The heroes of Fielding follow him down the high road of the picaresque; the heroines of Richardson are imprisoned and besieged by wicked wooers. And in the nineteenth century, the archetypes persist in masculine novels of education and feminine novels of manners. One moves with the hero from country to city—the green world of Pip's great expectations—while the other centers on the heroine in the closed world of the drawing room. The old plots keep turning up, as in *Pride and Prejudice,* which is *Much Ado* revisited. In our own literature, we have the closed circle of the Puritan community and mind in *The Scarlet Letter* and the escape down the green world of the Mississippi in *Huckleberry Finn.* In *The Ambassadors* and *The Wings of the Dove,* where innocent Americans enter the corrupt but magic world of European society, the patterns take on a Jamesian sophistication, while in *The Secret Sharer* and *The Heart of Darkness* Conrad is already translating them into the psychological, symbolic, and surreal modes that persist to our own day.

Drama exhibits a similar balancing of the two forms. Classical tragedy with its unity of place inevitably favors the closed world pattern. There is a literal siege in the *Seven Against Thebes;* more impressive is the spiritual assault upon a Prometheus or Philoctetes. To these heroes, nailed to a rock, abandoned on an island, come emissaries seeking to subdue their will by persuasion or by force. But the classical exemplar of closed world tragedy is the *Bacchae,* in which the rational and masculine mind personified in Pentheus and symbolized by his palace is invaded, possessed, and broken by the feminine and dionysiac forces it has denied. The *Oresteia,* as we might expect, synthesizes both forms. The symmetry of retribution makes the *Choephori* a reverse image of the *Agamemnon*: in each tragedy, a sinister homecoming reaches its climax with the actual entry into the house of Atreus, where man is slain by woman and woman by man. But the *Eumenides* takes Orestes on his quest for purification to Athens, city of light, and resolves the murderous dialectic of male and female in the person of Athena: it provides the green world exception that proves the closed world rule. The comedy of Aristophanes rectifies this imbalance in the patterns: its heroes escape from the unsatisfactory world of everyday to the heaven of the *Birds* or the Hades of the *Frogs,* or the purely mental utopias of the sophist and the jurist in the *Clouds* and the *Wasps.* But *Lysistrata* with its siege and its war between the sexes once more supplies the exception necessary to critical symmetry.

Classical drama is useful for our purpose by its relative clarity of outline and regularity of method. Renaissance drama offers a valuable corrective in its variation and diversity. As we draw nearer to Shakespeare and our topic, it becomes important to stress the versatility of the patterns and the freedom of the individual author. An archetype is not a stereotype. The Renaissance poet sought to "overgo" his models; imitation meant evolution, not mere repetition. Hence to analyse *Epi-*

coene and *The Changeling* as types of closed world comedy and tragedy is to discover the new and particular as well as the recurrent and archetypal. Setting *The Alchemist* beside *The Tempest* or *As You Like It* beside *Bartholomew Fair* shows how decorum shapes the varied potentialities of the closed and green world conventions to the opposed demands of romantic and satiric comedy. The closed world of *The Alchemist* is a green world seen from inside, a satiric inversion of *A Midsummer Night's Dream,* in which Subtle and Face, like Oberon and Puck, stage-manage a green (or golden) world of illusion for all who enter Lovewit's house. But here, as so often in life, the green world is a trap. Its magic is ingenious fraud, its enchanted forest a city house besieged by plague, its romantic passion the concupiscence of greed and lust. Nothing can transform that tawdry Queen of Fairy, Dol Common, into a Titania. Obviously the critical alchemy that would reduce Jonsonian and Shakespearean comedy to their archetypal first matter, or transmute one into the other, can only produce fool's gold.

The green and closed world patterns provide a basis for comparison, not a rule of conformity. They enable us to distinguish "naive" and "mannerist" versions: the green world patterning of *Mucedorus* and the closed world patterning of Fletcher's *Island Princess,* for example. They permit us to draw together for comparison motifs, structural outlines, entire plays of different periods. The ominous knocking at the gate in the *Choephori* echoes centuries later in *Macbeth.* Prospero's magic warps to tragic madness in Pirandello's *Henry IV;* Lovewit's house becomes the brothel of Mme. Irma in *The Balcony.* Extending the spectrum of examples in this way helps to correct notions based on the practise of a single period or writer. The closed world plays of Shakespeare's day, like his own, usually dramatize intrusion; modern dramatists show equal interest in the problem of breaking out of a drab or sterile or imprisoning environment. Dramas of intrusion alternate with dramas of escape or its frustration, while still others trace a complete cycle of arrival and departure, invasion and expulsion. Examples crowd upon the mind: the attempt to classify them would carry us beyond the limits of this essay and the reader's patience. But any exploration of closed worlds in Ibsen, Strindberg, and Chekhov—to say nothing of their successors—quickly shows that the possibilities of the pattern are limited mainly by the imagination of the artist. The reader is invited to try.

One returns with relief from these quests through world literature to the relatively closed world of Shakespeare's plays. But after even this brief survey of their variations, we will not expect to find the green and closed worlds restricted to the comedies. We can discern the green world pattern working through the tetralogy that begins with *Richard II*—most clearly in the comical-historical-pastoral of *Henry V*—but it is subordinated to chronicle history and Tudor myth. So too in several classical plays—*Troilus, Timon, Coriolanus, Antony*—the green and closed world structures are subordinate to what I can only call the pattern of the double world. Complementary or contrasted settings are juxtaposed, but neither really satisfies: the plays move from one to the other in a tragic dialectic by which the protagonists are destroyed—unless like Antony and Cleopatra they succeed in resolving and transcending it. But it is towards the four major tragedies that my discussion has been mainly directed. Analyzed in terms of our patterns, they divide with almost embarrassing neatness. *Hamlet* and *Macbeth* are closed world tragedies (though *Macbeth* does not observe the unity of place). Both Macbeth and Hamlet are cabined, cribbed, confined in the closed worlds of Dunsinane and Elsinore. But to these heroes there appear — for evil or for good — intruders from another world whose mortal agents they become. When, on the other hand Lear rushes out onto the heath — that tragic pastoral — or Othello and Desdemona take ship to Cyprus against her father's will, we have the familiar green world pattern. Both settings may be viewed as projections of the hero: the heath with its darkness and tempest reflects the passion and madness within Lear, tragically inverting the green world of wish and dream; Cyprus, the "warlike isle" threatened by the invasion of unbelief, is an emblem of Othello himself. But the green world of love and war becomes a closed world, invaded and possessed by the demonic spirit of jealousy and hate. Othello is thus a play that becomes tragedy by going on where comedy leaves off, a tragedy which evolves from comedy precisely as the later romances evolve from tragedy.[11] The detailed workings of these patterns in the tragedies is matter for a longer study, to which the present essay is by way of prologue. But perhaps enough has been said to suggest a theoretic frame within which Shakespeare's comedies and tragedies may be more coherently and systematically compared. For the two worlds of Shakespearean comedy are patterns to which that shaping imagination constantly returned, exploring and recreating them with ever increasing insight, subtlety, and power.

Notes:

(1) These investigations extend from "The Argument of Comedy" in *English Institute Essays* for 1948 through the *Anatomy* to *A Natural Perspective* (New York, 1965). My debt to Frye, both in substance and method, is very great and very obvious. My remarks on *Twelfth Night* are indebted to Robert Speaight's interpretation of the play as a comedy of privacy in a lecture delivered some years ago at Princeton. The notion of an "internalized" green world and the comparison of *The Alchemist* with Genet's *Balcony* I have stolen from two of my students, Stephen Nathan and Bruce Hardy. The concept of the "closed heart" is taken from *The Sense of Shakespeare's Sonnets* (Princeton, 1952) by Edward Hubler, to whose memory this essay is dedicated.

(2) This fact suggests a parallel modification of Frye's thesis that tragedy moves from liberty to bondage: in "redemptive" tragedy, the hero's doom becomes a liberation of the spirit.

(3) I am indebted for this point to Joseph H. Summers, "The Masks of *Twelfth Night*," in *Shakespeare: Modern Essays in Criticism*, ed. Leonard F. Dean (New York, 1957), p. 128. If other, equally definite obligations go unacknowledged, the fault is one of memory and not intention.

(4) Frye discusses Falstaff's expulsion as expelling humors of jealousy, lust, and greed from the characters, and as a folk ritual of "carrying out Death." Both observations are valid in their own way, but one is too narrowly moralistic, the other too anthropologically general to explain its thematic meaning.

(5) This may not seem true of Jaques. But Jaques and Duke Senior are clearly intended as doublets or complementaries: *il penseroso* and *l'allegro*, the weeping and the laughing philosopher. Jacques' melancholy is a plausible attitude for an exiled Duke (compare the choler of Prospero). But the

old Duke, finding "good in everything," aligns philosophic age with the youthful optimism of the lovers. Psychologically, then, Jaques stands for an attitude, a role, a potential self the Duke repudiates. Generically and archetypally, he expresses the opposition to love such a father would present (compare Prospero's deliberate adoption of the role of wrathful *senex* to test Ferdinand). In Arden, such opposition is only philosophic: there is no final resolution of the debate between the wisdom of experience and the wisdom of love; Signior Love and Monsieur Melancholy agree only to become better strangers. This archetypal role may explain why if Shakespeare ever intended Jaques to be Orlando's brother, he changed his mind; why Duke Senior so loves to "cope" his opposite and counterpart; why Jaques confronts both hero and heroine while the benevolent Duke is kept in the background; and why, at the happy ending, he shares with the Duke in the benediction on the lovers.

(6) For a fuller discussion of love and *concordia discors* in Spenser, see Thomas P. Roche, *The Kindly Flame* (Princeton, 1964), *passim*.

(7) See the final chapter of Cedric Whitman's *Homer and the Heroic Tradition* (Cambridge, Mass., 1963).

(8) I paraphrase—not without a sense of violation—a sentence from Trilling's introduction to *The Portable Matthew Arnold* (New York, 1949), p. 6., in which he speaks of "Achilles or Priam, each solitary under his doom, yet able for a moment to meet—the most terrible and most beautiful instant of community that literature has recorded—in the equal and courteous society of grief."

(9) The "thirteenth" book of the *Aeneid* by Maphaeus Vegius provides what many a Renaissance reader might regard as a proper ending of the poem. The "Iliadic" parallels are, of course, much more than literary pastiche. In *Virgil: A Study in Civilized Poetry* (Oxford, 1963), Brooks Otis shows that the first half of the poem enacts the purification and perfecting of the hero; the second half relates his heroic deeds. Aeneas' task is to restore Troy; he can do so only by undoing the moral tragedy of the Trojan War. Books VII-XII, then, are not so much the imitation as the reversal of the *Iliad*. Only by repeating the Trojan past in reverse can Aeneas bring back to the upper air of reality the vision of a Roman future granted him in the underworld. That is why he returns at the end of VI through the fictive gate of ivory. The struggles and sufferings of the remainder of the poem constitute his true reascent: *hoc opus, hic labor est.*

(10) The anonymous poet who completed Guillaume de Lorris' part of the *Romance* violates the pattern: he has Beauty come out of the castle and present the rose to the lover. This reminds us once again that archetypes are not easy: it demands a certain kind and degree of imagination to discern and carry out their inner logic.

(11) This statement directly contradicts Frye's position in *Anatomy of Criticism* (Princeton, 1957), pp. 215-216, and if true would seem to require significant revision in his theory of genres.

A Note on the Aural Errors in the First Quarto of King Lear

by Patricia Ingham

The nature of the copy for the First Quarto of *King Lear* and hence the precise relation of this copy to that behind the First Folio text remain unsolved problems. The Quarto's strange combination of gross errors and signs of foul papers has necessitated strange hypotheses. One salient piece of evidence is the group of supposed aural errors in the Quarto, but these do not seem to have been rigorously analysed in the light of contemporary Standard English pronunciation to discover whether they are erroneous, and, if so, whether they are distinctively aural errors of one particular kind. The following attempts such an analysis as a basis for further discussion.[1]

Most of the textual critics who produce theories about the nature of the copy for the Quarto make no attempt to give a comprehensive account of the aural errors. Two who have done so are G. I. Duthie and Madeleine Doran.[2] Duthie in his earlier[3] full discussion of the copy for the Quarto suggests that it was a memorial reconstruction by the entire company who "dictated their parts in turn to a scribe (perhaps the book-keeper) who wrote down what they said as fast as he could" (p. 78). Hence this scribe was the source of the aural errors. Duthie's grouping of the latter is as follows:

(1) "the most noteworthy . . . errors of hearing" (p. 79);
(2) "spellings which may perhaps be regarded as the result of mishearing, or as faithful reproductions of popular pronunciations" (p. 80).

Madeleine Doran's grouping is different. She believes that the copy for the Quarto was "the old manuscript, Shakespeare's original version of the play, containing all the additions and revisions he had subsequently made" (p. 136). She is inclined to think, therefore, that the supposed aural errors were made by the compositor. Her classification is as follows:

(1) "several undoubted" errors of mishearing (p. 124);
(2) "several more . . . perhaps due to mishearing" "although some of them may be misreadings or misprints" (pp. 124-5).
(3) "some spellings which suggest mishearing" "although it may be that they are merely ignorant spellings on the part of the printer" (p. 125).

These groupings seem ill-defined and the criteria on which readings have been assigned to one or other categories within them are not clear. I would suggest the following as more pertinent:

(1) mistakes not based on contemporary pronunciations. If these are aural errors then the writer (Duthie's scribe-book-keeper) simply did not hear what was said, but misheard

> *I apprehend* for *Ile apprehend* I.ii.79-80
> *doe* for *to* I.iv.168
> *weaknes* for *weakens* (unless this is, as seems more likely, mere transposition of type) I.iv.228
> *lethergie* for *Lethargied* I.iv.229
> *deed* for *need* II.iv.260
> *Hircanios* for *Hyrricanos* (none among the many variant spellings of this word ever seems to end in *-io*) III.ii.2
> *Mohing* for *Mowing* IV.i.61 (F. omits)
> *Argue* for *Agu* IV.vi.105

Possibly here belongs also *may know* for *make knowne* I.i.225: in this the omission of final *n* appears to have no phonological basis, but *may* for *make* may be due to the failure on the part of a listener to distinguish the final *k* of *make* from the initial *kn* of *knowne*, which was still pronounced with a [kn].[4] The *ay* might then be a reverse spelling of the infinitive such as would be used by the originator of the mistake *so bade* in group (2) below.

Miss Doran's theory should, presumably, compel her to ascribe these errors to careless reading of the copy by the compositor although, in fact, she includes some in her second group. It is, indeed, far from certain that these are aural errors of any kind, but only that they are mistakes. In any event none of them is based on an authentic representation of what was said either by the actor (or dictator) or by the compositor to himself in his head. They are therefore to be distinguished sharply from

(2) mistakes that represent contemporary pronunciations and are true aural errors depending on the fact that the presumed listener-scribe put down the wrong word, because for him it happened to be identical in sound with the actor (or dictator's) pronunciation of the right word (usually because the listener's pronunciation of the erroneous word was more vulgar or advanced than that current in Standard English at the time. A parallel in present-day English would be for a north-country speaker to mistake a Standard speaker's *room* for *rum*.) Doran, however, offers another explanation for the errors in this group: that the compositor "unconsciously substituted words similar in sound, just as now one sometimes writes *their* for *there*, *write* for *right*." (p. 125)

Either of these explanations accounts for the following mistakes:

ought for *oft* I.iv.347
where for *were* I.v.8
sight for *-cite* IV.iv.27
Bare for *beare* IV.vi.80
so bade for *'s obey'd* IV.vi.157-8
of for *haue* V.iii.306 (and possibly *haue* for *of* III.ii.33)
one for *owne* III.iv.23

If these are, as seems more likely in view of their number, the mistakes of a listening scribe rather than a compositor, then his pronunciations of *ought*, *where*, *sight*, *bare*, and *bade* were vulgar: he pronounced *ought* with [f] instead of the standard [χ] ; *wh* as [w] , although this was a vulgarism in Standard English until the eighteenth century; *sight* without the normal [χ]; and M.E. *a* as [ε:] , whereas [æ:] was standard. If *haue* (the man . . . shall *haue* a corne cry woe) is really an error for *of*, then he also used a vulgar pronunciation of *have*, but such a pronunciation cannot be inferred for him from *of* in V.iii.306 because there, presumably, he merely recorded what he heard. *One* for *owne*, although a mistake, merely means that he used a pronunciation of 'one' without an initial [w] , a fairly normal variant in Standard speech.

Under this hypothesis, of course, the actor (or dictator) not the listening scribe was responsible for the sounds given to the words actually intended and he happened to use pronunciations identical with the listener's pronunciations of the erroneous words. But if these are really compositor's errors, then for him each of these pairs of words were homonyms. We can therefore conclude that in addition to the non-standard forms listed above, he also used an advanced monophthongal pronunciation [ε:] for M. E. *ai* in *obey'd*.

> (3) Instances (not certainly to be regarded as errors) where the writer of the Quarto put the right word but used a spelling different from that of the Folio:
>
> > *aurigular* I.ii.94
> > *ruffen* II.ii.60
> > *caterickes* III.ii.2
> > *vaunt-currers* III.ii.5
> > *venter'd* III.iv.152
> > *cushings* III.vi. 34 (For *cushions*; F. omits)
> > *dungell* III.vii. 96
> > *Mobing* IV.i.60 (? for *mopping*; F. omits)
> > *Fauchon* V.iii.276
>
> It is by no means certain that these spellings are errors: *ruffen*, *caterickes*, *vaunt-currers*, *venter'd* and *Fauchon* represent accurately authentic vulgar pronunciations of the words in question. *Cushings* also depends on a vulgarism: it seems to reflect a speech in which [ıŋ] has become [ın], so that the listen-

ing scribe or compositor was able to spell a word ending in (n) with *ng*. Another possible explanation is that it is a hypercorrect pronunciation in [ɪŋ] used by the actor (or dictator) or the compositor. The word *dungell* also represents a contemporary pronunciation, in this instance probably one acceptable in Standard English. *Aurigular* and *Mobing* less certainly represent authentic pronunciations; both may be examples of the voiceless stops in intervocalic positions.[5]

If these are the spellings of a compositor then they are of a slightly different kind from the second group. There he knew two words pronounced identically; he memorised the sound of one and put down the other. Here, reading the words in the copy he merely substituted his own pronunciations, despite the plain discrepancy between them and the spelling in front of him and set up accordingly.

If, on the other hand, these are due to a listening scribe then they can be explained like Group (2) as an accurate account of what he heard. It is, theoretically, possible that he substituted personal spellings which did not represent the sounds he heard, but this seems less likely in view of the phonetic accuracy involved in the second group of readings.

However as indicated above, all but two of these spellings make sense and represent authentic pronunciations. It seems illogical, therefore, to regard them as necessarily errors, especially since they are the kind of pronunciation spellings which in "good" quartos are fairly readily ascribed to Shakespeare. Consistency requires that they should be similarly treated, and at least considered as possible evidence for foul papers as copy.

From the above examination two points emerge about the supposed aural errors in this Quarto: that those unmistakably aural are fewer than generally supposed, and that whoever was responsible for them used an advanced or vulgar form of speech.

Notes:

(1) Line references are from G. I. Duthie and J. Dover Wilson, *King Lear*, (Cambridge, 1960). Italics in textual citations are mine.

(2) *The Text of King Lear*, Stanford University Publications, Language and Literature, Vol. IV, no. 2 (1931). It should be pointed out that Miss Doran herself has since described this view of the copy for the Quarto as "dubious": RES, XVII (1941), 474.

(3) I.e. *Shakespeare's King Lear*, (Oxford 1949). In his edition (1 above) he modified his views to the more general statement that the copy was "transcription from foul papers by dictation, the persons involved having had some memorial knowledge of the play" (p. 135). The modification is not germane here.

(4) On the dating and status of pronunciations I accept throughout the views of E. J. Dobson in his *English Pronunciation 1500-1700*, (Oxford, 1957).

(5) See H. C. Wyld, *A History of Modern Colloquial English*, (Oxford, 1936), p. 312, where he cites examples of a similar voicing in other words.

Bond Slaves and Counterfeits: Shakespeare's Measure for Measure

by R. J. Kaufmann

Man is neither angel nor brute, and the unfortunate thing is that he who would act the angel acts the brute. *Pascal.*

So many base plated coins passing in the market, the belief is now become common that no gold any longer exists. *Carlyle.*

In the book of *Job* we find Job, stricken and misunderstood, striving to make clear to imaginatively restricted friends his own perceptions of divine quality,

> With Him is strength and effectual working;
> The deceived and the deceiver are His.
> He leadeth counsellors away [de] spoiled
> And judges maketh He fools.
> He looseth the bonds of Kings. *(Job xii.16-25)*

His speech constitutes a virtual thematic catalogue for *Measure for Measure*.[1] In Duke Vincentio there is invested "strength and effectual working," and, given the postulates of the play, "the deceived and the deceiver *are* His." Angelo, the deputized "judge," is led away "despoiled," but despoiled of his falsity, for in such happy alterations of stern injunctions comedy realizes itself. But, perhaps most important of all, there is a sense in which "He looseth the bonds of kings." For, *Measure for Measure* starts with all the citizens of its civic world variously in bondage. The play is literally and in many shadings of figure about bondage, but where bondage is psychic these bonds may not be loosed save by self-understanding. The intransigent Barnadine thus becomes thematically intelligible as an emblematic representation of the pure state of bondage. *Measure for Measure* is a play contrived to "unfold" (i.e., plumb and expose) the roots of a positive freedom. Such freedom must be imaginatively acquired by the characters, so that it is in some felt sense made their "own." In this magisterially controlled comic world, this liberation is effected through a set of contrived experiments in self-encounter at a level no longer captive to illusions of each captive character's particularized moral devising. In *Measure for Measure*, Angelo receives, *technically*, a large measure of freedom: he is transposed from subject to (deputized) sovereign. The departure of Duke Vincentio removes major legal constraints. Angelo remains, however, in a state of bondage to his false seeming. Moral and psychological enslavement nullify his political and legal freedom. Nowadays we have a rage to achieve authenticity of experience. Here the equivalent ruling figure is of counterfeit coinage;

the deep working metaphor is of minting valid selves in a world sleezy with "seemings." Each major character is helped to learn, if he can learn, the inner burden of St. Augustine's searching axiom in *De Doctrina Christiana*, "Everything which does not decrease on being given away is not properly *owned* when it is *owned* and not given."

There has been widespread uneasiness about the dramaturgical propriety of the play centering on the argued conviction that Shakespeare subverts the dignity of his own achievement by steadily arrogating to the Duke powers that rightly belong to characters whose independent moral dignity has been beautifully established in the early phases of the action. As, for example, Isabella who is made to descend from the poetic heights of

> Why all the souls that were, were forfeit once,
> And He that might the vantage best have took
> Found out the remedy. *(II.ii.80-82)*[2]

to the demeaning role of willing accomplice in the folk-worn bed-trick. Obviously, the mode of the play requires a strange sort of imaginative complicity on the part of the reader, but once we are in a secure relationship with the symbolic aura which develops round the Duke as he performs his morally proleptic functions, we should have no further disquiet about the efficient use to which Shakespeare puts him. These strong doubts about dramaturgical propriety arise from the "good ruler," Duke Vincentio, wandering about spying upon and deceiving his subjects, albeit manifestly for their own good. They are compounded by an unsteady association of Vincentio with Providence in the parabolic action which the play dramatizes. This affiliation of errant ruler and an animated Providence is unseemly and possibly radically incongruous to the contemporary mind.

It is comforting then to find in *Troilus and Cressida*, a near cousin in the canon, the reliable Ulysses making a neat and direct association of: Providence, spying, the good ruler and the proper functioning of the State. Ulysses, having told Achilles his secret love for one of Priam's daughters is known, the latter is incredulous, wondering how this information was discovered. Ulysses then explains,

> Is it a wonder?
> The providence that's in a watchful state
> Knows almost every grain of Pluto's gold
> Finds bottom in th' uncomprehensive deeps;
> Keeps place with thoughts and almost like the gods,
> Do thoughts unveil in their dumb cradles
> There is a mystery—with whom relation [i.e., report, gossip]
> Durst never meddle—in the soul of state,
> Which hath an operation more divine
> Than breath or pen can give expressure to. *(III.iii.196-205)*

Shakespeare, in the non-Christian context of *Troilus and Cressida*, felt obliged to furnish a rationalization for a form of behavior which might offend the integrity

86

of the mode he was then working in. This carefully argued rationalization is doubly helpful: 1) it spells out a dramatic nexus of terms to be used again in *Measure for Measure*; and 2) it permits us to infer that Shakespeare feared no such dislocation for readers who were properly attuned to the parabolic nature of his different dramatic enterprise in *Measure for Measure*. The Disguised Duke, released from his previously confining role, becomes less a phenomenal datum and is to be understood as conditionally different in quality as well as in name. We are not used to a *deus ex machina* entering so early into a play, but this is no argument for not comprehending the imaginative consequences when he does. The Duke in his disguise enacts with the fine literalness of the comic world, Hamlet's agonized endeavour, to "know not seems." He is moved to a vantage point of practical omniscience dramaturgically correlative to his state of self-knowledge. He precedes others into the world of "measure." This brings us to the title.

The title clearly derives from a concern for the two competing testamental laws of justice; the *lex talionis* and the Sermon on the Mount's more merciful reading, but as the action unfolds it comes to refer to "measure" in the sense of moderation. The characters find their proper repose in moderate conduct, save for Lucio who being incapable of moderation, finds no repose and therefore no freedom. He is thus publically identified with the self-enslaving principles he has chosen. Between the extremes of leniency and license; excessive restraint and compulsive indulgence—between Angelo and the earlier, too naively permissive Duke; between Isabella and Lucio there is a course where mens' lives run. Between the measure that measures arbitrarily and the measure that releases without severity, there is a practical ethic to live by, a mode of measuring human needs and of establishing a congruity between these and one's answering actions. In this decorum of practical moral behavior, social and personal authenticity is rooted. Understanding this redeems men from a counterfeited state, and the strong pun in the word "state" is critically indispensable. Shakespeare, like his contemporary Donne, puns with ideas.

Measure for Measure does not rely upon the normal process of character development. Instead there is a carefully paced liberation of the essential individual, through untarnishing his image, or uncovering ("unfolding") his light. Hence the evolution of the play is from unrecognized chaos to order as the Duke teaches each man his political function via honest commerce with his own residual nature. The Duke removes himself from his historically compromised role in the *vita activa* thereby releasing himself from captivity to a wrongly developed *persona*: the *pre-play* or *story* Duke shares with the other characters the general failure in perfect congruence with the obligations of his role; the Duke *of the play itself* does not. The force which sets in motion the parable we see enacted in his conversion, his self-liberation. *Julius Caesar, Henry V, Twelfth Night, Hamlet, Troilus* and *Measure for Measure* show a common preoccupation with *ceremony*. The earlier reluctance of the Duke to accept his own necessary symbolhood—to show himself willingly to crowds, so as to be a personified sanction for necessary public truths is related to Brutus' failure to grasp the consequences of transposing his self-governing code into a realm governed by a magnified rhetoric and a magnified style of behavior. It is also related to: Cassius' envious incomprehension of the ground of Caesar's greatness; to Henry V's necessary rejection of Falstaff as the concomitant to his acceptance of the role of King; and to Hamlet's quest for the exact quality of his composite identity as private person *and* king-figure. The whole play, *Troilus and Cressida,* is preoccupied with the regulative force of ceremony, with building communal truths and the costly epistemology of shared beliefs.

Shakespeare's concern with this cluster of themes shows itself well in his image choices, in his addiction to certain types of basic fable during the central period of his career. He was drawn to counterfeit images, those of borrowed robes and crowns, and to the imagery of the stage or theater itself as a place where systematic, public illusions are generated and sustained. In this most crucial period of Shakespeare's creative self-realization, we can observe his invention of artistic means to render that part of *religious* experience drama can successfully deal with through scrutiny of its renewal in the shared life of the community. *Measure for Measure* unfolds so as to infuse with reality what would otherwise be held in "opinion" or superficially, thus translating moral experience from the class of counterfeit objects or concepts to the genuine and known. Virtue must be tested against loss, against power, against possible advantage, and above all, against death. This last is the reason that the Claudio plot is so devotedly elaborated. De-Maistre asserted that social order rests ultimately on the executioner's axe. Perhaps the ordinary, untutored man's equivalent of the thoughtful man's *nosce teipsum* is the realization that his life can indeed be taken for his transgressions.

Let us now do some weighing and testing of our own by making a closer examination of the play's structure and language.

An observation by St. Thomas Aquinas in his *Summa* sharpens our sense of the thematic process of *Measure for Measure.*

> it belongs to the virtue of truth to show oneself outwardly by outward signs to be such as one is. Now outward signs are not only words but also deeds . . . dissimulation is properly, a lie told by the signs of outward deeds.[3]

Shakespeare's major works progressively expose the final inefficacy of mere *visual acuity.* These plays are testaments to the humanly contradicted necessity for a vision which sees deeply and clearly, for what Hamlet calls to "know not seems." Shakespeare's villains, Iago, Macbeth, Iachimo, and Angelo, place great if variably exploited faith in the trappings and outward manifestations of goodly seeming, and their actions reinforce their basic premise that man is easily deceived. This philosophical tradition of appearance and reality was hoary with use when it came down to Shakespeare, yet by assimilating it to his passionately grasping sensibility, he deeply enriched the concept.

Shakespeare, in his mature poetic, extended his means for controlling the viewer's response to the play through his compacting of metaphorical language; it is the critic's job to indicate closely the nature of the control he exercised in each play, to trace the essential metaphorical linkages which build and reinforce his themes; for Shakespeare's plays tend to germinate from radical metaphorical conceptions which "unfold" presentationally into the finished works of art. In *Measure for Measure* certain words possess what Ernest Leisi calls "elective affinities" for others. One such word-linkage in *Measure for Measure* is the habitual tendency for the terms of authority and governorship to be connected with those of clothing: the robes of authority motif. But this is a branching variant of a more basic habitual connection: that made between man's "mettle" and the terminology of coinage. Thus we find that the opening speeches of Act I tightly incorporate the tone and theme of the play. The Duke's opening speech is heavily imprinted with the imagery of economics.

> Of government the properties to unfold
> Would seem in me t'affect speech and discourse,
> Since I am put to know that your own science
> Exceeds, in that, the lists of all advice
> My strength can give you. Then no more remains
> But that, to your *sufficiency,* as your *worth* is able,
>   .   .   .   .   .
> And let them work. The nature of our people,
> Our city's institutions, and the terms
> For common justice, y'are as pregnant in
> As art and practice hath enriched any
> That we remember. There is our commission,
> From which we would not have you warp. Call hither,
> I say, bid come before us *Angelo.*
> What *figure* of us, think you, he will *bear?*
> For you must know, we have with special soul
> Elected him our absence to supply;
> Lent him our terror, drest him with our love,
> And given his deputation all the organs
> Of our own power. What think you of it?   (I.i.3-21, italics mine)

Leisi points out the obvious similarity between the departure of Duke Vincentio and that of the Master in St. Matthew's parable of the talents (*Matt.* xxv, 14ff). As in the parable which begins, "For the kingdom of heaven is as a man travelling into a far country, who called his own servants, and delivered unto them his goods," so in the play, the terms of material possession—the Duke speaks of "worth" and "sufficiency"—are used to represent the idea of spiritual "capital." With this in mind, Leisi attempts a persuasive emendation to fill the broken measures of lines eight and nine: "You add the talents of succeeding years." The words "figure" and "bear" in line sixteen provide a substantial continuation of the metaphor; as J. W. Lever points out, the words suggest "the ducal stamp on the seal of the commission.[4] Shakespeare further integrated Angelo into the coinage metaphor, for, "They have in England / A coin that bears the figure of an angel Stamped in gold." (*MV*, II.vii.56-57).

As the Duke continues his opening remarks to his old counsellor, Escalus, the imagery of coinage comes to a fuller fruition. The Duke notes, "spirits are not finely touch'd, / But to fine issues. . . ." (I.i.35-36). Lever points out, "'Touched' and 'issues', with 'fine' (= refined) suggest the 'touch' placed on gold coins of standard fineness before they were passed into circulation."[5] Finally, we see the culmination of the metaphor in the self-confident remark of Angelo:

> Now, good my lord,
> Let there be some more test made of my metal,
> Before so noble and so great a figure
> Be stamp'd upon it. *(I.i.47-50,*

Ernest Leisi comments on the use of the word "test" in this context: "Originally 'melting pot' (Latin *testa*) . . . the word acquired the force of a *nomen actionis* 'examination of precious metals by melting.' From this, the modern abstract meaning 'examination' developed."[6] In Elizabethan usage "metal" was interchangeable with the spelling and meaning of *mettle*. There are reinforcing usages in *Timon of Athens*: "They have all been touch'd and found base metal" (III.iii.6), and in *King John*: "Which, being touch'd and tried, Proves valueless." (III.i.101) The first fifty-one lines of *Measure for Measure* establish the basic terms of the play.

When John Calvin observed, "Satan is in many things a counterfeiter of God," he indicated in typically absolute terms what James I in his *Basilicon Doron* phrased more politically when differentiating a tyrant from a good ruler, "I shew how a Tyran would enter like a Saint while he found himselfe fast underfoot, and then would suffer his unrulee affections to burst forth." Both texts serve as a gloss for Angelo's dramatically contrived opportunity to gain moral freedom. It is the intention of *Measure for Measure* to place Angelo for the first time in his life above political contingency. He, unlike everyone else in the play save the Duke, is in bondage only to the laws of his own being. The robes of the Duke investing him with a roomy practical freedom, his own untested moral identity becomes the determinant of his behavior; there will "be some more test made of his metal" as he confronts himself in the unique conflict between his past and his newly precipitated role, until he reaches the terrifying question of Richard III: "What I is I?"

In Act II we see Angelo's concern for the outward, legalistic forms while he remains deaf to the music of the inner spirit. He intones, "It is the law, not I, condemn your brother." (II.ii.80) Isabella has, a few lines earlier, implied the defect in Angelo's brand of law:

> No ceremony that to great ones longs,
> Not the king's crown, nor the deputed sword,
> The marshal's truncheon, nor the judge's robe,
> Become them with one half so good a grace,
> As mercy does. *(II.ii.57-61)*

Angelo, dressed with the symbols of administration and execution of the law (ceremony, sword, and robe), has, like Richard II, mistaken the symbol for the substance,

90

the dress for the man. The more substantial quality, mercy, escapes him. James I stressed the necessity for *both* justice and mercy, stating, "for lawes are ordained as rules of vertuous and sociall living, and not to bee snares to trap your good subjects: and therefore the lawe must be interpreted according to the meaning, and not to the literall sense thereof."[7] Isabella's "man new made" will therefore temper the metal of justice with the warming heat of mercy. This is not to say the laws must not be enforced. For as James I noted, "what difference is betwixt extreame tyrannie, delighting to destroy all mankinde; and extreame slackenesse of punishment, permitting every man to tyrannize over his companion?"[8] The Duke has been guilty of a form of this slackness prior to his deputizing of Angelo. In the play as in Renaissance theory, the idea of a tempering, even an interfusion, of justice and mercy is established, for as Midrash in the Bereshith Rabbah observed: "Thus said the Holy one: 'If I create the world with mercy sin will abound: and if I create it with justice, how can the world exist? Therefore I create it with both mercy and justice, and may it thus endure.'"[9] One of the "problems" of this play results from its circumspect honesty in refusing to subordinate either justice or mercy. To see the play as a supersession of mere justice by mercy is to compromise the play's near tragic moral roundness. There is never an implication that the necessary mixture of these two qualities is an easy thing. Angelo, fails *as a ruler,* who must be the embodiment of mercy and justice; the robes of authority conceal an inward baseness which is redeemed only when he accepts his undisguised nakedness as a private individual in the last act. The play at numerous points prefigures the inner movement of Shakespeare's greatest play of moral testing, *King Lear.* When Isabella says,

> But man, proud man,
> Dress'd in a little brief authority,
> Most ignorant of what he's most assur'd—
> His glassy essence—like an angry ape
> Plays such fantastic tricks before high heaven
> As makes the angels weep. *(II.ii.118-123)*

her vision accords with Lear's in unfolding the inequity at the heart of Angelo's kind of justice.

Angelo also shares with Lear a fascination mixed with loathing for the act of sexual intercourse. He speaks of Claudio's getting Juliet with child thus:

> It were as good
> To pardon him that hath from nature stolen
> A man already made, as to remit
> Their saucy sweetness that do coin heaven's image
> In stamps that are forbid. *(II.iv.42-46)*

Angelo is talking of Claudio's begetting of a counterfeit, a bastard. We see this in the bawdy line from *Cymbeline:* "Some coiner with his tools made me a counterfeit" (II.v.5). A child is seen figuratively as a coin made either in legal or in forbidden stamps. This broadens the metaphorical development of the play. Also, Angelo's "life true made" must remind us of Isabella's earlier "man new made" by mercy. Thus, midway through the play, we see that *Measure for Measure* is about the making of a "true-made man," though not in Angelo's literal sense.

Angelo's lack of self-knowledge has caused him to forge his life through use of the stamps of appearance. His existence is just as much a spiritual lie as the sophistries with which he tries to make Isabella lay down her virtue to save her brother's life. The reader will remember that Angelo proposes:

> Might there not be a charity in sin
> To save this brother's life?   *(II.iv.63-64)*

Which brings us to Isabella. She has been treated rather harshly by the critics. Certainly she possesses a too categorically-imperative sense of moral law. She is also very inexperienced. Despite differences in practical alignment, her nearest kin in the Shakespearean canon is Troilus, another insistent, unemployed idealist. But still, Angelo's logic does not hold up, given the theocentric character of the play's universe. First, Angelo would not be committing a sin in granting mercy, since forgiveness—in appropriate cases—belongs to the nature of his office. The very title of the play militates against Angelo's heavy-handed (not even-handed) brand of "justice." Second, Isabella gives the only answer she can in her trying situation:

> Better it were a brother died at once,
> Than that a sister, by redeeming him,
> Should die for ever.   *(II.iv.106-08)*

Isabella's mettle, though yet brittle for lack of tempering, is far superior to Angelo's. Her most quoted speech on Christ as an intercessor,

> Why all the souls that were, were forfeit once
> And he that might the vantage best have took
> found out the remedy.   *(II.ii.80-82)*

shows that the *concept* of mercy is not foreign to her, it has simply not been practically annexed to her too private and vigilantly girlish convictions about purity. Mercy as a *practicum* of experience must be learned, most of all as it applies to the self. Further, Skulsky says that she all but allows that, in God's eyes at least, Claudio is a murderer. "'Tis set down so in heaven." But he does not add the end of her sentence, "but not in earth" (II.iv.50). What Claudio *is* a murderer of is what might be called the "ascetic fallacy:" that man can entirely "bate his natural edge." Isabella in the play escapes bondage to this fallacy; her frightened, inappropriate responses to Claudio in Act III are dramatically essential in showing that this bondage is genuine. The Duke's redemptive prescriptions apply in every case to well-diagnosed states of temporary moral captivity. It certainly applies to Isabella's brother, Claudio, who does not measure up to her high standard. As the Duke says to him:

92

> Thou are not noble
> For all th' accommodations that thou bear'st
> Are nurs'd by baseness. *(III.i.13-15)*

The Duke's "noble" is meant to awake a recognition of the mettle-metal imagery. A "noble" was the earlier name for the coin known as an "angel," and only a little later Isabella brings up the noble-base dichotomy in her remarks to Claudio.

> Yes, thou must die.
> Thou art too noble to conserve a life
> In base appliances. *(III.i.86-88)*

But the "baseness" in the genial but weak Claudio, who would sacrifice a sister's precious virtue, spills out. However, the slip is not total, and he soon vows to petition her no more. The moral assaying in the play is too precise to be ranged into neat polarities; Claudio is sympathetically human but soft—he absorbs a measure of stiffening nobility; Isabella is initially and partially unsympathetic in her humorless passion for spiritual nobility—she absorbs a requisite measure of softening generosity. The metal of true humanity is a special alloy. Angelo provides a further variation on the motif of nobility and baseness, and by the end of the play we see "to what metal this counterfeit lump of ore will be melted." (*All's Well,* III.vi.38ff.)

Thus Angelo is not the only one changed in the course of the play. Isabella, Claudio, and the Duke have gained from their experience. Isabella, with her strongly developed sense of sin and guilt, discovers the necessity of mercy. When, at the end of the play, she empathizes with Mariana and requests that Angelo be spared, her spiritual stiffness is emblematically rejected for a kneeling posture. The too docile Claudio, forced to confront the fact of his own mortality, learns the tenacity with which man clings to life. Everything in the play finally contradicts the sentiment that we must be "absolute for death;" the Duke's famous speech to Claudio on this text is drawn from his spiritual pharmacopia and acts as a specific against Claudio's slackened grip on his love of life. Like Angelo, Claudio and Isabella were linked together by the common factor of their inexperience. If maturation can be defined justly as a process of intelligent disillusionment, then both Claudio and Isabella mature in the world of the play. *Measure for Measure* is an unabashed parable of spiritual maturation in a mode less agonizing than *King Lear.*

But fullest growth in understanding belongs to that great stage-manager, Duke Vincentio. Prior to the play he had given his people too much "scope;" therefore *at the outset* of the play Vincentio, like his countrymen, is in bondage. For, he cannot yet reconcile knowledge with action. *Measure for Measure* is about his *becoming* the Duke *in fact* as well as symbolically. His growth can be seen as exemplifying the admonition of James.

> For it is not enough that ye have and retaine (*as prisoners*)
> within *your selfe* never so many good qualities and vertues,

except ye employ them, and set them on worke, for the weale
of them that are committed to your charge. *Virtutis enim laus
omnis in actione consistit.*[10]

The Duke's movement is from reluctant and hence marred sovereignty to effectual
working, from symbolic possibility to substantial reality.

Symbols of a poorly-run state abound in Vienna. The most significant break-
down manifests itself in the desuetude into which the institution of marriage has
fallen. No one in Vienna is married at the beginning of the play. Instead Mistress
Overdone and her bawd, Pompey, cater to the natural needs of the male citizens.
The language of illegitimacy and fornication crowds the play, reinforcing the
counterfeiting images. Licentious sexuality replaces the sacramental marriage
relationship. Claudio and Juliet at least have a *de praesenti* contract, yet they
still lack the sacramental sanction of the church.[11] Lucio, too, we find has gotten
a wench with child. And Angelo, although he had a *de futura* contract with Mariana
has abandoned her—for economic reasons, of course.

> She should this Angelo have married: was af-
> fianced to her oath, and the nuptial appointed.
> Between which time of the contract and limit of the
> solemnity, her brother Frederick was wrecked at
> sea, having in that perished vessel the dowry of his
> sister. *(III.i.213 ff.)*

And this was a signal for Angelo to desert her. Similarly, Claudio and Juliet fail
to solemnize their contract because of a tardy dowry. Ironically, the "play for pay"
business of Mistress Overdone is more honest than the mores of the gentlefolk.

Contrarily, another symptom of the break-down in this society occurs in the
denial of the flesh. Angelo seems a man who has bated his natural edge. Also,
Isabella seeks to live in a manner that is not of this world. Lucio, obviously not a
man troubled by the flesh-spirit dichotomy, tells her.

> I hold you as a thing enskied and sainted
> By your renouncement, an immortal spirit. *(I.iv.33-34)*

Whatever Shakespeare's attitude toward Roman Catholics might have been, we
can surely detect the thanatopic note in the nun, Francisca's, admonition to
Isabella.

> When you have vow'd, you must not speak with men
> But in the presence of the prioress;
> Then, if you speak, you must not show your face;
> Or if you show your face, you must not speak. *(I.iv.10-13)*

Costard in *Loves Labor's Lost* takes a much saner stance: "It is the manner of a
man to speak with a woman." (I.i.205-06) The societal situation pictured here by
Shakespeare resembles John Ford's in *The Broken Heart*, where the Spartans

must "send to Athens" for a philosopher to reacquaint them with human choices. Nature either operates completely released or completely repressed in Vienna.

For this reason the Duke leaves his society, so that he may best know how to deal with it when he "returns." The reliable Escalus calls the Duke, "One that, above all other strifes, contended especially to know himself." (III.ii.246-47) But the Duke ignored the "other strifes" which now threaten the very existence of his city. The Duke, in becoming an exemplar of self-governance, has slighted his practical and symbolic role. Just as the role of man *and* wife has been practically abolished, so the seat of justice *and* mercy has been abdicated.

When we perceive the play's pervasive concern with necessary acceptance of symbolhood as a factor of proper identity, the function of Lucio becomes clearer. There have been studies of the tongue-heart theme and several attempts to bind this "fantastic," Lucio, more tightly to the play. *Troilus and Cressida*, a play anticipating many of the themes and image patterns of *Measure for Measure*, throws light on Lucio. Thersites is a fractional forerunner of Lucio. Nestor describes him in terms recapitulated in *Measure for Measure* as, "A slave whose gall coins slanders like a mint." (I.iii.192-93) Lucio is also a master in the art of slander. He implies that the Duke indulged in fornication (III.ii.123ff.). And then he caps this with an absurd falsehood, speaking of the Duke as "A very superficial, ignorant, *unweighing* fellow." (III.ii.,136, *italics mine*) A little later, the Duke, echoing Nestor's statement in *Troilus*, observes:

> No might nor greatness in mortality
> Can censure 'scape. Back-wounding calumny
> The whitest virtue strikes. What king so strong
> Can tie the gall up in the slanderous tongue?   *(III.ii.179-182, italics mine)*

As we have said, Lucio alone at the end of the play, remains a slave. The reason for this lies in his galled, slanderous tongue. In the imagery of the play, this slander effaces the King's public image in a way exactly analogous to the defacing of the King's (or Duke's) head on the coins which circulate. By a required pun, the slanderer and the counterfeiter are two sides of the same coin. The slanderer, Lucio, violates necessary social faith, just as the counterfeiter subverts the economic confidence of society.

In this instance, Shakespeare shares a traditional nexus with Dante. Dante deals with the Counterfeiters in the eighth circle of the *Inferno*. There counterfeiters are seen as assassins of the King's reputation and murderers of the social and economic validity of the state. Dante's counterfeiter, Master Adam, like Shakespeare's Lucio, symbolically slanders the state in which he lived. Slander, issuing from a lack of temperance or self-governance, illustrates a failure of *caritas* while also destroying the faith necessary for *communitas*. The slanderer and the counterfeiter are yoked together by the similar consequences of their acts. Lucio offends against both justice *and* mercy, hence the parabolic appropriateness of his final assignment to a slavish condition.

Self-governance, being an individual act by definition, is not enough without acceptance of one's social and symbolic role. Not only can man not live alone, he cannot *signify* alone. Escalus tells us the Duke is "A gentleman of all temperance." "Temperance" in Shakespeare's time meant the same thing it now does, but it also possessed a deeper meaning: *O.E.D.* "temperance" II. 3. a., "The action or fact of tempering; mingling or combining in due proportion, adjusting, moderating." This usage carries on the metallurgical motif of weighing and testing. The Elizabethans were well aware of the analogies between man and metals current during the time. As Robert Steele tells us:

> Since the perfect proportion of the elements in the human body
> resulted in health, and in a metal made it gold, it followed that
> the less perfect proportion in other metals was a kind of disease,
> which could be remedied by an appropriate medicine.[12]

The Duke's function, then, is metaphorically alchemical. His "philosopher's stone" resides in his authority to temper the elements in Viennese society. That is, he can effect a proper disposition of roles.

The Duke in *Measure for Measure* responds to the necessity for reforming, and re-ordering his society. The nature of his *reform* is a reaffirmation of the equitability of the institution of marriage, a fact which makes his otherwise surprising marriage with Isabella at the end thematically *de rigeur*. *Measure for Measure*, with its bawds and prostitutes, shows the condition that obtains when sexuality lacks a creative channel for its energy. The institution of marriage, with its civic and sacramental sanctions, pays homage to the necessities of the blood while preserving, by its very existence, the fabric of society. James I in *Basilicon Doron* devotes several pages to the importance of marriage, saying "The three causes it was ordeined for, are, for staying of lust, for procreation of children, and that man should by his wife, get a helper like himselfe."[13] As the Duke warns Angelo:

> Look that you love your wife: her worth, worth yours.
> [i.e., become as worthy as she is]   *(V.i.495)*

But Mariana's worth is not the economic "worth" that Angelo was concerned with earlier.

In its diagrammatic, qualitative analysis of good and evil, of nature and supernature, of the individual and society, *Measure for Measure* sacrifices something of Shakespeare's normal structural elegance. Even though the Duke's role in the play has major justifications, he does not entirely escape the artistically subversive properties of the *deus ex machina*. No one is *entirely* satisfied with the play. Still the *fin-de-siècle* label of "problem play" can hinder critical inquiry if too rigidly adhered to. The basic honesty of the imaginative representation in *Measure* is the ultimate issue. Shakespeare, our greatest aesthetic genius, is also our most honest playwright. *Measure for Measure* serves as an eloquent primer to the themes of the great tragedies which surround it: the costly process of self-validation and its reconciliation with communal valuation; the moral psychology of enlightened political authority; and the secret mechanics for self-governance.

96

Notes:

(1) The nearly simultaneous appearance of two outstanding editions and of three thoughtful books about *Measure for Measure* prompts this essay. I am indebted to these works at several points, but no disrespect is intended when I say that they accentuate a feeling that modern discursive and exegetical criticism tends to disperse rather than concentrate the reader's moral and aesthetic responses. The critical works in question, all of high scholarly quality, are: Robert Grams Hunter, *Shakespeare and the Comedy of Forgiveness* (N.Y., 1965); Josephine Waters Bennett, *Measure for Measure as Royal Entertainment* (N.Y., 1966); and David Lloyd Stevenson, *The Achievement of Shakespeare's Measure for Measure* (Ithaca, 1966). The editions are the old-spelling one of Ernest Leisi (N.Y., 1964) and J. W. Lever's volume in the New Arden Shakespeare (Cambridge, 1965). Both are fine examples of enlightened modern editing. The extensive body of modern commentary on the play is conscientiously logged and evaluated in the endnotes to Bennett's book (pp. 161-191) and in Stevenson's third and fourth chapters (pp. 63-120).

(2) *MM.* I, 1, 64-65. The edition cited throughout is that by J. W. Lever for the New Arden Shakespeare. Other plays are quoted from G. B. Harrison, ed., *The Complete Works of William Shakespeare* (New York, 1952).

(3) Thomas Aquinas, *The Summa Theologica* (N.Y., 1922), XII, 100.

(4) Lever, *op. cit.*, p. 4.

(5) Leisi, *op. cit.*, 24.

(6) *Ibid.*, 45.

(7) James I, *Basilicon Doron* in *The Political Works of James I* (Cambridge, Mass., 1918), p. 38.

(8) *Ibid.*, p. 38

(9) See, Lever, *op. cit.*, p. lxiii.

(10) James I, *op. cit.*, p. 30.

(11) See, Ernest Schanzer, The Marriage-Contracts in *Measure for Measure*," *Shakespeare Survey*, XIII (1960), 81-89.

(12) Robert Steele, "Alchemy," in *Shakespeare's England*, I. 465.

(13) James I, *op. cit.*, p. 35.

The Marriage of True Minds: Truth and Error in Sonnet 116

by Hilton Landry

In the manner of its assertion the Sonnet [123] is in line with the more famous Sonnet 116 . . . a poem of which the difficulties have never, I think, been squarely faced. *L. C. Knights, "Shakespeare's Sonnets."*

Christian love grants the beloved all his imperfections and weaknesses, and in all his changes abides with him, loving the man it sees. *Kierkegaard, The Works of Love.*

I

It now seems clear that for modern readers Sonnet 116 must be among the least understood of Shakespeare's poems even though it is a hallowed anthology piece, is frequently quoted, and just as frequently praised. This Sonnet is usually taken to be an exalted celebration of love, or "perfect friendship,"[1] or the "unfailing constancy of true love,"[2] when in fact it celebrates none of them; it *celebrates* nothing at all. If we are to discover what Sonnet 116 does signify, to define its sense, feeling, and tone, we must consider it in its context.[3] But the larger context of the poem, consisting of those relevant Sonnets which surround it, is persistently ignored, and hence what passes for interpretation is actually misinterpretation, or at least serious distortion.[4] Not only are the general sense and intention of the poem misunderstood, but its details are often misread. For example, the couplet is sometimes cited as an instance of Shakespeare's tendency in the Sonnets to end weakly,[5] yet properly understood it is not deficient but rather an effective conclusion to a complex utterance. Perhaps Shakespeare himself is partly to blame for the traditional distortion of this Sonnet, for it has the grandeur of generality or a "universal significance," especially if one makes it "stand quite alone."[6] But however timeless and universal its implications may be, we must never forget that Sonnet 116 has a restricted or particular range of meaning simply because it does *not* stand alone.

Critics and scholars who are fully aware that the Sonnets fall into groups of related poems are not always willing to take such groups seriously; i.e., they do not allow the relationships among Sonnets to modify or control interpretation.[7] Or, if they do recognize the critical importance of the interrelations, they may still overlook or reject a genuine and evident connection. Such is the case in some typical treatments of Sonnet 116—those of Raymond Alden, J. W. Lever, and J. Dover Wilson.[8] Alden sees the connections among Sonnets 109-112 and 117-120 but leaves 116 in splendid isolation.[9] Lever puts Sonnets 109-112 and 117-120 into a group called "The Poet's Error" and 116 among those concluding his last group, "The Immortalization." The "underlying theme of these sonnets" comprising the

98

Immortalization group is "the conflict of Love with Time"; those "taken as a conclusion to the Immortality group celebrate the universal triumph of human love."[10] Dover Wilson, regarding 100-126 as a group, takes 116 to be a detached, universal, and "sublime declaration of perfect concord," and claims that 117 must be misplaced because there is no greater contrast or "contradiction" in the Quarto than the one it forms with the preceding sonnet.[11] Now it is precisely because they insist on its celebration of the "triumph of love over time" (Alden) or the *universal* triumph of human love that readers like Alden and Lever pluck Sonnet 116 from its natural context and either place it in another or make it completely independent.[12]

The natural context of 116 is a fairly large group of poems beginning with Sonnet 109, "O never say that I was false of heart," and ending with 121, "Tis better to be vile then vile esteemed," another Sonnet that may seem to be independent yet serves as a kind of generalizing conclusion to the group. Within this group, which I have labelled "the speaker's offense against friendship," are small clusters of closely related Sonnets: 109-112 (consisting of two pairs, 109-110 and 111-112), 113-114, 115-116, and 117-120.[13] The general subject of these Sonnets is the speaker's temporary offense against friendship, an offense which includes moral sin and was caused by, or resulted in, prolonged absence from the friend addressed. That he freely admits his errors, the speaker's many references to his sins make clear: "staine," "frailties," "stain'd" (109); "offenses," "blenches" (110); "harmfull deeds," "infection" (111); "shames" (112); "alters," "remouer," "remoue" (116); "wilfulnesse and errors" (117); "sick," "diseas'd" (118); "errors" (119); and "transgressions," "trespass" (120). But he also insists that these "worse essaies" proved the friend his "best of love" (110), that his love has been purged, renewed, and strengthened by his divagation:

> O benefit of ill, now I find true
> That better is, by euil still made better,
> And ruin'd loue when it is built anew
> Growes fairer then at first, more strong, far greater.
>   So I returne rebukt to my content,
>   And gaine by ills thrise more then I haue spent.[14]   (Son.119, 9-14)

These lines could be regarded as an appropriate epigraph to a full discussion of Sonnet 116, for they are more or less complementary to Shakespeare's view of the love relationship as presented in that poem. Here in Sonnet 119 the speaker is confidently giving us *his* side of the story, stressing the improvements wrought by bitter experience in his love for the friend. There what is in question is the effect of this experience on the friend's love for him. In short, what underlies Sonnet 116 is the fear that the friend's (former) love for the speaker may, with good reason, no longer exist.

Before examining 116 in detail, it is necessary to discuss briefly Sonnets 115 and 117 in order to determine their bearing on the intervening poem. A few local difficulties in 115 have received attention from critics and editors; the larger issue of its connection with 116 has been generally ignored or simply taken for granted.

According to J. B. Leishman, who treats it as one of the Sonnets on Love as the defier of Time, the theme of 115 is that "while Time is always changing, dimming and blunting, Love is always growing":[15]

> Those lines that I before haue writ doe lie,
> Euen those that said I could not loue you deerer,
> Yet then my iudgement knew no reason why,
> 4 My most full flame should afterwards burne cleerer.
> But reckening time, whose milliond accidents
> Creepe in twixt vowes, and change decrees of Kings,
> Tan sacred beautie, blunt the sharp'st intents,
> 8 Diuert strong mindes to th'course of altring things:
> Alas why fearing of times tiranie,
> Might I not then say now I loue you best,
> When I was certaine ore in-certainty,
> 12 Crowning the present, doubting of the rest:
>   Loue is a Babe, then might I not say so
>   To giue full growth to that which still doth grow.

The first quatrain, like the poem as a whole, asserts the speaker's error in former statements of the fullness and perfection of his love for the person addressed. But then he did not know why the flame of love should later burn more purely and intensely. For he was only taking account of Time's destructive changes in things which we would least like to see changed (ll. 5-8).[16] Fearing time's tyranny and the future, why shouldn't he have said "now I love you best," thus putting the crown of perfection on the present (ll. 9-12)? Because love is a child (like Cupid) that is always growing, he could not accurately make any such asseveration.

Paradoxically, what he feared is the very reason that his love burns clearer — the action of Time, whose "milliond accidents" affect a series of five things. Of these damaging changes wrought by time, the first, fourth, and fifth imply those sins the speaker has so freely admitted in Sonnets 109-121. He now knows from experience that time's accidents creep in between the making and carrying out of vows, weaken the firmest purposes, and turn determined souls into spiritual drifters who submit themselves to the stream of change. Yet the result has not been a falling off or a loss of love, as the speaker would have assumed in his naive past, or as it may now seem to an impartial observer and even the person addressed; the result has been a gain or increase of love, for his flame burns clearer. The course of love, after an apparent decline, has been ever upwards as it "growes fairer then at first, more strong, far greater."[17]

If Sonnet 115 looks forward, especially in the second quatrain, to the opening lines of Sonnet 116, Sonnet 117 looks back to that poem as a whole. It does so by presenting a bill of the errors of which the speaker may justly be accused and excusing them as the means by which he sought to test and to demonstrate what he hoped for or assumed in Sonnet 116 — the constancy and excellence of his friend's love.

Accuse me thus, that I haue scanted all,
Wherein I should your great deserts repay,
Forgot vpon your dearest loue to call,
4 Whereto al bonds do tie me day by day,
That I haue frequent binne with vnknown mindes,
And giuen to time your owne deare purchas'd right,
That I haue hoysted saile to al the windes
8 Which should transport me farthest from your sight.
Booke both my wilfulnesse and errors downe,
And on just proofe surmise, accumilate,
Bring me within the leuel of your frowne,
12 But shoote not at me in your wakened hate:
      Since my appeale saies I did striue to prooue
      The constancy and virtue of your loue

He invites his friend to accuse him of both sins of omission—neglecting the many duties of friendship and forgetting to invoke (in poems) the love to which he is bound—and sins of commission: intimacy with persons not worth knowing, resulting in the wasting of time properly his friend's, and deliberate spiritual adventuring at every opportunity.[18] He further invites the recording of his perversity and mistakes[19] and the addition of suspicious guesses to whatever can be proven against him. His friend may aim disapproval at him but must not go so far as to hate and reject him. For his plea in extenuation is that all the while he was attempting to test and demonstrate the constancy, the essence and the excellence[20] of his friend's love for him.

To J. W. Lever, and doubtless many others, this appeal (ll. 13-14) "is not very convincing and suggests a precarious relationship very unlike that of the early groups."[21] Whether it is convincing or not is quite beside the point, and of course the relationship is precarious when the speaker, looking at his past behavior from the friend's position, can draw up such a damaging bill of particulars against himself. But what is at stake here (and elsewhere in the series 109-121, as Shakespeare repeatedly suggests) is the *quality* or essence of the friend's love: does he still love the person though he hates the "vice"; does he love the sinner for the sinner's sake? That the speaker has tried severely the quality of that love is evident; that he has demonstrated its selfless constancy remains to be seen. For the worm at the heart of friendship is selfishness in some form. In the case of a friend,

it is possible in loving him to love only his friendliness toward us
in return. Then he is not loved *for his own sake*. He is loved for the
sake of his friendliness, for the sake of the benefits to be gained
from reciprocal friendship. Thus, very often, love for a friend
shows up as "enlightened selfishness"....In lower forms of friendship, for profit and for utility, a person really loves only himself;
this is fundamentally true also of the highest type of friendship
Aristotle could conceive of, friendship for the sake of the good.[22]

Needless to say, "friendship grounded either in selfish considerations of utility or in mutual love of 'the good' must change, as Aristotle saw so clearly, whenever the friend changes."[23] Now Shakespeare or the "I" of the poems takes a high view of friendship throughout the Sonnets: it is the art of "mutual render, onely me for thee" (125). A low prudential conception is attributed to the person addressed in Sonnet 87, only to be rejected by contrast with the speaker's ideal view. The speaker in 87 makes it clear that friendship is a free gift of one's self, and this ideal is implicit in the humble selfless love of Sonnet 88.[24]

There is nowhere any trace of a *quid pro quo* or *do ut des* attitude on the speaker's part, except in Sonnet 120, a poem which seems to balance the friend's fault in Sonnets 34 and 35 against the speaker's recent transgressions.[25]

> That you were once vnkind be-friends mee now,
> And for that sorrow, which I then didde feele,
> Needes must I vnder my transgression bow,
> 4 Vnlesse my Nerues were brasse or hammered steele.
> For if you were by my vnkindnesse shaken
> As I by yours, y'haue past a hell of Time,
> And I a tyrant haue no leasure taken
> 8 To waigh how once I suffered in your crime.
> O that our night of wo might haue remembred
> My deepest sence, how hard true sorrow hits,
> And soone to you, as you to me then tendred
> 12 The humble salue, which wounded bosomes fits!
> But that your trespasse now becomes a fee,
> Mine ransoms yours, and yours must ransome mee.

Even here one might point out that the stress is on regret for the suffering he may have caused and for delaying to offer the salve of humble penitence; but one could hardly join Lever in saying the poem is "a simple and direct appeal for human kindness."[26] There is still the opening line with its reference to the former trespass befriending the speaker to contend with, a notion most readily clarified by the rather crude equation of the last two lines of the poem.[27] Yet that earlier episode may also be said to console or befriend the speaker in this respect—he forgave his erring friend *freely,* though with some difficulty;[28] if he now asks for forgiveness in return, it is a mere afterthought which does not affect the quality of his past or present love. In fact, such a *quid pro quo* arrangement as the couplet proposes may well reflect not only the seriousness of his sins (which may be hard to forgive) but also doubts about the strength and nature of the friend's love. Both the seriousness of these sins and doubts about the friend's love are uppermost in the speaker's mind in the eloquent and misleading Sonnet 116.

II

Sonnet 116 begins with an optative definition negatively stated, elaborates on that definition in positive form in the second and third quatrains, and concludes

102

with a desperate paradox in the subjunctive mood. This rough sketch of its strategy will suggest my disagreement with Tucker Brooke's summary remarks on the poem, recently quoted with approval by J. Dover Wilson. There may be "nothing recondite, exotic, or metaphysical in the thought," and it may very well employ "one hundred and ten of the simplest words in the language," but it is hardly a poem which "has about it no strangeness whatever"[29] as analysis will make clear.

> Let me not to the marriage of true mindes
> Admit impediments, loue is not loue
> Which alters when it alteration findes,
> 4 Or bends with the remouer to remoue.
> O no, it is an euer fixed marke
> That lookes on tempests and is neuer shaken;
> It is the star to euery wandring barke,
> 8 Whose worths vnknowne, although his higth be taken.
> Lou's not Times foole, though rosie lips and cheeks
> Within his bending sickles compasse come,
> Loue alters not with his breefe houres and weekes,
> 12 But beares it out euen to the edge of doome:
> If this be error and vpon me proued,
> I neuer writ, nor no man euer loued.

Perhaps the most surprising feature of this remarkable Sonnet is the subject of the first sentence: "Let *me* not to the marriage of true mindes / Admit impediments." In view of the marriage metaphor and the nature of the understood obstacles to the ideal union of friendship, one would expect the speaker to say "Let *us*," or, more awkwardly but accurately, "Let *you*." As far as one can tell, all the impediments lie in the speaker's past; he refers to them repeatedly in Sonnets 109-115 and 117-121, explains that they have actually increased his love in 115, and in 117 presents them as a bill of particulars with an excuse appended. Thus, if anyone lets in impediments to the marriage of faithful and constant minds,[30] it will be the person who is addressed, not the unfaithful poet. The poet is the remover in question, the one who has changed his allegiance in the recent past, and the one in whom alteration is to be found. It is his friend's love for him which must not alter in the face of alteration or be inclined to seek a new object.

This opening quatrain is extremely important because how one takes it determines the way in which the remainder of the poem will be read. Even if one were to ignore the wider context, the connection with Sonnet 115, often though not always admitted, should be decisive. For the third and fourth lines of 116 are clearly related to the second quatrain of 115 where the speaker's confessed sins are implicit.[31] That he has been an inconstant remover may be attributed to time's accidents creeping in between vows and blunting the sharpest intents; his alteration may be described as the diversion of a strong mind to the course of altering things. How alteration and removing are to be distinguished is not precisely clear, but the remover is certainly one who has undergone a drastic change in feeling and attitude.[32] The broad psychological sense of "alteration" suggested by line eight of 115 ("Diuert strong mindes") would subsume removing (v. 93, ll. 3-4); the narrower sense suggested by the third quatrain of 116 would probably exclude it.[33]

The familiar parallel to lines 2-4 is from *Lear*: "Love's not love / When it is mingled with regards that stands / Aloof from th'entire point" (I.i.241ff.); the equally familiar parallel to the next two lines is from *Coriolanus*: "Like a great seamark, standing every flaw / And saving those that eye thee" (V.iii.74f.).[34] With the second quatrain the poet begins the positive elaboration of his hopeful definition of his friend's love, and he does so in images which emphasize its unshakable constancy and exemplary salvational virtue. It is commonly assumed, because of the analogue from *Coriolanus* and the phrase "seamark of my utmost sail" in *Othello* (V.ii.268), that the "euer fixed marke" must be a seamark or even a lighthouse;[35] but a passage in *Othello* which generally has been overlooked indicates that it may also be taken as the pole star, a traditional symbol of constancy.[36] Describing the storm which separates the Turkish fleet, a gentleman says, "The wind-shak'd surge . . . / Seems to cast water on the burning Bear / And quench the Guards of th'ever-fixed pole" (II.i.13ff.). Another passage in *Julius Caesar* on the proverbial stability of the north star also suggests that it may be identified with the "euer fixed marke":

> But I am constant as the Northern Star,
> Of whose true-fix'd and resting quality
> There is no fellow in the firmament.
> The skies are painted with unnumb'red sparks,
> They are all fire, and every one doth shine;
> But there's but one in all doth hold his place. *(III.i.60ff.)*

While storms or "flaws" of passion shake its object, this constant star of love looks on[37] without suffering any corresponding change. And because it is so firm and steadfast in devotion, it is both guide and shining example to every person who loses his emotional bearings, especially the "wandring barke" who is the speaker. Note, incidentally, that the "wandring barke" of line seven is given expansive treatment in lines 7-8 of Sonnet 117 ("That I have hoysted saile to al the windes / Which should transport me farthest from your sight"). In a less obvious way some of the implications of the difficult eighth line, "Whose worths vnknowne, although his higth be taken," are conveyed by the couplet of 117.[38]

The sense of this line obviously turns on the difference between known "height" and unknown "worth," between outward and inward, appearance and reality. What makes it appear difficult is a temporary separation of tenor and vehicle of a kind which is not uncommon in an extended metaphor. "Higth" is perfectly appropriate to the vehicle of the metaphor, to the star as star, but "worth" fits the tenor far better than it does the vehicle. Thus, although one may assign a meaning suitable to unknown worth as the possession of a star—e.g., immeasurable influence or riches, occult power—it is much easier to take it as a reference to distinctly human qualities. A glance at some typical Shakespearean contexts of "worth" should make this evident.

In Sonnet 16's "Neither in inward worth nor outward faire" (l. 11) and *Troilus and Cressida's* "And dare avow her beauty and her worth" (I.iii.271), the contrast between character and beauty emphasizes the inward nature of worth. Sonnets 38 (l. 9) and 39 (l. 1) use "worth" to signify the friend's general excellence; so do 80, 82, 83, and, in an ironic way, 87. Like 106, Sonnet 62 as a whole seems to stress worth as beauty, but it actually concerns various "worths," one of which is the essential quality of truth or fidelity.[39] Similarly, in Sonnet 37 the poet takes comfort in the friend's "worth and truth," and his worth includes both beauty and wit (ll. 5-8). ("Worth and truth," by the way, recalls "constancy and virtue" in the last line of 117, where Shakespeare might well have used "worth" in place of "virtue"[40] in view of their general meaning.) A final example from *Troilus and Cressida* will be particularly significant since it presents "worth" as the consequence of severely testing circumstances, a condition implicit in Sonnet 116 and explicit in 117. After telling the Greeks that their "checks and disasters" are the trials which test men's worth, reveal their persistive constancy, Agamemnon concludes with a wheat and chaff figure in which the winds of adverse Fortune winnow the light and worthless from what is "rich in virtue" and unadulterated. (Compare the conclusion of 117.) Nestor then illustrates this point by a comparison contrasting the shallow boat sunk or driven to harbor by a storm with the "strong'ribb'd bark" which "bears it out" (to use the idiom of 116, l. 12). He completes and applies the figure with the observation, "Even so / Doth valour's show and valour's worth divide / In storms of fortune" (I.iii.45ff.)[41] These lines may serve to remind us that "worth" is sometimes used to distinguish the real from the apparent as well as the internal from the external.

What, then, does unknown worth as a personal attribute signify in Sonnet 116? Adequate definition must begin with an attempt to explain how love's worth is, and is not, unknown, for the poet's use of "vnknowne" here has led to the charge of obscurity.[42] "Vnknowne" does not mean utterly unfamiliar or strange, or completely unknowable; on the contrary, it denotes what is not known completely, what cannot be fully grasped, what is immeasurable because infinite in value. It also suggests the difference between knowledge about and knowledge by experience or direct acquaintance, the difference, in short, between taken height and unknown worth. One may have some conception of the person and the person's love, but one cannot know the worth of that love until it has been experienced under circumstances which try it; and even then one cannot know it completely. (Compare *Ephesians* iii, 17-19 where through faith one may know the love of Christ which surpasses knowledge.) Unknown worth, then, points to the unfathomable depths of love, its infinite richness, especially as manifested in constancy, a quality which is known through, and *only* through, severest trial. Fidelity or loyalty without any obstacles to its continuation is simply truth; when it continues by overcoming obstacles it may rightly be called constancy. As for the inexhaustible bounty and rich worth of love, they are commonplaces or basic assumptions found everywhere in Shakespeare, but they are particularly well formulated in a few lines spoken by Juliet:

My bounty is as boundless as the sea,
My love as deep; the more I give to thee
The more I have, for both are infinite.   *(Rom., II.ii.133ff.)*

A further question about the second quatrain remains to be answered: why did Shakespeare choose the extended figure of star, storm, and wandering bark to define the character of the love between the speaker and the person he addresses? We know from the passages quoted from *Troilus* and *Julius Caesar* that he might have handled the difference between the inconstancy of one and the constancy of the other by comparing them to chaff and wheat, shallow boat and strong bark, wandering star and fixed star. Such comparisons would have the obvious advantage of putting them both in the same class and, in the first two cases, of subjecting both to the same storm, thus avoiding the charge that the star is too remote, too Platonic and transcendent.[43] Despite the apparent strength of this line of argument, I think one may dispose of it by simply listing Shakespeare's main reasons for using the star and bark metaphor. First, he wished to insist on the capacity of true love to serve as a perennial guide or saving example. Second, he wanted to "demonstrate" that the fidelity of this love is unimpeachable. Third, he did *not* wish to contrast openly the constancy of the friend with the inconstancy of the speaker. On the contrary, despite references to alteration, removing, and wandering, he wished to minimize inconstancy for reasons made clear in 115 and 119 (and implied in 117). He did this so successfully that most readers remain unaware of the speaker's flagrant sins against love. Finally, to add a minor point, the storm passage from *Othello* suggests that he did not think of the pole star as very remote; and in any case, one is at liberty to solve the problem of remoteness by regarding the ever fixed mark as a terrestrial object.

Apart from the concealed figure of the twelfth line, there is little in the third quatrain which requires comment. Love is not time's dupe or sport even though time will always destroy the freshness and beauty of the beloved. Time measures change but love never changes with time's paltry measures; it endures to the end of life or even to the end of the world. The assertion that love "alters not," of course, represents the speaker's earnest wish about his friend's love for him; it does not accord with his view of his own love for the friend in 115 and other Sonnets of this group, but it does agree with his position in Sonnets 123-125. "Beares it out even to the edge of doome" resumes the imagery of the second quatrain by comparing love to a ship which stays on course in spite of wind and sea and sails to the very edge of the flat world.[44] The decisive context for the meaning of "beares it out" is found in *Othello* (II.i.16ff.), a few lines after those on the pole star: "If that the Turkish fleet / Be not enshelter'd and embay'd, they are drowned. / It is impossible they bear it out." The Turkish fleet, like Nestor's shallow saucy boat, must find a harbor or be sunk; love, like a strong-ribb'd bark, fights through the storm with ease. In short, to "bear it out," by signifying both "to weather or ride out the storm" and "to steer a straight course,"[45] implies strength and control as well as sheer endurance.

These and other features of true love are knit up in "this" of the subjunctive couplet, as the poet, with desperate confidence, strives to maintain the accuracy of his declaration:

> If this be error and vpon me proued,
> I neuer writ, nor no man euer loued.

For Hallet Smith there is a "deceptive quietness and modesty" in the tone of line 13, culminating "in a total effect, for the couplet, of almost glib certainty" in the last line.[46] Sigurd Burckhardt finds that the "disputatious dare of the couplet is almost strident"; Shakespeare's conclusion "on the face of it . . . seems nonsense."[47] To Yvor Winters the conclusion does not *seem* nonsense; it is: "the concluding couplet is a mere tag, which has no dignity or purpose in relationship to the sonnet or within itself."[48] Many editors refuse to comment on the couplet, probably because they consider the sense, tone, and feeling self-evident. Those who are moved to gloss these lines usually say something quite misleading about the poet's undying love for his friend. For example, Martin Seymour-Smith says, "Shakespeare here testifies to his own constancy";[49] Ingram and Redpath state that "the poet is asserting not merely that his definition of true love is right but also that true love exists, as proved by his own case."[50] I think the most that we can say about the poet's view of true love is that he earnestly hopes it exists here and now in the friend's affection for him. It is doubtful that he cares much about true love in general, although he would be willing to grant its (rare) existence. If he is in error in all that he has hoped and said, it will unquestionably be proved against him by the friend's rejection of him, by the friend's failure to exhibit that extraordinary constancy which is now essential to their relationship. The strength of his hope for continued love, the intensity of his dearest wish, is to be measured by the last line. It is a valiant attempt to reduce the possibility of error to the absurd, the impossible, for obviously he has written and men have loved.[51] But the strength of his fear is to be measured by Sonnet 117, where he invites his friend to accuse him of neglect, book down his errors, disapprove of his behavior, but not to hate and reject him.[52]

Notes:

(1) Edward Hubler, ed., *Shakespeare's Poems and Songs* (New York, 1959), p. 124: "This sonnet, often taken to be a love poem, . . . for the more careful reader . . . remains a celebration of perfect friendship. . . ." See also his *Sense of Shakespeare's Sonnets* (Princeton, 1952), pp. 92-93, hereafter cited as Hubler.

(2) Thomas Tyler, ed., *Shakespeare's Sonnets* (London, 1890), p. 275, hereafter cited as Tyler.

(3) For comments on the order, contexts, and interpretation of the Sonnets, see my *Interpretations in Shakespeare's Sonnets* (Berkeley, 1963), pp. 3-6, 130-133, hereafter cited as Landry.

(4) Sigurd Burkhardt's "The Poet as Fool and Priest," *ELH*, XXIII (1956), 279-98, recently called a "splendid essay" by Murray Krieger, contains a splendid misreading of Sonnet 116 in the interest of loose "philosophical" generalizations (pp. 289-97).

(5) E.g. Raymond M. Alden, quoted in *A New Variorum Edition of Shakespeare. The Sonnets*, ed.

H. E. Rollins, 2 vols. (Philadelphia, 1944), II, 413, hereafter cited as *Variorum*.

(6)   Alfred Noyes, quoted in *Variorum*, I, 294.

(7)   See, e.g., Hubler on 94 (pp. 102-106); J. B. Leishman, *Themes and Variations in Shakespeare's Sonnets* (London, 1961), pp. 169-70, hereafter cited as Leishman; Murray Krieger, *A Window to Criticism* (Princeton, 1964), pp. 177-179 and *passim*, hereafter cited as Krieger.

(8)   See also Krieger, pp. 146-150.

(9)   Raymond M. Alden, ed., *Sonnets and A Lover's Complaint*, Tudor Shakespeare (New York, 1913), p. xiv; see also Alden's variorum edition, *The Sonnets of Shakespeare* (Boston, 1916), p. 431.

(10) J. W. Lever, *The Elizabethan Love Sonnet* (London, 1956), pp. 236, 246, 260, hereafter cited as Lever.

(11) J. Dover Wilson, ed., *The Sonnets*, New Shakespeare (Cambridge, 1966), pp. 207, 227, 229, hereafter cited as Wilson.

(12) C. F. Tucker Brooke in his edition, *Shakespeare's Sonnets* (New York, 1936), hereafter cited as Brooke, keeps 115 and 116 together but makes them 109 and 110 (after Sonnet 108 of the 1609 ed., Q) in his rearrangement; then he puts Q's 113 and 114 after them as his 111 and 112 and makes Q's 109-112 his 113-116. Sonnet 117 then takes its proper place. See his table on pp. 1-2. Martin Seymour-Smith, ed., *Shakespeare's Sonnets* (London, 1963), takes 100-115 as a series (p. 161) and 116-126 as another (p. 168); hereafter cited as Seymour-Smith.

(13) Landry, chart on p. 131.

(14) All quotations from the Sonnets follow the facsimile of the British Museum copy of the 1609 quarto (B. H. Bright, C. 21, C. 44), *Shakespeare's Sonnets*, Shakspere-Quarto Facsimiles, No. 30 (London: Charles Praetorius, n.d.).

(15) Leishman, p. 103. Neither the classification nor the theme is quite right.

(16) Since a full explanation of 115 is not intended, local difficulties are not glossed.

(17) Lever, p. 260, misses the point of Sonnet 115 and connects it with 60 and 124. Its relation to 60 is adventitious and general, to 124 more significant but not important for the interpretation of either poem.

(18) The sailing figure of ll. 7-8 clearly recalls the "wandring barke" of 116 rather than the opening figure of Sonnet 86 as Lever (p. 241) claims.

(19) By a kind of etymological pun, "errors" means "wanderings" as well as "mistakes." "Wilfulnesse and errors" may mean deliberate and inadvertent sins.

(20) "Virtue" nearly always has the sense "excellence, good quality" in the Sonnets, whatever others it may have. T. G. Tucker, ed., *The Sonnets of Shakespeare* (Cambridge, 1924), p. 194, wants to restrict its meaning here to "potency, essential value"; hereafter cited as Tucker.

(21) Lever, p. 241.

(22) Paul Ramsey, *Basic Christian Ethics* (New York, 1954), p. 96.

(23) *Ibid.*, p. 245.

(24) There is a short discussion of 87 in my essay "The Use and Abuse of Poetry: John Crowe Ransom on Shakespeare's Sonnets," *Paunch*, XXIII (April, 1965), pp. 25-26.

(25) On the connections among 34, 35, and 120, see Landry, pp. 153-54, n. 11. These connections may well constitute the chief support for the common assumption that the same person is addressed in Sonnets 1-126.

(26) Lever, p. 243.

(27) Tucker, p. 197, says "be-friends" is explained in ll. 13-14. See also Seymour-Smith, p. 172, on the couplet of 120.

(28) See the discussion of Sonnets 33-35 in Landry, pp. 56-63.

(29) Brooke, p. 7; Wilson, p. 227.

(30) "Impediments" is from the marriage service in the Elizabethan Book of Common Prayer. (For some reason, editors invariably quote the phrase "If any of you know cause or just impediment" which was not inserted until 1662.) See *Liturgical Services of the Reign of Queen Elizabeth*, ed. William Clay, Parker Society (Cambridge, 1847), p. 218.

(31) Tyler, p. 275, was one of the first to notice this obvious connection, although he wishes to limit the reference of "impediment" to "altring things" (115, l. 8). If one is willing to acknowledge that 115-116 constitute a proper pair, then even rearrangement would not have much effect on my interpretation of 116. Brents Sterling's "Sonnets 109-126," *The Centennial Review*, VIII (1964), 109-120, his latest attempt at rearranging the Sonnets, misses the drift of 116.

(32) Krieger, p. 147, n. 6, misreads the line when he speaks of "removal by death"; so does Hubler in his edition, *Shakespeare's Songs and Poems*, p. 124. The correct reading of the line and of "remoue" and "remouer" appears in W. G. Ingram and Theodore Redpath, edd., *Shakespeare's Sonnets* (London, 1964), pp. 268, 370, hereafter cited as Ingram and Redpath.

(33) Tucker, p. 192, wants the narrow sense, which would signify material or physical change in the beloved. But note that "alters" in the third quatrain, as in the second, has to do with *psychological* change (cf. "alter'd" in 93, l. 3).

(34) All quotations from the plays follow the text of G. L. Kittredge's edition, *The Complete Works of Shakespeare* (Boston, 1936).

(35) Tyler, p. 275, sees a lighthouse figure throughout the second quatrain; most editors refer to a seamark.

(36) Landry, p. 166. n. 37, points to the relations of *Othello*, II.i.13-19 and l. 12 of 116. C. K. Pooler's note in his Arden edition, *Sonnets*, 3rd ed. (London, 1943), p. 112, misses part of the significance of this relationship. Eyes are called "constant stars" in Sonnet 14, l. 10, and in *Phoenix*, l. 51, lovers are called "stars of love," partly because of their constancy.

(37) "Lookes on" also suggests a star since Shakespeare uses this verb with eyes or heavenly bodies (probably because of their light).

(38) Note also that "vnknowne" occurs only twice in the Sonnets, once in 116 and once in 117. Thus sense, imagery, and rare words indicate that, contrary to Brents Sterling, these sonnets belong together.

(39) See 62, ll. 5-8, especially l. 6 where "true" shape is to be distinguished from "truth."

(40) On "virtue," see n. 20 above.

(41) The value of tested virtue is a Shakespearean, as well as a Pauline and Senecan, commonplace.

(42) Yvor Winters, "Poetic Style in Shakespeare's Sonnets," *Discussions of Shakespeare's Sonnets*, ed. B. Herrnstein (Boston, 1964), p. 109, hereafter cited as Winters.

(43) For this charge, see Burckhardt, p. 290.

(44) Hallett Smith, *Elizabethan Poetry* (Cambridge, Mass., 1952), p. 175, hereafter cited as Smith, makes a similar point.

(45) M. M. Mahood, *Shakespeare's Wordplay* (London, 1957), p. 94, quite rightly says "*bear out . . .* might mean 'steer a course.'" The *Troilus* passage (I.iii.45ff.) on the strong bark also suggests steering a straight course.

(46) Smith, p. 175.

(47) Burckhardt, p. 290.

(48) Winters, p. 110.

(49) Seymour-Smith, p. 169.

(50) Ingram and Redpath, p. 269; their last phrase is quite ambiguous.

(51) Tucker, p. 193, has some interesting things to say about ll. 13 and 14, but he also inserts the customary misleading reference to the poet's constancy.

(52) Dowden is the one student of the Sonnets who grasps the general sense of 116 and its relation to 115 and 117, to judge from his very brief summaries in his edition, *The Sonnets of William Shakspere* (New York, 1887). Of 115 he says, "Shakspere now desires to show that love has grown through error and seeming estrangement"; of 116, "Admits his wanderings, but love is fixed above all the errors and trials of man and man's life" (p. 224). And of 117 he says, "Continues the confession of his wanderings from his friend; but asserts that it was only to try his friend's constancy in love" (p. 226).

The Masque of Greatness

by Ruth Nevo

Cleopatra dies with a deliberation unequalled among Shakespeare's tragic heroes. Though she proclaims "resolution and the briefest end" when Antony dies, an entire act goes by before the words are put into effect. What is happening, or being enacted, in this act? A recent study of *Antony and Cleopatra* conveniently juxtaposes two contrary possibilities of interpretation, thoroughly representative of the dialectically opposed positions which define the debate upon this strange final phase of the play:

> Egypt is the Egypt of the biblical glosses: exile from the spirit, thralldom to the fleshpots, diminution of human kindness. . . . The fourth and fifth Acts of *Antony and Cleopatra* are not epiphanies. They are the ends moved to by the process whereby things rot themselves with motion—unhappy and bedizened and sordid, streaked with the mean, the ignoble, the contemptible. Shakespeare may have his plays in which "redemption" is a theme (and I think he has), but *Antony and Cleopatra* is not one of them.

> If the desolation that begins to make a better life for Cleopatra (V.ii.1-2) does not take her away from the flesh-pots, if she does not undergo an ennoblement (if we prefer to confine the word 'redemption' to religious contexts) which carries with it an increase in human kindness and a diminution of selfishness and pride, and so is kindred to the change in Lear (a comparison which Professor Danby dismisses as blasphemous), it is difficult to see what Shakespeare was doing in the last act.[1]

It is indeed difficult to see what Shakespeare was doing in Act V so long as, in the heat of battle, Act V remains the last thing to be looked at; so long as judgement is made in terms of judgement already made of the power to save or corrupt of "Rome" or of "Egypt". What Shakespeare actually dramatises in Act V, I hope to show, is the working of Cleopatra's imagination as she moves towards the fulfillment of her resolve. It is of the most absorbing interest: not only what Cleopatra will do, but how she will do it, and it will affect retrospectively our entire view of the play. With a subtlety of insight and a richness of symbol unsurpassed perhaps even in his own work, Shakespeare exhibits the growth, the expansion, the completion of her great idea, its taking prossession of her to the point where she will be marble-constant in its service, and her final enacting of it, with a grand, triumphant, histrionic audacity.

He achieves this with the means of which in these late plays he has consummate mastery: successions of image-clusters or sequences, in which elements combine and recombine, relate and inter-relate, by analogy, contrast, counterpoint, or extension, to produce a fabric which beggars final analysis. Act V of *Antony and Cleopatra* is a *locus classicus* for the finding of what Middleton Murry described as "the greatest mastery of imagery":

> But the greatest mastery of imagery does not lie in the use, however beautiful and revealing, of isolated images, but in the harmonious total impression produced by a succession of subtley related images. In such cases the images appear to grow out of one another and to be fulfilling an independent life of their own. Yet this apparent autonomy is as strictly subordinated to a final impression as the stages of a logical argument are to their conclusion. Such triumphs of imagery are to be conceived as swift and continuous acts of exploration of the world of imagination.[2]

It is this world, these acts of exploration, that fill the strange hiatus of Act V. It can, I hope to show, be established that the main sequence of subtly related images —Caesar's Roman triumph—is related in a highly specific and illuminating way to Cleopatra's dream-vision of Antony and to her own final speech, and that the perception of this continuity not only in itself throws a central beam of light upon the play but also breaks new and fruitful ground for interpretation. Looked at from the standpoint of "the great mastery of imagery" displayed in its last act, the play is seen to possess richer poetic resources, a finer psychological portrayal and a grander and more inclusive theme than the current moralistic polemic would lead us to expect.

The triumph passages recur five times but there is nothing mechanical about their repetition. They operate as a kind of incremental refrain, and they mark the stages of Cleopatra's resolution. Their placing is always significant. The first occurs in Act IV after the second sea battle and the flight of the Egyptian ships. It is the occasion of the third and most violent of Antony's self-lacerating repudiations of Cleopatra. He knows himself "beguiled to the very heart of loss"; the shirt of Nessus is upon him, and in the anguish of his defeat and ignominy he turns upon her with a vengeful imprecation:

> Ah, thou spell! Avaunt!
> Vanish, or I shall give thee thy deserving,
> And blemish Caesar's triumph. Let him take thee,
> And hoist thee up to the shouting plebeians,
> Follow his chariot, like the greatest spot
> Of all thy sex. Most monster-like be shown

> For poor'st diminutives, for dolts, and let
> Patient Octavia plough thy visage up
> With her prepared nails.   *(IV.xiii.30-39)*

In his persuasion of Eros to save him, by death, from a similar fate, the tone is less violent but sufficiently emphatic in its insistence upon the humiliation, the unbearable dishonour, which the triumphal procession means to its victims:

> Eros,
> Wouldst thou be window'd in great Rome and see
> Thy master thus with pleach'd arms, bending down
> His corrigible neck, his face subdued
> To penetrative shame; whilst the wheel'd seat
> Of fortunate Caesar, drawn before him, branded
> His baseness that ensued?   *(IV.xiv.72-77)*

Cleopatra does not hear Antony's persuasion of Eros, but she remembers his previous words, and echoes them as she pleads the necessity of remaining within the monument:

> I dare not, dear,
> Dear my lord, pardon: I dare not,
> Lest I be taken: not the imperious show
> Of the full-fortune'd Caesar ever shall be
> Brooch'd with me, if knife, drugs, serpents, have
> Edge, sting, or operation. I am safe:
> Your wife Octavia, with her modest eyes,
> And still conclusion, shall acquire no honour
> Demuring upon me.[3]   *(IV.xv.22-29)*

This speech modulates remarkably from the extreme agitation of the refusal to descend, to the note of regal self-possession, not unmixed with the smaller pride of her rivalry with Octavia. The words follow Antony's, both those she heard and those which were addressed to Eros, with the kind of reciprocity of speech and idea between them of which the play is full. A single continuity of image is thus established: the chariot of the full-fortuned victor, the led captives, the watching wife, the whole imperious show. But when one compares Antony's speech in IV.xii.30-39 with Cleopatra's it becomes clear that she has not taken in to the full the degradation he depicts. The show is imperious, which is sufficiently galling, but she is not "shown monster-like, for poor'st diminutives, for dolts". In her imagination of the scene she is a brooch, an adornment, which, in her pride, she will deny to Caesar. Octavia does no more than to demure upon her, which again, sufficiently indicates the sense of an affront to her own pride of amorous conquest, but suggests nothing like the pitch of revulsion soon to be expressed. The violence and intensity of the next speech in which reference is made to Caesar's triumph provides a striking contrast:

> This mortal house I'll ruin,
> Do Caesar what he can. Know sir, that I
> Will not wait pinioned at your master's court
> Nor once be chastis'd with the sober eye
> Of dull Octavia. Shall they hoist me up
> And show me to the shouting varletry
> Of censuring Rome? Rather a ditch in Egypt
> Be gentle grave unto me; rather on Nilus' mud
> Lay me stark-nak'd and let the waterflies
> Blow me into abhorring; rather make
> My country's high pyramides my gibbet,
> And hang me up in chains!   (V.ii.51-62)

Octavia is demolished with a superbly vindictive adjective; but the brooch with which she would not adorn Caesar's triumph has been replaced by the image of an appalling desecration—an ultimate indecency of exposure: rather on Nilus' mud lay me stark-nak'd and let the waterflies blow me into abhorring. This hyperbolic exposure measures the horror of the other—the being made a motley to the view, hoisted up to the sound of the lewd jeering of the despised populace. The lines contain the most significant verbal echo:

> Let him take thee
> And hoist thee up to the shouting plebeans
>
> . . . . .
>
> Shall they hoist me up
> And show me to the shouting varletry
> Of censuring Rome?

The heroic view of life, the aspiration towards superior prowess or rare excellence, rests upon an aristocratic disdain for the common, or mean; a disdain which is exacerbated to abhorrence in the above passages. It is for the delectation of the rabble that the show is to be put on. Members of the multitude, the "many headed monster", increasingly figure in Act V: the Roman mechanics, the saucy lictors, the mere boys and girls who are level now with men, the beggar, the maid that does the meanest chores. These figures punctuate the long reverie of Cleopatra like the tolling of a bell, for they are the petty contemptible life from which either she and Antony will be marvellously distinguished, or by whom they will be mocked, derided, and debased.

To Proculeius' attempt to reassure her and to his offer to bear a message to Caesar her response is the obdurate "Say, I would die", a cry of mingled despair and defiance which is the aftermath of the passionate abhorrence expressed before. Then follows a short dialogue with Dolabella:

> *Dol.*   Most noble Empress, you have heard of me?
> *Cleo.* I cannot tell.
> *Dol.*   Assuredly you know me.

114

> *Cleo.* No matter, sir, what I have heard or known:
>   You laugh when boys or women tell their dreams;
>   Is't not your trick?
> *Dol.* I understand not, madam.
> *Cleo.* I dreamt there was an Emperor Antony.
>   O such another sleep, that I might see
>   But such another man!   *(V.ii.71-78)*

It is important to note this transition to the dream speech. She is rapt, abstracted, Dolabella cannot catch her attention. For the nightmare of humiliation with which she has tormented her imagination vanishes, and in its place is conjured up the dream of lost grandeur, of sovereign prodigality and colossal stature.

> His face was as the heavens, and therein stuck
> A sun and moon, which kept their course, and lighted
> The little O, the earth.
>   . . . . .
> His legs bestrid the ocean, his rear'd arm
> Crested the world: his voice was propertied
> As all the tuned spheres, and that to friends:
> But when he meant to quail, and shake the orb,
> He was as rattling thunder. For his bounty,
> There was no winter in't: an autumn 'twas
> That grew the more by reaping: his delights
> Were dolphin-like, they show'd his back above
> The element they lived in: in his livery
> Walked crowns and crownets: realms and islands were
> As plates dropp'd from his pocket.   *(V.ii.79-92)*

As we take in the extraordinary gigantism of the images, the distance from which they seem to be seen, the spectacular hyperbole, the processional, emblematic quality, the sense of the cosmic indeed, but a cosmic which is somehow contrived, we realise with a shock of recognition that it is precisely as a king in a pageant that she is envisaging him: the pageant of ignominy is exorcised in her imagination by the pageant of majesty.

Striking confirmation of this view of the effect made here is to be found in the 1794 commentary of that curiously neglected pioneer of image-critics — Whiter, whose observations, still rooted in the pre-industrial world, often possess a value to which no subsequent image-criticism can lay claim.

> The back of the dolphin is deeply associated in the mind of
> Shakespeare with the splendid scenery of the pageant or the
> procession. Would the reader believe that [the present passage]
> is to be referred to this source? There is nothing however,
> more certain and indubitable.[4]

Indeed, in all the similes throughout this dream Whiter discerned allusions to pageants and processions.

> Let it be remembered that an imitation of the sphere of the Heavens, with the attributes and ornaments belonging to it, the sweetness of its music, and the noise of its thunder, the Sun, the Moon, and the Earth, colossal figures, — armorial bearings, — a magnificent procession of monarchs and their attendants, — floating island, — and a prodigal distribution of wealth and honors, are the known and familiar material which formed the motley compound of the Masque, the Pageant, or the Procession.[5]

The "floating islands" to which Whiter refers are those presented in Jonson's *Masque of Beauty* of 1609, in which the "apparatus and cunning of the stage machinery" was, according to the Venetian ambassador "a miracle";[6] this was too late however to have been present to Shakespeare's mind during the composition of *Antony and Cleopatra*. But Whiter also quotes a "spectacle presented to Queen Elizabeth upon the water", in which one "*Harry Goldingham* was to represent *Arion* upon the DOLPHIN'S BACKE";[7] and in at least one royal procession in the time of Richard II, recorded in *Stowe's Annals,* the streets were hung with cloth of gold, and the citizens, all in livery, received costly and magnificent gifts of gold crowns, plate and coins.[8]

It is by now a commonplace that popular pageant and court masque — in its heyday in England at the time of Shakespeare's late plays — combined to form the theatrical imagination of the time. Yet, even when one is prepared to find the poet-dramatist and the masque-librettist sharing a world of symbols and images, the resemblance between Cleopatra's dream of Antony and Jonson's *Masque of Hymen* (written for the Twelfth Night of 1605 to celebrate the ill-starred marriage of Essex to the Lady Frances Howard) is startling. Whiter quotes the following description of it:

> No less to be admired, for the grace and greatness, was the whole Machine of the Spectacle, . . . a MICROCOSMOS, or GLOBE, filled with countries, and those gilded; where the sea was expressed, heightened with silver waves. This stood, or rather hung (for no axel was seen to support it) and turning softly discover'd the first Masque . . . which was of the men, sitting in fair composition, within a mine of several metals: To which the lights were so placed, as no one was seen; but seemed as if only Reason (mounted above their heads) with the splendour of her CROWN, illumin'd the whole grot. On the sides of this . . . were placed two great STATUES, feigned of gold, one of ATLAS, the other of HERCULES, in varied postures, bearing up the clouds, which were of releve, embossed, and translucent, as naturals.[9]

Allardyce Nicoll, in his *Stuart Masques and the Renaissance Stage* comments:

> The scene may readily be reconstructed—the vast globe (turned, tradition has it, by Ben Jonson himself) painted to represent the countries of the world, the sea blue with wavy silver lines, and the continents marked out in gold. . . . Since eight men were accommodated in it (the concave of the globe) we may imagine that the "microcosmos" must have been at least ten or twelve feet in diameter.[10]

Reason in this Masque was

> crowned with lights, her garments blue and semined with starres, . . . in one hand bearing a Lampe, in the other a bright Sword.[11]

Order too, who appeared later, had a "starre in his forehead".

In the Hercules scene of *Antony and Cleopatra* one of the soldiers asks, of the music, "It signs well, does it not?" and in the cloud scene, Antony says to Eros, "Thou hast seen these signs; they are black Vesper's pageants." Nicoll quotes a description of a masque by D'Avenant to the effect that the various personages were presented with "significant signes to express their various qualities", and comments upon these "court hieroglyphicks" as follows:

> the phrase is a key by which we may unlock the true secrets of those spectacles which so delighted the courtiers and their lords. This vast effort of the poets and the painters was more than a thing of immediate delight, a trivial titillation of the senses, to be forgotten when the last candles guttered and the palace halls had grown still . . . . The masques enshrined a philosophy of life; in them the conceptions of poetry took visible form, and the symbols through which current ideas became manifest assumed shapes of material loveliness . . . in the masque the fashion for the courtly *impresa* and for the emblem book reached its completest expression . . . In the *impresa* and in the masque alike the quality of *meraviglia,* or wonder, was called for—the exciting of that admiration aimed at in the entire spectacle.[12]

Meraviglia—is not this precisely the wonder, the admiration Cleopatra is "aiming at" in her speech to Dolabella—seeing in her own mind's eye an entranced vision of a man past the size of dreaming?

In another passage of *Antony and Cleopatra*, as Whiter noted, Shakespeare indicates the source of his imagery in so many words:

> Sometimes we see a cloud that's dragonish;
> A vapour sometime like a bear or lion,
> A towered citadel, a pendent rock,

> A forked mountain, or blue promontory
> With trees upon't that nod unto the world
> And mock our eyes with air. Thou has seen these signs;
> They are black Vesper's pageants. *(IV.xiv.2-8)*

Certainly rocks, mountains, promontories, citadels and towers form the staple scenery of the masque landscapes as we read of them in the designs and descriptions of the time. Inigo Jones' cloud machines were a byword. In *Hymenaei*, in the staging of which he co-operated with Jonson, the great gold statues of Atlas and Hercules bore up the "embossed, and translucent" clouds. Other clouds, however, were designed for movement by means of the machines so beloved by Inigo Jones, and at one point they opened, "and, the ayre clearing, in the top thereof was discovered Juno", while "round about her sate the spirites of the ayre in several colours making musique . . . above her, the region of fire with a continuall motion was seen to whirle circularly . . . and Jupiter, standing in the toppe . . . " brandishing his thunder. These deities then descend in "two great cloudes" which were seen to "stoupe and fall gently downe upon the earth". Later the whole scene was "cover'd with cloudes, as in a night".[13]

Thus both the mocking of Antony's eyes with air, and his abandonment by the god Hercules to the accompaniment of "music i' the air. . . . Under the earth" would seem to be indebted to the "insubstantial pageants" which had become the "necessary complements requisite for State and Greatness"[14] in the Stuart court. The splendour of the spectacle, the elaborate and sophisticated nature of the machines, the regal costuming, the wonder of the illusory effects which could be achieved were very much part of the magnificence demanded of the court Masque in England as upon the continent. But it is upon this issue of illusory effects that Ben Jonson quarelled with Inigo Jones and terminated their partnership. Jonson insisted that the design and the words of the masque, the "invention" in the poetic sense, were its soul, and an expression of ideal beauty and truth, while the spectacle, mime and dancing were the mere body. If the frequency of reference in Shakespeare's plays to problems of appearance and reality be an indication of a permanent interest, this platonic dispute concerning "Imag'rie" might well be supposed to have caught his attention. At all events there seems to be overwhelming evidence for the notion that the contemporary masque is what he had specifically in mind when he referred to the Fancy which outworks nature and which in turn is outworked by "nature's piece 'gainst Fancy."[15]

It is in fact historically possible for Shakespeare to have seen the *Hymenaei* and the *Masque of Blackness* before, or during the composing of *Antony and Cleopatra*, and even to have taken part in the controversy between Ben Jonson and Inigo Jones upon the rival claims to beauty and truth of poetry and carpentry. What is indubitable is the extent to which the masques and pageants had become the specific contemporary form of the theatrical mode of apprehension: the rich concretisation with which the masques indue the theatre metaphor enables it to become the key trope in the drama of Act V.

118

Not only is Cleopatra's vision of the Antony who "contemns shadows quite" formed in the image of the masque; so also is her imagination of what she will do. And this in its turn arises from the connection the context establishes between the masque-like vision which expresses Antony's magnificence and the indignity of Caesar's triumph which is its obverse, and as we have seen, its prelude in the play. The connection between the two—masque and triumph—is very close: it was indeed history's before it was Cleopatra's. "Pageant wagons", Nicoll informs us, "were the masque's original 'settings' and to the end of its career this type of court entertainment displayed a fond and almost nostalgic passion for triumphal chairs and chariots".[16] These served not only to draw the masquers into the dancing place, but were frequently introduced into the middle of the performance. In Edward VI's time a letter from the King's Lord of Misrule to his Master of the Revels refers to a performance arranged by the former which is called in the accounts "The triumph of venus and mars with their paiauntes maskes and other furniture";[17] while Bacon found it perfectly natural to link the two in the title of an essay—"On Masques and Triumphs". Thus the whole series of masque and pageant images provide the metaphors for Cleopatra's state of mind and thereby convey the essence of the drama Shakespeare is exhibiting. For Cleopatra's intense reverie in Act V—the forming and maturing of her heroic resolution—hinges upon the double image of the magnificence of Antony and the rival would-be magnificence of Caesar. She will out-do Caesar, out-triumph Caesar, leave him indeed "ass unpolicied", not merely by removing herself physically from the possibility of being exhibited in his triumph, but by a grand and queenly spectacle of her own. What she has realised as she weighed her possibilities, enacted in imagination her alternatives, is that it lies within her power to vindicate the passion which has ruined the triple pillar of the world; that it rests with her either heroically to affirm the rare quality of their love, its inalienable possession of heroic stature and value, of a supreme excellence among human things, or to leave it upon the pages of history as a royal strumpet's lust for an infatuated libertine.

Her final evocation of Caesar's triumph epitomises this decisive insight:

> Now, Iras, what thinkst thou?
> Thou, an Egyptian puppet, shall be shown
> In Rome as well as I. Mechanic slaves,
> With greasy aprons, rules, and hammers, shall
> Uplift us to the view. In their thick breaths,
> Rank of gross diet, shall we be enclouded,
> And forced to drink their vapour.

> *Iras.*   The gods forbid!

> *Cleo.* Nay, 'tis most certain, Iras. Saucey lictors
> Will catch at us like strumpets, and scald rhymers
> Ballad us out·of tune. The quick comedians
> Extemporally will stage us and present

> Our Alexandrian revels. Antony
> Shall be brought drunken forth, and I shall see
> Some squeaking Cleopatra boy my greatness
> I' the posture of a whore. *(V.ii.206-219)*

The horror of exposure to the leering, jeering, alien faces of the rabble, and the cold contempt of the Roman matron had come home to her before. But now the horror of exposure is transformed by her lordly scorn for the base, the vulgar, the gross, the low; that which produced a paroxysm of revulsion and abhorrence is now described with sovereign contempt. The last lines in particular measure the great distance she has come from that which will now never be, because now she knows what she will do. She has conceived of her own spectacle, her own triumph, her own way of affirming the truth that she was Antony's lass unparallel'd and not Antony's whore: a grand affirmation of his manhood, his valour, his virtue, and their greatness.

The forming of Cleopatra's idea of the "high Roman fashion" which will make death proud to take her has a psychological as well as a metatheatrical dimension. The bare notion of resolution and the briefest end, which had been present to her mind from the very moment of Antony's death, is acted upon by a growing sense of what is involved in the self-assertion of suicide. This is the process that gives power to the great speeches of lamentation in Act IV. Caesar's triumph functions, now, imaginatively, as an antimasque: that part of the spectacle which represents the obscene or antic grimaces of the ignoble and unworthy, prelude to the magnificence and dignity soon to follow in, by contrast, enhanced pride and splendour. Antony's death leaves the world "no better than a sty", levelled into insignificance:

> O, see, my women:
> The crown o' the earth doeth melt....
> O, withered is the garland of the war,
> The soldier's pole is fall'n: young boys and girls
> Are level now with men: the odds is gone,
> And there is nothing left remarkable
> Beneath the visiting moon.[18] *(IV.xv.62-68)*

The speech to follow continues with a revulsion against the universal commonplace anonymity of mere grief. As Antony dies, she faints, and Iras and Charmion attempt to rouse her, calling her "our Sovereign", "Royal Egypt", "Empress". To which she responds in evident repudiation of her royal titles, or at least, as the Arden editor suggests,[19] as "the outcome of a train of thought" suggested by them:

> No more but e'en a woman, and commanded
> By such poor passion as the maid that milks,
> And does the meanest chares. It were for me
> To throw my sceptre at the injurious gods,
> To tell them that this world did equal theirs,
> Till they had stol'n our jewel. All's but naught:

> Patience is sottish, and impatience does
> Become a dog that's mad: then is it sin,
> To rush into the secret house of death,
> Ere death dare come to us? How do you, women?
> What, what good cheer! Why, how now, Charmian?
> My noble girls! Ah, women, women. Look,
> Our lamp is spent, it's out. Good sirs, take heart,
> We'll bury him: and then, what's brave, what's noble,
> Let's do it after the high Roman fashion,
> And make death proud to take us. Come, away,
> This case of that huge spirit now is cold.
> Ah, women, women! come, we have no friend
> But resolution, and the briefest end. *(IV.xv.73-91)*

It is important to follow closely the movement of this speech, for it is the brief chronicle of what is to come: the outline of what in Act V is writ large. It is generally taken as Cleopatra's perhaps single motion of humility, and thus regarded as the basis for her "regeneration" to the better life: great grief breaks the proud spirit and she bows her head in an acknowledgement of her common humanity. The arresting idea that the meaning is quite contrary has been argued by Dorothea Krook in a recent study.[20] The reference then would be not primarily to her love for Antony, but to the fainting spell, a mark of physical or emotional weakness appropriate in a kitchen wench but outrageously humiliating and undermining of royal self-possession in a great Queen, for whom the demi-Atlas of the earth kissed away kingdoms and provinces. This, I suggest, is an overstatement but one which usefully calls attention to an undeniable ambiguity: the connotations of "poor" in "poor passion" are the crux of the matter. Poor as "pitiful" could express the humility of great grief; poor as "mean"—not. And it is in the latter sense that it occurs again and again in *Antony and Cleopatra,* particularly in one context where the idea of a transcendent excellence is involved:

> none our parts so poor,
> But was a race of heaven. *(I.iii.36-37)*

To register the ambiguity in "poor passion"—the hovering between the pitiful and contempt for the pitiful—is at once to perceive and to distance the emotion. What is exhibited is indeed a breaking down of Cleopatra's self-possession as her vulnerability to the anguish of loss floods her consciousness, but almost instantaneously the very notion of grief mastering her leads to a reflex of rebellion, a reaction against this great levelling power of sorrow, and her sense of her grief's incommensurability prompts her to the assertion of a mightily wounded greatness, a mighty deprivation. It is from this (in the first instance rhetorical) refusal to be humbled by the injurious gods that courage comes. The acting out of defiance, the expression of a profound scorn for her condition, for the world reduced to worthlessness by the theft of its jewel, and for all forms of behavior—patience and impatience, acquiescence or frenzy—which would be considered worthy or appropriate in an ordinary sorrow, produces the strength and the brave show of will of "what, what, good cheer!... Good sirs, take heart" and so on. The only possible response of honour is to repudiate the world which has lost that which alone made it worth living in. The speech is profoundly moving precisely because of the stamp upon it of a proud self-conscious encounter with sorrow. It is precisely the non-universal quality of the grief which is stressed: unshared, unsupported, because excessive and exceptional—registering the loss of something so uniquely valuable that only the final and greatest self-assertion possible to man is commensurate with it: the self assertion which chooses so to die as to "make death proud to take us".

This is her motive; this her need: not for fortitude or endurance, but for some gesture, some manifest demonstration of an unvanquished spirit. It is not a motive opposed to her love for Antony, but on the contrary derived from it and supported by it; the love and the pride are mutually sustaining. Such a quest for greatness is, of course, within the convention of the heroic death: a leave-taking from life which shall "become it", which shall make its mark upon the brute event. But the convention is here individualised to the highest degree, vitalised by the continuities of the imagery. This is evident in the speech upon the shackling of accidents; and the continuities of the imagery may suggest a conclusive solution to an old crux:

> My desolation does begin to make
> A better life: 'tis paltry to be Caesar:
> Not being Fortune, he's but Fortune's knave,
> A minister of her will: and it is great
> To do that thing which ends all other deeds,
> Which shackles accidents, and bolts up change;
> Which sleeps, and never palates more the dung,
> The beggars's nurse, and Caesar's. *(V.ii.1-8)*

That "a better life" can in no wise be taken in a Christian or quasi-Christian sense, would, on the reading of the drama suggested here, be self-evident. Shakespeare is consistently Roman, the entire direction of Cleopatra's thought is towards suicide, and the better life can only mean the growing ability to look upon life with the detachment and dispassion which gives a stoic his single recourse against Fortune. It is with a grim irony that she recognises the part played by "desolation" in this stoic progress. The speech's famous crux is in the last two lines, the interpretation of which, since Warburton's emendation of the Folio "dung" to "dug", has varied between the two readings with consequent effect upon the interpretation of Cleopatra's state of mind. The view presented here favours "dung", not only for the sake of the echo of Antony's "the nobleness of life" speech, important as that is, but because "dung" preserves the stringent tone of *contemptus mundi* where "dug" introduces a tender lassitude. Moreover the latter reading stresses the category—common humanity—which includes both beggar and Caesar, high and low, powerful and powerless; it therefore implies a perspective from which

122

humility is to be expected—the perspective of Alexander going a progress through the guts of a beggar. And critics indeed who favour this reading will be found to make much of Cleopatra's "humility" in "No more but e'en a woman" as well, as a stressing of "the common humanity that binds her to those who have served her".[21] But *common* humanity is the thing above all that Cleopatra repudiates. If the reading "dung" is kept, not only is the echo of Antony's defiant claim for their "nobility of life", their peerlessness, retained, but also the attitude to the inclusive category changes: the beggar and (now with audacious scorn) even Caesar, are both included in the category of all those, even the powerful, who are slaves to Fortune, as opposed to the better life of the only and truly great, those who attain power over mutability itself. The same continuity is what creates the possibility of a magnificently reserved irony in the scene immediately following:

> If your master
> Would have a queen his beggar, you must tell him,
> That majesty, to keep decorum, must
> No less beg than a kingdom. *(V.ii.15-18)*

And yet another echo reveals the insistent preoccupation when, startled, caught off her guard by her capture, it is again the image of the poor, the powerless, the inconsiderable which defines her self-assertion:

> Where art thou, death?
> Come hither, come; come, come, and take a queen
> Worth many babes and beggars! *(V.ii.47-49)*

Thus the linked sequences of images—Queen, woman; greatness, beggary; triumphal masque and antimasque—converge in an intimation of the means she will take in order to be noble unto herself, and so to give the world to know "We stand up peerless". What she is drawing upon is the power to affirm of the grand style when this is fully accredited by the deed. Their Alexandrian revels can be debased by scurrilous burlesque, or honoured by the "fine majesty of the heroic". Cleopatra has perceived that in her very renunciation of life she can strike again the high sumptuous note of the meeting at Cydnus; that, by enacting her idea, her spectacle, she can so refashion the story as to "steal away the spectators from themselves" in an obeisance to *meraviglia*.

> Show me, my women, like a queen: go fetch
> My best attires. *(V.ii.225-7)*

For the equivalent of such a "discovery" Allardyce Nicoll tells us,

> the entire masque was conceived; all the rest—the changing prospects, the descents of deities, the eccentric measures of the antimasque—was merely a framework and a preparation for the true masquing display when the noble courtiers, suddenly revealed in their glory, doffed their vizards and descended in solemn state from their thrones or triumphal chariots.[22]

And Shakespeare's stagecraft of juxtaposition leads him to introduce at this point his own contrasting "antimasque" in the shape of the clown, his own counterpoint of common humanity to the fire and air of Cleopatra, so that her transcendence of the baser life is given concrete dramatic representation. As to the final speech itself, nothing brings out with greater force the element of deliberately conceived performance in it than a comparison with the factual description of Cleopatra's end given in North's Plutarch:

> Cleopatra being layed upon a little low bed in poore estate, when she sawe Caesar come in to her chamber, she sodainly rose up, naked in her smocke, and fell downe at his feete marvelously disfigured: both for that she had plucked her hair from her head, as also for that she had martired all her face with her nailes, and besides, her voyce was small and trembling, her eyes sonke into her head with continual blubbering: and the most part of her stomake torn in sunder. To be short, her bodie was not much better than her minde: yet her good grace and comelyness, and the force of her bewtie was not altogether defaced.[23]

This description points up the fact that the question at issue is a question of style —entirely outside the realm of morality. North's Cleopatra, in "oughly and pitiefull state" is no doubt considerably less reprehensible than Shakespeare's vessel of pride. But she is an object of commiseration, not a figure of heroic grandeur. Shakespeare, as I have tried to show, has used the resplendent material images of a baroque-heroic theatrical grandeur as the very medium through which Cleopatra's vision of her role emerges, through which her conception of the "high Roman fashion" forms itself.

It is not perhaps the least of the triumph of it, the triumph which, as Bradley saw, is so much more than reconciliation, that it is the triumph of her own voluptuous "Egyptian" nature which is displayed. She may be another Venus, in her self-created masque, she may be Isis, goddess of love and the fertile Nile: her "sign" at all events, is the asp upon her arm, or upon her breast, the asp of the easy death —"as sweet as balm, as soft as air, as gentle". It is a grand performance in which she enacts, not the poor woman's passion of the milkmaid, nor the atoning virtue which could make a woman "a dish for the gods if the devil dress her not", but the *feliciter audax* which transforms death itself into a metaphor for love, an apotheosis of sensuality. In this she echoes Antony as in so much else. The kiss that is her heaven to have, the lover's pinch, the babe that sucks the nurse asleep, —in these garnerings of the heart the great contraries —valour and *voluptas*, the royal and the riggish, are resolved, and in their wake the antinomy between hero and fool obliterated. No wonder she is exultant, seeing Antony "rouse himself to praise her noble act", mocking the luck of Caesar, claiming her title of mate and match to the greatest soldier of the world. For it is a great act of the imagination. Antony died because, receiving news of her death, he knew himself bereft of the will to live. She is will and artifice to the end, and by her will and artifice she makes her view prevail. "Pleasure of life, what is it?" asks another Jacobean voice. "Only the good hours of an ague". What is celebrated in this masque of triumph is a pleasure of life which is not only the good hours of an ague; a pleasure of life to which life itself does homage, though, being both as constant as the sun and as changing as the moon, a new heaven and a new earth are required for its perpetuation.

And this observation brings me to one final aspect of the masque sequence which remains to be elucidated: its relation to the play's ambiguity. This feature of *Antony and Cleopatra* has been widely recognised in contemporary criticism. Mr. Schanzer has recently proposed that the special category of "problem play" include *Antony and Cleopatra* on the grounds of its ambiguity. But it is surely supererogatory to require a special classification for the drama because it embodies "differing and apparently irreconcilable evaluations of the central experience".[24] This is the nature of the tragic collision Shakespeare has chosen to dramatise in this play, though he has not chosen the theatre of the inner self and the soliloquy with which to do so. If Antony could reconcile himself to one or other of the irreconcilable evaluations of life with which he is faced he would solve his conflict and cease to be dramatisable as a man played upon by conflicting impulses. If he could either let Rome in Tiber melt or break his Egyptian fetters, he would be saved from the ruin which follows the decay of his will, the dissolution of his generalship, the defeat and disgrace of his arms. The oscillating structure of the play; the dialectic of contraries—nobleness, decadence, "women's maistry", world mastery; spontaneity, calculation; the ebb and flow of attraction and repulsion; the continual alternation of statement with subversive or counterstatement, of enhancement with exposure; the cluster of ironic reversals in Act III into which the Aristotelean peripeteia is broken up; the crucial figure of Enobarbus, paradigm of ruination through self-division; the imagery of varying tide and swansdown feather;—all are designed to exhibit the paradoxical co-existence of paralysis and hyperactivity of will in the absence of final choice, the ruinous sway of mind which the play dramatises. All are an index to the central controlling image of a man serving, or trying to serve, two masters, in full knowledge of their antithetical nature, and for this reason coming to grief. The mimetic power of this portrayal is such that when Antony, after Actium, when he is unqualitied with very shame, says nevertheless:

> Fall not a tear, I say, one of them rates
> All that is won and lost. *(III.xi. 69-70)*

anyone who has been responding to the play's antitheses and ambivalences is likely to be in real moral doubt as to whether he is watching the sublime or the ridiculous, a thing of beauty or an exhibition of besotted dotage. It is a total ambiguity of the order, as William Rosen has noted, of the couplet of Sonnet 129:

> All this the world well knows, yet none knows well
> To shun the heaven that leads men to this hell.[25]

125

What is distinctive and arresting about Shakespeare's handling of the story is that both masters, though their historical names are *virtus* and *voluptas*, synonyms for the heroic, *ex definitio*, and the arch anti-heroic, —both masters are of heroic pitch and magisterial power. Antony takes the same high heroic view of the pleasure of life which undermines his Roman virtue, as he does of the fame, honour, valour, which he jeopardises. Both epicurean and stoic aspirations make the highest kind of claim upon him. It is his tragic distinction indeed, that at its highest reach, his conception both of *virtus* and *voluptas* is larger and richer than anything his world can offer, and so he is exposed on both counts to the most grievous loss. In terms of the poetic drama this magnanimity of Antony is rendered by the grand scale and high hyperbole of both panegyric and lyric; both "in the name lay a moiety of the world" (V.i.18) and "Fall not a tear" (III.xi.69-70). And this is the source of the glow and glamour which lies upon the love and the valour which the play glosses also with a deflating irony.

It is Antony's magnanimity that Cleopatra recognises throughout; and it is her fidelity to her vision of it which affirms the truth at the end, of what she herself challenged, provocatively, at the beginning as "excellent falsehood!" But her affirmation is after all only of the order of spectacle, an insubstantial pageant which fades, leaving not a rack behind. No one remains alive who can report her rightly, no Horatio, no Edgar. Caesar's tribute,

> she looks like sleep,
> As she would catch another Antony
> In her strong toil of grace. *(V.ii.344-346)*

is already of a different order of imagination. Jonson's regretful description of the Masque of Hymen "whose grace in the execution left not where to add unto it with wishing" is curiously apposite:

> Such was the exquisite performance, as (beside the *pompe*, *splendor*, or what we may call *apparelling* of such presentments, that alone (had all else beene absent) was of power to surprize with delight, and steal away the *spectators* from themselves. Nor was there wanting whatsoever . . . eyther in riches, strangenesse of the *habites*, delicacie of *daunces*, magnificence of the *scene*, or divine rapture of *musique*. Onely the envie was, that it lasted not still, or (now it is past) cannot by imagination, much lesse description, be recovered to a part of that *spirit* it had in the gliding by.[26]

The total ambiguity of the action which has been imitated remains, therefore, so to speak, intact. Either it is true that the love between man and woman whose mark is reciprocity—a consonance of the imagination and the senses—is the gift of life which above all others has the power to neutralise the terror, the pain and the shame of life, or it is an illusion of illusions, a figment and a fantasy. There is nothing in the drama which conclusively forbids us, however ruefully, to adapt the wrathful irony of Ben Jonson, literary humanist, against Inigo Jones, master-designer, to the values affirmed in Cleopatra's final speech:

O showes, showes, mighty showes!
The eloquence of Masques![27]

For this reason no interpretation or judgement of the play based upon a moral position, whether condemnatory or exonerating of the grand passion it portrays, will fail to find sufficient evidence in the text. *Antony and Cleopatra* stands at a cross-roads of classification. It shares a pivotal ambiguity with its two companion tragedies of the Roman world: it is indeed an ambiguity inherent in a representation of Rome in the mind of a Renaissance Christian. With the later romances, on the other hand, it shares its preoccupation with the theme of the life and power of the imagination, the solving and saving truths of the imagination. It is the theatre-metaphor of the masque in the final Act which sets these elements into an illuminating relationship.

Notes:

(1) E. Schanzer, *The Problem Plays of Shakespeare* (London, 1963), p. 148. The citation from Professor Danby is from *Poets on Fortune's Hill* (1952), pp. 130, 148.

(2) *Countries of the Mind*, (1931), reprinted in *Shakespeare Criticism 1919-1935*, ed. A. Ridler (London 1936), p. 235.

(3) Sisson, in *New Readings in Shakespeare*, Vol. II (Cambridge, 1956) confirms Ridley's choice of "demure" rather than "demurr" in the Arden edn.

(4) *Specimen of a Commentary on Shakespeare* (London, 1794), p. 189.

(5) Whiter, p. 190 ff.

(6) Quoted by E. Welsford, *The Court Masque* (Cambridge, 1927).

(7) Whiter, p. 187.

(8) Whiter, p. 192 n.

(9) Whiter, p. 190 n.

(10) A. Nicoll, *Stuart Masques and the Renaissance Stage*, (London, 1937), p. 64.

(11) Nicoll, p. 183.

(12) Nicoll, pp. 154-5.

(13) *Ben Jonson*, ed. Herford and Simpson (Oxford, 1941), Vol. VII, pp. 217, 218, 223.

(14) Samuel Daniel, *Masque of the Twelve Godesses*, Preface.

(15) Once the connection is made, the stamp of the masque upon Shakespeare's imagination can be detected throughout the play. The details of the scene at Cydnus are, of course, given by Plutarch; but they are themselves assimilable to the splendid water-pageants of the Elizabethans. As Whiter again points out: "we may observe in general that these spectacles in different periods, and in different countries, have a wonderful resemblance to each other in all the particulars of cost and magnificence" (p. 192). It is perhaps not without point to note Enid Welsford's quotation of Usener upon the etymology of the word Carnaval: he derives it from *currus navalis*, the ship

car, and suggests its origin in a ship procession similar to that which figured in the cult of the goddess Isis (p. 13). At all events North's rendering of his Plutarch could have coincided most fruitfully in the imagination of a writer in 1606 with the *Masque of Blackness* which had been produced the previous year, and which is described by its author thus: "First, for the scene, was drawn a Landtschap [landscape] consisting of small woods ... which falling, an artificial sea was seene to shoote forth, as if it flowed to the land, raysed with waves, which seemed to move, and in some places the billow to breake, as imitating that orderly disorder which is common in nature. In front of this sea were placed six Tritons, in moving, and sprightly actions, their upper parts humane, save that their haires were blue, as partaking of the sea colour: their desinent parts, fish. . . . Behind these, a paire of Sea-maides, for song, were as conspicuously seated. . . . The masquers were placed in a great concave shell, like mother of pearle, curiously made to move on those waters, and rise with the billow; the top thereof was stuck with a chev'ron of lights, which, indented to the proportion of the shell, strooke a glorious beame upon them." (Jonson, *Works*, ed. Herford and Simpson [Oxford, 1925-41], VII, 169-171). Another MS has the shell guarded with dolphins and sea-monsters. The attire of these daughters of Oceanus, the light-bearers, was described by Jonson as 'Sea-greene, waved about the skirts with gold and silver; their haire loose, and flowing, gyrlanded with Sea-grasse, and that stuck with branches of corall' (p. 171). The touches with which Shakespeare embellished North's Plutarch are those which indicate the amorous desire of the elements themselves to gaze upon Cleopatra, and this kind of Renaissance animism provided a large proportion of the symbolical figures which appeared in the various Masques of the time.

(16) Nicoll, p. 127.

(17) Welsford, p. 146.

(18) Johnson's gloss upon the soldier's pole discloses a further link with the pageant imagery. He annotates: "he at whome the soldiers pointed, as at a pageant held high for observation". (*Variorum*, p. 322).

(19) New Arden edition, p. 201.

(20) D. Krook, "Tragic and Heroic in Shakespeare's *Antony and Cleopatra*", *Scripta Hierosolymitana*, Vol. XIX, ed. A. Sachs, (Jerusalem, 1967), p. 231.

(21) D. Traversi, *Shakespeare: The Roman Plays*, (London, 1963), p. 185.

(22) Nicoll, p. 214.

(23) P. D. Westbrook, "Horace's Influence on Shakespeare's *Antony and Cleopatra*", *PMLA*, LXII (1947), makes the interesting suggestion that some knowledge of Horace's Cleopatra Ode and Epode IX rather than Plutarch, might well have influenced Shakespeare's conception, since in these poems, despite their anti-Egyptian sentiment, is expressed in admiration for Cleopatra's noble and courageous end.

(24) L. C. Knights *Some Shakespearean Themes* (London, 1959), p. 144. Quoted in Schanzer, p. 5.

(25) *Shakespeare and the Craft of Tragedy* (Harvard, 1964), p. 148.

(26) Herford and Simpson, Vol. VII, p. 229.

(27) Quoted by Nicoll, p. 24.

Prince Hal and Francis: The Imitation of An Action

by J. D. Shuchter

The Francis scene in *I Henry IV* (II.iv.4-90, "Anon, anon sir") has received short shrift from editors, critics and directors alike, the last often simply omitting it as a piece of expendable comic byplay. I have seen the play produced some five times and have seen the Francis scene only once[1] (and not until I saw it did I begin to understand its significance). Editors and critics often apparently agree with Hal, who calls it merely a jest "to drive away the time till Falstaff come" (26),[2] though, as I shall show, their comments are self-contradictory. I want here to offer a reading of the scene that shows how it works in the play.

The consensus of commentary since Dr. Johnson, concerning the verbal substance of the scene, is that Hal is talking deliberate nonsense to Francis for no other reason than that of entertaining himself, Poins, and the audience with "the distraction of the drawer."[3] Johnson goes on to say that the slapstick aspect of the scene "may entertain upon the stage, but affords not much pleasure to the reader" (Johnson, p. 152). Even this recognition of the scene as good stage business is not allowed by a contemporary of Johnson, who characterises it as "too meanly farcical for the stage."[4] The same critic also says, "The passage is totally in the humbug style. We are to seek no meaning."[5] This is the dominant view, represented in the nineteenth century by the observation that the "Prince is amusing himself by obfuscating the tapster lad with some . . . rambling irrelevance."[6]

Some commentators have attempted to make dramatic or verbal sense of the scene. Kittredge, for example, says, "The Prince is talking incoherent nonsense to mystify Francis. One is tempted to make some sense of it, and perhaps Hal has some thought or other in the back of his mind: 'You'd better stick to your trade and learn to serve wine. If you rob your master you'll become a fugitive.'"[7] A recent editor quotes this passage and adds, "This is perhaps the best one can do" (Humphreys, p. 60). Another, making a commendable, though I think mistaken effort to see the scene in its place in the whole play, says of it that "the dramatic function of this episode seems apparent: the drunken buffoonery of the prince is used, hilarious as it is, as a foil to the brilliant and imaginative humor of Falstaff which follows hard upon it."[8] This is not the first time the scene had been used against Hal. Another partisan of Falstaff has said, "The Prince is inferior even to Poins in the imaginative design and execution of a jest. . . . The best he can do in this way is the perplexing of Francis, the drawer, which by no means satisfies the aesthetic requirements of a jest."[9]

The curious thing is that the very critics who stoutly declare that the scene is verbal nonsense are the ones who, like Kittredge, go right on to show that they understand perfectly well what it is that Hal is saying to Francis. Dr. Johnson's "The Prince intends to ask the drawer whether he will rob his master" (Johnson, p. 153), is representative, and a nineteenth century editor offers this paraphrase of Hal: "Will you rob your master by breaking your indenture and running away?"[10] These readings are quite correct, and in fact the several editors have among them explicated even the scene's most Nashean passages of raillery. And yet, as far as I know, and perhaps because of the almost exclusive editorial attention to the language, no one has gone on to point out the relevance of the scene to the play.

To put it succinctly, what Hal is doing in the scene is bringing poor Francis into a situation which mirrors the conflicts which plague Hal himself, and Hotspur also. Hal is subjecting Francis, in terms which the latter can comprehend, to the same kind of strain of conflicting obligations which he himself feels so keenly. (I do not of course mean that Francis can understand Hal's language, but only that he sees quite clearly what his problem is, namely that he must simultaneously serve Poins and stand still to listen to Hal). Hal and Poins are playing roles in the jest, and their roles with respect to Francis are functionally the same as those of Falstaff and King Henry with respect to Hal, and of Worcester and King Henry with respect to Hotspur. Hal, his natural youthful inclinations fed by Falstaff, is delinquent in the performance of his "job" as Prince, which happens, for the moment, to be a martial job (defined in I.i). Hotspur too is being incited, by Worcester's cultivation of his dominant humour, to act as the firebrand of a rebellion, and thus obviously to be delinquent in his duty. Both these situations are true of Francis as well. By Hal's insistence on verbal dalliance he is being kept from his job of serving wine, and at the same time, through the content of Hal's speeches, he is being mockingly incited to rebel against his master. Trying to obey two contradictory commands at once, shuffling back and forth between Hal's table and Poins' door, he is driven, as the pace of Hal's curiously compelling talk and Poins' summonses quickens, in ever-decreasing concentric circles until he is brought to a dead standstill, as the stage direction following line 77 indicates. He thus embodies the same stalemate that Hal is in at the very moment when the scene is being played. Francis enables us to perceive in an instant what is also being said by segments of plot too attenuated to be so apprehended. He is a kind of emblem of fruitless action consuming itself by its own energy, and one feels that he would have remained rooted to the spot forever, had he not been rescued by the spell-breaking entrance of the Vintner.

The structure of the whole scene, II.iv, of which the Francis bit is a part, gives us two clear indications that Shakespeare is deliberately drawing parallels between Francis and Hal. The most obvious is that the same sequence I have just described as ending the Francis scene is repeated a little later to end the mock-interview passage between Hal and Falstaff. Visually representing the essence of his character, Francis had stood "amazed", and the Vintner stepped in and galvanised him into action in the only terms possible for him—back to wine serving. At the end of the second mock-interview (l. 526), in one of those electrifying Shakespearean silences that tax the skill of actors to the utmost, Hal, almost by accident, reaches the moment of recognition of the essence of his fate—"Banish plump Jack and banish all the world." "I do. I will." The two stand face to face because there is nothing more to say, and nowhere to go. Then, after just an instant, and the always effective knock on the door, Bardolph bursts in, announcing the arrival of the Sheriff, breaking the spell and galvanising Hal into action—"Go, hide thee behind the arras; the rest walk above. Now, my masters, for a true face and good conscience" (ll. 549-552). And the long scene ends immediately with Hal's decisive "I'll to court in the morning. We must all to the wars."

If we are thus forced by the rhythm of the two sequences to think of the Francis scene and the mock-interviews in relation to each other, so also it is clear that the dialogue between Hal and Francis *plays* as an interview, and when one has seen it, it is hard not to think back to it when the mock-interviews with Falstaff come on. Hal's lines in the Francis scene combine biographical questions with subversive suggestions in such a way as to suggest that he is really trying to probe to the heart of Francis, to find out who he really is and of what he is capable. "Come hither, Francis." "How long hast thou to serve, Francis?" "Five year!" "How old art thou Francis?" The effect here is of combined catechism, lawyer's cross-examination, and temptation.

What then, if, instead of two mock-interviews in II.iv, we have three? My answer lies in the sequence of roles that we can see Hal playing out. It has long been a critical commonplace that the second mock-interview with Falstaff prefigures the rejection scene at the end of Part Two of the play. In the second mock-interview Hal becomes for a moment the King, and tells Falstaff the exact truth. It is no less true, but less noticed, that the first mock-interview prepares us for the second, because in the first (ll. 371-426) Hal plays himself. Thus, within the compass of some 100 lines we see enacted his change from Hal to King, a miniature of the change which actually requires the whole of the two Parts to accomplish. But the overall action of the two Parts is in three phases, not two, for before Hal is Prince he is tavern roisterer. It is the Francis scene which represents this first phase of Hal, for in it he is not only somewhat intoxicated but is the voice of the tempter, in the traditional locus of the tempter (the tavern), calling Francis to be "free." What we have then, in the three mock-interviews, is a three-act play-within-the-play which imitates, in almost farce terms, the steps of Hal's developmental action.

These are the things revealed by how the scene plays; what is understood about its "meaning" as it is watched. I should like now to push the investigation a little further, into what might be called the "literary-historical meaning" of the scene, and its "psychological meaning," significances that can only be perceived by reflection. Specifically, I think the scene tells us something in terms of the meta-phorical set-up of the play, and something about Hal's character.

Like so many Elizabethan plays in which the private and public spheres are connected because the fortunes of the state ride on the doings of the characters, this play makes considerable use of the "body politic" trope.[11] According to this familiar metaphor, the state is an organic being, in which all parts must perform their proper functions, the King, for example, being variously designated as the brain, heart, or even the body itself, of the state. Civil upheavals are spoken of in the metaphore as malfunctions of some part or parts of the body; as sickness. The opening of the play sets this metaphorical context for us, when King Henry describes in body terms the agony which grips the country. The sickness abroad in the land permeates all levels of society and manifests itself both in terms of feelings and of actions. In both respects the Francis scene plays a part.

If we glance back over the first four scenes of the play (I.i through II.i) we find that suspicion, guilt and anger move, like Wordsworth's "dissolution", from high to low. These are the symptoms of the sickness and we find them first with the King in the high court; second, transmuted into farcical but half-serious flyting, in the scene of the Prince at play; third, with the bickering and back-biting nobility; and fourth, in the other "court", the court-yard world of the Carriers and the Chamberlain. Take one step further, into II.iv, and we find that this social analysis has reached rock bottom, in the criminal element around Falstaff and in Francis, the lowest of the low. The sick atmosphere is already breeding the ultimate symptom, rebellion, at the higher levels, and Francis shows us that it is in a fair way to spread down to the lowest. In this sense the force of the scene lies precisely in the fact that it is Hal, the next-to-highest, who is tempting Francis.

The play invites us to see a variety of human responses to a world that is obviously in trouble. At one end of the spectrum of responses we might place the Lord Chief Justice, who, because the King is tainted, is the play's most imposing authority figure. At the other end would be Hotspur, who espouses disorder with all the relish of "a good plot, good friends . . . an excellent plot" (II.iii.18). All the other responses fall between these, including Falstaff's, which is too complex to be gone into here, and the reconciliatory ones of the King and Hal, which encompass diplomacy, force of arms, and Hal's interesting attempt to reconcile authority and license by embodying them both (about which I shall have more to say below). As I have already suggested, the raw nastiness of the Carriers and the Chamberlain is their emotional response to a world which just has not been right "since Robin ostler died (II.i.12). Francis gives us still another response to the national crisis as it touches him. It is the tragic-comic response of simple befuddlement and paralysis. Its effect, I think, is to give us a perspective in which to see the struggles of those who must cope with the crisis in its most threatening forms.

One of the good open questions in literary criticism is what constitutes literary character? Which lines, actions etc., are character and which are exposition, or poetry? I do not think we really know very well what we mean when we talk about Falstaff's "character" or Prince Hal's "character." In this century we have had something like a polarity come into being, with the Bradleyan idea of character as one pole, and as the other perhaps Wilson Knight and Tillyard, for whom characters tend to be counters in a dialectic of forces which is the real heart of the play. I do not intend to propound a theory of character here, but it is in the context of this question that I want to treat the Francis scene as a revelation of Hal's "character." My argument is this: the Francis scene is part of a large pattern of play-acting and impersonation by Hal, a pattern which is intimately connected

132

with Hal's problematical personal relationships (for instance, it is Falstaff's mention of Hal's coming "reckoning" to the King that triggers the second and third mock-interviews). This pattern is so strong that I believe it can be cited confidently as an aspect of Hal's character.

Our first insight into Hal is the "I know you all" soliloquy, and it is our first look at what later emerge as two of his habits, that of simultaneous participation in and observation of others' activities, and that of thinking and talking about himself in relation to others. We must remember that we are not yet talking about the question of how we are to react to the Hal of the soliloquy. To say immediately, on the basis of the soliloquy, "My, what a repulsive young man" is to define character as "what I feel about someone", an untrustworthily subjective criterion for drama, which so markedly consists of cumulative patterns and is without narrative guides to the feelings. What we are talking about now is what *Hal* thinks he means, and to return to the soliloquy, it is evident that Hal is thinking of himself as a performer, of life as a series of roles, and of another side of himself as spectator. Not long after the soliloquy he watches while Falstaff and the others rob, and then, though this time the idea is Poins', he watches with relish as Falstaff works himself ever deeper into the tale of the "eleven in buckram." In II.iv, we find that Hal participates in three "scenes", each time in a different role, but always a role he has known or is destined to know in "real" life. Hal's persistent theatricalising even dreams up a play that is never produced, when, at the end of the Francis scene he says "I prithee call in Falstaff; I'll play Percy and that damned brawn shall play Dame Mortimer his wife" (ll. 97-98). He has just been talking about Hotspur in relation to Francis and to himself, and immediately he wants to "play Percy."

Keeping in mind that it is Hal who proposes the Francis jest and Hal who proposes the mock-interviews with Falstaff, we may ask this question—what is the significance of what we may call Hal's theatricalising sensibility? The answer, I think, is that for Hal playing is a way of knowing; dramatising a situation is a way of clarifying the various positions within the conflict or of learning what the conflict really is. I think the three interviews in II.iv can be said to be cathartic for Hal, in that they take him through the current and conflict-ridden period of his life and into the future phase, kingship, where he symbolically resolves his conflicts. Thus the three interviews are, in the sharpest sense, *the imitation of Hal's action*. And the great moment at the end of it all, when Hal prophetically banishes Falstaff, is not merely unconscious foreshadowing. Its structure tells us that Hal sees the literal truth of the moment, and so the third of the Aristotelian triad of terms applies, for what Hal attains here is *anagnorisis*[12]—the recognition of the true nature of things. And if I must go on record about how I react to Hal, I would put this another way and say that at the moment of *anagnorisis* Hal is undeceived of the illusion he enunciated in the "I know you all" soliloquy, that to slough off the companions of his tavern days will be a simple matter that will cost him nothing. In other words, the play, up to II.iv, has represented this much of Hal's growing up. (It is also surely worth noting that the theatricalising outlasts Hal's youth, for in *Henry V* we find him, in the disguise-interview with the soldiers, still trying to define himself. What, exactly, *is* the King?).

Just as the structure of the Francis and Falstaff interview scenes tells us that a corner is being turned in Hal's understanding of himself, the overall rhythm of the play shows us the relationship between such understanding and necessary action. Much as Hamlet turns to decisive activity once his role is clarified for him on the trip to England, Hal, after II.iv, moves very quickly from pointedly doing nothing to just as pointedly doing everything, and the pace of the second half of the play quickens noticeably.

The process of learning by dramatising has a particular weight when it is Hal who does it, for Hal is the Prince, and I have already hinted that he is somehow trying to take the body politic trope very seriously by encompassing the whole state in his own person. This becomes clearest in the aftermath of the Francis scene, for it is here that his theatricalising sensibility reaches its fullest expression, and it is also here that he reaches a point of expanded consciousness in which he feels himself to be "of all humours" that have ever existed. Hal comes on in II.iv, in an excited state, caused partly by drink. One kind of character interpretation might want to say that he has a headful of the problems of father, duty, reputation, license, and so on, which he carries about with him. But we do not need to argue from such a naturalistic, or one might say novelistic theory of character, for, if we listen, we are told what has been put into his mind at the moment of his entering. Drinking with the tinkers, Hal has "sounded the very string of humility" (II.iv.5-7). Not only does this complete a pattern, begun in I.ii, in which he sounds the high string, comparing himself to the Sun, who will shine out from behind the "base contagious clouds" (l. 189), but it prompts the question: what is the sound made by the base string? It too is the sound of praise, for Hal reports that the drawers praised him most profusely. But Hal is more precise than that, for he tells us that what they did was to differentiate him sharply from "a proud Jack like Falstaff" (ll. 10-11). What they have done, in effect, has been to put Hal in mind of the one relationship that is more complicated and touchy for him even than his relationship with his father, of which the former is a kind of parody. And they have done so at the beginning of the very scene whose developing function it becomes to differentiate Hal from Falstaff ("I do. I will"). Thus the playing at being one of the tinkers has been instructive too, and we can now say of the interview portions of II.iv that all the themes and relationships that have been reverberating through the first six scenes of the play converge in Hal's mind and emerge therefrom as dramas. While Hal is waiting to view Poins' "Play of Falstaff the Liar", he devises the "Play of Francis the Rebellious Drawer", and when he has simultaneously attended it and performed in it, he meditates upon it.

What remains to be done here is to examine Hal's own thoughts on the Francis scene, for they are "drama criticism" and they tell us quite as explicitly as do the structural features, what Hal has done for himself in constructing this jest. The key line in the passage, between the rescue of Francis by the Vintner and the entrance of Falstaff, is line 90—"I am now of all humours that have showed themselves humours since the old days of goodman Adam." Hal is collecting humours, and what strikes him as Francis' humour is the drawer's non-verbal response, his absolute inability to cope with the situation, intellectually or even just physically. This is a useful specimen for Hal, who is caught in a bind himself, and it makes Hal think of the polar opposite, Hotspur, the man of words (though he claims not to be) and actions. And without explicitly saying so, Hal places himself in a spectrum between the two, so that the moral geography of his speech is closely parallel to that of the "I know you all" soliloquy, in which he had placed himself between court and tavern.

> That ever this fellow should have fewer words than a parrot, and
> yet the son of a woman! His industry is up-stairs and down-
> stairs, his eloquence the parcel of a reckoning. I am not yet
> of Percy's mind, the Hotspur of the north, he that kills me some
> six or seven dozen of Scots at a breakfast.   *(II.iv. 96-109)*

The Arden editor says that the "change of subject is surprising" (Humphreys, p. 62), but it is only the kind of sifting, sorting and comparing that Hal does all the time. All that is ellipsed is "*I am not like Francis, but on the other hand* I am not yet of Percy's mind." It is immediately after this speech that, as I have noted, Hal proposes to try being of "Percy's mind" by playing him.[13]

This account of Hal's method of finding his way to the center of a situation and his own place in it might open outward to a study of a particular class of Shakespeare's characters, for Hal is just one of several important characters who manifest a theatrical way of understanding life. One thinks quickly of Rosalind, in disguise, studying the phenomenon of love in *As You Like It,* of the Duke producing what might be called "The Temptation of Angelo" in *Measure for Measure,* and of course of Hamlet, trying to make his way toward understanding by playing and making plays. It could be said that for Shakespeare playing is a major way of knowing.

I do not think that what I have pointed out here changes the basic reading of *I Henry IV,* nor does it resolve the problem of how we are to respond to Hal. Since this problem is inescapable and since I have concentrated on Hal's symbolic action rather than his real action over the course of the two plays, I would like to say one or two things about the latter.

Clearly my reading of Hal is closest to that of Tillyard in *Shakespeare's History Plays,*[14] which says that everything in the plays, including Falstaff, is grist for Hal's mill as he learns what it means to be King. Toward this reading I would offer something that Tillyard did not say, namely that in my view the coronation-and-rejection scene itself, at the end of Part II, is a part of the theatricalising that I have been talking about. It is manifestly a set piece, and it is Hal *playing* the King. I do not think he is fully the King until *Henry V,* and even then the message of that play seems to be "The King is a man." Many of Shakespeare's plays suggest, or hope, that office, or "place" as they called it, was only a role, an external, and that in reality there is nothing but individual human beings. Falstaff, who places all principles of order and rule in perspective by ironically undercutting them, takes up the same position with regard to his conscripts. "Tush man. Mortal men, mortal men."

Yet the coronation scene and the rejection of Falstaff are good history[15] and sound Tudor morality doctrine, so the end of Part II may be "character" in a different sense from that in which I have been talking about it. But none of these possibilities makes Hal endearing, nor is it satisfactory to answer that Falstaff somehow "got away from" Shakespeare and usurped all the affection we have available. We cannot meet the problem head on by asking what Shakespeare wanted us to feel about Hal, for that is pure intentional fallacy, and frustration. I therefore offer the following suggestion. As a recent commentator says, the pattern of comedy ought not to conclude with the truncation of part of the hero's personality but with its augmentation;[16] therefore Hal is not a redemptive character. But if we look at the tradition of the redemptive morality comedy, to which the stage Hal is surely more or less in debt,[17] we find the following pattern: the hero first rejects Vice and then acquires some sign of his regenerate self; sometimes, as in *The Interlude of Youth,* the donning of a new white robe, and sometimes, as in the Wit and Science plays, the marrying of a virtuous lady. The redemption of the hero, then, involves not so explicitly a filling out of the personality as it does a restoration of the original purity that was distorted by sin (Youth speaks *argot* when he is in sin; Wit cannot recognize his face in a mirror when he is in sin). That Hal is rejecting sin in the rejecting of Falstaff is, quite apart from our feelings about it, indisputable. But I suggest that in the donning of robe and crown and the taking of a new station in life we have what is supposed to play as the iconography of regeneration.[18] What happens, I think, is that we find it impossible to accept the notion of kingship as the "objective correlative" for the regenerate state, and so it is only in *Henry V,* in the warm humanity of the King's scenes with the troops and with Kate, that we see evidence of the necessary finishing touches put to the character of the Christian Prince.

If this study has led to the question what is character, it also folds back upon itself, for the Francis scene, which I have been trying to illuminate, finds Hal asking that same question, along with a more pointed one, which he perhaps never quite answers—who am I?

Notes:

(1) In the 1962 production by the San Francisco Actors' Workshop.

(2) All citations from the play are from the Arden Edition, ed. A. R. Humphreys (London, 1960).

(3) *The Works of William Shakespeare*, ed. Samuel Johnson (London, 1765), IV, 152.

(4) Francis Gentleman, *The Dramatic Censor* (London, 1770), quoted by Hemingway, 129 (see below, n. 8).

(5) Gentleman, in his Introduction to the Bell edition of the plays, (London, 1773).

(6) C. Cowden Clarke, *The Shakespeare Key* (London, 1879), p. 99.

(7) *Five Plays of Shakespeare*, ed. G. L. Kittredge (Boston, 1941), p. 139.

(8) A New Variorum Edition of Shakespeare, *Henry the Fourth Part I*, ed. S. B. Hemingway (Philadelphia, 1936), pp. 129-130.

(9) W. W. Lloyd, *Essays on Shakespeare* (London, 1858), quoted by Hemingway, p. 134.

(10) *Shakespeare's History of King Henry the Fourth*, ed. William Rolfe (New York, 1885), p. 179.

(11) On the body politic trope, see Elyot, *Boke of the Governour,* I,i, and its background in T. Spencer, *Shakespeare and the Nature of Man* (New York, 1942). Also E. M. W. Tillyard, *The Elizabethan World Picture* (London, 1943), pp. 88-91.

(12) The fullest discussion of the Aristotelian terminology is still S. H. Butcher, *Aristotle's Theory of Poetry and Fine Art* (London, 1907).

(13) A different but complementary explanation of the change of subject is offered by Hemingway and Tucker Brooke in the Yale Shakespeare edition (New Haven, 1961). They share the Arden editor's "surprise" but suggest that it is precisely the frantic activity of Francis that reminds Hal of Hotspur (p. 143).

(14) Tillyard, *Shakespeare's History Plays* (New York, 1962), pp. 300-346. Tillyard does not deal with the Francis scene.

(15) Only the anecdote of the Lord Chief Justice and Hal is told by Elyot, but it was by his time only one excerpt from the firmly established tradition of the Chroniclers. Croft, in his edition of Elyot (London, 1883), II, 62, lists the story of Hal's wildness and reformation as available in Thomas of Walsingham, Thomas of Elmham, Thomas Otterbourne, Titus Livius, Capgrave, and Hardyng.

(16) J. Barish in *ShS*, I (1965), 9-17. In a 1964 BBC lecture J. B. Priestly resurrected the "gigantic Falstaff" position.

(17) As J. Dover Wilson shows in *The Fortunes of Falstaff* (Cambridge, 1944).

(18) The chroniclers are in complete agreement on their vision of Hal as the morality Youth figure, and they pointedly locate his reformation in the ceremony of accession. Croft quotes from John Hardyng: "The houre he was crowned and anoynt, / He chaunged was of all his olde condicyon; / Full vertuous he was fro poynt to poynt, / Grounded all newe in good opinyon; / For passyngly without comparyson, / Then set upon all ryght and conscyence / A newe man made by all good regimence" (Croft, p. 62).

The Stage in Robert Fludd's Memory System

by Frances A. Yates

I

In my book *The Art of Memory*[1] I discussed the theatre memory system in the second volume of Robert Fludd's *Utriusque Cosmi Historia* published by Johann Theodor De Bry at Oppenheim in 1619, and attempted to place it in the context of the history of the art of memory which was the main subject of the book. I devoted one chapter to arguing that the theatre alluded to was the second Globe Theatre. The argument had to be very compressed since I could not allow it much space in my general history of the art of memory. Obviously another book would be needed to develop the argument and to relate it to the theme, intrinsically even more important, of "Vitruvian influences in both Dee and Fludd"[2] to which I only briefly alluded. I am at present writing a book in which I hope to show that the reference to a contemporary theatre in Fludd's memory system is not merely a whim or an accident but provides a way in to the whole problem of the rise of the theatre movement in England, from the building of James Burbage's Theatre in 1576 onwards.

Meanwhile the Fludd engraving of a building which looks like a Jacobean stage has aroused a good deal of interest and was the subject of an article by I. A. Shapiro in the second volume of *Shakespeare Studies*.[3] Since readers of *Shakespeare Studies* ought to have an opportunity of hearing my reactions to it, I propose in the first part of this article to discuss it. In the second part I shall give a more detailed analysis of Fludd's memory system than I had room for in *The Art of Memory*.

I will begin with the pleasing task of noting the points on which Shapiro and I are in agreement. He has made a study of the memory system as a whole and looked at the illustrations in Fludd's books as a whole. He therefore knows that the legend started by Richard Bernheimer[4] according to which the German printer is supposed to have picked up some print which he had by him to illustrate the "theatre" in the memory system cannot possibly be true. "The briefest inspection of Fludd's *Historia*", says Shapiro, "makes it certain that the author himself must have supplied the material for its numerous and very detailed illustrations, most of which are elaborately keyed to the text."[5] I also emphasised that the illustrations for Fludd's books must have been supplied by himself and I pointed out that the five imaginary columns in the "theatre" engraving correspond exactly to the specifications given for them in the text.[6] Shapiro agrees with this. "Although it is possible that the German engraver was influenced by local fashions in some details of these illustrations, the basic design and material must always have come from Fludd, as the text postulates, and as the insertion of locations for the five imaginary columns proves in the case of this paticular illustration."[7] I may add that I shall bring evidence in my next book to demonstrate that the artist who drew the sketches for the engravings was almost certainly Fludd himself; this will make it possible to get rid of any German influences and to see the "theatre" as an engraving made from a sketch drawn by Fludd in England.

On the vital matter that this engraving reflects a stage in a real English theatre, Shapiro is in agreement with me. I quote the following from his article:—"that this illustration depicts a stage that actually existed, in or before 1619, is, I hope, now beyond reasonable doubt." And again:—"Miss Yates' assumption that the original of Fludd's stage illustration was English is undoubtedly justified by all the available evidence."[8] The Fludd engraving thus becomes a piece of evidence about the English stage which no theatre historian can ignore.

Another point on which Shapiro supports me is in the view that the Fludd engraving represents, not a whole theatre, but a stage. I said "the engraving does not represent a whole theatre. It represents a stage, or rather part of a stage"[9] and my subsequent argument is based on that assumption. Shapiro points out that the word *theatrum* which Fludd uses of the structures he describes and illustrates was commonly used for what we call a stage.[10] Further, and this is one of the most valuable things in his article, he reproduces an enlargement of the two small memory theatres which are shown in Fludd's diagram of the heavens (Fig. 1) on either side of the sign of the Ram.[11] As he rightly emphasises the illustration "dispels any possible doubt about Fludd's meaning because it shows both "theatres" as raised stages with the space below boarded up."[12]

Unfortunately in a note to this passage there occurs one of his confusing misrepresentations of my own remarks. This is what he says:—

> She states (p.330 of *The Art of Memory*) that the twin theatres shown in the sign of the Ram in this diagram are never referred to in the text. They are mentioned frequently, however, and are discussed in detail in the next chapter (Bk.I, chapter x), in Bk.II, chapters iii, iv, vi, and in Bk.III chapters ii, and vii. She was perhaps misled by observing that the twin "theatres" shown in the sign of the Ram differ from those in Fludd's other illustrations in having two doors in the lower stage front. That difference is explained by the tiny size to which the "theatres" had to be reduced in that diagram and the extreme difficulty in engraving more detail in such a small place."[13]

What I actually say is:—

> On either side of the sign Aries, two small buildings are shown. They are tiny "theatres" or stages. These two theatres, *in this form with two doors at the back of the stage,* are never illustrated again nor referred to in the text.[14]

I am not "misled" here. It is a correct observation. The three memory "theatres" illustrated and referred to in the text have either five or three doors, never two.

139

Moreover they are none of them identical in other respects with the two stages shown in the sign of the Ram in the diagram of the heavens. The discrepancy between the two stages shown in this diagram and those in the text seems to me a problem. Shapiro gets over the difficulty by assuming that the reduction in size accounts for the discrepancy. I do not accept this as a satisfactory solution. But the worst confusion is that he suggests that I have missed references to the stages in the heavens diagram in the passages which he cites. These passages[15] are about the memory theatres in the text the illustrations for which I have reproduced and discussed in my book.

The three engravings of what he calls "theatres" in Fludd's book are (1) the "theatre" (Fig.2) or stage with five doors on two levels, a terrace, and a bay window, that is to say the engraving which looks like a Jacobean stage, and which shows five column bases in the foreground (2) the "theatre" (Fig.3) with five doors all on one level and also showing five column bases in the foreground (3) the "theatre" (Fig.4) with three doors all on ground level and without column bases. Shapiro puts forward an interpretation of Fludd's memory system through which he argues that only (2) and (3) were intended by Fludd to be used in the mnemonics, one for what he calls his *ars rotunda,* the other for what he calls his *ars quadrata.*[16] The main "theatre", the one which looks like a Jacobean stage, Shapiro believes was not intended to be used in the memory system at all but was put in as a straight representation of the stage of the Blackfriars theatre. "Fludd did not expect his disciples to envisage for either of his methods 'theatres' like the stage shown in his first illustration. Why then did he insert this detailed representation of, apparently, an actual stage?"[17] Why indeed? Shapiro invents a change in Fludd's plans through which he decided to use only the two secondary "theatres" in his mnemonics but left in the first or main "theatre", perhaps because "he thought that his readers on the continent might be unfamiliar with what in England was meant by a 'public theatre' and that his illustration would explain what lay behind his modified versions".

I cannot agree to this. Because if any one thing is certain about Fludd's memory system, it is certain that the real "public theatre" shown in the engraving belonged into the system and was intended to be used in the mnemonics. More abundant evidence of this fact than I gave in *The Art of Memory* will be given in the second part of this article. In this part I shall confine myself to repeating the evidence, though with fuller quotations, which I used in that book.

For his *ars rotunda* Fludd uses memory theatres, or rather stages, which are to be placed in the heavens with the signs of the zodiac. It is a magical system in which the astral influences are supposed to organise the memory. In the text accompanying the diagram of the heavens (Bk.I, chapter ix) it is stated that these "theatres" are to be placed east and west of the signs; the eastern theatres are to be light in colour, the western ones, dark.

The immediately following chapter (I.x) is about these eastern and western theatres and contains an illustration of a specimen of one of them; this is the illustration of the Jacobean stage. The text accompanying it is as follows:—

140

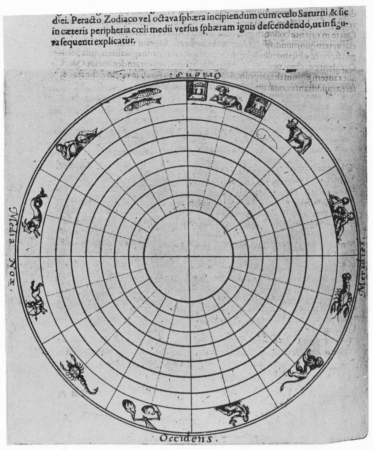

Figure 1: The Heavens. From Robert Fludd's *Ars memoriae*.

Figure 2: Theatre 1. From Robert Fludd's *Ars memoriae*.

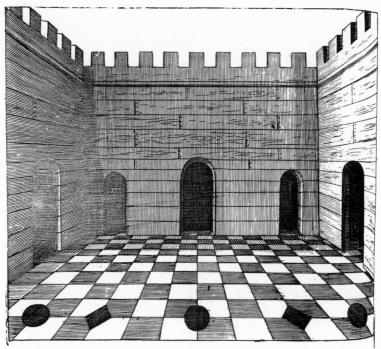

Figure 3: Theatre 2. From Robert Fludd's *Ars memoriae.*

Figure 4: Theatre 3. From Robert Fludd's *Ars memoriae.*

De theatri orientalis & occidentalis descriptione

Theatrum appello illud, in quo omnes vocabulorum, sententiarum, particularum orationis seu subjectorum actiones tanquam
in theatro publico, ubi comoediae & tragoediae aguntur, demonstrantur. Huiusmodi theatrorum *speciem unam* in puncto ori-
entis sitam esse imaginabimini; quae realis seu corporea, sed
quasi vapore aethereo consideranda erit: Sitque illa theatri
umbra similitudinibus spirittum egentum repleta. *Primum* ergo
theatrum habebit colorem album, lucidum & splendidum, prae
se ferens diem, diurnasque actiones. Quare in oriente collocabi-
tur, quia Sol ab Oriente se attollens diem incipit, claritatemque
mundo pollicitur: *Secundum* vero fingetur imbutum colore nigro,
fusco & obscuro: illudque in Occidente positum imaginaberis,
quia Sol in Occidente existens noctem & obscuritatem brevi
venturam denunciat. Quodlibet autem horum theatrorum habebit *quinque portas* ab invicem distinctas, & fere aequidistantes,
quarum usus postea demonstrabimus.

This theatre is stated to be representative of the eastern and western, light and
dark, theatres. It is evidently a light or eastern one; its dark opposite is identical
with it except for being in darkness. It is said to be like "a public theatre in which
comedies and tragedies are acted". It is stated that it has "five doors distinct from
one another and approximately (*fere*) equidistant, the use of which we will demonstrate later." We see in the engraving five doors or entrances onto the stage which,
if not quite exactly equidistant, are schematically arranged.

The opening phrase of the chapter quoted above would seem to translate as
follows:

> "I call that a Theatre, in which all actions of words, of sen-
> tences, of parts of speech or subjects, are demonstrated, as in a
> public theatre, where comedies and tragedies are acted."

This is the vital phrase which suggests that the engraving alludes to a "public
theatre".

I will now put forward a suggestion about the possible meaning of the phrase
as a whole which I did not make in my book.

In the memory tradition, artificial memory had two branches; memory for things
(notions or ideas); and memory for words, or the memorising of the actual words
used in a speech.[18] It would seem that the kind of artificial memory of which Fludd
is thinking in connection with this theatre is probably memory for words, since
"words, sentences, parts of speech" are specified.

There remains the word *actiones* to be explained, "all *actions* of words, of sentences, of parts of speech". I suggest that the use of the word *actio* here is probably an allusion to *actio* as one of the five parts of rhetoric, which in the classical

tradition were defined as *inventio, dispositio, elocutio, memoria, pronuntiatio.* The fifth part, *pronuntiato*, included *actio*, or gesture, not only the pronunciation of a speech but also the actions or gestures accompanying it. This is discussed by B. L. Joseph who in his book on acting and rhetoric[19] demonstrates that Elizabethan acting practise was guided by classical rules about *actio* or gesture. The Elizabethan actor combined *pronuntiatio* with *actio*, or "suited the action to the word", as Hamlet advised the players to do. The fifth part of rhetoric was particularly associated with actors. When Francis Bacon is listing memory images through which to memorise the parts of rhetoric, he chooses an actor as the image for action.[20]

My suggestion therefore is that in his phrase "all actions of words, sentences etc." Fludd may be thinking of actors, acting their parts with gestures as they pronounce the words of their speech. And that in this "theatre", human memory-for-words images will have expressive actions, like those with which actors underline the meaning of the words they pronounce. Such an association of the expressiveness, demanded of memory images in the classical rules for artificial memory, with acting seems also to have been present in antiquity.[21]

Fludd keeps his promise that he will explain later the use of the "five doors distinct from one another and approximately equidistant" which he shows in the engraving of the Jacobean theatre. This he does in Bk.II, chapter v. Opposite to the five doors are to be imagined five columns, the exact shapes of which are specified:—

> His pratis oppositae[22] fingantur *quinque columnae,* quae itidem debent figura & colore distingui; *Figura* enim *duarum extremarum erit circularis & rotunda, media* autem columna *habebit figuram hexagoneam,* & quae his *intermedia* sunt *quadratam* possidebunt figuram: Colore etiam hoc modo ab invicem different, ut colores earum relationem habeant cum coloribus portarum theatriis oppositatum.

The shapes of the five columns opposite to the five doors of the stage are here specified as round, square, hexagonal, square, round, in that order. Five column bases of these shapes and in this order are to be seen in the engraving of the Jacobean stage, which proves that that stage is to be used in the mnemonics with the five doors and the five columns described in this chapter. These five doors and five columns as memory places are to be imagined, says Fludd, as of different colours. Imagining memory places in different colours was a practise which was supposed to help memory; another example of the practise is to be found in the mnemonics of John Willis who recommends using sets of stages as memory rooms which are to be remembered in different colours.[23]

In view of the obvious fact that the presence of the five column bases in the engraving of the Jacobean stage alone proves that that stage was to be used in the mnemonics, how does Shapiro argue that it was not to be so used but was quite outside the memory system? He says that the five doors in the engraving of the

144

Jacobean stage are not equidistant, as stated in the text accompanying this engraving, and that therefore the "theatre" which Fludd intended to be used in the mnemonics was not this one but the theatre (number 2) which has five equidistant doors and is labelled *Figura vera theatri*, words which mean, according to him, that this is the true figure of the theatre to be used in the mnemonics. It too has column bases opposite the doors, but different from those in the main theatre (number 1) in that the central one is round, not hexagonal. Without explaining this difference, Shapiro insists that this alone was the theatre which Fludd intended to use in his *ars rotunda*. The other, smaller theatre (number 3) was to be used in his *ars quadrata*. The main theatre or stage, the Jacobean stage, was not to be used in either of these arts. It is simply put in, quite unaccountably, as a straight representation of the Blackfriars stage. In order to maintain this impossible theory, Shapiro naturally has to get rid of me, and after his brief, and to readers unfamiliar with Fludd's text, certainly incomprehensible statement of his theory, he briefly remarks that "It will be evident from the preceding account of Fludd's two types of "memory theatre" that Miss Yates has misinterpreted their significance."[24]

He never explains what the five column bases are doing in the engraving if this is a straight representation of the stage at Blackfriars. Surely there cannot have been five such columns right across the front of any stage, totally obstructing the view of the audience. The only possible explanation of the presence of such columns, impossible on a real stage, is that a real stage has been adapted for mnemonic purposes.

The reason why we can feel confident that it is the stage wall of a real theatre that we see in the engraving is because Fludd gives, in an earlier chapter of the *Ars memoriae*, a long discussion of fictitious places—that is places in buildings to be used in memory systems which are based, not on real buildings, but on imaginary buildings. Such imaginary or fictitious places are not, he says, to be used in the art of memory which must always be based on real places in real buildings. (The passage will be analysed and quoted more fully than in *The Art of Memory*, and with much other supporting material, in the third part of this article.) Since Fludd states that the building which he is using is like a "public theatre", it follows that the five memory places on the wall of the stage seen in the engraving are real. Many features of this stage—the bay window, the battlemented terrace, the differences in the five doors—are not mentioned in the text; they are real features of a real stage in a real public theatre which Fludd is memorising because real places are better to use in memory than imaginary ones. Shapiro tries to argue that the directions about using real places do not apply to the engraving of the Jacobean stage.[25] He does not seem to realise that he is thereby trying to destroy the guarantee that the stage in the engraving does show real places on a real stage wall.

I am sure that Shapiro genuinely believes in his impossible view that the Jacobean stage does not belong into the memory system, but a wish has been father to this thought. He wants to take that stage right out of the memory system so that he can treat it as a straight representation of the stage of the Blackfriars theatre, quite uncontaminated by astral mnemonics, and innocent of the mnemonic distortions which I assume in my reconstruction of the engraving as reflecting the stage of the Globe theatre.

The engraving having been withdrawn from the memory system becomes a document which he can use as a theatre historian, without worrying any more about mnemonics, and he settles down to his argument that the stage which it shows is that of the Blackfriars theatre.

One would expect, he says, a stage illustrated in a book published in 1619[26] to be that of the Blackfriars, for this was the most fashionable theatre in London at that time. "During the decade before 1619 the King's players were the most admired actors in London. The Blackfriars was their 'winter house' and seems to have been preferred to their other theatre, the Globe, by all who could afford its higher prices."[27] This fashionable theatre is therefore the one which Fludd would have chosen to depict. He believes that at the Blackfriars theatre there were boxes for the audience "contiguous to and on the same level as the stage"[28] which seems to him to confirm a resemblance to Fludd's illustration, where boxes seem to be placed on either side of the stage. The upper room or chamber in the Fludd illustration would be the music room at Blackfriars.

Noting that the boxes in the Fludd illustration have a space of plain wall above them, and not an upper row of seats, he takes this plain boarded space to be intended to keep out the light coming from the side windows in the great hall of the Dominican convent, which was adapted as the Blackfriars theatre.[29] Plays were performed by artificial light at Blackfriars, and these blank spaces above the boxes are, he thinks, a form of blackout. (The light could surely just as well have been kept out by having upper rows of seats constructed above the boxes.) He then allows his imagination to run riot over technical details whereby he constructs rooms behind the boarded spaces to be used by the actors. "We may safely conjecture that two such rooms were indeed constructed in the space above the boxes on each side of the stage. Since the floor of the upper room on each side would in any event have had to be put at about the level of the balcony floor, we may confidently assume further that the obvious advantages of having them at exactly the same level would have ensured that they were so constructed."

Shapiro is confidently assuming much more than we see in the Fludd engraving, that behind the side walls are the windows of the hall of the Dominican convent, that these are being blacked out by the blank spaces above the boxes, that behind these blank spaces are the rooms about which he knows so much. As long as a theatre historian is imagining purely technical details, however insufficient or non-existent the evidence for them may be, he feels that he is being sensible. Shapiro is trying to draw from the Fludd illustration technical evidence of a kind which it cannot give.

There are very serious objections to Blackfriars as the real "public theatre" alluded to in the Fludd engraving. Blackfriars was not a "public theatre" as Fludd states that his *Theatrum* is, but a "private theatre". It was the great wooden theatres, built as theatres, such as the Globe, which were called "public theatres". The Blackfriars which catered for more select audiences, and was adapted in the hall of an already existing building, was a "private theatre". This distinction was generally accepted and would certainly have been well known to Fludd who, as I shall show in my next book, was inside the theatre movement. He would certainly have been familiar with theatre interiors, whether the Globe, or Blackfriars, or others, and when he says that by *Theatrum* he means a "public theatre" he would have been precise in his use of the term.

The stage wall seen in the engraving with its battlemented terrace, its great, rough, central, hinged door, like that in some gatehouse of town or castle, is admirably suited for history plays and for scenes of siege or battle,[30] such as those frequently seen at the Globe when Shakespeare's history plays were being enacted. The stage at the Blackfriars was of a more refined type, probably more influenced by court practise and perhaps tending towards masque-like effects; its audiences preferred less boisterous plays than those given in the popular public theatres. The stage wall which Fludd shows is much more suited to be that of a public theatre like the Globe, than of a private theatre, like Blackfriars.

The argument about the fashionableness of Blackfriars as a reason for its being the theatre which Fludd would choose is, I think, quite mistaken. Fludd would choose a theatre which would suit his astral mnemonics, based on the round heavens, and this would be a round theatre like the Globe (round within and hexagonal without),[31] a theatre representing the world in its design, a *Theatrum Orbi(s)*, which is the title which we actually see written on the engraving as the title of the theatre. It is one of the precepts of the art of memory that quiet and unfrequented buildings should be chosen for memorizing, since crowds of people disturb the concentration needed.[32] An empty Globe would be more suitable for Fludd's purposes than a crowded Blackfriars. The stage shown in the Fludd engraving is empty; there are no actors, no audience; the central hinged door is open but no one comes out. We are in an empty building, being used for memorising, a *Theatrum Orbi(s)*, or Globe theatre, in which only the invisible memory artist is present, concentrating on his astral mnemonics.

Shapiro states that "the stage in Fludd's illustration is set in an obviously rectangular building", and that this would suit the Blackfriars hall.[33] He is here making an unconscious assumption. He is assuming that the side walls are to be continued forwards to form the sides of a rectangular building. There is no real ground for making this assumption. All we see is side walls which stop at the front edge of the engraving. If what we see is a stage, as Shapiro agrees, this stage may be set in a building of any shape.

One very great objection to the stage as we see it in the Fludd engraving, if interpreted literally, is that it is a very poor stage for acting purposes. The actors as they came out of the side entrances would practically touch the audience in the boxes. In this stiflingly confined space how could dramatic scenes be deployed? All would be confusion, both for the cramped actors and for the people in the boxes who would only see the actors nearest to them, not the whole scene.

147

In *The Art of Memory*, I emphasised that the boxes in the side walls shown in the engraving are never mentioned by Fludd in his text and were not used as memory places in the mnemonics. Only the five places or doors on the stage wall were to be so used (together with the five imaginary columns opposite to them). The reality of the position of the side walls with their boxes is therefore not guaranteed by the rule against using imaginary buildings in the art of memory.

The boxes however look real and must have been somewhere in the real theatre. My solution, which I worked out in *The Art of Memory* and illustrated with a reconstruction (Fig. 5), is that Fludd adapted the real stage, that of the Globe, behind a "memory room", and that in order to see the real stage, that of the Globe, behind the engraving we have to move the boxes into the side galleries of a public theatre.[34] The "posts" supporting the "heavens" in such a theatre would be about in the position on the stage where Fludd puts his imaginary columns. My reconstruction shows how, according to this interpretation, a possible stage for acting — a very good stage for acting — can be drawn out of the Fludd engraving, a stage in a public theatre, the stage of the Globe.

To those unfamiliar with the memory tradition, the "memory room" suggestion naturally sounds unconvincing. Nevertheless there is actually good warrant for this suggestion in Fludd's memory system, in passages which I did not draw in as

Figure 5: Sketch of the Stage of the Globe Theatre.
Based on Fludd. Drawn by R. W. Yates.

148

evidence in my book but which will be discussed in the second part of this article.

Even in the engraving itself there is, I believe, evidence that the position of the side walls cannot be relied upon as their position in a real theatre. In my book I said that the side walls in the engraving look structurally impossible. "And they do not fit on properly to the end wall, for they cut off bits of the battlements on the terrace."[35] This is a very important point. Minute examination of the engraving shows that the side walls join the back wall in such a way as actually to encroach on the geometrical forms which decorate the battlements. It is as though Fludd drew the back stage wall first, and then fitted the side walls onto it in this curious and unnatural way. (The rustication on the side walls also does not fit properly with that on the back wall.) In my reconstruction, the clumsiness through which the corners of the terrace are cut off by the side walls is cleared away, and the terrace is shown completed by the corners at its ends. The clumsiness would be accounted for if Fludd was tampering with a real theatre in order to close in its stage as a memory room.

The Blackfriars theory as to the meaning of the engraving rests entirely on the position of the side walls with their boxes. It is this which seems to point to the private theatre used by Shakespeare's company of players. Everything else, above all Fludd's own statement, points to their public theatre. And the position of the side walls is, I believe, the least reliable part of the engraving.

Leaving aside now all argument about the side walls, let us look only at the stage wall, for this we can be assured is real. And let us look at it without further argument as to what actual theatre it alludes to but in a more general way.

Comparison of the stage wall shown in the Fludd engraving with the stage wall of the Swan theatre, as depicted in the famous De Witt sketch[36] (hitherto our only visual representation of a theatre of the period) shows, as Shapiro says, certain resemblances.[37] The Swan stage has entrances with rough hinged doors, a little like the hinged door in the Fludd stage; it too has an upper gallery. But there are many differences. There are only two doors or entrances in the Swan stage, not five as Fludd shows. There is no upper bay-windowed chamber at the Swan, as in the Fludd engraving. The Swan's gallery is not open, like the terrace of the Fludd stage.

My view of the relationship of the Swan stage to that shown in the Fludd engraving is as follows. I am in agreement with those scholars who have argued that the Swan was a "dual purpose" theatre which could be used both for animal baiting and other sports or shows, and also sometimes for acting.[38] The trestles under the Swan stage indicate that it was a temporary stage which could be removed when the building was being used for bear baiting or other sports requiring the whole space of the arena. The fact that the Hope theatre, which we know was a dual purpose theatre, was, according to the contract for it, to imitate the Swan, confirms this argument.[39] It follows that the stage wall shown in the sketch of the Swan is not that of a public theatre designed especially for acting and with a permanent stage. We have in fact hitherto never seen a representation of the stage of one of the great public theatres, with stages carefully designed to meet the requirements of actors, of which the chief and most admired was the Globe. The great, the immense, importance of the Fludd engraving is that it shows us a type of stage wall used in theatres with permanent stages, designed for acting, a much more refined and better type than the rough Swan stage.

As Shapiro says, the stage wall shown by Fludd is much better suited for acting purposes than that shown in the Swan sketch. It contains five entrances, instead of only two. It shows how the terrace, or "tarras", or balcony had two entrances onto it, whereby actors entered above. It shows the position of the chamber or upper room as being placed in the centre of the terrace—a very satisfactory and symmetrical arrangement. It shows this chamber as a bay window projecting over the main stage. As Shapiro says:—"Fludd's balcony has a large corbelled bay window which projects forwards from its centre and, apparently, leaves the full width of the balcony behind it free for what architects call 'circulation'. The multifarious usefulness of this bay or 'penthouse' will be obvious to any student of Elizabethan play-texts and need not be dilated upon here."[40] He observes that the sides of the bay "appear to terminate flush with the stage front, and do not project backwards over the balcony."[41] I also had observed this feature and noted that it provided opportunity for circulation between the chamber and the terrace. As I have said:—

> The position of the chamber as shown by Fludd solves what has been one of the major problems of Shakespearean stageing. It has been known that there was a terrace on the upper level which was thought to run right across it, and known also that there was an upper chamber. It has been thought that this chamber was placed behind the terrace which with its railing, or balusters (or rather, as we now see, its battlements) would obscure the view into the chamber. Fludd shows us that the terrace ran *behind* the front of the chamber which projected beyond it over the main stage. The terrace as it were passed *through* the chamber which could be entered from it on either side. No one has thought of this solution of the chamber and terrace problem which is obviously the right one.[42]

Looking now at the Fludd stage as a general statement of the main features of the stage wall in a public theatre designed especially for acting, as was the Globe, I would not attempt to draw from it detailed technical information but more general views. Its most important revelation is that there were five entrances to the stage, as in the classical theatre, but adapted to a multilevel stage by being placed two above and three below. We can also see that the tiring house wall represents a great house or castle, with its gatehouse, or maybe a palace front (as in the classical stage), perhaps rather like the façade of Whitehall palace which faced the tiltyard,[43] where Queen Elizabeth used to sit at an upper window in a gallery to watch the tilting. The mixture of Gothic with classical elements—the Gothic battlements combined with the pseudo-classical effect of the painted rustication on

150

the canvas covering of the wooden walls—is what we should expect from the period.

The formula which we see here of the five classical entrances, combined with a bay window and a battlemented terrace, may well have been the standard type for a public theatre. This formula may already have been laid down in James Burbage's original Theatre of 1576. It would have assumed its most perfect form at the Globe, which was the Theatre re-erected in an improved and more splendid manner. The Fortune, as we know from its contract, was to copy the Globe except for being square; its stage may therefore have repeated the formula. And since the King's Men played at the Blackfriars theatre plays which they also performed at the Globe, it is probable that they would have needed to repeat in their private house acting facilities not basically dissimilar, though perhaps refined by courtly influences, to those to which they were accustomed in their public theatre, the Globe.

Professor Allardyce Nicoll has pointed out a resemblance between the Fludd stage and that shown in the illustrated edition of Settle's *Empress of Morocco* of 1673,[44] suggesting that the Restoration theatre may have been less different in design from that of the earlier period than has usually been supposed.

We are only at the beginning of a new era in theatre history which is opening up from the new information supplied by Fludd.

In view of the great importance of what we are learning about the Shakespearean theatre, those working on this new line of research must welcome one another's attempts. Shapiro's article is an advance on some previous attitudes to the Fludd theatre engraving. He has left behind him the era in which the German printer was supposed to have picked up any print which he had by him to illustrate what Fludd says is a public theatre. He takes the engraving seriously as a most important contribution to English theatre history. He realises that the memory system must be tackled before we can understand the engraving. Though his interpretation of the memory system contains bad mistakes which must be unpicked as quickly as possible before they mislead others, yet it has a certain value in showing where further analysis is needed. And his Blackfriars theory, if taken in a general sense and not in the literal way in which he tries to apply it, opens up a view of the subject with which I am in agreement, namely that Fludd's revelations are of the greatest importance, not only for any one particular theatre, but for the whole of the theatre movement initiated by Burbage.

II

Since the relationship of the Jacobean stage to the memory system in which it is embedded is crucial for its understanding, theatre historians and Shakespearean scholars will need to look into the memory system for themselves. The following notes are intended to provide a little guidance for its study.

The memory system is based, like all Fludd's works, on his philosophy of the Macrocosm and the Microcosm, the "histories" of which are the theme of the bulky tomes of the *Utriusque Cosmi Historia*. Man as Microcosm reflects the

Macrocosm; he is a "little world" which is an epitome of the "great world". Not only does his physical form and corporeal life repeat the elemental composition of the world of matter; his mental and spiritual life repeats the higher celestial world. The stars in their courses are "naturally" within his mind and memory. Fludd's two types of memory systems, the *ars quadrata* and the *ars rotunda,* the first of which memorises "corporeal" images, the second, celestial and spiritual images, express in terms of the "square" and the "round", the elemental and earthy, and the celestial and starry, aspects of the Macrocosm-Microcosm relationship.

The visual plan, itself a mnemotechnic using images on a wheel, which shows the contents of the section of the *Historia* which treats of the "technical history of the Microcosm" (Fig. 6), dominated by Man as the Ape of Nature, shows *Ars memoriae* as one of the subjects to be treated in the section. The art of memory is typified by a memory wall divided into five places based on three parallelograms, the central one undivided, the two at the sides divided into two halves. On these five places are five images. The title page of the treatise on the art of memory (Fig. 7), shows a memory wall divided into five places in exactly the same way, and also with five images on them. A man is imprinting these places and images on his imagination with the "eye of imagination". The theme of these five places runs all through Fludd's *Ars memoriae* like a leitmotiv. It is as it were stated in emblematic form in these two preliminary illustrations as a preliminary statement of how Fludd will use the places and images of the art of memory.

Memory treatises usually treat of "places" and "images" in two sections, following the classical pattern.[45] A good example, and one which Fludd probably knew, is Cosmas Rossellius, *Thesaurus artificosae memoriae,* Venice, 1578. Rossellius gives in his Part I, on places, a clear idea of the meaning of the term "common places" as used in the art of memory. Any system which includes within it a number of memory places is a common place, but these are in descending order of size and importance. The spheres of the universe are, says Rossellius, "most ample common places" because they include within them all the places in the universe. A city is a large common place, including many buildings and streets, all containing many memory loci. A building within a city would be a smaller common place; and a room or portion of a building a still smaller one.

Rossellius' Part II on images gives in a fairly straightforward way an account of the use of memory images, and distinctions between "memory for things" and "memory for words". He also abounds in "alphabetical orders", lists of names, animals etc. in alphabetical order to be used in memorising through attaching the word or letter to be remembered to a name in a list. Some of Fludd's images cover similar ground and he makes great use of "alphabetical orders".

But a fairly straightforward treatise like that of Rossellius, though a good introduction, is not sufficient for wrestling with Fludd who is engaged in astral mnemonics of the bewildering kind which is found in Giordano Bruno's works on memory. Magic mnemonics rests on the Macrocosm-Microcosm theory as to man's nature. By applying the principles of "artificial" memory to this "natural" foundation, the magic mnemotechnician hopes to systematise and make operative his

Figure 6: Title-page of Robert Fludd's
De technica Microcosmi historia.

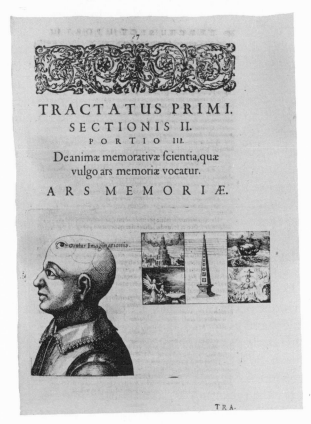

Figure 7: Title-page of Robert Fludd's
Ars memoriae.

natural cosmic memory. Bruno's attempts in this direction are of a frightful complexity. In one of his books, *De imaginum, signorum et idearum compositione*, Frankfort, 1591, he uses elaborate systems of memory rooms, atria, "fields", and cubicles, in association with a cosmological system based on the zodiac and the planets.[46] That Fludd knew this book is proved in Bk. I, chapter xi where he talks of memory cubicles containing sides schematically divided into five places and speaks of "thirty" in connection with them. Bruno uses thirty cubicles in his system.[47] Fludd's basic idea of using "theatres" or stages as memory rooms affiliated to the zodiac and planets was probably suggested by this book of Bruno's.

As memory treatises usually do, Fludd opens with some discussion of psychology of memory, based on the Aristotelian and scholastic "faculty psychology" according to which images from sense perception pass through the inner faculties into the storehouse of memory. He also repeats and elaborates the definitions of natural and artificial memory handed down from the classical sources. He then embarks on definitions of the two kinds of artificial memory which he will use, which he calls respectively *ars rotunda* and *ars quadrata*. The fantasy, he says, is operated in two ways in memory. One way uses "ideas" or "umbrae" which are forms of things separated from corporality, not composed of the elements, such as angels, demons, "effigies of the stars", images of gods and goddesses to which celestial things are attributed, images of virtues and vices which are also demonic. With such his *ars rotunda* is concerned. He is here again strongly influenced by Bruno who calls the magic images of the stars which he uses in his memory systems "ideas" or "shadows".[48] The other kind of memory, continues Fludd, uses images of corporeal things, and with these his *ars quadrata* is concerned. Of his *ars rotunda* Fludd says that it "miraculously assists the natural memory of the Microcosm". His *ars quadrata* is more suited to those unskilled in "astronomy" (read "astral magic") and is therefore preferred by most to the *ars rotunda*, though greatly inferior to it.[49]

It is important to remember the plan of memory treatises, how they divide into "places" first, then "images", when studying Fludd's *Ars memoriae*, for he is following the classical plan, though in a somewhat unconventional way and not quite consistently. Book I of his treatise is roughly speaking on places; Book II is, again roughly speaking, on the images to be used on the places described in Book I. And he adds a Book III on words, how different types of words are to be memorised in the two kinds of memory (I think that this means that both Fludd's systems are for "memory for words"). The student of Fludd's memory treatise must realise that he cannot understand it by reading it straight on in a word for word English translation of the Latin. He has to pick out from the three parts, the chapters which all apply to the same system, treated first in Book I with regard to places, secondly in Book II in regard to the images to be used on the places, thirdly in Book III in regard to the words to be remembered with the images on the places.[50]

Let us now take the *Ars rotunda* and study its appearances in all three books of Fludd's *Ars memoriae*.

Bk.I, chapter ix is entitled *De loco communis artis rotundae deque ejus parti-*

tione in propriis locis pro vocabulorum recordatione. It shows the great common place of the spheres of the universe with two small stages on either side of the sign of the Ram. It illustrates the principle of the *Ars rotunda* which will use stages (though not these actual stages) affiliated to the spheres of the universe in a magic memory for words system.

The following chapter x has already been quoted above. It contains the engraving of the Jacobean stage, the statement that it is an example of the theatres used with the zodiac, light or dark according to which side of a sign they are on.[51] The Jacobean stage is a light or eastern theatre. Its stage wall contains *quinque portae* as five memory places.

The Jacobean stage clearly belongs to the *Ars rotunda*; its place is in the round heavens; it will be used for the magical form of the art.

Book II, chapter iii is on the images or "ideas" to be used in the spherical art. These are either "principal" for all principal words; or "less principal". The example of a "principal" image given is the image of the sign Aries; if this image is not sufficient to express the "action" of the words you may add the image of Mars. the planet who rules that sign. "Less principal" images are of "histories" which may be used on the five places of the eastern theatre of the sign; such as Jason on the first place; Medea on the second; Paris on the third; Daphne on the fourth; and Phoebus on the fifth. In the western theatre the same images will appear but dark and obscure in this dark theatre.

It is clear that this is a reference to the eastern and western theatres in the zodiac, of which the Jacobean stage was one, and that these are magic images or "ideas" to be used on their five places.

Bk.II, chapter iv is entitled *De ordine principali idearum per sphaeras Planetarum.* The "ideas" are images of the seven planets in the twelve signs. The images are listed; the signs are represented by their characters.

Bk.II chapter v is entitled *De imaginibus minus principalibus.* It is the chapter which contains the description of the "theatre" with the five places of different colours and five columns opposite of round, square, and hexagonal shape. That is to say it is the second description of the Jacobean stage, here treated under "images", its first description in Bk. I chapter x having been under "places". It is concerned with images for words, for it is stated that animals signifying adverbs, prepositions, and conjunctions may be tied. to the columns, and if "significant" words are being memorised it will be necessary to use "principal" images or ideas, that is astral images of the kind listed in the preceding chapter.

Immediately following, in the same chapter comes the engraving of theatre number 2, the one with the five doors all on ground level and column bases like those in the engraving of the Jacobean stage, except that the central one is round not hexagonal. No directions are given as to the use of this theatre. That it comes immediately after the second description of the Jacobean stage seems to suggest that it is to be somehow closely associated with that stage.

Bk.II, chapter vi first discusses images in "empty places" (that is images not placed on architectural *loci*)[52] and then describes how celestial images or "ideas"

155

may be imagined *in pratis illis antea descriptis*, that is in the immediately preceding chapter v where the five doors of the Jacobean stage were described as *prata* or fields. It states that it is useful for the art to imagine in the zodiacal sphere "histories" of a kind which suit the signs. For example, in the sign of the Ram the story of Jason and Medea may be used. Five images of Jason and Medea are then listed. The first of these "ideas" is to be placed on the white door; the second on the red door; the third on the green door; the fourth on the gold door; the fifth on the black door. These colours correspond to those given for the five places in chapter v. This is therefore a list of images to be used on the *cinque portae* of the Jacobean stage.

We meet this stage again in Bk.III, on words, chapter ii of which is entitled *De vocabulorum significatorum recordatione in arte spherica*. "Significant words" were defined in the preceding chapter as nouns, verbs, adjectives and participles. We are told in this chapter how to record five such significant words, namely *liber, exaltabat, laetus, cultellus,* and *lux*. It is to be done with five images of Medea performing five different actions. These images are to be placed on the five doors of the theatres, the first on the white door. We are again in the Jacobean theatre with its five places on the stage wall memorised as of different colours, and Medea as a memory-for-words image is acting five parts on that stage. It is an "eastern" theatre for the last sentence of the chapter states that we may now proceed to the "western" theatre of the Ram (alluded to by the character for this sign) in which Medea's actions will be seen in the obscurity and darkness proper to western theatres.

The interesting appearance of Medea as a memory-for-words actress, suiting the action to the word on the five places of the stage, confirms the interpretation of "all actions of words etc." which I gave earlier.

This analysis of appearances of the Jacobean stage in all three books of Fludd's *Ars memoriae* proves up to the hilt (what was in any case obvious until unnecessary doubt was thrown on it) namely that the Jacobean stage belonged into the memory system and was to be used in the mnemonics. It is a specimen of an "eastern" theatre in the sign of the Ram. It belongs to the *Ars rotunda*, the magical form of Fludd's artificial memory which used magic images of the stars and other magicised images or "ideas" as its memory images in a magical memory-for-words system.

The common place of the other form of Fludd's art, the *ars quadrata* is defined in Bk.I, chapter xi, *De loco communi artis quadratae*.[53] It is a square cubicle. *Communis hujus artis locus erit conclave sive cubiculum, cujus latera sint aequaliter quadrata aut paralella.* There are apparently to be sets of these cubicles distinguished from one another by images on their exteriors. Their inner walls, or sides are to be divided into five memory places in the following manner. Each side is to be divided into three parallelograms; the two exterior ones are to be divided in half; the central one is to be undivided. The division is made clear by a diagram (Fig.8).

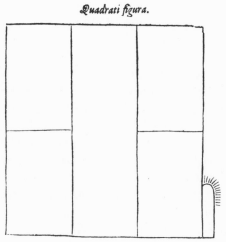

Figure 8: Diagram of memory places on cubicle wall.
From Robert Fludd's *Ars memoriae.*

This arrangement of five memory places on a wall corresponds to that shown on the title-pages where Fludd emblematised his art by a memory wall divided in just this way into five places, with five images on them.

The five places thus arranged on the side of a memory cubicle are, states Fludd, to be memorised in an order proceeding from east to west, following the motion of the sun. These directions infuse a slightly magical or cosmic character into the supposedly less magical *ars quadrata.* The interior of each cubicle is thought of as providing six sides, its four walls, its roof or "heaven", its base or "earth". Each of these sides is to be divided into the five places, giving thirty places in all, a number reminiscent of Bruno's cubicles.

The basis of the *ars quadrata* is thus sets of memory rooms or cubicles, with five places on their sides arranged in the manner specified.

Very closely attached to the cubicle basis of the *ars quadrata* is "theatre" number 3, the one with three entrances and without column bases which is illustrated in the immediately following chapter xii. The very short text accompanying the illustration of this theatre states that "we give to each of the aforementioned places the figure of a theatre containing 3 doors". The "aforementioned places" are the five places on the sides of a cubicle. Apparently the three-doored theatre is to be in some way affixed to these places, or is their form. This is rather baffling. I can only suggest that what may be going on here is the process (probably magicised) known in the memory tradition as "multiplication of places". To his already existing memory building the memory artist can add extra rooms, wings, or extensions, thus expanding the number of his places. The expansion of the five places on the sides of a memory cubicle by giving them the form of a three-doored theatre would increase the number of places available in it from 30 to 90.

The images recommended for the *ars quadrata* in Book II are always less magical or "spiritual" and more "corporeal" than those used in the *ars rotunda.* (The "alphabetical orders" for the two arts differ noticeably in this way.) There is probably a reflection of the three-doored theatre in the advice in Bk.III, chapter iii, that significant words are to be recorded in the *ars quadrata* through three different modes of association; and in Bk.III, chapter vi, where three places are specified for memorising proper names in the *ars quadrata*.

To sum up, both of Fludd's arts use sets of memory rooms. The *ars rotunda* uses sets of stages with five places on the stage wall, combined with five opposite columns. The *ars quadrata* uses sets of cubicles with five places on their sides.

The memory room technique was very ancient (I cannot go into this here). Fludd may have known Lambert Schenkel's memory treatise in which there is much discussion of memory rooms or cubicles[54] (the French translation of this book, published later than Fludd's work, sets out diagrams of memory cubicles[55]). He certainly knew of Bruno's magical use of memory rooms or cubicles. The closest analogy to his use of stages as memory rooms is John Willis's system which uses sets of stages memorised as of different colours.[56]

Theatres 2 and 3 are somehow closely associated with the memory rooms basis of the *ars rotunda* and the *ars quadrata*. Theatre 2 comes immediately after the second description of the memory stage with its five places used in the *ars rotunda*. Theatre 3 is to be directly attached to the five places used in the cubicles system of the *ars quadrata*.

III

How can we be sure that these fantastic systems can throw any light on a real stage? Because Fludd states that the five places which he uses in both his systems are real. I now collect the evidence about this, with quotations.

The long chapter (Bk.I chapter vi) against the use of imaginary buildings in the art of memory is unusual in my experience of memory treatises. The usual custom is to repeat the classical advice (in *Ad Herennium*) that if you do not know enough real places to use in artificial memory you may invent imaginary ones.[57] Fludd however discusses at length how injurious it is for memory to use imaginary places in imaginary buildings rather than real places in real buildings. Real places in real buildings must always be used; this is illustrated by analogies from optics and ends with a proof from "faculty psychology". The whole chapter is basic for the "reality" of stage; I have abbreviated it slightly in the following quotation.

> *De insigni nonnullorum in hac arte versantium errore, & prae-*
> *ceteris illi refelluntur, qui palatiis imaginariis utuntur*
>   Aliqui in hac arte versati voluerunt suam quadratam collocare in palatiis noviter imaginationis inventione fabricatis seu extructis: Quam autem inconveniens sit haec illorum opinio breviter explicabimus: Si enim imaginationis seu phantasiae operationes inprimis scientiae opticae comparaverimus, videbimus rem istam longe aliter sese habere: Nam si multa specula ita sibi ad invicem applicuerimus, ut alicujus in speculo primo

Figure 9: From Johannes de Witt, *Observations on London*.

visi objecti imago a primo illo speculo in secundum & iterum imago illa in secundo speculo visa in tertium reflectatur, atque illa ulterius imago speculi tertii in quartum, & sic in caeteris, percipiemus equidem imaginem speculi primi esse clariorem, perspicuiorem, & completiorem imagine speculi secundi, & hanc secundi illa tertii, & sic in quarto & quinto, ita ut ultima imaginis reflexio tandem obscura admodum & vix perceptibilis futura sit, id sane, quod fit propter debilitatem radiorum fractorum in multiplicatione reflexionum, ita ut prima reflexio sit fortior secunda, & secunda tertia, & sic in caeteris: Sic etiam dicimus, quod quo magis in hac arte opifex penetrat in phantasmatis penetralia, eo debiliores evadant imaginatiarum ejus iconum effigies: Et per consequens, magis manca atque deficiens erit imaginationis operativa virtus. Ex quibus sequiter, quod quo propinquius & magis immediate procedit imaginationis similitudo a realitate sensus, eo sit in hac arte, validior, durabilior & efficacior. . . . Non ergo erit conveniens nova palatia fingere, quae nunquam extiterunt uspiam, quoniam talis artificis fictio seducet mentem ejus a veritatis contemplatione, sed realis sit domus, aut castellum vel palatium, ut a loco communi sensibus suis bene cognito, tanquam fundamento opus tuum struendo, certiori ordine progrediaris: Et enim si fundamentum e memoria tollatur aut elabatur, totum corpus peribit, & subito evanescet: Quod quidem facillime fieri potest, si fictus sit primus locus communis. . . . Porro etiam, ut in speculorum reflexionibus dictum est, quo longius in multiplicatione rerum conceptarum distat earum imago a fundamento, eo debilior erit ejus impressio in memoria: Quare maxima erit fixionis prolongatio, primum imaginari palatium, deinde cubicula istius vel illius coloris, figurae rotundae, &c. postea quodlibet eorum latus in quinque partes dividere, ac mox quamlibet partitionem figuris etiam inventis implere, atque ultimo loco res retinendas iis alique actione imprimere: oblivione autem submerso palatio, reliqua etiam, videlicet cubicula, eorumque loci & imagines, ac res memorandae penitus auferentur. Praeterea, quam debilis erit ille actus (qui praecipuum & primum locum obtinet in hac arte) cujus vivacitate res in memoria conservari debent, tum quatenus ejus fundamentum est fictum, quatenus a veritatis fundamento per imtegrum gradum in fixione recedit. . . . Et proinde concludimus *quod a realibus incipiat & precedat phantasiae operatio non ab intentionalibus,* quoniam fortiores, certiores, & veritati propinquiores sunt actus ab iis egredientes, & in iis reconditi.

This text may be abbreviated in an English paraphrase as follows. Some people

160

use imaginary palaces in their *ars quadrata* (that is in their artificial memory). This is not advisable, for just as an image reflected from one mirror into another, and then into still others, loses its original clarity and strength, so an image of a place, reflected straight from reality is stronger and clearer than if reflected from an imaginary place. It is therefore not good to feign new palaces, which have no real existence, to use in the art of memory, for the fiction seduces the mind from the contemplation of reality. Therefore you should take for the common place of your art (of memory) a real house, or castle, or palace, well known to you. For if the first common place is fictitious it will not be stable in memory, just as reflexions in mirrors grow weaker the more distant they are from reality. And if you take as the foundation of your art of memory an imaginary palace, then cubicles in it, each of whose walls is divided into five parts, and then fill those parts with images, when the palace is submerged in oblivion, the rest of it, the cubicles and their places and images, and the things to be remembered will soon be carried away. For the original act of fixing a place in memory is weaker if its foundation is fictitious, and the farther it is from a foundation in truth the less fixed it is. Wherefore it is to be concluded that "the operation of the fantasy begins from real things, and not from intentions," and its acts are stronger and more certain when it proceeds from reality and returns to it.

The reader is here clearly warned that Fludd will use real, and not imaginary buildings in his art of memory, that cubicles within those buildings will be based on reality, and that five memory places on a cubicle wall will be real places on a real wall.

The phrase quoted at the end of the chapter refers to "faculty psychology" according to the theory of which images from sense impressions pass from the common sense to the imaginative faculty, thence to the estimative faculty, and finally to memory.[58] "Intentions" or resolves arrived at from the impressions are formed in the estimative faculty.[59] Fludd is saying that the imaginative faculty must immediately reflect the real places to be used in the art of memory without passing them through any later psychological processes. It is their closeness to reality which gives the images of the places their strength in the art. Looking now again at the man on the title page gazing with the eye of imagination at the five memory places, we realise that those five places must be real places on a real wall which the man is immediately reflecting in imagination (there is a diagram of the stages of faculty psychology in this man's head) as here advised.

We are now on the look out for a real building with five real places on its wall and as we turn the pages we soon come to the most prominent and striking feature of Fludd's *Ars memoriae*, the engraving of the stage with the five entrances in its wall. We learn that by this *theatrum* Fludd means a "public theatre". And we now know that the real, and not fictitious or imaginary foundation of Fludd's *ars rotunda* was the stage wall of a real public theatre on which he memorised five real places, just as they were in reality, a great hinged door with a bay-windowed room above it, two entrances flanking the central door, and two entrances above these giving on to a battlemented terrace.

And of course it is now obvious that the scheme of this stage wall fits exactly into the scheme of the five memory places. The central door and the bay window above it go into the central parallelogram. The two doors flanking it, and the two doors above these, go into the two side parallelograms divided into halves.

Turning the page showing the illustration of the theatre we come to the *ars quadrata* with the five memory places on the sides of its cubicles to be formed in exactly the same way, as the diagram for the *ars quadrata* places demonstrates.[60]

And we are again told that these places are real.

> Communis hujus artis locus erit conclave sive cubiculum, cujus latera sunt aequaliter quadrata aut paralella: Nec erit hujusmodi cubiculum fictum aut imaginatione sola conceptum, secundum illorum intentionem, qui palatia mente concipere solebant, quia confusio inde sequeretur, & obscuritas in phantasiae operationibus vim actionis obruentibus: Quare necessarium existimamus, ut cubicula realia eligantur, & ea quidem talia, quae ornatu, pulchritudine prospectu, aut re alique oculo sint jucunda . . .[61]

This is an echo of the earlier chapter against using imaginary palaces and imaginary cubicles. Fludd is telling us that the places on his cubicle walls are real, and not only real but also beautiful, attractive and pleasing to the eye. They are again the real places on the stage wall of a real public theatre.

The analysis of Fludd's *Ars memoriae* has led us to the point where we begin to wonder whether the whole of it, with its ever-recurring theme of the five memory places, was designed to allude to the real stage wall of a real public theatre.

The man on the title page was really gazing at the stage wall of a public theatre, and that theme was carried on throughout the treatise.

The more minute analysis of the memory system which I have made here confirms me in my view that the stage behind the Fludd engraving is the stage of the Globe theatre, which Fludd partially distorted to form a memory room suited to his astral mnemonics. Fludd was not a theatre historian bent primarily on leaving evidence about the theatre he knew for the benefit of future theatre historians. He was a Hermetic philosopher bent on constructing an astral memory system based on a real theatre. Standing in the Globe theatre he saw in front of him the stage wall; over the stage he saw the "heavens" painted on the under side of the inner stage cover. This gave him the magical roof for his memory room; the stage wall gave him his five places. He did not want his memory room to be open at the sides, like the real stage, and so he closed it with side walls which contained a feature of the real theatre, the boxes, but moved from their real position. He did not intend to use the boxes in the mnemonics and so their real position did not matter.

This interpretation I believe to be supported by the engraving itself. Every time I look at it, the side walls look to me phoney. They encroach on the breadth of the stage wall in an unnatural way and they look somehow wrong. They do not have the solidity and "reality" of the stage wall which can be relied upon absolutely as "real". It shows of course no details of stage furnishings, such as curtains, or the like, but it presents, I believe, with absolute reliability the basic scheme of the arrangement of entrances, upper chamber, and terrace on the stage wall of the Globe theatre. The title "Theatrum Orbi(s)" supports this identification, but that title would not of course have been written across the chamber in the actual theatre, which leaves scope for opening the chamber in the manner suggested in my reconstruction.

There remains the question of the reality of the theatres (2) and (3) which match the main theatre in their battlements but differ from it in being all on one level. These theatres should reflect some features of the real stage if they are following the rule against the use of fictitious buildings in the art of memory.

I suggested in *The Art of Memory* that these theatres may reflect screens used on the stage of public theatres.[62] They have the appearance of light screens covered with painted canvas. However the placing of such screens on the open stage to mark different localities, which was my original suggestion, presents difficulties. Placed so, they would obstruct the view of the audience.

I have been struck in making this new analysis of the memory system by the very close relationship of theatres (2) and (3) to the places in the main theatre. Theatre (3) is actually said to be the "form" of those places and was, apparently, to be thought of as fixed to its doors. Theatre (2) also seems to be in some very close relationship to the main theatre, the second description of which it follows immediately.

This has given me another idea as to the possible use of these theatres as screens. Could they have been placed exactly in front of the entrances on ground level in the stage wall to form scenes expanding out of those entrances? The central door of theatre (2) would fit fairly exactly over the central door of the stage to form a scene which actors could enter from the tiring house, passing from its doors through the doors in the screen without being perceived by the audience. Or two smaller screens, like theatre (3), could have been placed in front of the side entrances in the stage wall to form different scenes, say for the camps of rival armies, which again the actors could enter without being seen by the audience, passing from the entrances in the stage wall through those in the screen. If Fludd saw something real like this on the stage of a public theatre it might have given him his idea of using minor theatres, in close relationship with the main one, in his memory system.

Notes:

(1) London (Routledge & Kegan Paul), 1966; Chicago University Press, 1966; See also my article, "New Light on the Globe Theater", *New York Review of Books*, May 26, 1966, pp. 16-21.

(2) *Art of Memory*, p. 366.

(3) I. A. Shapiro, "Robert Fludd's Stage-Illustration", *Shakespeare Studies*, II (1966), pp. 192-209.

(4) Richard Bernheimer, "Another Globe Theatre", *SQ*, II (1958), pp. 19-29. Nothing further was published on the Fludd illustration until my book and article of 1966.

(5) Shapiro, p. 199.

(6) *Art of Memory*, pp. 324-325, 332.

(7) Shapiro, *loc. cit.*

(8) Shapiro, *loc. cit.*

(9) *Art of Memory*, p. 346.

(10) Shapiro, p. 193.

(11) Shapiro, p. 197.

(12) Shapiro, p. 193.

(13) Shapiro, p. 207, n. 7.

(14) *Art of Memory*, p. 330.

(15) For further discussion of these passages, see Part II of this article.

(16) Shapiro's observation that the *ars rotunda* and the *ars quadrata* use different theatres is, I believe, correct, and this is his most useful contribution to the interpretation of the memory system.

(17) Shapiro, p. 198.

(18) *Art of Memory*, pp. 11-15 and *passim*.

(19) B. L. Joseph, *Elizabethan Acting* (Oxford, 1951).

(20) *Art of Memory*, p. 371.

(21) *Art of Memory*, pp. 337-338.

(22) That is, opposite to the five doors as memory places. Memory places are sometimes spoken of as "fields" in the memory tradition, particularly by Bruno.

(23) *Art of Memory*, pp. 336-338.

(24) Shapiro, p. 196.

(25) Shapiro, p. 198. He quotes here only the last phrase of the chapter against using fictious places, and without understanding of its meaning; see below, pp. 158 ff.

(26) Since I wrote *The Art of Memory*, further evidence has come to light about Fludd's mode of composition of his books and about his relations with James I. The *Ars memoriae* may have been actually written a good deal earlier than 1619, the date of the publication of the part of the *Historia* in which it appears. Shapiro's hypothesis (pp. 206-207, n. 1) about the date of printing of this part ignores certain bibliographical considerations. A good deal is known about the publications of the De Bry firm, and this side of the problem will have to be studied in detail.

(27) Shapiro, p. 200.

(28) Shapiro, p. 201. He cites a recent article which gives new documentary evidence about the boxes at Blackfriars — Herbert Berry, "The Stage and Boxes at Blackfriars", *Studies in Philology*, LXIII (1966), pp. 163-86. The document is about a complaint made by occupants of a box at Blackfriars against a member of the audience who obstructed their view by standing on the stage. The document proves that there were boxes at Blackfriars, which in any case was known before; it is not explicit about where the boxes were placed.

(29) Shapiro, pp. 205-206.

(30) See *Art of Memory*, p. 352.

(31) One of Shapiro's careless misrepresentations of my arguments is the following:—"the foundations Mrs. Thrale saw were the reverse of those postulated by Miss Yates, being 'hexagonal in form without and round within'" (Shapiro, p. 208, note 17). In *The Art of Memory*, p. 355, I quote Mrs. Thrale correctly and my suggested ground plan of the Globe (p. 358, Fig. 11) is hexagonal without and round within. Another puzzling misrepresentation of the same sort is his note (p. 208) on how I am "doubly unlucky" in my suggestion that Fludd's diagram of the heavens might indicate the orientation of the theatre. My first misfortune is that Shapiro has not understood what I mean when I say (p. 330) "When the book is closed the heavens cover the theatre". My second misfortune is that in some copies of Fludd's book, "Oriens" is not at the top of the diagram. It very frequently happens that when the top of an illustration is not obvious (as in a round diagram like this one) the printer gets the block wrongly placed on the page. There are a good many inaccuracies of this kind in Fludd's books; in one of the copies of Fludd's *Historia* in my possession the visual alphabets (p.61 in the memory treatise) are printed upside down. Printers' errors are not guides to an author's meaning. However my belief that in a cosmically based building like the Globe, the stage would have been in the east rests on another line of argument to be developed in my next book.

(32) *Art of Memory*, pp. 7, 75-76.

(33) Shapiro, p. 199. He observes that the wall above and behind the stage front looks as though made of different materials from the stage front, and suggests that it is part of the stone walls of the Dominican convent, and that the two doorways in this wall are medieval and "what might be expected in a Dominican friary" (p. 201). It is true that the back wall looks different from the stage front; it looks to me like brickwork, not stonework. The two "medieval" upper doorways match, except for being smaller, the two doorways below them in the stage front.

(34) *Art of Memory*, pp. 346 ff.

(35) *Art of Memory*, p. 348.

(36) Reproduced in *Art of Memory*, Pl. 19 and in Shapiro's article, p. 202. The sketch of the Swan is so well known it seems unnecessary to reproduce it again here, but it appears in figure 9 for the convenience of the reader.

(37) Shapiro, pp. 201 ff.

(38) See especially C. W. Hodges, "The Globe Playhouse", *Theatre Notebook*, I, (1945-47), 111.

(39) E. K. Chambers, *Elizabethan Stage* (Oxford, 1923), II, p. 466.

(40) Shapiro, p. 204.

(41) Shapiro, p. 205.

(42) *Art of Memory*, pp. 350-351. Shapiro occasionally tends to apply these observations of mine to his own interpretation of the stage without recalling their source.

(43) See the correspondence in *The New York Review*, November 17, 1966, pp. 40-42.

(44) Quoted by Shapiro, p. 205.

(45) See *Art of Memory*, pp. 5-6.

(46) *Art of Memory*, pp. 293-297.

(47) G. Bruno, *De imaginum . . . compositione*, in *Opera latine*, II, iii, pp. 163 ff.

(48) See *Art of Memory*, pp. 215 ff.

(49) Fludd, *Ars memoriae*, Bk. I, chapters iv, v.

(50) Shapiro complains of Fludd's lack of systematic presentation. "He is liable to allude to features of his system before he has defined or explained them, and occasionally he puts an essential clue in a context remote from where it would be expected" (article cited, p. 192). This shows that he has not understood the system of presentation normal to memory treatises and which Fludd is following. Many of Shapiro's observations may derive from this misunderstanding.

(51) Shapiro states (p. 207, note 7) that I am wrong in putting the memory theatres only in the zodiacal sphere and that there should be such theatres also in the planetary spheres. But it is stated in Fludd's text that the theatres are in the zodiac, and moreover Shapiro's suggestion is astrologically impossible. Fludd is thinking, I believe, of horoscope "houses" which, though not identical with the signs, are associated with them, and of planetary images in such houses, turned into memory theatres. Bruno's magic memory systems have a similar kind of horoscope basis.

(52) Fludd had earlier expressed disapproval of "empty places" (Bk. I, chapter viii), that is, of using memory images in a vacuum, and not placed on memorised *loci*. Shapiro (p. 198) has not understood the point.

(53) This chapter is missed out by Shapiro who has not understood that the basis of the *ars quadrata* is the cubicles, with their sides divided into five places.

(54) Lambert Schenkel, *Gazophylacium artis memoriae* (Strasburg, 1610): on memory cubicles, pp. 193 ff. On Schenkel, see *The Art of Memory*, pp. 299-302, 338, 373-374, 380.

(55) Lambert Schenkel, *Le Magazin des Sciences ou vray art de memoire* (Paris, 1623). pp. 301 ff. Schenkel describes how the "frontispiece", or façade, of a chateau may be divided into memory places (pp. 284, 305). The method of memorising places in an order proceeding from east to west he calls the method of Ramon Lull (*ibid.*, p. 302). He describes how ambassadors multiply memory rooms through which to memorise the arguments of their opponents, and their own replies in opposite places. These techniques obviously have much in common with those of Fludd, who uses a stage front for his places, with columns opposite, and memorises the places in his cubicles from east to west.

(56) See *Art of Memory*, pp. 336-338 and Fig. 10.

(57) See *Art of Memory*, p. 8.

(58) For a diagram of "faculty psychology" in a memory treatise, see *ibid.*, p. 256, Fig. 9.

(59) On "intentions" in scholastic theory of memory images, see *ibid.*, p. 64. Shapiro (article cited, p. 198) quotes the phrase on the operation of the fantasy with no understanding of its meaning or of its relevance to the previous argument of the chapter.

(60) Fludd uses for memorising numbers the same diagrammatic lay-out of five places in his treatise *De Arithmetica memoriali* (*Historia*, Tomus Primus, Tractatus Secundus, pp. 153 ff). This is mentioned at the end of the *Ars memoriae* (Bk. III, chapter x) and may represent its missing books (on which see Shapiro, p. 208, note 12).

(61) *Ars memoriae*, Bk. I, chapter xi.

(62) *Art of Memory*, pp. 353-354.

166

The New Arden Henry VI, Parts I, II, and III: *Review Article*

by *Robert K. Turner, Jr.*

The new Arden Shakespeares are among the best editions now available for advanced students of the plays, and it is good to have these step-children of the canon in full Arden panoply.[1] Each volume is provided with the useful appurtenances which the earlier members of the series have made familiar—introductions which range over both textual and critical matters, copious glosses, and appendix collections relating to sources and other special problems. It is the texts of Dr. Cairncross's Henry VI plays, however, which are of particular interest.

The editor of the Henry VI trilogy has his work cut out for him. Although it is obvious that the three are very closely related, having been written at about the same time, on a single large theme, in much the same style, the textual strategy applied to them cannot be identical in all three instances. *1 Henry VI* is a single-text play, the Folio providing the only authoritative early version; but the Folio *2* and *3 Henry VI* are roughly paralleled by *The First Part of the Contention betwixt . . . York and Lancaster* (1594) and *The True Tragedy of Richard Duke of York* (1595), now generally thought (with some demurrers) to be memorial reconstructions of the plays more correctly represented in the Folio. Because bad quartos are not wholly without authority, *The Contention* and *The True Tragedy* provide potential sources of superior readings for Parts II and III as well as witnesses to the quality of the Folio versions, except in those places where F has been contaminated by Q. The only sources of emendations for Part I, however, are the learning and ingenuity of the editor and his predecessors.

The major difficulty the editor encounters, however, is the reconciliation of the inconsistent testimony of the texts themselves with a most uncertain body of external evidence. Some features of the texts point to one hypothesis of origin and transmission and others to quite others, which may or may not be consistent with what literary history tells us about the plays. It is a well known fact, for example, that Greene, writing just before his death in September, 1592, referred to Shakespeare in a contemptuous way and parodied a line from *3 Henry VI*, but the significance of that fact is so far from clear that Professor Dover Wilson (following Malone) is able to interpret it as Greene's angry attack on Shakespeare for having revised work by Greene and others (*The Second Part of King Henry VI* [1952], pp. xiv ff.) and Dr. Cairncross as an expression of Greene's dislike of Shakespeare's bombastic imitation of the classics in his own compositions (*2 Henry VI*, pp. xlii ff.). Or, to choose but one other series of problems, Nashe in August, 1592, alluded to the great popularity of a Talbot play, and Henslowe beginning on 3 March 1592 (that entry being marked "ne," presumably "new") recorded receipts from a play he called *Harey the vj*. Were *Harey the vj* and the play Nashe mentioned Shakespeare's *1 Henry VI*? If so, why was it being performed by Strange's Men when *The Contention* and *The True Tragedy* seem to have belonged to Pembroke's? And if *Harey the vj*, alias *1 Henry VI*, was new in March, 1592, and if the theaters closed to new writing in June, 1592, and yet if Greene knew *3 Henry VI* by the late summer, it would seem that Part I was written last in the sequence, for there would have been insufficient time between March and June for Parts II and III to have been mounted. If *Harey the vj* was not *1 Henry VI*, we can perhaps believe Dr. Johnson's conclusion: "It is apparent that [the second part of *Henry VI*] begins where the former ends, and continues the series of transactions, of which it presupposes the first part already known. This is sufficient proof that the second and third parts were not written without dependence on the first." But then we must ask, as Professor Wilson does (*The First Part of King Henry VI* [1952], p. xiii), why Gloucester forgets about Talbot when at the beginning of *2 Henry VI* (I.i.74-102) he enumerates the English sacrifices in France, and we may even vilely suspect that by Dr. Johnson's logic the second tetralogy could be set before the first.

So the questions multiply and no very strong case has as yet been made that answers them all. Faced with this situation the editor who is obliged to produce new versions of the Henry VI plays may adopt a conservative attitude toward the text, holding fast to the Folio and emending only when that text is clearly wrong. His position may be justified by the belief that the Folio, whatever its imperfections, is the best record we have of Shakespeare's contribution to these plays (whether his original writing, his reworking of his own earlier versions, or, as Professor Wilson would have it, his revision of the writing of others). Conservatism is further recommended by the general prudential rule of textual criticism: when in doubt, follow the copy-text. Or the editor may be persuaded that his interpretation of the internal and external evidence is good enough to warrant a liberal attitude toward the text, so that he may emend more frequently provided that his emendations are inherently plausible and consistent with a credible theory of transmission. Dr. Cairncross takes the latter position. After a survey of the evidence in which he tries to resolve the many conflicts and ambiguities, he concludes that Shakespeare wrote all three plays in 1590 in their sequential order and that the difficulties in the Folio texts are due not to Shakespeare's imperfectly revising his own or somebody else's writing but to the corrupting influence of various agents. Thus armed, he has produced texts of the plays that both in the number and the nature of their emendations differ greatly from the texts of other recent editors.

Dr. Cairncross believes that Shakespeare's autograph of *1 Henry VI* was partially annotated by a stage-adapter and later transcribed; and to Shakespeare himself, to the adapter, and to the scribe he attributes the irregularities and inconsistencies which to Greg suggested either "composite authorship or revision" (*The Editorial Problem in Shakespeare* [1954], p. 139). That authorial papers of some sort underlie the Folio text is reasonably evident, and in such a text loose ends may be expected. Dr. Cairncross, however, thinks that Shakespeare had a worse memory than other textual critics have been willing to suppose. Not only did he omit some necessary stage directions and change the designation of some characters,[2] but also he allowed Exeter to be surprised at seeing Winchester in his ecclesiastical dress (V.i.28) when Winchester had previously appeared in it,[3] and he placed Mortimer's death scene in the Tower (II.v) when in 2 Henry VI, written just after Part I, Dr. Cairncross tells us, he is said to have died in Wales (II.ii.38-41). The hypothetical stage-adapter can have worked only in a most irregular way if he were marking the autograph "in preparation for transcribing the 'plot' and the players' parts," effecting, or at least indicating, "adaptations in the cast" for "small economies, possibly for ease of doubling, if not for absolute reduction of numbers" (1 Henry VI, pp. xvi-xvii). In addition to misplacing stage directions (at II.i.7 and IV.i.181),[4] in getting rid of Sir William Lucy's part in IV.vii, he replaced this one character with a Messenger and a Herald. Small economy indeed. The scribe was even more a villain. He transposed Shakespeare's inversions, gave play to a rather delicate sensibility (at II.iv.91, finding "For Treason headed" in his copy, he wrote "For Treason executed," "headed" being too crude for him), made good pentameters hypermetrical by filling in ellipses,[5] was guilty of dittography and assimilation and misreading and omission. In short, he very often altered Shakespeare to the detriment both of good versification and good sense.

Dislocation of meter can indeed signal corruption, but the question is whether every dislocation of meter does so. Ignoring the possibilities of authorial carelessness and of attempts, whether successful or not, to vary meter for rhetorical effect, Dr. Cairncross seems to reason from a critical position to a textual one. If an examination of plot, style, theme, and character leads one to think that 1 Henry VI, and Parts II and III as well, "bears witness to careful planning and controlled design" (1 Henry VI, p. lii), evidence for non-sequential composition, revision, or multiple authorship must be put down at all costs. Hence the forgetful author and the desultory adapter. Moreover, because most of the play is in mechanically regular verse, the F lines that are irregular cannot be Shakespeare's. Hence the high-handed scribe, who, according to Dr. Cairncross's theory, "improved" the text in a way perhaps "not permissible in Shakespeare's lifetime" (p. xxvi).[6] Once such an agent is postulated, blame can be shifted to him for any reading that strikes the reason or the ear as unworthy or false. Emendation thus can proceed apace and so it does, with the result that Dr. Cairncross's text (not counting such non-substantive changes as relining, alteration in the designation of characters for consistency, and the expansion or contraction of verbal forms for metrical purposes) includes sixty-seven readings from earlier editions, twelve conjectures of earlier editors, and twenty-two original emendations. Of these 101 emendations, Professor Wilson's more conservative text admitted twenty-eight, and Professor C. J. Sisson's (in The Complete Works [1953]), hitherto thought by some to be about as daring as the law would allow, thirty-six. It is significant that a considerable number of Dr. Cairncross's changes originated with Rowe, Pope, and Theobald; in his 1 Henry VI we read correct, polished, eighteenth-century Shakespeare.

What we have then is a version of the play the liberality of which proceeds from a theory unable convincingly to account for some features of the text which have supported theories of revision or multiple authorship. Copy-text readings are abandoned in favor of guesswork, inspired guesswork though it very often is. And the edition contains a startling number of flat errors (or omitted notes, if emendations were intended):

> I.iv.58 Now *is it* supper-time (F: it is)
> I.v.20 I know not *what* I am (F: where)
> I.vi.3 Pucelle hath perform'd her *work* (F: word)
> II.iii.32 *thou art my* prisoner (F: then art thou)
> II.iii.37 *And* now the substance (F: But)
> II.v.75 Clarence, *the* third son (F: *omit*)
> III.i.71 my tender *tears* (F: years)
> III.i.98 father *to* the commonweal (F: of)
> IV.i.17 Thou *was* installed (F: was't)
> V.iii.152 bride *to* such a lord (F: of)
> V.iii.158 *these* two countries (F: those)
> V.iv.172 when *you* please (F: ye)
> V.v.18 with *a* humble lowliness (F: as)

In addition, one textual note is wrong (at III.ii.58 F reads *hot, Sir:* not *hot, Sir?*) and another is omitted (for the obvious emendation of F *modestie* to *modestly* at V.iii.179).

Dr. Cairncross's approach to Parts II and III is similar and equally open to question. There is, we are told, "no foundation for the idea that Shakespeare did not write the whole of *2* and *3 Henry VI*. And there is positive proof that he did" (*2 Henry VI*, p. xlii). This positive proof depends on three witnesses. First, there is Greene's attack, the precise meaning of which, as we have seen, has been differently construed, and about which all one can definitely say is that it links Shakespeare with Part III. It certainly does not allow the conclusion that he wrote Parts II and III in their entirety, and it says nothing at all on the subject of revision. Secondly, there is the sanction of Heminge and Condell. "They had been Shakespeare's fellows for over twenty years, and almost certainly from the date at which he wrote these plays" (*ibid.*). Thus, the argument seems to run, they can be counted on to have provided not only good texts but also ones wholly by Shakespeare. In fact, they seem to have located the best texts they could, but as long as Shakespeare's sole authorship of *Henry VIII* remains in doubt, we cannot say they never gave the publishers a collaboration. Finally, there is the pregnant nature of the epilogue to *Henry V* with its allusions to the broils of Henry VI's reign, "which oft our stage hath shown." To Dr. Cairncross these lines indicate either that Shakespeare wrote all *Henry VI* or that he did not write *Henry V*. By which reasoning we might also be able to prove Shakespeare's authorship of both *The Poetaster* and *Antonio and Mellida* on the evidence of *Troilus and Cressida's* prologue armed.

The textual history of *2 Henry VI* Dr. Cairncross believes to run as follows: Shakespeare's original version, cut for acting, was reported by a group of Pem-

170

broke's Men in 1593 or 1594 and printed as *The Contention*. The good version, Shakespeare's unblotted autograph, was censored for political reasons, the censorship causing Shakespeare to delete some passages and to rewrite others on slips of paper which he pasted over the original script. This manuscript became the prompt book. The Folio copy was an amalgamation of the prompt book and printed passages from *The Contention* Q3 and Q2 (probably), altered where necessary to bring them into line with the authoritative version. Thus two editorial attitudes are required: in "the larger part of the text, where Q copy was not used ... an editor's duty is to adhere as closely to F as possible," discounting the "peculiar habits and failings of the [F] compositors" (p. xlvii); but in those parts of the text set from Q copy latent corruption caused by imperfect amendment of Q as well as mistakes of the F compositors must be discovered by indirect means, among them again difficulties in sense and dislocation of meter (pp. xlviii-xlix).

Although one tires of the myth of the unblotted papers, there is nothing impossible in the main outline of Dr. Cairncross's theory, and his argument for Q copy, an important matter, deserves full and expert examination. If parts of F did derive from Q, common readings in these parts become suspect in a way they would not if F and Q were independent, for Q-F agreement may mean only that an error in Q went uncorrected. The application of the theory to the text, however, yields results similar to those permitted by the assumption of a naughty scribe in the textual history of Part I, for here if language deviates from facile idiom or meter from regular pentameter, Q copy can be cited to sanction emendation. Thus from I.i through II.i (as a sample), we find fifty-three emendations—twenty from Q, fourteen from earlier editors (again Pope quite often), and nineteen Dr. Cairncross's own or his adoption of earlier conjectures. Professor Wilson emended twelve of these readings, Professor Sisson fourteen, and the Pelican edition, conservatively edited by George Walton Williams, ten.[7]

Appropriately, Dr. Cairncross holds the textual history of Part III to be similar to that of Part II. *The True Tragedy* is a memorial reconstruction of the play as it was cut for acting and in response to censorship. F was based ultimately on Shakespeare's manuscript as annotated by a prompter and "slightly altered for various reasons of casting, censorship, and historical accuracy" (p. xxiii), but this time a transcript of the autograph rather than the autograph itself was sent to the printers. In the printing house the transcript served as copy for those sections of the play that differed greatly from Q, but, where practical, printed segments from Q2 and Q3, altered as necessary, were used to replace corresponding sections of manuscript. Editorial policy must, then, be about the same as in the case of *2 Henry VI*, except that the intervention of the scribe permits greater latitude throughout in emending suspect readings.

The application of this theory has the same effect as before. In Act IV, for example, Dr. Cairncross emends substantively twenty-six times: eight times from Q, twelve from earlier editors, and six originally or from previous conjectures. Professor Wilson emended the same readings nine times, Professor Williams seven, and Professor Sisson only six. Two of Dr. Cairncross's readings probably are mistakes.

IV.iv.30 trust not him that *once hath* broken faith (F: hath once)
IV.vii.46 *Out* title to the crown (F: Our)

There are more inaccuracies in the editions of *1* and *3 Henry VI* than one would expect to grow under the hand of an experienced textual scholar, but these presumably will be repaired when reprints are required. The important questions are, first, whether Dr. Cairncross's explanations of the characteristics of the early versions will stand up under examination and, secondly, whether his means of detecting corruption in the Folio are really satisfactory. Nobody should want to retain F readings that are manifestly wrong, but here we find a great many F readings that good scholars have thought defensible rejected in favor of readings from inferior texts or from the sense and sensibility of editors. However much one may admire the courage of conviction and canniness shown in handling isolated problems, it is difficult not to be suspicious of this smooth and tidy early Shakespeare.

Notes:

(1) *The First Part of King Henry VI* edited by Andrew S. Cairncross. The Arden Shakespeare. Methuen and Harvard University Press, 1962. Pp. lvii + 172. $3.85. *The Second Part of King Henry VI* edited by Andrew S. Cairncross. The Arden Shakespeare. Methuen and Harvard University Press, 1957 (reprinted with minor corrections 1962). Pp. liv + 197. $4.50. *The Third Part of King Henry VI* edited by Andrew S. Cairncross. The Arden Shakespeare. Methuen and Harvard University Press, 1964. Pp. lxiv + 187. $4.50.

(2) Richard Plantagenet's speech-prefixes are *Yorke* in II.iv and *Rich.* in II.v, not *Plant.* and *Rich.* as Dr. Cairncross says (p. xv).

(3) *Cf.* W. W. Greg: "... The author of V.i, in which Winchester has, it appears, only lately become Cardinal, can hardly have read, still less have written, I.iii, in which he already appears in full canonicals" (*The Shakespeare First Folio* [1955], p. 186).

(4) The stage direction appearing incorrectly in F at II.i.7 is *Their Drummes beating a Dead March*, which properly belongs at the beginning of II.ii. Like Dr. Cairncross, Professor Wilson (p. 138) thinks a prompter to have been responsible for misplacing it, but, as Greg pointed out, bookkeepers' phrasing would probably have been simply *Dead March* (*SFF*, p. 188).

(5) In the list of readings offered in support of this point (p. xix and fn. 2), the line cited at I.ii.28 is actually at I.ii.38 and the unnumbered line is I.iv.110. IV.i.72 is perfectly regular as it stands. In the list offered of other, unascertainable, scribal alterations (fn. 1), the following lines are more-or-less acceptable as pentameters: I.i.71 (read *Factions* with three syllables), I.iii.1 (read either *I'm* or *Tow'r*), and I.iii.8 (the first foot is an anapest).

(6) This hypothetical scribe rises to haunt the argument in a way Dr. Cairncross seems not to consider. Like Professor Wilson, Dr. Cairncross follows F in calling the Cowardly Knight *Falstaff* rather than *Fastolfe*. But if a man who changed so much were transcribing the play about 1623 (p. xxvi), which name would he have been the more likely to adopt?

(7) Because the volume under review is a corrected reprint, only I.i-II.i was checked against F. No error was found except the omission of a note supporting the emendation of F *Albones* to *Alban* at Part II, II.i.107.

Shakespeare's Other Ovid: A Reproduction of Commentary on Metamorphoses I-IV.

In Volume II, this space reproduced portions of texts which might have some bearing on our concept of "Shakespeare and Plato." To continue what will be an annual exploration of such material as may increase our understanding of well-known traditions influencing Shakespeare's art, the following pages reproduce George Sandys' commentary on Books I-IV of Ovid's *Metamorphoses*. If this commentary is relevant, however, it is not so because of any necessarily penetrating qualities of Sandys' intellect, but because the sources which he alleges may, in their totality, suggest once again that continuity between "Medieval" and "Renaissance" about which it is so difficult to make very positive or negative generalizations.

Sandys names a usual group of classical commentators, but he also refers to "Higinus" (presumably Hyginus 3), and to Macrobius whose commentary on the *Somnium Scipionis* influenced the many English Renaissance editions and translations of the only section from Cicero's *De Republica* known before 1820. And if there is Macrobius, it is not surprising that there is also Lactantius and Fulgentius who will be well known to students of Spenser and especially of Milton. Among the twenty-six authorities named on sig. D2^v are also some suggestive "moderns" ranging from Vives, Ficino, and Comes, to Francis Bacon. Many other authors are obviously drawn upon or specifically referred to in the commentary and in marginal glosses to the text (not reproduced here), and the whole thus constitutes another of those highly complex interweavings so characteristic of Renaissance intellectual endeavor.

A consideration of Sandys' Ovid will also rectify a possible imbalance in our assessment of specific influences upon the work of Shakespeare. "Shakespeare and Ovid," for example has been a concept tending to suggest an Ovid-via-Golding, and the consequence has frequently been an emphasis on Ovid/Golding not merely as Shakespeare's repository for myth, but as a frequent directive for his early style. It is true that an extremely good case has been built up since Malone for the influence of Arthur Golding's translation upon some of Shakespeare's writing, but Sandys may well serve as exemplar of other matters relevant to the Renaissance way with Ovid, a way which was not necessarily to be defined and delimited by the matter of diction. For T. W. Baldwin's observations (in fact, his whole chapter) on Shakespeare and Ovid, in *William Shakespere's Small Latine and Lesse Greeke* (Urbana, 1944), 417-455, need to be recalled. This is especially the case when Baldwin reminds us that the (Latin) *Metamorphoses* was "almost universally required" in the upper forms of the Elizabethan grammar school. Accordingly there is some danger in tacitly assuming—and few do—that Golding was to Shakespeare what Chapman was to Keats (or Shakespeare). Rather, if we assume from miscellaneous similarities of wording that there were attractions for Shakespeare in Golding's phraseology, we need not deny that Shakespeare's reading of sections of the *Metamorphoses* in Latin editions may have resulted in influences perhaps different, but of analogous strength. For if Golding rendered the text of the *Metamorphoses* into Elizabethan words, the Jacobean prose of Sandys, as it were, preserves for us some traditional ways of understanding what it was that Golding translated.

These traditional ways of understanding Ovid were embodied in the commentary on the Latin texts. Baldwin, in fact, has suggested (II,439-440) that Shakespeare's text might have been such a one as that with the explanatory notes of Raphael Regius which appear, for example, in a 1574 edition published in Venice. Whether or not this is so, the general point is valid enough, for the *Metamorphoses* could hardly have escaped expository interpretation with any more success than, say, the comedies of Terence. The title of an edition published in Cambridge, 1584 (STC 18951) is illustrative, *Fabularum Ouidii interpretatio ethica physica et historia*, as would be also the mere possibilities for interpretation inherent in any classroom where Ovid was being taught. And it is when we seek to determine what this interpretation would have consisted of that some one such as Sandys becomes, if not relevant, then perhaps indicative.

The point is a crucial one because the *Metamorphoses* is, of course, mythology, and our attitude towards the way in which Shakespeare uses mythology frequently affects our approach to his poems and to sections of his plays. It is therefore important to be reminded by Sandys that this mythology was to be interpreted in accordance with a tradition reviewed not when consulting Burckhardt, but in such a seminal work as C. de Boer's edition of the "Ovide Moralisé", the first volume of which appeared in 1915.

The studies of D. C. Allen, Bush, Chew, M. Hughes, Katzenellenbogen, Osgood, Panofsky, Praz, Saxl, Seznec, Tuve (most lately in her posthumous *Allegorical Imagery*, Princeton, 1966), Yates, and Wind will constitute sufficient reference to this tradition to obviate further discussion in this space, as will the four hundred-odd items appearing in the bibliographical lists of Panofsky's *Studies* and Seznec's *Geneology*, but several examples from what is reproduced here might be taken as suggestive of possibilities in Shakespeare's work.

The exposition of the myth of Actaeon, alluded to in *Twelfth Night* and discussed by Steadman breeds true in Sandys' commentary on the matter, for example, while Book IV, where we find Pyramus and Thisbe, and other Shakespearean gleanings, is suggestive in Sandys' commentary on Ixion (sigs. N3-N3^v) whose wheel is subject to reference by Lear. The various punishments in hell, observes Sandys, "*are allegorically referred to the perturbations of the mind*": he mentions Tantalus and "*Covetousnesse*" (hardly surprising students of Spenser), and then he compares "*Ixions wheele, to the desperate remembrance of perpetrated crimes, which circularly pursue, and afflict the guilty.*" We are referred to Macrobius for details, but we will readily enough recall Edmund's final remark about circles as well as

174

the pursuit of the Ixion concept in Lear's own imagery about the wheel of fire upon which he is bound and his remark about centaurs whose father Ixion was. Such aesthetic inferences are more easily made than demonstrated, however, and we are perhaps on more conservative ground by finally indicating Sandys' subscription to a traditional euhemerism according to which, for example, Deucalion's flood is regarded as a pagan recollection of Noah's inundation, a recollection reflected specifically in *Coriolanus* and therefore not necessarily anachronistically in *Julius Caesar* when Cassius refers to "the great flood."

Since the first edition of Golding's translation contained only four books, and given the restrictions of space in the present instance, it seems appropriate to make available Sandys' commentary only on these initial sections of the *Metamorphoses*. And since Golding himself alluded to the allegorical quality of his material, Sandy's own comments could be construed as detailed hypothesis about what Golding meant by "allegory," as a suggestion, if we will, regarding the cultural context of what it was that actually appeared in 1564. In any event, the reader is advised that the reproduction here is selective. Omitted is the verse-translation of Books I-IV with the often interesting marginal commentaries. What consequently appear are 1) all front-matter, 2) the illustration preceding each of the first four Books, 3) the body of commentary following each of the first four Books. Thus we reproduce sigs. A-C3^v (Book I illustration); D2^v-F3 (Book II illustration); G3^v-I2 (Book III illustration); K^v-L3 (Book IV illustration); M3-O^v.

The biographical and bibliographical studies and facts pertinent to Sandys and his Ovid are most conveniently assembled in the excellent study by R. B. Davis, *George Sandys, Poet-Adventurer* (London, 1955), Ch. VIII, while William A. Jackson, *Records of the Court of the Stationers Company: 1602-1640* (London, 1957), p. 201 and n.5 will serve as supplement. The present reproduction, from the 1640 edition (STC 18968) in the University of Cincinnati Library, is reduced from the original size and is in no way intended as an editorial effort. The reproduction is meant to be legible, but is otherwise subject, as concerns matters bibliographical, to the usual considerations governing photostatic copy. (J.L.B.)

Carmina quam tribuunt, Fama perennis erit.

Mercurius huius Decus fecerat Apollo
Omni qalí punctum, Vina & phebo gerens

PVBLIVS OVIDIVS NASO EQVES · ROMANVS POETARVM INGENIOSISSIMVS ·

The sweet tong'd Ovids Counterfeit behold,
Which Noblest Romans wor in rings of gold
Or would you ỹ, which his owne pensil drew,
The Poet, in his deathless Poems view.

OVIDIVS NASO   A Medall in Silver

S C   The reuers of ẙ Medall

OVID'S METAMORPHOSIS Englished, Mythologiz'd, And Represented in figures by G·S·

MDCXXXX

Francisco Clein Inv: Salamon Savery sculp:

OVIDS
METAMORPHOSIS
ENGLISHED,
MYTHOLOGIZ'D,
And

Reprefented in Figures.

An Eſſay to the Tranſlation
of VIRGIL'S ÆNEIS.

By G. S.

LONDON,
Printed by *J. L.* for *Andrew Hebb,* and are to be ſold at
the Signe of the *Bell* in S^t. *Pauls* Church-yard.
M. DC. XL.

Cum Privilegio ad imprimendum hanc Ovidii
TRANSLATIONEM.

THE MINDE OF THE
FRONTISPEECE, AND
ARGVMENT OF THIS
WORKE.

FIRE, AIRE, EARTH, WATER, all the Oppofites
   That ftrove in *Chaos*, powrefull LOVE unites;
And from their Difcord drew this Harmonie,
VVhich fmiles in *Nature*: who, with ravifht eye,
Affects his own made *Beauties*. But, our *Will*,
Defire, and *Powres Irafcible*, the skill
Of PALLAS orders; who the *Minde* attires
VVith all *Heroick Vertues*: This afpires
To *Fame* and *Glorie*; by her noble Guide
Eternized, and well-nigh Deifi'd.
But who forfake that faire *Intelligence*,
To follow *Paffion*, and voluptuous *Sence*;
That fhun the Path and Toyles of HERCULES;
Such, charm'd by CIRCE's luxurie, and eafe,
Themfelves deforme: 'twixt whom, fo great an ods;
That thefe are held for Beafts, and thofe for Gods.

PHŒBUS APOLLO (facred Poefy)
Thus taught: for in thefe ancient Fables lie
The myfteries of all Philofophie.

Some Natures fecrets fhew; in fome appeare
Diftempers ftaines, fome teach us how to beare
Both Fortunes, bridling Joy, Griefe, Hope, and Feare.

Thefe Pietie, Devotion thofe excite;
Thefe prompt to Vertue, thofe from Vice affright;
All fully mingling Profit with Delight.

This Courfe our Poet fteeres: and thofe that faile,
By wandring Stars, not by his Compaffe, faile.

To the moſt High and Mightie

Prince CHARLES, KING of
Great *Britaine*, *France*, and
IRELAND.

SIR,

YOur Gracious acceptance of the firſt fruits of my Travels, when you were our Hope, as now our Happineſſe; hath actuated both Will and Power to the finiſhing of this Peece: being limn'd by that unperfect light which was ſnatcht from the houres of night and repoſe. For the day was not mine, but dedicated to the ſervice of your Great Father, and your Selfe: which, had it proved as fortunate as faithfull, in me, and others more worthy; we had hoped, ere many yeares had turned about, to have preſented you with a rich and wel-peopled Kingdome; from whence now, with my ſelfe, I onely bring this Compoſure:

Inter victrices Hederam tibi ſerpere Laurus.

It needeth more then a ſingle denization, being a double Stranger: Sprung from the Stock of the ancient Romanes; but bred in the New-World, of the rudeneſſe whereof it cannot but participate; eſpecially having Warres and Tumults to bring it to light in ſtead of the Muſes. But however unperfect, Your favour is able to ſupply; and to make it worthy of life, if you judge it not unworthy of your Royall Patronage. To this have I added, as the Minde to the Body, the Hiſtory and Philoſophicall ſence of the Fables, (with the ſhadow of either in Picture) which I humbly offer at the ſame Altar, that they may as the reſt of my labours, receive their eſtimation from ſo great an Authoritie. Long may you live to be, as you are, the Delight and Glory of your People: and ſlowly, yet ſurely, exchange your mortall Diadem for an immortall. So wiſhes

Your Majeſties

moſt humble

Servant

George Sandys.

A Panegyrick to the King.

—— Materie respondet Musa. ——

IOve, *whose transcendent Acts the Poets sing,*
By Men made more then Man, is found a King :
Whose Thunder and inevitable Flame,
His Justice and majestick Awe proclaime :
His cheerfull Influence, and refreshing Showers,
Mercy and Bounty ; Marks of heavenly Powers.
These, free from Joves disorders, blesse thy Raign ;
And might restore the golden Age again,
If all men, by thy great Example lead,
Would that prepared way to Vertue tread.
Rare Cures, deep Prophesies, harmonious Layes,
Insphear'd Apollo ; crown'd with Wisdoms Raies.
Thy onely touch can heal : Thou, to thy State,
The better Genius, Oracle, and Fate :
The Poets Theam and Patron ; who at will
Canst adde t' Augustus Scepter Maro's Quill.
Our Worlds clear Eye, thy Cynthia, ever bright :
When neerest thee, displais her fairest light :
May her exalted Rayes for ever joyne
In a benevolent Aspect with thine !
Not Cupids wild-fires, but those Beams which dart
From Venus purer Spheare, inflame thy hart.
Minerva's Olive prospers in thy Land :
And Neptunes Ocean stoops to thy Command.
Like Bacchus thy fresh Youth, and free Delights ;
Not as disguised in his frantike Rites :
Such, as when he, with Phœbus, takes his seat
On sacred Nisa ; and with quickning heat
Inspires the Muses. Thou, our Mercury,
From shades infernall, wretches doom'd to dy,
Restor'st to light : thy prudent Snakes asswage
Hell-nourisht Discord, and Wars bloody Rage :
Thy Zeal to many Mercuries gives wing,
Who heavenly Embasyes to Mortals bring :

Thy

Thy Vigilance secure Repose imparts ;
Yet build'st no Counsels on his subtil Arts.
Those old Heroes with their Heroines,
VVho spangled all the firmament with Signes,
Shut out succeeding worthies, scarce could spare
A little room for Berenices *Haire.*
Great Julius, *who their Gods transcended far,*
Could rise no higher then a Blazing-star.
Others, whom after Ages most admire,
At Comets catch, or Stars new set on fire ;
VVhich, though Ætheriall, see not their event :
So soon, like sublunary Glories, spent !
These, whose Aspects gave laws to Destinie,
Before the luster of the Day-star flie :
Their lights prov'd erring Fiers, their Influence vain ;
And nothing but their empty N*ames remain.*
Those last immortaliz'd, whose dying breath
P*ronounc'd them* Men, *created Gods by Death ;*
VVhom fragrant Flames, Joves Eagles, Perjuries,
And Popular Applause, rais'd to the Skies ;
Down shot like Falling stars : more transitory
In their Divine, then in their Humane Glory.
These as the first, bold Flattery deifi'd :
Thou to whom Heaven that title hath appli'd,
Shalt by Humility, a Grace unknowne
To their Ambition, gain a heavenly Throne.
Enough my Muse : Time shall a Poet raise,
Born under better stars, to sing his Praise.

Urania

THE *Muses*, by your favour bleſt,
    Faire Queene, invite you to their Feaſt.
    The *Graces* will rejoyce, and ſue,
Since ſo excell'd, to waite on you.
Ambroſia taſt, which frees from Death;
And Nectar, fragrant as your breath,
By *Hebe* fill'd; who ſtates the Prime
Of Youth, and brailes the wings of Time.
Here in *Adonis* Gardens grow,
What neither Age nor winter know.
The Boy, with whom *Love* ſeem'd to dy,
Bleeds in this pale Anemony.
Self-lov'd *Narciſſus* in the Myrror
Of your faire eyes, now ſees his error;
And from the flattering Fountain turns.
The Hyacinth no longer mourns.
This Heliotrope, which did purſue
Th'adored Sun, converts to you.
Theſe Statues touch, and they agen
Will from cold marble change to men.
Chaſt *Daphne* bends her virgin boughs,
And twines to imbrace your ſacred brows.
Their tops the *Paphian* Myrtles move;
Saluting you their Queene of Love.
Myrrha, who weeps for her offence,
Preſents her teares; her Frankinſence
Leucothoë; the *Heliades*
Their Amber: yet you need not theſe.
They all retaine their ſence, and throng
To heare the *Thracian* Poets Song.
How would they, ſhould you ſing, admire!
Neglect his skill! as he his Lyre!
Contending Nightingals, ſtruck mute,
Drop down, and dye upon your Lute!
The Phœnix, from the glowing Eaſt,
With ſweets here builds her Tombe and Neſt:
Another Phœnix ſeene, ſhee dyes;
Burnt into aſhes by your eyes;
This Swan, which in *Peneus* ſwims,
His Funerall ſongs converts to Hymnes.
Theſe azure-plum'd *Halcyones*,
Whoſe Birth controules the raging Seas,

To

To your sweet Vnion yeild the praise
Of Nuptiall loves; of Peacefull Dayes.
Nymph, take this Quiver, and this Bow:
Diana such in shape and show;
When with her star-like train she crowns
Eurotas bancks, or *Cynthus* Downs.
There, chace the *Calydonian* Bore:
Here, see *Actæon* flye before
His eager Hounds. Wild Heards will stand
At gaze; nor feare so faire a hand.
There be, who our Delights despise,
As Shadows, and vain Phantasies.
Those Sons of Earth, inthrald to sense,
Condemn what is our Excellence.
The Aire, Immortall Souls, the Skyes,
The Angels in their Hirarchies;
Vnseen, to all things seen dispense
Breath, Life, Protection, Influence.
Our high Conceptions crave a Minde
From Earth, and Ignorance refin'd:
Crown Vertue; Fortunes pride controul;
Raise Objects, equall to the Soul:
At will create eternitie
Bestow on mortalls, born to die.
Yet we, who life to others give,
Faire Queene, would by your favour live.

TO THE READER.

SInce it should be the principall end in publishing of Books, to informe the understanding, direct the will, and temper the affections; in this second Edition of my Translation, I have attempted (with what successe I submit to the Reader) to collect out of sundry Authors the Philosophicall sense of these fables of Ovid; if I may call them his, when most of them are more ancient then any extant Author, or perhaps then Letters themselves; before which, as they expressed their Conceptions in Hieroglyphicks, so did they their Philosophie and Divinitie under Fables and Parables: a way not un-trod by the sacred Pen-men; as by the prudent Law-givers, in their reducing of the old World to civilitie, leaving behinde a deeper impression, then can be made by the livelesse precepts of Philosophie. Plato in his imaginary Commonwealth ordaineth, that Mothers and Nurses should season the tender mindes of their children with these instructive fables, wherein the wisdome of the Ancient was involved: Some under Allegories expressing the wonderfull works of nature: Some administring comfort in calamitie; others expelling the terrors and perturbations of the minde; Some inflaming by noble examples with an honest emulation, and leading, as it were, by the hand to the Temple of Honour and Vertue. For the Poet not onely renders things as they are; but what are not, as if they were, or rather as they should be; agreeable to the high affections of the Soule, and more conducing to magnanimitie: juster then either men or Fortune, in the exalting of Vertue and suppressing of Vice, by shewing the beautie of the one and deformitie of the other, pursued by the divine Vengeance, by inbred terrors, and infernall torments. For apparant it is, that They among the Heathen preserved that trueth of the immortalitie of the Soule: and therefore Epicurus, who maintained the contrary, dehorted his Scholars from the Reading of Poetry. In the Mythologie I have rather followed (as fuller of delight and more usefull) the varietie of mens severall conceptions, where they are not over-strained, then curiously examined their exact proprietie; which is to be born-with in Fables and Allegories, so as the principall parts of application resemble the ground-work.

I have also endeavoured to cleare the Historicall part, by tracing the almost worn-out steps of Antiquitie; wherein the sacred stories afford the clearest direction. For the first Period from the Creation to the Flood, which the Ethnicks called the Obscure, some the Emptie times; and the Ages next following which were styl'd the Heroicall, because the after deified Heroes then flourished; as also the Fabulous, in that those stories convayed by Tradition in loose and broken Fragments, were by the Poets interwoven with instructing Mythologies, are most obscurely and perplexedly delivered by all, but the supernaturally inspired Moses. Wherefore, not without authoritie, have I here and there given a touch of the relation which those fabulous Tra-Traditions have to the divine History, which the Fathers have observed, and made use of in convincing the Heathen. By this and the rest it may appeare, that our Subject, how ever slight in apparance, is nothing lesse both in use and substance, wherein, if my Intentions faile not, the matter and delivery is so tempered, that the ordinary Reader need not reject it as too difficult, nor the learned as too obvious.

To

To the Tranſlation I have given what perfection my Pen could beſtow; by poliſhing, altering, or reſtoring, the harſh, improper, or miſtaken, with a nicer exactneſſe then perhaps is required in ſo long a labour. I have alſo added Marginall notes for illuſtration and eaſe of the meere Engliſh Reader, ſince divers places in our Author are otherwiſe impoſſible to be underſtood but by thoſe who are well verſed in the ancient Poets and Hiſtorians; withall to avoid the confuſion of names which are given to one Perſon, derived from his Anceſtors, Countrey, Qualitie, or Achievements. The heads of the ſtories ſet in capitall letters in the Margent of the Tranſlation are the ſame with thoſe in the margent of the Commentary: by which you may readily finde the Mythologie peculiar unto every Fable.

And for the farther delight, I have contracted the ſubſtance of every Booke into as many Figures (by the hand of a rare Workman, and as rarely performed, if our judgements may be led by theirs, who are Maſters among us in that Facultie) ſince there is betweene Poetry and Picture ſo great a congruitie; the one called by Simonides a ſpeaking Picture, and the other a ſilent Poeſie: Both Daughters of the Imagination, both buſied in the imitation of Nature, or tranſcending it for the better with equall libertie: the one being born in the beginning of the World; and the other ſoone after, as appeares by the Hieroglyphicall Figures on the Egyptian Obeliſques, which were long before the invention of Letters: the one feaſting the Eare, and the other the Eye, the nobleſt of the ſences, by which the Vnderſtanding is onely informed, and the minde ſincerely delighted: and as the rareſt pieces in Poets are the deſcriptions of Pictures, ſo the Painter expreſſeth the Poet with equall Felicitie; repreſenting not onely the actions of men, but making their Paſſions and Affections ſpeake in their faces; in ſo much as he renders the lively Image of their Mindes as well as of their Bodies; the end of the one and the other being to mingle Delight with Profit. To this I was the rather induced, that ſo excellent a Poem might with the like Solemnitie be entertained by us, as it hath been among other Nations: rendred in ſo many languages, illuſtrated by Comments, and imbelliſhed with Figures: withall, that I may not prove leſſe gratefull to my Autor, by whoſe Muſe I may modeſtly hope to be reſcued from Oblivion.

Laſtly; ſince I cannot but doubt that my errors in ſo various a ſubject require a favourable connivence, I am to deſire that the Printers may not be added to mine. The literall will eaſily paſſe without rubs in the reading; the groſſe ones correct themſelves; but by thoſe betweene both the ſence is in greateſt danger to ſuffer. However, I have ſifted out all, or the moſt materiall, and expoſed them in the end of the Volume.

B 2

THE LIFE OF
OVID.

PUBLIUS OVIDIUS NASO, defcended of the ancient Family of the NASONES, who had preferved the dignitie of *Romane* Knights from the firft originall of that Order, was borne at *Sulmo* , a Citie of the *Peligni* , on the xiiii of the Calends of April , in the Conful-fhips of HIRCIUS and PANSA, both flaine at the battell of *Mutina* againft MARCUS ANTONIUS. While yet a boy, his quick wit and ready apprehenfion gave his parents an affurance of a future excellencie : in fo much as his father LUCIUS fent him to *Rome* (together with his brother, a yeere elder then he, and born on the fame day) to be inftructed by PLOSIUS GRIPPUS, that Art might perfect the accomplifhments of Nature. In his firft of youth he was much addicted unto Poetry , wherein he had an excellent grace and naturall facilitie. But continually reproved by his father for following fo unprofitable a ftudy , with an ill will he forfooke the pleafant walkes of the Mufes to travell in the rugged paths of the Law, under AURELIUS FUSCUS and PORCIUS LATRO; of whofe eloquence and learning he was a great Admirer. Neither attained he therein to a vulgar commendation, being numbred by MARCUS ANNÆUS SENECA among the principall Orators of thofe times. His profe was no other then diffolved verfe : his fpeech wittie, briefe, and powerfull in perfwafion. Having paft through divers offices of Judicature, and now ready to affume the habit of a Senator ; his elder brother and father being dead, impatient of toyle, and the clamours of litigious Affemblies, he retired himfelf from all publike affaires to affected vacancie and his former abandoned ftudies. Yet fuch was the mutuall affection between him and VARRO that he accepted of Command, and ferved under him in the warres of *Afia* : from whence he returned by *Athens* , where he made his aboad , untill he had attained to the perfection of that language. A man of a meane ftature, flender of body, fpare of diet ; and, if not too amorous, every way temperate. He drunk no wine but what was much alayed with water : An abhorrer of unnaturall Lufts, from which it fhould feeme that age was not innocent : neat in apparell ; of a free, affable, and courtly behaviour ; whereby he acquired the friendfhip of many , fuch as were great in learning and nobilitie ; among whom not a few of Confular dignitie : and fo honoured by divers, that they wore his picture in rings cut in precious ftones. One have I feene in a Cornelian, of exquifite workmanfhip, with his name ingraven on the one fide , and certain obfcure characters on the other, fuppofed as ancient as thofe times : I have alfo an old Medall of Silver ftamped with his image : both which are prefented under his Figure, with the Reverfe of the latter. A great Admirer , and as much admired , of the excellent Poets of thofe times , with whom he was moft familiar and intimate. Being perfwaded by fome of them to leave out three verfes of thofe many which he had written, he gave his confent, fo that of all he might except three onely : whereupon they privately writ thofe which they would have him abolifh, and he on the other fide thofe which he excepted ; when both their papers being fhown, prefented the fame verfes : the firft and fecond recorded by PEDO ALBINOVANUS, who was one of the Arbiters,

Semi-bovemque virum, femi-virumque bovem.
Sed gelidum Borean, egelidumque Notum.

Whereby it appeareth that his admirable wit did not want an anfwerable judgement in fuppreffing the libertie of his verfe , had he not affected it. An ample patrimony he had in the territories of *Sulmo*; with a houfe and a Temple in the Citie, where now ftands the Church of *Sancta Maria de Tumba* : and where now ftands the Church of *Sancta Maria de Confolatione*; he had another in *Rome* , not farre from the Capitoll ; with pleafant Hort-yards betweene the wayes of *Flaminia* and *Claudia* , wherein he was accuftomed to recreate himfelfe with his Mufes. He had three wives : whereof the firft being given him in his youth, as neither worthy nor profitable, foone after (according to the cuftome of the *Romanes*) he divorced : nor liv'd he long with the fecond, although nobly born, and of behaviour inculpable. The chaftitie and beautie of the third he often extolleth ; whom he inftructed in poetry , and to his
death

death entirely affected. Neither was her affection inferiour to his; living all the time of his banishment like a forrowfull widow, and continuing to the end exemplary faithfull. But in this every way happy condition, when his age required ease, and now about to imploy his beloved vacancie in the review and polishing of his former labours, he was banished, or rather confined to *Tomos* (a citie of *Sarmatia* bordering on the Euxine Sea) by AUGUSTUS CÆSAR, on the fourth of the Ides of December, and in the one and fiftieth yeere of his age, to the generall griefe of his friends and acquaintance: who sayled into *Thrace* in a ship of his own, and by land performed the rest of his voyage. The cause of this his so cruell and deplored exile, is rather conjectured then certainly knowne. Most agree that it was for his too much familiaritie with JULIA the daughter of AUGUSTUS, masked under the name of CORINNA. Others that he had unfortunately seene the incest of CÆSAR: which may be insinuated, in that he complaines of his errour, and compares himselfe to ACTÆON. But the pretended occasion was for his composing of the Art of Love, as intolerably lascivious and corrupting good manners. A pretence I may call it, since unlikely it is, that he should banish him in his age for what he writ when hardly a man, and after so long a connivence. Yet AUGUSTUS, either to conceale his owne crime or his daughters, would have it so thought: neither would OVID reveale the true cause, least he should further exasperate his displeasure. After he had long in vaine solicited his repeale by the mediation of GERMANICUS CÆSAR, and others that were neere unto the Emperour; or at least to be removed to a more temperate Clime; his hopes (as he writes) forsaking the earth with AUGUSTUS, he died at *Tomos* in the fifth yeere of the raigne of TIBERIUS; having lived seven yeeres in banishment. As TIBULLUS and he were born in one day, so he and LIVIE died on an other; that his birth and death might be nobly accompanied. He had so wonne the barbarous GET's with his humanitie and generous actions (having also written a booke in their language) that they honoured him in his life with triumphant garlands, and celebrated his funerals with universall sorrow; erecting his tombe before the gates of their citie, hard by a lake which retaineth his name to this day. His sepulcher was found in the yeere, MDVIII. with a magnificent coverture presenting this Epitaph.

FATUM NECESSITATIS LEX.

> *Here lies that living Poet, by the rage*
> *Of great* Augustus *banished from* Rome:
> *Who in his country sought t'interre his Age;*
> *But vainly, Fate hath lodg'd him in this tombe.*

ISABELLA Queene of *Hungary* in the yeere MDXL shewed to BARGÆUS a pen of silver, found not long before under certain ruines, with this inscription; *OVIDII NASONIS CALAMVS:* which she highly esteemed, and preserved as a sacred relique. Of the books which he writ, since most of them are extant among us, I will onely recite these following verses of ANGELUS POLITIANUS.

1	*From times first birth he chants the change of things;*	Metamorphosis.
2	*The flames of Love in Elegiacks sings,*	De Arte,& Amorum.
3	*With curses doubtfull Ibis he insnares,*	In Ibin.
4	*Epistles dictates fraught with Lovers cares,*	Epist. Heroidum.
5	*In Swan-like tunes deplores his sad exile,*	Trist.& de Ponto.
6	*His verse the* Roman *Festivals compile,*	Fasti.
7	*Of fishes sings unknown to* Latin *eares,*	Halieutica.
8	*Computes the stars that glide in heavenly spheres,*	Phænomena.
9	*His paper fils with Epigrammick rimes,*	Epigrammata.
10	*The tragick stage on high cothurnals climes,*	Medeæ trag.
11	*Whips Poetasters that abuse the times.*	In malos Poetas.

Yet leaves he out the *Remedy of Love*, a legitimate Poem (except he make it an appendix to the *Art*) and his *Consolation to* LIVIA for the death of DRUSUS: which SENECA hath
excerped

excerped and sprinkled among his severall *Consolations*. Among such a multiplicitie of arguments our gentle Poet did never write a virulent verse, but onely against CORNIFICUS; (maskt under the name of IBIS) who solicited his wife in his absence, and laboured against the repeale of his banishment. Concerning his Metamorphosis, it should seeme that he therein imitated PARTHENIUS of *Chios*, who writ on the same argument: as the *Latin* Poets even generally borrowed their inventions from the *Grecian Magazins*. I will conclude with what himself hath written of this Poem, wherein I have imployed my vacant houres: with what successe, I leave to the censure of others, which perhaps may prove lesse rigid then my owne.

> *I thanke your love : my verse farre livelier then*   Trist. lib. 1. Elegia. 6.
>   *My picture shew me ; wherefore those peruse :*
> *My verse, which sing the changed shapes of men ;*
>   *Though left unperfect by my banisht Muse.*
> *Departing, these I sadly with my hand*
>   *Into the fire, with other riches, threw.*
> *Her sonne* Althea *burning in his brand,*
>   *A better sister then a mother grew :*
> *So I, what should not perish with me, cast*
>   *Those books, my issue, in the funerall flame :*
> *In that I did my Muse my crime distast ;*
>   *Or that as yet unpolished and lame.*
> *But since I could not so destroy them quite ;*
>   *For sundry copies it should seeme there be :*
> *Now may they live, nor lazily delight*
>   *The generous Reader ; put in minde of me.*
> *Yet they with patience can by none be read,*
>   *That know not how they uncorrected stand :*
> *Snatcht from the forge, ere throughly anviled ;*
>   *Deprived of my last life-giving hand.*
> *For praise I crave thy pardon : highly grac'd,*
>   *If, Reader, they be not despised by thee :*
> *Yet in the front be these sixe verses plac'd,*
>   *If with thy liking it at least agree.*
>
> WHO *meets this Orphan-volume, poore in worth,*
>   *Within your Citie harborage afford.*
> *To winne more favour, not by him set forth ;*
>   *But ravisht from the funerall of his Lord.*
> *He, all the faults, which these rude lines deface,*
>   *Would have reform'd, had his mishaps giv'n space.*

OVID DEFENDED.

Since divers, onely wittie in reproving, have profaned our Poet with their faſtidious cenſures, we, to vindicate his worth from detraction, and prevent prejudicacie, have here revived a few of thoſe infinite teſtimonies, which the cleereſt judgements of all Ages have given him. I will begin with the cenſure of that accurate Orator,

MARCUS ANNÆUS SENECA,

Controv. 10

One of his frequent and admiring Auditors. *Naſo had a conſtant, becoming, and amiable wit. His Proſe appeared no other then diſſolved verſes.* And a little after. *Of his words no Prodigall, except in his Verſe :- wherein, he was not ignorant of the fault, but affected it : and often would ſay, that a Mole mis-became not a beautifull face, but made it more lovely.* Amongſt the excellent of his time, we may eſteeme

VELLEIUS PATERCULUS,

Hiſt. lib 2.

Who writeth thus in his hiſtorie. *It is almoſt a folly, to number the wits that are ever in our eyes. Amongſt theſe of our Age the moſt eminent are, Virgil the Prince of Verſe,* Rabirius, Livie *imitating* Saluſt, Tibullus, *and* Naſo *in the forme of his abſolute Poem.* Nor doth

LUCIUS ANNÆUS SENECA

Natur. Quæſt li. 3.

degenerate from his Fathers opinion : who to that Verſe, by him thus diſſolved, *The Rocks appeare like Ilands, and augment the diſperſed* Cyclades, annexeth this, *as ſaith the wittieſt of all Poets.* A conſtant Imitator of his, through all his Philoſophie ; but eſpecially in his Tragedies. Whereupon ſome have conjectured that *Seneca's* Medea belongeth to OVID. Whereof

QUINTILIAN

Lib. 10.

thus cenſures. OVID's Medea *ſeemeth to me to expreſſe how much that man could have perform'd, would he rather have reſtrained then cheriſhed his invention.* And

CORNELIUS TACITUS,

Dial. de O-rat.

Neither is there any compoſition of Aſinius, *or* Meſſala *ſo illuſtrious, as* OVID's Medea. The wittie

MARTIAL

Lib. 3. Epig. 38.

for the moſt part linkes him to incomparable *Virgil : as in this Epigram ;*
Th'art more then mad ! thoſe, whom thou ſee'ſt ſo bare,
With OVID's *ſelfe, or* Virgil *may compare*

And in that to *Inſtantius.*

Lib. 1. Epig. 7?.

Would'ſt thou adde ſpirit to my fainting Muſe,
And read immortall Verſes ? love infuſe.
Me, Mantua ; SULMO *mee ſhould ſtyle divine ;*
Were but Alexis, *or* CORINNA *mine.*

Recorded by

STATIUS PAMPINIUS,

Sylvar. l. 1.

amongſt the beſt Poets.
That honoured Day, the old Callimachus,
Philetas, *Umbrian* Propertius,
Prepare to celebrate with one conſent,
And NASO, *cheerefull though in baniſhment,*
With rich Tibullus.

Nor is he onely approved by prophane Authors. Thus learned

LACTANTIUS,

Inſtit. div. lib. 1.

OVID, *in the beginning of his excellent Poem, confeſſeth that God (not diſguizing his Name) ordained the world ; who calls him the Creator thereof, and Maker of all things.* In the following booke. *Which that ingenious Poet hath admirably deſcribed.* And

S. HIEROME ;

In Oſ. c. 1.

Semiramis, *of whom they report many wonders, erected the walls of* Babylon ; *as teſtifies that renowned Poet in the fourth book of his* Metamorphoſis. Nor is he forgot by

S. AUGUSTINE.

De Civ. Dei.

And NASO, *that excellent Poet.* Now deſcend we to thoſe, whom later times have preferred for

C

for learning and judgement. Thus fings the high prais'd

In Nuticia.

ANGELUS POLITIANUS.

'Tis doubtfull, whether He, whom SULMO *bore,*
The World-commanding Tyber *honour'd more,*
Then his foule exile thee defam'd, O Rome !
Whom Getick *fands (alas !) but halfe intombe.*
Perhaps obferved by Auguftus Spyes
To looke on JULIA *with too friendly eyes.*

In Ciceroni-
ano Dialogo.
Poetices. lib.
5. & 6.;

ERASMUS
crowns him with the perfection of Eloquence. And the Cenfurer of all Poets,

JULIUS CAESAR SCALIGER,
thus writes, when he comes to cenfure our Author. *But now we arrive where the height of wit,*
and fharpneffe of judgement, are both to be exercis'd. For, who can commend OVID *fufficiently ?*
much leffe, who dares reprehend him ? Notwithftanding , I will fay fomething ; not in way of detra-
ction, but that we alfo may be able to grow with his greatneffe. Then fpeaking of his Metamorphofis. *Books deferving a more fortunate Author ; that from his laft hand they might have had their*
perfection : which he himfelf bewaileth in luculent Verfes. Yet are there , in thefe well-nigh an in-
finite number, which the wit of another, I beleeve, could never have equal'd. And thus exclaimes

In Macrobius

againft Cæfar in the perfon of OVID.

Tyrant, with me I would thou hadft begun :
Nor thy black flaughters had my Fate fore-run.
If my licentious Youth incenft thee fo ;
Thy own condemnes thee : into exile go.
Thy Cabinets are ftayn'd with horrid deeds :
And thy foule guilt all monftrous names exceeds.
Divine wit, innocence, nor yet my tongue,
Next to Apollo's, *could prevent my wrong.*
I fmooth'd th' old Poets with my fluent vain ;
And taught the New a farre more numerous ftrain.
When thee I prais'd, then from the truth I fwerv'd ;
And banifhment for that alone deferv'd.

Præfat. in
Horatium.

Now heare we the much-knowing

STEPHANUS.
NASO, *in his Metamorphofis, may well be called the Poet of Painters ; in that thofe wittie defcrip-*
tions afford fuch lively patterns for their pencil to imitate. And

Difputat. de
Fabula.

MARCUS ANTONIUS TRITONIUS.
This divine worke is neceffary, and to be defired of all , that are addicted to Poetry , both for the grace-
fulneffe of fpeech, the admirable art of the Poet and delightfull varietie of the Subject. Neither was
there ever any , that diligently collected, or learnedly, elegantly and orderly expreffed the fables , but
OVID ; *who compofed out of* Orpheus, Hefiod, Homer, *and other the moft ancient Poets, fo ex-*
cellent and noble a Worke, that therein the learning of the Latines *may worthily glory.* And we
that of

Variar. Lect.
lib. 8.c. 18.

BERNARDUS MARTINUS:
I conceive the Poet of SULMO *did follow the induftry and advice of* Zeuxes, *in the compofure of*
that admirable worke of his Metamorphofis. For as that excellent Painter , about to draw the Picture
of Helena, *had affembled together the moft rare and beautifull Virgins of* Greece ; *that by exami-*
ning their feverall perfections and graces he might expreffe all in one with his curious pencill : fo he
out of the innumerable volumes of the Græcian Poets ; firft gathered thefe multiplicities of fables,
compofing the diffufed and varioufly difperfed into one body : and then diligently noting what in eve-
ry author was elegant and beautifull, transfer'd the fame to his own, that nothing might be wanting to
the enriching and adorning of his fo divine a Poem. I muft not omit this teftimony of the learned

Orat. 3. vo-
lum. 2.

ANTONIUS MURETUS.
The Metamorphofis, a divine Poem ; fhining through-out, with all the luftres of conceit and eloquence.
Nor this of

Præfat. ob-
ferv. in Me-
tam.

HERCULES CIOFANUS;
in that a Citizen of SULMO. *A wittie worke, repleat with folid and manifold learning. Who per-*
ufe it diligently , fhall finde fuch admirable fluencie, fuch fulneffe, fo great a gravitie of words and
fentences;

that few or none amongst the Latine Poets can be said to transcend him. What should I say of that singular, and well-nigh divine contexture of Fable with Fable? so surpassing, that nothing can be spoken or done, more artificially, more excellently, or, indeed, more gracefully. Who handling such diversitie of matter, so cunningly weaves them together, that all appeare but one Series. Planudes, well knowing that Greece had not a Poem so abounding with delight and beautie, translated it into that language. What should I say more? All Arts, which antiquitie knew, are here so fully delineated, that a number, expert in both tongues, of Prime understanding and judgements, admire it beyond all expression. The first that writ a Commentarie on this book (whereof fiftie thousand were vented, and that in his life time) was

RAPHAEL REGIUS:

In præfat. Comment.

who thus in his Preface. There is nothing appertaining to the knowledge and glory of warre, whereof we have not famous examples in the Metamorphosis of OVID; (not to speake of stratagems, nor the Orations of Commanders) described with such efficacie and eloquence, that often in reading, you will imagine your selfe imbroiled in their conflicts. Neither shall you finde any Author, from whom a civill life may gather better instructions. Conclude we with

JACOBUS MICYLLUS.

In Principio Additionum.

Hardly shall you finde a Poem, which flowes with greater facilitie. For what should I speake of Learning? Herein, so great, so various and abstruse; that many places have neither been explained, nor yet understood; no, not by the most knowing: requiring rather a resolution from the Delian Oracle, &c.

Let the ingenious that affect not error, now rectifie their own by the judgements of these. But incurable Criticks, who warre about words, and gall the sound to feed on their sores, as not desiring their sanitie, I forbeare to disswade and deliver them up to the censure of AGRIPPA.

C 2   QVOD

QVOD OLIM FACIEBAT

VOTVM GERMANICO OVIDIVS,
IDEM Augustissimo Carolo
Interpretis sui nomine faciunt
OVIDIANI MANES.

EXcipe pacato, Cæsar Britannice, vultu
    Hoc opus, & timidæ dirige navis iter.
Officicque, levem non aversatus honorem,
    Huic tibi devoto, numine dexter ades.
Huic te da placidum, dederis in carmina vires :
    Ingenium vultu statque caditque tuo.
Pagina judicium docti subitura movetur
    Principis, ut Clario missa legenda Deo.

197

A Lthough I conceived at the firſt, that it would ſeeme a vain oſtentation in me (who am onely a lover of learning) to ſtuffe the Margent with Quotations: yet upon ſecond thoughts, leſt it ſhould be objected how I make that my owne which I doe but borrow, and prove ungratefull to the lenders; I hold it not amiſſe in this empty Page, (ſo left by the overſight of the Printer) to mention thoſe principall Authors out of whom I have compiled theſe commentaries. The firſt place is due to diverſe of the Greek, and moſt of the Latine Poets, together with their Expoſiters. I am much indebted to Plato, the poeticall Philoſopher: not a little to Palaphates, Apollidorus, Aratus, Strabo, Diodorus, Pauſanias, Plutarch, and Lucian: among the Romanes chiefly, to Cicero, Higinus, Pliny, and Macrobius. Neither have I been ſparingly ſupplied by thoſe antient Fathers, Lactantius, Euſebius, Sᵗ. Auguſtine, and Fulgentius. Of moderne writers, I have received the greateſt light from Geraldus, Pontanus, Ficinus, Vives, Comes, Scaliger, Sabinus, Pierius, and the Crowne of the latter, the Vicount of Sᵗ. Albons: aſſiſted, though leſſe conſtantly, by other authors, almoſt of all Ages, and Arguments. Having beene true to my firſt purpoſe, in making choice for the moſt part of thoſe interpretations, which either bear the ſtampe of Antiquitie, or receive eſtimation from the honour of the Author.

VPON THE FIRST BOOK OF
OVIDS METAMORPHOSIS.

HIS *Argument first propounded, our Poet according to the custome of the Heroicall, invokes the divine assistance ;* Rather would we begin, saith *Livy ,* if it were our manner, as it is of the Poets, with our vows and prayers to the Gods, that they might give successe to so great a labour) *Then he proceeds to the description of that confused Masse, which the Platonists call the undigested World, as the world the digested* Chaos: *ordered, as they say, by* Love; *who raised the heavy, illuminated the obscure, quickned the dead ; gave forme to the deformed, and perfection to the imperfect : which was no other then that harmony in Nature created by the Almighties* Fiat. *And although by not expressing the originall he seemes to intimate the eternitie of his* Chaos: *yet appeares in the rest so consonant to the truth, as doubtlesse he had either seene the Books of* Moses, *or received that doctrine by tradition. He confesseth God, not disguising his name (as observed by* Lactantius) *to be the Creator of the World and Maker of all things : and by that word* Commanded, *so often reiterated, that he made them by his Word only. Whom he also calleth the* Better Nature ; *so named by the* Stoicke : Wilt thou call him Nature ? Thou offendest not: it is he by whose spirit we live, of whom all things were borne. *The better concludes a worse, which was* Chaos: *God they held to be the* Minde, *and* Chaos *the Matter : the* Minde *called by* Plato *the worlds* Architectresse.

CHAOS.

Chaos is first digested into the foure Elements. The Fire *exceeding the rest in drinesse, heat, and levitie, ascendeth next unto the Orbe of the* Moon ; *in forme sphericall, and turn'd about with the motion of the Heavens ; pure in his own Sphaere, not devouring, bright, giving light ; yet such as cannot be seene by reason of his tenuitie: dissipated, rarified, and consequently preserved by his circular motion. The next in levitie and place is* Aire : *moist, moderate hot ; filling whatsoever is not otherwise supplyed, as defending Nature from abhorred vacuitie ; which rather then suffer, heavy bodies will ascend, and the light fall down-ward: moderate hot, in regard of the vicinitie of the fire; moist, in that thin, fluent, and boundlesse ; the food of our spirits, without which the creature cannot subsist. Below the Aire the* Earth, *dry, cold, thick, solid and heavy ; dry, in that setled, and devouring all moisture ; cold, in that without motion, and farre removed from the fountain of heat : weight proceeds from densitie and soliditie, and therefore 'tis fixed in the midst of the world, as it were his Center. Last, he mentions the* water ; *as lowest in his superficies approved by the perpetuall descent of Rivers ; the shore being lower then the In-land, as the Sea then the shore. And although it seeme otherwise, yet is that but a deception of the eye, casting higher beames on places farre distant : so in a long Gallery the floore and seeling appeare to incline to each other. Yet is the water lesse heavy, moist, and respectively cold ; naturally pressing to the same Center with the Earth, imbracing, and running within it, as blood in the veines, which else would be barren: moisture being the mother of all generation. The forme thereof is sphericall, or equally distant from the Center ; making one Globe with the Earth, as is apparant at Sea by raising or laying the North-starre. And by loosing the shore by degrees, the lower objects first, and after the higher. So the mast is discovered before the Hull of a ship ; which if the Sea were levell (as* Patritius *will have it) would first appeare, as exceeding it so infinitely in magnitude. Neither is his argument weighty which he draws from water-levels, since that gibbositie cannot be discerned, nor taken by instruments, in so small a proportion ; rising but sixe foot in three miles, the space of a visible Horizon. This before he calleth* Amphitrite, *the feined daughter of* Oceanus *and* Doris, *and wife unto* Neptune: *in that he, as they held, was the spirit diffused through the universall masse of water ; and, as we may say, the soule of that Element :* Amphitrite, *that body and matter of all moisture, which imbraceth the Earth, or is imbraced by it. The name derived from the beating upon the incompassed Earth with her surges.*

THE 4 ELEMENTS
Fire.
Ayre.
Earth.
Water.

From the Elements he proceeds to the Ornament *of the Earth : made round, that it might be equall in it selfe ; and equally distant from the celestiall bodies, from whence it receiveth her vertue. That it is so, is apparent by the Eclipse of the* Moone, *for such as the substance, such is the shadow : effected by the naturall pressing of all parts to the Center ; if not of the World, yet of her own body. For the former is denied by* Copernicus *and his followers, who would rather place the Sunne in the Center : and alleadging the* Moone *to be a heavy body, with risings and depressions, like our vallies and mountains, as since discovered by* Galileos Glasses. *And perhaps to a Menippus in the* Moone, *the Earth, according to* Aristotle, *would appeare such another Planet. Our Poet before described the earth to hang*
THE
EARTH A-
DORNED.

in

in the Aire, ballanced with her own weight : and Lucretius *of the same under the name of* Cybel;

Hanc veteres Graium docti cecinere poeta
Sublimem in curru bijugos agi-
tare Leones :
Aeris in spatio magnam pendere
docentes
Tellurem, neque posse in terra si-
stere terram. Lib. 2.

The sage Greek Poets sung, that she was by
Yok't Lions in her Chariot drawn on high :
By which they taught that this huge masse of mold
Hung in the Aire ; nor earth could earth uphold.

Yet would the Aire give it way, were it not at rest in her proper Center. Some have marveiled that it fell not : but that fall would have proved an ascension ; for, which way soever, it must have fallen into heaven ; which our Hemisphere would have done as soone as the other. Yet Lactantius *and* St. *Augustine with acerbitie deride the opinion of the* Antipodes*, as if men could goe with their heads downward, and the rain upward.; but heaven is every where above us, and upward and downward are only words of relation in sphericall bodies, the superficies on every side, being the extreame, and the middle the Center. Yet* Virgilius *Bishop of Salsburg, was deprived of his Bishopricke for maintaining this opinion : now discovered by daily navigations, as long since by reason. The Sea-imbraced Earth is also inchased with Rivers which glide from their fountains : These are ingendred in the hollow cavernes below, by condensed aire which resolves into water, and increasing by degrees breake from under the ground ; maintaining their currents by a perpetuall accession. Some falling into bottomes, environed with hills, become lakes ; some are drunk up by the earth, as* Ladon, Lycus, Erasinus, &c. *almost all by the Sea ; which she through secret passages, sweetned, as some say, by a long progresse, repaies to new fountains : through which they have their recourse by a perpetuall vicissitude ; rising as high as they fall, and rather recoile then transcend their originall. Woods, Plaines, Mountaines and Vallies (not made, as some have dreamed, by the Flood) were created for beautie, use, and varietie. Neither makes it against the rotunditie of the Earth that some one Mountain aspires (as they report of* Teneriff*) fourescore furlongs above his basis ; being farre lesse then a wart on the face of man compared with the immensitie of the other, containing three thousand and sixe hundred miles in Semidiameter. But the best Geographers will admit of none above five miles high, which at Sea may be made threescore and sixe leagues off, being farther perhaps then any have been discerned.*

The five Zones, or divisions of Heaven and Earth, not reall but imaginary, were well devised by Astronomers to distinguish the motions of the Sunne, the Moone and the Starres, the vicissitude of times, the site and qualitie of Countries. The Torrid, so called of excessive heat, the Sunne being over it, is confined by the Tropicks of Cancer *and* Capricorne*, and parted in the midst by the Aequator ; containing in latitude seven and fortie degrees. This in the daies of our Author was held generally unhabitable. Yet* Lucan*, in the army of* Pompey*, musters the* Æthiopians : *and* Pliny *out of* Eratosthenes *describes* Taprobana, *under the line, (supposed the same with* Zumatra*) but elsewhere concurres with the former assertion : so* Ptolomie *makes a doubt thereof in his* Almagest*, yet in his* Geography *treats of the* Agisymban Æthiopians *on the South of the Equinoctiall. Thus hardly is an old opinion worn out though the arguments against it be never so forcible : found now by the Portugals and Spaniards not only populous, but healthfull, pleasant, and abounding with whatsoever the avarice or voluptuousnesse of man can desire. To them under the line the daies and nights are alwaies equall ; the heat of the one being qualified by the length of the other, and coole briefes continually blowing from nine of the clock untill the evening. All the Stars (even to the Poles) by turnes arise and set in their sight : though questioned by* Lerius Burgundus *and others. For in a free Horizon, as at Sea, we may see one halfe of the Heavens, or so insensibly lesse as cannot deprive the sight of a starre, the least farre exceeding the Earth in greatnesse, besides the refraction raises them halfe a degree. All within the Torrid Zone a part of the yeere have their shadows on their right side, and a part on the left, as the Sunne is either towards the Winter or Summer Solstice. Two Summers they have, and two harvests : the Trees ever greene, and bearing fruit continually. On each side of this lye the temperate Zones, confined by the Artick and Antartick Circles ; each containing fortie three degrees ; and of equall qualitie. As the Sunne at high neone is with us in the South, so is it North unto those who dwell in the other ; casting consequently contrary shadows, to the no small admiration of either who travell hither or thither.*

Ignotum vobis Arabes venistis
in orbem;
Vmbras mirati nemorum non
ire sinistras. Luc. l. 3.

The Arab in an unknown world now sees,
And wonders at the right hand shades of trees.

The Hebrews turning their faces to the East called the North the left, and the South the right hand;

contrary

Margin notes: Rivers. | Mountains. | THE FIVE ZONES. | The Torrid Zone. | The temperate Zones.

contrary to these souldiers of *Arabia* the happy who marched *Westward.* Their Winter beyond the Line being our Summer, and our Summer their Winter. The Frigid Zones, held inhabitable for extremitie of cold, by reason of the Suns distance from their verticall point, extend from the former circles to the North and South Pole; each three and twentie Degrees and a halfe in Latitude: yet this to the North is found within ten degrees of the Pole to be habitable. To them whose Zeniths are the Poles the Equator is their Horizon. The starres in their Hemispheres are ever in sight, and those neere the Line apparent to either. Halfe the yeere both have, but contrary to each other, one continued Day: and after for a certain season, they see by refraction the body of the Sun, though under their Horizon, through the thicknesse of Vapours; confirmed by the Hollanders, who have wintred neere unto that of the North. So if you put a peece of gold into a bason of water, and stand so farre off as not to see the bottome; yet will it shew you the gold at that distance. The rest of the yeere is a perpetuall twi-light, since the Sun is never below their Horizon above three and twentie Degrees; nor higher in the Summer; so that like Tantalus they starve for cold in his perpetuall presence; who wheeles their shadows continually about them, and hardly warmes them with his beames in regard of their obliquitie. By this division the extent of the Heavens between the two Poles contains one hundred and fourescore Degrees, which doubled for the other Hemisphere amount to three hundred and sixtie, the measure of the whole circuit. A Degree in Heaven is threescore miles on the Earth; so the Globe of the Earth is twentie one thousand and sixe hundred miles in circumference.

From Earth he ascends to Aire: how much thinner then Water the Optickes discover; the one causing a refraction but of halfe a Degree, and the other of fortie eight Degrees. Yet how much grosser then the skie, is by twilight apparent: the whole skie being all the night long in the beames of the Sun, (that little spire, the shadow of the Earth excepted) yet pitchy darke notwithstanding by reason of the transparent tenuitie, which gives no reflection. But Morning and Evening when the Sun shines on the Aire from under the Horizon, by the light thereof the starres are obscured: so that blew which we see in a cleere heaven is only the reflection of the Aire, thickned by the warme and moist vapours, drawn up by the Sun, and vertue of the Stars, which otherwise would be too subtill to breath in. Acosta writes, that upon the Andes high mountains of Peru, men and horses expire in that too subtile and piercing: and Aristotle, how those who ascended the top of Olympus (farre lower then the other) accustomed to carry wet spunges, to prevent the like mischiefe. These moist and grosse vapors, attracted as before, and condensed by cold, convert into clouds, which hang as if congealed together; and dissolving by the fervor of the Sun descend in fruitfull showres on the superficies of the Earth, not penetrating above the depth of ten feet, as observed by Seneca, a diligent digger in Vineyards. Here hot and dry exhalations, inveloped by watry Clouds, with motion or opposition of contrary cold, are inflamed: burning they rarifie; then struggle to burst forth, and at length force their way, darting down flames with horrible roarings. Although naturall, yet well tearmed a terror to man; nay, even to such who have slighted the Gods and contemned their power. Insomuch as Tiberius Cæsar when the aire grew troubled, was no lesse distempred in his minde, and would put on a Garland of Laurell, as a preservative against it. And Caligula, who usurped the title of Jupiter, and often bare a thunder-bolt in his hand, would shut his eyes, cover his face, and not seldome creep under bedsteeds and tables. But Dion writes that when it thundred and lightned aloft, he below would counterfeit the same by artificiall devices: following belike the example of Salmoneus, seene in Hell by Æneas,

Suffering dire punishment, who durst of late
Joves lightning, and heavens thunder imitate.
He, darting flames, through Greece and Elis rod,
Drawn by foure Steeds, in triumph like a God.
Mad man, the clouds, and lightnings matelesse force
To forge with brasse, and speed of horn-hooft horse.

-- Crudeles dantem Salmonea pœnas.
Dum flammas Iovis, & sonitus imitatur
Olympi,
Quatuor hic invectus equis, & lampada
quassans
Per Graium populos, mediaq; per Elidis urbem
Ibat ovans; divumq; sibi poscebat honorē.
Demens, qui nimbos, & non imitabile
fulmen
Ære & cornipedum cursu simul arat equorum. Virg. Æn. l. 6.

Next treats he of the winds, proceeding from abundance of hot and dry exhalations, which attracted by the Sun, and influence of particular Stars, are violently struck down by the cold and thick clouds of the third Region. But their naturall motion, which is to ascend, encountring with the violent, and neither prevailing, thrust them obliquely forward: when by meeting of like exhalations by the way their fury increaseth. Of these he mentioneth the foure cardinall only: calling them brothers; in that fained to be the sonnes of Aurora and the Giant Astræus. For by the Giants the Naturalists understand the included spirits of the Earth, of which the winds are ingendred; as the birth of Aurora in that they commonly rise in the morning; the aire being agitated by the approching Sun, the author
of

The Frigid Zones.

THE DESCRIPTION OF THE AIRE

Clouds.

Raine. Lightning and Thunder.

Winds.

of all motion. Their collaterall winds added, all amount on the Sea-mans Compasse *to two and thirtie. Their end is to agitate and purge the Aire, which otherwise would corrupt with too-much rest, and destroy the creature, to gather the clouds, to disperse them, to procure raine and faire weather, for the production and cherishing of vegetables.*

The
Heavens
and
their
Con-
tents.

    Now comes he to the Heavens; consisting of a pure and unmixed substance, held heretofore neither subject to corruption nor alteration. But late observations have proved the contrary: for Comets are now knowne to be above the Moone; nay higher then the least Parallax *can be discerned; generated, as* Tycho *conceives, of the Milky way; but according to* Kepler, *of a certaine thick matter, encompassing almost alwaies the body of the Sun. Howsoever, their dissipation must of necessitie contaminate the virgin puritie of* Aristotles Quintessence. *The Heavens being neither heavy nor light receive a sphericall figure, of all other the most perfect, capacious, and fittest for motion. Ten Spheres*

The Spheres.

there are including each other. The tenth moveth (or is moved by the finger of God) from East unto West, and finisheth its course in foure and twentie houres; making day, and night, and time, which is the measure of motion. The other nine, on another Axeltree twentie three Degrees from the first, move from West unto East. The ninth, which is the Chrystalline, turneth the eighth (wherein are the fixed Starres) about with it; both of a uniforme motion, and finish their course in twentie and five thousand yeares: which motion appeares not but by the observation of sundry Ages. In the daies of Meton, *foure hundred and thirtie yeares before* Christ, *the first Starre of* Aries *was in the vernall intersection, which still keepes that name, although now removed almost nine and twentie degrees. So that in more then two thousand yeares, the fixed Starres have not tra-*

The Planets.

velled from West to East, so much as one whole Signe in the Zodiack. The other seven being Planets, have varietie of motions: Saturne *finisheth his course in thirtie yeares,* Jupiter *in twelve,* Mars *in two, the* Sunne *and* Venus *in one,* Mercury *in eight and twentie daies lesse, and the Moon in eight and twentie daies. Yet all are violently turned about by the rapture of the tenth Sphere in foure and twentie houres; measuring with incomprehensible celeritie at least two hundred thousand miles every minute: which need not seeme incredible, if we consider the diffusion of light and motion of spirits, which either are or have many things analogicall to bodies, (not to speake of the passage of the glorified) performed in an instant: extolling rather (as doth this whole contemplation of Nature) the omnipotencie of the Creator.*

The Starres.

    The Earth being replenished with Beasts, the water with Fishes, and the Aire with Fowle; least the Heavens should only remaine emptie, our Poet faines that the Starres and Gods made that their habitation. By the Gods perhaps he intimates the Planets that carry their names: and the Ancient held that the Starres had life, and dominion withall, over our sublunary bodies. Nor have some Christians rejected this old opinion of the Philosophers, how certaine Angels, or Intelligences, assist and give motion to the Cælestiall Spheres. Insteed of which, the new refiners of Astronomy vouchsafe a kinde of soule to the Sunne, as requisite to those his notable effects of motion, generation, and influence. Plato *affirmes that at the first they adored no other: calling particular Starres by the names of their dead friends, and honouring them with Temples. If my mouth (saith* Job*) have kissed my hand to the Sunne or the Moone (so anciently hath the kissing of the hand beene a token of reverence) I should have denied God: and the Prophet complaines that the* Jews *not onely worshipped these, but the whole Hoast of Heaven, so taught by their idolatrous neighbours, who not only held that they had life and understanding, but saw whatsoever was done by mortals; hearing their praises and prayers, and accepting of their sacrifices. That the twelve signes in the Zodiack were directed by twelve superintendents:* Aries *by* Pallas, Taurus *by* Venus, Gemini *by* Apollo, Cancer *by* Mercury, Scorpio *by* Mars, Sagittarius *by* Diana, Capricornus *by* Vesta, Aquarius *by* Juno, *and* Pisces *by* Neptune. *Those ruling in the severall parts of the body, and these in the soule. And surely the Starres are not only ornaments; although exactly to discover their vertue in their aspects require a supernaturall knowledge: yet no otherwise incline or dispose the minde, then by working on our severall constitutions and complexions, nay many things concurre of farre greater efficacie, as parentage, education, discipline and custome. They consist of the more condensed part of the heavens: receiving all their light from the Sunne; especially the Planets, casting shadows in their opposition: and* Venus *by the new perspectives, found horned like the Moone. Yet unto the fixed Starres, besides their borrowed light, some attribute an innate splendor: supposing that the Sunne at so great a distance, appearing ten thousand times lesse unto them then to us, cannot communicate so great a light as they retribute to the earth. Yet still injoy he his title of the generall fountain of light, since his beames searching through the smallest cranny cast a greater lustre then all the Stars together in the Firmament. All that are seene in our Hemisphere, digested into Constellations,*

besides

besides the seven Planets, amount not to above one thousand and two and twenty : and in the other one hundred and one and twenty more have lately beene discovered : so in all there are eleven hundred fourty and three : however the glimmering and twinckling of so many make them seeme innumerable. And really so they are, though not by us to be discerned, as appeares by Galilæos Glasses.

Thus sprung this beautifull world out of the deformed Chaos ; and to Chaos (or rather into nothing) shall it againe returne, if this opinion erre not :

The aged world, dissolved by the last	——— *Sic, cum compage soluta*
And fatall houre, shall to old *Chaos* hast.	*Secula tot mundi suprema coegerit hora,*
Starres, justling starres, shall in the Deep confound	*Antiquum repetent iterum Chaos omnia ; mistis*
Their radiant fires : the land shall give no bound	*Sidera sideribus concurrent : ignea pontum*
To swallowing Seas : the Moone shall crosse the Sunne	*Astra petent : tellus extendere litora nolit.*
With scorne that her swift wheeles obliquely runne ;	*Excutietque fretum : fratri contraria Phæbe*
Daies throne aspiring Discord then shall rend	*Ibit, & obliquum bigas agitare per orbem*
The Worlds crackt frame, and Natures concord end.	*Indignata, diem poscet sibi : totaque discors*
	Machina divulsi turbabit fœdera mundi.
	Lucan. l. 4.

But many of our Divines doe beleeve that the world shall rather be renewed then annihilated, which opinion is strengthned by the eight of the Romanes, as by other places of the Scripture.

The last in act, but the first in intention, was the creation of Man, for whom the rest were created : extolled by our Poet as a sacred creature, and therefore not to be violated ; indewed with a Minde, which is, with Reason and understanding ; the Lord of the rest of the creatures, so deputed by his Creator, sprung of cælestiall seed, in regard of the essence of his soule, made of the earth, to teach him humility ; yet after the image of God : not onely in regard of his originall integritie (a good man, saith Plato, is like unto God) for that had beene lost by his fall, nor in the invisibility, eternity, and wonderfull faculties of the soule ; nor in his domination : but also (according to the opinion of the Jewes as appeares by Josephus : as of Zanchius, and many of our moderne Divines) in the symmetry and beauty of his body : Beauty is a quick and sprightly grace (as the Platonists hold) infused at first by a heavenly Ray ; shining in the Minde of man, the concinnitie of the body, and harmony of the voice : which by Reason, by the Eye, and the Eare, stirre-up, and delight, delighting ravish, and ravishing inflame us with ardent affection : by contemplating and affecting of this, we contemplate and affect the divine refulgency, as in that the Deity. But if this seeme incongruous in respect of our corruptible bodies, yet holds it well as they shall be glorified, and clad with a Sunne-like brightnesse. Lastly man was made with an erected looke to admire the glory of the Creator. What Theologian could have spoken more divinely ? Alone deceived in the name of the Artificer. Error is as full of contradiction as truth of conformity. A man to make the first man, and he Prometheus the sonne of Japhet. Lactantius writes that he lived in the daies of Jupiter, when Temples and Idols began to be erected, and was the first that ever made Statues. Saint Augustine reports him for a man of great wisdome, who informed the rude and earthly mindes of men with knowledge and understanding, and therefore was fained to have made them of clay : others, in that he taught the doctrine of the Creation. He is said to have fetcht fire from the Chariot of the Sunne by the counsell of Minerva ; because he first erected the mindes of men to cælestiall speculations. But to conforme the fable to the truth : Prometheus signifies Providence, and Minerva Heavenly Wisdome : by Gods providence therefore and wisdome Man was created. The cælestiall fire is his soule inspired from above : which the Philosophers themselves by the light of nature could discover. But nothing is here spoken of the creation of Woman. Aristophanes tells a fable in Plato how Man at the first was made double, after cut into two, and distinguished by their sexes ; an obscure notion of Eves being taken out of the side of Adam.

The fiction of the foure Ages degenerating from better to worse, I should have thought, with others, to have beene derived from that Image in Daniel ; where the first Monarchie is presented by Gold, the second by Silver, the third by Brasse, and the fourth by Iron : had not Hesiod long before (from whom our Poet takes his invention) by those names described them :

The Golden Race of many languag'd men,	*Aureum quidem primum genus diversi-loquentium hominum*
The Gods first made, who heaven inhabit, when	*Defecerunt, cælestium domorum incolæ :*
The Scepter Saturne swaid : like Gods they liv'd,	*Ii quidem sub Saturno erant ; cum in cælo regnaret.*
Secure in minde : nor sweat with toile, nor griev'd.	*Sed ut dii vivebant, securo animo præditi, Plane absque laboribus, & ærumna : neque molestia*

MAN
CREATED

THE
FOVRE
AGES.
The Golden
Age.

E   Age

Senecta aderat ; semper vere pedibus & manibus similes.
Moriebantur autem eeu somno dediti.
Hesiod. in Theog.

Age was no cumber; armes like vigor keep,
Feet equall speed: Death was as soft as sleep.

Then was there neither Master nor Servant: names meerely brought in by ambition and injury. Vnforced Nature gave sufficient to all; who securely possest her undivided bountie. A rich condition wherein no man was poore: Avarice after introducing indigency: who by coveting a proprietie, alienated all; and lost what it had, by seeking to inlarge it. But this happy estate abounding with all felicities, assuredly represented that which man injoyed in his innocency: under the raigne of Saturne, more truly of Adam, whereo the Sabbaticall yeare among the Jews was a memoriall: wherein they neither sowed their fields nor had a proprietie in the fruits of the Earth, which she voluntarily afforded. Saturne is fained to be the sonne of Cœlus, or Heaven, and Cybel, which is the Earth: so Adam had God to his Father, and the Earth, whereof he was made, to his Mother. Saturne was the first that invented tillage, the first that ever raigned; and so was Adam: Saturne was throwne out of Heaven, and Adam out of Paradise: Saturne is said to devoure his owne children, and Adam over-threw his whole posteritie: (perhaps the occasion of their sacrificing their children to Saturne or Moloch; for both were the same, as is apparant by their Idols and Ceremonies) Saturne hid himselfe from Jove, and Adam from the presence of Jehovah; Saturne being an Hebrew word which signifies to lie hid. But the actions of the first is referred to the latter Saturne (the Poets usually attributing the deeds of many unto one, and drawing them to their owne countrey-men) who was deposed by Jupiter his sonne, and driven out of Creete into Italy: said to be thrown into Hell, in that the West part of the world was called the Inferior, or Infernall, and under the Dominion of Pluto. But Astronomically, in that Saturne is the highest of the Planets; Tartarus signifying as well the heighth of Heaven, as the depth of Hell: nor can his motion be discerned; so slow, as seeming to stand still; and therefore faigned to be bound in fetters.

The Silver Age.

As the Westerne parts of the world were called the Inferior; so were the Easterne Heaven, or the Superior, being under the command of Jupiter.

Ille malum viris serpentibus addidit atris,
Prædarisq; lupos jussit,pontúmq; moveri.
Virg. Georg.

He poyson first to speckled Serpents gave:
Taught Wolves to prey, and made the Ocean rave.

And what was this but his connivency at wicked and licentious people, of whom he was glad to make use in the expulsion of his Father? Rebellion being alwaies accompanied by libertie and out-rage: when nothing can better resemble those golden times, then a free Common-wealth, ordered and maintained by well instituted lawes. But the silver Age is to be referred to the first Jupiter: which perhaps was Cain: A tiller of the Earth, the first that ever sacrificed, a shedder of bloud, a builder of Cities, the second that ever raigned, the husband of his sister, whose sonnes were the authors of various inventions, Tubal-Cain being Vulcan, Jabel Apollo, and Naamah Venus. Idolatry first began in his family; and finally he had his Sepulchre in the East: all which agree with the former. The Poets, saith Lactantius, did write the truth, though they writ it disguisedly. In his time the people first fell from the worship of God, and through feare or flattery worshipped their King: envy, malice, and oppression (the poison of Serpents, and rapacitie of Wolves) then entred the world, by his persecution of the good, and giving power to the evill: Warre and Avarice supplying the roome of exiled Religion. Thus infringing their former concord, and happy communitie; they began to circumvent, betray, and by blood-shed to purchase a misnamed glory.

The Brasen Age.

The Iron Age.

The Brasen Age succeeded the Silver: for man grew not instantly superlative wicked, but degenerated by degrees, till imboldned by custome, through his insolencie and out-rage, he affrighted Astræa or Iustice from the earth: (perhaps alluding to the righteous Henocks miraculous and early assumption) producing this Iron Age, which is here so accurately described by our Poet; and withall those miseries which pursue it.

Luctus & ultrices posuere cubilia curæ,
Pallentésq; habitant morbi, tristísq; senectus,
Et metus, & malesuada fames, & turpis egestas,
Terribiles visu formæ lethúmq; labórq;.
Virg. Æn. 1. 6.
But surely we slander this in calling it the Iron:
Aurea jam verè sunt sæcula,plurimus auro
Venit Honos, auro conciliatur amor.
Ovid. Am.

Dejected Griefe, revengefull Cares, the rage
Of pale Diseases, melancholy Age,
Base Beggery, ill-tempting Famine, Feare,
Toyle, Death, and Furies, ever wander there.

Now is the true styl'd Golden Age: for Gold
Honour is bought, and love it selfe is sold.

Nay,

Nay, of power to corrupt as many Magistrates as it hath made. We are honest for reward, and again dishonest for a greater.

It is said that the Earth, inraged with Jupiter for the slaughter of the Titans, in revenge produced Giants of a vast proportion: yet rather so called of their monstrous Mindes. For the statures of Men are now as heretofore: as appeares by the embalmed bodies of the Egyptians; and by the ancient Sepulchres in Judea. And as the former Ages have produced some of a prodigious Height, so also have the latter. Scaliger saw a Man at Millan, who hardly could lie on two beds, one set at the foot of another: and Goropeus, a Woman in the Netherlands, who exceeded ten feet. The Giant of Burdeux (of the Guard to Francis the first) was so tall, that a man of indifferent stature might have gone betweene his legges without stooping: Nor is there any mentioned in ancient History that exceeded sixe or seven cubits. The first Giants that we read off were begot by the sonnes of God on the daughters of Men: that is, by the sonnes of Seth on the off-spring of Cain. The name signifies to fall, in regard of their defection and apostasie from God and religion: tearmed in the Scriptures men of might and renowne, of their strength, and strenuous performancies: exceeding in pride and crueltie, and therefore said to rebell against Jove the counterfeit Jehovah. Such was the Giant Nimrod after the Flood; the ring-leader of those who built the Tower of Babel, whose height was intended to have reacht unto heaven, and to have prevented God in his future judgements. And what was that but the throwing of mountaine upon mountaine, to scale even heaven it selfe, and warre with the Gods? The one confounded with lightning, and the other by the confusion of languages. But those first are here most properly intended: who also are taken for too potent subjects, or the tumultuary vulgar; rebelling against their Princes, called Gods, as his substitutes: who by their disloyaltie and insolencies violate all lawes both of God and man; and profane whatsoever is sacred. The Giants were the sonnes of the Earth (for so they called of old the ignorant, and earthly minded: as those the sonnes of heaven, who were admired for their vertues) said to be of a huge proportion; in that commonly such are prone to intemperance, wrath, and injustice; seldome yeelding unto reason, but are carried with the swinge of their lusts and affections: to have many hands, in regard of their strength and atchievements, the feet of Dragons, for their wicked waies and divelish designes, supporting Rebellion, tyranny and impietie. Pherecydes the Syrian writes how the Divels were thrown out of heaven by Jupiter (this fall of the Giants perhaps an allusion to that of the Angels) the chiefe called Ophioneus, which signifies Serpentine: having after made use of that creature to poyson Eve with a false ambition. This battell is fained to have beene fought in Thessaly (the Poets still laying their Scenes in Greece, in which are the here mentioned mountaines of Pelion, Ossa, and Olympus) for the inhumanitie of those people, and their contempt of the Gods; and to be overwhelmed by them, for their flaming and sulphurous exhalations. Whereupon that naturall sense is given to this fable; how the Giants are those windes that struggle in the cavernes of the Earth; which not finding a way inforce it: vomiting fire, and casting up stones against heaven or Jupiter. The Earth, their mother, of their blood is here said to have renewed their race: in that succeeded by as cruell and wicked an off-spring: It is recorded that Faustina the wife of Marcus Aurelius, being desperately in love with a Fencer, was cured by the advice of the Mathematicians with a portion of his blood: who conceiving soone after, was delivered of Commodus; rather to be styled a Fencer then a Prince; whose only delight was in blood and murder. Plutarch writes that the ancient Kings of Egypt would drinke no wine untill the reigne of Psammetichus, nor offer it to the Gods: because they held the Vine to spring from the bloud of the Gyants that warred against them; whose juyce made those, who overlargely tasted it, like insolent and out-ragious. To prevent such disorders in his Ianisaries, the Grand Seigniour not seldome commands all the Wine in Constantinople to be staved: perhaps the politique intent of Mahomets prohibition. They attribute the Lightning unto Jupiter; not onely in that faigned to be the King of the Gods; but because he is the middle Planet betweene Saturne and Mars, participating of the cold of the one, and heate of the other: thunder and lightning proceeding from the conflict of those contrary qualities.

Jupiter now intending the destruction of Man-kinde for their sinnes, here calleth a Councell: to informe us how all humane affaires are governed by the certaine decree and providence of God; not by chance or Fortune, as the Tragedian complaineth.

O why shouldst thou that rul'st the sky,
And mov'd those Orbs so orderly,
Th' affairs of men so much neglect?
Nor raise the good, nor bad deject?

———— sed cur idem;
Qui tanta regis, sub quo vasti
Pondera mundi librata sui
Ducunt orbes; hominum nimium
Securus ades? non solicitus
Prodesse bonis, nocuisse malis.

The War Of The Gyants.

The Parliament Of The Gods.

Res humanas ordine nulla
Fortuna regit, spargitque manu
Munera caca, peiora fovens.
Vincit sanctos dita libido.
Fraus sublimi regnat in aula.
Tradere turpi fasces populus
Gaudet; eosdem colit, atque odit.
Tristis virtus perversa tulit
Præmia recti. Castos sequitur
Mala paupertas: vitioque potens
Regnat adulter.

O vane pudor, falsumque decus!
Sen. in Hipp.

No, Fortune without order guides
What ever mortall man betides:
Her bountie her blind hands disburse
At randome; favouring the worse.
Dire lust foil'd Chastitie profanes;
And fraud in Courts of Princes raignes.
Popular suffrages elate
Base men, who honour whom they hate.
Sad vertue the perverse reward
Receives of Truth: want presseth hard
On chaster mindes: th' Adulterer high
In vice commands. Vaine modesty!
Deceitfull excellence!

A mystery which David *could not conceive, till he had entred the Sanctuary. But by this we are admonished, that nothing in a Common-wealth is to be decreed unadvisedly or rashly; when* Jupiter*, who had all in his power, would determine of nothing of moment without the counsell and consent of the Gods: how much more men, who have so small a portion of that divine wisdome?* Iupiter*, that is a King, may of himselfe, saith* Seneca*, be beneficient, but not punish but by advice and approbation.*

The Milky way.

The Milky way which the Gods doe tread to this celestiall Senate, is the only reall and visible Circle in the Heavens. The poeticall and superstitious conceptions thereof, interwoven with the naturall cause, are thus expressed by Manilius.

Nec mihi celanda est fama vulgata vetustas
Mollior, è niveo lactis fluxisse liquorem.
Pectore regina divum, cælumque colore
Infecisse suo, quapropter lacteus orbis
Dicitur, & nomen causa descendit ab ista.
An major densa stellarum turba corona
Contexit flammas, & crasso lumine candet
Et fulgore nitet collato clarior orbis.
An fortes animæ, dignataque nomina cælo
Corporibus resoluta suis, terraque remissa
Huc migrant ex orbe, suumq; habitantia
* cælum*
Æthereos vivunt. animos mundosque fruuntur. In Astron.

Nor will we hide what ancient Fame profest:
How milke which gusht from Iuno's whiter brest
In heaven that splendent path and circle drew;
From whence the name, as erst the colour grew.
Or troops of unseene starres there joyne their light;
And with united splendor shine more bright.
Or Soules of Heroes, from their bodies freed,
Exchanging Earth for Heaven, (their vertues meed)
Shine in that Orbe, their proper place of rest;
And live ætheriall lives, of heaven possest.

This Parliament consists of Jupiter*, the King; of the Greater Gods, the Nobles; and of the inferiour, the Commons. Of the upper House there are sixe Gods, and as many Goddesses:* Jupiter, Neptune, Apollo, Mars, Vulcan, Mercury, *(the speaker)* Juno, Vesta, Minerva, Ceres, Diana, *and* Venus: *of the Lower, such whom the old world deified for their vertues. Thus by involving they abolished the truth, through the suggestion of the Divell, to make a confusion, and induce unto error: these multitude of Gods, with their regall* Jove*, so fained of the true* Jehovah*, the only Lord and Father of all, and of those cælestiall Spirits, his ministring Angels: as the other of his blessed Saints which in their puritie retaine his similitude. Neverthelesse by this example we may conclude with* Plato*, that the Monarchicall government is of all the best: the type of God, and desigured in the Fabrick of mans Body: thus preferred by* Homers Ulysses.

Non quidem ullo pacto omnes regnabimus.
Non bonum est multorum dominatus; unus
* dominus esto.*
Vnus Rex. Iliad. l. 2.

All cannot rule; for many Rulers bring
Confusion: let there be one Lord, one King.

In Jupiters *Oration our Poet describes the office of a good Prince in punishing offenders: wherein lenitie is to be preferred before severitie; that all remedies are first to be applyed ere inforced to the latter: and then to imitate the beginning of* Nero*, who wisht he had never known how to write, when he signed to the death of a* Romane*: or* Bias*, who alwaies wept when he pronounced that sentence. But if the disease grow uncurable, then are the corrupted members to be cut off, least they infect the whole body. A precept to be practised, as given by* Jove *in the cælestiall Assembly. Gods protection of the innocent, is here expressed in* Jupiters *care of the Semi-Gods; whom* Regius *conceives to be the Heroes: others cælestiall Spirits under humane figures, and procreated for the benefit of Man. But of these hereafter.*

Jove

Jove *illustrates the impiety of the world by the example of* Lycaon ; *who thus beginnes his relation.*

> The time's accus'd, and as I hope beli'd ;
> To try, I downe from steepe *Olympus* slide.

which Pontanus *the Iesuit takes to be derived from the eighteenth Chapter of* Genesis. *As* Vives *these following,*

> (A God transform'd like one of humane birth,
> I wandred through the many-peopled Earth ;)

From the bookes of the Sibyls ; *which can concerne no other then* Christ, *as by him alleadged.* Thus many Poeticall fables (saith *Tertullian*) have taken their originall from the sacred Scriptures: and what we write is not beleeved, because the same is written by the Poets. *This* Lycaon *was King of* Arcadia, *a cruell and inhumane Prince : who feasted the* Cretan Jupiter (*then with him on an embassy*) *with the flesh of a stranger. Which discovered, he overthrew the table ; and rushing into the streets, so incensed the Citizens, that they betooke them to their weapons, and by his conduct drove him out of the City : who living like an out-law in the woods, committing daily rapines and robberies, was therefore said, together with his sonnes, to have beene changed into Wolves : and* Jove *for expelling him was called* Lycæus. *Others say how he was the first that violated truces, and sacrificed his hostages to* Jupiter: *by his treachery drawing many into his power to their utter destruction: and therefore alluding to his name, which signifies a* Wolfe, *they fained him to be one. Yet* Evanthes, *no contemptible author, reports how the* Arcadians *accustomed to chuse a man out of the family of* Antæus; *who brought to a certaine lake, and forced to swim over, became forthwith a* Wolfe, *for nine years abiding with other wolves in the deserts. In which space if he had tasted no mans flesh, returning to the lake; and swimming back he recovered his forme.* It is wonderfull, *saith* Pliny, to consider how farre the Græcian credulity will extend: no lie so impudent that wanteth a witnesse. *But would he not retract his censure, were he now alive, and saw what is so ordinarily said to be practised by the witches of* Germany, *who take and forsake the shapes of wolves at their pleasure, and for which they are daily executed ? As we to magicall deceptions ; so he, a* Naturalist, *perhaps would ascribe it to that melancholy disease, or rather madnesse, of which the infected are called* Lycanthropi, *in that they imitate wolves, and think themselves such, leaping out of their beds in the night, and lurking about the sepulchers by day, with pale lookes, hollow eyes, thirsty tongues, and exulcerated bodies. But this fable of* Lycaon *was devised to deterre from impiety, treachery, and inhospitality ; as also to excite to the contrary vertues : since the Gods, though disguised, are alwaies present ; punishing, and rewarding, according to our actions. In this, as in the rest, our Poet proportions the transformation to the quality of the transformed.*

> A wolfe not much from his first forme estrang'd :
> So hoary hair'd, his lookes so full of rape ;
> So fiery-ey'd, so terrible his shape.

The Gods in this Councell are chiefly solicitous about the preservation of the divine worship : to informe how Religion *should be the chiefe and first care in all consultations : the World being made for man, and man for Gods service, as the divine Philosopher could instruct us.*

Jupiter *intending to burne the Earth, is restrained by that remembred destiny, how not onely Earth, but Heaven it selfe, should one day by fire be consumed. This is held to be but once revealed in the Scriptures, and that by* S[t]. Peter ; *how came it then to the knowledge of* Ovid, *who was dead before that Epistle was written ? It may be out of the Prophecies of the* Sibyls, *as in this.*

> These signes the Worlds combustion shall fore-run:
> Armes clashing, trumpets, from the rising Sunne
> Horrible fragors, heard by all : this frame
> Of Nature then shall feede the greedy flame.
> Men, Cities, Floods, and Seas, by rav'nous lust
> Of fire devour'd, all shall resolve to dust.

Igni flagrabit Mundus, signumq; dabunt hæc :
Enses atq; tubæ simul, & sole exoriente
Terribilem sonitum, mugituq; audiat omnis
Mundus, & exaret terram omnem torridus
ignis.
Hinc genus humanum postquam delerit, & omnes
Vrbes & fluvios exussent, atq; profundum,
Omnia sient hæc mixtus fuligine pulvis.
Orac : l. 4.

From hence perhaps the ancient Philosophers *derived their opinions, as* Seneca *a latter:* The stars shall encounter one another, and whatsoever now shines so orderly shall burne in one fire. *Who presume to ascribe it to a naturall cause : that the Sunne and the Starres, being fed by watery vapours,*

shall

shall set the world on a conflagration as soone as that nourishment is exhausted: when as the Starres are not fiery in their proper nature, and no vapours ascend above the middle Region of the Aire. Besides what sustenance can they receive from the humiditie of the Earth, when the least fixed starre which is observed is eighteene, and the Sunne one hundred sixty and seaventimes bigger then the Earth it selfe. But the immediate hand of God shall effect it, as it did this deluge; although this also the Naturalists impute to watery constellations.

DEUCALIONS FLOOD. The Sinnes of men drew on (in which our Poet concurres with Moses) the generall Deluge, although he transferre it to Deucalions, wherein most of Greece was surrounded; which hapned seaven hundred and fourescore yeares after the other: yet in this he describeth the former, as appeares by many particulars: which may serve to reconcile his Chronology, for many of these following stories were before the daies of Deucalion. There is no nation so barbarous, no not the salvage Virginians, but have some notion of so great a ruine. The naturall causes he alleadgeth of these accumulated waters. The North windes are shut up, the South set at liberty; the clouds descend in showres, which are

The Raine-bow. nourished by the Raine-bow: because the raine is increased by that dissolving vapour wherein it appeareth: so formed and painted by the reflected raies of the opposite Sun, on a dropping, darke, and hollow clowd. The upper-most colour in crimson, made by the stronger refraction on the darker part thereof; for light upon blacke produceth a red: the next is greene, proceeding from a feebler, on a part more remote and watery: the lowest is blew, created by the weakest rayes; so that the sight can hardly apprehend the reflected splendor, which therefore appeares more darke and obscure. The conjunction of these colours augment their diversitie, as red and greene ingender a yellow: yet all are onely in apparance, like those which are seene in a Mirror. To confirme what hath beene alleadged by a knowne experiment; if with a scoope, against the setting Sunne, you cast water circularly into the aire, a rainebow will appeare therein. This is called Iris, the daughter of Thaumas, or Wonder; Iris imports a message, because it presageth faire or foule weather, as it followeth the contrary; and therefore the messenger of Juno, who is taken for the aire, where clouds are ingendred. Moreover Neptune lifts up his floods, the commanded Rivers unlock their Fountaines; he strikes the Earth with his Trident, which is said to shake, in that the land which borders on the Sea is most subject unto Earthquakes; whose breaches give new ascents to subterren waters, or let in those of the Ocean. Some would fetch water from above the firmament to make enough for this Deluge (though that perhaps be meant by the clouds) lest God should be forced to a new creation after his Sabbath. And although the dissolution of the snow which perpetually covers the mountaines, especially of that huge accumulation from the beginning of the World beyond the Artick; and Antartick Circles; the rarifying of the frozen and universall Ocean (like a pot boyling over) as we see at full floods in a smaller proportion; the waters in the hollowes of the Earth, squiezed as out of a spunge, and supplied with aire, with those former concomitancies, might prove abundantly sufficient; yet is it safer to admire, then

Neptunes Trident. subject his miracles unto naturall causes. They attribute a Trident (a lance with three forkes) unto Neptune: which signifies the third site (according to Plutarch) of the Element of water, below the sky and the aire; whereupon the Sea was called Amphitrite, and the petty Sea-gods Tritons, or of the three parts of the World (the fourth then unknowne) imbraced by the Ocean: or of his triple power in enraging, asswaging, and bounding the surges. But Neptune was a mortall (as the rest of the Gods) to whom his brother Jupiter gave the Empire of the sea, with the Ilands, and Maritime cities: as was registred on a Pillar of gold in the Temple of Jupiter Triphylius.

DEUCALION AND PYRRHA. Deucalion and his wife Pyrrha, the Daughter of his brother Epimetheus, alone escaped (the reward of their piety) this generall destruction: he having made an Arke by the advice of his father Prometheus, in which he floated on the waters. Lucian reports that not onely they and their children entred the same, but all the creatures which the Earth sustained: comming unto him by paires, and deposing their naturall discord by the dispensation of Jupiter: and Plutarch, that he let forth a Dove, which returning oft, at length came no more: by which he knew that she had found footing: alluding all to the history of Noah: he is said to have beene King of Thessaly, the first founder of Cities, and erecter of Temples: in whose daies those parts abounded with men, as they with flagitious offences. For multitudes of people procure a scarcitie of all things, and necessity makes men more crafty, dishonest, and irregular. For these crimes, in those times (as our Poet here intimates) there fell such abundance of raine as drowned almost all Greece; Deucalion and Pyrrha saving themselves on the top of Larnassus, so called of their covered boate, and after Parnassus, a mountaine of Phocis:

Hesperio tantum, quantum semotus Eoo
Cardine, Parnassus gemino petit æthera
collo.

    From East and West alike removed lies
    Parnassus; whose two tops aspire the skies:

                          To

To *Phœbus* and *Lyæus* confecrate.
To both the *Theban Bacchæ* celebrate
The *Delphicke* third yeares-feaft. This did divide
Swoln Seas from Stars; the whole World drown'd befide.

Mons Phœbo, Bromioque, facer : cui nomine
mifto
Delphica Thebanæ referunt trieterica Bac-
chæ:
Hoc folum fluctu terras mergente cacumen
Eminuit, pontoque fuit difcrimen, & aftris.
Lucan. l. 5.

To apply the fable yet more to the hiftory. Both Noah *and* Deucalion *are celebrated for their
Iuftice and Religion* : Noah *was commanded to build an Arke by God* ; *and* Deucalion *advifed
thereunto by* Prometheus, *which is, the divine providence : both faved for their vertue, the
one on Mount* Ararat, *and the other on* Parnaffus, *while the vitious are fwallowed by their owne
impieties.*

Now Jupiter *diffipateth the clouds, fets the North-winde at libertie, and fhewes the Earth unto
Heaven* : Neptune *fuppreffeth the Seas with his* Trident, *and commands his trumpeter* Triton *to
found a retreat to the waters* ; *who is thus defcribed by* Virgil :

Whom mighty *Triton* beares, whofe fhells lowd blaft
Blew floods affright , his figure to the waft
Prefents a man, the reft a fifh; before
His monftrous breaft the foaming furges roare ?

Hunc vehit immanis Triton *& cærula con-*
châ
Exterrens freta, cui laterum tenus hifpida nâti
Frons hominem præfert, in pifcem definit al-
vus.
Spumea femifero fub pectore murmurat unda.
Æn. l. 10.

*Others defcribe him, perhaps more exactly, to have haire like water-parfely, a body covered
with fmall and hard fcale, gilles a little under the eares, the noftrills of a man, a wide mouth, with
Panthers teeth : blew eyes, hands, fingers, and nailes, like the fhell of a fifh, finnes under the breaft
like a Dolphin.* Pliny *writes how an* Embaffador *was fent of purpofe from the* Oliffiponenfi *unto*
Tiberius Cæfar *to tell him of a* Triton, *feene and heard in a certaine cave, winding a fhell, and in
fuch a forme as they are commonly painted. But I cannot omit what is written by* Alexander ab A-
lexandro, *who lived in the laft century, how he heard one* Draconet Boniface of Naples, *a foul-
dier of much experience, report in an honorable affembly, that in the wars of* Spaine, *he faw a fea
Monfter with the face and body like a man, but below the belly like a fifh, brought thither from the fartheft fhores of* Mauritania. *It had an old countenance ; the haire and beard rough and fhaggy, blew of
colour, and high of ftature, with finnes betweene the arms and the body. Thefe were held for Gods of the
Sea, and propitious to failers : Ignorance producing admiration, and admiration fuperftition. Yet
perhaps they erre not who conceived them to be onely Divells, affuming that forme, to nourifh a falfe
devotion.*

The defolate Earth now emergent, diftreffed Deucalion *and* Pyrrha, *purging themfelves with the
holy water of* Cephifus (*an ancient cuftome among the* Pagans) *repaire to the temple of* Themis ;
*with proftrated bodies and humble foules prefenting their prayers to the Goddeffe. Prayers inforce Cœ-
leftiall pitty, and pitty reliefe ; afforded in this anfwer.*

Goe from my Temple ; both your faces hide :
Let garments, all unbraced, loofely flow ;
And your great Parents bones behinde you throw.

*The Earth interpreted for our common mother, and the ftones for her bones, diffolved the ambigui-
tie of the Oracle. Such was that of* Apollo *to* Sextus *and* Aruns *the fonnes of* Tarquin, Junius Brutus *then prefent* : *Which of you firft kiffeth his Mother, fhall have the foveraign command of*
Rome. *The brethren caft lots who firft fhould falute her after their returne : but* Brutus, *a fuppofed
idiot, faining to ftumble, fell flat on the Earth and kiffed it : lighting on a true fenfe, as appeared by
the fequell. Like unto this was* Cæfars *dreame the night before he paffed over* Rubicon, *how he car-
nally knew his mother, which fignified his countrey. The fame is reported of our* Henry *the fourth
when he landed at* Ravenfpurge ; *both of them obtaining the Empire of either. As* Prometheus
before made men of Clay ; *fo now* Deucalion *his fonne, and* Pyrrha *his neece, by cafting of ftones behinde them : both including one morall ; that of falvage men they made civill, and imbewed their
mindes with cæleftiall knowledge : and that by the advice of* Themis, *which is the inbred law and in-
ftinct of nature. The congruity of the names gave birth perhaps to the fable : for* λᾶας *fignifieth a
ftone, and* λᾱός, *the common people. Or in that they drew the rude and ftone-like people in to the plains
from the rocks and caves of the mountaines firft after the Deluge, and gathered them into Cities. God
is faid in the Gofpell to be able of ftones to raife up children unto* Abraham : *the fenfe not unlike,
though*

Man-kinde
from
ftones.

209

though diviner ; meaning the ingrafting of the Gentiles into his faith, hardned in sinne through igno-
rance and custome. So the giving us hearts of flesh insteed of those of stone, *is meant by our*
our conversion. Themis *gave Oracles at the foot of* Parnassus, *long before* Apollo *gave any at* Delphos. *She is said to be the daughter of* Cœlus *and* Cybele, *commanding men onely to aske what
was just and lawfull, her selfe the same ; and her name signifying as much.* So *as those who forswore
themselves by the name of* Themis, *were held to violate all lawes both divine and humane ; and capi-
tally to sinne against either.*

PYTHON.

There was need of divine advice for the restoring of man : Heat and Moisture, *the parents of Generation, are fained here to have produced the rest : among which* Python, *a prodigious serpent,
whose bulke tooke up so much of the mountaine.* Although *this be allegoricall, yet read we of so
huge a Serpent by* Bograda *in* Africa, *that it deprived the* Romane army, *under* Attilius Regu-
lus, *of the use of the River, devouring many of his souldiers, and crushing many to death with his imbracements : whose body no dart nor weapon could penetrate : more terrible to the Legions and Co-
horts, then warre or* Carthage: *destroyed at last with milstones, and pieces of rocks, throwne out of
engines ; the stench infecting both the aire and armie. His skin was a hundred and twenty foote long.
But the sence of this fable is meerely* Physicall : *for* Python, *born after the Deluge of the humid Earth,
is that great exhalation which rose from the late drowned World, untill it was dissipated by the fervor
of the Sunne or* Apollo.

Tum tellus gravis imbre & adhuc stagnanti-
bus undis,
Humida, anhela,vagos tollebat ad æthera tor-
tus,
Involvent cœlum nube, & caligine opacau :
Hinc ille immanis Python.——*Pont. Met.*

The Earth then soakt in showres, yet hardly dry,
Threw up thicke clouds which darkned all the sky:
This was that *Python.*

*The word signifies putrefaction : and because the Sunne consumes the putrefaction of the Earth,
his beames darting from his orbe like arrowes ; with his arrowes he is said to have killed* Python.
So serpentine Errour by the light of truth is confounded. The Spirit which inspired the Priests of
Apollo *was called* Pytho, *as they themselves* Pythonists. *But, who will beleeve that the* Pythian
games had their originall from this fable? Strabo *relates that* Python *was a wicked and bloudy
theife, who infested all those parts with his outrages, and therefore was called* Draco. *He slaine by A-
pollo, the* Delphians *in gratitude for their recovered liberty, did institute those Games to his honour. During their fight the standers-by cryed* Io Pæan, *that is, shoote* Apollo: *which after grew a
customary acclamation in victories.* So the Græcians *sung the* Pæan (*a Hymne to* Apollo) *when
they went to the battell ; as we reade in* Thucydides *and* Xenophon. *These games were of all other
the most ancient : celebrated in the beginning of the spring, not onely by Greece, but by all the inhabitants of the* Cyclades.

DAPHNE.

Apollo, *elated with his victory, despiseth* Cupid: *yet escapes not his vengeance. He is here called a boy, by reason of the diversitie of affections which raigne in Lovers ; apt to beleeve, easily deceived, and refractary to reason : or that love is a childe in the heart of a lover, ever growing, and never waxing old ; though not still in apparance, yet alwaies in efficacie. For love is truely love no
longer then it increaseth : a deadly symptome is his standing at a stay ; and his first declination, a
downefall. He is said to be armed with fire, in that he inflames the heart with ardent desires : and as
fire is of all elements the most noble and active, even so is love of all the affections : to have wings in
regard of the inconstancy of love ; or of his swift desires and impatiency of delay : or rather of a lovers
celerity and industry in serving and deserving.* Cupid *drawes out of his quiver two arrowes of contrary effects : the one tipt with gold, the metall of the Sunne, who heats our blouds and fils with alacritie : the other with lead, belonging to* Saturne, *cold and melancholy : alacritie procures, and melancholy (not that which proceeds from extremity of heate, which hath a contrary operation) extin-
guishes desires.*

Mens erit apta capi tum, cum latissima
rerum,
Vt seges in pingui luxuriabit humo.
Pectora dum gaudent, nec sunt astricta do-
lore,
Ipsa patent : blanda tum subit arte Venus.
Tum cum tristis erat, defensa est Ilion armis:
Militibus gravidum læta recepit equum.
Ovid. in Art.

That mind is soonest caught which springs with mirth:
Like corne which riots on the lusty earth.
The heart that's free from sorrow, open lies
To *Venus* arts, and flattering loves surprise.
Sad *Ilium* repell'd the *Græcian* force:
But full of joy, receiv'd the fatall Horse.

Gold

Gold also is the symbole of Plenty, which nourisheth love ; and lead of Poverty, which starves it. Pliny also writes that a plate of lead applied to the breast suppresseth unchaste dreames. To love he attributes a double power of disdaine and affection, and Horace

> Who often unlike mindes and formes provokes
> To draw unequally in hated yokes,
> With cruell Mirth.

——— *cui placet impares Formas atque animos sub juga ahenea Sævo mittere cum joco.* Carm. l. 1.

But distinguished in person in that painted table at Elis. *Where the one (*Anteros*, or the love of vertue) endeavours to bereave the other of his Palme : by his name proclaiming defiance. Of whom perhaps our Poet in his Remedy :*

> Neere Port *Collina,* for devotion fam'd
> A temple stands, of lofty *Erix* nam'd :
> This shrines *Lethæan* love, who cures desires
> And powres cold water on his scorching fires.

Est prope Collinam *templum venerabile portam,* Imposuit templo nomina celsus Erix. *Est illic lethæus amor, qui pectora sanat,* Inque suas gelidam lampadas addit aquam. Ovid.de Rem. Amor.

Bow and arrowes are given to Cupid ; *in that beauty wounds a farre off ; and as an arrow the body, so peirceth it the heart through the eye : or of the wonderfull celerity of the minde, transfixing it selfe, and profoundly penetrating.* Daphne *affects* Diana, *which is chastitie ; preserved by solitarinesse, labour, and neglect of curiositie :* Apollo Daphne ; *drawne on with a barren hope. Lovers are great boasters. He brags of his temples, his parentage, his art of divination, (attributed, in that those, in whose nativitie that Planet predominates, are of the greatest foreknowledge : or that, as the eye of the World, he beholds things present, past, and to come) of his invention of musicke, which solaceth the minde, and removes our manifold cares with a sweete oblivion. The first instruments had but seven strings, in reference to the seven Planets : and because the Sunne is placed in the midst as Lord of the rest, whose motions (according to* Pythagoras) *doe make an incredible harmony, he therefore is said to have invented Musicke. As likewise Physick (his name is derived by* Festus *importing as much as to free and preserve from evill) in that the Sunne is so powerfull in producing Physicall simples, and to our bodies so salubrious. Yet heare we this great Physitian.*

> Ay me ! that hearbs can love no cure afford !
> That arts, relieving all, should faile their Lord !

Daphne, almost overtaken, invokes the deities of the River *and* Earth, *to devoure or transforme that beautifull forme which had so much indangered her : who assistant to distressed vertue, convert her into a laurell ; (expressed in her name) the image of her beauty and chastitie : innobled by her lover with addition of honours. This tree is consecrated to* Apollo, *or the* Sunne, *as agreeing with his nature ; being hot and dry, of great efficacy as well in divination as Physicke ; his Prophets crowning themselves with laurell, and eating of the berries. Nor wants it authoritie that the leaves thereof laid under the pillow will procure true dreames. The two Laurels here mentioned which grew before the Palace of* Augustus, *with an* Oake *betweene them, declare that the safety of a Prince is guarded by Vertue and felicitie : the one being the ensigne of Victory, and the other of a preserved Citizen. The originall of these there planted is thus related by* Suetonius, *and others : As* Livia *immediately after her marriage with* Augustus, *travelled to a Villa of hers in the* Veientine *territory, an Eagle soaring over her head, let fall a white hen into her lap, with a branch of laurell in her bill. Taken with the omen, she caused the one to be carefully kept, and the other to be planted. From the hen proceeded an infinite sort of the same colour ; in so much as that very house was diverse ages after called* Ad Gallinas: *and from the laurell a goodly row of bay trees, whereof the* Cæsars *made their garlands when they rode in triumph, and bare in their hands the branches : these, the solemnity ended, they stuck in the Earth by the rest of the trees, which augmented their number. But what was miraculous, when any one of them died, the trees which he had planted perished with him : and at the death of* Nero *(the last of the* Cæsars) *the whole grove withered. The Laurell, by reason of her native heate, is ever young and flourishing : here fained such by the gift of* Apollo, *in imitation of his eternall youth, and unshorne tresses : attributed to the* Sunne, *in that rising and setting he is ever the same, his faire haire no other then his long and beautifull beames. It was the custome of the* Græcian *youth not to cut their haire untill the downe appeared on their chinnes, and then to offer it at* Delphos *to* Apollo.

F   Daphne

Daphne is changed into a never-withering tree, to shew what immortall honour a virgin obtaines by preserving her chastitie. She is said to be the daughter of Peneus, *because the bankes of that river abound with laurel; to be beloved of* Apollo, *in that the fairest grew about his Temple of* Delphos; *to fly his pursuit, in that they affect the shadow; and to repell the fire of lust, in not being scorched by the Sun nor Lightning.*

10   *The neighbour and forraine Rivers now visite old* Peneus, *not knowing whether to condole or congratulate, for the losse, or noble transformation of his daughter. Onely* Inachus *was absent, lamenting the misse of his* Iö; *pursued, and comprest in a cloud by* Jupiter, *called the Thunderer, the ruler of the World, the giver of all good; yet introduced for an adulterer, a ravisher of virgins, and in himselfe a receiver of all evil. This* Inachus, *the father of* Iö, *was the first that ever reigned in* Argos, *accidentally drowned in* Carmanor, *which after was called by his name; and* Iö *faigned to be the daughter of that River.* Palæphatus *in his treatise of the convincing of fables, relating as incredible things, and more defacing the truth by professing it, (when fiction, that spar of Gold, is the art; and truth well counterfeited, the honour of the Poet) reports how* Iö, *the Priest of* Juno, *being got with childe, and fearing the fury of her father* Inachus, *fled out of the city: whereupon it was fained by the* Argives *that the mad Cow was broke loose, and delivered in* Egypt. *But* Herodotus, *how the* Phænician *Merchants sailing into* Greece, *and the women of* Argos *(among whom was* Iö*) coming a board to see their commodities, were surprized by them, and carried thither. Which more agreeth with the truth, since the ship that brought her was celebrated by the* Egyptians *in their festivalls.* Diodorus *writes how being the most beautifull woman of that age, she was married by* Osiris; *he called* Jupiter, *and she* Isis; *from whence the fable of* Jupiters *love unto* Iö *was derived. She teaching the* Egyptians *husbandry and many usefull knowledges, was after deified by them, and honoured with Temples and Altars. Most certaine it is that they worshipped* Osiris *in the likenesse of an Oxe, (and why not* Isis *in the forme of a Cow?) expressing agriculture (as they did) by the one; and the soile of* Egypt *by the other. Neither doubt I but that the* Israelites, *long sojourning there, brought from thence their superstition of the Golden Calfe; made after two by* Jeroboam, *who also had lived, as an exile in that Countrey. Concerning the naturall sense of this fable;* Iö *is taken for the Earth, the daughter of the River* Inachus, *or water in generall (as the sonne of* Oceanus *and* Tethys:*) in that the Earth a farre off appeares to rise from the Sea.* Jupiter *lay with her in a clowd; the æthereall heate, which is* Jupiter, *drawing vapours from the earth perpetually: fained to be turned into a Cow, for the industry of that creature in cultivating the Earth from whence she receives her fertility.* Jupiter *renders the Cow to approaching* Juno, *the milder temperature of the aire; the extreames of heate and cold being equally hurtfull to production: which she delivers to the custodie of* Argus. Argus *is taken for Heaven, his eyes for the starres, which continually behold the Cow, that is, the Earth, and by the varying of times by his motion procures her fertility. Halfe his hundred eyes are said to watch, while the other halfe slept: so halfe of them shine, the rest obscured by the splendor of the Sunne; here as usually, taken for* Mercury, *because that Planet is almost under his Orbe: thus expressed by* Pontanus.

'Tis said that *Mercury* exchanging name,
Did with his drowsie *Caduceus* tame
Forg'd *Argus* hundred eyes with sleepe, that slept
By halves, while he the snowy Heifer kept.
Argus is Heaven; æthereall fires his eyes,
That wake by turnes; and Starres that set and rise.
These sparkle on the brow of shadie Night:
But when *Apollo* reares his glorious light,
They, vanquisht by so great a splendor, dy;
And buried, in obscure *Olympus* ly.

Quin & Mercurium, mutato nomine dicunt Argum somnifero fictum stravisse Caduceo Insomnem, centumq; oculos & lumina centum
Pandentem & nivea servantem pascua vaccæ.
Argus enim cœlum est: vigilantia lumina flammæ
Æthorea & vario labentia sydera mundo:
Quæ passim multa sub lustru noctis in umbra
Collucent: sed Phœbo mox oriente perempta Torpent luce nova, & candenti lampade victa
Emoriuntur & obscuro conduntur Olympo.
Meteor.

The fable hath also an historicall allusion unto Argus, *that old and prudent* Argive *king, who was slaine by* Mercury, *in hope to succeede him: when banished for that fact by the* Greekes *he fled into* Egypt. *But allegorically: in that skill and industry is more available in husbandry then the influence of the starres. The Cow wandring through many Regions is the propagation of that knowledge: and in that* Egypt *exceeds all other in richnesse, and naturall bounty, there* Iö *is fained to recover her owne figure. Others have wrested this fable to mortality: That* Jupiter, *the minde of man falling from Heaven, and joyning with* Iö, *the body in a clowd is turned into a beast: as forgetfull of his owne originall; and captivated by his vices: when of more maturity in age and judgement,* Mercury *is sent to kill*

Argus,

Argus, *in that Reaſon bridles and ſubdues the exorbitancies of the affections. Then* Juno *lets looſe the* Furies, *the ſtings of the Conſcience.*

> A Hell on Earth : th'afflicted minde diſmaid,
> Full of foule crimes, and of it ſelfe afraid.
> Some ſafely ſin, none ſinne ſecurely beare ;
> But ſuffer ſtill the vengeance which they feare.

Quid pœna præſens, conſcius mentis pavor,
Animuſque culpa plenus, & ſemet timens.
Scelus aliqua tutum, nulla ſecurum tulit.
SentHipp.cætera in Epiſt.106.
Dat pœnas, quiſquis expectat,

This horror begets repentance, repentance reformation, by which he is reſtored to his former beauty, and becomes like the Gods through his ſanctity and integritie.

This fable is interwoven with that of Pan *and* Syrinx, Pan *was the firſt that invented the ſeven-fold Pipe : and for that cauſe is ſaid to have loved* Syrinx, *who when ſhe could not avoid his purſuit, was changed into Reeds by the Nymphs of the River.* Syrinx *ſignifies a reed, here fained the daughter of* Ladon, *in that there they grow in abundance. Of this Pipe, and how firſt found out thus ſingeth* Lucretius.

> By murmuring of winde-ſhaken reeds, rude ſwaines
> Learnt firſt of all to blow on hollow canes.
> Then pipes of pieces fram'd; whence muſick ſprung ;
> Playd on by quavering fingers as they ſung :
> Devis'd in ſhades and plaines, where ſhepheards graze
> Their bleating flocks, with leaſure-crowned laies.

Et Zephyri cava per calamorum ſibila primum
Agreſteis docuere canas inflare cicutas.
Inde minutatim dulces didicere querelas;
Tibia quas fundit digitu pulſata canentum,
Avia per nemora, ad ſylvas, ſaltuſque reperta,
Per loca paſtorum deſerta, atque otia dia,
Luce.l.5.

This was the Shepheard Pan ; *who for the ſame was eſteemed a God, as others were for other inventions. But of him hereafter. This tale is told by* Mercury *the God of eloquence ; whoſe winged feete declare his volubility of ſpeech ; his rod, the power of elocution in perſwading or diſſwading ; and his hat his diſguiſed art wherewith he covers the fallacies of his arguments.*

Now Epaphus, *the ſonne of* Iô, *attaining the government of* Egypt, *built the city of* Memphis ; *and cauſed his mother after her death to be adored for a Goddeſſe : who taxing* Phaeton *(as our Poet here faines) to be no ſonne to* Phœbus, *is the cauſe of his journey to his fathers palace ; and conſequently of the Worlds conflagration.*

F 2

OVIDS

Lib: 2.

VPON THE SECOND BOOK OF
OVIDS METAMORPHOSIS.

THE PA-
LACE,
AND
MAGNI-
FICENCE
OF THE
SUNNE.

THe entrance into this second booke is through the glorious Palace of the Sunne: wherein as *some conjecture, he intimates the temple of* Apollo; *with the Portico and Library, built by* Auguftus. *The materialls, gold, precious ftones, and ivory: the workman* Mulciber; *a name of* Vulcan, *which fignifies to mollifie; in that fire mollifies metall, and fubjects it to the will of the Artificer. In this defcription our Poet imitates* Homer *in the fhield of* Achilles; *and is imitated by the moderne in their Screenes and Arraffes. The Sunne is cloathed in a robe of fcarlet, onely proper to Princes and Magiftrates, expreffing their power of inflicting death by that bloudy colour; which private men were of old forbidden to weare, or refemble in any part of their garments. But he a King of the other Starres, from whom they receive their honour: his courtiers, the Houres, Dayes, Moneths, Yeares, and Ages; the Spring, Summer, Autumne, and Winter: being not onely their Lord and moderator, but their father; the meafure and viciffitude of Time proceeding from his motion.* Wherefore divine Reafon, faith Macrobius, and not fuperftition, made the Poets, who in their fables of the Gods did not fwerve from the truth of Philofophy, to referre all the reft that are under the skie to the various faculties of the Sunne, as infinuated by his feverall appellations; governing the cœleftiall lights, and difpofing of their influences: the multiplicitie of the Gods no other then the names of his particular vertues. *The erring World at the firft acknowledging thofe onely for Gods, whom they faw with their eyes, and of whofe glory and bounty they were fenfible.*

PHAETON.

Phœbus acknowledgeth Phaeton *for his fonne: he defires a confirmation: who bids him aske what he will; and bindes the performance by an irrevocable oath, the oath of the Gods, infernall* Styx; *here called their feare and terror: acknowledging therein a greater power then their owne, unto which they were lyable: and withall their mortality: for why fhould they feare what they never could fee, unleffe unto death obnoxious?* Why (faith Lactantius) fhould men caft their eyes unto Heaven, and fweare by thofe Gods who defcend themfelves into hell, and there found that which with terror they adored?

STYX.

Styx *is a fountaine in* Arcadia *at the foot of* Nonacris, *the water thereof is a violent poyfon, and fo corroding that nothing can containe it but the hoofe of a Mule. With this* Alexander (as is fufpected) *was made away, by the treafon of* Antipater; *not without fome afperfion upon* Ariftotle. *Nor is fuch a virulency incredible, contracted from the qualitie of the earth in her fubterrene current, whofe exhalations I have feene, in a dry and lightfome cave betweene* Naples *and* Putzoll, *to kill a dog in as fhort a time as I am in telling of it. From the fad effects of this fountaine, and as fad a name (for* Styx, *as* Regius *expounds it, fignifies forrow) was that fabulous River derived, which in winding mazes nine times infolds the infernall Monarchie. It is fained that* Styx *fent her daughter* Victory, *the joyfull iffue of a forrowfull mother, to affift the Gods in their warres againft the* Gyants: *in recompence receiving this honour from* Jupiter, *that whofoever forfwore themfelves by her name fhould for nine yeares be banifhed from their councels and feftivals. Thus interpreted by* Ariftotle, *that as water was held to be the firft and moft ancient of all things: fo nothing is to be preferred before, or is more holy and venerable, then the religion of an oath. But perhaps more accurately by the Vicount of* Saint Albons: *How leagues betweene Princes, though confirmed by oath, together with the bonds of merit, nature, or alliance, are commonly no longer of validity then they ftand with the Reafons of ftate, and peculiar utility. Onely the obligation of neceffitie (reprefented by* Styx, *that fatall and unrepreffable river) abideth firme and unviolable; fince the breach thereof is punifhed with a fufpenfion from the feftivalls of the Gods; under which, by the Ancient, the lawes, immunities, plenty and felicitie of a kingdome were deciphered.* Ambitious Phaeton *demands of his father the guide of his chariot for one day, and therein his owne ruine. God could not punifh a man more fometimes then in granting him his defires.*

――――― quid enim ratione timemus,
Aut cupimus? Quid tam dextro pede con-
cipis, ut te
Conatus non pœniteat, votique peracti?
Evertere domos totas optantibus ipfis
Dii faciles. Iuv. Sat. 10.

What juftly feare or hope we? what begunne
So well, or wifht for; but we wifh undone?
The eafy Gods by granting us our owne
Requefts, our fortunes oft have overthrowne.

To confirme an indefinite promife by oath is altogether unlawfull: for the breach thereof is a finne,
and

and the performance, not seldome a greater : *as* instanced by Jephta *and* Herod. *So here the father by his indulgencie destroyes his sonne, and grants what an enemy would have desired.* Phœbus *goes a-bout to deterre him by the difficultie, horror, and danger of the enterprise.* Seneca *makes the generous youth reply :* I like the way, and long to ascend : this, wherewith you thinke to affright, incites me : there would I stand where the Sunne himselfe trembles. *Vertue mounts aloft, it is the part of a poore and lazie spirit to pursue safe things. But those hot horses disdaine to obey so weake and un-skilfull a manager : they stray from their bounds, and follow their fury, till by their irregularity they had set the whole world on a cumbustion.* When Jupiter, *lest all should be devoured in one fire, stroke the Chariot and Charioter with lightning : who fell, like a falling starre, into* Eridanus.

Phaeton, *King of the* Thesports *and* Molossians, *was said to have beene the sonne of* Phœbus, *and to have fallen from his fathers Chariot, in that he first assayed to finde out the course of the Sunne ; but was by his death prevented. And in those dayes there fell such abundance of fire from heaven (which* Ficinus *conjectures to be the same that is mentioned by* Moses*) as destroyed many of the East-erne regions : whereupon it was fained that his misguidance had set the whole world on a conflagration. But physically he is said to be the sonne of* Phœbus ; *because* Phaeton *is, as the name it selfe signifies, a bright and burning inflamation, which proceeds from the Sunne :* Clymene, *or the water, his mo-ther ; from whom those exhalations are by the Sunne attracted. These set on fire procure a vehement heate : and therefore, the inflamation of those vapors is the sonne of these parents. Thunder and lightning necessarily succeed such excessive fervor ; for which cause he is said to be strook with light-ning by* Jupiter : *and to fall into* Eridanus ; *in that such droughts are commonly followed by inunda-tions : That River, for this good service, beeing made a cœlestiall Constellation.*

This fable to the life presents a rash and ambitious Prince, inflamed with desire of glory and domi-nion : who in that too powerfull, attempts whatsoever is above his power ; and gives no limits to his ruining ambition.

Prepar'd for vengeance, desperate men	*Audax omnia perpeti*
On crimes forbidden madly run.	*Gens humana ruit per vetitum nefas.*
From Heaven audacious *Iaphets* son	*Audax Iapeti genus*
To mortals fire convai'd by theft :	*Ignem fraude mala gentibus intulit :*
Pale troopes of new diseases then	*Post ignem ætherea domo*
Sad Earth of her sick sons bereft ;	*Subductum, macies & nova febrium*
And certaine Death, before but slow,	*Terris incubuit cohors :*
Did with a swifter motion goe.	*Semotique prius tarda necessitas*
Bold Dædalus through empty ayre	*Lethi corripuit gradum.*
With wings, not given by Nature, flew.	*Expertus vacuum Dædalus aëra*
Herculean labors Hell subdew.	*Pennis non homini datis.*
Hard nothing is t' adventrous man.	*Perrupitque Acheronta Herculeus labor.*
Even heaven it selfe affect we dare	*Nil mortalibus arduum est.*
By our vast follies : no, nor can	*Cœlum ipsum petimus stultitia ; neque*
Iove lay his vengefull thunder by ;	*Per nostrum patimur scelus*
Still urg'd by our impiety.	*Iracunda Iovem ponere fulmina.*
	Horat. l. 1. od. 3.

In that rash and unexperienced, he is said to be a boy, and refractary to counsell (without which, Power is her owne destruction) and therefore altogether unfit for government ; which requires mature advice, and supernaturall knowledge, it being of mortall things the most difficult. The first ascent is steepe and painefull ; the whole race full of care, of feare, and danger of precipitation ; pursued by envy, detraction, and practise ; encountering with Bulls, Centaures, Lions, Scorpions, and such-like mon-sters ; too powerfull subjects, who with their ambition and factions disturbe the publike tranquillitie. The Horses of the Sunne are the common people ; unruly, fierce, and prone to innovation : who finding the weaknesse of their Prince, flye out into all exorbitancies to a generall confusion. These, by the ad-vice of Phœbus, are rather to be curbed then incensed, not by cruelty, but a moderate severitie : well instituted and well executed lawes being the proper reynes to such horses. So Princes are to runne a re-gular course, and follow the steps of their noble Progenitors : neither to incline to the right hand, nor the left ; not to ascend too high, nor descend too low : (as Apollonius answered Adrian, that Nero lost his Empire by the sometimes over-straining, and sometimes too much slacking the strings of his in-strument) Pride diminishing love, and facility authoritie : or to attempt what is above their power, or to fall beneath it, the middle way being onely safe ; which not observed by our lusty Phaeton acce-lerates

lerates his ruine. This also may allude unto those, who straying from their proper spheares, their kingdomes; set the World on fire with the flame of warre, which seemes too little for their insatiate ambition.

Vnus Pellæo juveni non sufficit orbis :
Æstuat infælix angusto limite mundi,
Vt Gyaræ clausus scopulis, parvaque Se-
ripho.
Cum tamen a figulis munitam intraverit ur-
bem
Sarcophago contentus erit. Mors sola fatetur
Quantula sint hominum corpuscula ——
      Iuv. Sat. 10.

One World suffic'd not the *Pellæan* King:
Th'unhappy Youth sweats in that narrow ring,
As if to *Gyaros* sea-girt rocks confin'd.
But *Babylon* once entred, this great Mind
A little Urne contents. Death onely can
Define the true dimensions of a man.

To whom Cyrus, and Attila the Hun, *may be added, no lesse plagues to mankinde, then devasting conflagrations : all perishing in the end by the lightning of the divine vengeance.*

The Chariot of the Sun. *They attribute a Chariot to the Sunne in regard of the swiftnesse of his motion; and to expresse what is beyond the object of the sence by that which is subject unto it : they make it of Gold and reflecting stones, in regard of his splendor; and that Gold is the metall appropriated to that Planet, bestowing riches on those in whose nativitie he predominates. In the wheeles of the cælestiall chariots they placed eight spokes to declare how the cælestiall motions above the eighth spheare were beyond the extent of humane observation. His horses, as their name expresse, are no other then light and heate; whereof the Sunne is the fountaine. Wherefore horses and charriots were consecrated unto him by the Idolatrous Jewes; as the former sacrificed by the Persians and Lacedemonians. His horses are harnessed and brought forth by the houres, which are the ministers of time.*

The tract of his wheeles, is the Ecliptick line, and the beasts he incounters, the signes in the Zodiack. But this is his annuall course, and not his diurnall, wherein he describes almost a parallel to the Equinoctiall. He was held for a God, in that the author of life, of health, and producing whatsoever is beneficiall to man. Reputed by the ancient, The image of God in the world; inspiring our mindes with wisdome and justice : in himselfe an example of government, justice, and munificency.

Lucifer. Lucifer (*that is, a bringer of light*) *is here said to fore-runne* Aurora, *or the morning; and last of all to resigne his place, in that the last starre which shineth. This is the beautifull Planet of* Venus; *which, when it riseth before the Sunne, is the Morning starre, and setting after it, the Evening.*

Qualis est primas referens tenebras
Nuntius Noctis, modo lotus undis
Hesperus, pulsis iterum tenebris
Lucifer idem. Sen. in Hipp.

Now Sea-bath'd Hesperus, who brings
Night on, and first displaies his winges:
Now, radiant *Lucifer*; who day
Exalting, chases night away.

Aurora. *In regard that her course is sometimes swifter then the Sunnes, and at an other time slower; yet never farre off, and fulfilling the same period. A part of the yeare she is above him; and then most refulgent, in that halfe illuminated by his raies: shines to us-ward: and a part beneath, when appearing horned; as found out by the new perspectives. As Lucifer Aurora, so Aurora ushers the Sunne; which is the light reflecting from his orbs before he ascendeth our Horizon, upon the grosser ayre, and condensed vapors : and from thence throwne downe, as from a concave glasse, by repercussion. In winter, for want of heate to raise the low exhalations, the twilight is shorter : in Summer long; and longer as neerer to the Articke circle, by reason of the oblique descent of the Sunne : in so much as they then in* Scotland *have little night, and none at all farther Northward. Twilight begins with us for the most part when the Sunne is 19. degrees beneath our Horizon: which is about an houre and a quarter before, or after, his rising or setting.* Homer *calls the Morning rosy-fingered; and here our Poet strewes his purple gates and galleries with roses; (fained to spring from the bloud of* Venus, *in regard of their sweetnesse and beauty) yet is not really red, but so appeares through the imbecillitie of our sight, and interposition of thick rising vapors; light and darknesse procures a red, as formerly alleadged out of* Aristotle.

Falling Starres. *He resembles* Phaetons *fall to a falling starre, or that seemes to fall; which was timely added; although those fires which dart by night through the aire are so called. For one starre would overwhelme the whole Earth; which in his owne nature is weightlesse, and not subject to descend. These Meteors are round and compacted exhalations; which inflamed aloft, are strooke downe by the aeriall cold: and carry the name of starres, in that they resemble them both in forme and splendor; whose sloughs according to the vulgar receipt, we see often to lye on the ground like gelly.*

Phaeton

Phaeton *is said to be intombed by the* Naiades *; in that water extinguisheth fire. It was the custome of the Ancient not to bury those bodies which were slaine by lightning : but onely to intrench them about ; since no Beast nor Bird would feed on their flesh, and withall as they supposed not subject to corruption.*

PHAE-
TONS.
SISTERS.

The Heliades, *the daughters of the Sunne (for so the name signifies) with immoderate griefe bewaile the death of their brother ; and amidst the imbracements of their distracted mother are turned into Poplars. Great sorrowes stupifie, and we loose the apprehension of griefe by too much grieving : more deeply wounding women then men, in regard of their naturll imbecillitie. Two of these sisters he names :* Phaethusa, *which signifies ardor ;* Lampetia, *shining ; and here unnamed* Pasiphae, *which is all-inlightning. These are no other then the vertues and efficacy of the Sun in naturall bodies. They are said to have beene turned into trees ; in that by moisture, which is* Clymene, *and the heate of the Sun, all vegetatives are produced. The Poplar affects the water, and therefore the scene of this transformation is placed on the bankes of* Eridanus.

The teares of
Poplars.

The teares of these weeping trees convert into Amber : which is onely the gumme they expell by their inward vigour : and by the fine passage or straining of the juyce through the wood and barke, becomes so translucent and shining. But this by the scoffer Lucian *is exploded, who reports that he could neither there heare of Amber, nor see any Poplar trees by that River : although* Pliny *writes that the women there about accustomed to adorne themselves with the same. Yet if this be the marrow of a tree, then most likely of the Pine, in that they resemble one another in smell ; which falling on the ground, either thickned by heat or hardned by cold, is carried into the Sea by high-rising tides, or the swelling of Rivers, and cast upon foraine shoares : whereof no small quantitie is at this day found on our coasts. That it was liquid at first, is apparent by the flies and creeping things which therein are often inclosed. Whereof* Martial :

> The Bee which *Phethusas* teares inclose,
> As if intomb'd in her owne Nectar showes.
> The merit of so great an industry :
> For like enough she so desir'd to die.

And againe :

> The gem-like liquor on the viper fals,
> As on the Poplars weeping branch she crawles :
> While wondring how detain'd in that fat dew,
> Insensative in congeal'd Amber grew.
> Thine, *Cleopatra,* now no more preferre ;
> The Viper hath a nobler Sepulcher.

Et latet, & lucet Phaetontide condita gutta,
Vt videatur apis nectare clausa suo.
Dignum tantorum pretium tulit illa labo-
ram ;
Credibile est ipsam sic voluisse mori.
Lib. 4. Ep. 32.

Flentibus Heliadum ramis dum Vipera ser-
pit,
Fluxit in obstantem succina gemma feram :
Quae dum miratur pingui se rore teneri,
Concreto riguit vincta repente gelu.
Ne tibi regali placeas, Cleopatra, sepulchro,
Vipera si tumulo nobiliore jacet.
Epigr. 59.

More durable then the monuments and imbalming of Princes : for bodies prohibited, that they neither turn into ayre, being separated from the same, nor enter into the bodies adjacent, as of a contrary quality, nor have in themselves a circulation, will never change ; however in themselves corruptible. But Agricola *a diligent searcher into the nature of Minerals, will have it a kinde of Bitumen, rising out of the earth by the shoare : the yellow Amber being perhaps the one, and the white the other. The greatest quantities hereof is found about the Baltick Ocean, and those Northerne Regions.* Boetius *writes that in* Shutland *a peece was taken up as big as a horse : the Priest and his parishioners not knowing what it was, imploid it for Frankinsence.*

CYGNVS.

Cygnus *King of* Liguria *repaires to the Funerall of* Phaëton : *and while he bewailes the fate of his kinsman, is turn'd into a Swan ; delighting in the contrary Element to fire, and not mounting aloft, as detesting* Jupiter : *agreeing with the nature of this Fowle, wherewith that river aboundeth.* Pausanias *writes that he was a Prince much addicted to Musick (as all the* Ligurians *by his example) and therefore fained to have beene after his his death converted into the musicall Bird by* Apollo : *dedicated unto him, not onely for the harmony of his voice, but propheticall fore-knowledge ; who foreseeing his death, entertaines it with songs and rejoycings.*

> The dying Swan, adorn'd with silver wings,
> So in the sedges of Meander sings.

Sic ubi fata vocant, udis abjectus in herbis
Ad vada Maandri concinit albus Olor.
Ovid. Epist. Did.

But who ever heard a Swanne sing ? A fiction invented by Greece, *the mother of fables, perhaps to beautifie their Poems. For such is the sweetnesse and power of Poesie, as it makes that appeare, which*

H   *were*

were in profe both falfe and ridiculous, to refemble the truth ; and with fuch an incredible delight imprints it in the mindes of the hearers, as cannot be eafily out-raced. This muficall King informes us, that Princes fhould not like Nero *indeavour to perpetuate their names by fuch fciences (although commendable in their moderate ufe) lest they lofe their owne fhape, that is, the estimation of their wifedome which is onely to be preferved and exalted by a wife and temperate government.* Philip of Macedon, *when* Alexander *fung and plai'd curioufly on the Harp at a banquet, in this manner reproved him ;* Art not thou afhamed to have fuch skill in thefe trifles?

<table>
<tr><td>

Excudent alii fpirantia mollius æra;
Credo equidem, vivos ducent de marmore vultus :
Orabunt caufas melius, cœlique meatus
Defcribent radio, & furgentia fydera dicent:
Tu regere imperio populos, Romane, memento,
(Hæ tibi erunt artes) pacifque imponere morem;
Parcere fubjectu, & debellare fuperbos.
     Virg Æn.l.6.

</td><td>

Others can statues caft in breathing braffe,
And cut in marble ; which the life furpaffe :
Others can better plead ; defcribe the skies,
The Sunnes fwift courfe, and stars that fet and rife.
Doe thou the people rather, Roman, guide
With juftice, and for facred peace provide.
Be thefe the arts to purchafe thee renowne :
Protect the humble and the proud pull downe.

</td></tr>
</table>

Phœbus *ftomachs the death of* Phaëton, *and denies the world his light ; but is reduced by the intreats and threats of* Jupiter. *It is a winning way to defire what we may command : but if that faile, fubordinate powers are to be compelled by the fupreame ; or elfe the offence in either is equall.* Jove *like a common father, is folicitous in repairing the ruines of thefe diforders ; but cannot order his owne affections. He burnes in love with* Califto, *the daughter of* Lycaon *whom before he had turned into a Wolfe : and now turnes himfelfe into the figure of chaftitie ;* Diana, Califto's *Goddeffe. Vice is afhamed of vice : and fo ugly, that it cannot deceive but under the pretext of vertue ; as the Divell in the fhape of an Angell of light. The Virgin is devirginated, and caft by* Diana *out of her chafte affembly : whom* Cupid *in* Lucian *complaines that he never could wound, in that ever exercifed in hunting. But* Juno *(faid to be the wife of* Jupiter *in that the aire is fubjacent to Heaven; and his fifter, becaufe both, according to* Macrobius, *were ingendred of the fame fubftance) will not be fo pleafed. Jealoufie is unplacable ; as rafh as fire, and more cruell then the grave. She dragges her by the haire, beats her with her fift, and laftly converts her into a Beare. So loofe they their faire figures, and refemble deformed beafts, who abandon their chaftities : the excufe of ravifhment being convinc't by conception.* Califto *fignifies beauty : the more beautifull, the more perfpicuous their blemifhes.* Palæphatus *reports, how hunting in the mountains, fhe entred a Cave, and there was torne in peeces by a Beare : when her companions raifed this rumour of her change ; the Beare coming forth alone, and fhe never feene after. Others, how having vowed virginity, and guilefully deflowred by the Cretan* Jupiter, *fhe was expulfed by her fubjects : who fled into the woods, and there was delivered of* Arcas : *where they lived obfcurely ; till impatient of fo falvage a life, he attempted to kill his mother. She fled to* Jupiter, *who reconciled, and reftored them to their kingdome of* Arcadia. *From whence grew the fable, how, when ready to have beene flaine by* Arcas, *they were both affumed into heaven by compaffionate* Jupiter ; *and converted into neighbouring conftellations within the Artick circle. Thofe foure ftarres which make a quadrangle on the fide of the greater Beare, are called the Waine; The three on her taile, the horfes;* Boötes, *the Waggoner. The leffer Beare confifts of feven ftarres, in a like pofition : whereof the two formoft are called by Sea-men the Guards; as that on the tip of his taile the North-ftarre, in* Ptolomeys *time twelve Degrees from the Pole, but now within two, and yearely approaching neerer. Before the compaffe was found out, the Grecians failed by the greater Beare, called by them* Helice; *as the Phœnicians by the leffe, the more expert Mariners. And becaufe they never fet to thofe Regions, whofe elevation is greater then the diftance of thofe conftellations from the Pole, they are here faid to be interdicted the Ocean (the fetting ftarres fuppofed of old to defcend into the Sea, belike in that they held, as* S. Auguftine, *that all was Sea under us) at* Juno's *fuite to* Oceanus *and* Tethys, *by whom fhe was foftered : the Ayre which is* Juno, *being efpecially procreated by rarified Water.*

Juno *is drawne into Heaven by her yoaked Peacocks : in whofe traine, as formerly fained, fhe had fixed the eyes of* Argus. *And as his eyes were taken for ftarres ; fo hieroglyphically they expreffed night by the difplayed traine of that fowle. Sacred to* Juno, *in that firft feene in* Samos *her Iland : or rather in that a proud and ambitious creature, affecting high places, as of an aeriall temper : deciphering proud and ambitious men who attempt high things ; riches, which morally is* Juno, *being their tutelar Goddeffe ; having need of many eyes to fentinell their wealth, and prevent*
their

CALISTO.

Arcas.

Iuno's Peacock.

their downefall. The varietie of her colours shew the many vicissitudes of Fortune, which infest their mindes with cares and feares, who seeme to others so absolutely happy. The Emperour Adrian *dedicated to* Juno *a Peacock of gold and precious stones, in her Temple at* Euboea. *The* Romans *in the deifying of their Empresses, accustomed to let loose a Peacock from the top of the funerall pyle: making the vulgar beleeve that it was the soule of the deceased taken up into Heaven by* Juno. *And there are Coynes yet extant with the effigies of a woman on the back of an ascending Peacock, that bears the name of* Diva Paulina, *with this inscription* Consecratio. *It is no lesse true then wonderfull that the flesh of this fowle will never corrupt, as experienced for a twelve moneth by* S*t.* Augustine.*

Erichthonius *is here fained to have had no mother: for* Vulcan, *as they fable, intending to ravish* Minerva, *defiled the ground, from whence he had his beginning: expressed in his name which signifies* Earth *and* Contention. Minerva *being that pure elementary fire wherein nothing is ingendred, fained therefore a perpetuall Virgin, and to resist the contamination of* Vulcan, *our grosser fire (the son of* Juno *in that mixed with aire) which vainely strives to joyne with the other being clog'd and suppreft by the matter that feeds it; whose heate descending on the Earth begets a multiplicity of creatures. Others interpret* Minerva *for the industry of Nature, and* Vulcan *for an Art, in that fire is so usefull to the Artificer, who not by obsequiousnesse but violence indeavours to subdue what will not be constrained, and produceth thereby imperfect conceptions, as appeares by the vaine attempts of the Chymists, in their great Elixir. They give* Erichthonius *the hinder parts of a Dragon; some say in that he excelled in fortitude and wisedome: others, for introducing marriage among the* Athenians, *who before promiscuously coupled together: but chiefly in that he knew how to temper clemency with severitie, according to the times, and disposition of the people: in memoriall whereof the children of his posteritie were adorned with golden Serpents. He was the fourth King of the Athenians (who of him were called the issue of the Earth; or rather in that they knew not their owne originall, or scorn'd to acknowledge it) whereof the here-mentioned* Cecrops *was the first: said also to have a double shape; perhaps on the former grounds, or in that his magnanimous entrance was peeced out with craft and dissimulation, as the Lion with the Foxes tayle: or taken in the better sense, in that his courage was accompanied with fore-sight and vigilancie.* Pausanias *writes that* Erichthonius *was the first that invented Chariots to conceale his deformity: and* Virgil;*

<ERICH-THONIVS.>

First *Erichthonius* with foure horses drew
Swift Chariots; on hot wheele the victor flew.

Primus Erichthonius currus, & quatuor aufus
Iungere equos, rapidusque rotis insistere victor.
Georg. l. 3.

When newly borne, hee was hid by Minerva *in a basket; and delivered to the custodie of* Cecrops *daughters, with charge not to open it: but disobeyed, especially by* Aglauros, *it is said that shee and her sisters were vexed with Furies for a long time after; the terror of her inward guilt: to informe us that divine mysteries are not to be too curiously pryed into, nor the commands of God infringed without severe punishment. In some thing the fable alludes to the historie: for a childe being found at* Athens *in the Temple of* Minerva, *neere to that of* Vulcan, *with a snake wrapt about him (a presage of succeeding eminencie) it was fained to be the sonne of* Vulcan, *and to have beene fostered by* Minerva; *concealed in her Temple, perhaps for his safety, as* Joash *in the Temple at* Jerusalem; *and perfidiously discovered by her Priests, the here-mentioned daughters of* Cecrops. *But* Lactantius *will have* Erichthonius *to be the incestuous and long obscured issue of those forged Deities.*

The Crow *informes of the infidelitie of* Aglauros *and her sisters: Once a Nymph and changed into that bird by* Minerva, *to preserve her from the lust of* Neptune. *Chastitie miraculously protects her votaries. The losse of her faire forme is recompenced by her honourable dependency on the Goddesse. In* Corone, *a Citie of the* Messenians *in* Peloponnesius, *a Crow of brasse was placed on the fift of* Minerva's *statue; found in digging the foundation; of which is received that name: and from hence that bird perhaps was said to be sacred unto her. But now discharged her service for her unacceptable intelligence. Silence is secure, when speaking the truth is not seldome obnoxious to danger. The Crow is the symbol of garrulity; and therefore rejected by* Minerva: *because much talking interrupts the meditation of the minde, and is offensive to wisedome. Moreover no Crow comes neere unto* Athens; *so called of* Athenea, *the Greeke name of* Minerva, *of which Citie she was the Patronesse; perhaps the ground of that fable. Of this* Lucretius.

<CORONIS OF PHOCIS.>

H 2

To

*Est & Athenæis in Montibus, arcis in ipso
Vertice , Palladiæ ad Templum Tritonidos
alma,
Quo nunquam pennis appellunt corpora rau-
ca
Cornices, non cum fumant altaria donis :
Vsque adeo fugitant non iras Palladis acres,
Pervigilis causâ, Graium ut cecinere poetæ.
Sed natura loci hoc opus efficit ipsa sua vi.*
    Lib. 6.

To *Pallas* Temple, mounted in the hie
Athenian towre, no Crowes their wings apply,
Although the altars steame : not for the offence
Of too much diligence exil'd from thence
By th' angry powre ; as *Grecian Poets* sing :
For such effects from naturall causes spring.

**NYCTI-
MENE.**

As the lakes of Avernus *and* Asphaltis *were deadly to all foule that flew over them.* Antigonus, *in
his admirable Histories reports how* Coronis *for her ill newes (the persons of such being never acceptable ; when contrarily these who bring good are gracious :) of the discovery of* Erichthonius, *was banished the tower of Athens; and therefore fained to have beene changed into a Crow, since no Crow
approacheth it. A bird of bad presage, and pretending foule weather,*

*Tum Cornix plena pluviam vocat improba
voce,
Et sola in sicca secum spatiatur arena.*
    Virg. Georg. 1.

Th' unlucky Crow with full throat raine implores,
And struts alone upon the sandy shores.

For the Crow *rejoyceth in the moist and relenting Aire : in so much as she seemes to call on the Raine
which approacheth. It grieves her that the Owle should rise by her fall, having beene changed into
that deformed shape for her filthy incest. Yet no deformitie so ugly as her crime : wondred at like a pro-
digy in nature, and driven from the societie of others ; ashamed of her selfe, and sculking in the darke :
when vertue, though unfortunate, shunnes not the light ; a reward to it selfe, and never unpraised. The
Egyptians by the* Crow *and the* Owle *(to which this fable hath a reference) expressed two deadly enemies, pursuing one another with immortall hatred. For the* Crow *destroyeth the egges of the* Owle *by
day, and the* Owle *the others by night ; neither want there authors who write that their bloud will not
mingle. So the* Owle *is the hieroglyphick of death, and the* Crow *of long living. The* Owle *was sacred to* Minerva, *of which she was called* Glaucopis : *either for her gray eyes, in that those have the
best and acutest wits, who have eyes of that colour: or of her faculty of watching and musing; the powers
of the minde being in the silent night more recollected and vigorous : or that* Athens *her Citie so
abounded with Owles, whereupon it became proverbiall: or that the* Athenians *stamped their coyne
with that figure.* Demosthenes, *having escaped out of prison, and flying from* Athens, *is said to
look back on* Minerva's *tower with this exclamation : O* Pallas, *the Lady of this City, why tak'st
thou delight in three such unlucky beasts, as the* Owle, *the* Dragon, *and the* People ? *Intending
blindnesse by the one, by the other envy, and by the third instability.*

**CORONIS
OF LA-
RISSA.**

    The Crow *by way of advice relates these her infortunities to the* Raven : *who despiseth both counsell
and example, the wise directors of our humane actions, and informes* Apollo *of the secret imbracements of his beloved* Coronis *with the* Thessalian Ischyer. *Not the love of a God, and he of the rest
the most beautifull, could confine the wandring lust of an extravagant woman.*

*Crede ratem ventis, animam ne crede puellis.
Namque est fœmina tutior unda fide.
Fœmina nulla bona est, vel si bona contigit
ulli ;
Nescio quo fato res mala facta bona est.*
    Petronius.

Trust thy ship unto the winde ;
Not thy heart to woman-kinde.
Safer farre the faithlesse flood :
Bad, or ill made strangely good.

*So writes the Prose-satyre, yet spent his last breath in reciting amorous verses. The hate of a wronged
lover imitates the violence of his affection. Yet the one but momentary : he kills, and repents in an instant : love is revoked by pitty : whom he slew in his rage, now dead, he dotes on. This fable is parallel'd by that history of* Herod ; *who had no sooner put* Mariamme *to death, but his love increased with
his desperation ; and who could not live with her, could not live without her. The best therefore is not
to heare, what is a misery to know : the next to give time unto anger ; lest præcipitate rage leave
a way to repentance, but none to recovery.* Apollo *hates his intelligencer, and turnes his white feathers*

**THE RA-
VEN.**

*into black ; to shew how hatefull they are by whom we arrive at such knowledge, whereof love will be
ever doubtfull, how apparant soever. The* Raven *was sacred to* Apollo : *in regard of her colour, in
that the* Sunne *makes the complexion black ; whereupon in chiefe estimation with the* Brachmanes ; *so
innated in the* Raven *that her egges, as reported, will die the haire (and the teeth while a doing, if
not prevented by oyle) with that colour : but according to* Anaximander *in his* Horoscopes, *because
the voice of the* Raven *is of all other birds most significant, and therefore so accurately observed in*

Augury

Augury. *They alone use their throats as well as their tongues in the utterance of sounds, which become thereby more intelligible. A shoomaker in Rome had a Raven which would pearch every morning on the Rostra where they made their publique orations ; first saluting the Emperour Tiberius, Germanicus, and Drusus Cæsar, by their names ; then the people of Rome as they passed by : and that done, flie back to his Masters stall ; continuing this custome divers yeeres together ; untill in the end he was killed by the envy of another of that trade : which the Citizens so took to heart, that they drave him out of the street where he dwelt, and afterwards slew him. Then laying the dead Raven on a sumptuous bed, they carried him in great solemnitie on the backs of Æthiopians, to the funerall Pyle ; erected by the Appian way. Thus the people of Rome revenged the death of a bird, with the death of a Citizen: when in former time they not so much as enquired after the murder of Scipio Æmilianus, who had subverted Carthage and Numantia, giving it those rites of funeralls which they refused to bestow upon many of their bravest Commanders.*

AESCVLAPIVS.

Æsculapius is snatcht by Apollo from the wombe of his slaughtred mother : taken for the sonne of Apollo and Coronis ; in that Coronis is the moderate moist aire, which by the impression of the Sunne conceives Æsculapius, or the Giver of health. For if the aire be not rarified by the Sunne, or if contrarily overdryed by his fervor, there is no salubritie : and therefore Coronis is said to be shot to death by Apollo, when his over-violent rayes, which are resembled to arrows, do wound the aire with a mortall pestilence. Æsculapius was also called the sonne of Apollo, in that an excellent Physitian: and those who were the inventors of such Arts were acknowledged for Gods, or to be descended from them, as indued with divine inspirations.

CHIRON.

Æsculapius is delivered to Chiron : begotten, as they faine by Saturne on Philyra in the likenesse of a horse ; from whence he received his double proportion. A man abounding with wisdome and piety: skilfull in Astrology and Musique ; and the first that found out the qualitie of hearbs ; who after, for his knowledge in Chirurgery and light-handling of wounds, was called Chiron. He is said to be the sonne of Saturne and Philyra, that is of time and experience ; which chiefly conduce to the perfection of that Art : and to have the shape of a horse from the navell downward, since the cures of Chirurgery extend not onely to men but to cattell. His daughter is called Ocyrrhoe ; which is, swift-flowing, not onely in that born by the side of a swift River ; but because Chirurgery by incision opens a passage for corrupt humors, which by their speedier flowing from their wound accelerate the cure.

OCYR-RHOE.

Ocyrrhoe neglects the practise of her Fathers Arts to dive into the secrets of Destiny : who prophesies thus of by-standing Æsculapius :

> Health-giver to the World, grow infant, grow ;
> To whom mortalitie so much shall owe.
> Fled Souls thou shalt restore to their abôdds :
> And once, against the pleasure of the Gods.
> To doe the like thy Grandsires flames denie :
> And thou, begotten by a God, must die.
> Thou of a bloodlesse coarse a God shalt be :
> And nature twice shall be restor'd in thee.

He is said to restore the dead to life, in regard of his miraculous cures, when no hope was left of recovery : in so much that Pluto, as they faine, complained to Jupiter, how he would, if not prevented, dispeople his kingdome : and therefore upon the rejoyning of the scattered limbs of Hippolytus, as too audacious a performance, was stroke dead by his lightning. But Physically, Æsculapius, a giver of health proceeding from the bountie of the Sun, and temperature of the aire, is often destroyed by pestilent inflamations, or Jupiter ; falling out for the most part in the insalubrious seasons of the Spring and Autumne : when reviving, which is, purged from those infections, and assuming new vigor, he obtaineth a deitie. But the deification of Æsculapius should seeme to have been after the dayes of Homer, who maketh Pæon (the same with Apollo according to Macrobius) Physitian to the Gods, in the cure of Mars, then wounded by Diomed. He was fained to have been translated into Serpentarius ; a Constellation consisting of 24 Starres. In the yeere 1605, and in the moneth of October, a new Starre of the first magnitude was discovered in his foot ; which vanished again in February 1606.

Ocyrrhoe converts her prophesies to her father : said to be born immortall, in that knowledge is infinite, nor can by a mortall wit be had in perfection. That he should desire to die, out of the dolour of an incurable wound : which he after received in his foot, by the fall of one of Hercules arrows

dipt

dipt in the blood of Hydra. *Death is a happineſſe above immortalitie, if the immortall be ſenſible of pain or ſorrow : The Gods, by giving him leave to die, doe partly recompence his vertue; but fully, in placing him amongſt the ſtarres : now called* Sagittarius, *of the arrow he holds in his hand, as if newly extracted from his wound. And in that he was an adorer of the Gods, and a lover of goodneſſe, an Altar of ſtarres is placed before him, as a perpetuall monument of his religion and Pietie. By this the Ancient inferr'd, that the Good, though often exerciſed with afflictions, are never forſaken by God, who turns their ſorrow into joy, and crowns them in the end with never ending glory.* Ocyrrhoe *concludes her propheſie with her own approaching misfortune : like the Prophet at the deſtruction of* Jeruſalem; *who crying woe to the Citie, and then to himſelf, was ſlain with a quarry : She now repents thoſe curious Arts, which had drawn the divine vengeance upon her; and in ſo doing is converted into a Mare; to deterre from ſuch profane and interdicted ſciences.*

Apollo A
Heards-
man. Chiron *in vain implores the aſſiſtance of* Apollo; *who then was baniſhed heaven for a yeere, for killing the* Cyclops *who made the lightning which ſlew his ſonne* Phaeton, *who liable to humane neceſſities, was inforced to keepe the cattell of* Admetus *King of* Theſſaly: *or rather kept them for the love of his daughter, as is here inſinuated. This* Apollo (*for many there were of that name, the actions of all likely attributed to one*) *was King of* Arcadia, *expulſed by his ſubjects for his too ſevere government : who falling from a kingdome to a meane condition, was ſaid to have been baniſhed heaven. He flying to* Admetus *for ſuccour, received from him the command of thoſe people who dwelt about the river* Amphriſus. *And becauſe all Kings were called anciently* Paſtors, *he therefore was fained to have been his Heards-man. But rather incline we to the phyſicall ſence of this fable; ſaid to feed his cattell; in that the Sunne nouriſheth not only cattell, but what ever elſe is by the earth produced; and therefore called by* Homer *the univerſall Paſtor.*

Mercuries
theft. Mercury *is here introduced to ſteale away his oxen : which he did, according to* Homer, *the firſt day he was born.*

Editus in mane,citharam pulſavit eadem
Luce, boves Phœbo celavit veſpere raptoi.
    Hym. Mer.

     Born, in the morne upon the harp he plaid :
     At night from *Phœbus* his ſtolne ſteeres convaid.
And ſoone after his arrows :

Te boves olim niſi reddidiſſes
Per dolum amotas, puerum minaci
Voce dum terret, viduus pharetra,
    Riſit Apollo.
    Hor. l. 1. ode 10.

     While thee, ô boy, he threatned ſore,
     Vnleſſe thou would'ſt his ſteeres reſtore :
     His quiver ſeene without a ſhaft
           Apollo laught.

He is ſaid alſo to have ſtolne Vulcans *tooles out of his ſhop,* Venus *girdle from her waſt,* Jupiters *ſcepter, when yet a childe; and had ſtolne his lightning, but that he feared the burning of his fingers. This was deviſed, not only in that eloquence hath a bewitching power to deceive; but becauſe thoſe in whoſe horoſcope* Mercury *predominates, are craftie, ſubtill, and theeviſh; that hot and dry Planet having ſuch varietie of motions and tergiverſations : whereupon adored by Merchants, theeves and impoſtors. Nor wanted they a Goddeſſe to this cheating God.*

Iane pater,clare,clare cum dixit Apollo:
Labra movet metuens audiri; pulchra Laverna
Da mihi fallere, da juſtum ſanctumq; videri :
Noctem peccatis, & fraudibus objice nubem.
    Hor. Epiſt. 16.

     He, Father *Ianus,* bright *Apollo* praid :
     Then ſoftly mutters, Faire *Laverna,* aid
     My ſtealths; May I juſt and religious ſhow :
     Night on my crimes, clouds on my coſ'nage throw.

Battvs. Battus *for a double reward betraying* Mercury *to himſelf was transformed into a Touch-ſtone, (ſignifying in the* Latin, *an appeacher) the meed of his avarice and perjury. By* Battus *our* Ovid *intends a fooliſh Poet of that name, redounding with vain and tedious repetitions, whereof he here giveth an example : the like of him being called* Battologia.

Mercuries
Caduceus. Mercury *flies from hence unto* Athens, *bearing his Caduceus in his hand : a rod wound about with a male and a female Serpent, who gently neere the top convert to each other; ſignifying the aſſurance of peace and concord; as the wings above the velocitie of the minde. It is ſaid to aſſwage the rage of the Sea, in that contentions are appeaſed by the power of eloquence and the diſcreet negotiations of Embaſſadors. Of whoſe farther vertues thus* Virgil.

————hac animas ille evocat Oreo
Pallentes, alias ſub triſtia Tartara mittis :

     With this, pale Souls from *Erebus* he calls,
     And others in ſad *Tartarus* inthralls :

Procures,

Procures, and fleepe repels; fhuts dying eyes.
With this, through ftormes, and labouring clouds he flies.

*Dat fomnos, adimitq;, & lumina morte refig-
nat.
Illa fretus agit ventos, & turbida tranat Nubila.* Æn. l. 4.

For Mercury *taught that no man came into the World, or went out of it, without the divine appoint-
ment: and therefore was faid to paffe between* Jupiter *and* Pluto*; fetching Ghofts from the under-
fhadows, and carrying them thither. So in that dreames were held to be infpired from above, and calling that divine infpiration* Mercury *(the meffenger between God and man) they attributed this vertue to his rod, of producing and expelling them.*

Mercury *is in love with* Herfe*, folicites her fifter* Aglauros *for acceffe: fhe demands a maffe of* AGLAV-
ROS.
Gold*, and will be paid before hand; wherein as craftie as covetous: well knowing that ill deeds, when
done, are feldome rewarded. Covetoufneffe is unfatiable as the grave; without fhame, refpect, or naturall affections. But* Pallas *diverts her by* Envy*, a more Serpentine vice. Her Cave in the bottome
of a deepe Dale; to fhew how fhe dwells in bafe and abject Spirits, but never in the high and heroicall.
This her habitation is repleat with unactive cold, and a groffe humiditie. For fuch, as Phyfitians ob-
ferve, is the blood of the Envious; the caufe of that paleneffe and macilency in their looks and confti-
tutions. It is not lawfull for* Pallas *to enter her Cave; that is, for Vertue to commixe with* Envy*:
although* Envy *be alwaies a follower of Vertue. She forceth her doore with her Lance, nor intreats but
commands her; as a vaffall, and the executioner of the Divine vengeance.* Envy *is here faid to pur-
fue her with a wicked eye; for it was the opinion of moft of the Ancient that the eyes of the envious
doe not feldome fafcinate, by emitting malignant and virulent fpirits, which infect the fpirits of
another; of greateft force when the caft of the eye is oblique, as formerly infinuated by our* Author*:
and then moft dangerous when they glance at fuch as are full of joy, and in the height of their glory;
whofe fpirits come forth into the outward parts, and receive the percuffion at a neerer diftance: in fo
much as it hath been obferved, that they, when the triumphs were ended, have been ill difpofed for many dayes after. But the nature of* Envy*, her forme, and effects, are here fo painted to the life, as nothing can be added to her character.* Aglauros *infected with this poyfon, proves ingratefull both to
the God and her fifter, the unfeparable fymptome of that difeafe; and afflicts her felfe by comparifon:
who interpofing what her felfe difpaired of, is turned into a fpeckled ftone; the one prefenting the ftaines
of her minde, and the other her impudence. And it is a fad truth, that the advancement of a fifter or
a brother above one another either in love or fortune, is more envied then a ftrangers; and often produces cruell effects, efpecially if rivals. Cardinall* Hippolito d' Efte*, pull'd out the eyes of his brother*
Julio*, becaufe their fweetneffe pleafed too much the eyes of his Miftreffe: and how fifters have made
one another away upon the like occafion, is frequent in ftory. Now perhaps the body of* Aglauros *found
ftiffe with death, and freckled with poyfon, wherewith fhe defperately ended her tormenting envy,
might give invention to this fable of her transformation.* Apelles*, the firft that prefented paffions in
picture, which fince is grown to fo great perfection, expreffed in this manner thofe concomitant vices.
On a tribunall fate a man with the eares of an Affe, who beckned to approaching* Calumnie*: befides
him two attending hagges,* Sufpicion*, and* Ignorance*. The figure of* Calumnie *feemed full of haft;
and although neatly trickt, yet with fuch a looke and gefture as expreffed the wrath and rancor of her
bofome. In her left hand fhe held a flaming fire-brand; and haled a youth with the right by the haire,
lifting up his hands unto heaven, and calling, as it were, on the Gods to beare witneffe of his innocency.
Before, her ufher* Envy*, of an ugly feature and pale complexion; fharp of fight, and fo meagre, as if
worne to the bone with a long confumption: behinde her waited* Deceit *and* Treachery*. Then followed* Repentance *in mourning attire, looking over her fhoulder with an afhamed afpect, and eyes full
of teares, on revealed* Truth*, the conclufion of the worke, which reprefented his forepaffed troubles.*

Mercury *from hence afcending into heaven, is forthwith imployed by* Jupiter *as his faithfull Mef-* EUROPA.
fenger: fo not only called, in that elocution (which is Mercury*) reveales the pleafure of God unto
man, but alfo for that divine knowledge infufed from above, which is the rule and direction of our fo-
ber actions.*

But what a fenfuall God have we here? How un-majefticall is majefty where love hath a footing?

> The power from whom what ere hath being fprings,
> That King of Gods who three-forkt lightning flings;
> Whofe nod the worlds unfixt foundation fhakes;
> The figure of a fenfuall Bull now takes.

*The Gods themfelves at once cannot love and be wife. Love like an inchanter deludes the eye of the
minde*

minde with false apparitions : making that seeme noble , delightfull and profitable ; which is full of dishonour, affliction and ruine.

   ——This subjects their wills,
Even to affect their woes; the worst of ills.
Whose faithlesse eyes, suborn'd by false desire,
Vnto their hearts convay the cherisht fire ;
Which blindly creeps through every vein, and dries
The fluent blood, whence grosser vapours rise,
Which sad the soul with fearefull phantasies :
Then melancholy by adustion grows
To Madnesse, and doth all their powers depose.
Their thoughts are still abroad : those hale along
The captiv'd Soul; with it the Spirits throng.
Thoughts absence, cause distraction, and unrest ;
The Souls, debilitie, faint life opprest ;
The Spirits, sighs, frights, trepidations, teares.
O living death ! more then infernall feares !
Who in themselves, nor the beloved dwell ;
Are no where, and yet every where in Hell.
Nor can they so great miseries conceale,
Whose guiltie flames betraying signes reveale :
How pale they look, how wither'd, how forlorn :
Their bodies almost into shadows worn :
While their bewitcht intentions, busied still
On the affected, doe their stomachs chill ;
Their veines supply'd with little, and bad blood,
Extracted from the half-concocted food.
Observe but how their colours come and go ;
Their faltring tongues, their tossings to and fro ;
Their smotherd sighs, their tedious complaints ;
Blasphemous praises, rages, shamelesse vants,
Suspicions, cravings, levities ; all these
The symptomes be of that unchaft disease.
Who common Curtizans not seldome make
The objects of their sensuall loves, and take
Commandments from their eyes; with forfeiture
Of better fame : and what they hate, indure.
Who to the humors of the prostitute
Their language, habits, and behaviours sute ;
The slavish agents of their darker ends: (friends,
Neglecting heaven, themselves, their substance,
All laws, all dues ; and born with every tide
Of passion, wander as their errors guide. &c.

 And behold our Iupiter *becomes a beast to obtaine his bestiall desires : of whom the wittie* Martial;

  Father of Gods, this shape of Bull then thou   *Mutari melius tauro, pater optime divûm,*
  Should'st have assum'd, when Iö was a Cow.   *Tunc poteras, Io cum tibi vacca fuit.*
                      Mart. l. 14. ep. 180.

Who carries his rape on his back through the foming surges : which forth-with (as they fable) were composed , and the face of the Sea as smooth as a Virgins. The windes were rather spectators then actors. A thousand Cupids flew by, and often dipt their feet in the water, bright tapers ; and singing Iö Hymen. *The* Nereides, *halfe naked, on the backs of Dolphins, scoured along, with joyfull acclamations. The monsters of the Deepe deposed their terrors, and danced about them.* Neptune *ascending his Chariot, with pleasant* Amphitrite, *as the master of the solemnitie, drave before, and made*
                                    way

way as it were for his labouring brother. Venus *was drawn on a shell by two* Tritons, *who strewed the* Bride *with all sorts of flowres. This triumph continued to their arrivall in* Creet: *when* Jupiter *(the* Bull *no more seene) led* Europa *by the hand (now blushing and hanging the head, as well perceiving to what end she was brought thither) into the Cave of* Dicte. *Who for such pranks as these is thus rayled at by* Momus, *the Buffone of the Gods:* Thou, ô *Iupiter*, art the originall cause of our vices, and of the adulterating of our Senate, with such a multitude of Baftards: while thou forsakeft thy heaven, and in a borrowed shape committeft with mortals. Insomuch as we not a little feare that when thou art a Bull, one or other will facrifice thee: or when a golden showre, that some Gold-smith should melt thee, and for our *Iupiter* return us an Eare-ring or a Bracelet. *But to separate the history from the fable.* The Cretans *in revenge of the rape of* Io, *stolne before from* Greece *by the* Phœnicians, *sailed to* Phœnicia, *who surprising* Europa, *the daughter of* Agenor, *at* Sarepta, *a Village between* Sydon *and* Tyrus, *bore her away with them: and because the figure of a Bull was carved on the prow of the ship (or as others report, in that* Tauros *of* Gnoffus *was their Captain) it was fained that* Jupiter *stole her away in that likenesse: the* Sydonians *stamping the same on their Coine, either in flattery to their King, or to comfort him.* By Jupiter *she had* Minos, Radamanthus, *and* Sarpedon, *according to* Herodotus *and others: although* Homer *make the latter to be his sonne by* Laodamia *the daughter of* Bellerophon. *Of her name our part of the world was called* Europa. *By this it appeares that* Jupiter *was a mortall man, and none of the chaftest, though eminent in other vertues: withall exceeding ambitious, and affecting divine honours. For wheresoever he extended his conquests, or contracted friendship with Princes, he commanded Temples to be built by the one, and perswaded the other to erect them in memoriall of their amitie; which carried his name, and wherein, either out of observance or affection, they celebrated his memory with yearely solemnities. It is recorded that for many yeares he raigned in* Olympus: *to whom from all parts they resorted for juftice, being renowned for his equitie; and communicated such new inventions of theirs as were beneficiall to the life of man, which he had the honour to publish. And because the word* Olympus *is ambiguous, being a name of Heaven as well as of that Mountain; it was fained by the Poets, that he had the command of the cœleftiall Empire. So in regard of the height thereof, whose afpiring summit was crowned with his altar, it grew into a cuftome to facrifice unto the chiefe of the Gods on the tops of mountains (or perhaps in that neerer heaven, and more remote from worldly affaires) imitated by the* Jews *in their idolatrous High-places. Now* Jupiter, *dividing his Empire among his friends and kinsfolke; having fetled good laws, brought men to civilitie, and provided for their plentie; purchasing thereby an immortall praise, and leaving to his an eternall monument; retired in his old age into* Creet; *where he dyed, and was with all magnificency and rites of funerall intombed by his Sonnes in the Citie of* Gnoffus, *with this short infcription on his Sepulcher.* Jupiter the Sonne of Saturne. *After for the greatneffe of his actions and exemplary juftice deified by pofteritie, whereof in his life he had laid the foundation.*

OVIDS

Sa. Sadeler sculp.   Lib: 3.   F. Clein fe.

VPON THE THIRD BOOK OF
OVIDS METAMORPHOSIS.

CADMVS. Cadmus *is sent by* Agenor *in search of his sister* Europa; *either to bring her backe, or never to returne: in that one act an affectionate father, and a cruell.* Agenor *by interpretation is a valiant man: and* Cadmus *his sonne confirmes this assertion;*

Fortes creantur fortibus:
Est in equis patrum
Virtus: nec imbellem feroces
Progenerant aquila columbam.
    Horat. Ode 9

From strenuous Sires bold sonnes proceed;
Brave horses from a generous breed:
Nor doth that awfull bird of *Iove*
Beget a weake and fearefull Dove.

Who not degenerating, ascends that craggy and Herculean *path which leads to immortall glory. This is that* Europa, *in quest of whom he was sent by his father. For experience and renowne is not gotten by such, as affect their owne ease; but through painefull travell, and attempts of danger. True glory adheares to the Supreame goodnesse: and therefore* Jupiter *is fained to carry* Europa *away; whom to finde was a labour of excessive difficultie: which induceth* Cadmus *to consult with* Apollo; *since divine advice is the true Philosophie, and onely guide to noble indeavours; which is not to be disputed off, but effected. He is commanded to follow the conduct of a Cow (a creature expressing patience and labour) where she reposeth to build his City, and to call it* Bœotia. *Not unlike was the counsell of* Epimenides *of* Creet, *who advised the* Athenians *in the time of a great pestilence, to turne their cattle loose into the fields which they intended to offer; the Priests to follow, and where they stayed to sacrifice them unto the unknowne propitiatory Deitie. And* St. Paul *in that city saw an Altar with such an inscription. But the former Oracle is thus interpreted, that excessive labour was to be undergone in that journey; much to be suffered, and much to be done, ere he could attaine to the desired end: meane while by the continuall exercising of the minde, to indue it with such habituall fortitude as might inable him to subdue the Dragon; which is, intemperance, and all evill desires. This Dragon by* Cadmus *slaine was advanced to a constellation; placed betweene the two* Beares, *and consisting of one and thirty starres, incompassing the Northerne Pole of the Ecliptick. The sowing of the Dragons teeth in the earth (the mother of monsters) is to restore to every one his owne: true fortitude being alwaies accompanied with moderation and justice; ingendring love in the good, and envy in the bad; that earthly brood which thus prodigiously ascend (like upstarts on a sudden to honour and power) with weapons in their hands; which he by the advice of* Pallas, *or Wisedome, converts on their owne bosomes: wounding themselves in not wounding of others.* Palæphatus *gives this fable an historicall sense: how* Cadmus *slew* Draco *the sonne of* Mars, *then King of* Thebes, *in battle, and possessed his kingdome. The sonnes and friends of* Draco *drew to a head; but finding themselves too weake for so strong and couragious an enemy, disbanded; yet bore away much of his treasure, among the rest many* Elephants teeth; *dispersing themselves some in* Achaia, *others in* Peloponnesus, *many in* Phocis, *and in* Locris *not a few: from whence not long after with recollected powers they invaded the* Thebans, *maintaining a difficult; and a doubtfull warre: in so much as the* Thebanes, *ever after they fled with the* Elephants teeth, *accustomed to say, that such horrid mischiefes had befallen them for* Cadmus *killing of the Dragon; from whose teeth dispersed here and there, so many puissant enemies arose. But he rather sowing by his policy the seede of dissention amongst them, over-threw them by their owne power. Onely it should seeme he drew* Echion, *with other foure,* Cithonius, Udeus, Hyperener, *and* Pelorus, *men of principall qualitie, with their followers, to his party: perswaded thereunto by* Minerva, *or a prudent regard of their present condition.* Cadmus *was the first that invented letters, or rather the first that divulged them in* Greece; *who before, as the* Egyptians, *expressed their conceptions in hieroglyphicks:* Erasmus *expounds those serpents teeth, to be letters, in that the Authors of such wrangling and discord. The Consonants are interpreted for those souldiers who confounded one another: the Vowels, which render of themselves a sound, and give a power of expression to the Consonants, the same who joyned in mutuall amity. The* Phœnicians *writ, as all the Easterne Nations, from the right hand to the left: the reason why the outermost figure to the right hand in Arithmetick stands in the first place; they also being the inventers of that science.*

Cadmus, *after so many difficulties, advanced to a flourishing kingdome (Honour is to be courted with*

with *ſweat and blood, and not with perfumes and garlands) now ſeemeth happy in his exile : having*
beſides Harmione *to wife ; whoſe nuptialls were honoured by the preſence of the Gods, and their*
bountifull endowments. So beloved of them is the harmony of exterior and interior beauty eſpouſed to
Vertue. *She is ſaid to be the daughter of* Mars *and* Venus *; in that muſick not onely recreates the*
minde with a ſweet oblivion of former misfortunes, but alſo inflames it with courage, and deſire
of inſtant encounters, eſpecially the Dorick *and* Orthian *; the latter when* Alexander *at any time*
heard, as a man tranſported with fury, he would fly to his weapons. Cadmus *had but one ſonne by*
Harmione *called* Polidorus, *though here our Poet intimate many, and foure daughters ;* Ino, Semele, Agave, Autonoë. Athamas *by* Jno *had* Melicerta *and* Learchus ; Jove *by* Semele, Bacchus ; Echion *by* Agave Pentheus ; *and* Ariſtæus Actæon *by* Autonoë : *Whoſe ſucceeding ſto-*
ries are the arguments of as many Tragedies. To theſe enſuing miſeries, yet O fortunate Cadmus,
adde thine owne exile in thine old age : and then confeſſe with our Author, or rather with Solon, *from*
whom he hath borrowed it ;

> That man muſt cenſur'd be by his laſt houre:
> Whom truely we can never happy call
> Before his death, and cloſing funerall.

His grand-childe Actæon *was the firſt that made a breach into his felicities.* Diana *bathes her*
ſelfe in the Valley of Gargaphia *; attended by ſix Nymphs whoſe names ſute well with that ſervice.*
Crocale *ſignifieth pibble ſtones in the fountaine which ſerve as a ſtrainer to clarifie the water:* Nyphe
one that waſheth; Hyale *glaſſe, in regard of the cleereneſſe of the ſpring ;* Rhanis *ſprinkling ;* Phecas *a*
drop of dew ; and Phiale *a filling of water into lavers, as is here in the verſe expreſſed.* Actæon *by*
chance came hither and beheld her naked ; whom the bluſhing and angry Goddeſſe transformes into
the ſhape of a long-liv'd Hart : ſo called in that the longeſt liver of all that hath life : whereof
Auſonius :

The yeares that conſummate the age of men,	*Ter bines decieſque novem ſuper exit in annis*
Spin out to three times two and nine times ten :	*Iuſta ſeneſcentum quos implet vita virorum:*
The pratling Crow nine times as aged growes:	*Hos novies ſuperat vivendo garrula cornix,*
The Harts long life foure times exceeds the Crowes.	*Et quater egreditur cornicū ſecula Cervus.*

Juno in Lucian *upbraides* Latona *that her daughter* Diana *converted* Actæon, *having ſeene her*
naked, into a Hart ; for feare he ſhould divulge her deformitie : and not out of modeſty ; being ſo farre
from a virgin, as continually converſant at the labours of women, like a publike midwife. Actæon
thus transformed, is devoured by his own hounds. Steſichorus *writes that ſhe ſewed him within the*
skin of a Stag, *and ſet his dogges upon him : others, that he was neither turned into a Stag, nor clothed*
in his skin ; but that ſhe poſſeſſed his dogs in their madneſſe with ſuch an imagination. And perhaps
they ran mad in the Canicular *dayes through the power of the* Moone, *that is, of* Diana *; augmented by*
the entrance of the Sunne into Leo *: and then what force or knowledge could reſiſt their worrying of*
their maſter ? Scaliger *reports that the like befell to divers hunters of* Corſica *in his time : and ſome*
averre that Lucian, *the Apoſtata and Atheiſt, came to that end. Yet the* Tartarians *and* Hyrcani-
ans *left the dead bodies of their friends and kinsfolke to be devoured by dogges, eſteeming it the no-*
bleſt and moſt happy ſepulture. But this fable was invented to ſhew us how dangerous a curioſitie it is
to ſearch into the ſecrets of Princes, or by chance to diſcover their nakedneſſe : who thereby incurring
their hatred, ever after live the life of a Hart, full of feare and ſuſpicion : not ſeldome accuſed by their
ſervants, to gratulate the Prince, unto their utter deſtruction. For when the diſpleaſure of a Prince is
apparent, there commonly are no fewer Traitors then ſervants, who inflict on their maſters the fate of
Actæon. *Some ſuch unhappy diſcovery procured the baniſhment of our* Ovid : *who complaining of*
his misfortunes, introduceth this example.

Why had I ſight to make mine eye my foe ?	*Cur aliquid vidi ? cur noxia lumina feci ?*
Or why did I unſought-for ſecrets know ?	*Cur imprudenti cognita culpa mihi eſt ?*

Actæon

Inscius Actæon vidit sine veste Dianam;
Præda fuit canibus non minus ille suis.
Scilicet in superis etiam fortuna luenda est :
Nec veniam læso numine casus habet.
Trist.l.2.

Actæon naked *Dian* unaware
So saw ; and so his hounds their master tare.
The Gods sure punish fortune for offence :
Nor, when displeased, will with chance dispence.

Guard we therefore our eyes ; nor desire to see, or know more then concernes us : or at least dis-semble the discoverie. Julius Montanus *meeting with* Nero *in the darke, by his unsea-sonable respects upbraiding, as it were, his ruffianly licentiousnesse, was put to death :* The art was understood (*saith* Tacitus) *by* Mutianus *: but the disguising of his knowledge was a point of obedience. But why may not this fable receive a double construction ? Those being the best that ad-mit of most senses.* That Actæon, *neglecting the pursuite of vertue and heroicall actions, puts off the minde of a man, and degenerates into a beast ; while he daily frequents the wild woods to contend with such enemies. And some imagine how he was said to be devoured by his hounds, in that he impo-verished his estate in sustaining them. But what was that expence to a Prince ? I rather agree with those, who thinke it to be meant by his maintaining of ravenous and ryotous sycophants : who have of-ten exhausted the Exchequors of opulent Princes, and reduced them to extreame necessitie. Bounty therefore is to be limited according to the abilitie of the giver, and merit of the receiver : else it not easily ruinates it selfe, but loseth the name of a vertue, and converts into folly.* Plutarch *in the life of* Sertorius *makes mention of two* Actæons, *the one devoured by his hounds, and the other by his fa-vorites : not as if this latter were the Allegory of the former.*

SEMELE   Juno *for* Europa's *sake detesting the whole race, rejoyceth in the death of* Actæon. *None more jea-lous then she, nor more revengefull in her jealousie : in so much as she could not forbeare that* Dedalian *Statue which angry* Jupiter *threatned to marry : but upon their reconcilement caused it to be cast into the fire. Wherefore* Numa *made a law, that no harlot should enter her temple, or touch her altars. For no Goddesse was more injured with the continuall adulteries of* Jupiter *: late he ravished* Europa, *and now had got her neece* Semele *with childe. She frets and scoulds (a quality ever attributed unto her ; perhaps in regard of the turbulent agitations of the aire, which is* Juno) *and meditates on revenge : which the better to effect, converts her selfe into the shape of her nurse ; old* Beroe *of* Epidaur. *No treachery is so speeding as that which maskes under the visard of frienship.*

Tuta frequensque via per amici fallere nomen:
Tuta frequensque licet sit via, crimen habet.
Ovid. Art. lib. 1.

Under the name of friendship to betray,
A safe and usuall ; but a wicked way.

She begets in her a suspicion how she might be abused under the name of Iupiter, (*for to be imbraced by a God was held no impeachment to chastitie, but contrarily a high honour) as no extraordinary pra-ctice. And it is authentique in story, how* Paulina, *a chaste and beautifull Lady, made beleeve by the confederate Priest of* Serapis *that his God was in love, and desired to enjoy her ; was contaminated in his Temple by a gentleman of* Rome, *who acted his part. This discovered by him unto her, in hope to continue his possession ; and by her complain'd off with execrations and out-cries ; the Priest was put to death, the statue of* Serapis *reduced into powder and throwne into* Tyber, *and his Temple demolished; by the commandement of* Tiberius *: but the gentleman onely banished in that his offence was an over-violent affection. Too credulous* Semele *perswaded by the fraud of her supposed Nurse, asks a boone of* Jupiter (*who rashly before he knew it, confirmes the grant by an oath) that he would approach unto her, as he did unto* Juno, *with the ensignes of his deitie ; who burnes in his imbracements, as not able to en-dure the ætheriall tumults. Whereby the ancient taught that unlawfull requests were punished by the Gods in consenting. But more* Theologically, *how those who search too curiously and boldly into the divine Majesty, shall be oppressed with the glory and brightnesse of the same :* Jupiter *and* Juno *are said to couple with thunder and lightning ; in that lightning and thunder proceed from the conjuncti-on of ætheriall heate, and aieriall cold. Two sort of lightnings are here mentioned : the one called by the Philosophers fatall, that is, pre-appointed and mortall ; the other accidentall and lesse hurtfull. A third also there must be, expressed by the three-forked thunderbolt. The dryer dissipates, the more humid blasts ; the other melts money in bagges, and swords in scabbards ; instantly licking up liquor in vessels ; without breach or impaire to that which containes them.* Martia, *a noble Lady in* Rome, *had her infant slaine in her wombe by lightning ; without further prejudice then unto such as are deli-vered of abortives. So the lightning consumed* Mithridates *arrowes, as he lay asleepe, not so much as tainting the quiver : and, when an infant, his swadling-cloathes, without other hurt then leaving a firery marke on his forehead ; which he accustomed to cover with his haire. Vpon these accidents*

he

he was called Dionysius *which is* Bacchus : *if not better merited for ordaining prizes in his festivals for such as drunke stiffest, wherein he himself had commonly the victory.* By attributing varietie of lightnings to *Iupiter,* the Poets, saith *Seneca,* admonish us, how all offenders are not equally punishable : some only should be terrified, some chastised, and others utterly destroyed. *And as much was expressed by the rods and axes which were borne before the* Romane *Consuls : bound in bundles, to declare that Magistrates should not too hastily execute ; but while unbinding, to give time to their anger, which not seldome misinformes the judgement.* Joves *fearefull artillery he faines to be forged by the* Cyclops : *whereof* Virgil *more fully.*

Cyclops.

The *Cyclop's* in vast caves their anvills beat :
Steropes, Brontes, nak'd *Pyragmon,* sweat
In forging thunder : part now finisht ; *Iove*
This on affrighted earth hurles from above.
Part yet unperfect ; unto that aloud
Three lares of haile, three of a watry cloud,
Three of red fire, and stormy *Austers* wings ;
Terrible flashes, fragors, menacings,
Mixt with the same, and wrath pursu'd by flame.

Ferrum exercebant vasto Cyclopes in antro,
Brontesque, Steropesque, & nudus membra
Pyragmon.
His informatum manibus jam parte polita
Fulmen erat, toto genitor quæ plurima cælo
Dejicit in terras, pars imperfecta manebat.
Tres imbris torti radios, tres nubis aquosæ
Addiderant, rutili tres ignis & aliis Austri.
Fulgores nunc terrificos, sonitumq; motumq;
Miscebant operi, flammisq; sequacibus iræ.
Æn. l. 8.

The names of the Cyclop's *expresse their faculties : for* Brontes *signifies thunder,* Steropes *lightning, and* Pyragmon *a plyer of the fiery anvill. And ancient Authors affirme, that no mechanick Arts were invented before the finding out of fire, and the severall uses of the same : after which they increased daily, and daily grew to perfection by the industry of man to a publique utilitie. They were called* Cyclopes *of the imaginary round eye in their foreheads, so fained in regard of their fictitious imployment about thunder and lightning, forged in the aire, which is seated in the midst betweene earth and heaven : as of the circular motion of those vapours whereof these meteors are ingendred.* Cœlus *is their father, and* Tellus *their mother, in that such exhalations are attracted from the earth by the Cœlestiall fervor.*

But to returne to the sence of the story : Cadmus *according to* Sabinus *imports as much as Orientall, in that he came from the* East *: bringing with him both letters and learning.* Semele, *his daughter signifies an Image : and like enough he introduced some new superstition ; whereupon, in that delightfull and well accepted, it was fained that* Jupiter *was in love with* Semele. Ino, *another of his daughters, signifies Fortune : either a name imposed upon some new statue and ceremony ; or to declare that Empire depends not upon humane counsell, but on secret and fatall causes, whose events are so called. And probable it is, in that vines were first planted in the* East, *that* Cadmus *instructed the* Græcians *in that knowledge : wherefore* Bacchus, *because wine was held to be the gift of God, was said to be the sonne of* Jupiter *and* Semele ; *which is the divine worship. As for* Semele, *perhaps her aspiring to the divine honours of* Juno, *whom* St. Augustine *supposeth to be* Ashtoreth *the Goddesse of the* Sidonians, *as* Baal *or* Bell Jupiter, *who was* Belus *Grandfather to* Agenor ; *and some fatall accident upon her pride by lightning, might give a ground to this fable. And why might not she affect a deitie as well as her great Grandmother ?*

But as Bacchus *physically is taken for a vine ; so is* Semele *for the Earth ; and therefore called her sonne.* Jupiter *his father, in that wine hath in it a naturall heat ; nor ripens but in countries that are hot, or moderately warme. He is said to be taken from the ashes of his mother, in that ashes exceedingly inrich the soyle, and make it bring forth Grapes in abundance : to be sewed in* Joves *thigh ; because the vine delighteth in heat, nor will fructifie, or live without it, and lastly to be borne twice ; once out of the earth, and then from the thigh of the tredder ; since it is not wine before the grapes be trodden, for so they anciently prest them. The Nymphs are here said to have nurst him : because the vine, the moystest of all plants, is best nourished by moysture : and morally to informe us, that the malignitie of wine should be allayed with water. So of old they qualified the fury of* Bacchus *with the sober Nymphs ; as now the more temperate doe in hot Countries.*

Reconciled Jupiter *and* Juno *now highthen their delights with full boles of Nectar. The drinke of the Gods, importing a privation of death ; and therefore powred out by* Hebe, *the Goddesse of eternall youth. In their cups they talk wantonly :* Jupiter *would have the pleasure of women to exceed, and* Juno *of men.* Tiresias *is made their judge, who had tryed both sexes : his sentence is for* Jupiter, *how men had three ounces of the vigour of love, but that women had nine.* Juno *deprives him of his sight, which* Jupiter *supplies with the gift of prophesie. This* Tiresias *was the sonne of* Udæus,

Tiresias.

one

one of the five Captaites which survived that unnaturall warre; and assisted Cadmus in the building of his Citie. Women, if we give credit to histories either ancient or moderne, (whereof we shall treat in the transformation of Iphis) have often beene changed into men; but never man into woman. We therefore must fly to the allegory; not seldome among the Grecians as strange, as their fables stupendious. They allude Tiresias to the alternat seasons of the yeare: the spring called Masculine, because the growth of things are then inclosed in the solid bud; when every creature (expressed by these ingendring Serpents) are prompt unto Venus: but separated by his rod, the approaching fervor, he is turned into a Woman; that is, into flourishing Summer, defigured by his name: which season is said to be feminine, for that then the trees doe display their leaves, and produce their conceptions. The Autumne is a second time of generation, proceeding from the temperate qualitie of the aire; when he recovers his former sex by againe deviding the serpents; that is, by the approach of Winter, which deprives the Earth of her beautie, shuts up her wombe, and in that barren in it selfe is said to be Masculine. Iust was the judgement of Tiresias between Jupiter and Juno, that is, the two elements of fire and aire: for the aire conferres thrice as much as the fire to the generation of vegetables: which marries, as it were, the corne to the gleab, produces the blade, and swels it in the eare; whereas heat addes little to the materialls, though the maine in activitie, both producing the forme and causing maturitie. He is said to have beene bereft of his sight by Juno, in regard of the darke and clowdy aire of the Winter: when Jupiter by conceal'd heat infusing a conception of a future growth, is said to inspire him with the spirit of prophesy. But Lucian reports that the Grecians fained Tiresias to have beene sometimes a man, and sometimes a woman; because he first divided the wandring starres into Male and Female, in regard of their divers operations.

NARCIS-
SVS AND
ECCHO.

The first that made his Prophesies famous was the fate of Narcissus. His mother Liriope inquiring whether he should live untill he were old; Tiresias replied: If he know not himselfe. As strange as obscure; and seeming contradictory to that Oracle of Apollo. To know a mans selfe is the chiefest knowledge. The lack hereof hath ruined many: but having it must needs ruine our beautifull Narcissus: who onely is in love with his owne perfections; though not without store of despairing rivalls. Among whom the babling Nymph Eccho: who for being formerly Jupiters Property was deprived by Juno of speech; more then to reiterate the last word which she heard: and now despised by the froward boy, pines away with love, untill at length he consumes to an unsubstantiall voice. Well therefore was vaine-glory fained to affect selfe-love; who rejected, converts into a sound; that is, into nothing. Now Eccho signifies a resounding: which is onely the repercussion of the voyce, like the rebound of a ball, returning directly from whence it came: and that it reports not the whole sentence, is through the debilitie of the reverberation. Yet in the garden of the Tuillereis in Paris, by an artificiall device under ground invented for musick, I have heard an Eccho repeate a verse, not lowdly uttered, without failing in one syllable. Eccho is here said to conceale her selfe in woods and mountaines: but chiefely in winding vallies, rocky caves, and ruinous buildings. In many places three or foure answer one another: Lambinus writes, that at Charoune in the Ile of France he heard seven distinctly; and that there are not fewer then thirty to be heard at Pavia. The image of the voice, so often rendred, is as that of the face reflected from one glasse to another; melting by degrees, and every reflection more weake and shady then the former. Ausonius makes Eccho thus speake to the Painter that would have drawne her;

Vane, quid affectas faciem mihi ponere picton,
Ignotamq; oculis sollicitare deam?
Aeris & lingua sum filia, mater inanis
Iudicii, vocem qua sine mente gero.
Extremos pereunte modos à fine reducens,
Ludificata sequor verba aliena meis.
Auribus in vestris habito penetrabilis Eccho:
Et si vis similem pingere, pinge sonum.
Epig. 11.

Fond Painter, why wouldst thou my picture draw?
An unknown Goddesse, whom none ever saw.
Daughter of aire, and tongue: of judgement blind
The mother I; a voice without a minde.
I only with an others language sport:
And but the last of dying speech retort.
Loud Eccho's mansion in the eare is found:
If therefore thou wilt paint me, paint a sound.

Nemesis.

Thus she, thus many more were undone by the pride and beautie of Narcissus: when some one cryed out with eyes and hands erected to Heaven; So may he love himself, and so despaire! Whose curse is granted by Rhamnusia; a name of Nemesis in that she had her principall Temple at Rhamnus, a citie of Achaia; with her statue (so highly celebrated by Varro) of Parian marble, ten cubites high, and all of one stone: brought thither by the insolent Persians to set up for a trophy of the victory which they promised to themselves against the Athenians, but contrary in the event: and
therefore

234

therefore converted by Phidias, *that excellent statuary, into the Image of this Goddesse of Revenge, or Retribution, as her name importeth. Whereof* Ausonius *out of a* Greeke *Author.*

> I, by the *Persians* for a Trophy brought
> Then when a stone, am *Nemesis* thus wrought.
> I here a Grecian Trophy now reside :
> A *Nemesis* to scourge the *Persian* pride.

Me lapidem quondam Persæ advexere trophæum
Vt fierem bello : nunc ego sum Nemesis.
At ficut Græcis victoribus asto trophæum:
Punio sic Perfas vaniloquos Nemesis.

A Deitie severe and inexorable to the proud and arrogant, who are too much elated with the indowments of nature, or felicities of fortune. Her head he adorn'd with a crowne, impost with fearefull Harts, and figures of victory. Her shoulders were garnished with wings : in her right hand she held a Lance; and in her left a pitcher, including the little images of Æthiopians. *By her crowne presenting her universall Empire; as by the sculpture thereon the terror of her prevailing indignation: or expressing the malignant envy of the vulgar; who insult in the fall of the great and fortunate, crowning, as it were, the applauded Goddesse : by her wings declaring her swift, and unforeseene subversions; the potent and politick not seldome overthrown by what they contemned. By her Lance, her actuall inflictions, either through warre or their own temeritie : and by the* Æthiopians *in her pitcher, the farre extent of her vengeance; or in that she terrifies those, whom she confounds not, with black and ominous visions; as with the perfidiousnesse of friends, the circumventions of enemies, misfortunes, sicknesse, and death, which incounter them in the midst of their felicities. She is said to be the daughter of* Oceanus *and* Nox, *in regard of the vicissitude of things, and unrevealed secrecy of the divine judgement. For as the Ocean successively flowes and ebbs, so men in this interlude of life are exalted and cast down by a constant exchange, of which we need not seeke farre for examples : neither is the divine judgement agreeable with our humane; and therefore well fained the daughter of night, in that occult and separated from apprehension : which the* Ethnicks *themselves could observe;*

> Then fell *Ripheus*; none more just then he
> Of all the *Trojans*: but Cœlestialls see
> With other eyes——

—— Cadit & Ripheus, justissimus unus
Qui fuit ex Teucris, & servantissimus æqui.
Diis aliter visum. —— *Virg. Æn. l 2.*

So may we say of the death of Socrates, *esteemed the most innocent of men : and of the unparalleld calamities of the noble* Belisarius; *who having overcome the* Vandals *in* Africa, *triumphed over the* Persians, *and more then once delivered* Italy, *and* Rome *it selfe, from the bloody invasions of barbarous nations, for recompence had his eyes pull'd out by the Emperour* Justinian: *reduced withall to that povertie, as glad to shelter his age in a little shed by the high way, begging of those who passed by to* Give one halfepenny to the poore *Belisarius, whom envy and not error had bereft of his eye-sight.*

Narcissus, *pursued by the wrath of* Nemesis, *falls miserably in love with his own shadow, and dyes in doting on it. Nor are his eyes averted by death :*

> Who now eternally their gazes fix
> Upon the waters of infernall *Styx*.

To shew how punishments end not with life, but pursue the guiltie to an other world. The Naiades *strew his course with their haire; an ancient custome at funeralls. whereof* Homer *in the funerall of* Patroclus.

> His Corps with curles they covered;
> Shorne from each mourning Princes head.

Capillis autem totum mortuum tegebant quos injiciebant
Tondentes —— Iliad l. 23.

He is called their brother, in that fained to be begotten by a River *on a* Water-Nymph: *or because the flower into which he was changed, affecteth, and only prospers by the water. Whereof a moderne Poet.*

> Narcissus, *once a* Cupid, *adde but wings;*
> Who too-much trusted to deceitfull springs;
> A flowre, now to the flood inclines; that so
> He might by that which was his ruine grow.

Hic est ille suis nimium qui credidit undis
Narcissus, vero dignus amore puer.
Cernis ab irriguo repetentem gramine ripam,
Vt per quas periit crescere possit aquas.
Sabæus.

Narcissus

Narciſſus ſignifies ſtupid or heavy ; which hath a relation to the manner of his death : and there-fore his flower, which we call a daffadill, was dedicated to the infernall Deities.

S ome tract of Hiſtory I finde in Pauſanias. There is, *ſaith he ,* a place neere *Theſpia* which is called *Danacus :* in this is the fountain of *Narciſſus* ; wherein, they ſay, he beheld his own likeneſſe, and not conceiving that it was his ſhadow, or how himſelf was beloved by himſelf, pined away and dyed by the brinke of the fountain. But how abſurd is it to believe, that any ſhould be ſo diſtracted or beſotted with affection, as not to diſtinguiſh a ſhadow from a ſub-ſtance ? Yet ſomething like this is recorded, not vulgarly known. *Narciſſus* had a ſiſter born at the ſame birth, ſo exceeding like as hardly diſtinguiſhable ; alike alſo their haire in colour and trim, and alike their habites ; who accuſtomed to hunt and exerciſe together , with her brother fell violently in love : and ſhe dying, repaired oft to this fountain, much ſatisfying his affection in gazing therein, as not beholding his own ſhadow, but the image of his dead ſiſter. *Others write that he threw himſelf into the water out of impatiency to live without her. Of the miraculous likeneſſe of twins all ages have afforded examples. I have heard a Gentleman yet li-ving ſay, how his mother knew not his brother from him but by the treading of their ſhooes ; that both, when ſchollers, were likely whipt for the offence of one ; and that being bound Apprentiſes to two Mer-chants in* London, *they would ordinarily waite in one an others roome, undiſcovered by their Maſters, or any of the family. But now to the morall.*

Narciſſus, a youth ; that is, the ſoule of a raſh and ignorant man ; beholds not his own face, nor conſi-ders of his proper eſſence or vertue, but purſues his ſhadow in the fountain, and ſtrives to imbrace it ; that is, admireth bodily beauty, fraile and like the fluent water ; which is no other then the ſhadow of the ſoule : for the minde doth not truly affect the body , but its own ſimilitude in a bodily forme. Such Narciſſus, *who ignorantly affecting one thing, purſues another ; nor can ever ſatisfie his longings. Therefore he reſolves into teares and periſheth : that is ; the ſoule ſo alienated from it ſelf, and doting on the body, is tortured with miſerable perturbations ; and dyes, as it were, infected with that poyſon : ſo that now it rather appeareth a mortall body then an immortall ſoule. This fable likewiſe preſents the condition of thoſe, who adorned by the bountie of nature, or inriched by the induſtry of others, without merit, or ho-nour of their own acquiſition, are tranſported with ſelf-love, and periſh, as it were, with that madneſſe. Who likely ſequeſter themſelves from publique converſe and civill affaires , as ſubjects to neglects and diſgraces, which might too much trouble and deject them : admitting but of a few to accompany their ſolitarineſſe ; thoſe being ſuch as only applaud and admire them, aſſenting to what they ſay, like as ma-ny Ecchoes. Thus depraved , puſt up with unceſſant flattery, and ſtrangely intoxicated with ſelf ad-miration ; at length they contract ſuch a wonderfull ſloth, as ſtupifies their ſences, and deprives them of all their vigour and alacritie.* Narciſſus *is therefore converted to a flower of his name, which ſignifies ſtupid : flouriſhing onely in the Spring , like theſe who are hopefull in the firſt of youth , but after fall from expectance and opinion : the flower, as they, altogether unprofitable , being ſacred to Pluto and the* Eumenides: *for what bore of it ſelf no fruit, but paſt and was forgotten, like the way of a ſhip in the Sea, was conſecrated of old to the infernall Deities. But a fearefull example we have of the dan-ger of ſelf-love in the fall of the Angels ; who intermitting the beatificall viſion, by reflecting upon themſelves, and admiration of their own excellency, forgot their dependance upon their Creator. Our* Narciſſus, *now a flower, inſtructs us, that we ſhould not flouriſh too ſoone, or be wiſe too timely, nor over-love, or admire our ſelves : which although hatefull in all ages, in youth is intolerable. And therefore* Nemeſis *is introduced to revenge ſuch pride and inſolency ; and to make his vices his own deſtruction.*

BACCHVS *This wonderfull deſtiny gives wings to the fame of* Tireſias : *yet flouted , and upbraided with the loſſe of his eyes by violent* Pentheus, *of whoſe deſtruction he propheſies. This was the ſonne of* Echi-on *and* Agave *the daughter of* Cadmus ; *who now grown old, had reſigned unto him the kingdome of* Thebes. *A mortall enemy to the introduced Rites, and adoration of* Bacchus ; *which fill* Cythæron *with the ſhouts and clamours of frantick women, now a celebrating his Orgies : ſo called, either in that thoſe rites were celebrated on the tops of mountains, or becauſe his followers were wrapt with a kinde of fury. Three there were of that name, the* Lybian, *the* Ægyptian, *and the here mentioned* Theban : *who emulating the glory of the former, led an army into the Eaſt ; and left behinde him many trophies of victories : having multitudes of women in his train, as the former had* Amazons. *It is a traditi-on, ſaith the Athenian in* Plato, *that being diſturbed in his ſenſes by* Iuno ; *in revenge, he in-vented wine to infuriate the* Bacchæ. *Yet for this, and other behovefull inventions , he was ho-noured by men with Temples and Altars : in himſelfe made up of all contrarieties ; valiant and ef-feminate, induſtrious and riotous, a ſeducer to vice, and an example of vertue : ſo variouſly good and bad are the effects of wine according to the uſe or abuſe thereof. And becauſe the actions and inventions*

of

of the former grew now obscured by antiquitie, their fame and vertues were ascribed to the latter Bacchus: *especially by* Orpheus *in honour of the family of* Cadmus, *by whom he had been highly advanced. But heare we the* Thebans *sing of their* Bacchus; *since it gives no small light to what hath and is to be said hereafter.*

Thou who with Ivy deck't thy dangling haire;
We, arm'd with jav'lins, to thy Rites repaire.
Bright ornament of heaven, thy suppliants heare:
To thee their hands thy noble *Thebans* reare.
O favour! hither turn thy virgin face:
With thy syderiall looks disperse and chace
These lowring clouds, the threats of *Erebus*,
And rage of greedy fate, from ours and us.
It thee becomes to have thy tresses bound
With vernall flowres, with *Tyrian* miter crown'd,
And girt in Ivy wreathes: now liberally
Let flow, and now in knots thy tresses tie.
As when, of thy fierce step-dames wroth afraid,
With borrowed shape thou counterfet'st a maid.
Why art thou so effeminately drest,
VVith robes that sweep the earth, and naked brest?
Those Eastern nations who on *Ganges* drink,
And break the ice on cold *Araxis* brink,
Could not thy Lions for thy robe behold,
Drawn in a Chariot rooft with vines of gold.
Thee old *Silenus* on a long ear'd jade
Attends; vine-leaves his rugged fore-head shade.
Lascivious Priests thy Orgies celebrate:
Troopes of Bassarian frows upon thee wait.
Now on *Edonian Pangæus* tread;
Now on the *Thracian Pindus* loftie head,
Distracted *Mænas*, joyn'd with *Theban* wives,
To serve th' *Ogygian Iacchus* strives;
VVhose loynes a Panthers sacred skin invests:
VVith ruffled haire the matrons hide their brests,
And brandish leavy jav'lins lightly born.
Vnhappy *Pentheus*, now in peeces torn,
Relenting *Thyades*, their fury gone,
Behold with griefe; nor think that fact their owne.
Faire *Ino*, with the blew *Nereides*,
(Thy Aunt ô *Bacchus*) raignes in sacred seas:
The stranger Boy there makes his blest aboad,
Of *Bacchus* race, *Palemon*, no small God,
Thee, lovely Boy, the *Thuscan* rovers seiz'd:
Then *Nereus* the tumid maine appeas'd,
Blew seas converting into flowry meads:
The Plane-tree there his broad-leav'd branches spreads;
Greene Lawrel groves, belov'd by *Phœbus*, spring,
And chanting birds among the branches sing:
About the mast the youthfull Ivy twines,
The loftie toe imbrac'd with clustred vines:
Now in the Prow Idæan Lyons rore,
The trembling Poope *Gangetick* Tygres bore:
In seas themselves th' affrighted sailers threw;
VVho turn'd to *Dolphins*, flying ships pursew.
Pactolus wealthy streames thy burden tride,
Whose waters through a golden channell glide.

Effusum redimite comam nutante corymbo,
Lucidum cœli de[illegible]s, huc ades votis
Mollia Nysæis armata brachia Thyrsis,
Quæ tibi nobiles Thebæ, Bacche, tua
Palmis supplicibus ferunt.
Huc averte favens virgineum caput,
Vultu sidereo discute nubila,
Et tristes Erebi minas,
Avidumq; fatum.
Te decet vernis comam floribus cingi,
Te caput Tyria cohibere mitra;
Hederave mollem baccifera
Religare frontem:
Spargere effusos sine lege crines,
Rursus adducto revocare nodo.
Qualis iratam metuens novercam
Creveras falsos imitatus artus
Crine flaventi simulata virgo,
Luteam vestem retinente zona.
Vnde tam molles placuere cultus,
Et sinus laxi, fluidumq; syrma?
Vidit aurato residere curru,
Veste cum longa tegeres leones,
Omnis Eoæ plaga vasta terræ,
Qui bibit Gangem, niveumq; quisquis
Frangit Araxem.
Te senior turpi sequitur Silenus asello,
Turgida pampineis redimitus tempora sertu.
Condita lascivi deducunt Orgia mystæ:
Te Bassaridum comitata cohors,
Nunc Edonii pede pulsavit
Sola Pangæi; nunc Threicio
Vertice Pindi: nunc Cadmeas
Inter matres impia Mænas
Comes Ogygio venit Iaccho,
Nebride sacra præcincta latus.
Tibi commota pectora matres
Fudere comam: thyrsumq; levem
Vibrante manu, jam post laceros
Pentheos artus Thyades œstro
Membra remissæ, velut ignotum
Videre nefas.
Ponti regna tenet nitidi matertera Bacchi
Nereidumq; choris Cadmeia cingitur Ino.
Ius habet in fluctus magni puer advena ponti
Cognatus Bacchi, numen non vile Palæmon.
Te Tyrrhena puer rapuit manus,
Et tumidum Nereus posuit mare,
Cærula cum pratis mutat freta.
Hinc verno platanus folio viret,
Et Phœbo laurus charum nemus:
Garrula per ramos avis obstrepit.
Vivaces hederas ramus tenet.
Summa ligat vitis carchesia.
Idæus prora fremuit Leo.
Tigris puppe sedet Gangetica.
Tum pirata freto pavidus natat;
Et sequitur curvus fugientia Crabasa Delphin.
Divite Pactolus vexit te Lydius unda,
Aurea torrenti deducens flumina ripa.

Luxavit victos arcus Geticasq; sagittas
Lassa Massagetes qui pocula sanguine miscet.
Regna securigeri Bacchum sensere Lycurgi.
Sensere terræ Zedacum feroces:
Et quos vicinus Boreas ferit
Arva mutantes: quasq; Mæotis
Alluit gentes frigida fluctu:
Quasq; despectat vertice summo
Sidus Arcadium, geminumq; plaustrum.
Ille dispersos domuit Gelones:
Arma detraxit trucibus puellis:
Ore dejecto petiere terram
Thermodontiacæ graves caterva
Positis tandem levibus sagittis;
Mites factæ. Sacer & Cytharon
Sanguine inundavit,
Ophioniaq; cæde.
Pratides sylvas petiere & agros.
Præsidem Bacchum coluit noverca.
Naxos Ægæo redimita ponto
Tradidit thalamis virginem relictam,
Meliore pensans damna marito.
Pumice sicco
Fluxit Nyctileus latex.
Garruli gramen secuere rivi.
Combibit dulces humus alta succos,
Niveiq; lactis candida fontes
Et mista odoro Lesbia cum thymo.
Ducitur cum magno nova nupta cælo.
Solenne Phæbus carmen
Edit infusis humero capillis.
Concutit tædas geminus Cupido.
Telum deposuit Iuppiter igneum,
Oditque Baccho veniente fulmen.
Lucida dum current annosi sidera mundi,
Oceanus clausum dum fluctibus ambiet orbem,
Lunæq; demissos dum plena recolliget ignes;
Dum matutinos prædicet Lucifer ortus;
Altæq; cæruleum dum Nerea nesciet Arctos;
Candida formosi venerabimur ora Lyæi.
    Sen. Oedip.

Messagians, quaffing blood and milke, unbend
Their bowes; nor more with Getick shafts contend.
Thy powre ax-arm'd Lycurgus kingdome knows,
The fierce Zedacians; and where Boreas blows
On hoary fields; those climates who shake
With cold, that border on Mæotis Lake;
And those whose Zenith is the Arcadian Star;
The Northern Wagons, and flow Wagonar.
Scattred Geloni he subdued: disarm'd
The brave Virago's; Thermedonians warm'd
Cold earth with their soft lips; but pacifi'd,
Their moone-like shields and quivers laid aside.
Sacred Cythæron he imbrew'd with blood
Of slain Ophians. To the shadie wood,
And fields, transformed Prætus daughters run.
The pleased stepdame now affects her son.
Naxos, begirt with the Aegean wave,
A bridall bed to Ariadne gave;
Her losse repaired with a better friend:
Torrents of wine from barren rocks descend;
A flood of milke from silver fountains powres,
With Lesbian honey mixt, perfum'd with flowres,
Which through the meadows murmuring streams produce,
Whose thirstie banks suckt in the pleasant juyce.
The starry Bride to high-archt heaven is led:
Phæbus, his haire upon his shoulders spred,
Epithalamiums sang that happy night:
Both Cupids now the nuptiall tapers light:
Iove laid his wrathfull thunderbolts aside,
And hates his lightning, when he Bacchus spi'd.
While radiant starres shall run their usuall race,
While Neptunes armes the fruitfull earth imbrace,
While Cynthia shall her hornes together close,
While Lucifer the rosie Morne fore-shews,
While loftie Arctos shuns the salt Profound,
We Bacchus praise and beautie will resound.

But heare we him rail'd at as much by Momus. This your so generous Bacchus, is scarce a man, and no Grecian by the mother, but the nephew of Cadmus a Phœnician Merchant. I will not say what he is, now he hath aspired to immortalitie; nor tax him with his railing and drunkennesse: you all see how soft and effeminate in his pleasures; halfemad, and smelling early of wine: who hath brought amongst us his whole fraternitie, and declared them Gods: Pan, Silenus, and the Satyres; a rable of rusticks and Goat-heards, addicted to dances and gambols; and of shape as monstrous as their manners. One of these hath hornes on his fore-head, and nourisheth a filthy long beard; his lower parts like a Goat; and all over not differing much from a beast. Another, old, bald, and flat nosed like an Ape; for the most part riding on an Asse; who by birth is a Lydian. With those the prick-ear'd Satyres, bald also, and horned like late-falne kids, originally Phrygians. All of these have seemly long tailes. You see with what Gods we are furnisht with by this Gallant. I omit to speak of the brace of women which he hath brought us: the one his sweet-heart Ariadne, whose Crown is by him made a Constellation; The other daughter to Icarius the husband-man: and what, ô you Gods, is of all most ridiculous, Erigone hath brought her dog with her; least she should be sad, and want her old companion in heaven.

But now to be serious. Noah was he who immediatly after the flood first planted a vineyard; and shewed the use of wine unto men. Therefore some write that of Noachus he was called Boachus, and after Bacchus, by the Ethnicks; either by contraction, or ignorance of the Etymologie. The ignorance likewise of the truth hath begotten so many fables and allegories: he being neither the Lybian,

Ægyptian,

238

Ægyptian, *nor* Theban Bacchus, *but the ancient* Nyſæan; *who flouriſhed long before* Jupiter Hammon, *or the* Cretan Jupiter, *the ſuppoſed fathers of the other. Poſteritie divers waies celebrated this bountie of* Noah; *and therefore called him by ſundry names, as* Bacchus, Viniſer, *and* Oenotrius; *whereof* Italy *was after named* Oenotria, *of the excellent wines which that ſoyle produced.*

Now Pentheus *ſtrives to exaſperate the* Thebans *againſt* Bacchus. *He puts them in minde of their originall, their ancient religion, and what a ſhame to ſubmit to an effeminate boy, ſupported by frantick women and drunkards: ſhewing how eaſily reſiſted by the example of* Acriſius. *This* Acriſius *was king of* Argos, *the ſonne of* Abas, *and father of* Danae; *who in that he would not admit of his Rites, is ſaid to have chaſed him out of his kingdome.* Pentheus *ſends his guard to apprehend him: they wounded, return with one of his Prieſts, who tells the miracles of the ſhip ſticking faſt in the midſt of the deepe, and perjur'd ſailers converted into Dolphins. Yet the firſt is parallel'd by hiſtory; effected, according to* Pliny, *by a little fiſh; and therefore called by the* Romanes Remora: *which ſince ſo incredible, I will relate it in the words of the Author.* This fiſh frequenteth the rock, and is ſuppoſed by *Ariſtotle* to have many feet, in regard of the multitude of her finnes. Although the windes blow violently, and the tempeſts rave; yet commands ſhe their fury, and ſo curbs their power, that the ſhip continues immoveable; which neither cables nor anchors, though never ſo ſtrong and maſſie, could detaine: and that only by cleaving thereunto, without her own labour. But our Armado's are fortified with Caſtles; from whence they fight on the ſea, as from the walls of a Bulwark. O humane vanitie; when even thoſe ſhips, whoſe beaks are ſo armed with braſſe and iron to pierce through the ſides of ſuch as they encounter, ſhould be forced to obey the arreſt of a little fiſh not halfe a foot long! At the battell of *Actium* one detained, as they report, the Admirall, which carried *Antonius*, haſting to order his navy and incourage his ſouldiers, untill he was conſtrained to ſhip himſelf in another: upon which advantage the *Cæſarians* fell on with the greater violence. And in our memory *Caligula* was ſo checkt in his return from *Aſtura* to *Antium*. Nor long continued their admiration, having forthwith diſcovered the cauſe: for certain perceiving his Gally, which had five men to every oare, to be only detained of all the reſt of the navy, leapt preſently into the ſea; and ſearching about the keele of the veſſell, found this little fiſh faſt cleaving to the rudder. This ſhowne to the Emperor, with indignation he beheld what could ſtop his courſe, and reſiſt thoſe oares which were ſtretcht by the ſtrength of foure hundred ſea-men: renuing his wonder to ſee it loſe that vertue within, which it had when it cleav'd to the out-ſide of the veſſell. Thoſe who then, and after, beheld it, reſembled the ſame to a Snail, but not a little greater. *The like power he attributes to the* Purple fiſh, *annexing this ſtory out of* Titianus: Periander *diſpatching a mandate for* Gnidos, *to caſtrate all their boyes which were nobly deſcended, the ſhip was ſo long mored in the midſt of the ſea by this ſhell-fiſh, untill another arrived (the Prince repenting him of his crueltie) with a countermand. Wherefore the* Gnidians *to perpetuate the memory thereof, did conſecrate that fiſh to their* Venus. *But theſe ſtrange effects, which perhaps depend on no naturall cauſes, may rather proceed from the power of the* Divell. *I have heard of ſea-faring men, and ſome of that Citie, how a* Quarter-maſter *in a* Briſtol *ſhip, then trading in the* Straights, *going down into the Hold, ſaw a ſort of women, his known neighbours, making merry together, and taking their cups liberally: who having eſpied him, and threatning that he ſhould repent their diſcovery, vaniſhed ſuddenly out of ſight; who thereupon was lame ever after. The ſhip having made her voyage; now homeward bound, and neere her harbour, ſtuck faſt in the deepe Sea (as this of the* Tyrrhenians *) before a freſh gale, to their no ſmall amazement: nor for all they could do, together with the helpe that came from the ſhoare, could they get her looſe, untill one (as* Cymothoe *the* Trojan *ſhips) ſhov'd her off with his ſhoulder, (perhaps one of thoſe whom they vulgarly call* Wiſe-men, *who doe good a bad way, and undo the enchantments of others.) At their arrivall the* Quarter-maſter *accuſed theſe women: who were arraigned, and convicted by their owne confeſsions; for which five and twentie were executed. But to proceed with the fable.* Theſe Tyrrhenians *for their piracies and power at Sea, and for that they had tranſported divers Colonies to ſundry parts of the world, were ſurnamed Dolphins: whereupon this fable was by the* Greekes *deviſed; and withall to deterre from rapine and perjury, which ſeldome eſcapes the divine vengeance. The fantaſticall reſemblances of Lynxes, Tygres, and Panthers, are the terrors of conſcience, which drive the guiltie to deſpaire and ruine. They alſo are ſaid to have beene turned into Dolphins, becauſe thoſe fiſhes ſeeme naturally to affect the ſocietie of men; following of ſhippes, and ſporting about them, as they ſayle along: nay many, if we may give credite to credible Authors, have beene carryed on their backs to drie land;*

THE TYRRHEN PIRATS.

L 2 *and*

and therefore the ancient presented safetie by a bridled Dolphin. So give they warning of insuing tempests aud advise the mariners, as it were, to stand to their tacklings and take in their sailes. All which concurres with our Porpus, out of doubt the true Dolphin: wherein I am not only confirmed by the authoritie of Scaliger. For those that are called Dolphins by our East and West Indian Sea-men (who likely give known names to things which they know not) are fishes, whereof I have seene many, which glitter in the water with all varietie of admirable colours; and are hardly so bigge as our Salmon-trouts: too little by farre to beare those burthens wherewith almost all ancient authors doe charge them: besides none of these were ever seene in the Mediterranean sea, the scene of those stories. The credulitie of the old worlds superstition, was no lesse prodigious then their fables: for an instance, this fable we now treat of is yet to be seene in beautifull figures of mosaique painting (an antique kinde of worke, composed of little square peeces of marble: gilded and coloured according to the place that they are to assume in the figure or ground: which set together, as imbossed, present an unexpressable statelinesse) in S. Agnes Church at Rome, which was formerly the Temple of Bacchus.

God, in detestation of Atheisme, doth reward the devout, though in a false religion, with temporall blessings, as here Acætes advanced from a poore fisher-man to the pontificall dignitie: who now cast in prison and reserved for torments, the shackles fall from his leggs, and the doores unlockt themselves to afford a way to his safetie. This the more incenseth our violent Pentheus. There is no creature so immane and rabid, but anger addes to his naturall fiercenesse: Other affections have their apparant symptomes, but that of anger is eminent, whose fire inflames the looks and sparkles in the eye balls: proceeding from the sending forth of the spirits in a revengefull appetite: Good counsell converts into bad when unseasonably given; so the disswasions of Cadmus and Athamas exasperate his fury: who to chastise his kinsman, perhaps as much out of envy as zeale, ascendeth Cithæron. A mountaine of Bœotia, not farre from Thebes, which took that name from Orpheus his harpe, called alwaies sacred: in that there he first instituted the Orgies of the Theban Bacchus; transferred by him out of Egypt from the Ægyptian. For Cham and his accursed race; first inhabiting those parts, there planted Idolatry: which the Poets brought into Greece, who travelled thither to inrich their knowledge. For almost all Arts and Sciences had from them their originall: who had besides more impressions of antiquitie then any other nation; as appeareth by their Dinasteis, stretching beyond the generall deluge: who affirme that their first Kings lived twelve hundred yeares, and the latter but three hundred; comming neere the ages of man both before and after. But what Tradition delivers obscurely and lamely, is in the Scripture entire and perspicuous. Agave fulfills the prophecy of Tiresias in the slaughter of her sonne: who distracted with the fury of Bacchus, together with her sisters, supposing him a Bore, transfix him with their javelings, torne forthwith in peeces, for all his teares and submission, by the rest of the Bacchæ. There is nothing more plausible to the vulgar then the innovation of government and religion. To this they here throng in multitudes. Wise Princes should rather indeavour to pacifie, then violently oppose a popular fury: which like a torrent beares all before it; but let alone exhausteth it selfe, and is easily suppressed. Reformation is therefore to be wrought by degrees, and occasion attended: least through their too forward zeale they reject the counsell of the expert, and incounter too strong an opposition, to the ruine of themselves and their cause; whereof our Pentheus affords a miserable example. The blind rage of Superstition extinguisheth all naturall affection. Agave murders her sonne, and the aunts their nephew: nor have the latter ages been unacquainted with such horrors.

On the other side Pentheus expresseth the image of an implacable Tyrant; hating religion, and suppressing it in others: nor to be diverted by counsell or miracles; till his death approves that tyrants are no where safe; no not among their own kindred.

Discite justitiam moniti & non temnere divos. Virg. Æn. 6.   Admonisht, justice prize; Nor holy Gods despise.

The proud in prosperitie are the most dejected in adversitie. Who would not be intreated; now basely intreats for mercy: but could not obtaine what he never afforded. There is nothing more proud then man, nor more miserable.

OVIDS

Lib: 4

VPON THE FOVRTH BOOK OF
OVIDS METAMORPHOSIS.

ALcithoe *and her sisters will neither acknowledge the deitie of* Bacchus, *nor partake in his so-lemnities; which now are celebrated by the* Theban *women. Who hang the skins of spotted beasts on their shoulders; to expresse not only the varietie of colour, but the nature of wine; which makes the Salvage civill, and the civill Salvage, by the moderate, or immoderate use thereof. They dis-shevell their haire, as suting with the furious effects of wine, and crown it with Ivy : in that Ivy resembleth the vine, affording garlands, when the other is naked. Besides, the berries and leaves ine-briate alike, through their hot and dry qualitie : although others write that they preserve from drun-kennesse, resisting the fume of wine by their naturall coldnesse, and that therefore they were worne. Each held a Thyrsis in her hand (a Iavelin wreathed about with Ivy) to take away terror from their friends, and covertly to wound their enemies : or in that wine deluding with its naturall suavitie and specious apparance, ere aware overthrows the senses, and debilitates the body. Superstitious Antiquitie did beleeve that the Gods rejoyced in multiplicitie of names : either for their greater glory, or to ex-presse the varietie of their faculties. As called in this hymne* Lyæus, *because liberall cups exhilarate the heart, and free it from sorrow.*

All things are difficult unto the α ϒ:
Nor fretting cares would else from mortals fly.
Who whet with wine at warres, or want repine ?
Or praise not *Bacchus*, or thee *Erycine*?

Siecis omnia nam dura Deus proposuit, neque
Mordaces aliter diffugiunt solicitudines.
Quis post vina gravem militiam aut pauperi-
em crepat ?
Quis non te potius, Bacche pater, *teq; decent*
Venus? Hor. l. 1, Ode 10,

So Bacchus *of that fury and madnesse which flowes from excesse :* Nysæus *and* Dionysius, *of* Nysa *the top of* Cythæron, *where he was fostred by the Nymphs; or of* Nysæa *a citie of* India, *where the more ancient was said to have been born, and concealed in* Meros *an adjoyning Mountain.* Bromeus *of the roaring of thunder which was at his birth : or of the tumultuary noise of drunkards.* Evan, *a word used by the* Bacchæ *in their acclamations. Fire-got in that snatch from the fire of lightning, or of the fiery operation of wine. The sonne of two mothers; that is of* Semele *and the thigh of* Jupiter; *Twice borne, as produced by either : and historically said to be borne of* Jupiters *thigh, in that fostred in a Cave at the foot of* Meros *which was consecrated unto him. He is called* Eleleus, *because wine exciteth audacitie and courage.*

What will not wine ? It secrets brings to light:
Confirmes our hopes, and makes th'unarmed fight.

Quid non ebrietas designat ? operta recludit,
Spes jubet esse ratas,ad prælia trudis iner-
mem. Horat.

Thioneus, *of* Thione, *a name of his mother* Semele: *or of his sacrifices and Orgies.* Lenæus, *of the wine-presse;* Nyctelius, *in that his ceremonies were celebrated by night : and* Liber,*which is the same with* Lyæus. *For the inventer of wine, saith* Seneca, *was not called* Liber *of the libertie of the tongue, but that it frees the minde from the servitude of cares, assures, and makes it more lively and confident. But as of freedome, so of wine, the moderation is most health-full.* Solon *and* Arcesilaus *are said to have cherished their spirits with wine; and ebrietie is ob-jected to* Cato: *but the objector may more easily prove that vice is a vertue, then* Cato *to be vitious. Although not often to be used, least it induce an ill habit; yet sometimes prolonged, a little to exhilarate, and remove over-sad a sobrietie.* Bacchus *is said to be ever young in that wine refresheth the spirits with a youthfull vigour, for a time suppressing those infirmities of the minde which accompany age : and a naked boy, because drunkards reveale their own shame and nakednesse, as* Noah *did his. So the Prophet pronounceth woe unto him who makes his neighbour drunk to discover his nakednesse : as also because they betray their secrets like little children. For as the over charged with wine cast it up again, so do they their counsells : both boyling within, and labouring for a passage. They place him in* Heaven, *and give him the perfection of beautie : being taken for the Sunne by the ancient, as appeares by these verses in* Virgil :

Bacchus, and bountious Ceres, ô you cleare
Lights of the World; that guide the sliding yeare.

———— Vos o clarissima mundi
Lumina, labentem cælo quæ ducitis annum;
Liber & alma Ceres———— Geor. l. 1.

Presenting

Prefenting alfo the varietie of Stars by the spotted skins which were worn by his followers. So by their dances they imitated the motion of the Sun, and those vapours daily drawn up by his vertue, which falling in showres, give growth to whatsoever the earth produceth: wherefore the Phallus was carryed about in his solemnities, as the father of generation, that name perpetually given him. They arme his head with hornes perhaps in regard of his radiancy: or in that much wine makes men as salvage and as fierce as Bulls; Tunc pauper cornua sumit; that is, grows bold and foole-hardy: but chearefull and gentle when moderately taken, and therefore then said to have the face of a virgin: but this Macrobius ascribes to the Sunne as the rest of his properties. Historically he is said to be horned in that anciently they dranke in hornes, and that Bacchus was the first that plowed the earth with oxen: in imitation of whom the Frowes in his festivals bound hornes to their foreheads. Diodorus writes that he raigned in Nysa, a Citie of Arabia the Happy; where first he was concealed from the inquisition of Juno: whence marching Eaft-ward with a mightie army, consisting for the most part of women, he subdued all India to the uttermost bounds of the Earth: there erecting two pillars, beyond which no land was supposed to extend, after imitated by Hercules in the West: of which Dionysius in the situation of the World:

Hae & Thebani Dionysi terra columnas
Monstrat ad Oceanum, atq; extremi littora
Ponti,
Montibus Indorum, qua vasto gurgite Ganges
ÿn mare se volvit, Nyssaamq; impulit undam.

This shoare whereon the fartheft Ocean flows
The Columnes of the *Theban Bacchus* shows
On Indian hills, where gulphy Ganges sweeps
Nysæan waves in to the swallowing Deeps.

More probable that Noah (the true Nysæan Bacchus) there setled after the flood, the Arke refting (according to the opinion of Becanus, and others) upon the mountains of Margiana, called Ararat in the Scriptures: which hath been mistaken for the mountains of Armenia, because Armenia is sometimes so called: but indeed one continued ledge of hills; seeming to rise in Armenia, but running through many vast provinces: and losing in the course thereof that generall name of Ararat which it retaines in the Scriptures, and receiving according to the severall places, diversitie of appellations. Alexander having conquered these Countries, in imitation of Bacchus returned with his triumphant Army crowned with Ivy, and about Nisæa in Margiana feasted ten daies, there finding the most delicate wine: perhaps even then affecting the title of the sonne of Jupiter: informed by Leon the Egyptian Priest under the seale of secrefie, and that he should only communicate it to his mother Olympias, how all those Gods were but formerly men: which made his ambition to hope for like honours. The Thebans *sing of the miferable fate of* Lycurgus; the sonne of Dryas, and King of Thrace: who perceiving that the Thracians addicted themselves wholly to drunkennesse, commanded the vines throughout all his kingdome to be cut down: whereupon it was fained that he pursued Bacchus with such deadly hatred; killing his Frowes who lay hid in Nysa, and forcing the affrighted God to flie unto Naxos. For which fact deprived of his sences, in stead of a vine, he cut his thigh affunder: but according to Homer struck blind by Jupiter.

Neq; enim, neq; Dryantis quidem filius fortis
Lycurgus
Diu vixit, qui cum diis cœlestibus certavit.
Qui olim furentis Bacchi nutrices
Persequebatur per facrum Nyssaium: illi autem simul omnes
Thyrsos in terram projecerunt ab homicida Lycurgo
Verberata stimulo. Bacchus autem territus
Subit maris undam, Thetis autem excepit finu
Timente: vehemens enim tenebat tremor ob viri comminationem.
Huic quidem postea irati sunt dii facile viventes:
Et ipsum cæcum fecit Saturni filius, neq; omplius diu
Vixit: quoniam immortalibus invisus erat omnibus diis.

Nor *Dryas* son survived many howers;
Who waged warre with the Cœleftiall powers.
He furious *Bacchus* Nurses did pursew
Through sacred *Nysas* hills; to Earth they threw
Their leavy Javelins; whom his Goad deprives
Of life: in seas affrighted *Bacchus* dives;
Whom *Tethys* in her silver bofome took,
Trembling and panting with a gaftly look.
This vext the happy-living Deities;
Struck blind by *Iove*, by all abhord, he dyes.

Yet Diagondas the Theban *incurr'd no punishment for the like*; who by a perpetuall Edict abolished the beaftly night facrifices of Bacchus: suppreffed after by the Confuls, not only in the Citie of Rome, but through all their dominions. Plutarch *calumniating the* Jews will have their feaft of Tabernacles to be celebrated in the honour of Bacchus, and indeavours to parallell it with his frantick solemnities. Yet they had a meeting which they called Mifchte, of their free and more liberall drinking. They make his chariot to be drawn by Linxes: beafts with spotted skins, begotten between the Wolfe and Hyena: dedicated unto him (as others of that nature) for their immanitie and violence, much

affecting

affecting wine, and by that baite taken ; concurring with the affections and dispositions of drunkards : as also in that a creature of so short a memory ; insomuch as they forget the prey which they but turne their eye from, and seeke after other : to declare that nothing which is said or done in drinke should be remembred ; according to that saying, Odi memorem compotorem. *But contrary to the rule of* Pythagoras, *who would have their ridiculous words and actions continually repeated, as the onely cure of that evill. For what they were not ashamed to doe, they are ashamed to heare off. His solemnities are performed by women : being brought up, and accompanied by them in his Indian expedition : called* Bacchæ *of his name, and their frantick clamours : or said to be so associated, in that as* Plutarch *affirmes Women can beare more wine then men, in regard of their naturall humiditie ; or in that* Bacchus *is a friend unto* Venus.

Satyres.

The Satyres follow in the Reare : lasciviousnesse (for so the name signifies, perpetually attending on wine and effeminate immodesty. They are described to differ from the shapes of men in the lower parts only, which resembles a Goates, with long tailes, and hornes on their heads, their bodies all hairy. Pliny *affirmes that there were of them in the* Indian *mountains : and* Euphemus *of* Caria ; *how that sailing into* Spaine *he was born by the extremitie of weather through the wide Ocean to certain Ilands which were called the Iles of the Satyres : that the people were red of colour, and had long tayles like horses ; who coming aboard, without speaking one word offered violence to their women : when the terrified Mariners turned ashoare a Barbarian wench ; whom the Satyres following, contaminated with all varietie of beastlinesse. Some deny that such ever were. Although* Hierome *and* Athanasius *report that one appeared to* St. Paul *the hermit ; who said he was mortall, and an inhabiter of those Deserts.* Esay, *prophesying of the desolation of* Babylon, *saies that their houses shall be full of dolefull creatures, and that Satyres shall dance therein. So Fairy Rounds have therefore been much spoken off. I have heard of some who trade to* Ginny, *that they have seene, and had aboard, a beast (if I may so tearme it) that would goe on his hinder leggs, and use his former as hands : that it fed as we feed, would grieve, and weepe, and could not indure to be laught at. The* Moores *would say that they would assaile them in the woods, and beat them with cudgells. And perhaps the Baboone for his up-right posture, and witty imitation of man, might be mistaken for a* Laplander. *But I am confident that this conception of Satyres proceeded chiefly from salvage and wild men, discovered a farre off in the woods by the civill : wearing skins of beasts on their tawny bodies, with the taile hanging down behinde, and hornes on their heads for ornament or terror ; even yet in use among the* West-Indians. *Ignorance and Feare having anciently attributed to such a terrestriall Deitie.*

Silenus.

The Silenii were no other then old Satyres : but one here mentioned more famous then the rest : born in Indian Nysæa, *and tutor unto* Bacchus. Lucian *describes him to be old and bald, riding for the most part on an Asse : low of stature, unweildy fat, with an over-grown belly ; his eares long and erected ; never sober, and ever accompanied by the Satyres.*

Th' old drunkard reeles from his dull Asse : the cries
Of Satyres eccho ; Rise up, father, rise.

Ebrius ecce senex pando delapsus asello,
Clamarunt Satyri, surge age, surge pater.
Ovid. de Art.

He is fained an attendant on Bacchus, *big-bellied, reeling, and old : because immoderate drink puffs up the body, making the head light, and the feet inconstant, producing also untimely age, by extinguishing the naturall with adventitious heat ; according to the opinion of* Farnelius. *He is said to be the Foster-father of* Bacchus *in that wine is bettered by age : and to ride on an asse, because habituall drunkennesse besots the sences, and dulls the understanding. The Asse was placed among the starres for a memoriall of this : or rather, as they fable, for putting the Gyants to flight with his horrible brayings ;* Silenus *assisting the Gods in that warre. They give him a ferula in his hand (the stalke of a certaine weed) that as drunkards are ready to strike, so they should be unable to hurt : all offences being then to determine in mirth, and not to be the authors of tragicall consequences. The clamors loud instruments, and hurrying about in these frantick solemnities, decipher the confused noyses, and undecent behaviours, in such drunken assemblies.*

Dercetis.

The daughters of Mineus *follow their worke in contempt of this festivall, and lighten their labours by telling of stories. The eldest beginning, toucheth by the way the transformations of* Dercetis, *of her daughter* Semiramis, *and the transforming of* Nais. Dercetis, *the Syrian Goddesse, is said to have falne in love with a beautifull youth as he sacrificed unto her ; and by him had a daughter : when she, ashamed of her incontinency, put the youth away, exposed the infant in the deserts, and overcome with sorrow, threw her selfe into a lake neere* Ascalon ; *there changed into a fish, as beleeved by the inhabitants : for which cause the Syrians did abstaine from fishes, erecting hard by a magnificent temple,*

temple, with her image in the likeneſſe of a fiſh from the navill downward. But the report of Theon is more probable, how that falling into the Sea ſhe was ſupported by fiſhes to the ſhoare, and therefore wor-ſhipped in that forme. This was that Dagon the Idoll of the Aſcalonites: according to S. Hierome, (by interpretation the fiſh of ſorrow) which fell before the Ark of God; the head and hands broken off on the threſhold, (for which cauſe neither the Prieſts nor thoſe who entred the Temple would tread thereon ever after) ſo that nothing but the ſhape of the fiſh remained. At the ſhrine of this Idoll, they offered fiſhes of gold and ſilver. Moreover, the Syrians would eat no fiſh, in that they held it injuſtice to kill thoſe creatures which did them no harme, and were fed on rather for luxury then neceſſitie: from which, for the ſame cauſe the Grecian army on the Helleſpont, and Phæacians, though daintie in their diet, abſtained. Withall, conceiving the ſea to be the originall and father of all that had life; and that man was ingendred of a liquid ſubſtance, they adored fiſhes, as being of their own generation and ſubſtance.

SEMIRA-MIS. Her expoſed daughter in that fed by Doves was called Semiramis, which ſignifies a Dove in the Syrian language: who after became the wife of Ninus, and Queene of Aſſyria. Now when ſhe could no longer detaine the Empire from her ſonne (which ſhe had managed during his minoritie, and infinitely inlarged it by her conqueſts) not induring to ſurvive her glory, ſhe with-drew her ſelfe; and being ſeene no-more, was ſaid to have been tranſlated to the Gods, according to the Oracle. Others faine, as here our Poet, that ſhe was turned into a Dove: in memoriall whereof, or rather of her name, the Babylonians divinely honoured that bird; and gave it in their enſignes. Beſides they expreſſed the aire by the Dove, as by fiſh, the water: reverencing both as comprizing the nature of all things.

NAIS. Of this Nais there is elſewhere no mention, but only in Arianus: who writes of an Iland in the Erythræan ſea, called Noſola a hundred furlongs diſtant from the ſhoare, which thoſe inhabitants affirmed to be ſacred to the Sun, and how none ſailed thither who ever made return, in that poſſeſſed by a Nais, who having ſatiated her ſelfe with all that arrived, converted them into fiſhes; for which the incenſed Sun expeld her the Iland; yet granted her requeſt in the cure of her inexpleable luſt: converting thoſe, whom ſhe had changed by her inchantments, again into men; from whom proceeded that race of people called Ichthyophagi. But Ovid here writes that ſhe her ſelfe in the end was transformed into a fiſh: whereby her burning deſires were extinguiſhed. For perſecuted Venus is elſe-where ſaid to have hid her ſelfe in that forme: and where can that vanquiſhed ardor be better concealed, then in a creature of ſo cold a conſtitution, which affords neither food nor heat to re-incenſe it? Whereupon perhaps theſe vowers of chaſtitie are tied to that diet. From which rule all ſhell-fiſh is to be excepted: and therefore perhaps an abomination to the Iſraelites.

PYRAMVS AND THISBE. She reſolves on the ſtory of Pyramus and Thisbe: whoſe wretched ends upbraid thoſe parents, who meaſure their childrens by their own out-worne and deaded affections; in forcing them to ſerve their avarice or ambition in their fatall marriages, (aptly therefore compared to the tyranny of Mezentius, who bound the living to the dead till they periſhed by the ſtench) more cruell there to their owne, then either the malice of foes or fortune: yet undoing, are undone, and ſhare in the generall calamitie. Not conſidering that riches cannot purchaſe love; nor threats or violence either force or reſtraine it: which, free by nature, as proceeding from the freedome of the will, diſdaines compulſion; ſubduing all, unſubdued by any: and ſo generous, that whereas all other affections and actions aime at different rewards; love only is contented with love, holding nothing elſe a ſufficient recompence. On the other ſide this exemplifies the ſad ſucceſſe of clandeſtine loves, and neglected parents: to whom obedience is due, and the diſpoſure of that life which they gave them. The white Mulberies are turned into black by the blood of Pyramus and Thisbe. Yet are of both ſorts, the leaves of the white ſuſtaining thoſe little wormes which apparell the World in ſuch bravery. The Ægyptians expreſſed Wiſdome by this tree: for whereas others allured by the flattery of the inconſtant weather, thruſt forth their buds and bloſſomes, which after are nipt and violated by a ſudden alteration: the Mulbery knowing the froſt for her enemy, will not ſprout till it be utterly ſubdued by a more certaine temper; then buds almoſt in one night, and quickly brings her fruit to maturitie leaſt the violent fervour ſhould likewiſe indamage it.

MARS AND VENVS. The ſecond Siſter relates the love of the Sunne; inflicted by Venus for his diſcovery of her adultery with Mars. Which carries this Aſtrologicall ſence: that thoſe who are borne in the Conjunction of Mars and Venus are prone to inordinate affections. Mars ſometimes deſcendeth beneath the Sun, and Venus for a part of the yeare aſcendeth above him, as it were to meete with each other: whoſe conjunction may then be ſaid to be diſcovered by the Sun, when he ceaſeth to obſcure them by the proximitie of his greater ſplendor. Vulcan bindes them in a net: that is, with too much fervor ſubdues their operations.

For

For the starre of Mars *is hot*; and that of Venus *moderate moist*; and whereof generation consists: and therefore mutuall lovers: by Neptune *unbound*; in that water extinguisheth fire, which is Vulcan. This fable therefore was invented to expresse the sympathy that is necessary in nature. Proceed we a little with the influences of these Planets: Mars is malignant; but approaching Venus subdues his malignitie: Mars exciteth greatnesse of spirit and wrath in those in whose nativitie he predominates; Venus impeacheth not that vertue of magnanimitie, but the vice of anger: Venus ruling infuseth the effects of love; and Mars conjoyning, makes the force of that love more ardent: wherefore those that are born under that conjunction are most fervently amorous. Mars follows Venus: because audacitie is the page unto love; not love to audacitie: for none, in that valiant, are taken with love; but wounded with love become so, and undauntedly undergoe all dangers for the beloved. Mars likewise signifies strife, and Venus friendship; which, as the ancient held, were the parents of all things. But morally adulteries are taxed by this fable: which how potent soever the offenders, though with never so much art contrived, and secrecy concealed, are at length discovered by the eye of the Sun, and exposed to shame and dishonour.

> Ill deeds have ill successe : revenge, though slow,
> The swift ore-takes. Slow Vulcan catches so
> Fleete *Mars*, the fleetest of the Deities :
> Lame subtiltie doth nimblenesse surprise.

Non recte succedunt mala opera, assequitur tardus celerem:
Vt nunc Vulcanus cum sit tardus cepit Martē,
Qui est velocissimus deorum qui Olympium tenent,
Claudus inquam technis: Hom. Odys. l. 8.

Now Vulcan *was truely that* Tuball-Caine *recorded by* Moses; *there being no small conformitie in the name*; who invented the art of working in Brasse and Iron: the authors of such benefits by posteritie reputed the sonnes of Jupiter; he also being the grand-childe of Cain, the first Jupiter; and called the God of fire, because by fire they are forged. So Naama, his sister and wife, was this Venus; her name importing beautie or comelinesse: and intitled the Goddesse of love; in that beautie so powerfully swaies in our bloods and affections.

LEVCOTHOE. Venus revengeth her disgrace on the discoverer. The cælestiall heat is inflamed by a terrestriall: and he who should looke indifferently on all, now onely looks on Leucothoe: and descends so low as to assume the shape of a mortall. Love is a desire of beautie; implyed by Leucothoë, Beautie, a beame of the divine refulgency: and therefore no marvell if the lover neglect all things for the beloved; without whom there is nothing but darknesse and discomfort. His looks wax pale; a colour sutable to that disease; by which Erasistratus the Physitian discovered the concealed affection of Antiochus. This palenesse proceeds from a defect of heat and scarcitie of blood, when nature is too weake to performe at once two severall duties. For the intention of a lovers minde is continually exercised in contemplating the beloved; with it all the powers of the naturall complexion: which, besides the restlesse emission of the spirits, doth cause an ill digestion in the stomach, and as bad a concoction in the liver: so that the blood is but little and crude which flowes in their veines. The Sunne now neglecteth the rest of his loves: all former affections are buried in a new. But passionate Clytie repines to be thus despised. Iealousie rouseth at once affection and envy. She discovers Leucothoës scapes to her father, who buries her alive. When the Sunne unable to relieve her, besprinkles the place and her body with Nectar; from whence a frankincense tree ascendeth: aptly is he fained to be the author of this transformation. To have sprinkled her with Nectar, in regard of the sweet odor of incense, which feasts the Gods with perfumes: and to have produced that tree, because it growes in Sabæa, as naturally affecting immoderate fervor; and thereupon happily fained reciprocall lovers. Moreover, in that it delights in open places, and yeelds a gum so usefull in physick: nor sweet unlesse it be melted by the Sunne or fire; like prayers which in themselves have no savour, unlesse inflamed with zeale and devotion; which in the Ceremoniall law was expressed by the Censor. But historically Leucothoe perhaps was some vowed Virgin, buried alive, as the Vestals at Rome, for infringing her chastitie.

CLYTIE. Clytie, rejected for this discovery, pines away with griefe; and is changed into a flower which turnes about with the Sun: (because that part of the stalke is infeebled whereon his beames beateth) who retaining still her former affection, closeth her leaves when he sets, as bemoaning his absence. Wherein the nature of the Heliotrope is described, whose feeble leaves are shut up by the moisture and coldnesse of the night; but opened and cherished by the drinesse and warmth of the Sun, dispersed from the center to the circumference, receiving thereby an addition of lustre: which shews the concinnitie and temperature of earthly bodies with the Heavenly. So saith Lactantius, should we fix our thoughts upon Heaven, and follow the guide of the Cœlestiall light, by farre more glorious then that of the Sun; which will without error direct us to the port of eternall felicitie.

N   *Now*

DAPHNIS

Now Alcithoë begins her story; first passing over certaine obscure fables. As that of Daphnis *turned into a stone by a Nymph inraged with jealousie: so fained in that she stupified his sences with a love-cup. Such an one was given to the Emperour* Caligula. *Of this thus* Juvenall.

——*hic Thessala vendit*
Philtra, quibus valeant mentem vexare mariti,
Et solea pulsare nates. Quod desipis, inde est
Inde animi caligo & magna oblivio rerum
Quas modo gessisti. Tamen hoc tolerabile, si non
Et furere incipias, ut avunculus ille Neronis,
Cui totam tremuli frontem Cæsonia pulli
Infudit——   *Sat. 6.*

He Æmonian Philters sells, of wicked might
To vex the husbands minde, and lust excite.
The souls obscure eclyps, besotted sence,
And strange forgetfulnesse, proceed from thence.
Lesse horrid, if not madnesse there with all :
As did to *Neroes* unckle erst befall ;
To whom his wife *Cæsonia* gave the whole
Infectious front all of a trembling fole.

SCYTHON
SELMVS.

Eusebius *reports how the Poet* Lucretius *was so infuriated with a love-cup that he slew himself: and by the law it is death to administer them to any. Next mentions he* Scython, *sometime a man and sometimes a woman. Belike of both sexes, and committing with either. Then* Selmus *one of* Idæan Dactils, *who fostered* Jove *and was beloved by him: but after, for discovering his mortalitie, converted into an Adamant: or perhaps so fained in regard of his undaunted fortitude. The* Curetes *were said to spring from showres; in that mimicks, fooles, and jesters according to the proverbe,* It hath rained fooles, *when many are together. Called* Curetes, *because they were shaven like Idiots; as* Corybantes, *of their dancing with rattles and mimicall actions; attending on* Jupiter, *as their successors not seldome on Princes.* Crocus *and* Smilax, *mutually beloved of each other, when they could not injoy their affections, were turned into flowers which preserve their names. Of these a late Author.*

CVRETES.

CORVS
AND
SMILAX.

Formosi juvenes, sed iniquo sidere nati,
Hic Crocus, hæc Smilax; dignus utroq; Iove.
Nam pro Hebe Smilax poterat servire Tonanti,
Et Phrygio poterat pro Ganymede Crocus.
Qui legeris flores, horum cognoscite & ignes:
Tum flagrabat amor, quam modo fragrat odor.
    Sabæus.

Crocus and *Smilax*, lovelier then love ;
Borne under cruell starrs, yet worthy *Iove.*
She might have Nectar fild in Hebes stead ;
And he suppli'd the Idæan Ganymed.
Who gather flowres, know these, and know their fires :
Now fragrant, erst as flagrant their desires.

Crocus *is the same with our* Safforne, *though of different kindes. The* Smilax *resembles* Ivy, *bearing a flowre like our violet; some white, some yellow, some purple, some white and black, with varietie of mixtures. These flowres in regard of the infortunitie of those lovers, were consecrated to the* Eumenides: *nor worne in garlands by any, as ominous and fatall.*

SALMA-
CIS AND
HERMA-
PHRODI-
TVS.

The fine Nymph Salmacis *delighting only to adorne her person, to couch in shades, and bath in her own fountain, burnes in desire with the sonne of* Hermes *and* Aphrodite *partaking the names and beauties of either:* Mercury *being called* Hermes, *as the messenger of the Gods; and* Venus Aphrodite, *in that supposed to spring from the froth of the Ocean. Sensuall love is the deformed issue of sloth and delicacy: and seldome survives his glorious parents. Of which our Physitian.*

Ergo, ubi visus eris nostra medicabilis arte :
Fac moniti fugias ocia prima meis.
Hæc ut ames faciunt: hæc quæ fecere, tuentur :
Hæc sunt jucundi causa cibusq; mali.
Ocia si tollas, periere cupidinis arcus,
Contemptæq; jacent, & sine luce faces.
Quam Platanus rivo gaudet, quam Populus unda,
Et quam limosa canna palustris humo :
Tam Venus ocia amat, finem qui quæris amori,
Cedit amor rebus : res age, tutus eris.
Languor, & immodici sub nullo vindice somni,
Aleaq;, & vulto tempora quassa mero ;
Eripiunt omnes animo sine vulnere vires :
Affluit incautos insidiosus amor.
Desidiam puer ille sequi solet : odit agentes.
Da vacuæ menti; quo teneatur, opus.
    Ovid. Rom. amor. l. 1.

When thou art fit, and faine would physick take ;
First practise this : An idle life forsake.
What made thee love, makes thee a lover still :
The cause and nourishment of that sweet ill.
Shun Idlenesse, and Cupids bow will breake,
His slighted flames flie out, disarm'd and weake.
As reeds in marishes affect their Site ;
As Poplars in the running brooks delight ;
So Venus joyes in sloth : let Cupid be
By action tam'd ; live busie and live free.
Faint ease, long sleeps which no command controules,
Time spent in sport, and drencht in flowing bowles,
Without a wound th' infeebled minde surprize :
Then in unspide insidious Cupid flyes.
That sloth-affecting boy doth toyle detest :
Do something to imploy thy emptie brest.

           Salmacis

Salmacis clinges about the surprized youth like a serpent, till both become one body. The reason why lovers so strictly imbrace, is to incorporate with the beloved; which sith they cannot, can never be satisfied. Thus with the vanitie and vexation thereof to the life expressed by Lucretius.

The lovers ardor in inconstancy
Of error strayes, while they their loves injoy.
Their eyes and hands still shift from place to place:
Who hurt what they too eagerly imbrace,
Stifle with kisses, and their soft lips bite
With ravenous teeth, in that no pure delight.
Wherein those stings lye hid which urge them so
To hurt th' affected: whence their furies grow.
But Venus gently mitigates those ills:
And pleasant balme into the wound distills.
For hope, sprung from one fountain with desire,
Thinks with that beautie to asswage her fire;
Which natures self resists: The more possest,
The more deere love inflames the tortur'd brest.
For meate and drinke into the body ta'ne,
Because in proper places they remaine,
Our thirst and hunger easily subdew:
But in a humane forme and rosiat hew
The aery image is injoy'd alone:
Which by our vanisht hopes away is blowne.
As those who sleeping strive to drinke, yet get
No water to asswage their inward heat
But seek the shadow, labour in their dreams,
And thirst amidst th' imaginary streames:
So lovers love deludes with Imagry:
Nor can they satisfie their longing eye;
Nor yet their hands, still griping here and there,
One jot from that beloved body beare.
For this, when first they glow with heat of love,
And Venus mysteries desire to prove;
They greedily imbrace, joyne mouthes, inspire
Their souls, and bite through ardor of desire:
In vain; since nothing they can thence translate,
Nor wholly enter and incorporate.
For so sometimes they would, so strive to do:
And cleave so close, as if no longer two.

——— *etenim potiundi tempore in ipso*
Fluctuat incertú erroribus ardor amantum:
Nec constat quid primum oculi manibusq;
fruuntur.
Quod petiere,premunt arctè, faciuntq; dolorem
Corporis, & dentes inlidunt sæpe labellis,
Osculáq; adfigunt, quia non est pura Voluptas:
Et stimuli subsunt, qui instigant ladere idip-
sum.
Quocunque est, rabies unde illa germina sur-
gunt.
Sed leviter pœnas frangit Venus inter amorem,
Blandáq; refrænat morsus admista voluptas.
Namq; in eo spes est, unde'st ardoris origo,
Restingui quoq; posse ab eodé corpore flammã.
Quid fieri contra coram natura repugnat:
Vnáq; res hæc est,cui jus quã pluria habemus.
Tam magis ardescit dira cuppidine pestus.
Nam cibus atque humor, membris adsumitur
intus
Quæ quoniam certas possunt obsidere parteis
Hoc facile expletur laticum frugumq; cupido-
Ex hominis vero facie, pulchroq; colore,
Nil datur in corpus præter simulacra fruëdum:
Tenuia, quæ vento spes captat sæpe misella.
Vt bibere in somnis sitiens cum quærit,& hu-
mor
Non datur, ardorem in membris qui stinguere
possit,
Sed laticum simulacra petit,frustráq; laborat,
In mediog; sitit torrenti flumine potans.
Sic in amore Venus simulacris ludit amanteis:
Nec satiare queunt spectando corpora coram:
Nec manibus quicquam teneris abradere mem-
bris
Possunt,errantes incerti corpore toto.
Deniq; quem membris conlatis flore fruuntur
Aetatis: dum jam præsagit gaudia corpus,
Atq; in eo est Venus, ut muliebria conserat
arva:
Affigunt avide corpus junguntq; salivas
Oris & inspirant pressantes dentibus ora:
Ne quicquam quoniam nihil inde abradere pos-
sunt,
Nec penetrare,& abire in corpus corpore toto.
Nam facere interdum id velle, & certare vi-
dentur:
Vsq; adeo cupide Veneris compagibus hærent.
Rerum. Nat. l.4.

Plato *recites a fable, how man at the first was created double, and for his arrogancy dissected into male and female: the reason of their affected conjunction, as coveting to return to their originall: an obscure notion (as we have formerly written) of* Eva's *being taken out of the side of* Adam. *So* Hermaphroditus *and* Salmacis *retain in one person both sexes: of whom the like are called* Hermaphrodites. Aristotle *writes that they have the right brest of a man; and the left of a woman, wherewith they nourish their children. They were to choose what sex they would use, and punished with death if they changed at any time. One not long since burned for the same at* Burges: *who elected the female, and secretly exercised the male; under the disguize committing many villanies.* Caliphanes *reports, how among the* Nasamones *there were a whole nation of these; who used both with like libertie. There are many at this day in* Ægypt, *but most frequent in* Florida; *who are so hated by the rest of the Indians, that they use them as beasts to carry their burthens; to suck their wounds, and attend on the diseased. But at* Rome *they threw them as soone as born into the river; the Virgins singing in procession, and offering sacrifice unto* Juno. *It is here fained that* Hermaphroditus *by his prayers to his parents procured this qualitie to that fountain, that what man soever bathed therein should come forth halfe woman. Whereof thus* Strabo: *In* Caria *is the fountain of* Salmacis, *I know not how infamous, for making the drinker effeminate: since luxury neither proceeds from the qualitie of the*

N 2

ayre

ayre, nor water, but rather from riches and intemperance. *The* Carians *therefore addicted to floath and filthy delights were called* Hermaphrodites; *not in that of both fexes, but for defiling themfelves with either.* Hermaphroditus *is fained to be the fonne of* Mercury; *becaufe whereas the other are called either mafculine or fœminine, of their more or leffe vigour, heat, drouth, or humiditie; the Planet of* Mercury *participates of both natures; hot and dry, by reafon of his vicinity to the Sunne, removed never above 28 Degrees; cold and moift, by the neighbourhood of the Moone and the Earth: conforming himfelfe alfo to the aufpicious or malevolent afpects of thofe Planets with whom he joyneth his influence.*

MENEI-
DES.

But now approacheth the fate of the Meneides. *Thefe are named in hiftory* Leucippe, Arfione *and* Alcithoë: *who longing in their diftraction to feed upon humane flefh, caft lots among themfelves who fhould kill her childe; which fell on* Leucippe, *who rendred her fonne* Hippafus *to the flaughter. For this their husbands putting on black and fordid attire, were called* Phofoles, *which fignifies fmoaky; and the women* Oeonoloæ, *that is diftempered in fenfes; and fo were their pofteritie long after: whom the Prieft of* Bacchus *in his feftivals accuftomed to chafe with curfes in his mouth and a fword in his hand; nor held unlawfull to kill, if he over-tooke any of them. One flaine by* Zoilus *in the daies of* Plutarch, *as himfelfe affirmeth; but not unrevenged with fundry calamities. To this the fable may have fome allufion: the proceffe whereof, with their converfion into Bats may informe us, how the divine vengeance purfues the irreligious and profaners of fanctified dayes, with vaine difcourfe, or interdicted labours. Their flying in the twi-light deciphers fuch as fhun the light of truth to live in the ambiguitie of error. The Bat is the only foure-footed creature which flies: and therefore yet difputable whether a bird or a beaft, by which the* Ægyptians *prefented Neutralitie; hated, and not feldome obnoxious to both parties. Bats are chafed away, or killed with the fmoake of* Ivy, *which is confecrated to* Bacchus: *and therefore here introduced as an Antipathy in nature.*

IVNOS
DESCENT
TO HELL.

Still Juno *purfues the Houfe of* Cadmus *with inexpiable hatred: and now, to excite the Furies to the ruine of* Athamas *and* Ino, *defcends unto hell. The way thither, fteepe, too eafie; and gloomy with fhades of Ewe: a fatall and venomous tree; in fo much as in fundry countries they die that either folace or fleepe under it. Silence, Paleneffe, Cold, and Stupiditie (the fymptomes of Death) have here their refidence. But thofe ghofts only paffe the river of* Styx, *whofe bodies have their fepulture; and are reftored againe to their firft Originall.*

Hæc omnis, quam cernis, inops, inhumataq;
turba eft.
Portitor ille Charon: *hi, quos vehit unda, fe-*
pulti.
Nec ripas datur horrendas, nec rauca fluenta
Tranfportare prius quam fedibus offa quierint.
Centum errant annos, volitantq; hæc littora
circum,
Tum demum admiffi ftagna exoptata revifunt.
    Virg. Æn. l. 6.

All thefe you fee, poore fouls, are un-inhum'd.
  That Boat-man *Charon*: thofe he wafts, intomb'd.
This heavy flood unto that horrid fhore
None paffe, whofe bones are not at reft before.
A hundred yeares about thefe bancks they hover:
Then t'ane aboard, the wifhed ftrand recover.

Of the fame opinion was Plato, *and before him* Homer, *who makes* Hector, *terrified with that feare, to runne from* Achilles. *Which perhaps both the one and the other had learnt in* Ægypt: *the Kings of that countrey accuftoming to awe their fubjects, by threatning to deprive them of funerall.* Pluto's *citie hath a number of gates, which alwaies ftand open: there is but one paffage unto life, but to death a million. Yet for all this infinite concourfe it appeareth emptie: fo greedy is the grave, and hell fo infatiable. He introduceth the ghofts to exercife thofe functions which they followed in their life times: according to that of* Plato, *how the fame defires remained in the Soule which were either in her nature or affection when apparelled with the body. Thus followed by* Virgil.

——*qua gratia currum,*
Armorumq; fuit vivis, quæ cura nitentis
Pafcere equos, eadem fequitur tellure repoftos.
    Æn. l. 6.

The love of Chariots, of bright armes, the care
To feed their fleek-skinn'd fteeds; in death now are
As when alive.——

Which error of opinion (faith Cicero) *was much increafed by the Poets; who had and have, the libertie to faine what they lifted.*

Cerberus.

Cerberus, *the three-headed Hell-hound; barkes at the approaching Goddeffe. Belike contrary to his cuftome: for it is faid that he ufed to fawne on all that came thither; but affailed fuch, with horrible yellings, as endeavoured to returne.* Cerberus *fignifies the earth, which devoureth all flefh,*
                                          and

and from thence receiveth his name : said to have three heads, in regard of the triple division there-of : to flatter all commers, in that it giveth sepulture to all ; but to resist their retreat, since no travel-ler returnes from that silent Region. For this fained a three-headed Dog, and the infernall Porter.

Consonant to the truth was the opinion of the Poets, how vertue and vice in another world had their rewards and punishments : although erroneous in the distinction of the latter, that some were tempo-rary, and others eternall. From whence sprung their fictions of the infernall rivers, and abysse of Tartarus. Acheron (*according to* Ficinus) *corresponding with the ayre and Meridian, purging by sorrow and anxiety :* Phlegeton *with fire and the Orient, punishing wrath and concupiscence, by a more violent fervor :* Styx *and* Cocytus *with the Earth and Occident afflicting hatred by teares and lamentations. These were onely to purifie ; but the paines of* Tartarus *served not for physicke but example ; from whence there was no redemption. Before this Dungeon sate the daughters of* Night *; severe and implacable Deities, therefore named* Eumenides *; of their indignation :* Erinnyes *and* Fu-ries *of the terror wherewith they afflicted the guilty. These were said to be the Ministers of Divine vengeance upon flagitious offenders ; pursuing them not onely in this world, but the other.* Infernall punishments.

Among these the Gyant Tytius, *whose extended body covered nine acres ; his liver still fed on by* Vultures, *and never diminishing, for offering violence to* Latona. *But* Strabo *converts this fable to a history ; how* Tytius *was a tyrant of* Panopæa, *cruell, lustfull, and outragious, whom* Apollo *slew, as before he had* Python *: when to deterre others from like violence and impiety, it was fained that he suffered this infernall punishment. A conception translated from the fire of hell ; that ever feeds on the bodies of the damned, which suffer no diminution ; but afford unconsumable nourishment. He is said to bee the sonne of the Earth of his earthly affections ; and in opposition to the heavenly seede ; As the sonnes of men, in the Scripture ; Of so vast a proportion, in regard of the large exten-sion of lust.* Tytius.

Tantalus, *a friend to the Gods, admitted to their counsels and festivals, was thrust downe into Hell for revealing their secrets ; where he hungers and thirsts in the midst of aboundance, and as* Lucreti-us *faines, hath a massy stone hanging over his head, whose fall he continually feareth (like the sword which* Dionysius *with a slender thread, at a royal feast, hung over his flatterer* Damocles:) *Declaring hereby, how dangerous to know, and how fatall to discover the secrets of Princes.* Tantalus.

Sisyphus, *the most subtill of men, and one who infested the* Corinthian *Istthmos with his robberies ; being slaine by* Theseus, *was fained in Hell to roule a massy stone against a steepe hill ; which neere the top, tumbled downe againe, and eternally renewed his labour. The reward of treache-rie, injustice, and oppression.* Sisyphus.

So Ixion, *a favourite of* Jupiters, *for attempting* Juno, *(who insteed of her, imbraced a clowd in her likenesse) is turned on a restlesse wheele, in perpetuall memory of such treason and ingratitude. But histories report, how* Ixion *having slaine his father in law ; detested and avoided of all men ; forsooke his countrey, and came to a certaine King, by whom he was received with bounty, and made of his Councell. When* Ixion *not long after attempted the chastitie of his Queene ; wherewith she acquainted her husband. Who hard of beliefe, made her seeme to consent : and caused a wench called* Nephele (*her name signifying a clowd*) *to supply her place : whereupon he was said to have imbraced a clowd for* Juno. *For this, cast out of favour, and afflicted with the horror of so foule an offence, he was fained to suffer those infernall torments.* Ixion.

Lastly the Belides, *so called of their grandfather* Belus, *for killing their cosen germans and hus-bands the first night they lay with them, by the instigation of their father* Danaus, *are here made for ever to powre water into a vessell full of holes : to shew that the obedience to our parents will not ex-cuse us, when they command unjust things. These sisters are resembled to the life of man, and vanity of all humane endeavours ; which leave behinde them no impression, but are done and demolished together.* Belides.

But all these forementioned punishments are allegorically referred to the perturbations of the minde. As the Vulture which feeds on Tytius *liver to the cares of love (since love proceeds from the* Liver, *whose expense is daily repaired) or irreconciliable hatred. The famine of* Tantalus *to* Covetousnesse, *which starves it selfe in the midst of plenty, and may envy more happy* Poverty. Ixions *wheele, to the desperate remembrance of perpetrated crimes, which circularly pursue, and afflict the guilty.* Sisyphus *stone, to still-toyling and miserible* Ambition *: and the leaking urne of the* Belides, *to the inexpleable desires of the soule. And although* Lucretius, *a Pagan, and of the sect of* Epicurus, *held, as the* Sad-duces *among the* Jewes, *that the soule of man was annihilated by death, together with his body : yet may we recite his verses, as conducing to the interpretation of these fables.*

Looke

Respice item quam nil ad nos anteacta ve-
tustas
Temporis aeterni fuerit, quam nascimur ante,
Hoc igitur speculum nobis natura futuri
Temporis exponit, post mortem denique no-
stram.
Num quid ibi horribile apparet? num triste
videtur
Quicquam? nonne omni somno securius ex-
tat?
Atque ea nimirum quaecunque Acheronte pro-
fundo
Prodita sunt esse, in vita sunt omnia nobis.
Nec miser impendens magnum timet aere saxum
Tantalus, ut fama est, cassa formidine tor-
pens:
Sed magis in vita divum metus urget inanis
Mortaleis casusque timent, quemcumque fe-
rat sors,
Nec Tityon volucres ineunt Acheronte jacen-
tem:
Nec quod sub magno scrutentur pectore, quic-
quam
Perpetuam aetatem poterunt reperire profecto,
Quamlibet immani projectu corporis extat;
Qui non sola novem dispensis jugerit membris
Obtineat, sed qui terrai totius orbem:
Non tamen aeternum poterit perferre dolorem:
Nec praebere cibum proprio de corpore semper.
Sed Tityus nobis hic est, in amore jacentem
Quem volucres lacerant, atque exedit anxius
angor:
Aut alia quavis scindunt cupidine cura.
Sisyphus in vita quoque nobis ante oculos est,
Qui petere à populo fasceis, saevasque secures
Imbibit, & semper victus, tristisque recedit.
Nam petere imperium quod inane est, nec da-
tur unquam:
Atque in eo semper durum sufferre laborem:
Hoc est adverso nitentem trudere monte
Saxum, quod tamen à summo jam vertice rur-
sum
Volvitur, & plani raptim petit aequora campi.
Deinde animi ingratam naturam pascere
semper,
Atque explere bonis rebus, satiareque nunquâ:
Quod faciunt nobis annorum tempora circum
Cum redeunt: foetusque ferunt, vanosq; lepores
Nec tamen explemur vitae fructibus unquam:
Hoc, ut opinor, id est, aevo florente puellas
Quod memorant, laticem pertusam congerere
in vas:
Quod tamen expleri nulla ratione potestas.
Rerum. Nat. l. 3.

Looke back into eternall times survay:
It nothing us concerns till our birth day.
This mirror Nature us presents; which showes
That future state, when death our eyes shall close.
What in it horrid? or what tragicall?
Which more secure then sleep invelops all?
What of infernall *Acheron* was fain'd,
Is in our miserable life contain'd.
Nor wretched *Tantalus* doth ever dread
That falling stone which hangs above his head.
Vaine feare of Gods the living rather fright:
The feare of sad mishaps and fortunes spight.
Nor Vultures *Tityus* still in Hell infest:
Nor is there so much in his ample brest
As can perpetually their hunger feed;
Although his monstrous limbs in bulk exceed:
Though they, when stretcht abroad, not onely hide
Nine acres, but the spacious earth beside;
Yet could not he in endlesse torments lye,
Nor with his Liver ever food supply.
But *Tityus*, on whose brest the Vultures tire,
Is he who loves, and suffers through desire;
Or other cares, and curelesse discontents.
So *Sisyphus* unto our eyes presents,
One who in hope to honours highth aspires;
But evermore repulst, and sad, retires.
For Empire to affect, but not obtaine;
So sought with endlesse industry and paine;
Is to enforce a stone against the hill,
Which from the top roules to the bottome still.
Still to supply the ingratefull minde with store,
Which never hath enough, but thirsts for more;
(As doe those bounteous seasons of the yeare,
That liberally afford the fruit they beare,
Yet we unsatisfied still remaine)
Ment by these youthfull sisters, who in vaine
Still water powre into the fatall tunne;
Yet that as empty as when they begunne.

These Mythologies, with others of the like argument, are inlarged by Macrobius: *whereby the Epi-curians endeavoured to elude the truth of eternall punishments in confuting these fables, under which it was vailed by the more theologicall Poets. As the Sadduces, who not onely denied the Resurrection, but held that there were neither Spirits nor Angels: rejecting the Prophets with the rest of the Scriptures: save onely the five bookes of* Moses; *as the ancient Canons of their politicke government. This heresie, as their name, they derived from* Sadoc; *the Disciple of* Antigonus Sochæus *who succeeded* Simon *the* Just *in the Priest-hood. For when* Antigonus *taught that we should not serve God, as Servants their Masters, for hope of reward:* Sadoc *and* Baithus *misunderstanding, as if he had utterly denied the future rewards which attend on a good life, first broached those profane and impious opinions.*

The Furies.

Tisiphone, one of the Furies, ascending from Hell to execute the wrath of Juno, *carries Sorrow, Terror, Feare, and Frenzie along; who with snakes and infused poyson excites accursed mortals to horrible actions: scourging the guilty with whips, and affrighting with flaming torches. All well devised by the wiser Poet, from the contemplation of the divine anger, and causes of humane calamities. For what are the* Furies *but the wicked desires and commotions of the minde? Not unaptly expressed in their names. For* Megera *signifies Envy;* Tisiphone, *a desire of revenge; and* Alecto, *a mover of sedition and discord. These rages of soule are therefore those Furies who inflict so many*
calamities

calamities upon man ; attended by eternall feares, by forrow, horror, and diſtraction. The Serpents, *whips, and torches, are the ſtings and affrights of the afflicted conſcience ; which is her owne accuſer,* Iudge, *and* Executioner. *And therefore our* Ovid :

> No wound upon their bodies could be found :
> It was the minde that felt the deſperate wound.

The effects of the infernall poyſon being ſutable to the ingredients.

> She brought beſides from her abhorred home
> The ſurfet of *Echidna,* with the fome
> Of hell-bred *Cerberus,* ſtill wandring Error,
> Oblivion, Miſchiefe, Cares, infernall Terror,
> Diſtracted Fury, and affections fixt
> On Murder ; altogether ground, and mixt
> With blood yet reeking : boyld in hollow braſſe,
> And ſtir'd with Hemlocke. ――――

The Furies *are ſaid to be daughters of* Erebus *and* Night, *in regard of the blinde improvidence of man, who to ſatisfie his revenge, his luſt, or ambition, incurres thoſe miſeries that have no period : to be three, in that they afflict with the remembrance of what is paſt, with the preſent, and feare of the future : and laſtly to ſit before the infernall priſon, in that dying men are moſt ſolicitous, and moſt afflicted with their former offences.*

Inſuriated Athamas, *now miſtaking his wife for a Lioneſſe, and his children for her whelps, daſheth out the braines of* Clearchus : *when* Ino, *diſtracted with feare or fury, threw her ſelfe with* Me- INO AND
MELI-
CERTES.
licertes *from a* Rock *into the* Iōnian *Sea. Thus farre is in ſubſtance hiſtoricall. For* Ino, *a cruell ſtepmother to* Phryxus *and* Helle, *by laying many traines for their lives, inforced them to ſeeke for ſafety by flight. Her treachery diſcovered by* Athamas, *ſuppoſing the abſent to be made away , in a rage ſlew his ſonne* Clearchus, *and purſued the* Queene *with the other in her armes : who to avoide his fury, threw herſelfe with her burthen into the Sea ; from the rock* Moluris. *The body of* Ino *was taken up on the coaſts of* Megara, *and intombed by the daughters of* Celſus : *That of* Melicertes *being driven to the* Corinthian Iſthmos *where* Siſyphus *his unkle then raigned ; who dedicated thoſe games ; which before were ſacred to* Neptune, *unto the honour of his kinſman; and thereupon fained to have beene tranſlated into a Marine deity. So was his mother : it being the ambition of ancient times to deifie their dead anceſtors, as the flattering* Romanes *did their living Princes. But our Poet faines that this honour was given them at the ſute of their Grandmother* Venus ; *who the more to inſinuate with her unkle* Neptune, *profeſſeth her ſelfe to be borne of the froath of the Sea, and therefore named* Aphrodite : *ſo ſaid to be, in that the ſperme of man is no other then the ſpume of the blood ; and becauſe that ſalt ſo much conferres to fecunditie, provoking by the naturall heat, unto* Venus, *in this reſpect they anciently erected her Temples on the ſhore of the ſea.* Melicertes *was called* Palæmon, *and* Ino, Leucothea. *For it was their cuſtome, ſaith* Lactantius, *to change the names of ſuch as they deified, leſt in future times they ſhould be thought to have beene mortals. Whom the* Grecians *named* Palæmon, *the* Latines *called* Portunus : *painted with a key in his hand, as the protector of harbors : ſo called they* Leucothoe, Matuta, *or the* Morning. *Allegorically* Palæmon *is taken for the force of* Tempeſts : *the ſonne of* Leucothea, *in that the windes begin to ariſe with the* Morning, *and then deſcending from the mountaines are ſaid to have throwne themſelves headlong into the ſea : the* Morning *alſo, by her over-red complexion fore-ſhewing ſucceeding tempeſts. Theſe were held for the fautors of Seafaring men, in that they ſo much depend on the favour of the windes. This fable may likewiſe remember us to fortifie our ſelves in our afflictions with patience and expectance : when* Ino *ſo perſecuted by* Juno *for her naturall affection and piety to* Bacchus, *was after received into the number of the Gods, and made a partaker of their felicities. The transformation of the* Inos atten-
dance.
Theban *Ladyes , ſome into ſtatues , and ſome into fowle ; declare that neither our affections nor ſorrowes , ſhould urge us to blaſphemy, or cenſure of their actions, whoſe diſpleaſure is an implacable* Nemeſis.

Cadmus, *after ſo many calamities ſuſtained in his Family, as ominous abandons his city of* The- Cadmus and
Hermione.
bes *(or expulſed from thence, as others write, by* Amphion*) wanders with his wife* Hermione *to the confines of* Illyria : *there reſting where the ſtreames of* Drilo *divide it from* Liburnia. *The* Enchilenſes, *then infeſted by the* Illyrians, *had an anſwer from the Oracle : that they ſhould then prove victorious, when they were conducted by* Cadmus *and* Hermione : *who ſent unto, accepted of the*

charge ;

charge ; and gave the enemy a finall over-throw. So Cadmus raigned in Illyria : till changing his publique life for a private; by his obscure retirement, and politick submission to the laws & customes of those barbarous nations, he was fained with his wife to have beene turned into Serpents. And the rather in that the Illyrians were said to have two balls in one eye, and to be as sharpe sighted as dragons ; in so much as they killed, whom they long and fiercely beheld in their anger. It is fained that these Serpents were after transported into Elizium by Jupiter : intimating the excellency of Wisedome and fortitude, which not only carry us through the troubles and dangers of this miserable life, but rewards their dependants with eternall felicitie.

Here end the dysasters of Cadmus, and now convert we to the exploits of Perseus ; begotten by Jupiter on Danaë. For Acrisius the Argive king, being told by the Oracle that he should be slaine by the sonne of his daughter ; inclosed her to prevent his destiny, together with her nurse, in a tower of brasse: when Jupiter descending in a golden showre, was received into her lap, and then into her imbracements. Iupiter, saith Lactantius, endeavouring to violate Danaë, with store of gold corrupted her chastitie. When the Poets, to preserve the dignitie of Princes, attributed that to the Gods which was done by men ; and fained that he approacht her in a golden showre ; as we say a showre of steele, when darts and arrowes fall together in multitudes. Who with the like prodigality of gifts made all passages flye open.

Perseus
Danae.

Inclusam Danaen turris ahenea,	A towre of brasse, doores strongly barr'd,
Robustaque fores, & vigilum canum	Of wakefull mastiffes a fierce guard,
Tristes excubia, munierant satis	Had *Danaë* safely kept from her
Nocturnis ab adulteris :	Night-wandring adulterer ;
Si non Acrisium virginis abditæ	Had *Iove* and *Venus* not deluded,
Custodem pavidam, Iupiter & Venus	*Acrisius*, who kept th' included :
Risissent, fore enim tutum iter & patens	The way secure, and uncontroul'd
Converso in pretium Deo.	Unto a God transform'd to Gold.
Aurum per medios ire satellites,	Gold loves to force through guards ; then thunder
Et perrumpere amat saxa, potentius	More potent ; cleaving rocks a sunder.
Ictu fulmineo. ——	
Hor. l. 3. ode. 16.	

Another resembles Acrisius *to a man indued with excellent learning : that learning his daughter* Danaë, *shut up in a brasen towre ; in the head, the turret of the body, and seate of the soule : being there obscured, and sequestred from knowledge, untill Jupiter enters in a golden showre, and begetteth* Perseus : *that is, till the favour and munificencie of Princes inlarge it to the production of heroicall actions ; otherwise buried alive, and utterly uselesse.*

Haud facile emergunt, quorum virtutibus obstat	They hardly rise unto renowne,
Res angusta domi ——	Whose vertues poverty weighs downe.

Represented in the Emblematist by a student with one hand raised aloft with wings, and the other suppressed by a massy stone. Perseus *being borne ;* Acrisius, *not beleeving his daughter that he was begotten by* Jupiter, *put them both into an Arke, and commits them to the mercy of the sea; which drave them ashore on the Ile of* Scriphus. *There taken up, and knowne by King* Polydectes *to be of his kindred, they were bountifully entertained. But at length, attempting the dishonour of* Danaë, *he sent* Perseus *away, as fearing his presence, to warre with the* Gorgons; *from whence he returned victorious with the head of* Medusa : *of which we shall speak hereafter.*

Now with Mercuries *wings on his heeles, and girt with his fauchion ; defensively armed with* Pluto's *helmet, and the shield of* Pallas, *he flyeth over the* Lybian *Deserts : and the bloud that dropt from* Medusa's *head converting into Serpents ; so wittily fained of the infinity of Serpents which infest those Climates.* Perseus *is said to be the sonne of* Iupiter, *for his atchievements and perpetuall felicity : the wings of* Mercury *signifie celeritie ; which are tied to his feet, and not to his shoulders, to declare that in warlike affaires men should deliberate in the beginning, but be swift in the prosecution : his fauchion expresseth policy and circumvention :* Pluto's *head-peece, a concealement of counsells ; and the shield of* Pallas *a provident preservation : being all the necessary accomplishments of a Souldier.*

Atlas *the sonne of* Iapet, *inhabiting those westerne parts of* Africa *which bound on the great Ocean, being told by* Themis *that the sonne of* Iupiter *(prophecied by* Hercules*) should carry away the golden apples, which grew in his* Hesperian *Hortyard ; inclosed the same with a mighty wall, and*
committed

committed it to the custody of a sleeplesse Serpent : driving all forrainers from his confines. And now unhospitable unto Perseus, was at the sight of Medusa's head converted into that Mountain which carries that name, on whose high shoulders the starres are fained to take their repose. Some alluding this to a history, report that those apples were flocks of large and beautifull sheep belonging to Atlas, whose fleeces were of the colour of gold : and because a river invironed those pastures, they were said to be guarded by a Serpent : or in that they were kept by one Ladon, a churlish and inhumane shepheard. Or fained perhaps of the store of gold wherewith Mauritania aboundeth, digg'd up at the foote of that mountaine : the wakefull Dragon those restlesse cares which afflict the covetous in the tuition of their riches : a blessing to the liberall, but to the miser a punishment. Now Atlas flying thither from the invasion of Perseus, and there lurking, was said to have beene converted into that mountaine ; and in regard of the altitude thereof, to have sustained the heavens on his shoulders. But astronomically those apples are taken for starres, shining like gold, and in figure orbicular ; said to grow in the West, in that they appeare not before Sun-set ; the Zodiack, or our Hemisphæare, being the Serpent : all of them supported, in regard of his excellency in Astronomy, by Atlas. Some say, that ascending aloft, the better to observe the course of the starres, he fell headlong into the sea from this mountaine ; called for this by his name, as of that aspiring heighth the celestiall Columne.

Perseus *mounting through the ayre*, at length arriveth where the faire Andromeda *was chained* to a rocke ; who at the first sight is enamoured. For certaine subtill rayes expiring from within the heart, where the hottest and sweetest of the vitall blood hath a residence, dart from the eyes of the beautifull, into the eyes of the admiring beholder ; and penetrating from thence into the heart, inflames it forthwith with ardent affection ; wherein the sudden glances and dartings of the eye are more powerfull then long gazing. Andromeda *was here bound for the pride of her mother* Cassiope, who durst contend in beauty with the Nereides: *for which a sea-monster was sent by* Neptune *to infest that countrey, devouring both men and cattle.* In so much as Cepheus *consulting with the oracle of* Jupiter Hammon *(which signifies sand, in that his Temple stood in the Libyan Desert) to know the cause of that calamity, and way to remove it : was answered, how the daughter of* Cassiope *was first to be devoured by that monster : whom* Perseus *now slew, and freed the Lady* ; *the cause and reward of his danger.* By this the ancient reprooved their pride and ambition, who would be thought more then mortall ; when all humane beauty is worse then deformity, and all glory despicable, compared with the cælestiall : declaring besides that the offences of Princes are not seldome punished in their subjects and posteritie. Yet Andromeda, *innocent Vertue,* shall never misse of that sacred succour, which will not onely deliver her from the present danger, but match her to Perseus, that is, unto Honour and Felicitie : both after converted into glorious constellations. So Cepheus, *in that obedient unto the heavenly Oracle :* and so Cassiope, *but with her heeles upward, to deterre from the like preposterous arrogancie.* Joppa, *a city of Palestine, is said by* Pliny *and* Mela *to be the sceane of this tragi-comedy.* A city, *as supposed, more ancient then the Flood : where* Cepheus raigned, *as divers old Altars inscribed with his title (there preserved by the inhabitants) did testifie.* Scaurus in his Ædilship produced the bones of that monster, which he brought from thence, being fourty foot long, the ribs larger then an Elephants, and the back-bone a foot and a halfe thicker. Ovid here feares not to call Jupiter unjust, for so dooming the innocent Andromeda. Such estimation had the wiser Pagans of their deified Divels : nay many preferring mortalls before them. And surely Socrates would have made a better God of wisdome, Aristides of Iustice, Themistocles of warre, or Cato Vtican then the whole rabble ; with whom he is parallel'd by Lucan :

Those sea-weeds turned into Corall *alludes to the nature of that plant ; soft under water, but hard above :* *and therefore called* Gorgonia, *as if transformed by the head of* Medusa : *growing likewise in greatest plenty by those Ilands where the* Gorgons *were said to inhabit.* A greene shrub with white berries ; which forth-with hardens in the ayre and changes into red. They write that if it be but touched by man when it growes under water, it will turne to stone : and therefore they cut it up with sharpe hooks of iron; whereof it is called Corall. Of this plant thus writeth, I know not what Poet :

The wise by forraine countries are improv'd :
As tender Corall from the Sea remov'd.

Qui sapit ille animum peregrino obdurat in orbe:
Coralium extra undas sic abit in lapidem.

It is received for a truth that will not be rejected, how Corall sympathizes with the wearer ; and waxeth pale with his sicknesse : nor unprobable, since any distemperature of heat procures the like alteration.

Perseus *having sacrificed to his father* Jupiter, *his sister* Pallas, *and his brother* Mercury, *by*

O   whose

255

whose aid he had obtain'd so many, and so great victories; now celebrates his nuptiall feast in the court of Cepheus. Who importuned, relates his beheading of Medusa; sent thither by the treacherous Polydectes; or rather by the compassionate Pallas; in that she transformed who soever she lookt on, into marble. By the way he came to the Graeae, or Phorcides; two sisters, the daughters of Phorcus, both having but one eye, which they used in common: by the helpe whereof (having gotten it as they past it from one to another) he came to the habitation of the Gorgons: where spying Medusa a sleepe in the mirror of his shield, he cut off her head before her sisters could awake; from whose bloud up-sprung Crysaor, and the winged horse Pegasus. This fable declares that no great action should be taken in hand without the advice of Pallas, which is wisedome. That the equity of the cause is chiefly to be considered: for what more wicked then an unjust warre? or more noble then to suppresse a tyranny; under which the people lye prostrate; deprived of life and vigour, as under the aspect of of Medusa? He attempts her alone; in that she of all the Gorgons was onely mortall: to show that we should pursue what is fecible; and not such designes as are vast and endlesse. Yet first he diverts to the Graeae, interpreted for Conspirators; so named, in that old from their infancy; by reason of the cares and feares which accompany traitors. From these he takes their one eye, the secret intelligence that is betweene the factious, which shews him sleeping Medusa, or how to surprize his suspectlesse enemy: who striking looks on the sheild of Pallas; by providence preventing the instant danger and terror. Pegasus a flying horse, ascends from the bloud of Medusa: expressing that fame, which flyes through the mouthes of men, and celebrates victorious vertue. Perseus is also taken for the reasonable soule: the Graeae, for that knowledge and wisdome which is acquired by experience; without whose eye or conduction, Medusa, lust and the inchantments of bodily beauty, which stupefies our senses, make us altogether unusefull, and convert us, as it were into marble, cannot be subdued. Perseus is furnished with the shield of Pallas, the helmet of Pluto, the fauchion and wings of Mercury; because in all great difficulties perspicacity, policy, a quicknesse of wit, and deepe apprehension is required; without which no glorious action can be atchieved. Thus provided, Perseus kills Medusa, reason corporall pleasure: yet looks not on her, but onely sees her deformitie in the shield of Pallas (as we view without prejudice to our sight the eclipse of the sunne in the water) since it is not safe to behold what our hearts are so prone to consent to. From this subduing of our affections, an honest fame, our winged Pegasus, is produced. Pausanias reports this Medusa to be the daughter of Phorbus: who after the death of her father raigned over those people who border on the lake of Triton: whom she accustomed, with the neighboring Africans, to conduct to the warres; as then she did against the army of Perseus, and was slaine in the night by a stratagem. Perseus admiring her beauty in death, cut off her her head, and carried it with him into Greece for a spectacle: when such as beheld it, in that astonisht with the sight, were said to have beene turned into marble.

It is here fained that Pallas converted her faire haire into Serpents, for being vitiated by Neptune in her temple: declaring how infamy is the ugliest of deformities, especially in the beautifull. She therefore carries that figure in her shield, to affright such offenders. But her head is held by Perseus in the constellation: called the Divells head by the Hebrews, and Caput Algol by the Arabians: fatall in nativities, as too truely fore-told to the Duke of Biron.

Reviews

Shakespeare's Early Comedies: A Structural Analysis by Blake Odell Bonazza. Mouton & Co., 1966. Pp. 125. Gld. 18. *Reviewer: Paul A. Jorgensen.*

This slender but compact volume examines Shakespeare's comedies from *The Comedy of Errors* through *A Midsummer Night's Dream*. It is consistently and resolutely what its subtitle promises: an analysis of structure, with some occasionally excellent synthesis. However—fortunately, it seems to me—"structure" is interpreted to include more than plot and design. There is attention to character, language, and atmosphere, but principally as these bear upon form.

The book may best be characterized as methodical. Four types of plot are defined and their presence and interaction noted in Shakespeare's development as an architect of comedy. Some unpleasantness in reading, though doubtless also a schematic tidiness, results from Mr. Bonazza's labeling these plots A, B, C, and D. However, a methodical approach has more serious problems. The three earliest comedies are placed at a disadvantage in that they are used primarily to show what is missing in relation to the full tonal quality of *A Midsummer Night's Dream*, which has all four plots, expertly orchestrated. Though Bonazza disclaims the need for strict chronological placement, his thesis is certainly helped by the order he has chosen. It would be disastrous should his late (but generally accepted) placement of *A Midsummer Night's Dream* in the series be wrong, though only inconvenient if *Love's Labour's Lost* should turn out to have preceded *The Comedy of Errors*. In this latter respect, as in most of his scholarship (no reference is later than 1959), Bonazza has overlooked the latest evidence, e.g., Alfred Harbage's article, *"Love's Labour's Lost* and the Early Shakespeare," *Philological Quarterly,* XLI (1962), 18-36, which would date the play in 1588-1589, possibly preceding *The Comedy of Errors* by two or more years, even more if we accept Sidney Thomas' date of 1594 for *Errors*, proposed in *Shakespeare Quarterly,* VII (1956), 377-384.

On the whole, however, Bonazza's thesis, with its constantly stressed sense of movement toward greater complexity in Shakespeare's art, is tenable as well as attractive. And the three earliest comedies are not seriously misrepresented by a deprecatory treatment of their structural artistry. One acquiesces the more willingly in that Bonazza is always aware of what Shakespeare's novitiate is leading toward in the richer comedies. It is interesting to follow, from the point of view of the creative artist, some of Shakespeare's own perplexities and crossroads during a period that must certainly have been much concerned with the mechanics of structure.

And yet this is not really an enjoyable book. The author himself disarmingly, but wrongly, calls the major part of it pedestrian and tedious. Perhaps a book on structure runs this risk, with its long plot summaries and its analyses that read like more plot summaries. And yet Bertrand Evans' structural study, *Shakespeare's Comedies* (not mentioned by Bonazza), though several times the length of this volume, is not dull. Bonazza is emphatically not lacking in intelligence. What seems to go wrong is that he displays no comic feeling for the subject. Laughter and humor are occasionally mentioned and defined (pp. 30, 57, 58).

But consider the inadequacy of this accounting for laughter on one occasion in *The Comedy of Errors*: "Laughter results from the fact that the violation of commonsense expectations leads not to disaster but only to temporary discomfiture and distress" (p. 30). More, however, than comic theory is at fault. The book lacks humor. Although there is abundant talk of such matters as "comic reversal," there is no attempt to communicate by style the real reason why these comedies live: their funniness. And if a study of structure in comedy cannot communicate the quality as well as the outline of funniness, the methodology is imperfect. To be sure, most students of Shakespearean comedy have erred on the side of seriousness. The subject seems to attract sober men. But Bonazza's intent, mathematical style, joined with a disapproving attitude toward three of the plays, makes for an unusually cheerless reading. I personally do not want to look again at these plays for some time; and, I suspect, neither does Mr. Bonazza.

It is unfortunate that a book so meticulous in both method and style should suffer from numerous misprints (there is a major one on p. 23 and a catastrophic one on p. 49). But scholars are increasingly learning to bear these indignities as the low comic comments of a cruel world upon their seriousness.

The University of California, Los Angeles

The Dramatic Works in the Beaumont and Fletcher Canon, Volume 1, edited by Fredson Bowers. Cambridge University Press, 1966. Pp. xxxv + 670. $18.50. *Reviewer: Kenneth Muir.*

The first volume of what promises to be the standard edition of Beaumont and Fletcher contains five plays and a masque. Each has a separate editor: *The Knight of the Burning Pestle* (Cyrus Hoy); *The Masque of the Inner Temple and Gray's Inn* (Fredson Bowers); *The Woman Hater* (George Walton Williams); *The Coxcomb* (Irby B. Cauthen, Jr.); *Philaster* (Robert K. Turner); *The Captain* (L. A. Beaurline).

The general principles followed in this edition are those of the Bowers Dekker and the various editors, wherever I have checked their texts, have done their work with great accuracy. It is difficult to believe that it will ever have to be done again. The only comparable edition, published more than half a century ago by the Cambridge University Press, was by modern standards both unsophisticated and slapdash. Waller and Glover followed the text of the 1679 Folio. This in itself was a wrong decision and it led them to print many inferior readings, some of them impossible. The present edition is based in some cases on the First Quarto, in the case of *Philaster*, for good reasons, on the second Quarto, and in the others on the 1647 Folio. It need hardly be said that the text as a whole exhibits a substantial improvement on Waller and Glover's.

> By more than all my hopes I hold it

becomes

> (By more than all the gods) I hold it happy.

"And I vow" becomes "By all the gods". A third improvement in the same speech is not so obvious. The F2 reading "do I / opine myself most happy" is, at first sight, more attractive than "doe I, / Open my selfe most happy" but "open", meaning "declare" makes satisfactory sense.

Beaumont and Fletcher are second-rate dramatists and the full bibliographical treatment which has been accorded to them will not affect their reputations. What is still needed with them, as with Dekker, is a volume or two of annotations and a literary study of their work. Ideally, indeed, the same editors should provide the annotations, since no text can be established on bibliographical principles alone. When Marco Mincoff's book is eventually published we shall be in a better position to judge Beaumont and Fletcher as dramatists.

The cost of this volume puts it out of reach of most students, who need above all comparatively cheap but accurate reprints of Elizabethan plays. The various new series—Regents, New Mermaids, Revels—do something to satisfy this demand. But we used to be able to buy ten plays for a dollar; and it is to be hoped that university presses will remember that it is better to sell a book to an individual than to a library.

The University of Liverpool

Narrative and Dramatic Sources of Shakespeare, Volume VI, edited by Geoffrey Bullough. Routledge and Kegan Paul; Columbia University Press, 1966. Pp. xiv + 578. $10.00 *Reviewer: John W. Velz.*

The sixth volume of Geoffrey Bullough's nearly completed collection of the sources and analogues of Shakespeare's plays treats *Titus Andronicus, Troilus and Cressida, Timon of Athens,* and *Pericles, Prince of Tyre.* The juxtaposition is appropriate. Each has long been prey to the disintegrators because each has been thought unworthy of Shakespeare's talent. Yet, in the past twenty-five years, each has been subjected to aesthetic criticism which has ameliorated, somewhat, the categorical condemnations dominant from the time of Frederick Fleay. Of the four, *Tro.* now has attained some critical eminence, though scholars still are not agreed whether the play is "comicall satyre" or tragedy, and T. W. Baldwin's essays in the Hillebrand-Baldwin Variorum decline to dignify it with Shakespeare's name. The other three are still in limbo, but they are defended with increasing frequency; as long ago as 1930 Wilson Knight called *Tim.* the most massive and profound of the tragedies, and H. T. Price's brilliant exposition of the structure of *Tit.* (*Construction in Shakespeare,* 1951) is now commonly quoted as a classic of its kind.

Beyond these similarities, the four plays share common ground in that each evokes a classical world quite unlike anything found in the "Plutarch plays." Bullough calls them *Other "Classical" Plays,* and his quotation marks are significant, because in each of the four the ancient world is reflected in a distorting mirror. For *Tro.* the mirror may be topical (is loutish Ajax a burlesque of Ben Jonson, and/or Achilles a sardonic portrait of sulking Essex?); for *Tim.* the mirror may be allegorical (Apemantus' claim that Timon has never known "the middle of humanity . . . but the extremity of both ends" may indicate that the play is in the tradition of the Moralities and should be read as an alleogory of the *via media*); for *Per.* the mirror may be hagiographic (chastity and patience, the great virtues of the play, perhaps should be traced to the literature of Christian sanctity); for *Tit.* the mirror may be the Elizabethan notion that the history of declining Rome was a tumultuous succession of "garboyles" of the kind conveyed by Guevara's *Dial of Princes* (this view of the play is advanced with flair by T. J. B. Spencer in *ShS,* 1957, in an important essay which Bullough omits from his bibliography of commentary on *Tit.*).

Each of the four plays also presents a thorny problem for source-seekers. Did Shakespeare use the academic comedy on Timon? (Bullough convincingly reasons not.) By what route did he gain access to the Lucianic material in *Tim.*? Was either the prose tale of Titus or the ballad spoken by his ghost the major source of *Tit.*? (Both of these are now printed complete for the first time from the Folger chapbook.) Is Henslowe's allusion to the now lost "*Tittus and Vespacia*" of any relevance? Is Shakespeare's Cressida to be found whole in a combination of Chaucer, Lydgate, and Caxton, or is her lineage traceable through the Renaissance descendants of Henryson? (Bullough prints excerpts from *The Testament of Cresseid,* though he admits that only Cressida's statement in V.ii that she will "be plagu'd" justifies this inclusion.) Did Shakespeare use Chapman's Homer, or some other translation? (Bullough has "no doubt" that Shakespeare knew Chapman's translation and was ridiculing his hero-worship when he denigrated the heroic age in *Tro.*) What relationship ought to be postulated among *Per.,* Gower's *Confessio Amantis,* Twine's *Patterne of Painefull Adventures,* and the putative lost play which Shakespeare revised? (Bullough's careful comparison shows that Twine's contribution is not insignificant, though much smaller than Gower's.) The other three plays, no less than *Per.,* have traditionally been subjected to "lost-source-play" criticism. Indeed it was Edward Ravenscroft's comments on *Tit.* (1686) which founded the school of criticism in which one labels what does not appeal in a Shakespearean play "vestigial marks of the lost play."

The multiplicity of possible sources for these four plays has imposed some hard choices on Bullough. He includes some materials of strictly tangential relevance. Among these *The Testament of Cresseid* has already been mentioned; there is also the "Lamentable Ballad" on the "Heathenish Blackamore" who raped his master's wife and murdered both wife and children after inducing the husband to cut off his nose to save his family. This grotesque analogue to the story of Aaron and Titus is welcome, especially because it is printed complete. But some other decisions are less easy to justify. The academic play of Timon is reprinted in part, though Bullough argues that it postdates *Lr.* and that Shakespeare did not know it. The justification for including it would therefore seem to be making this rare text available to scholarship. But the deletion of the bulk of the bawdy subplot amounts to bowdlerization and obstructs any comparison between the hyperbolic sexuality of the academic play and the association in *Tim.* between misanthropy and carnal language. Then there is the case of Jasper Heywood's translation of *Thyestes,* from which about 250 lines are printed as "Source" for *Tit.* without cognizance either of Howard Baker's vigorous arguments against the influence of Seneca on *Tit.* (*Induction to Tragedy,* 1939) or of the fact that the most Senecan thing about *Tit.* is not the cannibalism or other horrors, but the pathetic fallacy which makes both Senecan tragedy and *Tit.* so melodramatic (compare lines 820-825, where the elements show their horror at Thyestes' meal, with II.iii.93-104, IV.i.53-60, V.ii.35-38, and other passages in *Tit.* where setting is made to conform to action).

This is not to raise major objections to Bullough's selections. One must be arbitrarily selective, willy nilly, and moreover, some of the choices are particularly felicitous. For example, Bullough includes part of Lyly's *Campaspe,* a play which shares with *Tim.* an Athenian setting, a railing cynic who is often called "dog," a painter-in-residence, and an emphasis on the theme of moderation (see, e.g., *Campaspe* I.ii "*Plures occidit crapula quam gladius*"). Bullough states his principle of selection clearly at the outset: "I have not sacrificed what Shakespeare may have used in order to include what he certainly did not." But perhaps he does not attach sufficient significance to the materials which Shakespeare omitted. Having the full text of the prose *History of Titus Andronicus,* for example, makes it apparent that Shakespeare's play is less "medieval" than the tale, where in Chapter IV "a Turnament at Justing" is mentioned and the sons of Titus, condemned for the murder of

260

"the Prince" (Bassianus in the play), "demanded the Combat against their Accusers, which by the Law of Arms they ought to have been allowed." If, indeed, this prose tale is the source of *Tit.*, it would appear that Shakespeare was at pains to make his play more "classical" than the materials he was basing it on. (This observation would accord with Bullough's view that Shakespeare drew on Plutarch's lives of Coriolanus and Scipio in an effort to enrich the Roman world of his play.)

Whatever their limitations, Bullough's selections would be revealing even if left to speak for themselves. But their value is greatly enhanced by a full commentary on each play. Some of this introductory material is little more than plot summary (on *Tro.* seven of the 29 pages are a *seriatim* rehearsal of the events of the play); but each introduction provides an informed survey of the main scholarly positions on source questions, and each of the introductions contains original suggestions of extraordinary percipience. The examples mentioned here are only representative of others like them.

Tit.: "The writing in the sand may come from the story of Io in *Met.* I. 649-50, where the woman transformed into a cow writes with her foot to let her father know who she is." (Bullough could have added that both Lavinia and Io have been ravished.) The human sacrifice in I.i *ad manes fratrum* is based on Seneca's *Troades*. The intrusive irony of Bassianus' and Lavinia's speeches in II.iii "recalls somewhat the hunting-scene in Marlowe and Nashe's *Dido Queen of Carthage*, into which Iarbas introduces a jarring note." The most valuable thing in the introduction on *Tit.* is Bullough's analysis of the rearrangements Shakespeare made in his materials to achieve greater credibility, concentration, and climax; he shows plainly that Shakespeare had a real sense of structure as he worked on the play. The defense of Shakespearean authorship and the comments on the use of Plutarch's "Coriolanus" in *Tit.* also are very good.

Tro.: Cressida has charm and is human as she recognizes her weakness and lives for the moment, but she is "shallower" than Chaucer's or Lydgate's portraits. Troilus' rejection of Pandarus in the fifth act recalls Hal's rejection of Falstaff in the fifth act of *2H4*—Pandarus and Falstaff both are misleaders of youth. The treachery with which Achilles kills Hector "foretells the destruction of Troy through intrigue and deceit." The antinomy of Greeks and Trojans is not between reason and intuition, but "between pride veiled with policy and pride openly admitted and glorified." Unlike the medieval and classical versions, *Tro.* omits the Chryseis story as a motive for Achilles' sulking, thus emphasizing "moral rot" in the Greek army. Perhaps Bullough's analysis attaches too much significance to the love theme: he does not note (as Baldwin does in the Variorum) that the lovers do not even appear in the second act. But his commentary on the tone and the characters is excellent.

Tim.: "The painted stones [probably referred to at III.vi.115] come from late Roman history, for it was a prank of the youthful Emperor Heliogabalus so to trick his guests." Shakespeare used the "Life of Marcus Antonius" extensively for *Tim.*, drawing from it six character-names, the motif of hedonistic luxuriance and sycophancy, the flamboyance of Timon's generosity,[1] Timon's misplaced trust in others (Plutarch discusses Antony as foolishly trustful), and the scene where Timon ignores Flavius' warning of impending ruin. Apemantus may be traceable to Cicero's *Laelius*, where Timon is mentioned as a misanthropist of the kind who needs "'one associate, at least, before whom he might discharge the whole rancour and virulence of his heart'." Bullough makes rewarding comments on shallow characterization and loose plot ends; the former he regards as a possible index to a purpose like that in the Moralities—the latter might be so regarded as well. The commentary on the ethics of the play does not recognize the importance of Timon's rejection of reciprocity in human and natural relationships (see IV.iii.439-449, "The sun's a thief . . . all that you meet are thieves."). And the suggestion that Shakespeare left *Tim.* unfinished to write a more manageable *Cor.* is unconvincing—if Timon's alienation makes his story intractable material, the same is true of Coriolanus, who also is alienated, and who is certainly no more pliable, psychologically and morally, than Timon.

Per.: The name of the hero may be traceable not to Pyrocles in Sidney's *Arcadia* nor to Plutarch's Pericles, but to the Latin *"pericula,"* alluding to the dangers through which the hero passes; this bit of onomastic etymology could have appeared in a now-lost Renaissance ballad on the Apollonius story. Similarities between *Per.* and the *Arcadia* "suggest that the tale of Apollonius of Tyre was one of the stories Sidney had in mind when writing. . . . They do not prove that the dramatist was thinking of Sidney's romance." The destruction of Antiochus and his daughter in II.iv "slightly resembles that of Antiochus Epiphanes in 2 *Maccabees* IX, 7-10."[2] Diana is in the play to focus attention on the chastity theme (Bullough might have noted that she had a famous cult at Ephesus, the setting of Shakespeare's denouement). The motif of chastity in a brothel appears in saints' legends, especially that of St. Agnes.[3] Bullough endorses the hypothesis that in the first two acts Shakespeare was merely a perfunctory reviser of an older play, but that he became interested in the task as he went along; this view of the problem of inconsistencies of style and quality in the play is at least as plausible as the alternatives.

Bullough's sixth volume is not consistent,[4] but at its best it is excellent indeed. Most scholars will disagree with some judgments and hypotheses in each of the four introductions; but all should accord Bullough respect for his perceptive approaches to these troublesome plays. And scholarship now has, for the first time, most of the materials it needs for consideration of source questions in Shakespeare's four "Other 'Classical' Plays."

Rice University

Notes:

(1) Bullough compares Timon's hyperbole with Cleopatra's: "Methinks I could deal kingdoms to my friends, / and ne'er be weary." (*Tim.* I.ii.223-224). "In his livery / Walked crowns and crownets; realms and islands were / As plates dropped from his pocket." (*Ant.* V.ii.90-92).

(2) For a fuller discussion of biblical and other analogues to this passage, see F. D. Hoeniger's note in the Arden edition.

(3) Bullough's emphasis on hagiography as a background to the moral values of *Per.* is an important scholarly contribution. It could have been supplemented by Hoeniger's discussion (in the introduction to the Arden edition) of the Miracle plays as a background to the flamboyant action, dangers, and miraculous rescues of the play. Hoeniger points to most interesting parallels between the Digby *Mary Magdalene* and *Per.* (in each play a woman dies in childbirth at sea and is cast away with her infant; in each play mother and child are later found alive).

(4) A reprint of this important book can remove three typographical errors: p. 44 notes at bottom of page are out of order (5 should be 1, 2 should be 3, etc.); p. 88, note 3, read: J. S. P. Tatlock; p. 371, line 23, read: Declamation 53.

262

The Strange Critical Fortunes of Shakespeare's Timon of Athens by Francelia Butler. Iowa State University Press, 1966. Pp. 188. $4.50. Reviewer: *Sylvan Barnet.*

The literature on Shakespeare is so voluminous that we must be grateful to any guide who picks his way through part of it and who accurately records his findings. *Shakespeare Studies, Shakespeare Survey, SQ, SNL, Abstracts of English Studies,* all deserve our gratitude for providing reviews of publications. Similarly, Mrs. Butler's study of the commentary on *Timon* might have allowed a reader to save an enormous amount of time.

Unfortunately, the reader does not get a good sense of the criticism, especially of the criticism of the last forty years, and it is probably this, rather than the work of Nathan Drake, Samuel Singer, J. M. Robertson, and even H. Dugdale Sykes (all given some space), that he cares about. For example, Mrs. Butler gives us a chapter on "Imagery and 'Thematic' Studies," but she does not mention (to name only a few critics that even the non-specialist in *Timon* knows and values) Edward Armstrong, Geoffrey Bush, Clifford Leech, John Danby, and Donald Stauffer. Possibly, too, this chapter should have discussed—or at least mentioned—the interest that Yeats and Pound showed in the play. Surely, a history of *Timon* that finds space for minor disintegrators but neglects major poets is an unbalanced history. I cannot see that these critics and creative writers are less worthy of note than many of those that Mrs. Butler discusses in her chapter. The next chapter, "An Empty Coffer: Structure and Meaning to the Audience," mentions a production in Prague in 1778 by one F. J. Fischer but does not mention any of the several productions by G. Wilson Knight, nor does it refer to Knight's chapter on staging *Timon,* in *Principles of Shakespearian Production.* Again, if there is a rationale, it has escaped me, but let us look at the inclusions rather than the exclusions. Mrs. Butler gives, for example, extracts from Muriel St. Clare Byrne and from Roy Walker on Richardson's Old Vic *Timon* of 1956-57. She incorrectly gives the page reference to a quotation from Miss Byrne's review; she incorrectly calls the reviewer Clare Byrne in the bibliography and index; she incorrectly says the Walker's review is of a production two years later; and she incorrectly gives (page 143) a quotation from Walker, omitting nine words and thereby changing the meaning. I quote Walker, italicizing the words Mrs. Butler silently omits: "Modern middle-class audiences have been indoctrinated with ideals of *prudence and economy and are, moreover, suffering the effects of* inflation and a credit squeeze." Most important, perhaps, is her decision of what to quote. One would think that a chapter on the stage history of *Timon* would, for example, take some notice of Walker's detailed remarks on the heavy cutting, but Mrs. Butler chooses to reproduce, incorrectly, a genial remark, where Walker begins to disengage himself from the play so that he can go on to a discussion of another play.

Perhaps this is the place to mention that a spot check revealed errors in half of the material checked. Examples: on page 14 Mrs. Butler says "Peter Ure complains of the 'static quality' of the second half of the play," but I find no such complaint on the page she cites; a footnote on page 57 to E. K. Chambers neglects to mention that the cited page is in the second volume of a two-volume work; a reference on page 63 to Hazlitt's *Characters of Shakespear's Plays* does not reproduce Hazlitt's spelling of the dramatist's name; page 76 gives William M. Merchant's middle initial incorrectly; page 88 quotes Traversi but neglects to indicate an ellipsis, thereby producing a distortion similar to the one in the passage from Walker. All of these errors were either immediately apparent or were noticed within a few moments of spot checking; it is not improbable that additional checking would reveal additional errors.

The writing throughout is undistinguished and sometimes inexact. The first sentence, in the Foreword, lets the reader know what he is in for: "Probably less is known about *Timon of Athens* than about any of Shakespeare's plays." (Of course Mrs. Butler believes *Timon* is by Shakespeare; of course she meant to write "any of Shakespeare's other plays.") As she works her way through her sources, she writes paragraphs like this one (page 12), from which I quote the initial words of each sentence: "Most editors agreed.... Some simply stated.... Many editors attempted.... A few theorized.... A large number of critics saw. ... Other critics argued.... Some critics—not many—thought...." Such sentences, however uninterestingly set forth, at least are clear, but what is one to make of this passage from page 46?

> In this first supporting essay, one can think along with Chambers as he rather naively progresses from a consideration of structure, to style, to divided authorship (which he rejects), to the idea that the play may be unfinished.

Does "think along with" mean "follow the argument," or "agree with"? Since Chambers' essay is said to be naive, presumably "think along with" has the former meaning, but why bother to tell us that we can "think along" with an author as he "naively progresses"? Perhaps, however, "think along with" and "naively" have meanings that I have not perceived. There is also a good deal of reference to "romantic," "objective," and "subjective," but none of these terms is adequately defined. Consider this passage from page 13:

> Critics who looked at *Timon* objectively were those who agreed with the Aristotelian concept of plot structure in tragedy which demands that the incidents in a plot should have an ordered interconnection or unity of action, so as to produce a plot with a beginning, a middle, and an end.

Apparently to agree with Aristotle is to be objective. After reading many pages of this sort of thing we are not surprised to encounter, on the last page of the final chapter, a paragraph that reveals puzzling critical assumptions:

> My own feelings about the play are that Shakespeare has attempted something unusual in it—the dramatization of an issue which is universal and consequently larger than characterization. Unfortunately, modernization of society has not yet evolved to a point where most people and their various spokesmen can be entertained by a dramatization of issues. Since this play is concerned with the true measure of man, can one expect that the issue will be interesting to the kinds of people who can sympathetically identify with Ann [*sic*] Frank but are unmoved by the issue involved in the slaughter of six million Jews?

The book began as a doctoral dissertation, and although inaccuracies and omissions are deplorable in a dissertation, the exercise was doubtless valuable for the student. But its value to others is severely limited: it summarizes the opinions of the older editors and critics whom most of us do not wish to read, but it is an unreliable guide to twentieth-century commentary on the play.

Tufts University

Paradoxia Epidemica: The Renaissance Tradition of Paradox by Rosalie L. Colie. Princeton University Press, 1966. Pp. xx + 553. $12.50. *Reviewer: Leonard Nathanson.*

Miss Colie's study of Renaissance paradoxy is indeed an ambitious undertaking. For she sets out to write comprehensively—engaging philosophical questions at a depth seldom encountered in literary criticism—about a subject long recognized as central to the thought and to the literary achievement of the Renaissance as a European cultural phenomenon. Paradox, in one or another of its senses, has figured in scores of books representing related interests in widely divergent disciplines: intellectual history (strategies of philosophic inquiry, development of modern scientific method, shifts in theological definition and religious sensibility); art and literary history (stylistic and thematic concepts of baroque, mannerism, etc. in painting, sculpture, architecture and the translation and extension of these concepts to literature); poetics (accounts of metaphysical poetry according to the definitions of the New Critical interest in opposed verbal mentionings and in the larger perspective of a renovated and critically focused historical scholarship). The confluence of interests such as these, applied to almost every artist and thinker of consequence, has given rise to enough hypotheses—from the glitteringly terse to the abstrusely turgid— to dazzle or stupefy students of the period. But this tendency to make the Renaissance serve as target for every hit-and-run aperçu and for many a ponderously expatiated thesis attests to its persistent relevance and to its power to arouse and tease the synthesizing instinct.

With full knowledge of the streams of contention rushing beneath and about her subject, Miss Colie nevertheless chooses to bypass controversial background and to launch straight out for the major figures and works that occupy the foreground of her interest. In her "Introduction," she does, however, set forth some very sensible reservations: that she does not offer paradoxy as an all-embracing intellectual formula for the age; that paradox cannot be regarded as congruent merely with "baroque," though significant relations clearly exist; and that paradox, though essential to the fiber of discourse about the mysteries of Christian faith, is not to be limited to religious subjects. There is no attempt to deal directly with the New Critical theory which values paradox, along with irony and ambiguity, as the peculiar source of poetic excellence, indeed as the trait that distinguishes poetry from other orders of discourse. But this book does demonstrate, implicitly yet quite cogently, that paradox is more profitably considered in relation to habits of thought, feeling, and expression deeply rooted in a cultural tradition rather than as the turn of mind of certain rare and poetically gifted individuals. Miss Colie possesses a fine verbal acuity and a considerable part of the book is devoted to close reading of poetic textures and structures. But she is too sophisticated ever to regard words as absolutes relative only to each other.

In a book of such scope organization is crucial not only for clarity and effectiveness of presentation but for the substance of argument too, since the subject, while "there," is at the same time being recreated in a new shape. Miss Colie acknowledges E. R. Curtius' *European Literature and the Latin Middle Ages* as an inspiration both for the "topical method" of her study and for its substantial concern with paradox. She confesses that various encyclopedic plans were tried but rejected. I find the plan she did settle upon altogether superior for her purposes and for those of her readers to an encyclopedic one such as served Northrop Frye well in *Anatomy of Criticism,* which aimed as a *summa literarum,* at a vast aerial perspective of all the continents of literary endeavor and not at the contours of individual works. Miss Colie seeks to engage finally the question of the excellence of the employment of paradox and therefore gives extended treatment to works as entities. She is able to adhere to her announced scheme of interest without grinding the individual work of art into grist for her mill. As a result, the reader interested in Donne or Milton, Spenser or Shakespeare will find much that is generally illuminating in Miss Colie's concise analyses, and not the abstract and reductive formulas that "topical" studies all too frequently produce. Moreover, while her approach springs from and is directed throughout by a strong historical sense, she does not lapse into the bland assumption that all tradition is good, that to explain the cause of some feature of a literary work is to establish its aesthetic success.

Miss Colie posits four broad kinds of paradox and partitions her study accordingly, progressing from relatively simple types to those of increasing complexity. Part I considers "Rhetorical and Psychological Paradoxes," with individual chapters on Rabelais, Petrarch, and Donne. Rhetorical paradoxes are "organized along the lines of traditional *encomia,* of an unexpected, unworthy, or indefensible subject" (p. 3) or defend "a proposition officially disapproved in public opinion" (p. 4). As such, they are inextricably involved in an "antic decorum" and in self-contradiction, since to praise what is unpraisable is either to undercut one's own logic or to challenge received opinion with an "oblique criticism of absolute judgment or absolute convention" (p. 10). This habit of mind and of discourse gives rise to what may be defined as an actual genre that in English literature is most successful and most familiar in Donne. The lighter of the *Songs and Sonets* along with the prose juvenilia revel in the triumphant misapplication of logic to undercut received values of constancy, beauty, and other virtues in love. The enterprise here involves less of a serious criticism of accepted ethical standards—essentially a reversal of the status of the one and the many—than a self-congratulatory pleasure in the poet-speaker's own witty impudence. In the love poems of earnest feeling, the paradoxes are psychological and approach the metaphysical as Donne ponders the "how" of the unity of two lovers, both when together and when apart. The ultimate problem of how love can be, and must be, at once physical and spiritual depends upon the paradoxes of the Incarnation, upon the collapsing and fusing of the one and the many.

The psychological perceptions of the experience of love as embodied in Petrarch and Donne often seek a larger basis of support in metaphysical definitions. The movement to Part II, "Paradoxes in Divine Ontology," thus seems a natural gradation. Here the authenticity of theological definition is emotionally confirmed in personal response, so that the interplay of continuity and of discontinuity between the divine and the human, the one and the many, achieves a cosmic resonance within the compass of individual sensibility. The three chapters Miss Colie devotes in this section to Traherne, *Paradise Lost,* and George Herbert are among the best in the entire study. The discussion of tautology in *The Temple* is especially fine ("In tautology, what is, is; in paradox, what is, is and is not." [p. 206], exposing, I believe, what lies closer to the center of this great poet's mind and art than does any previous criticism, including even Rosemond Tuve's superb treatment of the iconological dimension in Herbert. The sequence of chapters in this section in itself produces a significant pattern. For the retrograde chronology takes us from a rationalized principle of divine power and order in Traherne's "Affirmations in Negative Theology: the Infinite" to Milton's paradoxes of time and eternity and of divine omnipotence and human responsibility, finally back to Herbert's deeply personal yet fully sacramental approach to man's relation to God. This implicitly traced pattern, it is worth noting, confirms from a different standpoint Professor Martz's very interesting interpretation of the modification of religious sensibility during the seventeenth century.

Part III turns to "Ontological Paradoxes: Being and Becoming" and concentrates more on philosophical problems than on exegesis of the philosophical roots or import of literary works. A synoptic chapter introduces "Solutions to the Problem of Nothing," epitomized in Macbeth's "Nothing is / But what is not," which Miss Colie takes as the title for this chapter. Hamlet's teasing play with Ophelia about "Nothing" reverberates in the operations of his mind as he confronts his predicament and ponders the "extremes of the world's total significance and death's total oblivion" (p. 240). Iago, as a "self-made man" with no "recognized station," is a "nobody," who like the Nobody of pictorial tradition is to blame for the domestic chaos and ruin that overwhelm the master of the household. When Othello comes to recognize that "he has permitted 'nobody' to destroy his household" (p. 246), the lesson of the traditional paradox is completed as the householder is indicted for his own irresponsibility. Miss Colie's suggestive remarks about *Hamlet, Macbeth,* and *Othello,* while of peculiar interest to readers of *Shakespeare Studies,* will probably strike these readers as a good deal less convincing than her treatment of lyric, narrative, and discursive works elsewhere in this study. For in applying her interest in paradox to these dramas the author imposes a shape upon them that is not especially illuminating for their nature as dramatic entities. More valuable are succeeding chapters on Pascal, Dutch genre painting, and "Being and Becoming: Paradoxes in the Language of Things," which furnish an excellent and freshly focused overview of philosophical currents. The final chapter of this section assimilates recent critical opinion on *The Faerie Queene* to the author's scheme of interest in paradoxes of Being and Becoming, but in rather too abbreviated a compass. This approach to Spenser would repay more detailed development, which many, I should think, would like to see, especially if carried out by Miss Colie herself.

Part IV, "Epistemological Paradoxes," exhibits both the greatest strengths and the most obvious shortcomings of this book. An introductory general chapter—"'I am that I am' : Problems of Self-reference"—recapitulates and extends a number of strands of interest by applying the question of paradox to what is surely the acute issue of the late Renaissance: the problem of knowledge. This chapter appropriately concludes with a consideration of the most central figure in the perplexing "wars of truth" of the age: Montaigne. His "Apologie" covers all the planes of paradox from the calling into question of the accepted "Renaissance praise of man, of human dignity, and of human reason" (pp. 389-90) to the denial of the self that flaunts these unorthodox questionings. A chapter on "The Rhetoric of Transcendent Knowledge," marked by Miss Colie's usual penetrating command of intellectual history, discusses Sir John Davies' *Nosce teipsum* and Donne's *Anniversaries.* Perhaps the most consummately brilliant fusion of intellectual and literary analysis to be found in the entire study is the chapter on Burton's *Anatomy of Melancholy.* The exposition of the structure of thought informing this vast work takes us beyond its merely encyclopedic organization and beyond the kind of material interest that previous criticism has confined itself to.

It is the two final chapters, dealing respectively with *King Lear* and *Hamlet,* that are directly relevant to students of Shakespeare. Miss Colie analyzes the paradoxes of blindness and vision, reason and madness in *Lear,* relating them not only to the theme and action of the tragedy but to the larger contexts of Renaissance thought that she has previously established. Her comments are always sound and frequently incisive, and she is fully in command of the current state of critical discussion of the play. However, her results here, as with her briefer treatment of Shakespeare in an earlier chapter, are neither particularly

267

novel nor convincing, tending toward a recapitulation of what is by now a very standardized construing of the drama's thematic patterns and underlying "moral vision." The discussion of *Hamlet*—"Mine own Executioner"—in which the protagonist's dilemma is juxtaposed to the subject of Donne's casuistry and equivocation in *Biathanatos* is more profitable and seems to me more worth attending to than most attempts to apply intellectual history as an instrument of critical interpretation to Shakespeare. In the last analysis, though, one cannot help conclude that the author's scheme of interest supplies keys only to side doors, giving on rather misleading perspectives, of Shakespearean tragedy, whereas paradoxy takes us directly to the central chamber of the art of Donne or of Herbert. On the other hand, in view of how much Shakespeare criticism of this kind never manages even to get in the right neighborhood, Miss Colie's performance is quite commendable.

These chapters on Shakespeare are likely to prove of more enduring and profitable influence for certain procedural questions in Shakespeare studies than for interpretative ones. Miss Colie's discussion implies, I would say, strong support for the view that critics drawn to Shakespeare's reverberation of ethical and religious concepts would do better to seek out sources and analogues, as well as any background determinate of "meaning," in habits of thought and expression common to widely popular modes of discourse rather than in the formal systems of philosophy and of religious doctrine that such critics are prone to reconstruct at full historical length and then invoke—with strange consequences both for intellectual history and literary criticism—in the interpretation of plays. For ingrained habits of paradoxical thought—rhetorical and psychological, ontological and epistemological—made for widespread access (certainly too easy an access for paradox to be always effective and significant) to that irony and complexity which critics (both "new" and "historical") often overweigh and overvalue and therefore misjudge in the poetry and drama of the Renaissance.

In her "Epilogue" the author speculates about the reasons for the passing out of favor of paradox at the close of the Renaissance and the dawning of the age of Locke and Spinoza. Miss Colie's explanation inevitably recalls the account of the triumph of rationalism in intellectual inquiry that Basil Willey proposed more than thirty years ago in *The Seventeenth Century Background*. "Because paradox manages to be at once figure of speech and figure of thought, appropriate to a view of the universe profoundly metaphysical," it was, the author suggests, peculiarly suited "to mediate all sorts of ideas and things which, under strict categorical arrangements, do not at first glance appear to 'fit'" (p. 508). And though she avoids explicit reference to T. S. Eliot's "dissociation of sensibility" (surely the outstanding example of a private and poetic response successfully disseminated as a theory of history), Miss Colie's explanation of the demise of paradox carries a strong flavor of the same dubious idea. "In paradox, form and content, subject and object are collapsed into one, in an ultimate insistence upon the unity of being" (p. 518). Now this formula, as Miss Colie's excellent book demonstrates, clearly applies to Renaissance paradox, or at least to much of it. But even in this period, the fact that profound uses of paradox could be achieved both by the libertine naturalist Montaigne and the Protestant Platonist Milton must give us pause about narrowing this Protean mode of thought and expression to a single frame of philosophical reference, even to so capacious a one as the "medieval-Renaissance world view." And surely one should resist the temptation to extend such a formulation to a universal theory. After all, do not certain existentialist artists and thinkers of our own century, though they have completed the diametric reversal of ethical absolutes and personal contingency as orthodoxly conceived in the Renaissance, create richly paradoxical thought and expression out of their acceptance of individual reason as the only valid sanction for belief and conduct and yet as an absurdly inadequate one? Has not the celebrated "fragmentariness" of modern man given rise to as much and perhaps as great paradoxical expression of his condition as "unity of being" did for Renaissance man? Obviously, a study of paradox in modern literature would address itself to different forms of paradox, differently composed and aimed from those of the Renaissance. But surely the co-existence of psychological and ethical contraries fruitful for literary expression cannot be confined to any one period or to any given philosophic outlook.

Vanderbilt University

Norm and Form: Studies in the Art of the Renaissance by E. H. Gombrich. Phaidon Press, 1966. Pls. 186. Pp. viii + 167. $9.50. *Reviewer: J. M. Steadman.*

The eleven essays in this volume range in date from 1942 to 1963 and vary widely in subject and approach. Nevertheless they are linked by similar problems ("style, patronage and taste"), and they reveal a common theme—the influence that "the Renaissance climate of opinion . . . has exerted on both the practice and the criticism of art." Dr. Gombrich sets out to "study the explicit and implicit critical standards accepted within [the Renaissance] tradition by artists and patrons alike, and to ask what influence these norms may have on the forms produced by masters of varying gifts." In the course of this investigation he explores norms that underlay literature and the visual arts alike and theories that conditioned practice in the verbal as well as the visual arts. Though his volume is directed primarily to the art historian, it throws considerable light on the relation of Renaissance literature to art, and of both of these to the thought of the period. It should, accordingly, prove almost as useful to the literary historian and the historian of ideas as to the art specialist.

In his first essay ("The Renaissance Conception of Artistic Progress and its Consequences") the author finds the idea of progress largely responsible for the "mentality" that Ghiberti shared with other Renaissance artists—the tendency to conceive the development of art as a series of solutions to difficult technical problems. With this orientation, "the artist works like a scientist. His works exist not only for their own sake but also to demonstrate certain problem-solutions. He creates them . . . principally with an eye on his fellow artists and the connoisseurs who can appreciate the ingenuity of the solution put forward." In the "strangely elongated proportions of figures" from Ghiberti's second door for the Baptistry at Florence, Dr. Gombrich sees a conscious effort to emulate Lysippus' part in the progress of Greek sculpture. According to Pliny, Lysippus had contributed to the development of this art through elongating his figures in the interest of symmetry and appearance of reality; Pliny's account inspired Ghiberti to seek a comparable role.

The second study likewise turns to literature for the solution to a problem in art history. In the poetry of the Florentine humanist Ugolino Verino, Dr. Gombrich discovers evidence for identifying the so-called "Dido Master" as Apollonio di Giovanni, a fifteenth-century painter who specialized largely in the decoration of *cassoni*.

The third paper ("Renaissance and Golden Age") stresses "the rhetorical roots of that idolizing of Renaissance patronage so characteristic of the "Medici myth"—the convention that "makes the Medici in general, and Lorenzo in particular, directly responsible for a magic efflorescence of the human spirit, the Renaissance." The myth can be traced back to Lorenzo's age in poetry that extols him as the restorer of an age of gold. In Gombrich's opinion, it owes its currency partly to the fact that two other conventional topics of encomium—famous ancestry and heroism in battle—had been denied to poets who desired to praise Cosimo, "a mere banker and city boss . . . without ancestors and without claim to warlike prowess. . . ."

In "The Early Medici as Patrons of Art" the author attempts to uncover the "real events" that have been obscured by the Medici legend. Cosimo's "contribution to pious foundations" was (Gombrich argues) "a much more improvised and piecemeal affair" than Machiavelli and Vasari suggest. There seeems, moreover, to have been "a clear division of labour between Cosimo and his two sons in matters of patronage"—the father centering his interest on architecture and leaving "negotiations with painters and decorators to Piero and Giovanni." Emphasizing "how few works of art there are in existence which can be proved to have been commissioned by Lorenzo [il Magnifico]," Gombrich attributes "the paucity of documented commissions" not merely to shortage of money but partly to Lorenzo's pretensions as "an arbiter of taste": "Fastidious men make difficult patrons." In short, the Magnifico "may have seen his patron's role not as that of a 'regular customer' but—perhaps for the first time in history—as one who offers his influential support to advance the interest not of individual artists but of what he considered the interests of art as such."

In "Leonardo's Method for Working out Compositions," Dr. Gombrich emphasizes the novelty of da Vinci's drawing style. Unlike his fellow artists, who regarded themselves essentially as draughtsmen and whose standard was "the sure, unfailing line which needed no correction and no second thoughts," Leonardo worked out his design by a series of revisions, finally clarifying his idea by "using a stylus and tracing the line he finally chose through the paper to its reverse." "Like a sculptor modelling in clay," he refused to accept any form as final and preferred to go on creating, "even at the risk of obscuring his original intentions." Emphasizing invention over craftsmanship, Vinci agreed with the poet in giving priority to "the movements appropriate to the mental state of the creatures that make up [the] picture rather than to the beauty and perfection of their parts." The same predilection for the "indeterminate" that led him to exploit "the *sfumato* and the half-guessed form" characterizes his sketches; he used them to "help his 'invention' regardless of the subject." The sketch was "no longer the preparation for a particular work" but belonged rather to the process in the artist's mind; "instead of fixing the flow of imagination it [kept] it in flux."

The following essay interprets Raphael's *Madonna della Sedia* as a solution to a specific problem in composition, a response to the "challenge" of combining the "new-found freedom of movement" (characteristic of his Roman period) with "the strict discipline imposed by the tondo." Expressing a healthy skepticism towards two fashionable approaches in criticism ("that of the anecdote which sees in the picture the record of a casual encounter with life, and that of formal analysis which sees the secret of its unity and harmony in an interplay of curves"), Dr. Gombrich regards the painting as an "optimal solution" that does justice to "two mutually limiting demands—that of lifelikeness and that of arrangement." In the development of Raphael's conception for the picture he finds a "process, not of planning but of gradual adjustment." Raphael "never started with a schematic compositional sketch or with a study from life: he began somewhere in between, groping his way simultaneously towards those two mutually limiting orders"—"compact grouping and lifelikeness."

The title essay ("Norm and Form") explores the Renaissance origin of several of the major categories in art history. In the familiar "procession of styles and periods"—"Classic, Romanesque, Gothic, Renaissance, Mannerist, Baroque, Rococo, Neo-Classical and Roman-

270

tic"—Gombrich perceives "only a series of masks for two categories, the classical and the non-classical." The same passage in Vitruvius served as a pattern for Vasari in his description of Gothic, Bellori in his condemnation of the baroque, and Winckelmann in his attack on the rococo. Observing that all of these "various terms for non-classical styles" are actually "terms of exclusion," Gombrich criticizes the attempt to elevate these styles into "systems in their own right embodying alternative values, if not philosophies." In his opinion, art criticism would make greater "progress in the study of styles" if it "looked out for such principles of exclusion, the sins any particular style wants to avoid," than if it continued to look for "the common structure or essence of all the works produced in a certain period." The tendency to reduce "the idea of the classical and the non-classical to a mere morphological distinction of equally justified alternatives" blurs the really "vital distinction among unclassical styles: those which are unclassical from a principle of exclusion and those which are not"—the distinction (that is) between the "anti-classical" and the merely "unclassical." Inasmuch as "exclusion implies intention, and such an intention cannot be directly perceived in a family of forms," this distinction indirectly threatens the "whole idea of a morphology of styles." The remainder of this essay is devoted to a sympathetic but penetrating reappraisal of Wölfflin's method of "systematic comparison" and "morphology of style" in the light of this distinction.

"Mannerism: The Historiographic Background" treats the "idea of rescue and restoration" (the motif of the "return of the golden age") as a historiographic alternative to the pattern of "progress towards an ideal of perfection." Illustrating the restoration-motif by four texts ranging from Dionysius of Halicarnassus to Max Dvorak, Dr. Gombrich traces the same idea successively in the alleged restoration of Attic oratory from "Asiatic" extravagances, the Renaissance "restoration" of the arts after "Gothic" corruption, and Carracci's "restoration" of the arts after the "destructive vice" of Mannerism.

The following essay ("The Renaissance Theory of Art and the Rise of Landscape") argues that "landscape painting as we know it might never have developed without the artistic theories of the Italian Renaissance." Attributing its emergence as a new genre primarily to the interaction of Northern practice and Southern theory, Dr. Gombrich notes that "it is in Venice, not in Antwerp, that the term 'a landscape' is first applied to any individual painting." The development of landscape painting in northern Europe "followed a demand that existed in Southern Europe," and the demand itself was essentially a product of the Italian Renaissance, with its tendency to value art-works on aesthetic rather than utilitarian grounds, "for the sake of their artistic achievement rather than their function or subject matter." Italian theorists (he suggests) approached northern landscape paintings with preconceptions derived from the classics—the Horatian analogy between painting and poetry, Pliny's account of the Roman landscape painter Studius, and Vitruvius' emphasis on naturalistic prospects as subjects for mural decoration. Northern tradition and Southern theory combined to cast the Flemish painter in the role of a landscape specialist.

In "The Style all'antica: Imitation and Assimilation," the author stresses "the difficulty of defining the exact debt of Renaissance artists to antiquity" and the "increasing elusiveness in the style all'antica." Noting the value as well as the limitations of the "analogy between literary and representational styles," he explores the relation between antique invention and modern variation in the work of Giulio Romano (whom Aretino had praised for "the spirit of [his] conceptions—anciently modern and modernly ancient"). In both art and literature Gombrich emphasizes the distinction between imitation and assimilation. "Assimilation," he observes, "demands a degree of generalization. The artist must learn how to create

271

a figure that embodies his idea of the classical style," catching the "spirit" of the ancients and the "illusion of movement and life," and preferring to be "similar" to (rather than "identical" with) his classical models.

The final essay ("Reynold's Theory and Practice of Imitation") re-examines Sir Joshua's portrait of the Montgomery sisters *(Three Ladies adorning a Term of Hymen)* in the light of his principles of imitation, thus "narrow[ing] the rift which for many observers still exists between Reynolds the teacher and Reynolds the artist." In unravelling the various iconographical motifs in the painting, Dr. Gombrich finds "elements of Reynold's *Lady Keppel*, of Poussin's *Sacrifice to Hymen* and Rubens's *Three Graces*, of Poussin's *Bacchanal* and of an anonymous *Rape of Proserpina.*" The painting thus reveals the "same programmatic emphasis" on imitation as do the discourses; Reynold's doctrine and art alike represent a "conservative programme," an attempt to maintain the continuity of tradition by preserving "the artistic conceptions of the past, handed down in an unbroken chain from generation to generation." The impracticality of such a programme, the impossibility of retrieving the past by imitation, is reflected in the picture itself with its precarious balance between portraiture and history and its tension between the demands of individual realism and the ideal of classical beauty. Essentially the painting is less an "imitation" than an adaptation of the classical style.

Like the essays themselves, the illustrations and scholarly apparatus in this book are of high quality. The volume contains generous but indispensable notes and a list of illustrations. The index is devoted primarily to names, but also includes several of the more important topics. Typographical errors are few ("longt ime" on p. 108 and "oevre" on p. 126).

Ut pictura poesis. Dr. Gombrich's observations on the relationship between theory and painting in the Renaissance will be of great interest to literary scholars. In particular, his insistence on looking for the "principles of exclusion" instead of rival "systems" or "philosophies" in studying Renaissance and post-Renaissance styles provides a timely warning to the literary critic. (The latter is often all too prone to apply the categories of art history— "Renaissance, Mannerist, Baroque, Rococo, Neo-Classical," etc.—to prose or poetry without ascertaining what these terms meant for artists of the time or how far they can be legitimately transferred to literary styles.) Dr. Gombrich's suggestions and caveats will be as welcome to the student of Renaissance literature as to the art historian.

The Huntington Library

The Great Shakespeare Forgery by Bernard Grebanier. W.W. Norton & Company, Inc., 1965. Pp. xii + 308. $5.00. *Reviewer: S. Schoenbaum.*

The Ireland affair still fascinates, and rightly so. It is a rattling good story, with suspense, hilarity, and pathos. Instructive also, for it tells us something about an age which had not yet reconciled itself to the hard truth that there would be no intimate Shakespearean documents and which could discern the true lineaments of the Immortal Bard in the puerile effusions of an adolescent boy. For the modern, interest also attaches to the psychopathology of the relationship between Samuel Ireland and his neurotic son William Henry. The father —naive, kindly, and well esteemed as antiquarian collector, engraver, and author of volumes of *Picturesque Views*—was decently solicitous about the boy and a companion to him, but persuaded that the lad was witless. Stupid in school, William produced the forged

272

Shakespeare Papers, inscribed on antique paper with a special bookbinder's ink, to demonstrate his Chattertonian genius and to please his father, a great worshipper of the National Poet. The Papers made an enormous stir when displayed by Samuel Ireland at his home in the Strand in 1795: Boswell knelt before them and kissed them and said, "Well; I shall now die contented, since I have lived to witness the present day." Other intriguing characters played their parts, major or minor: Jordan the Stratford Poet, the playwright-manager Sheridan, Mrs. Jordan the actress, the eccentric Shakespearean editor Steevens, the formidable Malone. The drama moves inexorably towards the splendid climactic scene of the first—and last—night at Drury Lane of that previously unknown Shakespearean masterpiece *Vortigern,* at which Kemble sepulchrally intoned, "—and when this solemn mockery is ended," whereupon all hell broke loose. In his Foreword Mr. Grebanier says that he never before so much enjoyed writing a book. We can believe him.

His account begins inauspiciously with a ponderous similitude likening Shakespeare's reputation to that of the Alps, but he soon settles down to tell the story straightforwardly and with sympathy for his incredible hero. It is an entirely readable book—Grebanier writes with vigor—and the author has his own contribution to make to our understanding of the curious relationship that existed among Samuel Ireland, his housekeeper Mrs. Freeman (who is not implausibly suggested to be his mistress), and young William. But *The Great Shakespeare Forgery* does not qualify as the authoritative study of the Ireland affair. That is a pity, for such a study is much needed.

For any but the most lightbrained readers the value of the book is severely undermined by the absence of documentation and index (Mair's work on the same subject, *The Fourth Forger* of 1938, is also unannotated but at least has an index). For these deficiencies the publishers must share responsibility with the author. They were in a position to have one of their staff prepare at least a rudimentary index. Did they also discourage—or at least fail to encourage—notes, on the assumption that these would alienate the broad reading public to which a commercial publisher caters? If so, surely they were operating under a delusion: these days profitable books can also be scholarly and have scholarly apparatus; witness Ellmann's *Joyce.* For a subject such as Grebanier's, documentation is essential because the facts themselves have come down in conflicting versions. To cite but one instance: the author says (p. 286) that the Shakespeare Papers brought £130 at the Sotheby sale after Samuel Ireland's decease. The figure may well be correct, but where did Grebanier find it? Not long before his death William claimed that the Papers went for £640— a preposterous exaggeration—but in the nineteenth century Halliwell-Phillipps gave the sum as £300. A note is surely called for.

Such an objection voiced in the pages of *Shakespeare Studies* will, I suspect, leave Grebanier unmoved, for he seems to have it in for the scholars. How else can we take the following broadside: "Since modern scholarship has chosen to deny the validity of esthetic judgments, and thinks itself safe in relying upon dates above all other matters, the bulk of modern Shakespearean scholarship is merely vapid, esoteric, and false to the very fundamentals of literary creation" (p. 132). I must confess to puzzlement, not being conscious of any grave shortage of academic interpretative criticism of Shakespeare. Let Grebanier glance at Gordon Ross Smith's *Classified Shakespeare Bibliography* and be edified by a work representative of the sort of scholarship he sneers at.

This is not Grebanier's only curious statement. "It is a fact," he writes, "that the tamperings of the players with Shakespeare's text have sometimes found their way into the printed versions of his plays" (p. 114). Is he thinking of Jenkins on *Hamlet?* Not at all: "Indeed, there are a couple of such passages, peculiarly inane, allotted to the Fool in this very play [*Lear*]. But such interpolations are few, and the reader who knows his Shakespeare can identify them as readily as if they were printed in red ink." As though disintegration had not come and gone! Then, not everyone will share Grebanier's view that the bequest of the second best bed to Ann Shakespeare represents "one of the greatest and most grimly eloquent jokes in the annals of biography," although some no doubt will find such unorthodoxy refreshing.

Regrettably Grebanier's own scholarship is at times open to question. He nowhere tells readers that he has throughout lowered superior letters in quotations. The quotations themselves, and the citation of titles, are not impeccably accurate. For example, in a passage from Croft's epistolary novel, *Love and Madness,* which had an influence on young Ireland, Grebanier substitutes *ignoble* for *ignominious.* Through an error in spacing, the date of Shakespeare's promissory note to Heminges is made part of the receipt (p. 82). More serious is the misreading (twice) of *William* for *Willam* in the forged Southampton letter, an error repeated in the section of illustrations (where the correct spelling may be clearly seen). *Shakspeare* is incorrectly given as *Shakespeare* and *Shaksperian* as *Shakspearian* in several titles: William's *Authentic Account,* Samuel's *Miscellaneous Papers and Legal Instruments* and *An Investigation of Mr. Malone's Claim,* and Woodward's *Familiar Verses.* Malone's christian name is variously given as Edmund and (correctly) Edmond. Grebanier unhappily misspells *Bidford* in a sentence disparaging Jordan's misspellings.

On substantive matters of fact and interpretation, as on the accidentals of spelling, Grebanier is not always trustworthy. Shakespeare's will was not found in 1747 in Somerset House, as he states, but in Stratford, where Joseph Greene came upon a copy of it in that year. Grebanier does not, like Mair, fall into the error of seeing Malone, a notably generous man, as the vindictive persecutor of the Irelands; but he misunderstands that great scholar's achievement. Malone, Grebanier tells us, introduced 1654 emendations into his 1790 Shakespeare. A major achievement of Malone's edition—as Grebanier would have grasped had he attended more carefully to the preface—is that he purged the text of unwarranted emendations: he *restored* 1654 readings. Like Mair before him, Grebanier relates that Ireland got the idea for his first Shakespeare forgery from encountering the Blackfriars Gatehouse mortgage deed in the Johnson-Steevens Shakespeare, and that the forger traced the dramatist's signature to the deed as reproduced in that edition. Grebanier is here following William's own account in the *Confessions* (1805); but although Ireland's title-page motto is "The whole truth, and nothing but the truth," he should never go unquestioned. The deed does not appear in the Johnson-Steevens Shakespeare. Acquired by Garrick, it came into the possession of his widow and was communicated to Malone on 13 February 1788 through the good offices of Horace Walpole. Malone first published it in his 1790 edition, and there Ireland found it. He would give the man who exposed him credit for nothing.

The book has other limitations. Grebanier appears to be unacquainted with Malone's detection of the Macklin forgery of 1748 (see Shakespeare, *Plays and Poems,* ed. Malone, Vol. I, Pt. 1, pp. 386-414), and he too readily accepts the view, first propounded by Isaac Disraeli, that Steevens was responsible for the fabricated letter, dated 1600, from George Peele to "Henrie Marle," and first published in the *Theatrical Review* of 1763: Steevens might be expected to know that by 1600 Marlowe and Peele were dead. It is an hypothesis (however plausible), not a fact—as Grebanier puts it—that Shakespeare collaborated with Fletcher on *Henry VIII.* More than once Grebanier refers to the "old Jordan" who escorted the Irelands round Stratford in 1793; but Jordan was then forty-seven—younger than his client Samuel. I do not believe, with Grebanier, that Jordan cooked up the dramatic revelation at Clopton House of the destroyed Shakespeare papers in collusion with the farmer occupant, Williams. Such a trick would be beyond the cunning of Jordan, described by Wheler as "one of those humble geniuses, to whom a little learning, if not a dangerous thing, proved almost useless" (*Guide to Stratford-upon-Avon,* 1814, p. 139); and we know that Malone, informed of the episode by Jordan himself, took it seriously enough to complain to Williams' landlord.

Although Grebanier has consulted numerous sources for his book, he has missed some important ones. Apparently he does not know *Ireland's Shaksperian Fabrications,* in Harvard College Library, which includes William Henry's *Authentic Account,* with numerous— and sometimes revealing—annotations by the author. Also bound into the volume is a manuscript attributed to Ireland's mother. Harvard College Library possesses, moreover, a copy of the Sotheby auction catalogue of 1801 with Ireland's notes. Grebanier acknowledges that the *Miscellaneous Papers and Legal Instruments* of 1796 does not contain texts of all of the forgeries, but he seems to be unaware that in the nineteenth century Halliwell [-Phillipps] published the omitted documents in *A Descriptive Catalogue of a Collection of Shakspeariana . . . Including a Remarkable Series of the Ireland Forgeries* (London, 1866), an edition limited to fifty copies. Halliwell [-Phillipps] reproduces several letters to Heminges in which the Bard begs his friend "to speake toe Masterre Johnsonne who hathe treatedde mee mouste hawtylye," confesses that "onne cannotte bee wise atte alle tymes evenne soe was itte withe myselfe atte Bitteforde," and complains of "myne olde syckness."

The illustrations amount to a curious mélange. We are shown the amphitheatre for the 1769 Shakespeare Jubilee and Grebanier's own mulberry cup, but none of Ireland's forged sketches. Nor does the author reproduce the touched-up portrait of Shakespeare in the part of Bassanio, which the credulous Samuel thought once hung in the Green Room of the Globe.

To sum up: Grebanier has written an entertaining and informative book that fails rather markedly to meet scholarly standards. But, then, he has apparently written off the scholars anyway.

Northwestern University

Christian Rite and Christian Drama in the Middle Ages: Essays in the Origin and Early History of Modern Drama by O. B. Hardison, Jr. The Johns Hopkins Press, 1965. Pp. xvi + 328. $7.50. *Reviewer: Norman Sanders.*

Perhaps the first thing that should be said about this book, before any examination of its details is attempted, is that it is one of the most important works of scholarship on the origins of the English drama that has appeared for many years. Certainly, it is a part of the fresh examination, which has been taking place recently, of the documents and materials dealt with some fifty years ago by Chambers and Young, whose work has long stood unchallenged, except in its details, as the orthodox view of the emergence of drama in England. However, Mr. Hardison's work differs from the researches of such scholars as Prosser, Salter, Wickham, and Gardiner, in that it does not so much force us to reject certain long-held assumptions about various segments of mediaeval drama as question the very basis on which the received history has been built.

This is not to say that Mr. Hardison attempts to supersede Chambers' and Young's histories; for his approach is exploratory and suggestive rather than comprehensive. The book comprises a series of essays on topics of central importance in the early drama, not a continuous account of its development. Nevertheless, it does offer a sustained argument in that it moves (as did the drama itself) from pure Christian rite through dramatic representation within the context of the liturgy and on to secularized recreation of religious event.

The whole study is prefaced by that all-too-rare exercise—a good essay on the intellectual climate surrounding scholarly work: in this case that of Chambers, Young, Manly, and Symonds. While most students of the drama quickly become aware of the influences exercised on even the greatest critics by the assumptions and preoccupations of the ages in which they lived, they are generally less cognizant of the pressure of such forces in the work of historical scholars as they deal with their more scientific data. Mr. Hardison argues in this first essay that behind Chambers' interpretations of the historical and documentary evidence he amassed there lie the patterns of thought and theories developed by the evolutionary biologists. This discussion is a necessary lead-in to the book's thesis, as much of its importance depends not so much on new discovery as on a searching re-examination of already available materials. In general, his point is well made:

> the standard historians of medieval drama have followed the procedure used by early evolutionary anthropologists in connection with the study of myth. They have attributed present concepts and attitudes to a culture of the past. They have assumed that medieval man thought like nineteenth-century man, or ought to have done so. The result has been serious distortion. History has become teleological, interpreted intentionally and unconsciously in terms of what texts anticipate rather than what they are.

However, in his eagerness to make his point, Mr. Hardison sometimes tends to overstate his case (perhaps with deliberate polemical intent?); and one is occasionally stopped short by the implications of some of his attitudes. An example may be seen in his discussion of Chambers' reactions to the Church's role in early dramatic ventures:

> The clergy is consistently cast in the role of the villain who opposes the "mimetic instinct" which is associated with such terms as "healthy," "human," and "pagan." Classical drama was, by definition, "pagan." Christians, allied with "barbarian invaders," attacked the theater. By the seventh century, "the bishops and the barbarians had triumphed." Yet the mimetic instinct lived on. Minstrels "braved the ban of the church, and finally won their way." Folk plays, "the last sportive stage[s] of ancient heathen ritual," were enacted, although they "remained to the last alien and distasteful to the Church."

There is a good deal of truth in this, even as there is in F. P. Wilson's gibe that Chambers wrote about religious drama and left out religion. Nevertheless, there is plentiful evidence that the early Church did oppose secular dramatic activity and vigorously discriminate against its practicioners, presumably believing them to be a danger to the true faith and a living remnant of the paganism it sought to overcome. In his account of "The Mass as Sacred Drama," Mr. Hardison argues that

> the "dramatic instinct" of European man did not "die out" during the earlier Middle Ages, as historians of the drama have asserted. Instead, if found expression in the central ceremony of Christian worship, the Mass. This being the case, an understanding of the medieval interpretation of the Mass should illuminate many hitherto obscure aspects of the history of European drama.

If this is true, one wonders why Amalarius in his *Liber officialis* found it necessary to draw from a satisfying well-established ritual an allegory which is (in Mr. Hardison's own contention)

> closer to literary criticism than to theology. [Amalarius and his followers] sought to express the felt significance of an event which is at the center of Catholic life in language which would both explain it and make it ever more widely available to the *simpliciores*.

Do even *simpliciores* requre an "explanation" of a fully satisfying dramatic experience? particularly one which resorts to the methods of literary criticism? It is, one would have thought, at least possible to see the *Liber officialis* as an attempt to emphasize the dramatic elements of the Mass so as to make it as rewarding a mimetic event as it was a religious celebration.

This second section of the book however, does demonstrate convincingly that while the Mass as a sacred drama embodies in its structure the central pattern of Christian life, its celebration also contains all elements necessary to secular performance. Mr. Hardison uses to great effect his knowledge of the ninth-century Mass with its focal point in the Resurrection rather than in the Crucifixion, the association of the initial ceremonies of the Communion with the actions of the three Mary's at the sepulcher, and the linking made by Amalarius between the paten and the ointment box of the Mary's. This essay also constitutes as fine a discussion of Amalarius's allegorization as one could wish for, and has some searching comment on the concept of "sliding time". Here again, however, I think the author occasionally pushes his arguments too far. For example, we find this on the subject of Dürer's 1511 woodcut on the *salus animae theme*:

> Is Dürer's woodcut an image of truth, a record of an hallucination, or a piece of late medieval didacticism? The question is irrelevant. It is asked from the point of view of the detached observer, and the detached observer is, by definition—by the fact of his detachment—incapable of the experience against which the validity of the answer must be tested. To criticize the allegory or to explain it on grounds alien to the Catholic faith is to eliminate all possibility of understanding the Mass as a cultural and historical institution. It is also, incidentally, to eliminate the possibility of understanding the relation of the mass to liturgical drama.

The final sentence here is intellectual sleight of hand; religious commitment can be as blinding as detachment, though perhaps not in the same way.

Perhaps the most original sections of the book are those on the "Lenten Agon" and *"Christus Victor"*. Here Mr. Hardison examines the Easter Liturgy as a total dramatic structure rather than isolating, as is usual, individual ceremonies like the *Elevatio Crucis* or the *Visitatio Sepulchri*. Like the Mass, the Easter cycle is dramatic and non-representational in mode; but, unlike the Mass, it includes representational episodes, of which one important characteristic is the use of chronological or linear time rather than the "eternal present". In these essays also the argument is presented that the *Quem Quaeritis* was not composed to be used as a complement to the *Resurrexit* Antiphon but was associated with the Easter Vigil Mass.

In his subsequent examination of the earliest extant documents relating to the *Quem Quaeritis* tropers, in the fifth essay, Mr. Hardison develops this point in greater detail and argues against the Chambers-Young hypothesis that the simplest version must be the earliest, and that greater complexity always implies a later date and development. He offers the following conclusions based on his own chronology of the extant *Quem Quaeritis* manuscripts: (1) the *Quem Quaeritis* dialogue originated not as an Introit Easter troper associated or in connection with Matins, but as a ceremony associated with the Vigil Mass; and (2) its subsequent displacement and modification are explained by three factors: the anticipation of the Vigil Mass to a time no longer even approximately coincident with the Resurrection, the characteristics of monastic as against secular worship, and the special requirements of those ceremonies with which the *Quem Quaeritis* became associated in the tenth century. This means that between the eleventh and twelfth centuries at the time when the *Quem Quaeritis* was becoming codified, the dialogue of the piece was simplified along the lines found in the St Gall manuscript. It is difficult to argue with Mr. Hardison's closely reasoned upsetting of the traditional ideas about the troper, except to admit to some slight doubts about the Aquileia version with its evidence of a much freer treatment. The less fully developed argument that the Christmas play was produced by analogy to the Easter play is equally acceptable.

So far as the history of the secular drama is concerned, the section of the book on the Resurrection play is the most rewarding. Analyses of the Aquileia and St Lambrecht texts amply demonstrate the author's contention that liturgical drama is the outcome of the search for representational modes which employed historical amplification, improvisation, verisimilitude, and linear time, yet preserved the vital relationship with ritual.

But while liturgical drama represents the first sustained crossing of the boundary between ritual and representation in the Middle Ages, the plays in the vernacular tradition like *La Seinte Resureccion* were conceived from the outset as representational. After a detailed analysis of this play (which includes a new possible arrangement of the necessary *sedes* which is very different from those of Chambers and Wright and is in keeping with Amalarius's church locational symbolism), Mr. Hardison posits that the liturgical drama, somewhere before the middle of the twelfth century, branched off in two directions: first, towards the complex Latin plays of the thirteenth century like those of Fleury or Benediktbeuern, which preserved the ritual ceremonial features of the Easter plays; and secondly, towards works like *Le Mystère d' Adam* and *La Seinte Resureccion*, vernacular plays which reached a complex level of development a century before Latin drama but remained localized in Norman England.

The implications of the existence of a highly conventionalized vernacular tradition in the twelfth century raises important questions about the dependence of later vernacular drama on the liturgical tradition. As Mr. Hardison notes:

> The first definite record of an English cycle is 1377. Yet we have clear proof that the basic problems of representational drama were solved in England by 1175. What happened to this drama during the intervening two centuries? Was the tradition entirely lost, or has preoccupation with the liturgical tradition simply caused the evidence of its survival to be ignored? If it survived, what influence did it have on the cycles? . . . The chief difference between the staging of the *Resureccion* and that of the English guild cycles two hundred years later is that in the fourteenth century the stage has been enlarged to include the entire town, and the stations have been mounted on pageant cars. If the Norman French drama of the twelfth century did not prepare the way for the later religious drama of France and England, one would like, at the very least, to know what happened to it. The fact that the Canterbury manuscript of the *Resureccion* dates from around 1275 suggests, however, that Anglo-Norman influence may have persisted

even as the language of the popular drama of Britain was changing from French to English.

No one with any knowledge of the mature Elizabethan and Jacobean drama can read about the ritualistic elements of the early secular drama without the mind leaping ahead to speculate on their later manifestations and implications. And it is a measure of the importance of Mr. Hardison's book that the reader is continually indulging in such speculation. For example, it is difficult not to pause and think hard about Shakespeare's Romances in the light of a passage as the following:

> the ritual structure characteristic of the Mass and the Church year carries over unchanged into representational plays. This structure is comic, not tragic. The mythic event celebrated is rebirth, not death, although it is a rebirth that requires death as its prelude. The experience of the participants is transition from guilt to innocence, from separation to communion.

In his "Epilogue", Mr. Hardison unpretentiously offers a series of observations on some of the later implications of his study. He dwells on the general connections between the liturgy and the great vernacular cycles, and concludes that the latter

> must ... be considered a fusion of the techniques of representation derived from vernacular tradition with the ritual form characteristic of Latin religious drama. The combination accounts for both their episodic quality and their larger unity.

Perhaps the most tantalising of his speculations, as he argues for the importance of recognising the persistence of ritual form, is that contained in his final pages, where he touches upon the possible implications of his work so far as Shakespeare's tragic form is concerned. It is to be hoped that he develop at greater length in the future his suggestion that it is possible to speak of "the comic structure and tragic tonality in *Romeo, Hamlet,* and *Othello*". That indeed would be scanned.

The University of Tennessee

Italian Tragedy in the Renaissance by Marvin T. Herrick. University of Illinois Press, 1965. Pp. viii + 315. $6.75. *Reviewer: Maurice Charney.*

The bathetic high point of Italian Renaissance tragedy is reached in Antonio Decio's *Acripanda* (1591) when the queen opens the linen bundle containing the severed arms of her slaughtered son and daughter:

> Ch' io non vi riconosco,
> E quand' io bacio, e palpo
> Qualche lacero membro,
> Non so se palpo e bacio
> Qualche membro, che sia
> Parte di te, figliuolo,
> O di te parte, o figlia;
> E non posso distinti
> Pianger là il figlio, o la figliuola quivi [4.3].

I do not recognize you, and when I kiss and touch some mangled limb, I do not know whether it is part of you, my son, or part of you, O daughter; and I cannot distinguish to mourn for my son there or for my daughter here.

The difficulty may be complicated by the fact that the children are twins, but the queen's "irritable reaching after fact and reason" seems disturbing in a passage of such putative passion. The problem extends to other Italian tragedies of blood and revenge, since the wildness of the emotions aroused is tempered by the embellishment of the rhetoric and by the ever-present assumption that savage passions make one a more fluent and inventive speaker. Mr. Herrick never explores the subject of rhetoric, but I should think that he would have wanted to point out how the artfulness of the discourse in Italian Renaissance tragedy undercuts the cruelty of the subject matter, and makes it seem merely an imaginative flight.

One of the most influential plays of the sixteenth century, and one that did most to establish the tragic genre of blood and revenge, is Giraldi Cinthio's *Orbecche* (1541), which is largely an adaptation of Seneca's *Thyestes* through the medium of Cinthio's own *novella* in *Hecatommithi*, an important source of plots for Shakespeare and the Elizabethan dramatists. *Orbecche* may be considered in relation to Cinthio's theory of tragedy, the topic of what is probably Herrick's best chapter. The chief character of the play is a young woman, Orbecche, daughter of Sulmone, King of Persia. The setting and costumes are exotic, and the supernatural solicitings of Nemesis, Furies, and the Ghost of Selina (Sulmone's murdered wife) are used to give a sense of dark and fateful necessity to the plot. The action is concentrated within one natural day (sunrise to sunset). As in Seneca, there are long soliloquies, debates, and narrations of messengers. Cinthio puts particular stress on the emotional possibilities of the *nuntius*:

> Hence he, as though smitten with fury, cannot help uttering great words full of the horror he has in his mind, and he ought to amplify in narration the wretched and horrible mishap by showing the actions, the wailings, the words, the cruelty, the desperation, the manner in which the wretched victim fell.

The "horror" of this narration is very close to the effect of wonder or amazement *(maraviglia)* that is so important in the theory of tragicomedy; it is a necessary third emotion that must be added to Aristotle's pity and fear.

Everything in *Orbecche* builds toward the gruesome murder of Oronte, the secret husband of the heroine, and their two little boys. Her enraged father, King Sulmone, throws the corpse of Oronte to vultures and dogs, after placing its head and hands in a silver vessel covered with a black silk veil. He strips the bodies of the two children, being careful not to disturb the daggers still sticking in them, then places them both in silver vessels. These offerings are presented to Orbecche as a sardonic, belated wedding gift. She recoils with appropriate horror at this fiendish revenge, but she has the presence of mind to drive one of the knives into her father's breast, then later to kill herself with it. The details are all carefully worked out, and there is a strong sense that the revenge must be esthetically appropriate to both its cause and to the magnitude of the doers. There is a law of poetic justice (or, more accurately, poetic injustice) that must be satisfied. As Cleopatra says in a play of Spinello (1550): "Great cruelty ought to be avenged with greater cruelty."

Cinthio's *Orbecche* serves as a model by which we may understand such plays as Speroni's *Canace* (1542), Dolce's *Marianna* (1565), and Groto's *Dalida* (1572). Groto's frenetic play attempts to outdo *Orbecche* in its spectacular revenge scenes, reported, of course, by a messenger nearly crazed with horror. The injured queen, Berenice, beats her rival, Dalida, with iron rods until a shower of blood falls, and then, forcing a knife into Dalida's helpless hand, guides it to cut her wailing children to pieces. Berenice proceeds to stab Dalida through the left breast until the point of the knife snaps on her shoulder blade. There is a competition of ingenuity in these horrors, and, since they are not shown directly on stage, the playwright has scope to indulge his imagination through the persona of the messenger. In Francis Berry's terminology, these narrative "insets" permit the kind of passionate effects that would not be possible in conventional dialogue drama.

On the face of it, it would seem that Italian Renaissance tragedy must have exerted a strong influence on Elizabethan revenge drama, which makes frequent use of Italian settings and Machiavellian villains, but the actual sources for many of these plays are Italian short stories from the collections of *novelle* that were translated into English (for example, those of Boccaccio, Cinthio, and Bandello). The only English translations or adaptations of Italian Renaissance tragedies are George Gascoigne and Francis Kinwelmershe's *Jocasta* (1566) from Dolce's *Giocasta* (1549), and William Alabaster's *Roxana* in Latin, acted about 1592, from Groto's *Dalida* (1572). This is not a very impressive record of literary influence.

Herrick tends to exaggerate this influence by the repeated use of vague and exclamatory comparisons. This is particularly true of his final chapter, "Italy's Contribution to Tragedy." At one point he takes four Italianate English tragedies (*The Spanish Tragedy*, '*Tis Pity She's a Whore*, *Hoffman*, and *Orestes*) and says of them:

> In discussing the Italianate qualities of these four plays I cannot possibly discriminate very often between the influence of *novelle* and the influence of tragedies. No one can. But I have selected qualities that could have come from the Italian plays, qualities that are especially prominent in the Italian tragedies of the sixteenth century.

This is bad logic, especially because Herrick has himself argued that the direct influence comes primarily through the *novelle*. The same faulty reasoning may be seen in Herrick's treatment of Pescetti's *Il Cesare* (1594) as a source for Shakespeare's *Julius Caesar* (1599):

> I am not insisting, with Boecker, that there must have been some connection between the Italian *Cesare* and the English *Julius Caesar*, but I am not altogether satisfied that there could not have been any connection. A negative can hardly be proved, but present-day Shakespeareans may be right in ignoring Pescetti.

This is an intellectual muddle, and we need to turn to Geoffrey Bullough's *Narrative and Dramatic Sources of Shakespeare*, Volume V (1964), to make some sense out of Pescetti's play as a possible but by no means necessary source for Shakespeare, since it is likely that both drew their material from the same historians.

Herrick's style is full of obvious flaws, and his attempts to be chatty often produce examples of banality and bad taste: "Latin, as students of history and literature know, was indispensable in medieval and Renaissance education"; "Pistoia was no Dante. He could not make *terza rima* the right vehicle for tragic emotion on the stage. Perhaps no one could, not even a Dante"; "The characters in Shakespeare's *Hamlet* are Christians while those in *King Lear* are pagans, yet *Lear* is a greater tragedy"; "Some readers today may question the statement that ancient tragedy was religious; but it is true." These are only a few samples of the simple and propaedeutic heartiness that runs throughout Herrick's book. At least half of it is devoted to what the dust-jacket calls, pleasantly, "analyses of plot," which turn out to be plot summaries. *Italian Tragedy in the Renaissance* offers a useful introduction to its subject, although it is the sort of book that could immediately be made superfluous by reading the plays.

Rutgers University

Psychoanalysis and Shakespeare by Norman N. Holland. McGraw-Hill Book Co., 1966. $9.95. Pp. xi + 412. *Reviewer: Alvin B. Kernan.*

"So have I heard and do in part believe," says Horatio when told on the battlements of Elsinore that during the Christmas season the cock crows all night long. Literary critics, at least those sympathetic to psychoanalytic theories of personality, are likely to respond in the same way when told about Hamlet's unresolved Oedipal conflict, Desdemona's penis envy, and Antonio's passive homosexual feelings for Bassanio and Shylock.

Such tales may not be literally true, but they do phrase and focus dimly known, partly suspected forces at work within the plays. But the greater part of the literary critic's willingness to believe comes from a recognition of definite similarities in the operational methods of psychoanalysis and modern literary criticism at its best. The manner in which a psychoanalyst approaches and understands personality resembles, at least surfacely, the way in which a critic perceives and understands a work of literature. The objects of understanding are, of course, very different: in one case a living human being with a past and a complete psyche, in the other an artifact, a symbolic representation of an unknown. But the assumptions about how the person and the work of art are to be understood have much in common: (1) economy is assumed, *all* actions and *all* phrasings are expressive and significant; (2) the meaning and value of any individual expressive form is best understood not in isolation but as a part of a larger complex structure; (3) the totality—of personality or of play—is finally not to be taken as simply a phenomenon, but rather as the outer manifestation of a complex reality lying below and behind the surface and expressing itself in the only way it can, through visible and audible forms.

Sharing such crucial assumptions, the literary and psychoanalytic critics ought to produce complementary readings of plays and poems. But the sad truth is that the purely literary critics and the psychoanalytic critics have never really been easy with one another, and their readings of literature have been widely divergent. The trouble seems to have started almost with the beginnings of psychoanalysis, for Freud, despite his wide though curiously undiscriminating reading of literature, both admired writers of fictions and disliked them as competitors who are free to invent behavior, while the psychoanalyst is bound to the wheel of fact. His fascination with and antagonism towards Shakespeare was particularly strong, and this astute man, so determined to be scientific and precise, held until the end of his life the view that the plays he referred to frequently were written by the Earl of Oxford.

Norman Holland, now chairman of the English department at Buffalo, is primarily a literary critic, who has had extensive training in the theories and methods of psychoanalysis. His allegiance to both disciplines is strong, and *Psychoanalysis and Shakespeare* traces the development of the psychoanalytic theory of literature, shows where it has triumphed and where it has gone astray, and suggests ways in which conventional and psychoanalytic criticism can ultimately be reconciled. The book is divided into three parts, of which the third containing Holland's conclusions "Logical" and "Not So Logical" is by far the most interesting. Part I is a good explanation of the nature of the psychoanalytic view of the origins and function of literature as developed and employed by Freud and some of his successors. No matter how much the "conventional" critic—like myself—may object to the particular bias of Freud's scheme, it still stands as a nearly perfect model of what literary criticism still lacks: a general theory which explains how and why literature is written, why it takes the particular forms it does, how it affects its audience, and why it is, therefore, so fundamental in all human societies. Holland is better on pure Freud than on his successors, and Chapter 5, where ego psychology's modifications of the basic Freudian theory of literature is explained, is too thin and too filled with jargon. This chapter particularly contains a number of sentences which seem to have come from Book III of *Gulliver* or *A Tale of a Tub*: "Ludwig Jekels has studied pity and shown its relation to fear, and Dr. Daniel Schneider has expounded the dynamics of catharsis as a sequential process." (p.47)

Holland is in general hampered by inclusion of references to enormous numbers of psychoanalytic investigations of literature, without having the space to give many of these the extensive explanations they require. In many cases he does not himself agree with these theories, and it is difficult to see why he clutters an argument, which is difficult enough to follow anyway, with such unneeded and unwanted material.

The catalogue method, however, works extremely well in Part II, where Holland provides a collection of Freud's statements about Shakespeare and his works, a résumé of subsequent psychoanalytic studies of Shakespeare the man—"Shakespeare creates in his plays an oedipal world (rather than one primarily oral or anal, like Marlowe's or Jonson's)"—and a long section in which all of Shakespeare's works appear alphabetically and the major psychoanalytic interpretations of each are noted and summarized. This section and its excellent supporting bibliography provide a superior reference work for any Shakespearean critic concerned with psychoanalytic interpretations of particular plays.

In Part III, "Psychoanalysis, Shakespeare, and the Critical Mind," Holland turns away from summarizing and cataloguing the views of others and begins to offer his own theories. Psychoanalytic criticism has been confused, he argues, because its practitioners have not made it clear exactly which mind they are analyzing: the mind of the author whose id and ego interact to project the inventor's desires and defenses? the minds of the characters in the fiction whose patterns of action and thought suggest psychic patterns observed in actual people in clinical practice? the minds of members of the audience which respond to the disguised desires acted out before them? In a curious piece of byplay, Holland then proceeds to argue that since deductions about the mind of the author can never be proven, and since the characters are fictional rather than real persons psychically complete, the only mind which the psychoanalytic critic can meaningfully discuss is that of the audience, which is real and observable. But having said this, Holland disavows his conclusion as only an exercise in false logic, and proceeds to the first of his two main points, that the mind of the author, the psychic lives of the characters, and the responses of the audience form a continuum, and the critic who focuses on one aspect of the totality is necessarily speaking of the others. "When the critic of character finds homosexual jealousy in Iago, and oral identity crisis in Coriolanus, or an oedipus complex in Hamlet, he necessarily implies that these states of mind were possible for Shakespeare and also that they are possible for us in the audience." (p. 322) Conventional critics will scarcely be surprised by this point, but they may retain their doubts about the possibility or value of knowing with any accuracy the mind of the author or the response of the audience—doubts which have necessitated the present concentration on the work itself without worrying about the intention of the author or the adequacy of responses from the audience.

This leads directly to Holland's second point: the relationship of the "social, moral, aesthetic, religious, or intellectual themes" which the conventional critic finds in a literary work, and the "unconscious themes" which the psychoanalytic critic discovers. Holland's method of closing the apparent gap is a compromise which tries to preserve the validity of both the psychoanalytic insights and the more conventional ones. The energy which is the source of the work remains, as in Freud, "grotesque unconscious fantasies" which are transmuted (by methods which Holland never specifies very clearly) "into a meaningful social, moral, or intellectual wholeness." The conventional critic proceeds to read literature in terms of these "social" and "moral" forms, while the psychoanalytic critic breaks through to a more direct perception of those unconscious energies originally present in the mind of the author, still schematically present in the activities and interactions of the fictional characters, and latent in the minds of the audience until released and satisfied by the spectacle. There is no doubt that Holland believes that the psychoanalytic critic is closer to the essential energies of literature; but there really is, he argues, no absolute incompatibility between the perceptions of the psychoanalytic critic and those of the conventional literary critic. When they are accurate—and Holland allows for failures of both types of criticism— the two types of critics are merely using a different terminology to describe the same set of phenomena perceived at different levels.

> The man who tells us the skulls in that Danish graveyard are testicles or that Desdemona suffers from penis envy meets not unsurprisingly a certain amount of puzzlement if not downright scoff. And yet *Othello* is very much a play of love and war, in which heterosexual love is replaced by a conflict between men; the Turkish navy or Iago's cynicism interrupts the marriage of the general and his "fair warrior." Is, then, a notion of penis envy or something like it so far-fetched? ["A question to be asked" as Falstaff once said.] *Hamlet,* we have seen, is a play about the ways in which an inner problem makes the outer world weary, stale, flat, and unprofitable. In that very graveyard Hamlet finds the outward visible signs of his inward resignation—is it so far-fetched that he should also find there external symbols for those parts of his body so deeply involved in his disillusionment? (p. 323)

These lines, which are intended to be conclusive, are, for me at least, loaded with unanswered questions and inaccurate statements. If we were to grant, for example, that sex and death are closely related in *Hamlet* would we still be entitled to say that the skulls represent testicles? Couldn't they equally well represent anything else associated with the death theme during the course of the play? poison? ghosts? love? self-interest? Are we free to assign *any* value to an object simply because that value happens to correspond with the object in question in our particular symbology?

But what is chiefly troubling in Holland's examples, here and elsewhere, is his reduction of the meaning of the play in "conventional" terms to a point where it can come close to squaring with the meaning as revealed by psychoanalytic criticism. To say that *Othello* is a play about "love and war" is certainly true, and such an interpretation does get the play somewhat into line with an interpretation centering on penis envy; but it is certainly not an adequate statement of the subject of *Othello.* Holland is uneasily aware of this problem, and in part I suppose he has purposely chosen for his examples some of the wilder interpretations of psychoanalytic criticism. In the remainder of the book he makes use of much more restrained psychoanalytic theories to demonstrate the complementarity of psychoanalytic and literary criticism in brief analyses of eleven Shakespearean plays as seen from the two critical points of view. But even the use of milder, more generally acceptable psychoanalytic theories still forces him to do considerable violence to the "conventional" interpretations of the plays in order to fit them to the psychoanalytic views. *Romeo and Juliet,* for example, is reduced to "the quintessential tragedy of opposites," love and hate, in order to accommodate the conventional view to the psychoanalytic view of the play as a defense against ambivalence "by splitting or isolation," which fails when the defense breaks down and the opposites engulf one another.

Holland's attempt to bring psychoanalysis, literature, and literary criticism into a close functional relationship is admirable and interesting, the best piece of writing I know of on this subject. But it is not entirely convincing. To tell the analysts and the literary critics that they have a semantic problem, that they have all along been talking about the same thing in different terms, is not going to bring the long antagonism to a close. The literary critic remains baffled, even outraged, when told, for example, that *Othello* is really all about an Iago who is homosexually in love with Othello and the other men of the play and defends himself psychically by aggression and by accusing Desdemona of loving the men with whom he is himself in love. Baffled and outraged in turn by the critic's response to his offerings, the psychoanalyst responds by charging that the literary critic refuses to see the obvious because of his own defense mechanisms or his overdeveloped sense of propriety. It is not, however, the neurotic or the prude in each of us which resists the psychoanalyst's over-simplifications of Shakespeare's plays. It is not because we do not believe in penis envy or oedipal complexes, not because of our own defense mechanisms, not even, finally, because we believe there is a difference between a fictional character and a living person, that literary critics boggle at most psychoanalytic criticism. It is rather because such interpretations as that of the homosexual Iago violate the most fundamental rules of evidence, the psychoanalyst's as well as the literary critic's. The key to this particular interpretation of *Othello* is provided by nothing more than Iago's invention of a night in a shared bed with Cassio when Cassio in a dream throws a leg over him and kisses him. The remainder of Iago's activities, it is then argued, are explained by this one revelation. Similarly, the putative penis envy of Desdemona is ultimately based on nothing more than the lady's wish "that heaven had made her such a man," a line which itself is at the very least ambiguous.

The regular method of most psychoanalytic critics of Shakespeare is to focus on some small part of the play which fits into an already known theory of human behavior, and then to impose that entire theory upon the remainder of the play. Used in this way, psychoanalytic criticism becomes but the latest and the most fashionable version of a familiar but largely discredited critical approach. The critic begins with a theory—"Shakespeare was a conservative who wrote his plays to prove the dangers of political and social disorder," "Bacon wrote Shakespeare and the plays are a coded message recording this fact," "Shakespeare struggled throughout his life with an unresolved oedipal complex and his plays are attempts to dramatize this neurosis"—and the plays then become a demonstration of the particular reality already known to the critic.

Approached in this way, Shakespeare's plays become secondary documents—in Platonic terms, imitations of imitations of an idea. Truth, says the critic with this type of bias, is best known and most clearly stated in the direct theoretical terms of political philosophy or psychoanalysis; the plays are but fancy dress (displaced, disguised, sugar coated) versions of these more fundamental statements. The best of literary criticism replies by arguing that the plays are themselves primary documents in the continuing investigation of political, social, and psychological reality. They are not properly to be taken as decorated dramatizations of some flat-footed political maxim, nor are they to be seen as the vague poetic fumblings of a seventeenth-century precursor to Freud feeling his way in the imprecise language of drama towards what the psychoanalyst was to state with scientific precision. The playwright and the psychoanalyst are, of course, trying to understand and

285

describe the same mysteries, and in many places their insights are strikingly similar. (Indeed, it would be most surprising and discouraging if they were not.) But the Shakespearean formulation of reality is not a Newtonian physics to the atomic physics of psychoanalysis, any more than it is a popularized and easy version of philosophy, sociology, or Christianity: it is a different and competing way of knowing the truth, making its statements in a unique and highly refined language and grammar.

This is true of literature in general, but it seems particulàrly true of drama, which is marked by a peculiar transcendence of any single theoretical position. The perspective of drama, and particularly Shakespearean drama, is such that it constantly calls into question the very kind of explanations the psychoanalytic critics so confidently offer. The foreground of a play is occupied by men of various persuasions confidently saying "This must be so," certain of themselves and their views of an immutable reality. But even as they speak their language is reflecting unknown powers at work within them, other characters are moving in unanticipated directions, the forces of society and history are beginning to exert pressure, and the familiar surface of the world is beginning to bubble and break into new shapes. The scene of Shakespearean drama is somewhat wider and more comprehensive than the scene of psychoanalysis, with its narrow focus on the individual, but playwright and analyst would, of course, be at one in their understanding of the sudden eruption of unknown inner forces through the surface of familiarity. But where the analysts believe that the nature and origin of the dark forces can be known, stated, and codified, the dramatist by the very nature of his medium realizes man acting in front of a mystery, desperately trying to understand and formulate reality, while being swept along by a fate outside his control. The essential "action" of all drama, and particularly Shakespeare, is man *trying* to understand his fate; the essential "action" of psychoanalysis is the analyst *understanding* man's fate.

Put in another way, we can say that the nature of dramatic form allows characters to present and speculate about their own motives and those of other characters but does not allow complete exposure of "true" motives. Motive is not only ultimately indeterminant in a play, it is sadly irrelevant. The plot sweeps forward and a character finds himself defined by what he does, not what he wanted, consciously or unconsciously, to do. The Player King in *Hamlet* speaks for all players when he says, "Our thoughts are ours, their ends none of our own." No doubt the harder-minded psychoanalysts would agree, but when the analyst functions as Shakespearean critic he assumes, mistakenly I believe, that he can know and phrase the thoughts of the characters and by doing so reveal the meaning of a play. The play, however, to sum up, questions the possibility or value of knowing motive, while the psychoanalyst assumes that motive can be known and that it shapes the future. There is, finally, a most important difference between psychoanalytic and dramatic ways of approaching and understanding reality.

Yale University

The Second Part of King Henry IV *edited by A. R. Humphreys. The Arden Shakespeare. Methuen and Harvard University Press, 1966. Pp. xci + 242. $4.50. Reviewer: G. Blakemore Evans.*

This is a notable edition and a worthy companion to Professor Humphreys' earlier New Arden *I Henry IV*. The ninety-one page introduction covers in skillfully selected detail the all-too-numerous problems, critical and textual, which *II Henry IV* raises, and evaluates with a sure touch the significant criticisms of the play that have appeared in recent years, especially those since the publication of M. A. Shaaber's standard Variorum edition (1940).

Considerable attention is given to the much debated question of whether *II Henry IV* was originally planned as a sequel to *I Henry IV* or was written as an afterthought merely to capitalize on the popularity achieved by the figure of Falstaff. The case against those critics who consider *II Henry IV* as an "unpremeditated addition" is (and to me persuasively) dealt with at some length (pp. xxii-xxiv). Professor Humphreys' own verdict arises in many essentials from the view of Professor Harold Jenkins (*The Structural Problem in Shakespeare's "Henry IV,"* 1956), who argues that Shakespeare decided on a second part after Act III. Agreeing that Shakespeare had such a second part in mind while at work on Part I, Professor Humphreys, nevertheless, believes it better "to assume that at the outset, or at least very soon after, Shakespeare envisaged two plays, both of which would deal with the traditional story of the Wild Prince reformed, but one of which would aim at Shrewsbury and Valour, the other at Westminster and Justice" (p. xxvii). Here he seems to me very close to Tillyard and Dover Wilson, though he concludes that "one must reject the idea that the two parts reveal an embracing ten-act-cycle form" (p. xxviii).

The several recognized sources for the play are thoroughly and interestingly analyzed. Briefly put, to Daniel's influence is credited the tone and attitude that "control the emotional timbre of the play" (p. xxxiii); to Holinshed (and Stow) the essential historical facts. Hall is declared "probably not a source" (Appendix II). Selections from the pertinent sources are contained in Appendix I. I could wish that Professor Humphreys had chosen to quote directly from the 1587 edition of Holinshed rather than from the 1807-8 reprint. There is a misprint of 'or' for 'of' at the bottom of page 189.

Under "Themes and Their Treatment" (pp. xliii-liv) Professor Humphreys gives a beautifully succinct and balanced treatment of seven themes that he feels create a "nexus" through which *II Henry IV* achieves its own special kind of unity and "is hardly less powerful [than Part I] as an act of the imagination" (p. xliv): (i) Ricnard and Henry ("As between Richard and Henry, the position the play expresses is that God approves the king whose rule best satisfies the needs of his subjects. That rule is Henry's."); (ii) Henry and Necessity; (iii) Statecraft and Morality; (iv) Miscalculation; (v) Anarchy; (vi) Age and Disease; and (vii) Life in Place and Time. Discussions on Falstaff and his Rejection (pp. liv-lxi) and on "Style and Its Functions" (pp. lxi-lxviii) complete the critical introduction.

Professor Humphreys' text is a model of accuracy. He accepts the Quarto (1600) as the primary text, one set directly from Shakespeare's original draft. His view of the relation between the Quarto (Q) and the First Folio (F1) texts leans toward the use for F1 copy-text of some form of transcription, prepared either from an augmented and "corrected" copy of Q, or (a view he feels to be more likely) from a manuscript with some theatre connections by a scribe who kept his eye on Q as he worked. The first of these views is very close (as he notes) to that advanced by Professor Fredson Bowers in 1953; the second, so far as I know, is original with Professor Humphreys. Both views differ from M. A. Shaaber's, who would argue for a manuscript independent of Q, and from Alice Walker's, who supports the direct use of an annotated copy of Q without an intermediate transcription. Of the four, I find Professor Humphreys' extension of Bowers' transcript theory the most convincing.

On the matter of editorial choice of certain readings between Q and F1, there will probably always be room for disagreement. But given Q as the basic copy-text and the general agreement that whatever its origins F1 is a "literary" and considerably sophisticated text, I cannot help wondering why Professor Humphreys chooses F1 over Q in the following cases: I.i.28 'whom' (F1) for 'who' (Q); I.ii.97 'time' (F1) for 'time in you' (Q); I.iii.78 'not be dreaded' (F1) for 'not to be dreaded' (Q); III.i.16 'leau'st' (F1) for 'leauest' (Q); IV.iv.94 'heauen' (F1) for 'heauens' (Q). I would also suggest that the Q speech-prefix *'Offic.'* at II.ii.54 if expanded to *'Officers.'* makes better sense in the context than the F1 assignment of the line to Fang and indicates a combined outcry by both Fang and Snare. One Q reading (or rather spelling) retained at I.ii.21 ('off' in "I will sooner have a beard grow in the palm of my hand than he shall get one off his cheek;") seems less desirable than Collier's conjecture 'of', since 'of' seems to be supported by I.ii.243: "the first white of my chin." Certainly F1 interprets both passages in the same way, reading 'on' in both cases, and the confusion between 'off' and 'of' is common enough in Elizabethan spelling.

The textual notes are carefully done and offer a complete record of the substantive variants between Q and F1. Where they occasionally fail is in an inadequate record of semi-substantive Q variants and a silent acceptance of F1 or later editorial pointing. For example: Induction, l. 8 'Reports:' (F1), 'reports,' (Q), where l. 8 in Q can go with either l. 7 or l. 9; I.ii.13-14 'iudgement. Thou horson Mandrake, thou art' (F1), 'iudgement thou horeson mandrake, thou art' (Q), where the Q pointing throws 'thou horeson mandrake' with the preceding clause and perhaps makes rather better sense, since it seems to attach the following reference to 'something fitter to be worne in my cap' to an 'agot' rather than to a 'Mandrake' as in F1; II.i.15 'doth, if his weapon be out. Hee will' (F1), 'does, if his weapon be out, he will' (Q), where the Q reading makes it possible to take 'if his weapon be out' with either the preceding or following clauses; II.iv.311 'Not?—to' (Humphreys, after Capell-Malone), 'Not to' (Q, F1), where the Q, F1 reading makes perfectly good sense without any repointing; IV.v.59 'hence: / Goe seeke' (F1), 'hence go seeke' (Q), where Q 'hence' might be taken with 'go'; V.i.14 'cook—are' (Humphreys, after Theobald), 'Cook: are' (F1), 'Cooke are' (Q), where the dash (after F1 colon) substantially changes the meaning. I am not arguing here that the F1 (or other editorial) pointing is wrong, merely that the Q pointing (and in one case the Q, F1 pointing) should not be silently set aside as unimportant.

One policy which Professor Humphreys follows is, I believe, unfortunate because it tends in the direction of the kind of sophistication already discernible in the F1 text. He ignores most of the elided forms in Q (and sometimes F1) prose passages (none of the following is recorded in the textual notes): Q 'rob'ry' becomes F1 'Robbery' (I.ii.60); Q, F1 'falne' becomes 'fallen' (I.ii.106, 117); Q, F1 (subs.) 'list'ning' becomes 'listening' (I.ii.120); Q 'follow'dst', F1 'followd'st' becomes 'followedst' (II.iv.226); Q 'destny' becomes F1 'destinie' (III.ii.231); Q 'tempring' becomes F1 'tempering' (IV.iii.128); and Q 'marvailes' becomes F1 'maruellous' (V.i.32). On the other hand, he is careful in prose to preserve the Q 'th'' forms (as at I.ii.49 'th'unquiet' or II.i.129 'th'effect').

Some good Elizabethan forms, which according to the principles of modernization here generally adopted could not perhaps have found a place in the text, should, nevertheless, for the student, have been recorded in the textual notes: Q 'Iarman' (II.i.143), a rare form of special interest because of its appearance in the manuscript fragment of *Sir Thomas More* now generally accepted as being in Shakespeare's hand; Q 'kinreds' (II.ii.26); Q, F1 'idlely' (II.ii.29); Q 'Heicfors' (II.ii.149); Q, F1 (subs.) 'pruins' (II.iv.143); Q, F1 (subs.) 'haber de poiz' (II.iv.252); Q, F1 'vildly' (II.iv.297); Q, F1 'commandement' (III.ii.23); Q 'huswiues' (III.ii.311); Q 'ruffin' (IV.v.124); Q 'Cursie' and 'cursy' (Epilogue, 1, 2).

Professor Humphreys' original pointing and explanation of the difficult lines 171-77 in IV.i deserve special notice, but two other new emendations seem to me open to some question. In II.iv.331-33 ("For the boy, there is a good angel about him, but the devil attends him too.") 'attends' has been substituted for Q 'blinds' and F1 'outbids', an emendation which he suggests is attractive on the evidence of a quarto reading in *Merry Wives,* I.iii.50-51 ('she hath legians of angels. *Pis.* As many diuels attend her.'). Apart from the fact that Q of *Merry Wives* is a 'bad' quarto and that F1 reads 'entertaine', it appears to me that Q 'blinds' is perfectly defensible (even without Sisson's emendation of 'too' to 'to't') in view of a passage in Webster's *Duchess of Malfi,* II.i.97-98 (F. L. Lucas ed.): "You would looke up to Heaven, but I thinke / The Divell, that rules i'th'aire, stands in your light." That is, like Bosola, the boy has good inclinations, but the devil, who had special power below the moon, sometimes shuts out (and thus blinds him) the influence of heaven (his good angel). The second emendation occurs at IV.iii.40-42: "that I may justly say, with the hook-nosed fellow of Rome, three words, 'I came, saw, and overcame.'" Here Professor Humphreys substitutes 'three words' for Q 'there cosin' (catch-word 'their'; both words omitted in F1) on the evidence of a marginal gloss and a passage in North's Plutarch ("Life of Caesar"). This is certainly tempting, but there appears to me to be more difficulty than he admits in supposing a compositorial misreading of 'words' or 'wordes' as 'cosin'. Again, I suggest that the Q reading makes possible sense if we read the passage as "that I may justly say, with the hook-nosed [Q hook-nos'd] fellow of Rome, 'There cousin, I came, saw, and overcame.'" The word 'cosin' thus refers in typically Falstaffian bombastic fashion to Caesar, with whom he identifies himself, and not to Prince John. As Professor Humphreys rightly says not even Falstaff would be impudent enough for such familiarity.

What criticisms I have offered in the last part of this review are nearly all matters of editorial opinion on particular textual decisions—matters on which, if scholarship is to remain alive and challenging, there must always remain a healthy area of disagreement. I would like, therefore, to return to my opening sentence: "This is a notable edition . . ."

Harvard University

Measure for Measure edited by J. W. Lever. The Arden Shakespeare. London, Methuen and Harvard University Press, 1965. Pp. xcviii + 203. $4.50. *Reviewer: Cyrus Hoy.*

"An editor of *Measure for Measure* has only one text to go upon, that of the Folio, and he could wish for a better," wrote Dover Wilson when he edited the play for the New Cambridge Shakespeare in 1922. He continued: "In places, not a few, it is 'maimed and deformed' beyond all hope of recovery, while its corruption frequently suggests the carelessness of some hasty transcriber concerned to catch the general sense but scarcely to preserve verbal accuracy." The case is no longer considered to be quite so desperate. Copy for the Folio text is now generally held to have been a transcript of Shakespeare's foul papers prepared by the scribe Ralph Crane; and while Crane was a somewhat fussy and pedantic workman, much given to imposing his own preferences on to his text in matters of spelling and punctuation, he was by no means a careless one. Textual anomalies such as inconsistencies in the details of time-scheme and plot, the presence of mute or near-mute characters, and the assumed presence of "verse fossils" embedded in passages of prose, all of which editors of another generation looked upon as certain evidence of abridgment, or revision by a non-authorial hand, or both, are now recognized as the characteristic features of an author's rough draft. Thus the much disputed passages in the second scene of Act I, wherein at lines 56-74 Mistress Overdone reports having seen Claudio arrested and why, but in lines 79-85 is ignorant of his offense when Pompey announces that "yonder man [presumably Claudio] is carried to prison", are far more likely to represent (as Mr. Lever cogently argues) duplicate versions of the scene, one of which (lines 79-85) was imperfectly marked for omission in Shakespeare's foul papers, than non-authorial tampering with it, as Dover Wilson suggested.

The one point in the text which Mr. Lever finds corrupt beyond the possibility of recovery occurs in the Duke's soliloquy which ends Act III. Here Mr. Lever suggests that one of the octosyllabic couplets may be missing after the line "Making practice on the times". The loss of a soliloquy by the Duke at IV.i.60ff. may have occasioned the transfer to that point of the opening six lines which (as Warburton suggested and all editors, including Mr. Lever, agree) once stood at the head of the soliloquy that now begins with the line "No might nor greatness in mortality" at III.ii.179. Something is needed in IV.i to fill the interval while Isabella and Mariana withdraw to discuss the assignation with Angelo; six lines are hardly sufficient to the purpose, and as Mr. Lever observes, "the actor taking the Duke's part must have been required to deliver [them] with exceptional slowness and deliberation."

The textual problem of *Measure for Measure* is not, then, so very formidable. Mr. Lever has emended the reading of the Folio text in only some forty instances; of these, ten are emendations of his own devising. The most interesting reading he has to propose is "head-strong jades" for Folio "headstrong weeds" at I.iii.20, this chiefly on the analogy of Marlowe's similar phrase in *II Tamburlaine*, IV.iii.12. At other times, however, Mr. Lever's emendations suggest an editor who, having found disconcertingly little to do in the exercise of his function, tends to tamper with his text in order to leave his mark on it. Of emendations thus prompted, I would include his reversal of the words "place" and "time" at III.i.247,248; the emendation of Folio "and have" to "and so have" at IV.i.54; the alteration of Folio "Where prayers crosse" to "Where prayer's [i.e. prayer is] cross'd" at II.ii.160, which is certainly subtle, I suspect over-subtle. Emendation is required at V.i.14, where Folio reads "Give we your hand", but Mr. Lever would have done better to follow the third Folio (and all editors) in reading "Give me your hand" instead of his strained "Give we our hand".

The reading above all others which, according to the present reviewer, cries out for emendation in the text of *Measure for Measure*, Mr. Lever like most editors refrains from emending. This is the close of Angelo's great soliloquy at the beginning of II.iv, where Folio —and most editors, including Mr. Lever—read:

> Let's write good Angell on the Deuills horne
> 'Tis not the Deuills Crest:

Dover Wilson suggested emending "not" to "now", which is surely the true reading, but even he refrained from accepting his own conjecture into the text of the play. Editors stick doggedly to the Folio reading, and then try to make sense of the passage by means of an explanatory note, of which Mr. Lever's is a fair example:

> Angelo will reveal the diabolical side of his nature, "the devil's horn", while designating it with his own name "angel", though this is not his real title.

To which one can only reply, "Of course it's not." Any fool knows that the style "good angel" is not the devil's crest, and any one who has been following the play with half an ear knows that Angelo, by now, is no angel. If the line means what Mr. Lever says it means, it is one of the most anticlimactic in Shakespeare.

The text of Mr. Lever's edition is not free from errors. I have noted the following: II.ii.8 ("I not" for Folio "not I"); II.ii.186 ("Even" for Folio "Ever"); II.iii.20 ("same" for Folio "shame"); II.iv.109 ("you not" for Folio "not you"); III.ii.118 ("I have never" for Folio "I never"); IV.ii.88 ("must he" for Folio "he must"); V.i.10 ("O, but your" for Folio "Oh your").

The University of Rochester

English Humanists and Reformation Politics Under Henry VIII and Edward VI by James Kelsey McConica. The Clarendon Press, 1965. Pp. 340. $7.20. *Reviewer: Alice Lyle Scoufos.*

Perhaps a more exact title for this detailed study of early humanistic STC items would be *Erasmianism and the English Press, 1500-1553,* for James McConica has chosen as the thesis of his work (synthetic in approach) to the influence of Erasmian humanism upon the development of English thought during the reigns of Henry VIII and his son Edward VI. In his search for evidence of English commitment to the Erasmian *philosophia Christi,* the author surveys extensively the published materials of the period to reveal the patterns of humanistic patronage in the Court, in the universities, and in the city of London itself. The book is valuable in its broad survey: not only is the influence of the members of the More-Colet-Fisher circle examined, but also placed under scrutiny are the writings of the professional members of Doctors' Commons, the literary productions which came from the religious houses at Syon and Shene, the textbooks sold at Oxford and Cambridge, and the strong financial influence of the Mercers' Company and the Merchant Adventurers upon the schools. Such research has led to the author's general conclusion that "widespread Erasmian activity in educated circles" was "much greater than has been commonly supposed." The dissemination of Erasmian humanism is then traced through the crisis years into the Cromwellian period where the Erasmian ideals, so the author proclaims, influenced governmental policy; the post-Cromwellian England of Henry's reign is described as a place where occurred "the most complete fulfilment of the Erasmian programme which Europe has yet seen." In the last years of the Henrician reign the fragmented humanistic party, now identified by the author as a tripartite grouping of liberals, moderates, and conservatives, continued to be influential and moved into the reign of Edward VI, still motivated by Erasmian policy, a policy which was "a capacious mansion which could contain most opinions except the extremes of Protestantism and a rooted attachment to Rome."

In spite of its valuable abundance of details, this study has a serious basic weakness: unfortunately, the Erasmian philosophy has been so broadly defined that the English Renaissance fits readily into its pocket. If this book is placed in its context of modern historical scholarship, the obliqueness of its slant becomes apparent. McConica has created a counterattack against the work of such scholars as Albert Hyma (whose insistence upon the small effect of Erasmus's ideas on the development of English humanism was itself an attack upon the older intrenched position which emphasized the binding relationship between the famous Netherlander and the English intellects) and Roberto Weiss whose work with the emergence of humanism in fifteenth-century England is well known.[1] What McConica refuses to face is the fact that a Thomas Linacre (who learned his Greek from Politiano in Florence with the two sons of Lorenzo de Medici) would have published

291

his *De Emendata Structura Latini Sermonis* and the *Progymnasmata Grammatices Vulgaria*, and would have assisted Aldus with the first edition of Aristotle's works in the original Greek even if there had been no Erasmus of Rotterdam. The same is true of the English humanists' love of Lucian: satire and wit were sharp in the age of John Skelton (whom McConica does not mention). We may speculate even further with some safety that Tyndale would have been a compulsive reformer and pietism would have characterized English humanism had Erasmus remained isolated with the Augustinians at Steyn. Furthermore, Henry in all probability would have divorced Catherine had there been no Erasmian statements on divorce,[2] and the expedient Cromwell would have found propaganda materials for Moryson and Starkey to English had Erasmus printed nothing of his own work. It is also quite probable that Catherine Parr would have established her royal nursery school and that humanistic studies would have been taught there even if Erasmus had lived a century before or a century after his time.

McConica's research has been diligent, but his emphasis is misplaced. An example of this misplacement is the author's selection of the *Enchiridion* as the "centre-piece" of Erasmianism. He chooses this work because of its popularity: after its first printing in 1503 it quickly went through twenty-three editions and was translated in the sixteenth century into Czech, German, English, Dutch, Castilian, French, Italian, Portuguese, and Polish. Erasmus's enemies asserted "that there was more holynesse sene in the lytell booke than in the hole authoure and maker thereof."[3] But if the modern scholar opens the popular little book, what does he find? Paradoxically enough, he finds, not humanism *per se*, but rather a storehouse of medieval exhortation to the good life: Chapter One is a warning, "We muste watche and loke aboute us euermore whyle we be in this lyfe." Chapter Two describes "the weapons to be used in the werre of a christen man." Chapter Seven deals with the medieval tripartite human being: "Of the thre partes of man / the spyrite / the soule / and the fleshe." There are compact chapters on "specyall synnes" such as "bodily lust," "auaryce," "ambycion or desyre of honoure and auctorite," and there is a lengthy discussion of the dangers of "elacyon / otherwyse called pryde or swellyng of the mynde." It is this pious folk wisdom which accounts for the popularity of the *Enchiridion*, and to place such an early work at the center of (and as it were make it the soul of) Erasmianism is to take a simplistic view of the mind of the famous scholar from Rotterdam.

Even more disconcerting is the labeling of Erasmus's early work in the medieval *ars moriendi* tradition as a humanistic product; the *De Praeparatione Ad Mortem* follows a pattern which enjoyed tremendous vogue during the later middle ages. This death literature became a commonplace long before Caxton published in 1479 the *Cordiale Siue De Quatour Nouissimis* which Lord Rivers had translated from the French of Jean Mielot.[4] A medievalist would quickly have recognized that Erasmus was writing in a well-worn tradition when he informed his reader that "by the contẽplation of thinges eternal and heuenly, we may lerne the despising of temporal and erthly [things]."[5] This admonition toward renunciation, this return to the old abnegation is the antithesis of humanism. The instructions in this early work contain the traditional statements concerning man's innate depravity: "Add to all these, the mynde of man alwayes decayinge and drawyng downewarde to worse and worse. For thoughe not in al, yet surely in the most part of men, the saieng of Austyne is true. *Qui maior est etate, maior est iniquitate.* He that is greater in age, is greter in wickednes" (sig. B5ᵛ). And even more medieval is the morality play context of the "disputation betwixte the diuell and the syche man" which appears near the end of the book (sigs. F2-F3ᵛ).

As equally disconcerting is the inclusion among the humanistic influences Erasmus's work in the *de contemptu mundi* tradition. This early book was written before Erasmus made his first trip to England, and it is deeply imbued with the monastic ideals. The advice to a young man concerning the withdrawal from secular life is stern: "If all thy care be to lyue rightously / loke than that thou gete the lightlye out of this worlde / for the worlde & vertue wyll in no wyse agree to gether."[6] The secular values are again and again decried: "the honours of this Worlde be vayne or foolyshe and unstable." And so it goes.

What has happened in McConica's book is, of course, an indiscriminate use of labels and a casual interpretation of Erasmianism. It is difficult to recognize in the Erasmian works just cited the mind to which Pope Paul III addressed his plea for assistance against heresy in 1535: "Nor are we ignorant how much your extraordinary learning conjoined with an equal eloquence, can help us in rooting out these new errors from the minds of men." McConica knows of the "aenigma Termini" but he does not consider the paradox of the Erasmian intellect.

Concedo nulli, we must admit, is an insigne which reverbrates beyond Terminus and echoes ironically today to haunt alike the Erasmian biographer and the Renaissance historian. For the ambiguity of that personal motto (its arrogance seems to have appealed to the young Erasmus just as its incisive grotesqueness implemented the pietism of his mature years) also characterizes the mysterious qualities of that famous humanistic scholar from Rotterdam. If McConica had surveyed more carefully the modern scholarship which centers on Erasmus, he would have found a warning in the plethora: ambiguity resides in the series of contradictions. The leading Christian humanist of the early sixteenth century is depicted in one recent study as a rebel who consciously and subconsciously set about to attack the sacramental structure of the orthodox Catholic faith.[7] Yet in another recent study Erasmus's devotion to Roman Catholicism is seen as a pioneering force which helped to set in motion the Counter-Reformation.[8] And still another modern scholar has depicted Erasmus as a figure too complex to fit into the conception of Christian humanism as that term is defined in our age.[9] Moreover, it has been only with the completion in 1958 of P. S. Allen's eleven volume edition of the correspondence (*Opus Epistolarum Des. Erasmi Roterodami*) that scholars have begun to place the multi-faceted figure of the Renaissance humanist within perspective.[10] Had McConica paid heed to the wealth of research being done on his major figure, he would have avoided, I think, the simplicity with which he approaches his terms. As it is, his work must be used selectively: the author's research is reliable; his conjectures, unfortunately, enervate his book.

The California State College at Fullerton

Notes:

(1) See Albert Hyma, *The Christian Renaissance* (New York, 1935); "The Continental Origins of English Humanism," *HLQ,* IV (1940), 1-25; Roberto Weiss, *Humanism in England During the Fifteenth Century* (Oxford, 1957).

(2) Erasmus wrote to Vives in 1528 that he intended to stay out of the Jove-and-Juno affair, the great matter of the king's divorce. His statements on divorce were known, but they were not translated into English until mid-century. See *The Censure and iudgement of the famous clark Erasmus of Roterodam: Whyther dyuorsemente betwene man and wyfe stondeth with the lawe of God* (London, 1550?).

(3) *A Booke Called in Latin Enchiridion Milites Christiani / and in Englyshe the Manuell of the Christen Knyght* (London, 1533), sig. A2.   •

(4) For a survey of the *ars moriendi* literature of the later middle ages and the Renaissance, see Sister Mary Catherine O'Connor, *The Art of Dying Well* (New York, 1942).

(5) Erasmus Roterodame, *Preparation To Deathe* (London, 1543), sig. A5.

(6) Erasmus Rot., *De Cõtemptu Mundi*, trans. Thomas Paynell (London, 1533), sig. G2.

(7) E. V. Telle, *Erasme de Rotterdam et la Septième Sacrament* (Geneva, 1954).

(8) Louis Bouyer, *Autour d' Erasme* (Paris, 1955). McConica seems not to have had recourse to this study.

(9) Siro A. Nulli, *Erasmo e il Rinascimento* (Turin, 1955). This work was apparently not used by McConica.

(10) The broader perspective is apparent in the work of Karl H. Oelrich, *Der späte Erasmus und die Reformation* (Münster, 1961). McConica does not have recourse to this work.

The Rhetoric of Tragedy: Form in Stuart Drama by Charles Osborne McDonald. University of Massachusetts Press, 1966. pp. vi + 346. $7.50. Indices. *Reviewer, Adolph L. Soens.*

McDonald performs a valuable service for students of Elizabethan and Stuart drama in this book. He delineates a tradition of sophistic rhetoric, and demonstrates its influence on the chief sources of Renaissance pedagogy. He describes the way in which the poets became versed in this tradition and analyzes the way in which it influenced their plays. He demonstrates the structural relevance of this tradition of rhetoric to Stuart drama. Finally, he shows the value of knowledge of this tradition in analyzing Stuart drama. Since McDonald has accomplished so much that has not been done before, and his successful demonstration of rhetoric's structural relevance is a real service, it seems almost ungrateful to remark that he makes two errors in investigative technique which prevent him from doing as much as he might have done. These two errors prevent him from analyzing the semantic as well as the structural significance of the tradition he studies.

McDonald, since he is studying a tradition of rhetoric which extends from Greece to Stuart England, should have studied all of the divisions of rhetoric. He does not. He deals with Invention, Disposition and Style. He neither investigates the relevance, nor demonstrates the irrelevance, of two other divisions, Memory and Delivery. Second, he does not investigate the modifications which the middle ages imposed upon the tradition, nor does he demonstrate the non-existence of such modifications. Such investigation might have enabled him to study the semiotic, as well as the structural relevance of the tradition of rhetoric he uses ably.

McDonald first identifies and analyzes a tradition of rhetoric which he identifies as sophistic. He discriminates this tradition from the tradition represented by, say, Cicero, and he relates the tradition to the pedagogy of Rome, as well as to the plays of Euripides and Seneca. He then describes the tradition as it reached Stuart dramatists, and uses this tradition to analyze *Hamlet, Sophonisba, The Malcontent, The Revenger's Tragedy, Bussy D'Ambois,* and the plays of Webster and Ford.

The chief analytic concepts which this tradition offers him are the antilogy, related to invention, disposition and style; ethopoetic and pathopoetic methods of developing character; and the figures of diction and the narrative methods characteristic of the Senecan *Declamationes*. He demonstrates the structural relevance of these concepts as figures of thought to Stuart drama. McDonald is the first student of Renaissance rhetoric to demonstrate the systematic practical relevance of sophistic rhetoric to the structure of Renaissance drama. He has also shown how to use rhetorical concepts successfully in the analysis of Renaissance genres without getting bogged down in lists of figures or getting side-tracked into using figure-frequencies as an earmark to identify authors.

Both the list of figures, and the figure-frequency count are characteristic of formulary rhetorical analysis. McDonald is quite aware of the difference between a formulary rhetoric, such as Peacham's and suasive rhetoric, such as Cicero's or Aphthonius'. McDonald is also careful to study rhetoric as Renaissance poets learned it; from the practice of teachers, and the textbooks which reveal this practice.

McDonald first describes the tradition of sophistic rhetoric in Greece, and then uses this tradition to analyse the plays of Euripides. Sophistic rhetoric trained students to argue both sides of a question. It thus developed figures of thought, such as antilogy, forms such as *laus* and *vituperatio*, formal and balanced arguments, and figures of diction useful in developing these forms and figures. McDonald illuminates Euripides' plays by applying these figures of thought, and their emphasis on balanced argument to the structure of the plays. A purist might argue that the tradition which McDonald develops need not be attached to Protagoras, but might rather be attached simply to Pedagoge. Such an objection would miss the value of McDonald's work, for it is not the attachment to Protagoras that is valuable, but the demonstration that figures of thought can be used to analyze the plays, and that the plays can be considered fruitfully as a series of verbal encounters governed in part by devices and situations drawn from a rhetorical tradition. McDonald next describes the evolution of sophistic rhetoric in Rome, and applies this rhetoric to the plays of Seneca. By pointing out the similarities between the plays of Seneca and the rhetorics such as Aphthonius' *Progymnasmata*, *ad Herrenium*, and the *Declamationes*, he has prepared his ground for his analysis of plays by authors who studied Aphthonius, the *Declamationes*, and the plays of Seneca in the Renaissance.

McDonald then describes the tradition as it was available to the authors he analyzes in the Tudor and Stuart periods. He skips lightly over what did or did not happen to the tradition during the middle ages. Since he describes the effects of pedagogy on the tradition, and since this tradition can be discriminated from some of the more theoretically biased rhetorical techniques, it seems probable that medieval homiletic, which was concerned with semiotic as well as formal structure, might have influenced some of the rhetorical practice taught school-boys in the Renaissance. Semantic concern certainly influenced commentaries on the authors studied by Renaissance school-boys.

One or two examples will illustrate my discontent with the extent of McDonald's investigation. McDonald analyzes brilliantly the formal part played in the *Revenger's Tragedy* by image motifs, and relates these motifs to the antilogic structure he discerns in the play. He does not discuss the semantic significance of the particular images in any connected way. He notices the structural significance of image patterns in *Hamlet*, but does not relate this structural significance to any semantic pattern. Had he analyzed *Macbeth*, he would doubtless have noticed the bird imagery, and would have related it to an antilogic rhetorical pattern. It is, however, quite clear that "owl" images and "falcon" images are related semantically as well as formally, and that they are related within a structure, not merely incidentally. McDonald describes the structure, without exploring its meaning, so to speak.

Two areas which he does not explore would seem to offer possibilities for providing semantic explanations. Frances Yates' recent book on Memory, one of the divisions of rhetoric taught school-boys, points out the use of semantically appropriate signs to mark the *topoi* orators used. The semantic connection made the job of memorizing simpler than it would have been were the signs chosen simply arbitrary earmarks. Medieval homiletic was concerned with the semantic analysis of images and image patterns which might appear at first arbitrary. Whether or not these two disciplines, Memory and homiletic, did in fact influence the tradition of sophistic rhetoric, and the plays influenced by this rhetoric is unexplored. McDonald should have demonstrated the irrelevance of Memory, at least, if it is indeed irrelevant. The cavil should be weighed according to the merits of the book however. The fact that McDonald does not explore the implications of memory simply makes him one of that class of scholars who write on Renaissance rhetoric without exploring two of the major divisions of rhetoric, Memory and Delivery. The class is large, and there is only one memorable scholar in the contrasting class, Frances Yates.

McDonald next analyzes Hamlet, and the brilliance and deficiency of his method show in his analysis. He uses the rhetorical concepts of *ethos, pathos,* and *illustratio* to define the development of Hamlet's character and the structure of the play, and manages to do away with the rather overworked dilemma of Hamlet's hesitation without involving himself in the contradictions which have beset every analysis based on humours or decorum. On the other hand, as McDonald himself points out, the rhetorical pattern which he discerns requires that the *illustratio* of Fortinbras' march to fight the Poles bear a disproportionate emotional weight in this pattern. One is still left wondering what *pathos* exists in Fortinbras, off to a small and bloody scuffle, which did not inhere in a murdered father, a debauched mother, and an apparently treacherous sweetheart.

McDonald himself suggests the area in which he might have found an answer. He centers his analysis on the ethopoetic and pathopoetic elements in Hamlet's character, and uses the player's Hecuba speech, and Hamlet's reaction to it, to delineate the concepts he develops. Yet much of the player's speech, and Hamlet's associated speeches, relate to rhetorical delivery. This coupling opens a wider problem, for in many of the commentaries studied by Weinberg in his history of Italian criticism in the Renaissance, and in commentaries on the classics from other than Italian sources, the threefold definition of "imitation" contains elements which are related to delivery. McDonald is not alone in his indifference to one of the major divisions studied by Renaissance rhetoricians. His merits simply point up this deficiency more clearly than do other books of less merit.

McDonald's analyses of *Sophonisba* and *The Malcontent* are thorough and perceptive. Since Marston is less a poet than Shakespeare, and thus less able to integrate structure and semantic development, McDonald's analysis of the structure of these plays raises few unanswered questions. His analysis of their rhetorical development, the relationship of figures of thought to balanced, scenes, arguments and characters is extremely enlightening to read, and gives the reader the pleasure, as well, of watching a job very well done.

McDonald's analysis of *Bussy D'Ambois* is even more satisfying than his work with Marston. He successfully relates the ambiguous moral posture of the hero to the rhetorical structure of the play. He demonstrates the consistent use of antilogies in the matched scenes, debates, and even image patterns within the play. He demonstrates the persuasive function of the rhetoric when he shows Chapman using antilogies sophistically to force the audience to adopt a standard differing from either of the members of the antilogy. McDonald is especially interesting in his analysis of Chapman's use of image patterns.

He shows that they are essentially formal rather than semantic.

McDonald's analysis of the *Revenger's Tragedy* is his most elegant piece of work. He accounts for the image motifs of the play, the exaggerated Senecan devices, and the structural function of these and other antilogistic figures. He relates all these to their background in sophistic rhetoric, and he demonstrates the close inter-relation of theme, technique, device and structure. He also shows clearly the influence of Marston, and the evolution which Marston's technique has undergone at the hands of Tourneur. Finally, McDonald examines Ford and Webster as examples of sophistic rhetoric overblown. He finds that they become interested in the immediate, not the structural, antilogies, and as a consequence present a series of disjunct brilliances. He presents instances in which devices of sophistic rhetoric distort scenes from their structural functions. He shows how figures of thought, in effect, degenerate in these plays to ornament, and his demonstration makes clear what happened to these plays.

McDonald concludes with a study of cultural elements which may or may not have produced the effects he discerns by applying the tool of sophistic rhetoric. One of his tools is Ong's analysis of rhetoric, another the method of McLuhan. I feel that McLuhan's relevance is so remote that it disfigures the book to bring him in. The medium may very well be the message, or something approximate thereto, but the medium of these plays was neither a series of dots, nor a picture tube. It was rather the actor on a relatively bare stage. I wish that McDonald had examined delivery, rather than packaging, in his last chapter.

University of Notre Dame

The Elizabethan Dumb Show: The History of a Dramatic Convention by Dieter Mehl. Harvard University Press, 1966. Pp. xiii + 207. $5.50.

Die Pantomime im Drama der Shakespearezeit: Ein Beitrag zur Geschichte der 'Dumb Show' by Dieter Mehl. Quelle & Meyer, 1964. Pp. 160. DM 20. *Reviewer: Rolf Soellner.*

The English version of this book is a free translation, with some additions and revisions, of the German study, which grew out of a doctoral dissertation, directed by Professor Wolfgang Clemen of the University of Munich. The author is clearly a disciple of this leading German Shakespeare scholar. Like Clemen's *Die Tragödie der Shakespearezeit* (translated as *English Tragedy before Shakespeare*), Dr. Mehl's study analyzes a definable element in the general context of dramatic development. And like Clemen's excellent *Kommentar zu Shakespere's Richard III* (unfortunately not yet translated), the present study works from a close scrutiny of texts outward to form and function.

Dr. Mehl gives a broad definition to "Elizabethan": his examples stretch from *Gorboduc* to Fletcher's tragicomedies and include works of Marston, Middleton, and Rowley that fall in the Jacobean period. He adopts an equally broad definition of dumb show as "a part of a play which presents by means of action without speech an element of the plot that would be more naturally accompanied by speech." He goes beyond this definition by including a scene like that in Greene's *Friar Bacon and Friar Bungay* (II.iii) in which the Prince and Bacon observe through a magic glass Lacy's wooing of the maid of Fressingfield; although the latter pair speaks, Dr. Mehl claims the scene, not quite convincingly, as a dumb show since the observers do not hear the conversation. Mr. Mehl gives relatively little space to the origins and beginnings of the dumb show, on which previous studies have usually focused; in agreement with recent trends, he derives it more from native sources than from foreign models, from pageants, mimes, and the like, and also from emblems. In discussing form and function of the dumb shows, he distinguishes an amazing variety of uses in the about thirty works which he considers in detail, proof of the versatile and experimental character of Elizabethan drama. There are some extraordinary uses of the dumb-show device, such as that in *Hamlet*, which Dr. Mehl discusses thoroughly and judiciously and the uniqueness of which becomes apparent when seen in the context of the whole tradition. The general development of the dumb show he discerns is one from being at first an only loosely connected, sometimes extraneous, and often allegorical addition to becoming an increasingly integrated part of drama, telescoping actions extending over long periods and creating strong visual impressions of incidents the dramatists wished to emphasize.

While this is a useful little book, one might wish it had been more concise in its presentation and wider in its view. There was hardly a need for such lengthy reproductions and large excerpts of so many dumb shows. But Dr. Mehl does not go far afield in connecting changes in this device with changes in dramatic styles or acting styles. In this respect the relative scarcity of dumb shows in the 1590's and their sudden resurgence in generally more realistic form around 1608 gives much food for thought. As it is, Dr. Mehl's is a helpful guide to a strange and fascinating ingredient of Elizabethan drama. The usefulness of the book is increased by an appended bibliography listing and briefly describing the known dumb shows from the Elizabethan through the early Stuart periods including some not noticed before, although these are mostly transitional forms.

The Ohio State University

John Webster and His Critics, 1617-1964 by Don D. Moore. Louisiana State University Press, 1966. Pp. x + 199. $4.00. *Reviewer: Charles R. Forker.*

This monograph, as its title suggests, undertakes to survey comprehensively and systematically the numerous and varied critical responses to Webster from his own time to the present. Because his place in English literature has been a matter of recurrent dispute—at least since Charles Lamb's nearly worshipful rediscovery of him at the beginning of the nineteenth century—Moore's task has been sizeable; and in addition to assembling the far-flung evidence for the study of Webster's reputation (not omitting a valuable account of how the plays have actually fared on the professional stage since their inception), Moore attempts to account for different critical reactions not only in terms of individual biases and predilections but also in terms of the history of taste itself. The result is a useful contribution to scholarship. This book will save modern investigators a good deal of bibliographical spadework; it will also provide important sources for anyone interested in the history of Elizabethan dramatic scholarship.

To read Moore's survey is to be struck instantly by the variety and number of famous men who have either written on or otherwise had to do with Webster. The list begins with his collaborator-friends, Rowley, Middleton, and Ford, who all wrote commendatory verses for *The Duchess of Malfi* (the last named contends that no classical poet surpasses Webster's achievement in that play); it then goes on to include Pepys (who, like many a later writer, preferred his Webster in the study), Nahum Tate and Lewis Theobald (who both "corrected"

Webster for the eighteenth-century theatre), Lamb, Hazlitt, Kingsley, R. H. ("Orion") Horne (who again rewrote Webster for the stage), George Henry Lewes, Swinburne, James Russell Lowell, George Saintsbury, William Archer, J. A. Symonds, Shaw, Edmund Gosse, Rupert Brooke, T. S. Eliot, and Edmund Wilson.

The early sections of the book are organized historically, while the later chapters depart to some extent from strict chronology in order to group critics according to movements, schools, or particular prejudices. A disappointingly thin first chapter (twenty-one pages merely) brings the chronicle of Webster's reputation up to Lamb and the Romantic revival. Of course the available seventeenth- and eighteenth-century material on Webster is notoriously meagre, and quite properly Moore does not try to make his bits and pieces look like a banquet. Nevertheless, since his work is willy-nilly a history of scholarship as well as a study of reputation, one could wish that his coverage had been a little fuller. Though their interest is more historical than evaluative, it is a pity that he neglects to record the attacks of Thomas Hall and his nameless ally on John Webster of Clitheroe (a popular preacher unrelated to the poet), whom the attackers ignorantly or maliciously confused with Webster the dramatist, and whom one of them called a "Quondam Player" (in *Vindiciae Literarum*, 1655), as well as those by John Stephens and two of his Lincoln's Inn cronies who also railed at the playwright, apparently without realizing his identity (in *Essayes and Characters*, 1615). Moore also overlooks (perhaps deliberately) at least two minor allusions to Webster in John Phillips' *Wit and Drollery* (1656) and William Winstanley's *Lives of thy Most Famous English Poets* (1687). Although the book went to press too soon to notice my own arguments for Webster's influence on the style of Shirley's *Cardinal* (in my 1964 edition of that play) or the extensive plagiarisms of Webster by Robert Baron, which I recently documented in an article for *Anglia* (LXXXIII [1965], 176-198), Moore might interestingly have considered the matter of Webster's influence on later seventeenth-century writers, since imitation is, among other things, a form of literary criticism. He notes that, generally speaking, Webster was highly regarded in his own century though he seems to have ranked behind Shakespeare, Jonson, Beaumont and Fletcher, and Chapman. It is interesting to be reminded that he was recognized even in his own day as a laborious playwright who wrote slowly and with difficulty, and that his reputation as an important writer has rested from the beginning almost exclusively on the two Italian tragedies for which all but specialists now read him.

As soon as Moore gets to the nineteenth century he has more substance to chew upon. Not surprisingly the earlier, impressionistic critics of Webster tend to divide neatly into extremes of partisanship and detraction. Hazlitt and Swinburne line up solidly behind Lamb in their enthusiasm, the first asserting that Webster's two best-known plays "perhaps come the nearest to Shakespeare of anything we have on record" (p. 36) and the second insisting (without a trace of irony) that Euripides is to Webster "as a mutilated monkey to a well made man" (p. 51). The puritanical Kingsley, whose attitude toward drama reminds one of Stephen Gosson's, scarifies Webster for his attraction to vice in words that partly explain why he was so little performed in Victorian times:

> We should not allow these plays to be acted in our own day, because we know that they will produce their effects of sin. We should call him a madman who allowed his daughters or his servants to see such representations. (p.47)

Towards the close of the century the Ibsenites, Archer and Shaw, are no less severe with Webster, though of course their objections were aesthetic rather than moralistic, founded as they were on the self-limiting canons of late nineteenth-century realism. Nearly all the

Victorians, whether enthusiasts or debunkers, seem to have been most impressed by Webster's "horror," his "moods," and the intermittent rather than sustained effects of his verse.

With the twentieth century, of course, comes a body of more balanced and historically better informed criticism. Though modern commentators have not altogether dispelled earlier objections to Webster's sins of construction, they have naturally perceived new sources of unity in the interconnections of theme, imagery, tone, and symbol, and in a fresh appreciation for parallels and contrasts of character and scene. Webster's "metaphysical" verse has been much better understood since T. S. Eliot, the "new critical" revolution, and recent studies of Renaissance rhetoric. The main contention among modern critics seems to center on opposing definitions of Webster's moral climate. One school, represented by writers such as Una Ellis-Fermor, M. C. Bradbrook, Clifford Leech, Travis Bogard, Robert Ornstein, and Gunnar Boklund, sees Webster's world as unified only by a pervasive despair —a world in which the frequent moral aphorisms to which so many of the characters give expression are either intrusive or ultimately irrelevant. The other school consists of those (like C. V. Boyer, F. P. Wilson, Lord David Cecil, and Irving Ribner) who do discern moral order in Webster's universe—usually of a more or less traditionally Christian kind. The nature of this critical division, a little over-schematic in Moore's restatement of it, is conveniently suggested by two differing interpretations of the Duchess of Malfi's line "I could curse the stars" and Bosola's comment thereon: "Look you, the stars shine still" (IV.i.96-100). Leech regards this passage as the "completest assertion in Jacobean drama of man's impotence, of the remoteness, the impersonality of the cosmic powers" (pp. 125-126), while Ribner sees the stars as a symbol of hope, permanence, and the "illuminating beauty which persists in spite of all" (p. 145).

The titles of two of Moore's chapters, "Webster in the Study" and "Webster and the Modern Stage" indicate another well-nigh incurable split, for even the playwright's most sympathetic admirers have usually been happier with Webster the poet than with Webster the practical dramatist. The lamentable truth is that his reception on the boards has been nearly as ill-starred as his hapless characters. Webster himself complained about the failure of an audience to appreciate The White Devil despite superior actors, and there have been alarmingly few successful performances of his plays since then. Not that this is wholly the dramatist's fault of course. Both the Italian tragedies were revived at the Restoration with some success, but the calendar of eighteenth- and nineteenth-century performances taken as a whole makes a depressing chronicle indeed. Tate's revision of The White Devil in 1707 (under the revealing title Injured Love) purged Vittoria of any taint of sin, removed all references to sex, and (perhaps luckily) was never actually performed at all. Theobald's version twenty-six years later of The Duchess (retitled The Fatal Secret) ran for a grand total of two performances. It changed the ending ludicrously so that the Duchess emerges alive from the tomb, Ferdinand having been tricked by means of a wax dummy into believing in her death, while Antonio lives to become Lord Protector and divide his wealth with Bosola. Horne's adaptation of the same play in 1850 (Moore gives no real indication of how extensive the alterations are, for Horne rewrote roughly a third of the play) was somewhat more successful owing to impressive performances by Samuel Phelps and Isabella Glyn, but even the most sympathetic witnesses remained doubtful about Webster's stageworthiness. When William Poel resurrected The Duchess in 1892 in a cut version more faithful to Webster's original than any that had been seen for over two centuries, he succeeded only in provoking Archer's vitriolic denunciation of Webster. More recent productions have been both luckier and more numerous, but very few have triumphed. George Rylands' London production of *The Duchess* in 1945 with John Gielgud and Peggy Ashcroft hit its mark with an audience for whom the Nazi concentration-camp atrocities were topical, but W. H. Auden's Broadway version of the same play failed disastrously the following year despite (or perhaps because of) a cast that included John Carradine, Elizabeth Bergner, and Canada Lee (the last in white makeup!). Jack Landau has twice directed modern-dress productions of *The White Devil* in New York (1955 and 1965), both with brilliant success. Such productions have reassured us that Webster can be satisfying in the theatre, but Moore's discouraging account is a salutary reminder that poetic and dramatic values are not necessarily the same, and that Webster's macabre ironies can only too readily turn to embarrassment or silliness when they are transferred to the stage without sufficient subtlety and imagination. Moore's survey of performances is too sketchy in production details to satisfy most historians of the theatre, but he does append to his bibliography a very useful list of newspaper and periodical reviews, thus pointing the way to fuller information.

In reviewing the whole course of Websterian scholarship and criticism Moore occasionally seems to ignore or at least to understress the importance of the more technical aspects of his subject. He fails even to mention, for instance, William Hazlitt's four-volume edition of 1857, which must have done much to make the dramatist available to Victorian readers, and he shows himself insufficiently aware of the effect on modern critics of such important recent scholarship as R. W. Dent's collection and analysis of Webster's borrowings, of J. R. Brown's studies of the printing of Webster's plays, of R. G. Howarth's important researches into Webster's obscure biography, especially his conclusions about Webster's learning, and of Boklund's significant discussions of Webster's use of sources. This unawareness seems to be responsible for his two references to F. L. Lucas's admittedly indispensable edition of 1927 as "definitive" (pp. 93 and 95) and his apparent acceptance of Sir Sidney Lee's biography of Webster, written in 1899 for the *DNB*, as the "best we know" (p. 67). Moore also slights continental criticism of Webster and totally ignores the importance of foreign translations (there are interesting ones in German, French, Italian, Spanish, Serbo-Croatian, and Russian as well as a scholarly edition of one of the plays in Japanese).

Mr. Moore can be careless or uninformed about details. He repeats Webster's reference to "Alcestides" from the preface to *The White Devil*, apparently failing to recognize the dramatist's blunder (because of his insecure Latin) for "Alcestis" (p. 7). He misleadingly reports that Gildon in *The Lives and Characters of the English Dramatic Poets* confuses the dramatist "with a religious writer of the same name" (p. 11), whereas Gildon's claim that Webster was a clerk of the parish of St. Andrews in Holborn implies nothing of the sort, and in fact R. G. Howarth (see *Notes and Queries*, IX [1962], 334-336, and X [1963], 193) casts the gravest doubt upon the existence of such a Webster, for we know that others occupied the office between 1612 and 1648 and no such name appears in the surviving registers of parish clerks or other relevant documents for the period in question. The "H. M." whose essays on Webster in *Blackwood's Magazine* (1818) have a significant place in Moore's treatment of Romantic criticism has been identified as John Wilson (1785-1854), one of the most prolific contributors to that periodical, by A. L. Strout in *A Bibliography of Articles in Blackwood's Magazine* (Lubbock, Texas, 1959), p. 38.

Apart from a number of typographical errors which a more scrupulous proofreading might have caught, there are numerous inaccuracies of quotation (e.g., pp. 8, 33, 75, 83, 88, 89, 119); the author consistently misspells the title of Edward Phillips' well-known compendium as "*Theatrum Poetarium*" (pp. 170 and 192); and he has a way of getting names wrong, as, for instance, when he mistakes "Thomas" for William Warburton (p. 15) and William "Minton" for William Minto (p. 54 and throughout). The bibliography and all-important footnotes (inaccessibly huddled together at the rear of the volume) contain some annoying inconsistencies. For instance, the place of publication of Bogard's *Tragic Satire of John Webster* is variously given as Los Angeles (p. 172) and Berkeley (p. 189); the date of Parrott's famous edition of Chapman's tragedies is given as 1961 (the date of the reprint) rather than as 1910 (the original, and therefore proper, date); and Moore oddly does not distinguish books published at Cambridge, England, from those published at Cambridge, Massachusetts.

Although Moore occasionally forgets to credit his necessarily specialized audience with the fundamentals of literary history (he will digress to give us Pope's dicta on Shakespeare, Thomas Warton's and Bishop Hurd's responses to *The Faerie Queene*, or a potted summary of the rise of naturalism in the nineteenth century), his motive is obviously and rightly to prepare the reader for specific reactions to Webster and to illustrate the milieu that allowed Theobald to mangle him with notions of poetic justice or Shaw to sneer at the "Tussaud laureate." I find Moore's own critical judgment usually cool, balanced, and just, though of course one may reasonably disagree with him on any number of specific points. He avoids siding with critics who by implication still regard Webster as grandly semi-barbarous, without rushing headlong into the arms of those who exhaust ingenuity in order to explain away his every weakness. He is especially acute, for instance, in his discussion of Rupert Brooke's youthful, bumptious, charming, irritating, and still important pioneer study of the dramatist, and in his penetrating analysis of the assumptions (some of them surprisingly untenable) that underlie the enormously influential statements of T. S. Eliot. If criticism of criticism does not make for the liveliest reading, it is nevertheless true that Moore performs a needed labor with intelligence and tact; his volume is therefore both welcome and serviceable. It would be pleasant to hope that its appearance will encourage similar studies for some of Webster's celebrated fellow dramatists.

Indiana University

Lute Music of Shakespeare's Time. William Barley: A New Booke of Tabliture, 1596 edited by Wilburn W. Newcomb. The Pennsylvania State University Press, 1966. Pp. xxxviii + 115. $9.50. *Reviewer: Carol MacClintock.*

According to Chappell's *Popular Music of the Olden Time*, the plays of Shakespeare contain thirty-one references to songs which were current at the end of the sixteenth century and of which the music and the words are known to scholars. As it happens, the *New Booke of Tabliture* of William Barley, transcribed and reproduced by Mr. Wilburn Newcomb in his volume *Lute Music of Shakespeare's Time*, contains none of these but it does have several others, together with twenty-four lute compositions contemporary with them.

Barley's book, historically important because it is the first anthology printed in England to contain music exclusively by English composers, is a relative late-comer in the field of such publications. The sixteenth century was the "Golden Age" of the lute: every court, every noble house in Europe had its professional lutenist, and talented (and not-so talented) amateurs abounded, for the lute held a position comparable to that of the piano in the nineteenth century. Great quantities of music were composed and numerous "tutors" were written. The first printed music for lute appeared in Italy in 1507, and not long thereafter the first instruction book was printed (in Germany, Virdung's *Musica getutscht*, 1511), followed by others in France, Germany and Italy. For the next two centuries an absolute flood of music for lute was written, both original pieces for the instrument and arrangements of vocal music for it.

It is curious that the first English treatise on lute playing did not make its appearance until 1568—and was merely a translation of the 1567 edition of Adrien Le Roy's *Instruction de partir toute musique facilement en tablature de luth*, "englished by J. Alford Londenor", with the title *Brief and easye instruction*. Another such translation of a French work appeared in 1574, then no further publications until 1596, when William Barley printed *A new Booke of Tabliture, Containing sundrie easie and familiar Instructions shewing howe to attaine to the knowledge, to guide and dispose thy hand to play on sundry Instruments, as the Lute, Orpharion, and Bandora*, the first of the numerous English lutebooks which were to be published in the next several decades.

Barley's book consisted of two parts—an instruction for the amateur and an anthology. The instruction part is a partial translation and adaptation of a French work, and it is regrettable that Mr. Newcomb has not pursued this matter further. The anthology, or "lessons" (i.e. solo pieces) has compositions for the Lute, the Orpharion and the Bandora. The Orpharion and Bandora were both related to the Lute, having six or seven courses of strings, fretted, and tuned similarly to the Lute. The Bandora, having a somewhat lower range, was useful as a bass instrument in a consort, while the Orpharion seems to have been a solo instrument. There are pictures of them in the text and Mr. Newcomb provides technical details in his prefatory chapters. He also has a brief biography of William Barley and a discussion of the musical forms of the compositions.

The transcriptions include 7 pieces for lute, 12 for Orpharion, and 10 for Bandora. Four composers chiefly are represented: John Dowland, the great English lutenist whose fame was international, Francis Cutting, of purely English renown, Philip Rosseter, known also for his "Ayres" and for his association with the poet-musician Thomas Campion, and Anthony Holborne, Oxford gentleman, musician and composer for the Citthern. There is also a single composition by one Edward Johnson. The composers of the other selections are unknown. Four of the pieces for Bandora are songs—the first to be published in England with such accompaniment. *Those eyes that set my fancie on a fire* and *How can the tree but waste and wither away* have complete texts; of the other two only incipits are given. No clues are offered as to either author or composer of any of these.

The instrumental pieces fall into dance forms of the day—Alman, Pavan and Galliard (also called *cinquepace* in Shakespeare's time)—and variations on tunes popular during Elizabeth's reign. It is regrettable also that Mr. Newcomb does not include a discussion of such popular tunes. For instance, "Goe from my window," one of the songs sung in Beaumont and Fletcher's *Knight of the Burning Pestle*, is here in John Dowland's lute version, as is "Fortune my foe", alluded to by Shakespeare in *Merry Wives of Windsor* (II,sc. 3) and by Ben Jonson in *The Case is altered* and in his masque *The Gipsies metamorphosed*. Beaumont and Fletcher, too, refer to "Fortune" in three of their plays. "Beckington's Pound", better and more generally known as "Packington's Pound", is given in Francis Cutting's version. This air was used by Ben Jonson in *Bartholomew Fair* for one of his songs, and it seems to have been so popular that the many songs written to that tune have never been entirely enumerated. "Walsingham," a tune belonging to the time of Henry VII, found in Barley's *New Booke* in Cutting's arrangement, was frequently mentioned by Beaumont and Fletcher and other writers. The melody destined to become one of the most famous of all, often referred to in plays and poems, the "Lacrime pavan", was not of popular origin but composed by John Dowland. Barley's publication of this work (without Dowland's knowledge or consent) was its first appearance in print.

All the music in Barley's *New Booke of Tabliture* is delightful. Mr. Newcomb has transcribed it into modern keyboard notation on two staves, thus enabling one to play it on the piano or, preferably, the harpsichord. He has also included the original lute tablature for the benefit of scholars who like to see the original form and for the growing number of lutenists who prefer to play from tablature. The music is written in a fairly clear and legible manuscript hand and the volume as a whole is beautifully printed and a pleasure to use. More exhaustive discussion of the musico-social background and more thoroughgoing critical notes would have made the volume more useful to scholars. Nevertheless, Mr. Newcomb's publication now makes a portion of the instrumental music so often mentioned by writers of Elizabethan times but unknown to the twentieth century accessible and possible of performance.

The University of Cincinnati

Shakespeare's Occasional Plays: Their Origin and Transmission by J. M. Nosworthy. Arnold (London), Barnes & Noble (New York), 1965. Pp. 238. $7.95. *Reviewer:* R. W. Dent.

This study examines four plays, three of which have been commonly but not universally regarded as written for special occasions: *Hamlet, The Merry Wives of Windsor, Troilus and Cressida,* and *Macbeth*. Mr. Nosworthy believes all four were occasional in origin, and that problems such as dating, collaboration, adaptation, revision, and textual variation can in part be resolved by proper recognition of that fact. After a brief introduction defending the choice of these four while excluding others (the validity of the exclusions lies beyond the scope of this review), Nosworthy devotes three chapters to each play, usually moving from problems to "occasion" to solutions. A concluding chapter usefully summarizes what he considers the significance of his principal proposals for the biographer, critic, producer, and, above all, the textual scholar. One must always remember the concession he makes in that conclusion but occasionally appears to forget in the preceding chapters: ". . . remarkably few of the resultant proposals are anything more than partial or speculative" (p. 216).

As the sub-title implies, this is primarily a study aimed at Nosworthy's fellow bibliographers. Its strictly textual portions deserve careful evaluation by his peers in that field. I am not one of them, and I shall not make myself one of Pope's "fools" by rushing in. Let us hope his painstaking examination of problems will not be neglected merely because some of his solutions and some of his non-textual arguments prove unpersuasive.

For partly rhetorical reasons, Nosworthy treats the plays non-chronologically, in order to conclude where he expects the greatest resistance—on *Hamlet*. This review follows his order. Necessarily, my summary of his thesis for each play oversimplifies his position.

Macbeth: Written and produced for the court in 1606, *Macbeth* was from the first a very short play, its brevity imposed by the short time at Shakespeare's disposal and by either censorship or the fear thereof. Shakespeare was sole author both of the original play and of a revised version about 1612, employing for the latter songs and properties from Middleton's *The Witch*, itself a borrower from Jonson's *Masque of Queenes*. This second version of *Macbeth*, preserved in the Folio, converted the play's original 'nymphs' to 'hags,' was modeled to suit 1612 tastes, and was fundamentally quite as spectacular and "operatic" as

304

Davenant's famous adaptation. The Folio was probably printed not from a transcript but from a "fairly orderly set of foul papers, edited systematically but not exhaustively," and consisting essentially of the 1606 version with additions as used for prompt copy.

One must consider some of the arguments on which Nosworthy's elaborate hypothesis depends. First, dating. Many will deny that 1607 is "the absolute forward limit of dating" for *Macbeth's* initial production. Leeds Barroll may be extreme in asserting "there is no reason why *Macbeth* might not have been written as late as 1611" (*Essays in Shakespeare,* ed. Gordon Ross Smith [1965], p. 153), but his grounds deserve attention; if accepted, Nosworthy's entire hypothesis of early and late Shakespearean versions of course collapses. Certainly— although this might be made compatible with Nosworthy's essential view—the influence of Plutarch's "Antony" on *Macbeth* can more plausibly be explained by the supposition that *Macbeth* was written after, not before, *Antony and Cleopatra.*

Secondly, the date of *The Witch* cannot so casually be assumed merely because it fits one's theory. The Harbage-Schoenbaum *Annals,* its reviser a Middleton specialist, continues to date the play 1615, although allowing limits of c.1609-c.1616.

Thirdly, as the arguments of Farnham, Muir, and McGee can show, Simon Forman's allusion to 'feiries or Nimphes' in 'a wod' does not by itself warrant the assumption that he must have seen a production without bearded hags. Here, Nosworthy thinks Peter Heylyn's *Microcosmus,* with its 1625 allusion to 'Fairies' and 'forrest' gives possible support. The contrary is true. Heylyn can scarcely be assumed to have seen a production of *Macbeth* prior to his twelfth birthday.

Lastly, on the vexing authorial problem of the Hecate scenes, I find little significance in the supposed parallels to *A Midsummer Night's Dream* (following Knight), or in the additional parallels to *Titus Andronicus.* On the basis of such recurrences as ravens, owls, or yew trees it is foolish to suggest that Middleton could not have written Hecate's speech in III.v without having also written parts of *Titus.* Arguments supporting Shakespeare's hand in IV.i.39-43 are similarly vulnerable, whatever one's views on the authenticity of these lines. In short, Nosworthy scarcely demonstrates for me his "inevitable conclusion" (p. 31). Others may disagree, however. His arguments based on parallels, whether as here to earlier Shakespeare or later in the book to Lyly or Porter, seem to me perilously forced much of the time.

Troilus and Cressida: Asked to provide a comedy for the 1603 Revels of one of the Inns of Court, Shakespeare inserted comic material, topical allusions, and some concluding burlesque scenes into a half-finished tragedy which he had planned to have culminate in the death of Troilus. A transcript of this version, made by a pedantic transcriber (possibly Jonson) who "assumed the role of censor," provided copy for the 1609 Quarto. The 1603 Revels prologue, slightly adapted, became the controversial Bonian-Walley address to the reader. At some time subsequent to the Inns of Court production, Shakespeare began a revision of his foul papers for a version, probably never performed, which would emphasize his original tragic intention. This uncompleted revision provided copy for the Folio. Future editors must prefer the "Quarto version, *qua* version," but must allow the Folio far greater authority on variant readings than has been customary.

"It may be protested," Nosworthy concedes, "that the argument presented here heaps conjecture upon conjecture" (p. 84). It may indeed. But the play is one that proliferates conjectures almost as readily as does *Hamlet.* Regrettably, the present speculations went to press before Kimbrough's or Coghill's quite different ones appeared (although Kimbrough's basic view had been published in 1962), and of course they were already in print before the

Coghill-Alexander-Empson-Cook-Bowers-Maxwell exchange in *TLS* (Jan.-May, 1966; Nosworthy's proposals go unmentioned). Suffice it to say, even more than in the past there are alternative interpretations of Roberts' 1603 entry, of the Prologue's absence in the Quarto, and, of course, of the play's genre. Most critics will probably think Nosworthy's serious-comic-burlesque scene-by-scene analysis an oversimplification; few will believe "the only conceivable explanation, however unpalatable, is that Shakespeare changed his horses in mid-stream" (p. 74). I, for one, can apparently "believe anything," for I do not find V.viii.1-2 (Hector on the 'putrified core') unmistakable "conscious burlesque" or "palpably the work of the man who devised the 'very tragicall mirth' of Pyramus and Thisbe" (p. 73). To be less subjective, Shakespeare's sources simply will not support so simple a statement as that "the circumstances attaching to the death of Hector in the play held, in reality, for Troilus" (cf. Bullough, VI, especially pp. 177-179); the few source details apparently transferred from Troilus' death to Hector's do not establish that an original tragic intention was transferred to Hector and burlesqued. If this "transfer" and "burlesque" are indeed "the clearest indication of Shakespeare's changed purpose" (p. 75), small wonder the entire hypothesis appears strained.

"Of the various new theories propounded here," Nosworthy also concedes, "those relating to the Epistle as refashioned prologue and to Jonson as transcriber and factor are perhaps the most vulnerable, but neither invalidates the main thesis" (p. 84). Given this concession, it may be superfluous to object to either, but it is difficult to resist objecting to both.

First the Epistle (pp. 55-57). It seems to me that Nosworthy exaggerates the extent of its legal quibbles and of their obvious association with an Inns of Court production, whether of 1603 or 1609. At any rate, it is surely an exaggeration to claim that with "one or two trivial changes" the 1609 Epistle makes better sense as a 1603 prologue. Moreover, its "Euphuistic touches" are neither Euphuistic, strictly, nor out of date in 1609 (they are no more conceited, incidentally, than those of the Bonian-Walley 1609 Epistle for Ravenscroft's *Pammelia,* a genre-establishing preface somewhat akin in that respect to the one provided for *Troilus* or provided by Fletcher for Bonian-Walley's *The Faithfull Shepherdess*). Too, the *O.E.D.* examples will not support Nosworthy's interpretation of 'possessors' as more than remotely possible. As for 1609 being too late for commendation of Shakespeare's 'sauored salt of witte' or of his comedies, one must at least recall 1 *Henry IV's* third Quarto (1608) plus the fact that our scant records scarcely imply any disappearance of Shakespeare's comedies from the stage during these years.

The Jonson theory (pp. 69-71) is infinitely weaker. One is first asked to believe that Jonson would have functioned as transcriber, and then that he would have taken the transcript with him after his "break" (imaginary?) with the King's Men. Too, even if *Poetaster* were the later play and if *Neoptolemus* rather than *Pyrrhus* were its quarto reading, the appearance of *Neoptolemus* in *Poetaster* IV.iii.24 (not IV.i) should scarcely "suggest" Jonson's "familiarity" with *Troilus and Cressida* (see the end of the Variorum's long note on IV.v.161). Nosworthy's whole theory was apparently encouraged by an improper inference from the few Bonian-Walley entries in the Stationers' Register—where a Chapman poem "stands out in honorable isolation" with Jonson's *Masque of Queenes, The Case is Altered,* and *Troilus.* Had Nosworthy checked Morrison's *Index of Printers, Publishers, and Booksellers,* he would have gained a quite different impression. In addition to three of the four works just named (*The Case is Altered* was not printed for them), their ten publications included *The Faithfull Shepherdess,* Ravenscroft's songbook, Stephen Hobbs' long medical treatise, and at least two volumes devoted to the saving of Christian souls. Bonian-Walley were far more respectably engaged than Nosworthy implies, and at the same time Jonson's relationship with them was less than remarkable. On the latter, moreover, Nosworthy has conveniently ignored the prevailing view, one he readily accepted in his 1952 *JEGP* article (vol. LI, not XV), that Jonson was not responsible for the 1609 publication of *The Case is Altered*. This whole Jonson proposal—like a few others noted in this review—undermines one's confidence in arguments Nosworthy has prepared with infinitely greater care and expertise. It is a pity.

The Merry Wives of Windsor: When asked on short notice to present for the queen a play on Falstaff in love, Shakespeare hastily revised or adapted a pre-existing comedy, most plausibly Porter's *Two Merry Women of Abingdon*. The *Merry Wives* in its Folio form was the result. There are no substantial grounds for postulating later revision, although a few minor alterations were made by someone, possibly Shakespeare, to avoid censorship. The Folio *Wives* suffers in part from compositorial errors and from occasional misreadings and omissions in Crane's transcript. The Quarto, bad as it is, provides correction for some of these faults. But many "irregularities" in the Folio can best be explained as relics of otherwise discarded episodes in the source play. Part of the Quarto derives from manuscript fragments of that play; these included "the final scene, together with one or two fragments, of a play that depicted the gulling of a 'metamorphosed youth'." These fragments, containing Shakespeare's own markings and working notes, combined with a debased memorial report of *Wives* to serve as Quarto copy.

Most of my objections concern the Porter hypothesis and are in some degree peripheral to the essential argument. One cannot help wondering, however, if the vehemence with which Nosworthy rejects 1597 as a possible date for *Wives*, or the casualness with which he dates 1 and 2 *Henry IV* 1597 and 1598 respectively, was not affected by his having as source-play candidate a possible 1599 composition by the dramatist in whose influence Nosworthy has long been interested. While it may perhaps be "legitimate" to claim "that *The Merry Wives*, in its broad outlines, comes very close to *The Two Angry Women*," surely it is a bit strong to assert "that no other known play written before 1600 resembles *The Merry Wives* in any way" (p. 94).

The professed verbal similarities to Porter's one extant play seem to me especially forced. Take a few from p. 95. *Aqua vitae*, used at least three times before *Wives*, is not "rare." Shakespeare allusions to butter or cheese, on the other hand, may indeed be "rare" outside *Wives*, but of the three Porter resemblances quoted, Hart established the commonplaceness of one with parallels not to be found in Porter, Tilley (B768, 780) establishes the proverbial quality of a second, and the third seems insignificant. One may similarly discount a majority of the supposed resemblances on pp. 95-96, especially those found also in the other Falstaff plays (e.g., 'Butter' in 1 *Henry IV* or 'Cock and pie' in 2 *Henry IV* [p. 96[n]6 mistakenly says *Romeo and Juliet*]). Hart's old Arden edition is richly filled with evidence on the colloquial and proverbial richness of *Wives*, and later scholarship has supplemented this. Tilley, himself incomplete, records 102 proverbs and proverbial phrases in *Wives*. Is it surprising that a few of these appear also in Porter? This is not to deny that *The Two Angry Women of Abingdon* may have been a popular and influential play throughout the 1590's (the last revision of the *Annals*, while retaining the entry under 1588, extends the limits to c.1585-1598). On this matter, A. C. Partridge has usefully supplemented Nosworthy's earlier Porter studies (*Orthography in Shakespeare* [1964], pp. 16-23). But such similarities as those discussed above, plus others in incident and plot, scarcely make *The Two Angry Women* appear "inevitable" as Shakespeare's "model" for the Folio *Wives*. Nosworthy goes further, however. Examining the Quarto, he deduces, after "a little guarded speculation," that Shakespeare instead employed the somehow available foul papers of Porter's "finished, or nearly so" *Two Merry Women of Abingdon*. One grows nervous.

On February 28, 1599, Porter received forty shillings in exchange for a promise to deliver all his future plays to Henslowe and "in earneste of his boocke called ij mery wemen of abenton." Four days later, Henslowe paid Chettle ten shillings "in earneste of his boocke, wch harey porter & he is a writtinge . . . called the spencers." On March 22, Porter received five pounds, ten shillings for the latter play, and three April entries indicate the completed "spencers" reached the stage. Is it at all conceivable, given Henslowe's spellings, that this lost play was not a chronicle on the Spencers, as is generally assumed, but a comedy called *The Spinsters*, as alternate title to *Two Merry Women*? Is it much less a Henslowe spelling than *Jeffa/Jephthah, henges/Hengist*, or *weascheaster/Westchester*? I mention the possibility, perhaps a readily rejectable one, because if valid it negates much of Nosworthy's argument, and if invalid we have little reason to think *Two Merry Women* approached completion at all, let alone that Shakespeare might somehow have had access to the foul papers.

But let that go. In 1940, Nosworthy wrote as follows: ". . . one imagines that two plays must have sufficed to exhaust the possibilities of the two ladies of Abingdon, and that a third play about them is unlikely. There is no first-rate testimony that this play really belonged to the Abingdon set. The authenticity of the interpolated 'of Abenton' has never . . . been questioned, but it is, in any case, an obvious afterthought" (*MLR*, XXXV, 519). Nosworthy has the right, of course, to change his mind. But he scarcely has the right totally to ignore his previous argument while basing his hypothetical reconstruction of the lost play on contrary assumptions.

As for the implications of the Quarto, Quickly's reference to a 'metamorphosed youth' (sig. G2^v) need not "prove conclusively that this section belonged to a play that had nothing to do with Falstaff" (p. 103), nor does that portion corresponding to the Folio's V.v.107-259 seem much marked by "tokens of Porter's style" (pp. 104-108). Thus I feel unready to concede the "one absolutely certain conclusion," that the Quarto derives in part from a non-Shakespearean manuscript source play.

Hamlet: Even more than with the other portions of the book, these much longer chapters can scarcely be summarized in all their complexity. According to Nosworthy, *Hamlet* was probably designed from the outset for an academic presentation. This accounts for its extraordinary length, its emphasis on characters with university backgrounds, and for much of its sophisticated content. Prior to transcription of his foul papers, Shakespeare marked several passages for deletion and made one or two additions. The transcript itself served as prompt copy for the tragedy's initial performance (at Oxford or Cambridge) and rarely, if ever, thereafter; it was then later used, concurrently with Q2, for the Folio. The foul papers (so difficult as to require frequent consultation of Q1) were the basic copy for Q2. Passages peculiar to Q2 were probably never spoken on the stage in Shakespeare's lifetime. The Folio, on the other hand, represents a stage version, "quite certainly the original one." Q1, in turn, reflects Shakespeare's cut version prepared for the Globe; it "is throughout a memorial reconstruction of an official abridgement of the Folio version, with cuts, amendments and replacements for which Shakespeare was himself responsible." In emending the Folio, which is theatrical and therefore authoritative, Q1 should receive somewhat more respect, Q2 somewhat less, than has been traditional.

On p. 1, Nosworthy concedes that the evidence for *Hamlet*'s being occasional "is perhaps sufficient but certainly no more than that." The bibliographical value, and even the critical value, of these chapters should not depend on our accepting the "occasion" hypothesis. But the hypothesis is central, nevertheless, and one may begin with examining some of the assumptions with which the "occasion" chapter (XI) opens:

> . . . the Folio *Hamlet* runs to approximately 3,700 lines, and that figure alone must surely establish that the extant authentic versions cannot have been intended for the Globe. *Hamlet* is, in fact, the longest play in the canon by several hundred lines, and it is not without significance that the play which runs it a very poor second, *Troilus and Cressida*, was itself a *piece d'occasion* which never reached the public theatre, whose normal requirements apparently amounted to something between 2,700 and 3,300 lines. (p. 164)

We can ignore the question of *Troilus'* theatrical history for the present. But not the rest. How can Nosworthy leap into his hypothesis while ignoring statistics so painstakingly presented by Alfred Hart, years ago, in *Shakespeare and the Homilies*? With respect to average play lengths (far lower than Nosworthy's above) and the implications of *Hamlet's* length, Peter Alexander remains as relevant now as two decades ago: ". . . [Hart] has discussed with patience and lucidity a body of fact that must be properly allowed for . . . in all subsequent discussions" (*RES*, XII [1935], 343). How would Nosworthy explain Jonson's exceptional length, even in plays for the King's Men? or Shakespeare's so frequently exceeding the length required by what Nosworthy calls his "workaday needs" or "basic requirements" at the Globe? Too, should he ignore the implications of title-pages such as that for *The Devil's Charter* ('augmented . . . for the more pleasure and profit of the Reader') or *The Duchess of Malfi* (only 3037 lines, but 'with diverse things printed, that the length of the Play would not beare in the Presentment')? As for that "poor second," *Troilus*, it is barely a poor third, not materially longer than a half dozen of Shakespeare's plays. *Richard III*, the actual "second" and not so "poor," exceeds *Troilus* by 300 lines and was not "occasional."

So far as I know, there is no surviving evidence that either university in Shakespeare's day ever requested of a professional company an "occasional" play such as Nosworthy postulates. Alton's *Academic Drama in Oxford* (pp. 29-95 of which are cited on p. 4) only barely supports the much milder position that "various colleges certainly made payments to professional entertainers and sponsored public performances." For the period of 1590-1620 Alton records just one payment to actors (identity unspecified); the records generally are for expenses incurred in student performances of academic plays, "not works of art" in Alton's phrase. Under what circumstances *Volpone* was performed at Oxford and Cambridge we do not know, but public success appears to have preceded private performance. Evidence must be strong indeed before one will feel ready to accept the hypothesis that *Hamlet* was designed from the first for a university audience.

It is not that strong. This is true even if one accepts all Nosworthy's arguments, including the significance of Polonius having once attended a university, or 'keep' as having a "colloquial university sense" which it did not have in 1600. The relevance of Hamlet's own Wittenberg background has long been emphasized by many critics, none of whom saw any need to infer an "occasional" inspiration for its presence. That Hamlet's friends, true or false, share that background is not surprising (if anything, one might rather be surprised at the absence of references to "school days"). The play is not thereby "made to centre upon what are, in effect, the activities of a group of students" (p. 181). Comparison with *"Tom Brown at Oxford and The Adventures of Mr. Verdant Green"* (p. 173) seems to me less relevant than, for example, comparison with Marlowe's Doctor Faustus, or Webster's Flamineo and

Bosola, or Ford's Giovanni and Orgilus. Nosworthy does mention Faustus, but only to dismiss what seems to many an essential aspect of his tragedy. Undeniably, much in *Hamlet*—even Hamlet's quatrain to Ophelia, which goes unmentioned—would be especially appealing to a university audience, or to any sophisticated and intellectual audience. But that is another matter.

The final *Hamlet* chapter (XII) seeks to establish Q1 as a memorial reconstruction of an abridged Folio version used at the Globe. Like Chapter X ("The General Textual Problems"), except to the degree that the theses in XII depend on the preceding "occasional" hypothesis, Nosworthy must here be judged by his bibliographical peers. I was aware only occasionally of objections, all minor: e.g., 'cinquepace' need not imply that "the offending clown had a stock of five jokes" (p. 193); if 'by chance, as the blinde man catcheth a hare' is "above ordinary prose level" and has "even a touch of distinction" (p. 194), Philip Stubbes deserves equal praise (see Tilley, M81); Horatio's knowledge of King Hamlet's armour need not imply his presence at the battle (p. 200); the couplet repeated from *Twelfth Night* II.iv.119-121 seems scarcely plausible as Shakespeare's own addition to *Hamlet* in revision (p. 204); and Anne of Denmark seems no stronger an explanation for Q1's altered Gertrude (p. 214) than Prince Henry seemed for an absent "mad Prince of *Wales*" in the Folio *Wives* (p. 121). My objections to Chapter X, except for the first, are similarly minor: the implications of Q1's 'To be' soliloquy (pp. 133f.) might be severely complicated, I believe, by echoes recorded in *SQ*, XIV (1963), 87-89; possible verbal or stylistic indebtedness to the *Ur-Hamlet* is too casually set aside (pp. 130f.); that the Pyrrhus speeches parody Aeneas' account in *Dido* is not "almost certain" and cannot legitimately be used to support the *Ur-Hamlet* argument (p. 177's further treatment of *Dido* combines improbability with conjecture disguised as fact); with respect to the 'scarse . . . a blot in his papers' tradition, if the *Sir Thomas More* manuscript is irrelevant to Hamlet's "complexity of utterance" (p. 138), it should not have been relevant to the similarly complex *Troilus and Cressida* (p. 62); Horatio's lines at I.iv. 75-78, deleted in Q2, seem to me far from "pointless except as a preparation for the suicide" of Ophelia (pp. 141f.); 'He keepes them like an Ape' (IV.ii.19) implies no "extraordinary gastronomical process" (p. 161).

According to p. 201, ". . . scraps of evidence, though individually vulnerable, have cumulative weight." This can be true. But occasionally Nosworthy appears to have relied on this assumption to his own disadvantage, rhetorically if not logically. A few ill-considered "scraps," especially if treated as of equal validity with far stronger evidence, impair the effectiveness of the latter. One inevitably feels that what appears sound may to a more qualified reader appear equally vulnerable. I remain convinced, however, that this book has infinitely greater value for Shakespearean textual studies, especially when Nosworthy is himself criticizing current theories, than my largely negative and non-bibliographical focus implies. Thus I reiterate my initial hope: that this provocative book will receive from Mr. Nosworthy's fellow bibliographers the careful consideration and evaluation it appears to deserve.

The University of California, Los Angeles

Shakespeare's Romantic Comedies. The Development of their Form and Meaning by Peter G. Phialas. The University of North Carolina Press, 1966. Pp. xvi + 314. $7.50. *Reviewer: Peter Ure.*

M r. Phialas affirms that Shakespeare's comedies, "*though not sermons*, express fundamental moral convictions" (my italics). We have come a long way from Dr. Johnson, who thought that in his management of his material Shakespeare sacrifices virtue to convenience and "is so much more careful to please than to instruct, that he seems to write without any moral purpose." Nowadays we have no difficulty in discovering "systems of social duty", as Johnson called them, in Shakespeare's plays. When they have been exhibited, these systems turn out to have an unsurprising likeness to those most favoured by twentieth-century academics and professional critics. Mr. Phialas often tells us that the nine comedies which are the subject of his book (*The Comedy of Errors* to *Twelfth Night*) are concerned to find a way of presenting "an ideal attitude towards life and love" (p. 213) and point to "an ideal view of love and life's processes" (p. xvi)—"ideal" meaning "the best possible in our world as we know it." Shakespeare is preoccupied with different and often conflicting conceptions of "man's ideal relationship to woman" (p. 262); he wanted to explore and expound "the ideal attitude towards the experience of being in love" (p. 114). It is far from astonishing that this ideal turns out to be, in the chapter on *As You Like It*, a "balanced attitude to life and love"; Rosalind is the "ideal comic heroine" because she expresses the "perfect equilibrium" between the "idealism of romance and the realism of the working-world." In the chapter on *Much Ado* we learn that "the thought which underlies [Shakespeare's] whole work" is that "love is the only means of achieving harmony and happiness and salvation" (p. 150). The assumption of this study is that the "larger theme" is Shakespeare's first and last interest, and that the more abstractly moralistic the terms in which that theme can be stated the more obviously worthy of the attention of Shakespeare's genius it can be presumed to have been. We are again reminded of an elder critic, Matthew Arnold this time: "what would [Shakespeare] say at seeing his easy morality erected by Germans & others into a system of life, & a thing to be held in view as an object for inward disciplining of oneself towards. He would say—You fools—I have walked thro: life ἐπί ξυροῦ 'ακμῆς God knows how."

Modern criticism, with its far greater knowledge of the official moralisms of Shakespeare's own time, has got very near to presenting us with the kind of Shakespeare whom the Victorian sages might have been able officially to approve for all practical purposes of moral instruction but whom they were unable to discover for themselves, not only because of their ignorance but because of their wild, romantic souls. For Mr. Phialas, Shakespearian comedy is a process whereby various extreme attitudes towards love are juxtaposed and thereby mutually qualify one another by gentle mockery; in so doing, they "point to an optimum, a best possible attitude", one that brings together "realism" and "idealism" (see pp. 214-5). Shakespeare works always at the behest of this shadowy "optimum." One must admit that he would doubtless have claimed, if you had been by to ask him, that comedies taught "amendment of life"; but Mr. Phialas's account of his motivation makes it more unprofessional, more unindividuated—and, above all, much duller—than the plays themselves might lead us to infer that it was. After all, they contain large elements of excess, extravagance, danger and sheer uncovenanted charm. It is all, no doubt, a question of emphasis and tastes. But Mr. Phialas seems uninterested, in the main, in the fact that Shakespeare was devising theatrical artefacts, and that his work, in all its aspects, including the homiletic one, must often have been affected, if not controlled, from moment to moment by his understanding of what would "go" in the theatre. In the case under review, they were *comical* theatrical artefacts as well. "Laughter," as we have bitterly learnt, is a question-begging term, but at the very least the plays studied in this volume were meant to keep actors satisfied and give audiences a good time: man cannot always be a virtuous twentieth-century academic. There are no theatres, no laughs, no lords of misrule, nothing unregenerately destructive or delightfully frightening, nothing at all from the fairground, in Mr. Phialas's version of Shakespearian comedy. All is brought imperturbably into balance, as by the smoothest of moral counsellors. There is a kind of stunning, academic naïveté— not, I think, untypical of the general approach—in one of his remarks about Falstaff: "What Falstaff says and does in *Henry IV* is most carefully calculated by the poet for its comment upon the main action, and this comment is the chief reason for Falstaff's presence in the play" (p. 146). It is with some desperation that one wonders whether Mr. Phialas has ever observed what actually happens to an audience when "Falstaff" is upon the stage, even when the Falstaff is, as so often nowadays, of the gloomy, German, alienated sort. To assume that a true account of Shakespeare's motives in writing comedy can ignore *that* is to be widely astray. But Mr. Phialas, except momentarily in the chapter on *Much Ado,* finds it uncongenial to write in terms of actors, scenes, visual devices and so forth; with his eye fixed on the "ideal," he might as well be writing about novels, treatises or sermons.

If the account of Shakespeare the idealist and moralist seems uncongenial, it cannot be said that the related notion of Shakespeare the artist is any more pleasing. Writing of *A Midsummer Night's Dream,* the author says (p. 114): "Shakespeare began to work on the play by first selecting the idea he wished to dramatize and then choosing the fables and characters accordingly." Some readers will find this sort of Shakespeare not the easiest to imagine; but it is a Shakespeare of that kind who is the driving-force of the "development" which is called attention to in the sub-title of this book and may be said to supply its motive power. Its author is trying to describe what in one place he calls Shakespeare's "search for a comic form which would best incorporate a love-story" (p. 148). Throughout, Shakespeare is seen making efforts to develop this comic form; he searches, plans, explores themes, sets out on a conscious programme (or is it "perhaps unconscious in the beginning"—see p. 217?) of artistic self-improvement, reaches significant milestones and looks round for somewhere else to go on to, and so on. Mr. Phialas's descriptions of Shakespeare's plays are so muddled up with decisions and motivations imputed to the playwright himself that it is hard for the ordinary reader to fight free of this imaginary Shakespeare who is being created on every page, and to remind himself that he is after all only an invention and a metaphor. It is a defect of the author's qualities. Mr. Phialas has seen no way in which to gratify his ambition to write about "development" except by positing a developer and calling him Shakespeare. It is odd how precisely this fictional character corresponds, in manners, motivation, style of thought, terminology, assumptions about and knowledge of his age, to a learned and intelligent commentator of the mid-twentieth century. Did Mr. Phialas never catch a glimpse of his own face in the glass?

The method, though not of course new, is still irritating, partly because it is the commentator who seems to be in charge of designing Shakespeare's plays. It is also hard, if one wishes to describe where the real value of the book lies, to disentangle what this "Shakespeare" is said to *do,* from what Mr. Phialas says is actually *there* in the plays— the latter being a far more useful aspect of his undertaking. The difficulty doubtless arises from taking nine comedies (which comprise all the solid evidence we have about anything) and trying to link them in a continuous chain of development, rationally explicable in the terms of twentieth-century criticism. Mr. Phialas, therefore, has necessarily imposed upon himself the task of inferring the nature of a chain from its links; he need not, though, have appeared so confident about his knowledge of the chain-maker. It is perhaps at all times insufferably rash to infer an artist's development, in the broad sense in which the term is used in this book, from the evidence yielded by a comparison of his works written at different times, when there is no other evidence (such as statements *in propria persona* or by contemporaries, letters and journals). When even basic dates are uncertain, it is rasher still, and Mr. Phialas is several times constrained to argue circularly on this account. The present state of our knowledge may be such that, with very careful work (none of which has as yet been properly done), we might learn to describe "Shakespeare's development" in respect of a few fairly simple technical devices, such as Rhyme or Disguise; although even in tackling some apparently simple task of that sort we should have to guard against anachronistic Darwinian assumptions. But the attempt to describe his total moral and artistic evolution, with all the relatedness that that involves, even (or perhaps more especially) over only a segment of his work, mainly leads, I think, to our seeing our own faces in the glass.

Once the reader has, so far as is possible—and it is not wholly possible—emancipated himself from the phantom Shakespeare, he can plainly see that Mr. Phialas has plenty that is suggestive and interesting to say, although he does not seem to succeed in producing a complete and satisfying account of any one of the nine plays as a work of theatrical art. In the earlier part of the book, the account of *The Taming of the Shrew* is very selective (the taming process itself is virtually omitted) and that of *The Two Gentlemen of Verona* is too preoccupied with the final scene. Later, the concept of "symbolic structure"—also, if I understand the matter rightly, called "analogical structure"—is an interesting one; but when it is applied to the relations between pastoralism and romantic love in *As You Like It*, or between extravagant loving and extravagant speaking in *Love's Labour's Lost,* or between fairies and humans in *A Midsummer Night's Dream*, it does not seem to throw any *new* light on the various relatednesses and dimensions of those three plays; whether or not "analogical structure" is a useful idea in itself, we have long known about what it seems to be pointing at.

Mr. Phialas has a very good chapter on *The Merchant of Venice,* with an admirable account of Shylock (pp. 159 ff.). He has much that is sensible and true to say about *Much Ado,* although it seems an index of a rather unsubtle reading of that portion of the play to declare *tout court* that Benedick and Beatrice "begin by scorning love and each other." For some reason, he is extremely interested in the songs in the plays; into them he reads manifold significances—but this merely draws attention to his relative indifference to other theatrical devices. He is illuminating on *Love's Labour's Lost* in general (pp. 86 ff.), but the chapter illustrates, perhaps in inevitably extreme form, what seems to be a general fault of presentation: the quest for completeness, of a kind usually associated with the doctoral student, has induced the author to spend many pages at the beginning of each chapter discussing dates and sources, retailing various information, refuting Dover Wilson, and engaging in other majestical pastimes which don't seem particularly fresh or relevant to the reader who wants a new account of the comedy. *Shakespeare's Romantic Comedies* could easily have been 100 pages shorter. No use, either, is served by prodigious notes like number 68 on p. 297 or number 10 on p. 286. These exhausting lists of articles and books on a particular sub-topic certainly assure us, as do the notes in general, that the author has done his reading; but such assurances can safely be reserved for exacting examiners by nervous candidates. The University of North Carolina Press would have done better to spend their money not on spattering the book with vignettes—pleasant though the spatter is—but on printing the notes and references at the foot of the pages.

It has not been possible to see this book except as a quantity of by no means despicable ingredients floating about in a content of highly questionable assumptions. But *Shakespeare's Romantic Comedies* is a thoughtful and earnestly composed undertaking. In so far as it is a worthy attempt to investigate the Shakespearian fusion of comedy with romantic love, it gets some way forward with the important task of defining more clearly what, apart from genius, separates Shakespeare's comedy from that of his contemporaries. The more's the pity that Mr. Phialas, even if only for purposes of contrast, doesn't go beyond a bare mention of the names of Lyly or Chapman or Middleton or Dekker.

University of Newcastle upon Tyne

The English History Play in the Age of Shakespeare by Irving Ribner. Second Edition. Barnes & Noble, 1965. Pp. xii + 356. $6.75. *Reviewer: John R. Elliott, Jr.*

When it originally appeared in 1957, under the imprint of the Princeton University Press, Irving Ribner's *The English History Play in the Age of Shakespeare* was the first full-scale study of that genre since Schelling's *The Elizabethan Chronicle Play* in 1902. Following the conclusions reached by Lily B. Campbell and E. M. W. Tillyard in their studies of Shakespeare's historical drama, Ribner rejected the earlier notion of the history play as an episodic pageant, lacking in coherent form and serious intent, and sought to define the genre in the light of Elizabethan political doctrine and historical purpose. The book surveyed in detail the various forms taken by the history play throughout the Tudor and Stuart period, including analyses of the development of the history play from medieval religious drama, the Senecan and nationalistic plays of the 80's and early 90's, the adaptation of history to tragedy, the biographical play, the legendary play, and the historical romance. It contained as well two chapters on Shakespeare and an introductory account of Tudor historical writing and its relation to drama. In an appendix, Ribner furnished a chronological list of English history plays from 1519 to 1653, together with a bibliography of relevant primary and secondary materials.

A revised edition of *The English History Play* has now been issued, this time by Barnes and Noble. The apparatus of the book has been brought up to date, so that footnotes and bibliography now include references to work done on the subject of the history play since 1957. Professor Ribner explains the more substantive revisions in the text of the work as follows:

> Although the point of view of the study, as explained in the Preface to the first edition, has not been altered or modified, a good many paragraphs have been rewritten, largely for the sake of greater clarity. It seemed to me in going over the work after some lapse of time that, as in almost any historical study of limited and circumscribed scope, it left various matters either unsaid or merely touched upon so lightly that there was a danger of conveying to the reader too narrow a view of some of the plays under discussion. Where it seemed to me that some further exposition or qualification might be of value, I have here tried to supply it.

Readers uncertain as to exactly what these changes entail may gain some idea of their extent and importance from the following summary of a collation of several chapters of the revised edition with the corresponding chapters in the original one. Chapter I, "History and Drama in the Age of Shakespeare," is reprinted without change, except for a few additional footnotes. In Chapter II, "The Emergence of a Dramatic Genre," three paragraphs (on pages 31, 47, & 48 of the new edition) have been reworded, without substantial change, and one new paragraph (p. 55) added, incorporating Spivack's analysis of the role of the Vice in *Cambises.* Chapter IV, "The Early Shakespeare," contains two new paragraphs (pp. 95-6 & 118), one emphasizing the thematic unity of the *Henry VI* plays, the other allowing for the challenge posed by Richard III's cynical humour to the orthodox moral universe of that play. In Chapter VIII, "Legendary and Anglo-Saxon History," Ribner adds two passages (pp. 248 & 258-9) qualifying his earlier emphasis on the importance of the political issues in *King Lear* and *Macbeth,* although he maintains his claim that each play "is firmly linked to the history play tradition." The most considerable changes in the new edition occur in Chapter VI, on "Shakespeare's Second Tetralogy." Several pages in Ribner's earlier discussion of *Richard II* and *Henry IV* have been rewritten and added to, with the apparent purpose of toning down the claims made there for Shakespeare's sense of *realpolitik.* Ribner now admits, with Traversi, that in the victory of Henry IV "there is a sense of human loss which makes the tragedy of the play;" and, with Sen Gupta, that "Shakespeare in his history plays never limits his attention to the mere political roles of his characters . . . Shakespeare's histories are the expression of a profoundly moral view of human relations which does not differ essentially from that which he expressed in his non-historical plays" (p. 158). At the same time, however, Ribner strengthens his argument in support of Shakespeare's sympathy for Bolingbroke's rebellion, and in his "Note on Tudor Political Doctrine" at the end of the volume adds some new material on the difference between the theory and the practice of absolute obedience in the sixteenth century.

In sum, while the value of *The English History Play* as a work of reference has been enhanced by its up-dating of notes and bibliography, the extent and importance of the revisions in the new edition are minimal, affecting the book's basic argument only in very minor ways. As Professor Ribner notes, the "point of view" of the study has not been altered. As a result, scholars owning the first edition may well continue to consult it without undue fear of remaining ignorant of significant new discoveries or opinions. But if the book's original strengths thus remain the same, so, naturally, do its weaknesses, and it may not be out of place at this late date to reconsider exactly what Ribner's study has contributed to our understanding of the history play, and what it leaves yet to be done.

The main problem in dealing with the history play is to define it. The term itself is a modern invention applied to a large and amorphous group of plays to which the Elizabethans themselves gave a variety of theatrical designations. The value of Ribner's study therefore depends very largely, as the author recognizes, on its "point of view," that is, on the criteria which it establishes for the definition of the genre. While the new volume's dust jacket claims that the book furnishes "a definition of the history play as a distinct dramatic genre," Professor Ribner himself is more modest. In his opening chapter, "History and Drama in the Age of Shakespeare" (which, as I have noted, is reprinted without change from the first edition), Ribner declares that he has sought only a "workable definition" of the history play, assuming that it consists, at most, only of an adaptation of the traditional dramatic genres to a new subject matter and purpose. For Ribner, the history play is not a distinct genre at all, but a very large grouping of plays of every possible shape, united only by the supposed truth of their contents and their fulfillment of one or more of the recognized purposes of history (Ribner enumerates seven such purposes). In short, Ribner has merely expanded upon the definition of the history play originally proposed by Hardin Craig as "a grouping of dramas, not on the basis of form, but of subject matter and purpose" (*J. Q. Adams Memorial Studies,* Folger Library, 1948, pp. 55-64).

Now, one implication of this definition is that for the Elizabethans the purposes of history must have been sufficiently like the esthetic and moral purposes of drama to enable the forms of the traditional dramatic genres to be adapted to historical subject matter. That this was so would seem to be proved by the emergence of early history plays such as *Kyng Johan* and *Gorboduc* from both the medieval religious drama and Senecan tragedy, as well as by the comfortable co-existence between the history play and the traditional genres throughout the period, a co-existence which produced such mixed bags as "Comical Histories," "True Tragedies," and "Merry Comedies . . . drawn out of the most famous History." Indeed, the very possibility of a history play would seem to depend upon a conception of history as being sufficiently universal in scope and meaning to make it a fit subject for art. Such a conception was largely lacking in classical thought, with the result that Aristotle firmly rejected history as a basis for drama. It is, however, a marked feature of Christian theology, based as it is on the incarnation of God in history, with the result that the first Christian dramas—the medieval Biblical cycles—are in every sense of the term, history plays. In view of the homogeneity of the historical, theological, and esthetic purposes of such a drama, Ribner's insistence that a play must, in order to qualify as a history play, have as its *major* goal the fulfillment of a specifically historical or political purpose seems unnecessarily restrictive. Plays which "may have serious political undertones, as does *Hamlet*," Ribner writes, "cannot be called history plays, for their political implications are secondary to the dominant purposes of the plays" (p. 25). The arbitrariness of such a rule is apparent in the inconsistency with which Ribner himself applies it. For instance, while he excludes *Hamlet* from the genre of history play, he includes *King Lear,* in spite of his explicit qualification in the new edition that "in *King Lear* Shakespeare was not primarily concerned with political problems" (p. 248). Ribner's reason for including *Lear* is that it "is a great personal tragedy with deep ethical concerns, but in so far as it involves the collapse and restoration of order in the state it is a political play as well, firmly linked to the tradition of historical drama" (p. 248). The recognition implied here that a play may be significantly historical without being predominantly political certainly seems an advance over Ribner's earlier and narrower definition of the genre; it remains unclear, however, why such a description is not as applicable to *Hamlet* as it is to *Lear.* In fact, there are very few Elizabethan plays which do not have some political "undertones," which are not set in some distinctive historical milieu, and which do not depend upon the audience's awareness of social and political norms for their effect and their meaning. One suspects, sympathetically, that Ribner has introduced his distinction between "dominant" and "secondary" political implications, inconsistent as he is in applying it, in order to save himself from having to treat nearly every Elizabethan drama as, in one way or another, a history play.

A case might well be made, then, for an even broader approach to the history play than Ribner has taken, a study, let us say, simply of the historical elements in Elizabethan plays of all kinds. In part, Ribner's book does accomplish this, in spite of its self-imposed restrictions, for the author takes note of a number of plays—biographical, legendary, and romantic dramas—only tangentially connected with the history play proper, as he has originally defined it. At the same time, however, an equally strong case might be made for a more specific definition of the genre. Having recognized that there is scarcely a play in which the acute Elizabethan consciousness of history and politics is not in some way reflected, we can also recognize, as the Elizabethans themselves seem to have, that there are some plays that reflect this consciousness more acutely than others, and, more importantly, that do so in ways which alter the form as well as the purpose of the traditional dramatic

316

genres. From the very beginnings of dramatic production in the Middle Ages, Englishmen wrote plays which derived their structure not from other dramatic models but from the patterns inherent, or supposed to be inherent, in history itself. The form of the Corpus Christi play is the form of Christian history as it was set forth by the exegetes and in the liturgy of the Church. The structure of *Kyng Johan* is the pattern of English history as Bale conceived it, a pattern which he set forth in identical form in his non-dramatic historical writings and which is also to be found in Foxe's *Book of Martyrs*. And it may be significant, in spite of the vagaries of Elizabethan dramatic nomenclature, that the first use of the word "history" as a specifically theatrical designation occurs on the title-page of the Quarto *1 Henry IV*, a play which resists classification either as tragedy or comedy and whose complex form reflects the more secular analysis of political forces typical of late sixteenth-century historiography.[1] Precisely what this Quarto editor, and the later Folio editors, had in mind when they designated plays as "histories" we may never know with certainty, but it seems clear that they meant by it something quite distinct from other dramatic genres. Might we not, then, attempt to distinguish between those history plays which derive their form at second hand, so to speak, by borrowing it from other dramatic or literary genres, and those which take their form directly from the patterns of history itself, as these patterns were variously conceived in the sixteenth and seventeenth centuries? Even if Ribner is correct in asserting that "the history play cannot be defined on the basis of dramatic form, for the forms in which we find it are many" (p. 7), might we not possibly come closer to the Elizabethans' own understanding of their art if we were to inquire further into what happens to these dramatic forms under the impact of political and historical subjects, particularly in the hands of such an imaginative and creative historical dramatist as Shakespeare? The history play is, in Una Ellis-Fermor's phrase, one of the "frontiers" of drama, that is, it is an attempt to convert into drama material which is, by nature, ordinarily unsusceptible of dramatic treatment. The answer to the question how such a conversion is possible would seem to lie as much in the relationship between the form of history and the form of drama as in the content or purpose of either.

When all this is said, however, Ribner's study of the Elizabethan history play remains a substantial achievement. It is a book which, like many pioneering works of scholarship, has opened up a field of investigation in a way that alone makes possible the very corrections and refinements which future scholars may bring to it. If one wishes that the opportunity of a new edition had stimulated the author to a reëxamination of some of his basic premises, one must also recognize that the charting of so wide an expanse demands above all the steering of a safe course. And if one hopes that more adventurous explorers will follow in Ribner's wake, one hopes equally that their discoveries will be based on the same judgment and breadth of knowledge that he has brought to the study of the English history play.

University of California, Santa Barbara

Notes:

(1) The structure of the Corpus Christi play and its historical basis have been discussed in two recent studies: O. B. Hardison, Jr., *Christian Rite and Christian Drama* (Baltimore, 1965); and V. A. Kolve, *The Play Called Corpus Christi* (Stanford, 1966). Bale's conception of English history is studied in William Haller, *The Elect Nation: The Meaning and Relevance of Foxe's Book of Martyrs* (New York, 1963), pp. 60-71. The use of the word "history" as a theatrical designation has been traced by Allardyce Nicoll, "'Tragical-Comical-Historical-Pastoral': Elizabethan Dramatic

Nomenclature," "Bulletin of the John Rylands Library, XLIII (1960), 70-87. Late Elizabethan historiography has been studied by F. Smith Fussner, *The Historiographical Revolution: English Historical Writing and Thought, 1580-1640* (New York, 1962). (None of these works is listed in Ribner's revised bibliography.)

"The Giant Race Before The Flood": Pre-Restoration Drama on the Stage and in the Criticism of the Restoration by Gunnar Sorelius. Studia Anglistica Upsaliensia, 4, Acta Universitatis Upsaliensis, 1966. Pp. 227. *Reviewer: Charles H. Shattuck.*

For the last forty years, students who have wanted to know what happened to Shakespeare during the Restoration period have turned to Hazleton Spencer's *Shakespeare Improved* (1927)—a book still useful as a running introduction to the subject but sadly dated by its almost comical outbursts of bardolatry. Spencer's ridicule of the Shakespeare adaptations—his battery of synonyms for "bad," "worse," and "worst"—does not amuse us any longer quite as Spencer meant it to. Of the adaptations as a whole he concluded flatly: "I am not aware that anything good can be said."

By the 1920's bardolatry had slowly won its victories and seemed an assured faith. Except for an occasional echo of Cibber's *Richard III*, all vestiges of the old corruptions had been extirpated from the stage. Under the scholarly direction of Bridges-Adams, Stratford-upon-Avon was gathering momentum. Pure Shakespeare lay ahead.

Spencer had probably never heard of Komisarjevsky, and though he spat the word "precieux" at contemporary stage designers who concerned themselves too much with scenery and lighting, he could not have dreamed of what the oncoming generation of stage directors would do to Shakespeare in the way of "interpretation." If Tyrone Guthrie can drop the clown out of *All's Well*, how shall we scorn Nahum Tate for dropping the Fool from *Lear*? Robert Graves revises the language of *Much Ado* for modern ears and Franco Zeffirelli stages it as a Sicilian folk festival. David Warner acts Hamlet as a limp-wristed anti-hero who dies snickering. A production of the *Dream* last year was billed as a "psychedelic voyage into the sexy world of Shakespeare." I mention but a few most recent of the hundreds of "interpretations" of Shakespeare which since the 1930's have killed bardolatry dead and totally demolished the Spencerian arrogance toward staged Shakespeare of the past. Who can any longer give low marks to the Davenants, Drydens, and Cibbers who in their day and way sought also to make Shakespeare "say something" to their people?

Better historians than Spencer then was have taught us to look upon the old adaptations soberly and try to understand what made them what they are. A decade ago, for instance, George Branam in his *Eighteenth-Century Adaptations of Shakespearean Tragedy* studied Shakespeare in the Augustan age with admirable sympathy and sense. Two years ago, in *Five Restoration Adaptations of Shakespeare*, Christopher Spencer provided us what Hazleton Spencer would not have thought worth the bother—five of the most famous Restoration versions worked up under painstaking disciplines of textual scholarship—together with the injunction to read them not as butcherings of Shakespeare but as plays in their own right, as authentic Restoration art.

The Swedish scholar Gunnar Sorelius has now undertaken to reassess the status and progress not only of Shakespeare but of all the pre-Commonwealth drama as it survived on the Restoration stage and in Restoration criticism. When the Flood receded, the theatre artists stood in a bare and empty place where they were to build a drama of their own. Two new technical instruments lay to hand which would both inspire and confuse them: changeable scenery and women to play the women's parts. Three strong impulses rose among them or were put upon them, which likewise both hurt and helped them: *rationalism*, which insisted upon almost mathematical clarity of purpose, form, and language; *moralism*, which demanded the suppression of obscenity and the restoration of the stage as a school of conduct; and *patriotism*, which directed the artists to look to the native tradition for exemplars.

In their books and in their memories lay the relics of what Sorelius calls "the greatest drama ever created," what Dryden would call "the giant race before the flood." They took up the old drama exactly as the Cavaliers had left it in 1642. Thus the tragi-comedies of Beaumont and Fletcher, instinct with courtly wit and sentiment, were at first their overwhelming favorites. A few of Ben Jonson's comedies which demonstrated his principles of unity came next in their esteem. Shakespeare, old-fashioned and irregular, ran a poor third. Within the forty year period this order would be exactly reversed, but the victory of "Shakespeare" was not entirely a victory of Shakespeare. Many of his plays did not please at all, and many came through only in versions scraped clean of poetry as well as ambiguity, or in versions rebuilt from the ground.

For the first time England was seriously infected by Criticism, which the English playwrights were not sturdy enough to resist. Dryden they could have coped with, for Dryden was a playwright himself and had to keep an open mind. The *Essay of Dramatic Poesy* juggles and plays with ideas rather than imposes them; and as the years went on, Dryden could accommodate his theories: lean toward French practices, abandon them; subscribe to rhyme, abandon rhyme; overpraise Jonson at the expense of Shakespeare, reverse that stand. But there were harsher arbiters to reckon with—among them Thomas Rymer, a strident, bullying sort of umpire, whose *Tragedies of the Last Age* (1677) enforced the ideas of decorum and poetic justice. Decorum limited characters strictly to those kinds of language and action ideally suited to their social status. Poetic justice compelled all plots to reward the virtuous and punish the wicked. As Sorelius says, "Poetic justice is the death of tragedy." Rymer eventually lost credit because of his ridiculous abuse of *Othello* (*A Short View of Tragedy*, 1692), but the main rules he had formulated stuck firmly, and thence began the two-hundred year decline of English drama into sentimentality, dullness, and melodrama. The tragic writer who was so bold or so inept as to kill off his virtuous characters had to apologize for his "Opposition to a known Rule in Poetry."

In a chapter devoted to Comedy, Sorelius explains how the native art developed from native tradition rather than by borrowings from the French. Jonson's rules of order, Beaumont and Fletcher's courtliness, and Shakespeare's variety of invention were the springs which fed the main stream of comedy. Romantic comedy and shapeless "dull follies" of fantastic adventure were rejected; but Fletcherian love stories were welcome as carriers of sentiment and elegant behavior. Satire was embraced for its educative power—to whip knaves and fools, to encourage manners and wisdom and virtue. From the Jonson bequest came all that was needful in lessons of form: the unities of time, place, and action, and the techniques of connecting scene to scene. Unity of action strictly enforced might have drawn too tight a net, but Jonson's own practice proved the value of a numerous *dramatis personae*, and excuses were readily available to justify the English habit of multiple plotting. In the art of character portrayal, native models of both wit and humor were drawn upon, the higher value being placed upon wit (freed of puns) as a means of improving·conversation among gentlemen.

The case for native origins of Tragedy is muddled with controversy, and is perhaps less interesting anyway because of the comparative failure of the age to achieve so much in that genre. The false start into heroic tragedy in rhymed couplets was spurred initially by the frenchified taste of the King: Orrery testifies that he wrote *The General* "because I found his majty Relish'd rather, the French Fassion of Playes, then the English." Yet, as Richard Flecknoe observed and modern scholars have confirmed, the heroic style had been antici- pated by Beaumont and Fletcher and refined by Suckling and other Cavalier poets. Preciosity of style and the Love and Honor theme were common enough in England well before 1642. The heroic fad diminished in the later 1670's, and something like a Shakespearean revival set in. The rediscovery of Longinus' *Of the Sublime* encouraged an appreciation of the Shake- spearean variety of passions and vividness of depiction, of the Shakespearean modes of dis- order and metaphor. But ingrained habit, the temper of the age, and Thomas Rymer stopped the revival from taking hold. Just at that time, in 1677, Rymer loosed his blast against the old English tragedies and issued the catch-phrase "poetic justice." Four years later the greatest of English tragedies was rewritten to prove "that Truth and Vertue shall at last succeed."

The chapter devoted to Restoration adaptations of the older drama does not go into minute analysis of every play that was given a new face, but is concerned rather with the basic purposes that underlay the work. Adaptation was on the whole, barring an occasional cheap plagiarism, "an honourable undertaking." The new versions, many of them made by the best dramatists of the day, were "deliberate and serious endeavours to make the necessary adjustments in what they recognized as great masterpieces." Could the Restoration artists have heard a certain nineteenth-century bardolator's cry of "Withered be the hand, palzied be the arm, that ever dares to touch one of Shakespeares plays!" they would have thought him mad. Sometimes they altered the plays simply to enrich them with the splendid new technical facilities of the Restoration playhouse: music, scenes and machines, actresses. Always they clarified language. Sometimes they strengthened faltering plots, pruned out vulgarities, improved moral tone. Davenant's *Law Against Lovers* was, among other things, an attempt to salvage Beatrice and Benedick from a "bad" play and give them significant work to do in a good one. The Dryden-Davenant version of *The Tempest* was by no means an exercise in bawdry, as has long been insisted, but a playful (innocent and loving) exten- sion of the theme of "Innocence and Love," a study of "natural man." In his *Troilus* Dryden undertook by honored principle to transmute a chaotic text into perfect tragedy, and in the Troilus-Hector scene to emulate the friendship theme of the Brutus-Cassius scene in *Julius Caesar*. Shadwell's *Timon*, besides underscoring political ideas of contemporary relevancy, aimed for heightened pathos and unity though the invented love stories.

Three centuries later, thanks to generations of scholarship, it is our privilege to under- stand the Elizabethans and Jacobeans on their own terms better than Dryden's generation could, and for the most part to prefer the originals to any adaptations—at least in the study. What happens to the old plays on our stages is another matter. Our adaptations do not get printed. But if they are remembered at all in times to come, they too will surely seem to distant observers irreverent, ignorant, perverted, and absurd; will need a new Sorelius to explain them.

The University of Illinois

The Achievement of Shakespeare's Measure for Measure by David Lloyd Steven- son. Cornell University Press, 1966. Pp. 169. $5.75. *Reviewer: Herbert Weil, Jr.*

For David Lloyd Stevenson, *Measure for Measure*, "an intellectual tour de force," is Shakespeare's "greatest comedy." It is both "Shakespeare's most ingeniously constructed comedy" and "finally, a comedy which unlocks our most profound awareness of the nature of an ineluctable evil in man." As readers of Professor Stevenson's excellent article, "Design and Structure in *Measure for Measure*" (*ELH*, 1956), might expect, his book proves far more successful in establishing some aspects of the play's ingenious construction than in probing the nature of "ineluctable evil in man."

In fact, this essay, which offered a much more careful and thorough exposition of the play than many better-known, anthologized pieces, provides the substance for most of the argument in the book, not only for its initial chapter predictably titled "Design and Structure: *Measure for Measure* as Intellectual Comedy." The second chapter, "The Substratum of Meaning" offers "A Scene by Scene Interpretation of the Action." Then come two chapters describing criticism of the play, and a summary. The first stresses the resistance to the play of those who feel "its fundamental intentions are blurred by a faulty construction" and the next discusses the advocates of "Theological Exegesis." In these chapters the author adds many examples to those in his earlier article, impressively establishing his point that, unlike more recent scholars, 18th and 19th century critics—even when "provoked to comment on *Measure* in opposite ways . . . would have agreed that the play was not obscure." An appendix reprints "with a few minor differences in wording," Stevenson's 1959 *ELH* article, "The Historical Dimension in *Measure for Measure*: The Role of James I in the Play." This essay stresses the court performance of the play in 1604 and alleged references to the *Basilicon Doron*. Rather startlingly it ignores the context—Angelo's soliloquy describing his newly awakened lust—for the supposed compliment to James I (II.iv.24). Because the author confesses that the matter of this essay "does not really fit into a critical evaluation of the play," and because his arguments are developed much more fully by Robert G. Shedd in his 1953 University of Michigan dissertation, I shall not discuss them further here.

In a book almost half of which is devoted to brief summaries of criticism, it is surprising to find missing so many of the better and more influential critics of *Measure*. Among those never discussed are Rossiter, Ure, Schanzer, Ornstein, Leech, Evans, the major introduction by Lever to the new Arden edition, and the relevant discussions of distinct types of Elizabethan marriage contracts. Stevenson gleans phrases and sentences from many critics and scholars, but he never deals in any depth or detail with the shortcomings he alleges. Even when one agrees with his reservations, one recognizes that Stevenson—much like his subjects—asserts his conclusions without adequate supporting evidence. These two chapters, coming as they do after Stevenson's own scene-by-scene-interpretation, need less attention than his own explication.

Because Stevenson combines sharp perceptions with misleading claims, his reading deserves careful evaluation by students of *Measure*. Yet almost every major assertion in the book requires a more precise formulation if it is to become accurate for the many perspectives demanded by the play.

The primary argument of the book claims that critics have refused to consider *Measure for Measure* as "a brilliant self-contained artistic achievement which carries its meaning within its own dramatic design" (p. 5). So far, so good. But the next sentence of the introduction goes on to declare, "The impulses it teases alive strike deeply, and with great subtlety and range, into our covert, wordless knowledge of the role of sex in men's lives, into our sense of the human being's endless liability to desire, our sense of the devious ways in which physical lust interpenetrates and controls other more apparent motives, and dominates rational thought." Several lines later, the author forecasts his conclusion, "I should call *Measure* an intellectual comedy with a clear, firm dramatic structure designed to release or unlock our inner world of sexual 'knowing' and our inner world of non-institutionalized moral cognition and judgment." However suggestive the play and its critic may be, I suspect that few of its admirers would willingly base their appreciation of *Measure for Measure* on the sexual discoveries released by its action. What do we learn about the lusts of Angelo or of Lucio that is not clear on our first reading? What depth or subtlety is attempted in representing the sexual desires of Claudio, of Mariana, or of Kate Keepdown? And if some revelation of hidden sexual "knowing" is the *purpose* of the play, how can we explain its lack of development in the final acts?

When Stevenson is discussing the design of the play, valid observations abound. Even here, however, the author has a tendency to push too far, to promote the partial truth to an excess (pp. 9-10):

> *Measure for Measure* . . . as its title suggests, is overtly almost grossly, schematic in its architecture. The arbitrary contrasts in moral attitude and moral decision among the principal characters in the play are precisely balanced and intentionally evident. The plot movement is made equally schematic. By the play's special dramatic ordering we are made fully aware that we are witnessing a repetitive plot movement in which the second half of the play is a replaying of the situation discussed in the first half, but to a contrasting conclusion.

Once again, there are potentially profound insights here—but the balance is hardly so precise, the comparison of plot and character are hardly measurable as "equal." The author insists that the characters "are deliberately simplified and made less interesting in themselves than is Hamlet, for instance, or Falstaff" [!] and are sacrificed to exciting lines and "coldly comic irony and paradox." When it fails to be alert to tone or dramatic emphasis, this approach may lead to readings at best only partially valid, such as: "We have not been called upon to evaluate Isabella's chastity any more than we have been called upon to evaluate that of Elbow's wife" (p. 31).

Never clearly defined is the way in which the second half of the play repeats and alters the first. Very few of the play's critics, much less its directors, spectators, and readers have been "fully aware" that its second half "replays" the first. In what senses is this true? Only in the loosest and most general ways are the pattern and situations repeated. Stevenson bases his "crucial turning point" between the two halves of the play on the major change he finds in Isabella. But her line to the Duke, "I have the spirit to do anything that appears not foul in the truth of my spirit," cannot bear the weight of Stevenson's interpretation as "the dramatically effective beginning of the dissolution of her overweening 'goodness,' the beginning of her redemption into actual livable goodness." Even more important for Stevenson's claim that a carefully planned order is achieved is his exaggerated description of "the woman who emerges from her [Isabella] to conduct the Mariana episode, the woman who in Act III puts on the 'destin'd livery' of secular femininity" (p. 27). Few readers will take so seriously a role that is barely represented on stage. Nor should we ignore, in order to find such a clear transformation, the first appearance of the novice Isabella expressing her compassionate sympathy for the pregnant Juliet.

Stevenson stresses very heavily the symmetry of the play which becomes for him the primary determinant of moral and emotional character. He himself structures his analysis not by themes, language, plot or ironies, but through consideration of characters in three main groupings: 1) the Duke of Vienna, viewed as "spokesman for the audience, its articulate representative in the play"; 2) Claudio and Juliet; and 3) Angelo and Isabella. He finds that Claudio and Juliet are "placed by Shakespeare at dead center and not themselves subjected to the reversals of the play, but are the causal agents of such reversals in others (p. 14) . . . [and again] Claudio and Juliet are central to the play as the paired and parodied representatives of a kind of norm of sensual behavior" (p. 16). Yet it is Angelo and Isabella whose "actions and decisions" are the main ones in the play. "Quite unlike the protagonists in Shakespeare's romantic comedies, Angelo and Isabella exist in *Measure for Measure* to demonstrate the ironies in which they are involved" (p. 18).

The author's strategy tends to eliminate any integrity of individual character. He writes that:

> Isabella's virtue . . . flourishes in an intellectual comedy carefully kept in equilibrium. . . . She is a kind of obverse to Angelo, in which the ironies of attitude and decision by which she exists in the play are complementary to those of her opposite. Just as Angelo turns out to be infinitely more depraved than the lovers he condemns, so too the 'enskied and sainted' Isabella is revealed to be totally merciless in her reviling of her brother, for whose life she had so arduously pleaded mercy. And to keep the reversals which flow from this pair of rhetoricians in complete equilibrium, the play is allowed to come to an end only at the moment of exact equivalence between Isabella and Angelo (pp. 23-5).

This argument helps correct a fairly general tendency to ignore the qualities Isabella and Angelo share, while emphasizing the distinctions between them. But once again, Stevenson tends to distort his insights by reducing these major distinctions between them to little or no significance. The author is led by his conception of schematic neatness to advance as supporting evidence dubious readings of individual passages:

> In order to heighten the audience's sense of the linked relation of these two in the structure of *Measure for Measure*, both Angelo and Isabella, on their first appearance in the play, make public boast of the virtues with which they are to be identified. Angelo, having been cited by Escalus as the only man in Vienna worthy to exercise ducal power, self-righteously demands:
>
> > Now, good my lord,
> > Let there be some more test made of my metal
> > Before so noble and so great a figure
> > Be stamp'd upon it. (I.i.48)
>
> Isabella's first words in the play, interlocking her role with that of Angelo, are a contentious quibbling that the order of Saint Clare does not have strict enough rules (p. 17).

Stevenson observes correctly that Isabella's first lines, "wishing a more strict restraint / Upon the sisterhood," suggest a proud speaker, but surely he exaggerates in describing the heroine here as "a woman in love with an image of herself in the role of a legendary saint." How many members of the audience would remember Angelo's first speech after more than 300 lines, comprising three expository scenes that introduce Claudio, Lucio, many other characters, the central plot situation, present the return of the Duke, and his donning the disguise of a friar? And why—except to fit the scheme—are Angelo's lines "self-righteous" rather than an appropriate, modest response to his ruler's praise? Four pages earlier Stevenson has referred to the "intellectual-moral experiment . . . by which Angelo, hitherto virtuous in name only, must translate his theoretical rectitude into action." But what evidence is there that Angelo has been "virtuous in name only?" And if this were true, why should the respected Escalus (in the speech Stevenson cites but leaves apparently inexplicable) unreliably praise him as the only man in Vienna worthy to serve as deputy?

Although this may seem to place undue emphasis on what some might consider relatively minor points, it does permit us to see in relatively brief compass the sort of interpretation of discrete passages that is only too typical in the book. Again and again, the lines of the play are distorted, are reduced to a single meaning that must fit a readily recognizable scheme. And this scheme too often seems to become for Stevenson the primary end of Shakespeare's dramaturgy.

Furthermore, such an emphasis on "equivalent" design may show very well some ways in which the audience is prepared, but it misleads by leaving no room for surprise even on initial exposure to the play. In discussing "Isabella's ferocity toward her brother," Stevenson argues (pp. 28-29):

> The whole play up to this point has prepared us for it by Isabella's initial self-righteousness. . . . Moreover, we would surely be totally unprepared for a display of tender solicitude on the part of Isabella toward Claudio, for any 'gracious denial of him,' in the Duke's damning phrase. We have difficulty conjuring up such a picture of her. It would be a devastating violation of the paradoxical structure of the play.

Here once again, a fine analysis of the temper of Isabella's language is marred by a failure to accept another dimension in her extreme—if temporary—vindictiveness. Surely we should feel surprise when the religious novice prays to Heaven that Claudio prove illegitimate:

> Heaven shield my mother play'd my father fair!
> For such a warped slip of wilderness
> Ne'er issu'd from his blood.

and then continues:

> Take my defiance!
> Die, perish! . . .
> I'll pray a thousand prayers for they death,
> No word to save thee.

But Stevenson's major untested premise comes in his absolute acceptance of the Duke as both omniscient and completely reliable. "As F. R. Leavis has put it, 'the Duke's attitude, nothing could be plainer, is meant to be ours—his total attitude . . . is the total attitude of the play'" (p. 13). Like many other critics who laud the Duke's morality and practice, Stevenson ignores the tone for such lines of clumsy, pompous self-description as, "Let him be but testimonied in his own bringings-forth, and he shall appear to the envious a scholar, a statesman, and a soldier." Treating such a response to the badgering of Lucio as a convincing compliment to James I based on the *Basilicon Doron*, Stevenson does not show how such a speech can be made dramatically effective. It of course can be played to suggest an ironic criticism that the speaker himself does not recognize. But no room for such innuendo is possible with Stevenson's basic assumptions about the reliability of Duke Vin-

324

centio, a character so prominent that he speaks more lines than any other in Shakespeare's comedies. Although he does notice the Duke's "final, highly personal, intemperate outburst against Lucio," Stevenson never comes to terms with the ways in which the ruler often proves unable to cope with Lucio, Barnardine, or Pompey. The whole group of broadly comic characters is discussed only incidentally, finding no place of their own in the careful, overt design. Because he does not include any detailed analysis of their roles and critical comments, the author leaves incomplete many of his points concerning the "intellectual comedy" of hidden desires.

The validity of Stevenson's argument rests primarily upon his claims that an "exact equivalence" exists between Isabella and Angelo and upon his identification of the Duke's attitude as our total attitude toward the play. From his treatment of the Duke in particular we can deduce the major weakness in his conception of "intellectual comedy." Because he does not recognize the flaws of the Duke, he cannot notice the many echoes of Angelo's weakness in the speeches of the ruler. Stevenson's conception of comedy in this book is handcuffed to his conception of the controlling character in the play. Because Vincentio has no major flaws and because in every way he acts as "spokesman" for the audience, we too, it must follow, become like "the detached, rather aloof Duke of Vienna." But this is only part of the truth of the play. Comedy need not leave us aloof and detached. *Measure for Measure* is a forerunner of plays by Pirandello and Giraudoux in its shifting perspectives and its unreliable exposition. If we must share the perspective of a reliable Duke, we are left with no bridge to the moral, sexual, emotional, and intellectual turmoil and revelation that Stevenson rightly says the play should produce. Samuel Johnson, Clifford Leech, A. P. Rossiter and others have recognized shifty, pompous, and rather vacuous qualities of the Duke. When we combine these with his good intentions and his ability to avert all serious harm, we have a mixture—one that does not seem to me to conform with any schematically rigid design of the play.

Stevenson's assumptions do not permit him to explicate the profound problematic side of *Measure for Measure*. He aptly recognizes "the arousal in an audience of an uneasy awareness. . . . [*Measure*] suggests no serious realizable solution to the moral dilemma it has dramatized, but it comes to an end by implicating all of us in the perception that moral dilemma is a part of the human situation (p. 128). . . . It is a deliberately 'uncomfortable' play, one which carefully exploits our own easy, surface response to its substance by forcing us to adjust to a level of apprehension of motives for human actions which lie far deeper than we are usually willing to go" (p. 131). But so intent is he on the moral and structural equivalence of contrasting characters and the reliability of the dominant Duke that he creates a conceptual balance that permits little play to the pendulum-swing of the disturbing moral and sexual suggestions.

However imprecise, partial, and repetitive are many of the observations in this book, it compares favorably with most criticism of *Measure for Measure* and deserves careful consideration by students of the play. Unlike the other two books devoted to the play, Stevenson's does attempt to discover the coherence of the play in the text itself. Like too many directors, he may omit discussion of passages—particularly those in which the Duke confronts Lucio and Barnardine—that do not jibe with his over-view. But he does not, as does Mary Lascelles, add stage business that reconciles Isabella to Claudio, thereby violating both her bitter vituperation and her striking silence to him after the last lines she speaks to her brother, "O fie, fie, fie! / Thy sin's not accidental, but a trade. / Mercy to thee would prove itself a bawd; / 'Tis best that thou diest quickly." Nor does he, with Josephine

Waters Bennett, derive much of the major accomplishment of the play from conjectures of innuendoes based upon Shakespeare's acting the part of the Duke. If Professor Stevenson does not exhaust "The Achievement of *Measure for Measure*," he does often set us on the path toward a more thorough appreciation, and he often provokes us to a more lucid formulation of the alternatives posed by this vastly underrated play.

The University of Connecticut

Shakespeare's Problem Plays: Studies in Form and Meaning by William B. Toole. Mouton & Co., 1966. Pp. 242. Gld. 18. *Reviewer: James L. Calderwood.*

One of the aims of this book is to put its own title out of generic business; thus after an extended analysis of the plays grouped by Boas and Tillyard in the "problem play" category —*Hamlet, All's Well, Measure*, and *Troilus*—Mr. Toole concludes that the term is, after all, a "poor designation for this group of plays. The phrase is probably best regarded as ... a convenient tag for four plays that have provoked much critical controversy" (p. 237). So the problem-play genre disappears in the process of expanding to embrace the entire Shakespearean corpus. But Mr. Toole gives as well as he takes generically, for if the plays are not "problem plays" they still merit being studied side-by-side because of their common reliance upon "the pattern of temptation, sin, remorse, repentance, penance, and pardon" that is mapped out in *The Divine Comedy* and that "comes to Shakespeare through the framework of the mystery cycle and the morality play" (p. 231). As this would suggest, Shakespeare is once again to be confronted by the critic in the role of scourge and minister, after the manner of Roy Battenhouse, Paul N. Siegel, J. A. Bryant, Irving Ribner, and G. R. Elliott. An opening chapter on the "major critical approaches to the problem plays" passes up the great chain of Christianizing criticism from Boas and Lawrence to Tillyard and especially Nevill Coghill, whose articles deriving Shakespearean comic form from Dante prepare the route teleologically for the present study. The second chapter lengthily demonstrates that Dante's poem, the miracle cycles, and the morality plays are indeed saturated with Biblical typology and structured on the notion that life is a pilgrimage through this vale of tears toward beatific visions and eternal felicity. Then, guided by Coghill's "main conclusion—that the great cosmic Christian pattern of distress through sin and redemption by the grace of God is mirrored in the framework of Shakespearian comedy" (p. 35)—individual chapters are accorded each of the four plays so needful of the redeeming grace of Christian allegorical criticism.

The analyses that follow are both pretentious and humorless. The chapter on *Hamlet* is typical. It begins, like the others, with a review of earlier criticism as seen from the perspective of Chaucer's Troilus in the eighth sphere. From that altitude, a certain tolerance is possible. We are assured, for instance, that though Bradley operated without benefit of *The Elizabethan World Picture* and the new awareness of Shakespeare's medieval Christian legacies, his insights "have not, by any means, been absolutely nullified as a consequence of the new understanding" (p. 98). Maynard Mack is given a pat on the back for referring to "most of the important raw material of the biblical allusions Shakespeare weaves into" *Hamlet* but is rebuked for not doing the critic's job of work; he "does not probe into the way" these allusions work, failing, for instance, "to be aware of the implied connection between the sins of Gertrude and Eve" (p. 102, note). As the Gertrude-Eve parallel suggests, Mr. Toole, a registered practitioner of Biblical typology, is an expert in pumping up surface observations to the status of critical epiphanies. Still, he is wary of the term "allegory," if not the practice, and hence is quick to say, for instance, that Hamlet is not really "meant to be an allegorical representation of Christ any more than Denmark in pre-Claudian times is meant to represent allegorically the Garden of Eden" (p. 105). Gertrude-Eve, Claudius-serpent-Cain, pre-Claudian Denmark-Garden of Eden, poisoning-original sin, Hamlet-Christ: these are not allegorical equations, Mr. Toole argues, but "parallels" and "analogues." Without endorsing the "parallels," one can applaud the impulse to escape from a cramped critical position. The trouble, though, is that while asserting that the play is the metaphoric "tenor" of certain Biblical "vehicles" (in I. A. Richards' terminology), Mr. Toole really treats it as the allegorical "vehicle" for a Biblical "tenor." Thus he repeatedly assumes that *Hamlet* has evaded the understanding of critics to the extent that they have failed to register the ultimate and binding significance of its Biblical dimension, which he construes less analogically than anagogically. It is rather as though Cleanth Brooks had analyzed *Macbeth* as a sustained metaphoric illumination of certain higher truths about clothes.

These typological elements of *Hamlet* are embedded within a morality play structure based upon sin and salvation. Hamlet casts off everything that makes him uniquely Hamlet and becomes the Christian Everyman, all his dilemmas neatly reduced to a hyperconsciousness of "original sin" that transforms him from his normally "sanguine" disposition into that fearful "adustian state" of Lily B. Campbell fame. Passion—undefined but ultimate—spins both the plot and the plotter's reason: "Hence the terrible unrest of his mind and soul" (p. 108). Neglecting his Christian duties, the hero incurs the possibility of damnation by killing Polonius, but fortunately repents in time, the turning point of the play occurring when he points to Polonius' body and says, "For this same lord, / I do repent." (His pious "I'll lug the guts into the neighbour room" is left discreetly unmentioned.) Full illumination, however, comes only during the sea voyage when Providence manifests itself. Now "he accepts his task and waits the outcome of his destiny, the fires of adustian passion having subsided" (p. 117). And so on.

The route through sin to salvation is even more vital to *All's Well* and *Measure* since these two plays, "we may say categorically, must be interpreted in the light of Dante's concept of comedy to be understood and appreciated" (p. 36). Bertram and Angelo now become Everyman, and Helena in the one and the Duke (who is also "suggestive of" God) and Mariana in the other begin to shine with inner light of Christological symbolism as they reënact the Atonement in their individual fashions. It is not necessary to fill in the details; the analyses are machine-"tooled" on the same pattern as that of *Hamlet*. Indeed, as a final chapter of conclusions makes clear, all four plays can be made to shrivel into thematic uniformity provided we adopt a kind of intellectual tunnel-vision that causes thirteen ways of looking at a blackbird to dwindle into one.

The University of Califoria, Irvine

A Humanist's "Trew Imitation": Thomas Watson's Absalom: A critical edition and translation by John Hazel Smith. (Illinois Studies in Language and Literature, LII) University of Illinois Press, 1964. Pp. 293. $6.00. *Reviewer: W. F. Staton.*

John Hazel Smith's edition of Bishop Thomas Watson's *Absalom* is a distinguished addition to the work done at the University of Illinois on humanist drama. Watson's Latin tragedy, which survives in B. M. Stowe MS. 957, has been accessible to students heretofore only in the summaries of Boas and of Churchill and Keller, so that the present edition with full introduction, English translation, and apparatus fills a real need.

This is especially so because Watson's play is both good and important. Smith has not been able to narrow the 1535-1544 date limits given in Harbage's *Annals*, but these limits place *Absalom* very close in time to Buchanan's *Jepthes* and Giraldi's *Orbecche* and a generation earlier than *Gorboduc* and Garnier. Since *Absalom* shows a very intelligent humanist's "trew imitation" of classical precept and practice in the writing of tragedy, its date shows a development of neo-classical tragedy at Cambridge at least comparable to that at Bordeaux, Ferrara, and Paris.

Smith has had better luck with the question of authorship than with that of date. F. S. Boas, who in *University Drama in the Tudor Age* treated *Absalom* more fully than anyone else before Smith, denied Bishop Thomas Watson's authorship of the play. He had to work from a MS. of an Absalom play and a laudatory reference by Roger Ascham to Bishop Watson's play of that title, both of approximately the same date, but he felt that the MS. play was not good enough to warrant Ascham's praise. (In another place in the same book, however, Boas compared the Latin *Absalom* to Peele's *David and Bethsabe* and concluded "in dexterous arrangement of material, in concentration of interest, and, above all, in psychological insight, *Absalom* is the work of an abler and more original playwright than Peele"; Boas, his benighted age conceded, had a strange penchant for not letting his right hand know about his left.) Nonetheless, the evidence for Watson's authorship was stronger than that for many a confidently attributed sixteenth-century play: just to stay with Boas, we might mention *The Spanish Tragedy* and pass over in silence *Soliman and Perseda*. Fortunately, however, Smith has demonstrated Watson's authorship conclusively by a comparison of the handwriting in the MS. with that in two other documents signed by Bishop Watson; photographs of all three are included in his edition.

The most interesting thing about Watson's *Absalom* is its dramatic structure. The play begins after Absalom has returned from the exile which was his punishment for murdering his brother Amnon in revenge for Amnon's rape of their sister Thamar. Absalom's disaffection toward his father David is shown to grow through his rebellion to his taking of Jerusalem and his defiling of his father's concubines in Act III. As Smith shows in his analysis of the play's structure, Watson, who generally follows the Biblical order of the story, holds back David's countermoves against Absalom until after he has brought his tragic hero to this high point. The action is thus allowed to turn completely on the last scene of Act III, when Absalom accepts the wrong advice which leads to his overthrow by David. Following T. W. Baldwin, Smith plausibly relates this neat handling of the action to the Donatus-derived notion of the five act structure. But I think he underrates the force of the Renaissance tendency toward the non-classical, chronological structure which Madeleine Doran and others have emphasized. Smith writes: "There is no question that he deliberately altered his source to achieve unity of action. First, he limited his play to the single action of Absalom's revolt. The background of the rebellion (Amnon's rape of Thamar and murder by Absalom, Absalom's exile in Gessur and long seclusion in Jerusalem), as well as the ultimate cause of it (David's murder of Urias), is merely recalled by characters in the play" (p.62). My guess is, however, that the reason Watson did not include a prologue about his murder by the ghost of Urias or a long descriptive lament of her rape by Thamar or a chorus account of either or both of these events was more his tendency to follow the chronology of his source than his desire for unity of action.

Another interesting aspect of *Absalom* is its skillful combining of Roman and Judeo-Chris-

328

tian thought and motifs. The chorus at the end of Act II, for example, commenting on David's forbearance toward Absalom cites the forbearance of Isaac, Joseph, Gideon, and Miriam and concludes with the Senecan sentiment (in Smith's translation): "Only a spirit which is good under adversities revives; only a mind which is patient under difficult circumstances makes for peace. In prosperous times the result for man is—sweet delight. A temperate mind endures all things calmly; a temperate mind lightens lean poverty." Smith's identification of Watson's scriptural and Senecan sources makes this amalgamation abundantly clear. I wonder, though, whether earlier critics' practice of dividing Renaissance classical tragedy into Greek and Roman camps has not caused him to overlook the possibility of Greek influence on Watson; a passage like the following certainly sounds to me as if Watson knew the *Antigone:* "Your father is dear, but my country is dearer: I would not place a friend, however dear, above the king; a private citizen must always be held secondary to the ruler." (Smith's translation, p. 183.)

Smith's translation is very literal. The following is not too unfair a sample. When Absalom is reflecting on his past murder of Amnon and his projected rebellion against David, he says:

Delictum adhuc quodcumque factum est dicitur
Graviora factis non rudis mens concipit.

Smith translates: "That which has been done up to now is called a crime. But my not inexpert mind conceives graver ones than those already performed." (pp. 104-107.) A Dudley Fitts type of translation might read, "If they think what I've done already is bad, wait till they see what my little old brain will cook up next." Something somewhere between these two would be nice, but failing that, for the present purpose I much prefer Smith's method.

Purdue University

The Art of Memory by Frances A. Yates. University of Chicago Press, 1966. Pp. xv + 400. $8.95. *Reviewer: Charles K. Hofling.*

This intriguing volume has as its central theme the account of the development of systems of memorization from the Greeks to Leibniz. The story is told in a scholarly fashion, yet one which is simple, unpretentious, and, at times, even lively. The bulk of Miss Yates's effort is directed toward a consideration of the art of memory during the late Middle Ages and the Renaissance. The author's extensive knowledge of the cultural history of these periods enables her to bring her primary subject into relationship with a number of other subjects of great intellectual significance. As Hugh Trevor-Roper has said, "Wherever she looks, she illuminates."

An example is worth presenting in some detail. In the minds of scholars of the Middle Ages, Miss Yates tells us, Cicero, who was greatly venerated, was considered to be the author not only of his own work on rhetoric, *De Inventione,* but of another's work, *Ad Herennium.* In his own essay, Cicero speaks of virtue's having four parts, Prudence, Justice, Fortitude, and Temperance. These qualities are further subdivided, and one of the divisions made of Prudence is memory. In *Ad Herennium* instructions are furnished for an artificial memory system. This system involved the imagining of a large building or structure which must include a number of quite specific and readily identifiable architectural features (loci). The memorizer was to imagine that he had placed certain persons or objects in juxtaposition to each of these features, having chosen the persons or objects which would remind him of either the ideas which he wished to recall or of the very words which he intended to use. It was generally agreed that the symbolic figures (*imagines agentes*) should be imagined in as striking and vivid a manner as possible in order to make them unforgettable.

As a result of the medieval confusion as to the authorship of *Ad Herrenium* and of Cicero's great influence upon Albertus Magnus and Thomas Aquinas, there emerged from the writings of the two great religious figures the compound idea that the acquisition of Prudence, one of the Cardinal Virtues, required the cultivation of memory and that this task was best accomplished through the development of such an artificial memory system as has just been described.

Miss Yates connects all of this with Dante and the Divine Comedy in a tentative, but most interesting way.

> the places of Hell, varied in accordance with the nature of the sins punished in them, could be regarded as variegated memory *loci*. And the striking images on those places would, of course, be the images of the damned. . . . That Dante's *Inferno* could be regarded as a kind of memory system for memorizing Hell and its punishments, with striking images on orders of places, will come as a great shock, and I must leave it as a shock. It would take a whole book to work out the implications of such an approach to Dante's poem. . . . If one thinks of the poem as based on orders of places in Hell, Purgatory, and Paradise, and as a cosmic order of places in which the spheres of Hell are the spheres of Heaven in reverse, it begins to appear as a summa of similitudes and examples, ranged in order and set out upon the universe. . . . In this interpretation, the principles of artificial memory, as understood in the Middle Ages, would stimulate the intense visualization of many similitudes in the intense effort to hold in memory the scheme of salvation, and the complex network of virtues and vices and their rewards and punishments—the effect of a prudent man who uses memory as a part of Prudence.
>
> The *Divine Comedy* would thus become the supreme example of the conversion of an abstract summa into a summa of similitudes and examples, with Memory as the converting power, the bridge between the abstraction and the image.

That a memory scheme of the sort just described can be of value in certain situations is well known to most professional performers of "mental magic." The entertainer is, for example, shown two numbered lists randomized on the spot, the one of objects and the other of places. Within a matter of a few moments he associates every object with the place of corresponding number. Then, as members of the audience, given the same lists, call out the names of the objects, the performer gives the names of the corresponding places.

When questioned as to the technic of such feats, the magicians usually say that they make merely attempt to *visualize*, briefly but very vividly, each object in its assigned place. They say that the more peculiar and grotesque the combination ("the gorilla in the refrigerator," "the cat in the revolving door," "the necktie in the oven") the easier is the task. Moreover, the master lists, from which the randomized ones are freshly made for each performance, are constructed of the names of objects and places which lend themselves to vivid visualization.

With the recent work on the relationship of ribonucleic acid and the synthesis of specific protein in neurons to the establishment of memory traces and with the investigation, through the electron microscope, of the "synaptic knobs," which appear quite strongly to be related to the development of specific neural circuits, it may well be that medical science is on the threshold of a workable explanation of remembering and forgetting in neuro-physiological terms.

It will, however, in all probability, continue to prove useful to consider remembering and forgetting from the standpoint of psychoanalytic theory, the modern classic on the subject being David Rapaport's, *Emotions and Memory* (Baltimore, 1942). Two ideas of especial significance are (a) that the great preponderance of all remembering and forgetting is motivated rather than chance-directed and (b) that the most powerful motivations are likely to be unconscious and linked, on the one hand, to fantasy gratification of basic libidinal and aggressive strivings and, on the other, to the avoidance of painful inner conflict.

Viewed in this light, the basic elements of an art of memorization as propounded by Cicero and those who learned from him—which Miss Yates merely presents, neither praising nor depreciating from the standpoint of efficacy—appear to be reasonable in certain situations. In cases in which the professional lecturer or orator was interested in his subject and in the specific outcome of his presenting the material to his audience, it appears highly unlikely that tricks of the trade would have been needed or used. On the other hand, in cases in which the subject and the communication had no personal significance for the speaker aside from the seeking of a purely professional gratification in a job well done, the "art of memory" might well have been of value. If the speaker could find vivid associations ultimately linked to his own motivations (and not productive of excessive conflict) for the several elements of the pedestrian speech he was called upon to deliver, his recall might well be facilitated.

The University of Cincinnati

Something of Great Constancy: The Art of "A Midsummer Night's Dream" by David P. Young. Yale University Press, 1966. Pp. 190. $5.00. *Reviewer: Gates K. Agnew.*

It comes as no particular surprise that Edward Dowden exhausts in fewer than six of more than four hundred pages the contribution of *A Midsummer Night's Dream* to the development of Shakespeare's mind and art. Dowden's book was published in 1872, almost a century before the outburst of interest in comedy we have but begun to witness. But it may serve to jog the memory that as late as 1954 an estimable practitioner of the new criticism referred to *Dream* without the slightest self-consciousness as "barely more than a delicate, tenuous piece of decoration." Derek Traversi did not argue in behalf of his observation (*An Approach to Shakespeare*, p. 17), and it is instructive that he did not feel obliged to. David P. Young's study will not put all things right, but it is a graceful and helpful reflection of the new tastes and techniques which in shedding light on the comedies of the 1590's promise new insight into the whole question of the dramatist's development. The shortcomings of this book are no less instructive than its excellences, for they proceed from an undue deference to the critical preconceptions which have long enshrined tragedy as the most significant of dramatic forms and alternately from lack of rigor in pursuing his promising approach.

That approach is announced as a "vertical" analysis of *Dream*, concentrating extensively on one play at the expense of a broader survey and synthesizing the author's own findings with the work of other commentators. This is a useful and much-needed method in so far as it enables Young to avoid the all but inevitable disintegration of the "horizontal" study into a self-verifying demonstration of an inadequate thesis about the nature of Shakespearean comedy (as in H. B. Charlton's *Shakespearian Comedy*) or a thematic study which minimizes the dramatic integrity of the individual play (e.g. J. R. Brown, *Shakespeare and his Comedies*) or a series of unrelated essays which never really grapple with the tough critical issues raised by any play (J. D. Wilson, *Shakespeare's Happy Comedies*). Of course the "vertical" organization has its own imperatives and temptations. It stands or falls on the seriousness with which the author pursues a critical synthesis as distinguished from employment of straw men or the creation of a merely eclectic casebook transcribed into the first person and held together with rhetorical finesse. Young comes out well in regard to straw men, but he seems as unable to learn anything from the older critics of *Dream* as he is unwilling to doubt anything in the newer views he has espoused. The result is a controversial thesis rather than a synthesis, which argues in effect that because Traversi's conception is insufficient it is irrelevant, neither a revealing if partial insight nor a necessary element in the construction of a more sophisticated view of the play.

The first of three main sections, that on backgrounds, is by all odds the most successful because it does not raise the issue of confronting and synthesizing a broad spectrum of previous critical thought. Young's exposition of the non-dramatic background ("three kinds of celebration—royal marriage and the May and Midsummer holidays") and the dramatic background (sharply contrasted versions of the popular and coterie dramas) is enclosed in a happy discussion of the meeting of Bottom and Titania which nicely draws attention to the decisive critical question source studies pose, the "difficult question of the response of the audience as a group to the effective manipulations of the dramatist" (p. 16). The aristocratic world of Titania and the popular world of Bottom meet and fuse without incongruity, indeed with a "sense of inevitability" which makes for both good fun and "substantial art."

The second and third sections of *Something of Great Constancy* take up respectively style and structure, and the intellectual content of the play. Young shows how the gorgeous variety of styles in *Dream* is a means of characterization and a device for pointing up groups and themes, and after defending the comedy against charges of weak characterization in the lovers and against the insinuations of textual disintegrators, he elaborates on the stylistic elements which perform a reconciling and unifying function: iterative imagery, "picturization" and panorama, and profusion (i.e. amplification, especially in the phenomena of the natural realm). There is a weakness here, nothing to do with the sensitive and full appreciation of Shakespeare's wide world of styles, which increasingly inhibits the rest of the book. Young is bent on asserting the harmony Shakespeare produces from disparate stylistic elements, "The Concord of·this Discord" as his section is titled. But what is the harmonizing power of amplification of natural details; simply that everyone does it? It may be suggestive to write that "the panoramas become a kind of metaphor for the play," and that "like reiterated images they serve to create a fully realized world" (p.83). And it is certainly true that "Listening . . . is one way of bringing an audience seated in a theater into contact with nature, stimulating and awakening the sensuous memory" (p.84). But it begs the question to argue that the union of diverse materials is achieved in displays of myriad, profuse, diverse nature, and in the end Young seems only to repeat the point as a handy organizing device.

The fact is that Shakespeare's integration of hitherto alien dramatic elements cannot be accounted for on the level of style, and perhaps in recognition of this Young completes his section with a passage on dramatic structure. It begins by restating the admirable thesis that effect on the audience is the proper and profitable subject of an inquiry into structure, and it then lists schematic models for describing the progress of the morality play, the romance, and the pastoral romance. We are still on the right track with the statement that it is "the characters and, by imaginative extension, ourselves who alter as we move through the worlds in question, discovering their interaction" (p. 91). Yet rather than analyze the dramatist's purpose in celebrating physical nature during this process of alteration in character and spectator alike, Young reverts suddenly to a description of the relative ontological statuses of the different realms in *Dream,* and he does so in a manner which precludes effective discussion of the dynamic interaction of those spheres. From a horizontal pattern of narrative progress he turns abruptly to the image of concentric circles, maintaining that our consciousness of the four groups of characters is "essentially spatial" (p. 92). I confess I do not understand how the experiences of several groups of characters on a stage may be said to occur "simultaneously," nor how the fact that the audience is "conscious of the location of each group" can be translated into geometrical, spatial metaphors. From Athens the play transports us into a magical wood only to return us to Athens with Oberon's blessings. The journey through symbolic space brings a resolution of the two worlds in the present experience of the young lovers, and to an even greater extent in the experience of Theseus, Hippolyta, and the participating audience. The static figure of concentric circles does not lend itself to explaining the nature of that resolution. Since he chooses to think in such terms, it is perhaps inevitable that Young should ultimately defend *Dream* as a dramatic apology for one circle (the world of imaginative apprehension) at the expense of another (the world of rational comprehension) and then employ the divisions he has created as evidence of "the philosophical divisions of the time" (p. 153).

The last section, "Bottom's Dream," is thus influenced by the author's failure to establish a language and metaphor for discussing comic form. A negative logic quietly prevails throughout: *Dream* is not "thoughtless" (p. 111), it is not divorced from the intellectual issues of the day, it is not purposeless. Having rejected the old conception of *Dream* as an insubstantial decorative piece, Young can only insist on the play's intellectual pithiness and contemporaneity until he finds in them with the aid of Elizabeth Sewell a new purposeful form: "this is Shakespeare's ars *poetica*" (p. 179). To a critic who does not seem to have read Susanne Langer or Northrop Frye or very much of C. L. Barber, Sewell's *The Orphic Voice* (New Haven, 1960) arrives as a sort of critical panacea despite its evident tendentiousness. Miss Sewell puts us on guard early in her study by asserting her freedom "to draw out from half-forgotten or ill-interpreted authors . . . whatever they can offer us, not worrying (beyond the straightforward claims of integrity and logic in these matters) whether we are falsifying them in the process" (p. 22). Her loyalty is to a thesis, but if Young's "vertical" approach is meaningful, his first loyalty must be to the play as a play. In fact he has disposed of one kind of disintegrator only to embrace another, who can distinguish sagaciously between the utterances of "Bacon-Theseus" and "Shakespeare-Theseus," and who claims "the sole purpose" of Bottom's company is to portray a "mechanical experiment" (pp. 116, 128). It may be illuminating, in conclusion, to examine the interpretation which results and sketch briefly an alternative which seems to be more faithful to the received text.

The interpretative crux of *Dream* is still the speech of Theseus in the last act which pits the strong imagination of the lover, the madman, and the poet against "cool reason" (V.i.2-22 in the Kittredge edition). Young objects to these lines being quoted out of context as if they embodied the dramatist's views, but he then proposes to analyze them "with the notion that Shakespeare's views can be determined only, if at all, by differentiating them from what Theseus says" (p. 137). That little qualifying phrase "if at all," which represents the sum of Young's advance over his predecessors, turns out to be an empty rhetorical gesture, and he proceeds to argue that Hippolyta rather than Theseus "has the last word"—meaning that it is she who speaks for Shakespeare. According to this argument, Lysander had been "ludicrously wrong" in rationalizing his new-found affection for Helena, and now "Theseus is also wrong." What the lovers and Hippolyta attempt in vain to account for is "not a dream" because we, the audience, have seen it happen, and Theseus' reason is "overmatched by the facts of the context in which he attempts to exercise it." The real problem is that "well-meaning reasonable men like Theseus" cannot get it into their heads that the experience of the lovers constitutes "a potential defense of the poet's art," and they cannot because "they do not know how to value the imagination" (pp. 139-141). The value of the imagination and poetry to Young and Sewell is that they come "closer to the truth" than reason and philosophy (p. 149).

For my own part, I cannot "almost hear [in Theseus' speech] the dry voice of Bacon appealing to the dry light of rationality" (Sewell, p. 115). I much prefer her earlier statement in regard to such verbal antitheses as reason and imagination: "they are old, they are tidy, they are mistaken" (p. 19). What then are we to make of the last scene of *Dream* if we view Theseus' speech as a gesture integral to a dramatic process moving in both time and space? First, Theseus' person and words seem above all the dramatist's means for establishing a firm sense of symbolic place. The court of Theseus does not breed an atmosphere of dry, prosaic, philistine rationality; it is rather what Dowden calls "the positive, social world" of historical experience (*Shakspere: A Critical Study of his Mind and Art*, p.73). What Costard in *Love's Labour's Lost* describes as "the day of wrong" has given way to a night of dreams emancipating magical and fantastic powers, and now through the dominant person of Theseus, the fabled ruler of antique story, Shakespeare returns his audience to a world approximating actual experience, in which the governing principles of order and form are manifested and displayed in an expressed reliance on rational comprehension over imaginative apprehension. The world of the fifth act is to the magical wood what the world of the spectator is to the play as a whole, and the pervasive fairy power of earlier acts must be emphatically placed by the dramatist precisely because it is his ultimate intention to celebrate the meaning and power of the imagination *within* the daylight kingdom of Theseus, itself now shaded in night. A character who allows himself to comprehend the bringer of a joy merely because he apprehends that joy (V.i.18-20) manifestly cannot perform this placing function, but that does not necessarily leave us with a coldly rationalizing Bolingbroke. Theseus is not to be identified with either, and it is through him more than any other character (including Puck) that Shakespeare shapes our response to his play.

To inquire after the status and potency of imagination in the world of Theseus is to explore the relevance of *Dream* for its audience. It is not very helpful to conclude with Young that the bewitched wood is real because we have seen it in the play (p. 139). The play itself, as distinguished from actors and props, is an illusion. From the Theseus-world of practical authority, public business, and moral responsibility, the happenings in the wooded night and in romantic comedy itself are necessarily "strange," to borrow Hippolyta's word. The common experience of the lovers "grows to something of great constancy," but the most we and Theseus can comprehend about that "something" is that it is admirable, and inexplicable except in terms of effect on the lovers. Theseus never denies that effect. Without violating his symbolic identity, Theseus can and does comprehend and validate the *fait accompli* whose source and motive power are strange. He finds the lovers in a daylight, demythologized green world (IV.i), but overbears the will of Egeus as he had refused earlier to do, thereby witnessing in deed to the authenticity of the lovers' achieved affections. Later, when Hippolyta reiterates her wonder in response to his practical scepticism, Theseus by way of reply turns to greet the lovers "full of joy and mirth" which events have wrought.

334

Furthermore, Shakespeare devotes the remainder of the scene to showing various ways in which Theseus does in actuality value the imagination and its products. He chooses a play, an antique fable if there ever was one, as a reasonable (i.e. appropriate and fitting) means of gracing his nuptial celebration, rejecting both a rationalizing satire and a riotously emotional Bacchanalian device (V.i.32-84). Then he recounts at length how the exercise of the imagination is really an integral part of his rational exercise of authority (V.i.91-105). Finally, he guides the unwilling and sceptical Hippolyta—so recently an appreciative spokesman for the marvelous which men of affairs can neither refute nor afford to rely upon—to an understanding of imaginative response in a theatrical audience, a response similar to the imaginative amendment practiced by the ruler on his progress. Predicated on the assumption of the players' good will, this response gives life to the dramatic illusion which at a fitting moment and place recreates the "strange and admirable" within the Theseus-world. To the comprehension, Bottom's play remains "nothing" and "the silliest stuff." But Theseus reminds us that from the point of view of public, social experience, "the best of this kind are but shadows," and in this controlled courtly setting it is appropriate to "apprehend some joy" from incomprehensible shadows. Under his tutelage, Hippolyta learns to find grace in Moon and pitiable pleasure in the passion of Pyramus, and her imaginative amendment of these shadows is not a way of escaping to or from reality. It is a way of celebrating the benevolent providence apprehended by imagination, which reflects and reenforces the celebration of harmony, fruitfulness, and love that society comprehends in the institution of marriage. In her willingness to amend, Hippolyta is enhanced in our eyes, and we further identify with her response.

Theseus proves to be a valuable guide to the role of the imagination exactly because he does not champion its cause at the expense of a reasonable pursuit of justice and love. To rephrase my point in homely and heretical terms, I would argue that Theseus functions not unlike the powerful modern administrator who refuses to accept poems in place of required annual reports, but who thrives on poetry and makes possible the existence of a local theater. If such a man seems more strange than admirable to us, it may be because we have all done too much thinking in concentric circles.

Indiana University

Significant Articles, Monographs, and Reviews

January, 1967—December, 1967
By J. Leeds Barroll

When presenting our second annual article in this series last year, we observed in this space that while the existence of at least two admirably thorough Shakespeare bibliographies made further such compilation superfluous, a selected listing of certain material might have its own uses. The response from scholars has been such as to suggest the continuation of this series, and, for the benefit of new readers, it might therefore be well to reiterate some principles of selection. A selected listing of significant material may have its uses if the term "significant" bears some relationship to whether an article or a monograph seems to enlarge the sum of factual knowledge concerning Shakespeare's life, immediate artistic milieux, or media. There is also "significance" in some efforts to explore the nature of the art-entities themselves with which Shakespeare challenges our comprehension. It is not simple, after all, to maintain the necessary distinction between two verbal structures, differentiating that verbal description which is "criticism" from the plays and poems which are themselves structured through words. When criticism, therefore, through consistent argumentation and an acute sense of the relativity of the verbal, succeeds so as to alter or at least to modify existing views on the nature of Shakespeare's art, those instances certainly warrant notice. It is also extremely important to follow reviewings, for they are the complements, the Aristotelian end, as it were, to that beginning represented by the scholarship under scrutiny. And if we assume that scholarship is essentially a social act whereby knowledge is increased through the interchange of information and ideas, then investigation is meaningless when deprived of a reasoned and careful response. It seems important to note responses of this nature when they occur. We also refer to "Ancillary Studies" in a third section, for although the reviewing-portion of *Shakespeare Studies* is properly the place for noting books, there are some, which though not directly pertinent, may contain material of possible relevance to matters Shakespearean, but which sometimes may not have too obvious a bearing upon the subject: in the latter case, the presumed relevance is indicated.

Significant work in all areas has doubtless been omitted: "to err" etc. Much of the correspondence received, however, has adverted to certain kinds of omission which represent editorial principle rather than neglect. It does not seem appropriate to include in this listing either work by the Editor, or, more important, articles and reviews appearing in previous volumes of *Shakespeare Studies* itself. This matter apart, however, and in the hope of avoiding serious omission, the Editor would be grateful for a continued reception of offprints and possible ancillary books published *since January 1st, 1968.* It only remains for us to thank the community of Renaissance scholars as well as the publishers for their very generous response to our similar request last year: it is only human for this writer to wish that all such material could have been noted below.

M. C. Bradbrook, "The Comedy of Timon," *Renaissance Drama,* IX (1966), 83-103.

This article discusses the untitled anonymous manuscript play on Timon of Athens (Dyce 52.25F) which Dyce edited for the Shakespeare Society in 1842. The author's contention is that the play may be a law students' burlesque of Shakespeare's *Timon;* if so, then, of course, the relevance of this manuscript to the date of Shakespeare's play is obvious. One problem, however, is that the dating of the manuscript must be speculative. The article itself should nevertheless be consulted, especially in that section entitled "The Shakespearean Connections," for these possible connections suggest the need for more attention to this subject than has been bestowed upon it in the recent past. Cf. also *Shakespeare Studies,* II (1966), 35, for reference to Bradbrook's previous observations on *Timon.*

Jan Harold Brunvand, "The Folktale Origin of *The Taming of the Shrew,*" *SQ,* XVII (1966), 345-359.

The author argues that Shakespeare's play is a "good literary version of the northern-European subtype of Tale Type 901—the kernel narrative of the Taming of the Shrew Complex of traditional Indo-European folktales." (see his n. 1, p. 345 for the classification here). The significance of the study lies in the author's suggestion that whatever relationship *A Shrew* had to Shakespeare's play, *The Shrew* conforms much more closely to elements of the oral tradition. Clearly, this fact may not eliminate the problem of *A Shrew,* but it does establish some new and perhaps definitive distinctions between both plays which could conceivably indicate separate authorship more clearly than heretofore. The fact that the "Shrew" concept was dramatized twice—or at least in two versions—within Shakespeare's dramatic milieu can hardly be coincidence, no matter how widespread the folktale itself may be. Brunvand's article strongly suggests either that Shakespeare became more conversant with well-known oral traditions after having written *A Shrew,* or that, more conversant with oral traditions in the first place, he reworked someone else's play not only according to his own techniques, but also in the light of his own broader folktale information.

Louise George Clubb, "Pictures for the Reader: A Series of Illustrations to Comedy, 1591-1592," *Renaissance Drama,* IX (1966), 265-277.

The author here supplements the work of Helen M. C. Purkis by demonstrating that a number of the woodcuts in Gonzaga's *Gli inganni* (Venice, 1592) were used a year previously, in the second editions of Castelletti's *I torti amorosi* (Venice, 1591) and Oddi's *Prigione d'amore* (Venice, 1591). Clubb's important contribution is to bring a series of woodcuts together, some not being common to all three editions, and to reproduce them ("in their natural size" for *Gli inganni*). Since the author is careful to note that any knowledge of the full extent of this series, and of the range of effects it may have offered (presumably through juxtaposition of particular woodcut to portion of text, bibliographical considerations being equal) must await further investigation, it may be useful here to summarize the series as she presents it. We are dealing with a total of 29 separate woodcuts spread over the three different books and often used more than once in the same book. 14 of the 29 woodcuts *all* appear in all three books, while the other 15 are distributed (and re-used) variously. If we employ the letters of the alphabet, A(14) represents that nucleus of 14 woodcuts common to all three books, while the next 15 letters of the alphabet (B through P) can each stand for one of the 15 remaining *individual* woodcuts, no matter how often used. Hopefully without distorting the author's intent, the tally below depicts the distribution, not indicating how *often* a particular woodcut is reproduced in a given book. The figures following the = sign, however, will total: number of *individual* woodcuts/total number of woodcuts in the volume. Clubb herself does indicate which woodcuts are repeated.

Inganni	(8⁰)	: A(14) B C D E F G		[Q] [R]=20+[2]/30*
Torti	(12mo):	A(14) B	H I J K L M	=21/47
Prigione	(12mo):	A(14) C D E F G H I J K	N O P	=26/52
		*See Clubb's n.3		

The analysis of the repetitions would itself be useful, this being outside the scope of Clubb's article. The work may be complemented with T. E. Lawrenson and Helen Purkis, "Les editions illustrées de Térence" in *Le lieu théâtral à la Renaissance,* ed. Jean Jacquot (Paris, 1964), pp. 1-23. Clubb's work also offers suggestions about conventions of character-grouping as well as about the scenic possibilities of the Serlio vista, common to all the woodcuts. See also Melzi below.

Nevill Coghill, *et al., "Troilus and Cressida," TLS,* Jan. 19-April 6 (1967), *passim.*

This series of letters debating the veracity of the second title-page of Q1609 involves several scholars whose arguments cannot, within the scope of the letter-columns, be developed with requisite rigor. Bowers (16 March) and Cook (9 March) are to the point, while Maxwell (6 April) is useful debating what indeed are the "known facts" about the play with Coghill who had listed these "facts" (30 March). To Maxwell's questioning about the first "known fact," we might add a query regarding Coghill's sixth: to the effect that Shakespeare necessarily garnered Thersites from Homer. It would be useful if more students of *Troilus* would recall, for example, the interlude *Thersites* (c 1537) and what the existence of this interlude may imply about traditional knowledge.

Madeleine Doran, "Good Name in *Othello,*" *SEL,* VII (1967), 195-217.

Although one might not necessarily agree with the implicit interpretation of the play which informs this review of the problem of, as it were, "Reputation, reputation, reputation!" in *Othello,* the article restores for us an ideological vocabulary in terms of which the human issues suggested by this drama can be viewed in sharper perspective. The study of the tradition of Roman *fama* as it modulates into Medieval and then Renaissance ways of thinking about "good name" which can be destroyed by Slander and Envy culminates in such interesting *aperçus* as that of Iago frequently being given the epithet "dog," the animal itself most frequently associated in literature with Envy. And, of course, when the observation is made that "in Shakespeare slander is one of the worst of evils," the reader after pertinent recollections, may possibly understand the Duke's severity towards Lucio in *Measure* as more indicative of Shakespearean ethical propensities than definitive of meretricious behavior by Vincentio (my suggestion; not Miss Doran's). Finally, through this article, Othello's last speech gains depth, but the very gain achieved through the benefit of the author's observations may enable one to disagree with her conclusions here. For Othello may not necessarily have achieved his *"restitutio in integrum",* as Doran suggests, by his final action; may it not be conceivable, rather, that within the context established here, Othello's last act becomes more deeply ironic? "All that's spoke is marr'd," observes Gratiano. However, this is not the place to revive argumentation about the ethical implications of Othello's suicide.

W. R. Elton, ed., *Shakespearean Research Opportunities,* III (1967).

Shakespearean work in progress is again listed by the names of reporting scholars (pp. 25-63). A new feature (pp. 64-91) is a selected list of materials published, 1966-67, on works "concerning Renaissance intellectual currents of contextual relevance to Shakespearean interpretation." History, Economics, and Science may be topics indicative of the many categories within this section. *SRO* may be obtained by writing the editor, care of the Department of English, University of California, Riverside, California 92502, U.S.A.

Doris V. Falk, "Proverbs and the Polonius Destiny," *SQ*, XVIII (1967), 23-36.

It is from the viewpoint of those studying the quartos of *Hamlet* that this article might be most useful, for while it devotes much space to tracing the *sententiae* and their metaphors which might apply to Polonius, it also offers an accounting for the name *Corambis* which Q1 has given Ophelia's father. Briefly, the Elizabethan version of a line from Juvenal had become proverbial: *"Crambe bis posita [or cocta] mors est"* : Cabbage twice served (or cooked) is death. The proverb was explained by Taverner whose commentary suggests the meaning: that the phrase refers to a situation in which one heard "a thinge againe, and againe repeted not without tediousness and greuaunce." *LLL*, IV,ii.19-20, refers to the second part of the phrase, *"bis coctus,"* and in the same context. The similarity of phrases would, the author indicates, have made the name "Corambis" appropriate, but the case needs to be made with more attention to the nature of the text. It may—or may not— be significant, for example, that Q1 carries on its title-page the indication of Oxford and Cambridge performance: the audiences there might have been more sensitive to the hint than those at the Globe. How often, too, and in what forms does *Corambis* occur in Q1? As long as the article alludes to the quotation-marks in Corambis' speeches as indicative of *sententiae* in hand, it seems worth the effort to exhaust the textual situation first, before studying the implications. But the significance of name may have only been a point in passing as Falk goes on to discuss the tradition of the father-son advice-scenes in quasi-satirical writing.

Elaine W. Fowler, "The Earl of Bedford's 'Best' Bed," *SQ*, XVIII (1967), 80.

This brief note provides further support for those who argue that Shakespeare's disposition of his second-best bed was not necessarily an indication of marital ill-feeling.

Bridget Gellert, "The Melancholy of Moor-Ditch: a Gloss of *1 Henry IV*, I.ii.87-88," *SQ*, XVIII (1967), 70-71.

This brief note supports and adds documentation to Kittredge's observation that Moorfields itself was not only metaphorically, but specifically, associated with melancholy and especially, as Gellert suggests, with the melancholy of decayed soldiers and beggars—who in their youths had lived like the proverbial grasshopper? The passage quoted suggests this, but the author does not, possibly because the parallel seemed too obvious for comment.

Rudolph E. Habenicht, ed. "Shakespeare: An Annotated World Bibliography for 1965," *SQ*, XVII (1966), 213-341; ". . . for 1966," *SQ*, XVIII (1967), 207-334.

Although this annual section of *Shakespeare Quarterly* is well known, attention should be called to the more extended indexing, and the adduction of such special features as a separate section for the listing of reprints. With a section also devoted to listing the reviews of "non-current" books, this annual bibliography continues to be refined as the superb instrument of reference which it has come to be. One would wish that it were possible, in 1968, for the bibliographies to be combined, with their indices, as a natural complement to Gordon Ross Smith's listings which, we recall, end at 1958.

E. A. J. Honigmann, "On the Indifferent and One-Way Variants in Shakespeare," *Library*, XXII (1967), 189-204.

This article represents the kind of logical development which one would hope to observe, now that the study of Shakespeare's text has reached a certain degree of sophistication. For the question propounded by the author is this: given a situation where one play survives in two independent or substantive texts, what kind of methodology should be brought to bear when an editor must choose between such indifferent variants as *my/mine, spoke/spake,* etc. Recourse to what has been established as the "better" text—a frequent response—is not necessarily valid procedure, the author reminds us, for he recalls the warning of Greg in this matter. To say that one text contains twice as many errors as another tells us little about their relative accuracy, Greg observed, unless we also know the frequency of variation. For even if there were, on an average, one variant in every blank-verse line (of, say, about eight words), the texts would still have respectively 96 and 92 per cent of their actual words correct. Their relative accuracy would therefore not be in the ratio of 2:1, but of 24:23. Therefore, Honigmann reminds us, we cannot assume, in the case of *Othello*, for example, that taking our indifferent variants from F which has only half as many rejected readings as Q, we will have a 2:1 chance of potential accuracy; the odds are rather like 24:23. After justifying the statement with a brief sampling from *Othello*, the article proceeds to its point anent indifferent variants by studying about fifteen of them including "the Folio's peculiar prejudice against the word *yea*" in the matter of *Yea/Yes* variants.

The implications of the results are manifold, since it is clear from Honigmann's examples that there are pronounced patterns of "one-way" variance, situations where the Folio demonstrates a distinct preference for one specific form of a particular word. Clearly, if Folio prejudice has been determined in the case of one indifferent variant, then the principle of choosing the variant from the "better text," when that text is F, is not necessarily the safest method. Again, when we encounter such "one-way traffic" in one text or one group of Folio texts, and encounter reverse changes (that do not appear insignificant) in a second text or group, the identifiable habits of compositors or correctors, or even scribes may emerge. The author's conclusion is therefore hardly an overstatement. "Before editing any single play surviving in two good texts, one must check on all its indifferent variants in the other Quartos and the whole Folio and, if necessary, in other books produced by the printers of the two substantive versions." The only question which might be raised here has to do with the determination of the "indifference" of the variants themselves. Variants (iii) and (x) in Honigmann's article (A/he; Ah/Oh) may, for instance, bring us into the realm of slang and interjection, crucial elements in the scrutiny of strictly dramatic language. How do we determine whether 'a is really an "indifferent" variant of *he* or an indication of the level of conversation. Are modern "huh," "hmm," "Ah hah!" the same, different, or opposite from Elizabethan *Ah, Oh, Ha*, and even *Well, well* and, in any event, how do we distinguish these words from each other, once spellings (and compositorial preferences) have been established? A study of this dimension of language has long been needed. Compare Kable below.

Richard Hosley, "How Many Children had Lady Capulet?" *SQ*, XVIII (1967), 3-6.

The fine hand of Rowe is always with us, and this article is salutary if only by reminding us that Lady Capulet is never referred to as such in Q2 where she is designated six times as *Old Lady*. *Mother* occurs more than sixteen times, and *Wife, Lady, Capulet's Wife*, or *Lady of the house* occur according to varying proportions in speech-tags or stage-directions. The point the author wishes to make is that this, and other evidence are only counterbalanced by the lines included in I.iii.69-74: "Ladies of esteeme, / Are made alreadie mothers by my count. / I was your mother, much upon these yeares / That you are now a maide, . . ." The article adverts to other *old* designations in other plays where the character is indeed old, but the direction of attack is upon the lines themselves. The author proposes the following emendation: ". . . By my count / I was *a* mother, much upon these yeares / That you are now a maide, . . ." Compositor-substitution caused by eyeskip to the line below where *you* might have influenced substitution of *your* for *a* before a noun is suggested as the basis for the emendation, bibliographically, while other lines are adduced to show that Lady Capulet and Capulet seem to refer to other children who have since died. It would be interesting to see this matter pursued further: the aesthetic case is good; textually, it would have been useful to determine compositor-habit in this kind of error, if the compositor could be isolated.

T. H. Howard-Hill, "Shakespeare: The Clarendon Press Concordance,"
Shakespeare Newsletter, XVII (1967), 35.

See below: Marder.

G. K. Hunter, "Seneca and the Elizabethans," ShS, 20 (1967), 17-26.

This is significant reminder of the influence of Ovid as well as a brief re-examination of the myth, popular among many scholars, that Seneca was a central influence upon English Renaissance tragedy. The essay is most notable for its discussion of the whole *Quellenforschung* concept and for its n.13 which effectively demonstrates the occurrence of stichomythia as early as in the Wakefield cycle. Methodologically, however, some distinction between Seneca the dramatist and Seneca the philosopher would have been useful, while the distinction between Seneca the dramatist and the problem of *sentences* from various pseudo-Senecas perhaps complicates the question. Pseudo-Seneca's (my phrase) imply some feeling about Seneca in the first place, while early examples of stichomythia may do little more than, e.g., suggest an earlier date for Seneca's influence on drama. Generous in its references to *Induction to Tragedy*, but more informed than Baker, this useful article does leave us with certain questions.

William S. Kable, "The Influence of Justification on Spelling in Jaggard's Compositor B," SB, XX (1967), 235-239.

Investigation of the Pavier quartos has obvious importance because these quartos operate as a control-group by which to determine how Jaggard's Compositor B (better known for his Folio work) set text from Shakespeare quartos not for F, but for the Pavier printings in 1619. The author reports that a comprehensive spelling analysis of the Pavier quartos has produced a significant body of evidence which suggests "the remarkable influence of justification" on B's compositorial spellings. From almost every linguistic group observed in the Pavier quartos, for example, the majority of exceptions to B's well-known spelling-patterns arise in lines which have presumably been justified, the influence of justification exerting itself even upon the spellings for which B has otherwise displayed the strongest preference. In his work, for instance, B characteristically altered the 315 *doe* spellings of the Pavier quartos to *do* in 303 cases. Since no compositor is likely to observe a superhuman rigidity in his preferences, the remaining 12 cases could conceivably be taken as human inconsistency, despite B's spelling-preference. But the author observes that one in four of the *doe*'s coming through from copy (3 out of the 12?) occurs in justified lines. More importantly, there are eight apparently "aberrant" changes of *do* to *doe* in all of the Pavier quartos, and five out of these eight changes occur in lines which have been justified. The article goes on to indicate some other kinds of change, such as ampersand for *and*, the spellings of *clock* and the use of the tilde to shorten *from*. Several interesting conclusions are accordingly indicated. Justification, for Compositor B, ranked ahead of his tendency to set preferential spellings. Therefore, justification becomes an important element in compositor studies based on spelling analysis which may otherwise be contaminated by "justified" spellings. But one might take as an equally important point what is presented almost as a subordinate element in this study, for the author adduces examples which warn us against carelessness in our assumptions as to what may indeed constitute a "justified" line. We observe what might be termed "anticipatory justification" which can often result in the execution of a short line rather than of a long, crowded one: comparison with copy-text is therefore essential in these matters. Compare Honigmann above.

Stanley J. Kahrl, "Medieval Supplement," Research Opportunities in Renaissance Drama, X (1967), 123-166.

This section, new this year, reports the proceedings of Conference 15 of the MLA : "Medieval Drama."

James G. McManaway, "John Shakespeare's 'Spiritual Testament'," SQ, XVIII (1967), 197-205.

Speculation on the possible recusancy of Shakespeare's father has always been reinforced by the "Spiritual Testament" of John Shakespeare. This material came into the hands of Edmund Malone who, we will recall, printed it in his 1790 edition. But Malone's material consisted of only the last five leaves of a six-leaf manuscript, plus, finally, only a transcript of the contents of the missing first leaf, obtained in time to be included among "Emendations and Additions" of this same edition of Shakespeare. Whatever manuscripts did exist are now lost, but in 1923 a quarto (1661) agreeing closely with the Malone "testament" was discovered. Written in Spanish, published in Mexico City, and giving Carlo Borromeo (d.1585) as the author, this quarto led to the discovery of other Mexican editions of the "testament" which therefore seems to have been especially popular among Spanish Catholics as a devotional formulary wherein the "testator" delcared his intention to live and die a Catholic. McManaway's article carries us much further in this whole matter, not only by listing three more Mexican editions, but by presenting for the first time the only known text in English, an item which is also the earliest (1638) surviving text of the Borromeo testament now in hand. It is therefore possible to do more than guess at the accuracy of the transcript sent to Malone as the contents of the missing first leaf. Accordingly, McManaway reprints the material as follows. The 1638 text (a 32mo, possibly published on the Continent) is reprinted up to the point where Malone's last five manuscript-leaves began. At this point, McManaway continues the 1638 edition but, at the same time, indicates in brackets where Malone's version (spelling aside) differs.

Whatever differences do occur are strikingly negligible so that it seems safe to assume that we have here, in effect, the missing first leaf which includes Article I, the most explicit statement of Catholic belief (my opinion; not McManaway's). The author rightly calls attention to the great inferential importance of the missing manuscript itself, and his last paragraph needs careful scrutiny. The only reservations one might have about this significant contribution is a regret that the Spanish versions of "Leaf 1" material were not alluded to, but space-limitations may have precluded the luxury.

Louis Marder, "Shakespeare Concordances: 1787-1967," *Shakespeare Newsletter,* XVII (1967), 33-35.

See also above: Howard-Hill.

Robert C. Melzi, "From Lelia to Viola," *Renaissance Drama,* IX (1966), 67-81.

This is a thorough and careful review of the discussions about source generated by Manningham's statement regarding *Twelfth Night*—that it was "most like and neere to that in Italian called *Inganni.*" While accuracy in studies of multiple sources is always, by its very nature, difficult to assess, this article must be used as a supplement to Bullough and has the further utility of associating Shakespeare more plausibly than heretofore with the *commedia dell'arte.* See also Clubb, above.

H. J. Oliver, "An Alleged Variant in *As You Like It,*" *N&Q,* XIV (1967), 136.

This article conclusively dismisses the validity of the Furness statement that *AYL,* II.iii.60, in his copy of F, read *neede* (for F: *meede*). Examination of the Folger copies and of the Rodd-Corser-Smith-Furness copy shows, in the former, *meede* throughout, and in the Furness, the following: "the paper before the 'n' is different in colour and that the space between 'neede' and the preceding word is greater than average by 'just about the space that would be required by the first stroke of an original 'm.'" On the relatively sophisticated stage at which the study of F is now being conducted, any variants as among copies need to be taken seriously indeed, and it therefore seems important to refer to this brief but well-documented note.

Rodney Poisson, "'Which Heaven has forbid the Ottomites'", *SQ,* XVIII (1967), 67-70.

Two interesting points are raised here in connection with the scuffle arranged by Iago. A footnote refers to a contemporary account describing the habits of drunken Englishmen going up to belfries to ring the bells "for hours together," while the body of the brief article alludes to the opinion which the Turks were said to hold about duelling. It was forbidden them by Mahomet, and, in armies, it was

342

foreign to the "equisite order" of their "martiall" discipline. Othello's reference would therefore convey some irony of effect, especially in the context of Jacobean court problems about single combat, as described, e.g., by Akrigg.

L. G. Salingar, "Time and Art in Shakespeare's Romances," *Renaissance Drama*, IX (1966), 3-35.

This is a suggestive essay which contrasts the final comedies with *Errors* by stressing the deliberate archaisms which characterize the last plays. If *Errors* appears to have been written strictly according to the tradition of Roman comedy, Shakespeare, in his final plays, would seem to have accepted the difficulty of "giving imaginative reality to the movement of time," a technical problem which "neither the classical convention nor the medieval one, even in its more sophisticated Elizabethan form" could really solve when long time-spans were involved. Most striking is the author's adduction of Middleton's *Hengist* (c 1618) wherein Ranulph Higden occupies a position analogous to that of Gower's in *Pericles*, with both plays thus presenting those "consciously antiquarian touches" which reveal "the Jacobean, as distinct from the Elizabethan, theatre." What might be added to this argument may not necessarily have been meant to lie within the scope of this provocative essay, but it seems important to observe that not only the Gower prologues, but also the many rhymed lines which occur in the speeches of *Pericles* have led scholars in the past to nudge the play into the twilight fringes of the Shakespeare apocrypha. Yet if the 1609 quarto was indeed a "corrupt" version (textually-demonstrable errors aside), there must have been a sufficient number of poetasters for the "pirates" to evade one with a penchant for writing medievalist and especially 1580-ish verse such as appears in Hamlet's "Mousetrap" (cf. Wood below). Finally, though not wishing to carp with the author's careful section I, it would seem a trifle misleading to call New Comedy, if only in metaphor, "Euripidean." L. Vives spoke of the New Comedy as the comedy of Menander, and although the influence of Euripides is manifest in Menander's work, it was perhaps Menander to whom Plautus and Terence felt they were indebted. Erasmus rated Menander over Aristophanes, Homer, and Euripides, even though acknowledging that his works were no longer extant; J. Rainoldes equated Menander with comedy in 1599. The argument may seem labored, but "Menander" implied Plautus and Terence. When one acknowledges Plautus as the source for *Errors*, meanwhile recalling the fishermen's chorus of Plautus' *Rudens* when contemplating the fishermen-scene in *Pericles*, a seemingly pedantic objection to speaking (for the English Renaissance) of "Euripidean comedy" might acquire some small justification.

S. Schoenbaum, ed. "Current Projects," *Research Opportunities in Renaissance Drama*, X (1967), 93-121.

This listing is subdivided into I. Medieval, and II. Renaissance. *RORD* may be obtained by writing the editor at Northwestern University, Evanston, Illinois, 60201, U.S.A.

James H. Sims, *Dramatic Uses of Biblical Allusions in Marlowe and Shakespeare* (University of Florida Monographs: Humanities, No. 24, 1966).

Work on Biblical allusions in Shakespeare is useful where it offers insights into aesthetic process, and it is to be hoped that the study of Shakespeare as a discipline has proceeded well past the point now where discussions about the possible relevance of Renaissance theology to the drama of the period are dismissed, *a priori*, as "allegorical." For this would be to say no more—in fact, even less— than if one were to observe that Greg's studies of Elizabethan drama have been "merely verbal." It might even be suggested that the tendency to dismiss particular studies as "allegorical readings of Shakespeare" performs an intellectual disservice, not only to the discipline as a whole, but to those very writings which themselves use "allegorical reading" as a pejorative term by which to describe any work which seeks to investigate the influence of sixteenth-century Christianity on Renaissance art-forms. For any nomenclature, when used as a dismissively reductive term, must fail, by definition, to delineate and examine underlying assumptions which, in this case, imply at least three generalizations: 1) that any conceded relevance of Renaissance Christian ideas or motifs to Shakespeare's dramas distorts their meaning and/or reduces their artistic value; 2) that the more "normal," the more "natural," the more "theatrical", the more "common-sense" ideas (i.e. non-Christian and/or post-eighteenth-century) are more suitable and relevant to recovering the value-orientations by which one is to understand the structure of a Shakespeare play; 3) that any study of the relevance of Renaissance Christianity to an understanding of ideational organization in a Shakespearean play is a study of "allegory".

After reminding ourselves that even "allegory" is itself a simplistic term to apply to the complexities and diversities of Renaissance representational modes, the study of Renaissance theology and its popular traditions remains a highly exacting discipline: no single book or article on the subject achieves validity *sui generis*. The study of Shakespeare's Biblical allusions, for example, is itself a special problem in definition. What, after all, is a "Biblical allusion"? Is it a reference, in a play, to some article of Christian faith ultimately derived from the Bible? Is it the dramatic use of an English proverb possibly pre-dating any Renaissance translation of the Bible and drawn upon by translators as the most idiomatic rendering of a Hebrew, Greek, or derived Latin passage? Is it a reference in a play to the Patristic commentary (and the accompanying iconological tradition?) bearing on a particular Biblical passage? And how does "Biblical allusion" enter a play: as a value-statement by a particular character? as a series of events recalling a series of events in Biblical narrative? as an evocation of Biblically-significant locales with an assumed ideological context? Is, in fact, "Biblical allusion" so difficult an element to define that, until a careful study in procedure is forthcoming, the safest temporary definition might restrict itself to specific references regarding specific stories and names comprehended in the parables and annals of the Old and New Testament as well as of the Apocrypha. If so, then one might subsequently proceed from such a tabulation to other matters which could be inferred, all other artistic considerations being equal. Foakes, in his Arden edition of *Errors* (pp.113 ff.) considers, for instance, the relevance of *Acts* xix, and of Paul's Epistle to the Ephesians, while we might ourselves be curious, in *Pericles*, about the presence of that Antiochus, villain of the Apocrypha, as well as the shipwreck of the hero in such a place as Tarsus.

In any event, a work on Biblical allusions in Shakespeare is a difficult undertaking, and readers of this monograph need to bear these difficulties in mind, for they may be concerned about the completeness here of the (working) repertoire of published scholarship from which some important elements are absent. Ultimately, one might say of studies on Shakespeare's Biblical allusions what one might say about bibliographies. Both are useful, by definition, if they yield only a few items (or allusions) which a reader might not otherwise have garnered. The discussion of Jephthah (p.56) in the *Homilies* is a case in point.

John Hazel Smith, "Seneca's Tragedies: A Tentative Checklist of Fifteenth-, Sixteenth-, and Seventeenth-Century Printings," *Research Opportunities in Renaissance Drama*, X (1967), 49-74.

Joseph Westlund, "Fancy and Achievement in *Love's Labour's Lost*," *SQ*, XVIII (1967), 37-46.

This essay argues that the ethical thrust of this play (my term) is to present the conflict between fancy and achievement. Separation from reality, through words and through ways of thinking, causes lack of discernible achievement except in the telling case of Armado whose plainness of speech may seem ludicrous, but who remains the only successful wooer in the comedy. This mode of viewing the play enables the article to relate the last song, as well as the news of death, to the structure as a whole, since the former favorably contrasts winter with summer, and the latter is a reminder of reality. Finally, the Show of the Worthies is taken by the author to summarize thematic elements in the play because the real achievement of the Worthies themselves contrasts with the failure of the wooers and also emerges, in its bombast, "as a humorous statement of the breakdown in communication which is

344

implicit in the main action of the play." In connection with the Worthies, however, the author makes some debatable points. The choice of the term "labour" in the title of the play is said to probably be related to the frequent references to the Worthies and their labors, and especially to the labors of Hercules whose inclusion, with Pompey, among the Worthies is unorthodox, although the heroes included varied a great deal. Actually, the problem is that Shakespeare has not adhered to the usual general formula: three Jews, three Gentiles, and three Christians (for the tradition, see p.336 n.1 of my article in *MLR*, LIII [1958], 327-343). Shakespeare was aware of the formula, since Judas Maccabaeus is present in the show (for Maccabaeus, cf. John Conley in *N&Q*, XIV [1967], 50-51), but four pagans are presented. Since Hercules had the reputation of evading his labors for love, and since Hector had no such problems, it is interesting though not baffling, that Moth, the page, represents Hercules, and Armado represents the Trojan, just as it is interesting that Pompey, instead of his conqueror, the more usual Julius Caesar, is defined as a "Worthy." Whatever the aesthetic significance, the show warrants closer attention than it is given here. Furthermore, until the point is proved, it seems dangerous to mingle twentieth century poetic practice with Renaissance aesthetic when it comes to titles, especially as concerns plays. There is no proof that play-titles were meant to be organically meaningful parts of the art-offerings (cf., e.g. *"Henry IV,"* or, simply, *"Cymbeline"*) or that the titles were even necessarily conferred by the author, or even consistently used as labels, (e.g. in Stationers' entries and court payments). But this is to carp at an otherwise useful analysis.

Christopher Whitfield, "Anthony and John Nash; Shakespeare's Legatees," N&Q, XIV (1967), 123-130.

This article explores the Stratford background and connections of the above-mentioned persons, and although the work is sufficient unto itself, it might be added that there are implications for the student of Shakespeare's life. It is significant that Anthony and John Nash were so closely associated with the life of Stratford because their presence in Shakespeare's will might suggest the continuing dynamism in the poet's relationship to Stratford throughout his career, a dynamism implied by other evidence, in any event. Here we need merely recall that Shakespeare left 26/8 to Anthony and John for memorial rings, and that this is just the same sum left for the same purpose, to presumably closer associates: Burbage, Heminges, and Condell. The article itself should be used in connection with Whitfield's previous work discussed in *Shakespeare Studies*, II, (1966), 45.

James O. Wood, " 'Pericles,' I.ii," and "Notes on 'Pericles,' Acts I and II," N&Q, XIV (1967), 141-143.

Both of these notes cast some light on the 1609 quarto of *Pericles* by assessing the degree of supposed "corruption" in the early parts of the play. I.ii.35-36 need not be considered "corrupt" in the light of the Wilkins background which suggests that I.ii. of Q 1609 lacks "not textual integrity" but perhaps "dramatic expertness and finish." The second, somewhat diffuse article, approaches the problem of "corruption" by suggesting that some of the words may be Northern and/or obsolescent, but not, therefore, necessarily misreadings. Some characteristic Shakespearean usages are alluded to from other plays in this connection. The reader may wish to compare this article with Salingar, above.

Akihiro Yamada, "Bibliographical Studies of George Chapman's *An Humorous Day's Mirth* (1599) Printed by Valentine Simmes," ShStud (Tokyo), V (1966/67), 119-149.

Yamada's collation of the fifteen known copies of a Chapman quarto printed by Valentine Simmes not only provides a good model of what such a study should be, but also furnishes information of potential importance to editors of the various Shakespeare quartos printed by Valentine Simmes. It will be sufficient here to indicate subdivisions in the article: I. The Nature of the Printer's Copy; II. Press-Variants in Q (1599); III. Compositorial Analysis; IV. The characteristics of the Compositor. Although the author indicates that he has used spelling, punctuation, speech-prefix, running-title, as well as examination of the measure of the composing-stick and the number of lines to a page—all as criteria to suggest the involvement of only one compositor—it would have been useful to have had a more extended statement on the subject in the way of statistics. Certainly the basic statistics are provided, but since the author concludes that the compositor's punctuation-habits appear to differ even from those other compositors who worked for Simmes, those concerned with Shakespeare's plays would be more than a little interested. However, the author's purpose was to analyse Chapman, and it is ungrateful to complain. See also *Shakespeare Studies* II (1966), 45-46.

Reviews

W. E. D. Atkinson, ed., *Acolastus* (University of Western Ontario Studies in the Humanities, 1964). See John Hazel Smith in *JEGP*, LXVI (1967), 444-447.

Paul Bacquet, *Un Contemporain d'Elisabeth I : Thomas Sackville* (Geneva : Droz, 1966). See Jean Robertson in *RES*, XVIII (1967), 315-317.

Paul Bertram, *Shakespeare and "The Two Noble Kinsmen"* (Rutgers University Press, 1965). See Arthur Brown in *Library*, XXII (1967), 268-270.

William H. Bond, ed., *Records of a Bibliographer. Selected Papers of William Alexander Jackson* (Harvard University Press, 1967). See *TLS*, Nov. 30 (1967), 1172.

Fredson Bowers, *Today's Shakespeare Texts, and Tomorrow's*, SB, XIX (1966). See J. C. Maxwell in *SQ*, XVIII (1967), 184-185.

Fredson Bowers and Lyle H. Wright, *Bibliography* (University of California Press, 1967). See "Bibliography and Dr. Bowers," *TLS*, April 27 (1967), 362.

Fredson Bowers, *Bibliographical and Textual Criticism* (The Clarendon Press, 1964), See J. K. Walton in *N&Q*, XIV (1967), 147-153.

Ernest Brennecke, *Shakespeare in Germany, 1590-1700* (University of Chicago Press, 1964). See G. I. Duthie in *Anglia*, LXXXV (1967), 101-104.

Peter H. Brieger, *The Trinity College Apocalypse* (Eugrammia Press, 1967). See *TLS*, May 25 (1967), 476.

Stella Brook, *The Language of the Book of Common Prayer* (André Deutsch, 1965). See C. G. Harlow in *N&Q*, XIV (1967), 106-108.

Howard Mayer Brown, *Instrumental Music Printed Before 1600. A Bibliography.* (Oxford University Press, 1965). See A. Hyatt King in *Library*, XXII (1967), 154-158.

O. J. Campbell and Edward G. Quinn, *A Shakespeare Encyclopaedia* (Thomas Y. Crowell, 1966). See J. B. Fort in *Études Anglaises*, XX (1967), 299-300.

Nevill Coghill, *Shakespeare's Professional Skills* (Methuen, 1966). See Arthur Brown in *Library*, XXII (1967), 163-165.

G. I. Duthie and J. Dover Wilson, eds., *King Lear* (Cambridge University Press, 1960). See Mary Lascelles in *RES*, XVIII (1967), 322-326.

Ludwig Edelstein, *The Meaning of Stoicism* (Harvard University Press, 1967). See *TLS*, July 20 (1967), 629-631.

William R. Elton, *"King Lear" and the Gods* (The Huntington Library Press, 1966). See G. I. Duthie in *Renaissance Quarterly*, XX (1967), 377-380.

D. V. Glass, *London Inhabitants within the Walls 1695* (London Record Society, 1966). See M. H. Port in *N&Q*, XIV (1967), 354.

W.W. Greg and Charlton Hinman, eds., *Richard II (1597; I Henry IV (1598).* Shakespeare Quarto Facsimiles, Nos. 13, 14. (The Clarendon Press, 1966). See James G. McManaway in *SQ*, XVII (1966), 429-430.

Rudolph Hirsch, *Printing, Selling and Reading: 1450-1550* (Otto Harrassowitz, 1967). See *TLS*, Sept. 21 (1967), 848.

A. R. Humphreys, ed., *The Second Part of King Henry IV.* The New Arden Edition. (Methuen, 1966). See James G. McManaway in *SQ*, XVIII (1967), 83-85, and T. H. Howard-Hill in *RES*, XVIII (1967), 456-458.

Jean Jacquot, ed., Le lieu théâtral à la Renaissance (Centre National de la Recherche Scientifique, 1964). See M. C. Bradbrook in *MLR*, LXII (1967), 509-510, and Bodo L. O. Richter, "Recent Studies in Renaissance Scenography," *Renaissance News*, XIX (1966), 344-358.

Harriet Joseph, *Shakespeare's Son in Law: John Hall* (Archon Books, 1964). See Mark Eccles in *SQ*, XVII (1966), 432-433.

Faye C. Kelly, *Prayer in Sixteenth Century England* (Univ. of Florida Monographs: Humanities, No. 22, 1966). See Rosemary Freeman in *N&Q*, XIV (1967), 476-477.

Clifford Leech, *"Twelfth Night" and Shakespearean Comedy* (University of Toronto Press, 1965). See James Hisao Kodama in *Shakespeare Studies* (Tokyo) V (1966-67), 150-156.

J. F. Nims, ed., *Ovid's Metamorphoses: The Arthur Golding Translation* (The Macmillan Company, 1965). See T. W. Baldwin in *JEGP*, LXVI (1967), 124-127.

Otto Pächt and J. J. G. Alexander, *Illuminated Manuscripts in the Bodleian Library* (The Clarendon Press, 1967). See *TLS*, March 16 (1967), 228.

John Pope-Hennessy, *The Portrait in the Renaissance* (The Phaidon Press, 1967). See *TLS*, Oct. 19 (1967), 981-982.

Gilbert Ryle, *Plato's Progress* (Cambridge University Press, 1966). See T. M. Robinson, "Plato Oxoniensis" in *UTQ*, XXXVII (1967), 90-102.

S. Schoenbaum, *Internal Evidence and Elizabethan Dramatic Authorship* (Northwestern University Press, 1966). See Arthur Sherbo in *JEGP*, LXVI (1967), 127-129.

Shakespeare Jahrbuch (Weimar) 1964/65. See Karl P. Wentersdorf in *SQ*, XVIII (1967), 91-93.

N. D. Shergold, *A History of the Spanish Stage from Medieval Times until the End of the Seventeenth Century*. (The Clarendon Press, 1967). See *TLS*, Oct. 19 (1967), 986.

Irwin Smith, *Shakespeare's Blackfriars Playhouse* (New York University Press, 1964). See T. J. King in *Renaissance Drama*, IX (1966) 291-309. (Review Article).

Marion Bodwell Smith, *Dualities in Shakespeare* (University of Toronto Press, 1966). See Paul A. Jorgensen in *Renaissance Quarterly*, XX (1967), 63-66.

Carl J. Stratman, *Bibliography of English Printed Tragedy: 1565-1900* (Southern Illinois University Press, 1967). See *TLS*, March 30 (1967), 276.

John Taylor, *The Universal Chronicle of Ranulf Higden* (The Clarendon Press, 1966). See Anne Hudson in *RES*, XVIII (1967), 185-187.

Joan Thirsk, ed., *The Agrarian History of England and Wales, Volume IV: 1500-1640* (Cambridge University Press, 1967). See *TLS*, Dec. 14 (1967), 1212.

Rosemund Tuve, *Allegorical Imagery* (Princeton University Press, 1966). See D. C. Allen in *JEGP*, LXVI (1967), 118-120.

Henry J. Webb, *Elizabethan Military Science* (University of Wisconsin Press, 1965). See T. R. Henn in *MLR*, LXII (1967), 111-113.

David P. Young, *Something of Great Constancy: The Art of "A Midsummer Night's Dream"* (Yale University Press, 1966). See Sidney R. Homan, Jr., in *JEGP*, LXVI (1967), 578-582.

Walter Whiter, *A Specimen of a Commentary on Shakespeare*, ed., Alan Over and Mary Bell (London: Methuen; New York, Barnes & Noble, 1967) See Mary Bell, "Walter Whiter's Notes on Shakespeare", *Sh.S*, XX (1967), 83-94, for a discussion of Whiter's critical ideas.

Ancillary Studies

R. L. Anderson, *Elizabethan Psychology and Shakespeare's Plays.*
Russell and Russell, 1966.

The author, in the "Preface to the Second Edition" of this well-known work would, however, seem to make it clear that we are dealing with a reprint here, using that word herself as she indicates what, given the leisure for it, she might have done by way of revision. One may accordingly take issue with her conclusion to this Preface : that, nevertheless, "the exposition of Elizabethan faculty psychology I have made is sound; it remains the most comprehensive treatment of the subject that exists." Far too much has been written on the subject to render this a fair statement of the situation, especially if a number of unpublished dissertations be taken into account, those of J. V. Cunningham and of R. Soellner, for example, no article in Anderson's bibliography being later than 1926. However, the usefulness of this reprint is not therefore vitiated, for Anderson's important monograph has always needed to be more accessible than heretofore.

Aristotle, *Poetics*, tr. Gerald F. Else. The University of Michigan Press, 1967.

This translation, with introduction and notes by the well-known author of *Aristotle's Poetics : The Argument* (Cambridge, Mass., 1957), is based on the Oxford Classical Text edition by Rudolf Kassel (1965). Useful for critical theorists rather than for literary historians — since Else is not orienting himself towards, say, Weinberg's subject (Renaissance interpretations of the *Poetics*) — this carefully annotated text is an inexpensive and important resource for any student of tragic theory. The translation differs somewhat in details of wording, rather than syntactically, from that in the 1957 publication.

Hugh Aveling, O. S. B., *Northern Catholics.* Geoffrey Chapman, 1966.

This is a detailed study which continues investigations carried out by the author in *The Catholic Recusants of the West Riding* to determine just what was the relationship between the authorities and the Catholic recusants between 1558 and 1790. Here with the Catholic recusants of the North Riding, the author carries on his important methodological premise that the behavior of both recusants and authorities could be judged more clearly in the light of rather detailed information about such groups within specifically delimited geographical areas. The third in a series of four studies, this work cannot be ignored by those who continue to investigate the nature of Shakespeare's formal religious affiliations, for, as the author points out: "the more one becomes familiar with the documents of recusant history — even, or especially, those of the central government surveying the country-wide recusant problems from Westminster — the more sharply one sees that a multiplicity of local and domestic details (family relationships, the lay of the land and of local jurisdictions and franchises, the *minutiae* of local administrative methods and of the land law and economic conditions) alone explain the behaviour of recusants and of the authorities towards them."

Calendar of the Patent Rolls: Elizabeth I (Volume V: 1569-1572).
Her Majesty's Stationery Office, 1966.

This volume continues the Calendar of Patent Rolls on the plan indicated in the preface to the first volume of the calendar for this reign. Although any attempted "description" of such a mass of information in the space here would be an absurdity, the many documents relating to the Northern Rebellion are worth mentioning, as is, e.g. the exclusive licence granted Thomas Marsche by the queen on 29 Sept., 1572, to print and sell twelve standard and specified school books.

O. J. Campbell and E. G. Quinn, eds. *The Reader's Encyclopedia of Shakespeare.*
Thomas Y. Crowell Company, 1966.

Unlike many such compilations, this book can be used as an aid not only to the undergraduate, but to the memory of the professional scholar. Given the inherent limitations of such "encyclopedias", it is an ideal work of its kind, ranging through stage-history, criticism, and reproductions of the title-pages, say, of both quartos of the *Merchant of Venice,* to an entry on George Bryan, one of the actors whose names appear in the "plot" of *Seven Deadly Sins.*

Caxton's Aesop, ed. R. T. Lenaghan. Harvard University Press, 1967.

The relevance of Aesop to Shakespeare's own probable training in school has been dealt with at some length by T. W. Baldwin, *Small Latine,* I, ch.27, and Baldwin has argued that Caxton's Aesop was not Shakespeare's. Nevertheless, Caxton's translation was the only one in existence in Shakespeare's youth, and this edition, with Lenaghan's introduction describing the nature of the medieval/Renaissance *Aesop* will be valuable to scholars who have noted the many references to quasi-Aesopian material in Shakespeare's plays.

"Directory of Scholars Active," *Computers and the Humanities,* II (1967), 77.

Work in progress is not generally described in *Shakespeare Studies,* but scholars may wish to consult *L125: "An Index to the Stationers' Register," the proposed scope of which is "to index all proper names and titles in the Eyre and Rivington volumes of the *Stationers' Register,* and, hopefully, to then form a similar index for the Arber volumes."

Richard J. Durling, compiler, *A Catalogue of Sixteenth Century Printed Books in the National Library of Medicine.* U. S. Department of Health, Education and Welfare, 1967.

This catalogue lists and describes all sixteenth-century imprints held by the History of Medicine Division of the National Library of Medicine, but it should be consulted with special reference to p. 693 where the NLM numbers are "translated" to STC numbers and where eighteen titles not in STC are indicated.

Julia G. Ebel, "A Numerical Survey of Elizabethan Translations," *Library,*
XXII (1967), 104-127.

This is useful material for those concerned with subjects where translations might provide pertinent data. The divisions are according to the languages, and the listings refer either to STC numbers or to numbers from other relevant catalogues. Lathrop has, of course, been consulted.

W. W. Greg, *Collected Papers,* ed. J. C. Maxwell. The Clarendon Press, 1966.

Although the title of this work may speak for itself, readers may wish to consult Maxwell's Preface which, i.e., indicates which of the thirty articles was revised by Greg in any significant way since their origianl publications.

350

Sir Paul Harvey, ed. *The Oxford Companion to English Literature.*
Fourth Edition. The Clarendon Press, 1967.

Useful, among other things, for the fact that the article on the English Calendar has been revised by
C. R. Cheney so that this material, with calendars, is now more easily available than heretofore.

Marvin T. Herrick, *Italian Plays, 1500-1700, in the University of Illinois Library.*
University of Illinois Press, 1966.

In this listing of over five hundred plays, none written in Latin by Italian dramatists has been included.
The listing is arranged by author and there is an index by play-title. There are no bibliographical
descriptions, but Herrick does indicate the number of acts in each play and whether each drama is
in verse or prose. Pp.91-92 list eleven *intermedii* which the author defines as "brief dramatic or musical
entertainments bound with, included in, or written for particular plays."

W. J. Jones, *The Elizabethan Court of Chancery.* The Clarendon Press, 1967.

Since information about dramatists of the period is often available to literary historians through records of litigation, Jones's study of the Chancery as a court of law at a time when both its officials and
procedures were subjected to a process of definition has an obvious relevance. The first section of
this study is devoted to those who staffed the court, the second, to the growth of procedural rules,
along with extensive discussion of terminology. A final section discusses the relation of the Court of
Chancery with other courts of the period such as the Court of Wards which had responsibility for
idiots and natural fools. The relationship between the two Courts in this area which could concern
orphans too, may, for example, interest students of the children's dramatic companies.

John Lyly, *The Complete Works,* ed. R. Warwick Bond. The Clarendon
Press, 1967.

This lithographic reprint makes Bond's three volumes again available not only to students of Lyly,
but to those scholars who might wish to reconsider Bond's voluminous and careful (but dated) commentary for its possible bearing on such early Shakespearean work as *LLL.*

A. W. Pollard and J. Dover Wilson, *Shakespeare Problems.* Cambridge
University Press, 1967.

The item is entered as the title-page reads, but it will be more familiar to scholars as the Cambridge
University Press Library Edition of *Shakespeare's Fight with the Pirates* and of *Shakespeare's Hand
in the Play of Sir Thomas More.* Both works are here made available again in the one volume at a
price of 60s. The "Library Editions" are defined by the Press as a series of reissues of out-of-print
standard works from the Cambridge catalogues. "The texts are unrevised; apart from minor corrections these editions reproduce exactly the last normal printing. Where desirable or possible the author
has provided a short prefatory note." Comments here will, of course, be unnecessary except by way
of welcoming further reprints of this sort.

Jacques Ramel, "Biographical Notices on the Authors of 'The Misfortunes of
Arthur' (1588)," *N&Q,* XIV (1967), 461-467.

By studying what is known of Thomas Hughes, John Penruddock, John Lancaster, Francis Flower,
and Nicholas Trotte, this article offers some wider insight into the role of Gray's Inn as a medium for
drama, and suggests the range of participation by reminding us of the disparities in the ages of these
authors.

Lawrence J. Ross, "Symbol and Structure in the *Secunda Pastorum*", *Comparative Drama*, I (1967), 122-149.

This article, appearing in the new quarterly journal *Comparative Drama*, does not have a direct bearing on Shakespeare, but a reading of it will indicate the possibilities inherent in a tradition which, as Hardin Craig has pointed out, persisted through the 1590's, and it does suggest something about the sophistication of a dramatic structure which was part of Shakespeare's cultural heritage. The study of the relation of a farcical action to the totality of a play within the English cycle drama is not wholly irrelevant to such problems as those posed by the relation of a Falstaff to *1, 2 Henry IV*, as long as one does not confuse analogy with identity.

Allan Stevenson, (Letter), *TLS*, June 1, 1967, p. 492.

This brief note reminds us of some of the problems involved in the use of the beta-radiographic process for detecting early English watermarks.

D. L. Stevenson, *The Love-Game Comedy*. Barnes & Noble, 1966.

Originally published in 1946, this study of *LLL* has been extremely difficult to find in many libraries.

John Webb, ed. *Poor Relief in Elizabethan Ipswich*. Suffolk Records Society, 1966.

Wishing to show how one leading provincial town dealt with the problem of poverty during the period between the accession of Elizabeth I and the passing of the Poor Law Act of 1598, Webb has been able to gather records which can focus attention on 1577-79 and 1596-98. To specify the value of any records is to court absurdity, but students of *Lear* may wish to peruse, for example, the humane treatment accorded to "innocents", while historians of drama in the provinces may find some indicative value in the plague relief accounts, along with Webb's own references.

Lynn White, Jr., ed. *The Transformation of the Roman World*. The University of California Press, 1966.

A series of essays arising from lectures given by historians associated with the Center for Medieval and Renaissance Studies of the University of California, Los Angeles, the volume is the third publication contributed by this Center. Relevant here is VII, "The Continuity and Preservation of the Latin Tradition" by Philip Levine, a useful supplement to the work of C. N. Cochrane.

Edgar Wind, *Pagan Mysteries in the Renaissance*. Penguin Books with Faber and Faber, 1967.

This is an inexpensive Peregrine edition of Wind's well-known work but it is not merely a reprint. "Although the argument of this book remains unchanged from what it was . . . the documentation has been increased substantially," to increase the value of what is still one of the most significant studies of Renaissance Neoplatonism.

L. Wittgenstein, *Lectures and Conversations on Aesthetics, Psychology and Religious Belief*, ed. Cyril Barrett. Basil Blackwell, 1966.

Although containing nothing written by Wittgenstein himself, this compilation of notes taken down by his students specifies the principles of *Philosophical Investigations* to discussions of such problems as that of talking about "imagery".

Directory

I

Gates Kennedy Agnew, *Department of English, Indiana University, Bloomington, Indiana 47405.*

G. P. V. Akrigg, *Department of English, The University of British Columbia, Vancouver 8, British Columbia, Canada.*

John A. Allen, *Department of English, Hollins College, Hollins College, Virginia 24020.*

Mrs. Mark W. Ammons, *520 E. Buffalo Street, Ithaca, New York 14850.*

John S. Anson, *Department of English, The University of California, Berkeley, California 94720.*

James Applegate, *Department of English, Wilson College, Chambersburg, Pennsylvania 17201.*

Mark Ashin, *Department of English, The University of Chicago, Chicago, Illinois 60637.*

W. E. D. Atkinson, *Department of English, The University of Western Ontario, London, Ontario, Canada.*

Warren B. Austin, *Department of English, Stephen F. Austin State College, Nacogdoches, Texas 75962.*

Wallace A. Bacon, *School of Speech, Northwestern University, Evanston, Illinois 60201.*

Kennith R. Balsley, *The Episcopal Academy, Philadelphia, Pennsylvania 19131.*

Betty Bandel, *Department of English, The University of Vermont, Burlington, Vermont 05401.*

Jonas A. Barish, *Department of English, The University of California, Berkeley, California 94720.*

Sylvan Barnet, *Department of English, Tufts University, Medford, Massachusetts 02155.*

Mrs. T. C. Barnum, *Department of English, Syracuse University, Syracuse, New York 13210.*

Mrs. J. Leeds Barroll, *416 South Carlisle Street, Philadelphia, Pennsylvania 19146.*

E. Beatrice Batson, *Department of English, Wheaton College, Wheaton, Illinois 60187.*

Roy W. Battenhouse, *Department of English, Indiana University, Bloomington, Indiana 47401.*

John S. Baxter, *Department of English, Queen's University, Kingston, Ontario, Canada.*

Bernard Beckerman, *Department of Drama and Speech, Hofstra University, Hempstead, New York 11550.*

A. C. Begor, *Department of English, University College, The University of Toronto, Toronto 5, Ontario, Canada.*

John Benedict, *W. W. Norton and Company, 55 Fifth Avenue, New York, New York 10003.*

Josephine Waters Bennett, *Department of English, Hunter College, New York, New York 10021.*

G. E. Bentley, *Department of English, Princeton University, Princeton, New Jersey 08540.*

Rev. Miguel A. Bernad, S.J., *Ateneo de Manila, P.O. Box 154, Manila, Philippines.*

Dennis Biggins, *The University of Newcastle, Newcastle, N.S.W., Australia.*

William B. Bjornstad, *Department of English, Drake University, Des Moines, Iowa 50311.*

Ben Black, *Department of English, The University of Kentucky, Lexington, Kentucky 40502.*

Grace T. Blakey, *Department of English, The University of Michigan, Ann Arbor, Michigan 48104.*

C. I. C. Bosanquet, *The Vice-Chancellor, The University, Newcastle-upon-Tyne, England.*

Hoyt Edwin Bowen, *Department of English, Pfeiffer College, Misenheimer, North Carolina 28109.*

George C. Branam, *Office of Academic Affairs, Louisiana State University, New Orleans, Louisiana 70122.*

Ernest Brennecke, *Department of English, Columbia University, New York, New York 10027.*

John Britton, *Department of English, Fordham University, Bronx, New York* 10458.

Harriet D. Broeker, *Department of English, Knoxville College, Knoxville, Tennessee* 37916.

Charles B. Brooks, *Department of English, California State College at Long Beach, Long Beach, California* 90804.

Arthur Brown, *Department of English, University College London, Gower Street, London, W.C.1, England.*

William J. Brown, *Department of English, Southern Illinois University, Carbondale, Illinois* 62903.

Edward S. Brubaker, *Department of English, Franklin and Marshall College, Lancaster, Pennsylvania* 17603.

Albert H. Buford, *The Graduate Office, Villanova University, Villanova, Pennsylvania* 19085.

Paulina Buhl, *Department of English, Shorter College, Rome, Georgia* 30161.

C. O. Burgess, *Department of English, Old Dominion College, Norfolk, Virginia* 23508.

Andrew S. Cairncross, *Department of English, Texas Technological College, Lubbock, Texas* 79409.

Roger W. Calkins, *Department of English, Mt. Allison University, Sackville, New Brunswick, Canada.*

Louise Callison, *Department of English, Alderson-Broaddus College, Phillippi, West Virginia* 26417.

Mrs. Martin Cannon, *9662 North 29th Street, Omaha, Nebraska* 68152.

Otis G. Carnes, *Division of Languages and Communication, Pembroke State College, Pembroke, North Carolina* 28372.

Félix J. Carrère, *2 Chemin des Fenouillères, Aix-en-Provence, France.*

James E. Carver, *Department of Languages and Literatures, St. Andrews Presbyterian College, Laurinburg, North Carolina* 28352.

Joseph S. M. J. Chang, *Department of English, The University of Wisconsin, Milwaukee, Wisconsin* 53211.

David R. Cheney, *Department of English, The University of Toledo, Toledo, Ohio* 43606.

H. E. Childs, *Department of English, Oregon State University, Corvallis, Oregon* 97331.

Clarence L. Cline, *Department of English, The University of Texas, Austin, Texas* 78712.

Eileen Z. Cohen, *Department of English, Temple University, Philadelphia, Pennsylvania* 19122.

Mr. and Mrs. William Collins, *9 Interwood Place, Cincinnati, Ohio* 45220.

David B. Comer III, *Department of English, Georgia Institute of Technology, Atlanta, Georgia* 30313.

Mrs. Milton Kay Conver, *1228 Dean Court, Cincinnati, Ohio* 45230.

Archibald C. Coolidge, Jr., *Department of English, The University of Iowa, Iowa City, Iowa* 52240.

Jackson I. Cope, *Department of English, The Johns Hopkins University, Baltimore, Maryland* 21218.

P. L. Cornett, *Department of English, Wayne State University, Detroit, Michigan* 48202.

L. G. Crossman, *The University of Saskatchewan, Regina Campus, Saskatoon, Saskatchewan, Canada.*

John Crow, *Department of English, King's College, The University of London, London, England.*

Miss Elizabeth Cummings, *La Salle-Peru-Oglesby Junior College, La Salle, Illinois* 61301.

Giles E. Dawson, *The Folger Shakespeare Library, Washington, D. C.* 20003.

Dayton N. Dennett, *Department of English, Massachusetts State College, Fitchburg, Massachusetts* 01420.

Robert W. Dent, *Department of English, The University of California, Los Angeles, California* 90024.

Alan C. Dessen, *Department of English, The University of Wisconsin, Madison, Wisconsin* 53706.

Noyes Devor, *Central College, McPherson, Kansas* 67460.

David O. Dickerson, *Department of English, Greenville College, Greenville, Illinois* 62246.

Thomas P. Donlon, *50 New Park Road, Black Rock, County Dublin, Ireland.*

Madeleine Doran, *Department of English, The University of Wisconsin, Madison, Wisconsin* 53706.

R. J. Dorius, *Department of English, San Francisco State College, San Francisco, California* 94132.

Alvin W. Druhman, *Department of English,*

St. Joseph's College, Rensselaer,
Indiana 47978.

K. C. Eapen, 1111 Second Street, Charleston,
Illinois.

K. R. Eissler, 300 Central Park West,
New York, New York 10024.

Mrs. Frank R. Elder, 785 Greenville Avenue,
Cincinnati, Ohio 45246.

William R. Elton, Department of English, The
University of California, Riverside,
California 92502.

William A. Elwood, Department of English,
The University of Virginia, Charlottesville,
Virginia 22903.

English Department, The University of
California, Riverside, California 92502.

English Department, The University of
Jyväskylä, Finland.

English Department, Miami University, Oxford,
Ohio 45056.

English Department Library, Ohio State
University, Columbus, Ohio 43210.

R. O. Evans, Department of English, The
University of Kentucky, Lexington,
Kentucky 40506.

Sylvia D. Feldman, Department of English,
Douglass College, Rutgers University,
New Brunswick, New Jersey 08903.

S. T. Fisher, 53 Morrison Avenue,
Montreal 16, Canada.

Robert E. Fitch, Pacific School of Religion,
Berkeley, California 94709.

H. Fluchère, Faculté des Lettres,
Aix-en-Provence, France.

C. L. Ford, 2718 Drake Avenue, Costa Mesa,
California 92626.

Charles R. Forker, Department of English,
Indiana University, Bloomington, Indiana
47405.

Joseph Barthélémy Fort, 7 Rue Monticelli,
Paris 14, France.

Levi Fox, The Shakespeare Birthplace Trust,
The Shakespeare Centre, Stratford-upon-
Avon, England.

Russell A. Fraser, Department of English,
Vanderbilt University, Nashville,
Tennessee 37203.

Raymond M. Fredman, Department of English
and Speech, Cuyahoga Community College,
Cleveland, Ohio 44115.

Dean Frye, Department of English, McGill

University, Montreal 2, Quebec, Canada.

Northrop Frye, Department of English,
Victoria College, The University of
Toronto, Toronto 5, Ontario, Canada.

Roland Mushat Frye, Department of English,
The University of Pennsylvania, Philadelphia,
Pennsylvania 19104.

Mary N. Gailbreath, Department of Health,
Education and Welfare, Washington, D. C.
20202.

David Galloway, Department of English, The
University of Waterloo, Waterloo, Ontario,
Canada.

Lloyd Graham Gibbs, Department of English,
The University of South Carolina,
Columbia, South Carolina 29208.

John N. Gill, Department of English,
Wartburg College, Waverly, Iowa 50677.

Albert Gilman, Department of English,
Boston University, Boston,
Massachusetts 02215.

Robert Hillis Goldsmith, Department of
English, Emory and Henry College, Emory,
Virginia 24327.

R. Dorset Graves, Division of Languages and
Literature, Chadron State College,
Chadron, Nebraska 69337.

Thelma Greenfield, Department of English,
The University of Oregon, Eugene,
Oregon 97403.

Albert J. Guérard, Department of English,
Stanford University, Stanford,
California 94305.

Ann Haaker, Department of English,
California State College, Fullerton,
California 92631.

Margie M. Hankinson, Department of English,
Texas Woman's University, Denton, Texas
76204.

Alfred Harbage, Department of English,
Harvard University, Cambridge,
Massachusetts 02138.

Donald E. Hayden, College of Liberal Arts,
The University of Tulsa, Tulsa,
Oklahoma 74104.

Ray L. Heffner, Brown University,
Providence, Rhode Island 02912.

Robert B. Heilman, Department of English,
The University of Washington, Seattle,
Washington 98105.

Tinsley Helton, Department of English,

355

The University of Wisconsin, Milwaukee, Wisconsin 53211.

Miss V. W. Henley, The University College of Fort Hare, Alice, Cape Province, South Africa.

George R. Hibbard, Department of English, The University, University Park, Nottingham, England.

Archibald A. Hill, Department of English, The University of Texas, Austin, Texas 78712.

Addie Suggs Hilliard, Western Kentucky State College, Bowling Green, Kentucky 42102.

Charlton Hinman, Department of English, The University of Kansas, Lawrence, Kansas 66045.

Charles K. Hofling, 300 Warren Avenue, Cincinnati, Ohio 45220.

Allan Holaday, Department of English, The University of Illinois, Urbana, Illinois 61803.

Lilla M. Holliday, 370 Probasco, Cincinnati, Ohio 45220.

Irvin B. Horst, The University of Amsterdam, Amsterdam, The Netherlands.

Frank L. Hoskins, Jr., Department of English, Newberry College, Newberry, South Carolina 29108.

T. H. Howard-Hill, Brigg's Cottage, Noke, Oxford, England.

Mrs. H. W. Hunsiker, 5622 Northumberland Street, Pittsburgh, Pennsylvania 15217.

Mrs. Donald F. Hyde, Four Oaks Farm, RFD 3, Somerville, New Jersey.

Reginald W. Ingram, Department of English, The University of British Columbia, Vancouver 8, British Columbia, Canada.

Maurice Jacobs, 1010 Arch Street, Philadelphia, Pennsylvania 19107.

Mrs. Elizabeth T. James, Danbury State College, Danbury, Connecticut.

Hobart Jarrett, Department of English, Brooklyn College, Brooklyn, New York 11210.

Sears R. Jayne, Department of English, Queens College, Flushing, New York 11367.

S. F. Johnson, Department of English, Columbia University, New York, New York 10027.

James H. Jones, Department of English, Northern Michigan University, Marquette, Michigan 49855.

M. T. Jones-Davies, 80 Boulevard de la Duchesse Anne, Rennes, France.

Stanley J. Kahrl, Department of English,

The University of Rochester, Rochester, New York 14627.

J. A. Kemen, 2871 Almester Drive, Cincinnati, Ohio 45211.

Paul Murray Kendall, Department of English, Ohio University, Athens, Ohio 45701.

William H. J. Kennedy, Department of English, Queensborough Community College, Bayside, New York 11364.

Harry Keyishian, Department of English, Fairleigh Dickinson University, Madison, New Jersey 07940.

Arthur F. Kinney, Department of English, Yale University, New Haven, Connecticut 06520.

John P. Kirby, Department of English, Randolph-Macon Woman's College, Lynchburg, Virginia 24504.

Joseph P. Klatzkin, 209 Academy Street, Trenton, New Jersey 08618.

J. W. Knedler, Jr., Department of English, University College, New York University, Bronx, New York 10453.

James Hisao Kodama, Department of English, Gakushuin University, 5 Mejiro 1-chome, Toshima-ku, Tokyo, Japan.

Joseph E. Kramer, Department of English, The University of California, Berkeley, California 94720.

David Laird, Department of English, Los Angeles State College, Los Angeles, California 90032.

Edward A. Langhans, Department of Drama, The University of Hawaii, Honolulu, Hawaii 96822.

President Walter C. Langsam, The University of Cincinnati, Cincinnati, Ohio 45221.

Ruth M. Levitsky, Department of English, St. Jerome's College, Waterloo, Ontario, Canada.

John S. Lewis, Department of English, The University of Texas, Arlington, Texas 76010.

Vernon E. Lichtenstein, Department of English, Coe College, Cedar Rapids, Iowa 52402.

J. I. Lindsay, Department of English, The University of Vermont, Burlington, Vermont 05401.

Philip W. London, Department of English, The University of Windsor, Windsor, Ontario, Canada.

W. B. Long, Department of English, The City College of the City University of New York,

New York, New York 10031.

Clifford P. Lyons, *Department of English,
The University of North Carolina,
Chapel Hill, North Carolina 27515.*

Michael Manheim, *Department of English,
The University of Toledo, Toledo, Ohio
43606.*

Derick R. C. Marsh, *Department of English,
La Trobe University, Melbourne, Victoria,
Australia.*

Mary H. Marshall, *Department of English,
Syracuse University, Syracuse, New York
13210.*

Mr. and Mrs. Noel Martin, *6226 Robison Road,
Cincinnati, Ohio 45213.*

Charles D. McCloskey, *Department of English,
La Salle College, Philadelphia,
Pennsylvania 19141.*

Robert McDonnell, *Department of English,
Ohio University, Athens, Ohio 45701.*

James G. McManaway, *The Folger Shakespeare
Library, Washington, D. C. 20003.*

George J. Merrill, *Department of English,
Lakehead University, Port Arthur, Ontario,
Canada.*

C. William Miller, *Department of English,
Temple University, Philadelphia,
Pennsylvania 19122.*

Samuel J. Miller, *1525 Joseph Street,
Cincinnati, Ohio 45237.*

J. L. Mills, *611 East Franklin Street,
Chapel Hill, North Carolina 27514.*

June J. Morgan, *Department of English, Kansas
State Teachers College, Emporia, Kansas
66802.*

Ruth Mortimer, *20 Prescott Street, Cambridge,
Massachusetts 02138.*

Miss Nancy Muhleman, *19 Belmont Avenue,
Winchester, Kentucky 40391.*

Kenneth Muir, *Department of English,
The University of Liverpool, Liverpool 3,
England.*

Garry N. Murphy, *Department of English,
Southern Illinois University, Edwardsville,
Illinois 62025.*

Armour H. Nelson, *Department of English,
California Lutheran College, Mountclef
Village, Thousand Oaks, California 91360.*

Benjamin Nelson, *Department of English, State
University of New York, Stony Brook,
New York 11790.*

Lawrence G. Nelson, *Department of English,
Sweet Briar College, Sweet Briar, Virginia
24595.*

Miss Nora May Nolan, *3547 St. Charles Place,
Cincinnati, Ohio 45208.*

Mrs. Robert L. Nutt, Jr., *RFD, Elliston,
Virginia 24087.*

Zelma Odle, *849 E.N. 16th, Abilene, Texas 79601.*

Francis R. Olley, *Department of English,
St. Joseph's College, Philadelphia,
Pennsylvania 19131.*

Linwood E. Orange, *Department of English,
The University of Southern Mississippi,
Hattiesburg, Mississippi 39401.*

Tucker Orbison, *1402 Jefferson Avenue,
Lewisburg, Pennsylvania 17837.*

Jiro Ozu, *Department of English Literature,
Tokyo University, 7-chome, Hongo,
Bunkyo-ku, Tokyo, Japan.*

Edward B. Partridge, *Department of English,
Tulane University, New Orleans,
Louisiana 70118.*

Robert D. Pepper, *Department of English,
San Jose State College, San Jose,
California 95114.*

Eugene V. D. Perrin, *Institute of Pathology,
Western Reserve University, Cleveland,
Ohio 44106.*

Margaret I. Pfau, *Department of English,
Youngstown University, Youngstown, Ohio
44503.*

Rodney Poisson, *Department of English,
Huron College, London, Ontario, Canada.*

Burton R. Pollin, *Department of English,
Bronx Community College, Bronx,
New York 10468.*

Lawrence J. Pontrelli, *52 76th Street,
Brooklyn, New York 11209.*

William Michael Poslaiko, *15810 Murray Hill
Drive, Detroit, Michigan 48227.*

W. W. Powell, *Department of English, Georgia
Southern College, Statesboro, Georgia 30459.*

Moody E. Prior, *Department of English,
Northwestern University, Evanston,
Illinois 60201.*

Eleanor Prosser, *657 Los Ninos Way,
Los Altos, California 94022.*

George Foster Provost, Jr., *Department of
English, Duquesne University, Pittsburgh,
Pennsylvania 15219.*

Edward Quinn, *Department of English, City*

College of the City University of New York, New York, New York 10031.

Norman Rabkin, *Department of English, The University of California, Berkeley, California 94720.*

Donald Radin, *3875 Dakota, Cincinnati, Ohio 45229.*

Margaret Loftus Ranald, *Department of English, Queens College of the City University of New York, Flushing, New York 11367.*

Mr. and Mrs. William Ransohoff, *3536 Biddle Street, Cincinnati, Ohio 45220.*

H. H. Ransom, *Department of English, The University of Texas, Austin, Texas 78712.*

Robert R. Reed, Jr., *621 East McCormick Avenue, State College, Pennsylvania 16801.*

Ernest L. Rhodes, *Department of English, Old Dominion College, Norfolk, Virginia 23508.*

Townsend Rich, *Department of English, State University of New York, Albany, New York 12203.*

Mildred Riling, *Department of English, Southeastern State College, Durant, Oklahoma 74701.*

William A. Ringler, Jr., *Department of English, The University of Chicago, Chicago, Illinois 60637.*

Frederick J. Rogers, *Department of English, Western Michigan University, Kalamazoo, Michigan 49045.*

Mr. and Mrs. J. R. Rogers, *P. O. Box 7785, Leopoldville, Republic of Congo.*

Philip H. Ropp, *Department of English, Hampden-Sydney College, Hampden-Sydney, Virginia 23943.*

William Rosen, *Department of English, The University of Connecticut, Storrs, Connecticut 06268.*

Mrs. George S. Rosenthal, *3523 Biddle Street, Cincinnati, Ohio 45220.*

Sally Ross, *425 Rawson Woods Lane, Cincinnati, Ohio 45220.*

James E. Ruoff, *Department of English, The City College, New York, New York 10031.*

Andrew J. Sabol, *Department of English, Brown University, Providence, Rhode Island 02912.*

Alexander Sackton, *Department of English, The University of Texas, Austin, Texas 78712.*

Norman Sanders, *Department of English, The University of Tennessee, Knoxville, Tennessee 37916.*

Frank R. Saunders, *65 Westbrooke Avenue, West Hartlepool, Co. Durham, England.*

William O. Scott, *Department of English, The University of Kansas, Lawrence, Kansas 66045.*

Alice Lyle Scoufos, *Department of English, California State College, Fullerton, California 92631.*

Daniel Seltzer, *Loeb Drama Center, Harvard University, Cambridge, Massachusetts 02138.*

I. A. Shapiro, *The Shakespeare Institute, The University, Birmingham, England.*

John Shaw, *Department of English, Hiram College, Hiram, Ohio 44234.*

Neille Shoemaker, *Department of English, Baldwin-Wallace College, Berea, Ohio 44017.*

Howard Siegel, *Ventura College, Ventura, California 93003.*

Carl W. Siegrist, *1552 Glen Keith Boulevard, Baltimore, Maryland 21204.*

Gordon Ross Smith, *Department of English, Temple University, Philadelphia, Pennsylvania 19122.*

George Soule, *Department of English, Carleton College, Northfield, Minnesota 55057.*

Christopher Spencer, *Department of English, Illinois State University, Normal, Illinois 61761.*

Judah L. Stampfer, *Department of English, State University of New York, Stony Brook, Long Island, New York 11790.*

Richard Stensgaard, *Department of English, California State College, San Bernardino, California 92407.*

F. W. Sternfeld, *Faculty of Music, Oxford University, Oxford, England.*

David L. Stevenson, *Department of English, Hunter College of the City University of New York, New York, New York 10021.*

Frank Sullivan, *Department of English, Loyola University, Los Angeles, California 90045.*

G. T. Tanselle, *Department of English, The University of Wisconsin, Madison, Wisconsin 53706.*

Henry ten Hoor, *Hope College, Holland, Michigan 44932.*

Bert A. Thompson, *Kearney State College, Kearney, Nebraska 68847.*

James L. Titchener, 4021 Rose Hill, Cincinnati, Ohio 45229.

B. H. Trask, 21 East 90th Street, New York, New York 10028.

Robert K. Turner, Jr., Department of English, The University of Wisconsin, Milwaukee, Wisconsin 53211.

Peter Ure, Department of English, The University, Newcastle-upon-Tyne, England.

Linda van Norden, Department of English, The University of California, Davis, California 95616.

John W. Velz, The Folger Shakespeare Library, Washington, D. C. 20003.

John B. Virtue, Department of English, Eastern Michigan University, Ypsilanti, Michigan 48197.

Eugene M. Waith, Department of English, Yale University, New Haven, Connecticut 06520.

Frederick O. Waller, Office of the Dean of Undergraduate Studies, Portland State College, Portland, Oregon 97207.

S. Warhaft, Department of English, The University of Manitoba, Winnipeg, Manitoba, Canada.

C. R. Wasserman, Department of English, Indiana University, Bloomington, Indiana 47403.

Herbert S. Weil, Jr., Department of English, The University of Connecticut, Storrs, Connecticut 06268.

A. H. Weinhold, 257 North Erie Avenue,

Wichita, Kansas 67214.

Mrs. Richard Wellman, 203 Farragut Road, Cincinnati, Ohio 45218.

Karl P. Wentersdorf, Department of English, Xavier University, Cincinnati, Ohio 45207.

Robert H. West, Department of English, The University of Georgia, Athens, Georgia 30602.

Mr. and Mrs. Harris K. Weston, 565 Woodbrook Lane, Cincinnati, Ohio 45215.

John W. Wieler, Department of English, Hunter College, New York, New York 10021.

George Walton Williams, Department of English, Duke University, Durham, North Carolina 27706.

Marilyn L. Williamson, Department of English, Oakland University, Rochester, Michigan 48063.

Graham C. Wilson, Department of English, San Francisco State College, San Francisco, California 94132.

William C. Wolff, Jr., Department of English, Fordham University, Bronx, New York 10458.

Anthony Wolk, Department of English, Portland State College, Portland, Oregon 97207.

James O. Wood, 1056 Carolyn Avenue, San Jose, California 95125.

Thomas E. Wright, Department of English, San Fernando Valley State College, Northridge, California 91324.

R. Zimbardo, Department of English, The City College, New York, New York 10031.

II

Adrian College, Shipman Library, Adrian, Michigan 49221.

Agnes Scott College, Decatur, Georgia 30030.

The University of Akron, Akron, Ohio 44304.

College of The Albemarle, Whitehurst Library, Elizabeth City, North Carolina 27909.

Albion College, Albion, Michigan 49224.

The University of Albuquerque, Albuquerque, New Mexico 87105.

Alvernia College, Reading, Pennsylvania 19607.

American International College, McGown Memorial Library, Springfield, Massachusetts 01109.

American University, Washington, D.C. 20016.

Amherst College, Amherst, Massachusetts 01002.

Angelo State College, San Angelo, Texas 76901.

Anna Maria College, Paxton, Massachusetts 01612.

Antioch College, Olive Kettering Library, Yellow Springs, Ohio 45387.

Aquinas College, Grand Rapids, Michigan 49506.

The University of Arizona, Tucson, Arizona 85721.

The University of Arkansas, Fayetteville, Arkansas 72701.

Arlington State College, Arlington, Texas 76010.

Armstrong State College, Savannah, Georgia 31406.

Asheville-Biltmore College, Asheville, North Carolina 28801.

Ashland College, *Ashland, Ohio 44805.*

Athens College, *Athens, Alabama 35611.*

Atlantic Christian College, *C. L. Hardy Library, Wilson, North Carolina 27893.*

Augsburg College, *Minneapolis, Minnesota 55404.*

Augusta College, *Augusta, Georgia 30904.*

Augustana College, *Denkmann Memorial Library, Rock Island, Illinois 61201.*

Augustana College, *Sioux Falls, South Dakota 57102.*

Austin College, *Hopkins Library, Sherman, Texas 75090*

Babson Institute, *Babson Park, Massachusetts 02157.*

Baldwin-Wallace College Bookstore, *Berea, Ohio 44017.*

The University of Baltimore, *Baltimore, Maryland 21201.*

Barnard College, *New York, New York 10027.*

Beloit College, *Beloit, Wisconsin 53511.*

Bethel College and Seminary, *St. Paul, Minnesota 55101.*

Birmingham-Southern College, *M. Paul Phillips Library, Birmingham, Alabama 35204.*

Black Hawk College, *Moline, Illinois 61265.*

Bob Jones University, *Greenville, South Carolina 29614.*

Boise College, *Boise, Idaho 83707.*

Boston College, *Chestnut Hill, Massachusetts 02167.*

Bowdoin College, *Brunswick, Maine 04011.*

Bowling Green State University, *Bowling Green, Ohio 43402.*

Brandeis University, *Waltham, Massachusetts 02154.*

Briar Cliff College, *Sioux City, Iowa 51104.*

The University of Bridgeport, *Bridgeport, Connecticut 06602.*

Brigham Young University, *Provo, Utah 84601.*

Bronx Community College, *Bronx, New York 10468.*

Brooklyn College, *Brooklyn, New York 11210.*

Brown University, *Providence, Rhode Island 02912.*

Bryn Mawr College, *Bryn Mawr, Pennsylvania 19010.*

Bucknell University, *Lewisburg, Pennsylvania 17837.*

Butler University, *The Irwin Library, Indianapolis, Indiana 46207.*

Cabrillo College, *Aptos, California 95003.*

California Institute of Technology, *Pasadena, California 91109.*

California Lutheran College, *Thousand Oaks, California 91360.*

California State College, *California, Pennsylvania 15419.*

California State College at Los Angeles, *Los Angeles, California 90032.*

The University of California, *Berkeley, California 94720.*

The University of California, *Davis, California 95616.*

The University of California, *Irvine, California 92650.*

The University of California, *Riverside, California 92502.*

The University of California, *Santa Barbara, California 93106.*

The University of California, *Santa Cruz, California 95060.*

Calvin College, *Grand Rapids, Michigan 49506.*

Canisius College, *Buffalo, New York 14208.*

Cardinal Cushing College, *Brookline, Massachusetts 02146.*

Cardinal Glennon College, *St. Louis, Missouri 63119.*

Carnegie Institute of Technology, *Hunt Library, Pittsburgh, Pennsylvania 15213.*

Carroll College, *Waukesha, Wisconsin 53186.*

Catherine Spalding College, *Louisville, Kentucky 40203.*

Central College, *Pella, Iowa 50219.*

Central Missouri State College, *Warrensburg, Missouri 64093.*

Centre College, *Danville, Kentucky 40422.*

The University of Chicago, *Chicago, Illinois 60637.*

Chicago City Junior College, *Wright Branch Library, Chicago, Illinois 60634.*

Chicago Teachers College North, *Chicago, Illinois 60625.*

Chico State College, *Chico, California 95927.*

Church College of Hawaii, *Laie, Oahu, Hawaii 96762.*

The University of Cincinnati, *Cincinnati, Ohio 45221.*

The Cincinnati Bible Seminary, *Cincinnati, Ohio 45204.*

City College, *New York, New York 10031.*

Claremont Graduate School, *The Honnold*

Library, Claremont, California.

Clemson University, Clemson, South Carolina 29631.

Colby College, Waterville, Maine 04901.

The University of Colorado, Boulder, Colorado 80304.

Colorado State College, Greeley, Colorado 80631.

Columbia College, Columbia, South Carolina 29203.

Columbia University, New York, New York 10027.

Concordia College, Bronxville, New York 10708.

Concordia Teachers College, Klinck Memorial Library, River Forest, Illinois 60305.

Concordia Teachers College, Link Library, Seward, Nebraska 68435.

Connecticut College, New London, Connecticut 06320.

The University of Connecticut, Wilbur Cross Library, Storrs, Connecticut 06268.

Cornell College, Russell D. Cole Library, Mount Vernon, Iowa 52314.

Cornell University, Ithaca, New York 14850.

Crosier Seminary, Onamia, Minnesota 56359.

Dartmouth College, Baker Library, Hanover, New Hampshire 03755.

David Lipscomb College, Nashville, Tennessee 37203.

The University of Dayton, Albert Emanuel Library, Dayton, Ohio 45409.

The University of Delaware, Newark, Delaware 19711.

Denison University, Granville, Ohio 43023.

The University of Denver, Denver, Colorado 80210.

De Paul University, Chicago, Illinois 60604.

Dickinson College, Carlisle, Pennsylvania 17013.

Dominican College, Racine, Wisconsin 53402.

Don Bosco College, Newton, New Jersey 07860.

Drake University, Des Moines, Iowa 50311.

Drew University, Madison, New Jersey 07940.

Drexel Institute of Technology, Philadelphia, Pennsylvania 19004.

Duke University, Durham, North Carolina 27706.

Duquesne University Bookstore, Pittsburgh, Pennsylvania.

Earlham College, Lilly Library, Richmond, Indiana 47374.

East Carolina College, Greenville, North Carolina 27834.

East Texas State University, Commerce, Texas 75428.

Eastern Illinois University, Booth Library, Charleston, Illinois 61920.

Eastern Washington State College, Hargreaves Library, Cheney, Washington 99004.

Elmhurst College, Elmhurst, Illinois 60126.

Elmira College, Elmira, New York 14901.

Elon College, Elon College, North Carolina 27244.

Emory & Henry College, Emory, Virginia 24327.

Erskine College, Due West, South Carolina 29639.

Fairfield University, Fairfield, Connecticut 06433.

Florida Southern College, E. T. Roux Library, Lakeland, Florida 33802.

Florida State University, Tallahassee, Florida 32306.

Folger Shakespeare Library, Washington, D. C. 20003.

Fordham University, New York, New York 10458.

Furman University, Greenville, South Carolina 29613.

Gannon College, Erie, Pennsylvania 16501.

Gardner-Webb College, Boiling Springs, North Carolina 28017.

George Mason College of the University of Virginia, Fairfax, Virginia 22030.

Georgetown University, Washington, D.C. 20007.

Georgia Institute of Technology, Atlanta, Georgia 30332.

Georgia Southern College, Rosenwald Library, Statesboro, Georgia 30458.

Georgia State College, Atlanta, Georgia 30303.

The University of Georgia, Athens, Georgia 30601.

Goucher College, Julia Rogers Library, Towson, Baltimore, Maryland 21204.

The Great Neck Library, Great Neck, New York.

Grinnell College, Grinnell, Iowa 50112.

Guilford College, Guilford College, North Carolina 27410.

Gustavus Adolphus College, St. Peter, Minnesota 56082.

Hamline University, St. Paul, Minnesota 55101.

Harding College, Searcy, Arkansas 72143.

The University of Hartford, Hartford, Connecticut 06117.

Hastings College, Perkins Library, Hastings, Nebraska 68901.

Haverford College, *Haverford, Pennsylvania 19041.*

Heidelberg College, *Tiffin, Ohio 44883.*

The Henry E. Huntington Library and Art Gallery, *San Marino, California.*

Hofstra College, *Hempstead, New York 11550.*

Hollins College, *Fishburn Library, Hollins College, Virginia 24020.*

Hood College, *Joseph Henry Apple Library, Frederick, Maryland 21702.*

The University of Houston, *Houston, Texas 77004.*

Howard Payne College, *Brownwood, Texas 76801.*

Hudson Valley Community College, *Troy, New York 12180.*

Huron College, *Ella McIntire Library, Huron, South Dakota 57350.*

Illinois State University, *Milner Library, Normal, Illinois 61761.*

The University of Illinois, *Urbana, Illinois 61803.*

The University of Illinois at Chicago Circle, *Chicago, Illinois 60680.*

Immaculata College, *Immaculata, Pennsylvania 19345.*

Incarnate Word College, *San Antonio, Texas 78209.*

Indiana University, *Bloomington, Indiana 47405.*

Indiana University of Pennsylvania, *Indiana, Pennsylvania 15701.*

Indiana State University, *Cunningham Memorial Library, Terre Haute, Indiana 47809.*

Indiana-Purdue Regional Campus Library, *Fort Wayne, Indiana 46805.*

Iona College, *Ryan Library, New Rochelle, New York.*

Iowa State University, *Ames, Iowa 50010.*

The University of Iowa, *Iowa City, Iowa 52240.*

Ithaca College, *Ithaca, New York 14850.*

Jarvis Christian College, *Hawkins, Texas 75765.*

John Carroll University, *Grasselli Library, Cleveland, Ohio 44118.*

Johns Hopkins University, *Baltimore, Maryland 21218.*

The Josephinum, *Worthington, Ohio 43085.*

Judson College, *Bowling Library, Marion, Alabama 36756.*

Kansas State University, *Manhattan, Kansas 66504.*

Kansas State College of Pittsburg, *Porter Library, Pittsburg, Kansas 66762.*

Kent State University, *Kent, Ohio 44240.*

The University of Kentucky, *Lexington, Kentucky 40506.*

Keuka College, *Keuka Park, New York 14478.*

Knollcrest Calvin Library, *Knollcrest Campus, Grand Rapids, Michigan 49506.*

Kutztown State College, *Rohrbach Library, Kutztown, Pennsylvania 19530.*

LaGrange College, *William and Evelyn Banks Library, LaGrange, Georgia 30240.*

Lake-Sumter Junior College, *Leesburg, Florida 32748.*

Lamar State College of Technology, *Beaumont, Texas 77704.*

LaSalette Seminary, *Altamont, New York 12009.*

Lehigh University, *Bethlehem, Pennsylvania 18015.*

Le Moyne College, *Syracuse, New York 13214.*

Lewis College, *Lockport, Illinois 60441.*

Lewis and Clark College, *Portland, Oregon 97219.*

Little Rock University, *The John A. Larson Memorial Library, Little Rock, Arkansas 72204.*

Lock Haven State College, *Lock Haven, Pennsylvania 17745.*

Long Island University, *Brooklyn, New York 11201.*

Loras College, *Wahlert Memorial Library, Dubuque, Iowa 52001.*

Louisiana State University, *Alexandria, Louisiana.*

Louisiana State University, *Baton Rouge, Louisiana 70803.*

Louisiana State University, *Earl K. Long Library, New Orleans, Louisiana 70122.*

Louisiana Polytechnic Institute, *Prescott Memorial Library, Ruston, Louisiana 71270.*

The University of Louisville, *Louisville, Kentucky 40208.*

Lowell Technological Institute, *Lowell, Massachusetts 01854.*

Loyola College, *Baltimore, Maryland 21210.*

Loyola University, *E. M. Cudahy Memorial Library, Chicago, Illinois 60626.*

Loyola University, *New Orleans, Louisiana 70118.*

Lynchburg College, *Lynchburg, Virginia 24504.*

Macalester College, *Weyerhaeuser Library, St. Paul, Minnesota 55101.*

362

MacMurray College, *Pfeiffer Library,*
Jacksonville, Illinois 62650.
Madison College, *Harrisonburg, Virginia 22802.*
The University of Maine, *Orono, Maine 04473.*
Maria College, *Albany, New York 12208.*
Maria Regina College, *Syracuse, New York*
13208.
Marietta College, *Dawes Memorial Library,*
Marietta, Ohio 45750.
Mars Hill College, *Memorial Library, Mars Hill,*
North Carolina 28754.
Marshall University, *Huntington, West Virginia*
25701.
Marycrest College, *Cone Library, Davenport,*
Iowa 52804.
Marygrove College, *Detroit, Michigan 48221.*
Marygrove College, *Monroe, Michigan 48161.*
Mary Holmes Junior College, *West Point,*
Mississippi 39773.
The University of Maryland, *McKeldin Library,*
College Park, Maryland 20742.
Mary Manse College, *Toledo, Ohio 43620.*
Marymount College, *Palos Verdes Estates,*
California 90275.
Maryville College, *Lamar Memorial Library,*
Maryville, Tennessee 37801.
The University of Massachusetts, *Amherst,*
Massachusetts 01002.
The University of Massachusetts, *Boston,*
Massachusetts 02116.
Massachusetts Institute of Technology,
Cambridge, Massachusetts 02139.
Memphis State University, *John Brister*
Library, Memphis, Tennessee 38111.
Mercy College of Detroit, *Detroit, Michigan*
48219.
Miami University, *Oxford, Ohio 45056.*
The University of Michigan, *Ann Arbor,*
Michigan 48104.
Michigan State University, *East Lansing,*
Michigan 48823.
Middlebury College, *Middlebury, Vermont*
05753.
Middle Tennessee State University,
Murfreesboro, Tennessee 37130.
Millersville State College, *Millersville,*
Pennsylvania 17551.
Mills College, *Oakland, California 94613.*
The University of Mississippi, *University,*
Mississippi 38677.
Mississippi State University, *Mitchell*

Memorial Library, State College, Mississippi
39762.
Mississippi State College for Women, *J. C. Fant*
Memorial Library, Columbus, Mississippi
39701.
Missouri State Library, *Jefferson City,*
Missouri 65102.
The University of Missouri, *Columbia,*
Missouri 65201.
Monmouth College, *Guggenheim Memorial*
Library, West Long Branch, New Jersey
07764.
The University of Montana, *Missoula,*
Montana 59801.
Montgomery County Community College,
Conshohocken, Pennsylvania 19428.
Moravian College, *Harvey Memorial Library,*
Bethlehem, Pennsylvania 18018.
Morris County Free Library, *Morristown,*
New Jersey 07960.
Mount Holyoke College, *South Hadley,*
Massachusetts 01075.
Mount Mary College, *Milwaukee, Wisconsin*
53222.
Mount Mercy College, *Catherine McAuley*
Library, Cedar Rapids, Iowa 52402.
Mount Mercy College, *Pittsburgh, Pennsylvania*
15213.
College of Mount St. Joseph-on-the-Ohio,
Mount St. Joseph, Ohio 45051.
Mount St. Mary College, *Hooksett,*
New Hampshire 03106.
College of Mount St. Vincent, *Elizabeth Seton*
Library, Riverdale, New York 10471.
Mount Union College, *Alliance, Ohio 44601.*
Mount Vernon Seminary, *Washington, D. C.*
20007.
Mundelein College, *Chicago, Illinois 60626.*
Muskingum College, *New Concord, Ohio 43762.*
Joint University Libraries, *Nashville, Tennessee*
37203.
National College of Education, *Evanston,*
Illinois.
Nazareth College, *Rochester, New York 14610.*
The University of Nebraska, *Lincoln, Nebraska*
68508.
Newberry College, *Newberry, South Carolina*
29108.
The Newberry Library, *Chicago, Illinois 60610.*
The University of New Hampshire, *Durham,*
New Hampshire 03824.

New Haven College, *West Haven, Connecticut 06516.*

New Mexico State University, *Las Cruces, New Mexico 88001.*

Newton College of The Sacred Heart, *Newton, Massachusetts 02159.*

State University College, *E. H. Butler Library, Buffalo, New York 14222.*

State University College, *Milne Library, Geneseo, New York 14454.*

State University College, *New Paltz, New York 12561.*

State University College, *Oneonta, New York 13820.*

State University College, *Benjamin F. Feinberg Library, Plattsburgh, New York 12901.*

State University College, *Potsdam, New York 13676.*

State University of New York, *Binghamton, New York 13901.*

State University of New York, *Lockwood Memorial Library, Buffalo, New York 14214.*

State University of New York, *Stony Brook, New York 11790.*

Niagara University, *Niagara University, New York 14109.*

The University of North Carolina, *Chapel Hill, North Carolina 27515.*

The University of North Carolina, *Greensboro, North Carolina 27412.*

North Carolina Wesleyan College, *Rocky Mount, North Carolina 27801.*

Northeast Louisiana State College, *Sandel Library, Monroe, Louisiana 71205.*

Northeast Missouri State Teachers College, *Pickler Library, Kirksville, Missouri 63501.*

Northeastern Illinois State College, *Chicago, Illinois 60625.*

North Park College, *Chicago, Illinois 60625.*

Northwestern University, *Evanston, Illinois 60201.*

Northwestern State College, *Russell Library, Natchitoches, Louisiana 71475.*

Notre Dame College, *St. Louis, Missouri 63125.*

Notre Dame College, *Staten Island, New York 10301.*

The University of Notre Dame, *Notre Dame, Indiana 46556.*

Oakland University, *Rochester, Michigan 48063.*

Ohio University, *Athens, Ohio 45701.*

Ohio State University, *Columbus, Ohio 43210.*

Ohio Wesleyan University, *Delaware, Ohio 43015.*

Oklahoma City University, *Oklahoma City, Oklahoma 73106.*

The University of Oklahoma, *Norman, Oklahoma 73069.*

The University of Omaha, *Gene Eppley Library, Omaha, Nebraska 68101.*

Oregon State University, *Corvallis, Oregon 97331.*

College of Our Lady of Mercy, *Burlingame, California 94011.*

Parsons College, *Fairfield, Iowa 52556.*

Paterson State College, *Wayne, New Jersey 07473.*

Pennsylvania State University, *University Park, Pennsylvania 16802.*

Pennsylvania State Library, *Harrisburg, Pennsylvania 17126.*

The University of Pennsylvania, *The Charles Patterson Van Pelt Library, Philadelphia, Pennsylvania 19104.*

Philadelphia College of Pharmacy and Science, *Philadelphia, Pennsylvania 19104.*

The University of Pittsburgh, *Pittsburgh, Pennsylvania 15213.*

Point Park College, *Pittsburgh, Pennsylvania 15222.*

The University of Portland, *Portland, Oregon 97203.*

C. W. Post College, *Greenvale, Long Island, New York 11548.*

Arcadia Public Library, *Arcadia, California 91006.*

Bexley Public Library, *Columbus, Ohio 43209.*

Brooklyn Public Library, *Brooklyn, New York 11238.*

Buffalo and Erie County Public Library, *Buffalo, New York 14203.*

Carnegie Library of Pittsburgh, *Pittsburgh, Pennsylvania 15213.*

Charlotte and Mecklenburg County Public Library, *Charlotte, North Carolina 28202.*

Chicago Public Library, *Chicago, Illinois 60602.*

Cincinnati Public Library, *Cincinnati, Ohio 45202.*

Columbus Public Library, *Columbus, Ohio 43215.*

Detroit Public Library, *Detroit, Michigan 48202.*

East Meadow Public Library, *Long Island, New York 11554.*

Erie Public Library, *Erie, Pennsylvania 16507.*

Fort Wayne and Allen County Public Library,

Fort Wayne, Indiana 46802.

Fullerton Public Library, Fullerton, California 92632.

Gail Borden Public Library, Elgin, Illinois.

Gaston-Lincoln Regional Library, Gastonia, North Carolina 28052.

Jeffersonville Township Public Library, Jeffersonville, Indiana 47130.

Kansas City Public Library, Kansas City, Missouri 64106.

Los Angeles Public Library, Los Angeles, California 90017.

Milwaukee Public Library, Milwaukee, Wisconsin 53233.

New York Public Library, New York, New York 10018.

Providence Public Library, Providence, Rhode Island 02903.

Queens Borough Public Library, Jamaica, New York.

Roanoke Public Library, Roanoke, Virginia 24011.

Tampa Public Library, Tampa, Florida 33602.

Teaneck Public Library, Teaneck, New Jersey 07666.

Toledo Public Library, Toledo, Ohio 43624.

Warren Public Library, Warren, Michigan 48092.

Worcester Public Library, Worcester, Massachusetts 01608.

Purdue University, Lafayette, Indiana 47907.

Queen of the Apostles, Harriman, New York 10926.

Quincy College, Quincy, Illinois 62301.

Quinnipiac College, Hamden, Connecticut 06517

Radford College, Radford, Virginia 24141.

The University of Redlands, Redlands, California 92373.

Regis College, Denver, Colorado 80221.

Regis College, Framingham, Massachusetts 01701.

Regis College, Weston, Massachusetts 02193.

Rhode Island School of Design, Providence, Rhode Island 02903.

Rice University, The Fondren Library, Houston, Texas 77001.

Rio Grande College, Davis Library, Rio Grande, Ohio 45674.

Ripon College, Lane Library, Ripon, Wisconsin 54971.

Roberts Wesleyan College, Roberts Memorial Library, North Chili, New York 14514.

The University of Rochester, Rochester, New York 14627.

Rochester Institute of Technology, Rochester, New York 14608.

Roosevelt University, Chicago, Illinois 60605.

Russell Sage College, Troy, New York 12180.

Rutgers University, New Brunswick, New Jersey 08901.

Sacred Heart College, Cullman, Alabama 35055.

St. Ambrose College, Davenport, Iowa 52803.

St. Andrews Presbyterian College, De Tamble Library, Laurinburg, North Carolina 28352.

St. Benedicts College, Abbey Library, Atchison, Kansas 66002.

College of St. Benedict, St. Joseph, Minnesota 56374.

College of St. Elizabeth, Santa Maria Library, Convent Station, New Jersey 07961.

St. Francis College, Biddeford, Maine 04005.

St. Francis College, McGarry Library, Brooklyn, New York 11201.

St. Francis College, Loretto, Pennsylvania 15940.

St. Francis Seminary, Salzmann Library, Milwaukee, Wisconsin 53207.

St. John Fisher College, Rochester, New York 14618.

St. John's University, Jamaica, New York 11432.

St. Joseph's College, East Chicago, Indiana 46312.

St. Joseph's College, North Windham, Maine 04062.

St. Joseph's College, Rensselaer, Indiana 47978.

St. Joseph Seraphic Seminary, Callicoon, New York 12723.

St. Louis University, Pius XII Memorial Library, St. Louis, Missouri 63103.

St. Mary's College, Notre Dame, Indiana 46556.

St. Mary's Dominican College, New Orleans, Louisiana 70118.

St. Mary's Seminary, Perryville, Missouri 63775.

St. Mary's University, San Antonio, Texas 78228.

St. Mary of the Lake Seminary, Chicago, Illinois 60631.

St. Michael's College, Winooski, Vermont 05404.

St. Norbert College, West DePere, Wisconsin 54178.

St. Paul's College, Concordia, Missouri 64020.

St. Procopius College, Lisle, Illinois 60532.

College of St. Teresa, Winona, Minnesota 55987.

Salem College, Winston-Salem, North Carolina 27108.

Salisbury State College, *Salisbury, Maryland 21801.*

The University of San Diego, *College for Men, San Diego, California 92110.*

San Francisco State College, *San Francisco, California 94132.*

The University of San Francisco, *Richard A. Gleeson Library, San Francisco, California 94117.*

Santa Barbara City College, *Santa Barbara, California 93105.*

The University of Santa Clara, *Orradre Library, Santa Clara, California 95053.*

Sarah Lawrence College, *Bronxville, New York 10708.*

Seattle University, *Seattle, Washington 98122.*

Seton Hill College, *Reeves Memorial Library, Greensburg, Pennsylvania 15601.*

Shippensburg State College, *Shippensburg, Pennsylvania 17257.*

Shreveport Bossier City Southern University, *Shreveport, Louisiana.*

Siena College, *Loudonville, New York 12211.*

Siena College, *Memphis, Tennessee 38117.*

Skidmore College, *Saratoga Springs, New York 12866.*

South Bend Campus of Indiana University, *South Bend, Indiana 46615.*

South Dakota School of Mines and Technology, *Rapid City, South Dakota 57701.*

The University of South Florida, *Tampa, Florida 33620.*

South Texas Junior College, *Houston, Texas 77002.*

Southeast Missouri State College, *Kent Library, Cape Girardeau, Missouri 63701.*

Southern Illinois University, *Edwardsville, Illinois 62025.*

Southwest Missouri State College, *Springfield, Missouri 65802.*

Southwestern at Memphis, *Burrow Library, Memphis, Tennessee 38112.*

Stanislaus State College, *Turlock, California 95380.*

Stephen F. Austin State College, *Nacogdoches, Texas 75962.*

Stephens College, *Columbia, Missouri 65201.*

Stetson University, *DeLand, Florida 32720.*

College of Steubenville, *Starvaggi Memorial Library, Steubenville, Ohio 43952.*

Stonehill College, *Cushing Martin Library, North Easton, Massachusetts 02356.*

Suffolk University, *Boston, Massachusetts 02114.*

Swarthmore College, *Swarthmore, Pennsylvania 19081.*

Sweet Briar College, *Mary Helen Cochran Library, Sweet Briar, Virginia 24595.*

Syracuse University, *Syracuse, New York 13210.*

The University of Tampa, *Tampa, Florida 33606.*

Taylor University, *Upland, Indiana 46989.*

Temple University, *Philadelphia, Pennsylvania 19122.*

The University of Tennessee, *Knoxville, Tennessee 37916.*

Tennessee Polytechnic Institute, *Cookeville, Tennessee 38500.*

The University of Texas, *Austin, Texas 78712.*

Texas A & M University, *College Station, Texas 77843.*

Texas Christian University, *Mary Couts Burnett Library, Fort Worth, Texas 76129.*

Texas Technological College, *Lubbock, Texas 79409.*

Texas Woman's University, *Denton, Texas 76204.*

Towson State College, *Albert S. Cook Library, Baltimore, Maryland 21204.*

Trinity College, *Deerfield, Illinois 60015.*

Trinity College, *Hartford, Connecticut 06106.*

Tufts University, *Medford, Massachusetts 02155.*

Union Junior College, *Arthur L. Johnson Library, Cranford, New Jersey 07016.*

Union University, *Emma Waters Summar Library, Jackson, Tennessee.*

United States Air Force Academy, *Colorado 80840.*

United States Military Academy, *West Point, New York 10996.*

Upsala College, *East Orange, New Jersey 07019.*

The University of Utah, *Salt Lake City, Utah 84112.*

Utica College of Syracuse University, *Utica, New York 13502.*

Valdosta State College, *Valdosta, Georgia 31601.*

Valley City State College, *Allen Memorial Library, Valley City, North Dakota 58072.*

Vassar College, *Poughkeepsie, New York 12601.*

The University of Vermont, *Burlington, Vermont 05401.*

Villa Maria College, *Buffalo, New York 14225.*

Virginia Military Institute, *Preston Library, Lexington, Virginia 24450.*

The University of Virginia, *Charlottesville, Virginia 22901.*

Wadhams Hall Seminary, *Ogdensburg, New York 13669.*

Washington University, *St. Louis, Missouri 63130.*

Washington University, *Seattle, Washington 98105.*

Wellesley College, *Wellesley, Massachusetts 02181.*

Wells College, *Aurora, New York 13026.*

Wesleyan University, *Middletown, Connecticut 06457.*

West Chester State College, *Francis H. Green Library, West Chester, Pennsylvania 19380.*

Western Kentucky State College, *Bowling Green, Kentucky 42101.*

Western Maryland College, *Westminster, Maryland 21157.*

Western Michigan University, *Kalamazoo, Michigan 49001.*

Western Reserve University, *Cleveland, Ohio 44106.*

Wheaton College, *Norton, Massachusetts 02766.*

Wichita State University, *Wichita, Kansas 67208.*

College of William and Mary, *Williamsburg, Virginia 23185.*

Wilson College, *Stewart Memorial Library, Chambersburg, Pennsylvania 17201.*

Winthrop College, *The South Carolina College for Women, Rock Hill, South Carolina 29733.*

The University of Wisconsin, *Madison, Wisconsin 53706.*

The University of Wisconsin, *Milwaukee, Wisconsin 53211.*

Wisconsin State University, *Stevens Point, Wisconsin 54481.*

Wittenberg University, *Springfield, Ohio 45501.*

Wofford College, *Spartanburg, South Carolina 29301.*

The College of Wooster, *Andrews Library, Wooster, Ohio 44691.*

The University of Wyoming, *Laramie, Wyoming 82071.*

Xavier University, *Cincinnati, Ohio 45207.*

Yale University, *New Haven, Connecticut 06520.*

Yeshiva University, *Pollack Library, New York, New York 10033.*

Youngstown University, *Youngstown, Ohio 44503.*

III

Adelaide, The University of Adelaide, *Barr Smith Library, Adelaide, South Australia.*

Antigonish, St. Francis Xavier University, *Angus L. MacDonald Library, Antigonish, Nova Scotia.*

Arhus, Statsbiblioteket, Tidskriftafdelingen, *Universitetsparken, Arhus C, Denmark.*

Armidale, The University of New England, *Armidale, N.S.W., Australia.*

Auckland, The University of Auckland, *Auckland, New Zealand.*

Basel, Englisches Seminar der Universität, *Augustinergasse 19, 4000 Basel, Switzerland.*

Bellville, The University College of the Western Cape, *Bellville, South Africa.*

Berlin, Deutsche Akademien der Wissenschaften, *Unter den Linden 8, 108 Berlin 8, Germany.*

Besançon, Bibliothèque de l'Université, *Besançon, France.*

Birmingham, The City of Birmingham Reference Library, *Ratcliff Place, Birmingham 1, England.*

Birmingham, The University Library, *Edgbaston, Birmingham 15, England.*

Birmingham, The Shakespeare Institute, The University of Birmingham, *Birmingham 15, England.*

Bordeaux, Faculté des Lettres, *Section d'anglais, 20 Cours Pasteur, Bordeaux, France.*

Brandon, Brandon University, *Brandon, Manitoba, Canada.*

Bristol, Bristol Public Libraries, Central Library, *College Green, Bristol 1, England.*

Burnaby, Simon Fraser University, *Burnaby, British Columbia, Canada.*

Cambridge, Cambridge University, *Cambridge, England.*

Campsie, Canterbury Municipal Library, *139 Beamish Street, Campsie, N.S.W., Australia.*

Canberra, National Library of Australia, *Preparation Branch, Canberra, A.C.T., Australia.*

367

Canterbury, The University, Canterbury, Kent, England.

Cardiff, The University College of South Wales, Cathays Park, Cardiff, Great Britain.

Clayton, Monash University, Clayton, Victoria, Australia.

Colchester, The University of Essex, Wivenhoe Park, Colchester, Essex, England.

Copenhagen, Det Kongelige Bibliotek, Tidsskrifter, Christians Brygge 8, Copenhagen K, Denmark.

Dijon, Université de Dijon, Faculté des Lettres et des Sciences Humaines, Section d'anglais, 6 Boulevard Gabriel, Dijon, France.

Dublin, The University College, Earlsfort Terrace, Dublin 2, Ireland.

Dublin, The University of Dublin, Trinity College. Dublin, Ireland.

Dunedin, Otago University, Dunedin, N.1, New Zealand.

Durham, The University Library, Palace Green, Durham, England.

Edinburgh, The National Library of Scotland, Edinburgh 1, Scotland.

Edmonton, The University of Alberta, Edmonton, Alberta, Canada.

Edmonton, Edmonton Public Library, Macdonald Drive, Edmonton, Alberta, Canada.

Exeter, Devon County Library, Barley House, St. Thomas, Exeter, England.

Exeter, The University of Exeter, Prince of Wales Road, Exeter, England.

Florence, The British Institute of Florence, Palazzo Lanfredini, 9 Lungarno Guicciardini, Florence, Italy.

Fredericton, The University of New Brunswick, Bonar Law-Bennett Library, Fredericton, New Brunswick, Canada.

Freetown, Fourah Bay College, The University College of Sierra Leone, Freetown, Sierra Leone, West Africa.

Genève, Librairie de l'Université Georg & Cie S.A., Corraterie 5, 1211 Genève 11, Switzerland.

Georgetown, The University of Guyana, Queens College Compound, Georgetown, Guyana.

Giessen, Seminar fuer Englische Philologie der Universität, 63 Giessen, Bismarckstrasse 4, Germany.

Glasgow, The University, Glasgow, W.2, Scotland.

Halifax, The University of King's College,

Halifax, Nova Scotia, Canada.

Hamilton, McMaster University, Mills Memorial Library, Hamilton, Ontario, Canada.

Hobart, The University of Tasmania, Hobart, Tasmania, Australia.

Hull, The University, Hull, England.

Jerusalem, The Hebrew University, Jerusalem, Israel.

Jyväskylä, The University of Jyväskylä, Department of English, Jyväskylä, Finland.

Kensington, The University of New South Wales, P.O. Box 1, Kensington, N.S.W., Australia.

Kingston, Queen's University, Douglas Library, Kingston, Ontario, Canada.

Lausanne, Bibliothèque Cantonale et Universitaire, 6, Place de la Riponne, 1000-Lausanne, Suisse.

London, Bedford College, York Gate, Regents Park, London, N.W.1, England.

London, Goldsmiths' College, New Cross, London, S.E.14, England.

London, The London Library, St. James's Square, London, S.W.1, England.

London, The University College, Gower Street, London, W.C.1, England.

London, The University of London, Senate House, Malet Street, London, W.C.1, England.

London, Westfield College, The University of London, Hampstead, London, N.W.3, England.

London, Orthological Institute, 3, Lincoln's Inn Fields, London, W.C.2, England.

London, The University of Western Ontario, London, Ontario, Canada.

Louvain, Bibliothèque de l'Université de Louvain, Place Monseigneur Ladeuze, Louvain, Belgique.

Manchester, Manchester Public Libraries, Central Library, St. Peter's Square, Manchester 2, Great Britain.

Manchester, The University of Manchester, Manchester, England.

Manchester, De La Salle College, Middleton, Manchester, England.

Manila, Ateneo de Manila University, P.O. Box 154, Manila, Philippines.

Marburg/Lahn, Englisches Seminar der Universität, Marburg/Lahn, Landgraf-Philipp-Strasse, Germany.

Mona, The University College of the West Indies, Mona, Jamaica, West Indies.

Montreal, McGill University, 3459 *McTavish Street, Montreal 2, Canada.*

Montreal, Sir George Williams University, *Montreal 25, Canada.*

Muenchen, Shakespeare-Bibliothek beim Englischen Seminar der Universität München, *8 Muenchen 22, Geschwister-Scholl-Platz 1, Germany.*

Münster, Universitätsbibliothek, *Postfach 1521, 44 Münster/Westf., Germany.*

Newcastle, The University of Newcastle, *Newcastle, N.S.W., Australia.*

Nottingham, The University of Nottingham, *University Park, Nottingham, England.*

Oslo, The British Institute, The University of Oslo, *Blindern, Oslo 3, Norway.*

Oslo, Universitetsbiblioteket, *Tidsskriftkontoret, Drammensveien 42B, Oslo 1, Norway.*

Ottawa, Carleton University, *Colonel By Drive, Ottawa 1, Ontario, Canada.*

Ottawa, National Library, *Public Archives Building, 330 Sussex Drive, Ottawa 2, Ontario, Canada.*

Oxford, Bodleian Library, *Oxford, England.*

Pavia, 1st Lingua e Lett, *Inglese, Universita, Pavia, Italy.*

Rondebosch, The University of Cape Town, *J. W. Jagger Library, Rondebosch, C.P., South Africa.*

Saarbrücken, Anglistisches Institut der Universität des Saarlandes, *66 Saarbrücken 15, Germany.*

St. Andrews, The University, *St. Andrews, Fife, Scotland.*

St. Catharines, Brock University, *St. Catharines, Ontario, Canada.*

St. John's, Memorial University of Newfoundland. *St. John's Newfoundland, Canada.*

Santurce, College of the Sacred Heart, *Box 12383, Loiza Station, Santurce, Puerto Rico 00914.*

Saskatoon, The University of Saskatchewan, *Murray Memorial Library, Saskatoon, Saskatchewan, Canada.*

Sheffield, Central Library, *Surrey Street, Sheffield 1, Yorkshire, England.*

Sheffield, The University, *Sheffield 10, England.*

Singapore, The University of Singapore, *Bukit Timah Road, Singapore 10, Malaysia.*

Southampton, The University, *Southampton, England.*

Sudbury, Laurentian University, *Sudbury, Ontario, Canada.*

Sydney, The Public Library of New South Wales, *Sydney, N.S.W., Australia.*

Sydney, The University of Sydney, *Fisher Library, Sydney, N.S.W., Australia.*

Toronto, Toronto Public Library, *College and St. George Streets, Toronto 2B, Ontario, Canada.*

Toronto, The University of Toronto, *Toronto 5, Ontario, Canada.*

Toronto, Trinity College, *Hoskin Avenue, Toronto 5, Ontario, Canada.*

Toronto, York University, *4700 Keele Street, Toronto, Ontario, Canada.*

Trichur, Sree Kerala Varma College, *Trichur 4, India.*

Tübingen, Universitätsbibliothek, *74 Tübingen, Germany.*

Uppsala, Universitetsbiblioteket, *Uppsala, Suède.*

Valletta, Royal University of Malta, *St. Paul Street, Valletta, Malta.*

Waterloo, St. Jerome's College, *Waterloo, Ontario, Canada.*

Waterloo, Waterloo Lutheran University, *Waterloo, Ontario, Canada.*

Wellington, Alexander Turnbull Library, *Box 8016, Wellington, New Zealand.*

Windsor, The University of Windsor, *Windsor, Ontario, Canada.*

Winnipeg, The University of Manitoba, *Elizabeth Dafoe Library, Winnipeg 19, Manitoba, Canada.*

York, The University of York, *Heslington, York, England.*